ECONOMIC GROWTH OF COLOMBIA

ECONOMIC GROWTH OF COLOMBIA: PROBLEMS AND PROSPECTS

Report of a mission sent to Colombia in 1970
by the
World Bank

Chief of Mission and Coordinating Author
Dragoslav Avramovic

THE JOHNS HOPKINS UNIVERSITY PRESS
Baltimore and London

FOREWORD

This Report on Economic Growth of Colombia is the first Country Economic Report to be published by the World Bank.

In earlier years, the Bank published a number of general survey mission reports on particular countries. These were produced by special missions made up in varying proportions of Bank staff members and independent experts, and were designed for publication. This series has now been discontinued.

In support of its own operations, the Bank has also prepared periodic reports on borrowing countries. These have not been intended for publication. They have been written mainly as a basis for decisions on Bank policy and for discussions with the government of the country. In the last few years, the number and depth of coverage of these reports has increased. Many of them have been used by consortia and consultative groups organized among all the governments providing assistance to a particular country.

Three of these reports have ultimately been published by the governments concerned, and one by the Bank, but most have remained unpublished. They have, however, been available to the Executive Directors of the Bank, and through them to member governments, and have been increasingly used by those with access to them as basic sources of information and analysis.

It has now been decided to publish a selection of the Bank's Country Economic Reports, with the agreement of the government concerned, in order that they may be more generally available. The Colombia Report was chosen as the first partly because of an initiative by the Government of Colombia, partly because it is a relatively comprehensive report dealing with a number of long-term issues.

Hollis B. Chenery
Economic Adviser to the President
International Bank for Reconstruction and Development

TABLE OF CONTENTS

STATISTICAL ANNEX

TABLES

MAPS

PREFACE

This report was prepared by a Bank economic mission which visited Colombia in February-March 1970. The draft was completed in July and discussed with the Colombian authorities in September. The report was circulated in mimeographed form to the Bank Board of Executive Directors, other international agencies and the Consultative Group for Colombia — consisting of major donor countries and international agencies interested in assisting the development of Colombia — in November. It served as a background document for the Group's meeting held in Paris in February 1971, which decided to extend the required external support to the Colombian Economic and Social Development Plan 1970-73.

The present published version is the same as the November 1970 mimeographed report with three exceptions. First, descriptive material easily found in other documents was deleted. Second, an attempt was made to eliminate duplications and repetitions in the different parts of the report. Third, the statistical material bearing on the economy as a whole, e.g., national accounts, fiscal developments, foreign trade, balance of payments, etc., was brought up to date wherever possible, and this provided an opportunity to comment on the report's projections in the light of actual developments in the last 18 months.

It would not have been possible to prepare this report without the wholehearted support of the Colombian authorities. They placed at our disposal all necessary factual and analytical material and were always prepared to discuss their views with us and to comment on our findings.

The mission's efforts were greatly facilitated by the cooperation received from the International Labor Organization team sent in early 1970 to study unemployment in Colombia. This report draws heavily on their findings. The mission worked closely with the United Nations Development Program resident staff in Colombia. Their help was especially valuable in the preparation of the Preinvestment Study Program, Chapter 5. This is the first time such a program has been undertaken by a Bank mission. The draft of the report has benefited greatly from the comments and suggestions of the secretariat of CIAP (Inter-American Committee on the Alliance for Progress).

The report consists of 25 chapters. The different strands of the argument are pulled together in Chapter 1 which presents the conclusions of the report. Chapters 2-5 analyze the issues which cut across particular sectors: employment, investment, public finance, regional development, planning; these chapters also contain the projections of growth, external capital prospects of specific sectors. Chapters 6-13 discuss the process of industrialization, mining and energy supply. Chapters 14-18 analyze the situation in agriculture and its principal problems. Chapters 19-21 discuss transport, telecommunications and tourism. Chapters 22-25 are devoted to the social sectors: education and training, water supply, and public health.

The following Bank staff and consultants participated, full or part-time, in the mission. The chapters to which they made their main contribution are also indicated.

Balkind, J.	20
Calvo, D. - Consultant	21
Darnell, G.	14,17,18
Dorich, L. - Consultant, Pan American Health Org.	4
Douglas, A.	20
Duarte, I. - Consultant, Pan American Health Org.	23
Dublin, T. - Consultant, US Public Health Service; Health, Education, and Welfare	24, 25
Dumoulin, J.	14, 18
Engelmann, P.	4, 5
Germanacos, G. - Consultant	22
Gillman, H. - Consultant	16
Glenshaw, P.	9, 10
Hurlebaus, J.	23
Hyde, G.	2, 3, 14, Statistical Annex
Isla, M.	13
Jaffe, J.	9, 12
Lehbert, B.	14, 18, Statistical Annex
Lipkowitz, S.	6, 8, 9, 10
McGarry, M.	14, 17
Minton, A.	20
Myren, D. - Consultant, Ford Foundation	14, 18
Naylor, G. - Consultant	8
Neufeld, H.	6, 7, 8, 11
Paschke, J.	8
Shields, B.	19, 20
Teigeiro, J.	6, 7, Statistical Annex
Van der Meer, S.	20

The published version was edited by T. H. Silcock.

The Coordinating Author is responsible for the scope and overall conclusions of the report.

August 31, 1971

ECONOMIC GROWTH OF COLOMBIA

CHAPTER 1
THE OVERALL VIEW

The Problem

As a result of several factors operating in the internal economy and its international economic relations, Colombia has achieved in recent years rates of growth in real income considerably above the historical average. The gross domestic product rose by 6.1% in 1968, 6.5% in 1969 and approximately 7.0% in 1970, compared to less than 5% per annum during 1950-67. At the same time there has been a growing concern, within the government administration and in public opinion generally, for the high level of urban unemployment and the low standards of welfare in rural areas—a major cause of urban drift. The question is whether the recent acceleration of economic activity can be sustained and used to the best advantage for employment growth at a rapid rate. The alternative is a temporary cyclical upswing, much of it absorbed by rising personal consumption, to be followed by a settling back of the system to a relatively low rate of growth and labor force absorption.

The next section reviews the circumstances that have brought about the recent acceleration. This is followed by the discussion of the employment challenge and of the rural problem. The remaining three sections analyze the issues of resource allocation and resource mobilization.

Bases for Growth

Two factors have led to the acceleration of growth: expansion of investment, and alleviation of the foreign exchange constraint.

Investment

A sharp increase has taken place in recent years in Colombia's capacity to undertake development projects. This has been reflected in an upward shift in the aggregate rate of investment, in a particularly sharp rise in public investment, and in a dramatic increase in the flow of projects submitted for financing to international lending agencies.

The proportion of fixed capital investment to GDP in the last three years of around 19% is much higher than the historical average (Table 1-1). It was attained before the effects of the upward movement in coffee prices of late 1969 were felt, moreover.

Table 1-1: GROSS INVESTMENT IN FIXED CAPITAL, 1950-69
(as % of GDP)

	Average
1950-54	15.0
1955-59	16.5
1960-64	17.4
1965-66	16.2
1967-69[1]	19.1

[1]Estimated for 1969.

Source: Banco de la Republica.

This increase in aggregate investment was primarily a function of an upward shift in public investment (Table 1-2).

1

Table 1-2: PUBLIC AND PRIVATE INVESTMENT, 1966-69
(Indices, in constant prices, 1966 = 100)

	1966	1967	1968	1969[1]
Public Investment, (Public Finance Definition)	100	131	158	178
Public Investment, (National Accounts Definition)	100	132	151	169
Private Investment (National Accounts Definition)	100	100	115	115
Public Investment as Percent of Total (National Accounts Definition)[2]	20.3	28.3	26.3	28.7

[1]Provisional.

[2]The national accounts understate public investment. They include only expenditure on buildings and other construction in the public sector; all expenditure on machinery and equipment is assigned to the private sector for national accounts purposes.

Source: Banco de la Republica; Statistical Annex

The increased capacity to prepare investment projects satisfactorily, from the engineering and economic viewpoints, has been reflected in a sharp upswing of project commitments of external lending agencies in recent years (Table 1-3):

Table 1-3. COMMITMENTS OF FOREIGN ASSISTANCE FOR DEVELOPMENT PROJECTS, 1961-69
(In millions of US$)

Year	Value of Project Commitments
1961	103
1962	89
1963	127
1964	91
1965	42
1966	89
1967	86
1968	179
1969	233

Source: Departamento Nacional de Planeacion.

The prospects for future project availability are excellent. Through a special office in its Planning Department, the government has placed project preparation work and associated studies on a systematic and well-coordinated basis. This office, FONADE, has been well financed by the government and by the Inter-American Development Bank. The 1970 IBRD

Economic Mission, jointly with FONADE and the UNDP Resident Representative Office in Colombia, has prepared a draft preinvestment study program. The total investment which may be initiated on the basis of all proposed studies could range in the order of US$2-3 billion. During the 1970's, public investment should show an improvement in quality and expansion in scope. If the acceleration of growth in real income is sustained, prospects for private investment should also be very good, particularly as full capacity utilization is approached.

A major problem which can now be foreseen concerns the availability of local finance for investment, particularly in the public sector. In 1950-66, public savings averaged 4% of GDP. In 1967-69, they reached 6% of GDP, as a result of a sharp increase in public revenue (almost 40% in real terms in 1966-69). Despite this increase in savings the government had to resort to external borrowing to finance part of the local currency cost of projects; and the latter has taken the form, in part, of program loans. In the last four years program loans have financed 15% of public investment, on the average.

As public investment expands the need for public savings will expand correspondingly; in particular, with the level of project commitments now being contracted the demand for local savings to support the foreign-financed projects will increase sharply.

Foreign Exchange Supply

Two developments have led to alleviation of the foreign exchange constraint to growth: expansion of non-traditional exports and a sharp upswing in the world coffee market (Table 1-4).

Table 1-4: MERCHANDISE EXPORTS, 1960-70[1]
(In millions of US dollars)

	Non-Traditional Exports	Coffee	Petroleum	Total
1960	52.3	332.2	80.0	464.6
1961	58.4	307.8	68.2	434.5
1962	70.8	332.0	60.6	463.4
1963	66.5	303.0	77.2	446.7
1964	78.9	394.2	74.9	548.1
1965	107.1	343.9	88.2	539.1
1966	108.7	328.3	70.6	507.6
1967	126.3	322.4	61.2	509.9
1968	170.6	351.4	36.3	558.3
1969	207.2	343.9	56.7	607.8
1970	225.0[2]	467.1	55.8	748.0[2]

[1]Customs clearance basis.

[2]Provisional.

Source: Departmento Administrativo Nacional de Estadistica (DANE).

In the three years 1966-69 non-traditional exports doubled—an average annual growth rate of 24% on a base which is not insignificant.

Non-traditional exports consist of a large variety of items, both agricultural commodities and manufactures. Among the former, the most important are cotton, bananas, sugar, tobacco, and livestock; among the latter, textiles, leather, glass, wood products, cement, and paper. Lately, machinery, chemical products, and pharmaceuticals have been exported. One of the most impressive achievements of the Colombian economy has been the speed with which new products have been added to the export flow (Table 1-5).

Table 1-5: GROWTH OF NON-TRADITIONAL EXPORTS
(In thousands of US$)

		1963	1966	1969
Commodities existing in	1955-57	24,967	49,714	68,989
Commodities initiated in	1959	5,184	12,251	27,015
	1960	6,212	4,954	36,413
	1961	3,210	4,548	16,021
	1963	3,323	4,872	31,441
	1964	–	2,449	909
	1966	–	–	9,224

Source: Banco de la Republica.

The Colombian authorities' target for non-traditional exports in 1974 ranges from a minimum of US$380 million to a maximum of US$600 million—annual average growth rates of 15% to 30%. The results in 1970 were disappointing—the value of shipments rose by 8% and registrations only 4%. It is of critical importance for the process of growth and diversification that this setback prove temporary. Since the world market outlook is not bright for bananas, sugar, and cotton (which account for 30% of non-traditional exports), it is other agricultural products and manufactures which have to expand very rapidly.

One promising source of foreign exchange earnings that has been neglected in the past is tourism. In 1969 Colombia received 140,000 visitors and $16 million in exchange earnings; this compares with $65 million in Bermuda and $94 million in Jamaica. With 1,000 miles of Caribbean coast, Colombia has the potential for international tourism development on a substantial scale. It has the same characteristics as the rest of the Caribbean: short distance from the U.S. supplier market and therefore relatively cheap air fares, reverse climatic seasons, and exceptional beach assets. In addition, it has historical and cultural attractions, particularly in Cartagena, and ethnic and cultural ties with neighboring Venezuela, another supplier market. As a South American country, Colombia forms part of package tours to the area, and Bogota can offer additional tourist circuits—the archeological remains in San Augustin, and the Popayan and Boyaca areas. Prices in general and hotel prices in particular are at incentive levels compared with other Caribbean resorts. Recently, with the introduction of group inclusive tour fares, Colombia has become competitive in air fares with the rest of the Caribbean. A strong impetus to tourist development in the Santa Marta area will be given by the opening in late 1971 of the Caribbean Trunk Road linking Venezuela with the Colombian coast. Public sector support to tourist development would have to include improvement of infra-structure, particularly water supply and sewerage, on the coast and on the island of San Andres. Tourist development will contribute, at a relatively low investment cost, to alleviation of unemployment which is particularly high in the coastal area (18% in Barranquilla).[1]

The coffee upswing took place in the fall of 1969, with world market prices rising 40-50% in six months. Since coffee still accounts for a third of Colombian agricultural production, a tenth of gross domestic product, a tenth of central government revenue, and 60-65% of merchandise exports,[2] the impact on the economy was pervasive.

The immediate cause of the upswing was the frost which severely affected the Brazilian output of 1970/71. The underlying cause was the turn in the postwar world coffee cycle.[3]

1. See Chapter 21, *Tourism*.
2. See Chapter 15, *Coffee*.
3. Since the turn of the century, the world coffee economy has displayed distinctive wavelike movements, each lasting about 20 years, in which brief periods of shortages, high prices and excessive investment have been followed by prolonged periods of over-production, low prices and destruction of capital stock, leading to a new shortage and thus beginning of a new cycle.

Following its downward phase from the mid-1950s to the late 1960s, characterized by an avalanche of supplies, surplus stock accumulation and depressed prices the world coffee economy has been experiencing deficits of current production in relation to current consumption for a number of years and on a substantial scale (Table 1-6). The 1970/71 production deficit was the largest in recorded coffee history, equivalent to 24% of world consumption (Chart 1-I).

Disposals from stocks filled the production deficits and dampened the rate of price increases. These disposals were accelerated sharply in late 1970, following a decision by the International Coffee Council in August requesting the producing countries to increase substantially the export quotas. World coffee prices immediately turned downward. The New York price of Colombian coffee which averaged 42.6 cents in 1968 and had risen to 60 cents in early 1970, fell to 47.6 cents by mid-1971.

The official projections made in early 1970 anticipated the price decline but were wrong in its timing: it was expected that the price will remain unchanged in 1970 and 1971, and then fall gradually (by some 20% by 1975) as Brazilian production recovered and new output likely to be generated by higher prices reached the market. On these assumptions earnings from coffee were estimated to average US$500 million annually in 1970-72, compared to US$340 million in 1967-69—an increase of almost 50%. Actual exports in 1970 were US$467 million—see Table 1-4—quite close to the projection, but those for 1971 will be substantially lower. The level after 1971 will be determined by the manner in which the remaining world coffee stocks are handled, and by coffee production policies. The first issue very much depends on the position taken by the major consuming countries in the International Coffee Council, as demonstrated during the last year. Adequate stock management would strengthen prices in the short run. The second issue is in the hands of the producing countries: if major new investments in coffee plantings can be avoided—through coordinated export tax policies, price policies, credit restrictions, administrative measures or a combination—world coffee prices over the long-run would be considerably above the historical average. Colombia, which accounts for 14% of world coffee sup-

Table 1-6: COFFEE, WORLD CONSUMPTION AND PRODUCTION[1]
(In millions of bags of 60 kgs)

	Consumption			Production	Surplus (+) or Deficit (−)
	Imports into Consuming Countries	Consumption in Producing Countries	Total		
1961	44	13	57	67	+10
1962	47	14	61	73	+12
1963	49	14	63	69	+ 6
1964	49	14	63	66	+ 3
1965	47	15	62	59	− 3
1966	50	16	66	82	+16
1967	49	17	66	58	− 8
1968	56	17	73	69	− 4
1969	53	18	71	61	−10
1970	53	18	71	65	− 6
1971	53[2]	19[2]	72	55	−17[2]
1972	54[2]	19[2]	73	67-71[3]	-2 to -6[2]

[1]Calendar year for consumption; preceding crop year for production (i.e., 1971 means crop year 1970/71).

[2]Estimates.

[3]Preliminary for crop year 1971/72.

Source: U.S. Department of Agriculture, *World Agricultural Production and Trade,* for production; George Gordon Paton & Co., *Complete Coffee Coverage,* for consumption.

CHART 1-I

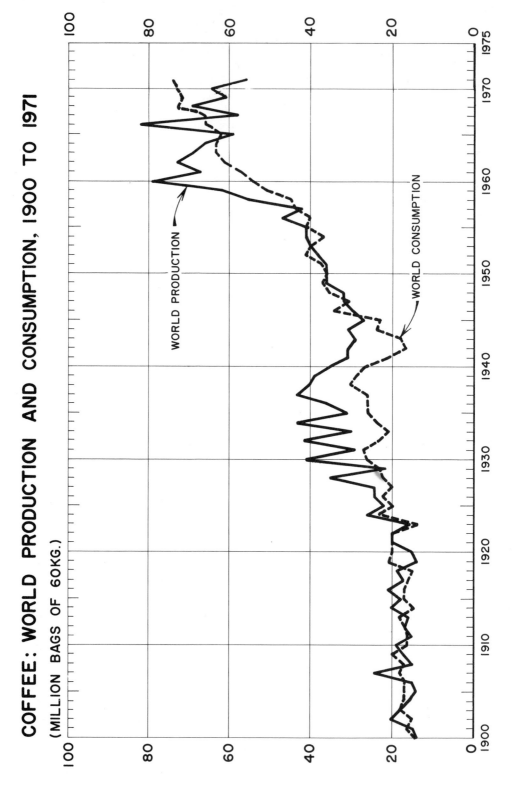

COFFEE: WORLD PRODUCTION AND CONSUMPTION, 1900 TO 1971

(MILLION BAGS OF 60KG.)

WORLD PRODUCTION

WORLD CONSUMPTION

NOTE: Before 1921, exportable production and net imports.

IBRD – 4156(2R)

ply, has been in the forefront of international efforts to control the world coffee market in a coordinated manner. Success in these efforts, which only partly depends on Colombia, accompanied by vigorous expansion of non-traditional exports, would mean that for the first time since the mid-1950s growth of domestic output and investment would not be seriously constrained by a shortage of exchange. Conversely, a prolonged slump in the coffee market and mediocre results in non-traditional exports, would make it very difficult to raise the economy's growth rate significantly above the historical average.

The Employment Challenge

Urban Unemployment

In its recently published study,[4] the ILO Inter-Agency Team has estimated open urban unemployment at 14% of the labor force in 1967. This is an average of sample surveys in eight cities, including the largest four.

In addition, there is underemployment and "disguised" unemployment—persons without work who would probably seek it if open unemployment were lower. The ILO Team estimates these groups at 12% of the urban labor force on a full-time equivalent basis, again in 1967 (Table 1-7).

Table 1-7: URBAN UNEMPLOYMENT AND UNDEREMPLOYMENT, 1967
(Percentage of active urban labor force)

		Total	Males	Females
1.	Open Unemployment –– persons without work and seeking it	14	12	19
2.	Disguised Unemployment –– persons without work and who would probably seek it if unemployment were much lower	(7)[3]	10	n.a.[2]
3.	Open Underemployment[1] –– persons working less than 32 hours per week and seeking to work longer	2	2	1
4.	Disguised Underemployment[1] –– persons working less than 32 hours per week, and who would probably seek longer hours if the opportunity were available	3	2	4
	TOTAL	(25)	25	(25)[3]

[1]The proportion of the labor force working less than 32 hours a week is larger than this figure which is obtained by expressing the number of hours of underemployment in units of 48 hours (i.e. in its full-time equivalent) before the percentage is worked out.

[2]No estimate possible but probably substantial.

[3]Incomplete total; see footnote 2.

Source: ILO, op. cit., p. 15.

Partial evidence suggests that open urban unemployment has declined since 1967 (Table 1-8).

4. ILO, *Towards Full Employment, A Programme for Colombia,* May 1970. The Inter-Agency Team was headed by Prof. Dudley Seers, Institute of Development Studies, University of Sussex.

Table 1-8:   UNEMPLOYMENT RATE IN BOGOTA, 1963-70 (%)

1963[1]			1967		
March		8.4	April		16.0
June		8.7	June		12.7
September		7.4	September		10.6
December		7.1	December		9.5
Average	7.9		Average	12.2	
1964[1]			1968		
March		6.7	March		13.5
June		7.2	June		11.6
September		7.4	September		11.2
Average	7.1		December		9.8
			Average	11.5	
1965			1969		
April		9.2	March		11.0
June		8.8	June		11.6
September		9.7	September		8.9
December		8.0	December		6.9
Average	8.9		Average	9.6	
1966			1970		
March		10.1	March		8.8
June		11.5			
September		9.7			
December		9.1			
Average	10.1				

[1]In 1963 and 1964 the labor force includes persons of age 14 and over; in other years, 10 and over.

Source: Centro de Estudios sobre Desarrollo Economico (CEDE), Universidad de los Andes.

There are no recent unemployment surveys for cities other than Bogota. On the average, their unemployment in the past was higher by 2-3 percentage points. If they have experienced a similar movement but of a lesser magnitude than Bogota, open urban unemployment in Colombia now may average 10% to 12%.

The massive increase in unemployment in the mid-1960s was associated with low output growth rates and depressed investment:[5] the apparent improvement in the late 1960s coincided with acceleration in output growth and investment.[6]

5. In 1965-67 aggregate output rose at 4.4% per annum, industrial production at 5%, and gross fixed investment averaged 16.7% of gross product, all three below historical trend values.

6. In 1969-70 aggregate output rose at 6.5% to 7.0%, industrial production at 8.0%, and investment reached 20% of gross product, all three above historical trend values.

Labor Force Growth

For the next ten to fifteen years Colombia's labor force is projected to grow at 3.5% per annum, one of the highest rates in the world.

The expected labor force growth rate is higher than in the past, primarily because of an acceleration of population growth. Even if the latter, at present estimated at 3.3% per annum, were to fall off in the immediate future because of a reduction in the birth rate the growth of the labor force would be unchanged for the next fifteen years, since the expected entrants into the labor force have already been born. But unless the birth rate falls faster than the death rate, the problem, already grave, will be compounded in later years.[7]

During the last two decades employment rose by 2.2% per annum. This was associated with an output growth rate of less than 5% per annum. Continuation of these trends would lead to staggering numbers of unemployed, in view of the prospective labor force growth of 3.5% per annum.

With an average productivity (output per man-year) growth of 3.2% per annum, output has to increase at 6.7% to absorb new entrants into the labor force. Output has to increase at 7% to 8% if unemployment is to be reduced. This is a challenge common to most Latin American countries—see the Prebisch Report.[8]

The Rural Problem

Urban unemployment results in part from massive migration of the rural population. Between 1951 and 1964 the three largest cities grew at 7% per annum, more than double the rate of natural increase; all cities grew at 5.4%, while population in the rural areas increased at only 1.3%. More than one-half of the total population now lives in cities.[9]

A massive exodus from agriculture, in the face of insufficient employment opportunities in urban centers, is explained by poor living conditions for much of the rural population. It has been argued that agricultural real wages have changed little since 1935—a fall in the following 15-20 years being made up by a rise which ended in 1963, and that the bottom third of the rural population is probably no better off than in the 1930s.[10] The supply of basic facilities—water, health care, electricity—are vastly inferior in the rural areas.[11] Almost two-thirds of the schools in the rural areas provide only one or two years of schooling. As a result, of the total number of children enrolled in the first grade of primary schools, only 3% complete the fifth grade of such schools, while secondary education and vocational training facilities are virtually non-existent in the rural areas.[12]

Low incomes in agriculture reflect low productivity and the extremely small size of the vast majority of farms *(minifundias)*. In 1960 a fourth of all farms enumerated contained only one-half of a hectare (1.25 acres) and half had less than three hectares. Many of these were un-doubtedly part-time farmers relying on other employment to assure livelihood. In contrast, three-and-a-half percent of large owners were recorded to hold two-thirds of all the farm area. Some of the largest holdings are in frontier areas which are not accessible for near-term development (Table 1-9).

7. The other factor determining growth in labor supply is the degree of participation of population in active labor force (participation rate). This rate has fallen in Colombia to a very low level of below 30%, partly as a result of changes in the demographic structure of the population (rising proportion of the very young) and partly as a result of growing unemployment (reducing the incentive to seek work and thus be counted as a member of the active labor force). A further fall is not anticipated; on the contrary, participation rates are now expected to start increasing. Hence, growth in labor supply exceeds the rate of population growth over the next fifteen years. (For detailed analysis see Chapter 2, *Population, Employment, and Unemployment;* ILO, *op. cit.;* and CIAP, *Domestic Efforts and the Needs for External Financing for the Development of Colombia,* Volume II, Appendix A, February 1970.)

8. Raul Prebisch, *Change and Development, Latin America's Great Task,* Santiago 1970.

9. Cities are defined here to include centers of 1,500 and more inhabitants. For discussion of urban and regional problems see Chapter 4, *Regional and Urban Development.*

10. Unpublished estimates by Prof. Albert Berry.

11. For details, see Chapters 13, *Power,* and 23, *Water Supply,* and 24-25, *Public Health.*

12. Chapter 22, *Education and Training.*

Table 1-9:   PATTERN OF LAND DISTRIBUTION BY FARM SIZE, 1960[1]

Farm Size (Hectares)	Number of Farms	Percent of Total Number of Farms	Total Area (Hectares)	Percent of Total Area
less than				
1.0	298,071	24.7	131,993	0.5
1-3	308,352	25.5	545,964	2.0
3-5	150,182	12.4	561,019	2.0
5-10	169,145	14.0	1,164,749	4.3
10-20	114,231	9.4	1,572,076	5.8
20-30	44,049	3.6	1,043,554	3.8
30-50	42,740	3.6	1,595,147	5.8
50-100	39,990	3.3	2,680,471	9.8
100-500	36,010	3.0	6,990,471	25.6
500-1,000	4,141	0.3	2,730,704	10.0
over 1,000	2,761	0.2	8,321,619	30.4
Total	1,209,672	100.0	27,337,287	100.0

[1]Since 1960, 2 million additional hectares have been put under cultivation and 300,000 farms established.

Source: Agricultural Census, 1960.

According to officials of INCORA (the land reform agency), the figures in Table 1-9 tend to exaggerate the proportion of the land held in very large holdings: some 3-4 million hectares should be deducted from the category above 1,000 hectares and registered as reverted to the public domain, and under INCORA's control. This was mostly poor land deserted by the owners. The quality of the land varies greatly, and while some of the large holdings are good arable land, it is maintained that the majority are not. Drainage and irrigation are apparently needed in many holdings.

The problem is compounded by the improper utilization of good land, largely because of historical patterns of land ownership and use.[13] Livestock raising goes on in large holdings in fertile valleys that should presumably be planted to crops, while steep mountain slopes are frequently worked on and found denuded of their natural forests and therefore exposed to erosion. Many family farms are simply too small to support a decent level of living even where operated with reasonable efficiency. These issues are discussed more thoroughly in the next section and in Chapter 14, *Structure and Problems of Colombian Agriculture.*

Major Issues of Resource Allocation

A continuing emphasis on export diversification and a systematic policy of containment of the coffee sector represent necessary but not sufficient conditions for high rates of growth and employment. Rates of growth in industry and non-coffee agriculture will have to be stepped up substantially, infrastructure facilities will have to be created, and there is a great need for new facilities in education, health, and water supply. There is also a need for reasonable balance between capital and current expenditures. Public policy influences resource allocation decisions in three ways: through capital and current expenditures of the government and its decentralized agencies: through the management of credit; and through price policy, including here tariff protection, price support, subsidies, tax incentives, and foreign exchange arrangements. The Colombian authorities have made extensive use of all three devices. The latter two—price policy and credit management—have been particularly important in the commodity producing sectors—agriculture and industry.

13. See on this ILO, op. cit., pp. 59-63.

Commodity Producing Sectors: Costs and Prices

In relation to international prices, the cost and price levels of Colombian production at present broadly fall into three categories.

(a)   Coffee is produced and sold on the world market at an effective exchange rate of Col$11 per US$ (compared to the over-all exchange rate of Col$18 per US$).[14] The effective coffee exchange rate results from export taxes of 40%.

(b)   A variety of agricultural products and manufactures enter the export market at an effective exchange rate of Col$20 per US$ or are competitive with imports at an effective exchange rate up to Col$23 per US$. Among agricultural products, lowest cost items are bananas, cotton, soybeans, timber, and fish. Among manufactures, lowest cost are textiles, cement, glass, paper products, some chemicals, and processed foods. The effective export exchange rate results from the application of an export subsidy on non-traditional products,[15] and the effective import exchange rate reflects a comparison of domestic and foreign prices for a large number of products.

(c)   Two staple foodstufs, wheat and corn, have support prices 40-50% above world market prices, i.e. an effective exchange rate of Col$25-27 per US$. (The situation in rice, the third major staple, is complex.[16]) Among manufactured products, prices of consumer durables are very high; this partly reflects high duties on imported inputs, but it also results from low production volumes and perhaps high assembly costs. Some chemicals also have high prices—an effective exchange rate above Col$27 per US$. Domestically produced capital goods have an average duty of 40%, i.e. an effective exchange rate of Col$25 per US$; this again is influenced by duties of similar magnitude on imported inputs.

It would follow from the above that Colombia has a clear comparative advantage in coffee production since it can export coffee at an effective exchange rate of Col$11 per US$, while almost all other activities call for an effective exchange rate above Col$20 per US$. The implication is that, in relation to international price, costs in coffee are about one-half of costs in other sectors, or less. This comparative advantage cannot be realized and may be illusory, however; because of slow growth in world demand, the large Colombian share of the market, and quota arrangements which help maintain the world price, Colombia can channel only very limited additional resources into coffee production. The major outlets to growth have to be sought in other sectors.

Can Columbia achieve full employment on a sustained basis by channeling its resources into the next best group of activities—those under (b) which are competitive with foreign producers at an effective exchange rate range of Col$20-23 per US$? This question cannot be answered satisfactorily at the present time, but it is possible to suggest ways in which solutions can be sought.

Agriculture

The Colombian agricultural resource base is such that, judging from recent experience, it can assure satisfactory supply of most products both for home and export markets within the indicated price range. This is possible because of the extraordinary variety of soils and climates

14. Rates as of mid-1970. The findings also apply to the situation in 1971.

15. Subsidy in the form of tax certificates equal to 15% of the value of exports, less a discount for one-year mandatory waiting period (20% of the value of the certificates), applied to the overall exchange rate of Col$18 per US$, equals an effective exchange rate of Col$20 per US$.

16. The support price, at the overall exchange rate, is US$191 per metric ton, but the domestic market price is $150 (1970). The world market price in 1968-1969 averaged $185, but is expected to fall to $125 per ton by 1975.

and cheap labor supply. It is puzzling why long-run output growth has been so sluggish (3.4% per annum). With proper incentives since 1966, it has accelerated to more than 5.5%. Agricultural trade balance (excluding coffee), on the average a negative US$25 million per annum in 1960-66 turned into a positive US$55 million in 1969; agricultural exports other than coffee have lately been increasing at 25% per annum. Output expansion has been particularly rapid in grain sorghum, soybeans, cotton, sugar, and rice.

The key problem of Colombia's agriculture is low average yield. Its potential is indicated by high yields achieved on successful farms, yields which compare favorably with yields achieved in other developing countries, even those which have specialized in particular crops (see Chapter 18, *Unemployment, Labor Absorption and the Future Possibilities in Agriculture*).

Two main policy questions loom very large in agriculture:

(a)   Which crops should be stimulated, through price support, credit, and government investment and research?

(b)   At what speed should land reform be carried out?

In principle, the decisive considerations in answering the first question are the differences in time and costs involved in raising yields of different crops: those crops should be stimulated for which time and cost requirements are likely to be lowest. A complication arises because property relations in agriculture differ considerably for different crops: stimulation of a promising crop grown primarily by large commercial farmers would not help the large majority of small farmers. And the other way around: a crop may not be particularly promising over the short run, but if grown primarily by large numbers of small farmers, might merit support on social as well as economic grounds. In some cases the conflict can be avoided: grain sorghum, output of which has increased rapidly, and which is badly needed as input for meat production, is primarily grown by small farmers; cocoa, which has excellent natural growing conditions and which is needed as a substitute for imports, is grown on medium-sized farms and its expansion is likely to be concentrated there as well (Table 1-10). But cotton, a very rapidly expanding crop, is primarily grown by large commerical farmers; while corn and wheat, the least competitive of all crops, are found primarily in smaller farms. (There is, however, no reason why cotton cannot be grown by smallholders or corn or wheat on commercial scale farms.)

Table 1-10:   CROP AREA IN RELATION TO FARM SIZE
(Percentages)

Crop	Farms 0-5 Hectares	Farms 5-50 Hectares	Farms 50-200 Hectares	Farms over 200 Hectares	Total
Cotton	3.9	18.8	28.6	48.7	100.0
Rice	7.1	26.2	28.2	38.5	100.0
Sorghum & Millet	35.3	41.3	14.3	9.1	100.0
Cocoa	17.1	53.8	18.6	10.5	100.0
Corn	26.2	42.3	18.0	13.1	100.0
Wheat	30.6	52.5	12.3	4.6	100.0

Source: Chapter 14, Structure and Problems of Colombian Agriculture.

These circumstances preclude ideal solutions, but they still allow for intelligent solutions. Situations should be avoided in which support prices lead to such output expansion of a non-competitive crop that large financial losses are sustained by the government in exports, as happened with rice in 1969. Similarly, the objective of corn price support policy might not be to generate export surpluses, but to meet the rapidly rising domestic demand for feed (together with sorghum). While support to domestic wheat production will continue to be needed, it is debatable whether Colombia should strive for self-sufficiency if non-traditional exports grow rapidly (and therefore imports can be paid for). It is doubtful whether the policy of subsidized credit should continue with respect to large commercial farmers: social objectives would be adequately served if subsidized credit is available only to small farmers. (A dual support price system—higher prices for small farmers and lower for large ones—is difficult, but dual credit conditions are feasible.) Commercial farming appears sufficiently profitable to be able to afford the full cost of credit.[17]

The second question concerning the speed of land reform has been discussed extensively, most recently by the ILO team. A powerful agency, INCORA, has taken a leading role not only in agrarian reform but in rural development generally: it is engaged in supervised agricultural credit, in large-scale irrigation and drainage works, colonization, and preparation of preinvestment studies.[18] Further preinvestment studies, one covering an entire region, are proposed.[19] The organization is now able to carry out land redistribution and to support the beneficiaries much better than several years ago.

Over the long run, there is no reason to think that agrarian reform would adversely affect output. An individually operated farm is likely to enjoy a much larger labor input and can be planted to higher value crops than the farm worked by tenants and hired labor.[20] Over the short run, the critical question is how adequate are supporting services following the reform. The experience thus far is encouraging: the yields on small holdings in the INCORA projects, where adequate technical assistance and credit are provided, compare favorably with yields on large commercial farms.[21] If this pattern can be maintained fears of a short-run decline in output would not be justified, while social benefits of agrarian reform would be enormous. Income distribution in agriculture, which is more skewed than in the urban areas,[22] would improve, and so would rural living standards; while the migratory flow off the land would be slowed down, relieving the pressure of unemployment in the cities.

As pointed out by various qualified observers, a major constraint on acceleration of the pace of land redistribution and colonization in Colombia is the government's ability to provide adequate supporting services after settlement. The research, manpower training, and financing efforts needed to make land transfer an effective vehicle for rural improvement may already be near short-run limits. To step up the tempo of land distribution far beyond the country's ability to furnish these essential services could result in the creation of thousands of new subsistence farmers barely able to eke out a living from their new plots. Since this is not a pleasant prospect, it must be concluded that Colombia will do everything possible to train and recruit new agricultural extension people, soil scientists, crop experts, education and public health specialists, and, in short, do what is necessary to permit a more rapid and equitable utilization of the country's land resources.

17. In a sample survey of fourteen export products in 1968, the highest profit margins were recorded in bananas and cotton, the chief non-coffee farm exports. Margins amounted to 16% of sales.

18. See Chapter 14. (Drainage and irrigation works have proven to be quite expensive per family benefited.)

19. See Chapter 5, *Preinvestment Study Program*

20. ILO, *op. cit.*, pp. 64-65. There is an apparent inconsistency between the evidence shown in Chapter 14, which indicates that yields per hectare in a number of crops increase with farm size, and the evidence quoted by ILO which states that gross value of output per hectare on the sub-family farms is much higher than on the very large farms. One possible explanation may be that the very large farms normally use a large proportion of land for livestock grazing (which has low output value per hectare) or leave part of the land unworked, while sub-family farms use all the land for growing the highest value crop that is technically possible. The result would then be that even if large farms achieve higher yields in individual crops, they obtain lower gross value per hectare owned, on the average.

21. See Chapter 14.

22. In 1960 the 5% of the population in agriculture with highest incomes received 40% of total farm income, and had an average income which was twenty times as high as the median income of the agricultural population. In the cities in 1964, the corresponding figures are one-third and nine. (Albert Berry, *The Distribution of Agriculturally Based Income in Colombia,* 1960; Miguel Urrutia y Clara Elsa Villalba, *"La distribucion del ingreso urbano para Colombia en 1964,"* Revista del Banco de la Republica, September 1969.) It is unlikely that the situation has changed radically since.

Industry

Tariffs for Colombian manufacturing are relatively high: two-fifths of the items carry duties above 45% implying an effective exchange rate in excess of Col$25 per US$ for the products concerned. It is questionable, however, how representative this is for the cost and price level of the industrial sector as a whole. About one-half of Colombian manufacturing still consists of non-durable consumer goods (Table 1-11) where economies of scale are not important and where prices do not compare unfavorably with foreign prices at the exchange rate range of Col$20-23 per US$. Another third of industrial output consists of intermediate goods where economies of scale are relevant: in several major product groups in this category Colombia has become an exporter at the exchange rate of Col$20 per US$. The key issue for Colombian manufacturing is not that the present industrial structure is inefficient and high-cost, although inefficiencies exist, but what policies would have to be pursued in the future to avoid major misallocations of resources while still assuring rapid industrial growth. This question is particularly relevant for the intermediate and capital goods industries.

As for intermediate goods, Colombian prices are reasonably competitive with import prices in steel, for the limited range of products that are domestically produced, although this may be less so when the world market weakens as is now expected. Steel consumption is of the order of 600,000 tons and is projected to increase to close to 1 million tons by 1975. It is of crucial importance for the future of the Colombian engineering industries that they obtain as low-cost steel as possible, and the issue of phases of development and location of an integrated industry

Table 1-11:   STRUCTURE AND GROWTH OF MANUFACTURING OUTPUT

	Gross Value Added, 1967[1] (Col$ million)		Annual Growth Rate 1953-1967
Non-durable consumer goods		8,430	5.3
Food	2,442		
Beverages	2,072		
Textiles	1,001		
Clothing and footwear	644		
Pharmaceuticals	1,183		
Other	1,088		
Durable consumer goods		1,004	8.0
Intermediate goods		4,940	8.7
Textiles	1,001		
Chemicals	866		
Non-metallic minerals	794		
Metal products	674		
Petroleum and coal products	572		
Paper and products, basic metals, leather, and wood	1,034		
Capital goods[2]		621	11.5
Other		412	13.3
		15,406	6.7

[1] For conversion into dollars the 1967 exchange rate of Col$ 15 per US$ should be used.

[2] Except appliances and motor vehicles.

Source: Chapter 6, *Role and Characteristics of Colombian Manufacturing,* and *Statistical Annex.*

(interior versus Atlantic coast) is suggested for a priority preinvestment study. Domestic production of fertilizer, another key intermediate product, appears competitive with import prices, but distribution costs are very high and there is great uncertainty regarding specific mixes needed for the different crops in the highly varied soils and climates of Colombia. This complex of issues and the associated further development of the industry also call for urgent detailed investigation. In other chemicals the production is new, technical efficiency is below international standards, and the scale of output too low. Prices are particularly high in synthetic fibers. It is suggested that further development of the petrochemical industry be planned in the context of the Andean regional market.[23] Production of construction materials such as cement and asbestos products is quite competitive: these materials enter the export market. Also competitive are petroleum and coal products, paper, wood products and textiles.

The Colombian market for capital goods is now of the order of US$400 million per annum, and it should grow rapidly. The development of the domestic engineering industries would be stimulated if present high duties on imported inputs for these industries were reduced.[24] Given the relatively small size of the market, the industry would find it useful to specialize in particular products and in parts of particular production lines—perhaps in interchange with major international manufacturers—to the maximum extent possible. Planning growth of a domestic engineering industry and associated adjustments in domestic tariff, licensing, and credit arrangements will be a novel experience. It is suggested that a special unit be established in the government to carry out the needed market and production studies and to make recommendations concerning policy changes and specific licensing decisions.

The introduction of the flexible exchange rate and the across-the-board export subsidy on non-traditional products in 1967 has played a crucial role in shaping the Colombian industrial structure. By this measure Colombia has taken a major step to insure not only that rising domestic demand for imported industrial inputs will be matched by an expansion of industrial exports and thus of import capacity needed to sustain rapid industrial growth, but also that specialized production for the world market can compete for productive factors with production for the protected domestic market, thus raising the efficiency in resource use all-around. It is of fundamental importance that this policy be continued, in one form or another. Thus, if in order to accelerate industrial growth it is necessary to raise effective protection on engineering and/or intermediate goods and this cannot be achieved by reducing duties on imported inputs, the increase in protection should be accompanied by an increase in the export subsidy. This would obviate the need for extremely high protection and the associated increases in real costs and disincentives for capital investment, while still achieving the objective of rapid industrialization.

One of the major problems which will face industry in Colombia, in common with other developing countries, is trade restrictions in major foreign markets. Colombia has developed an efficient, high-quality textile industry, based on domestic raw materials, which is now emerging as a major exporter. Its export effort can be supplemented by a massive expansion of ready-made clothing, a field where other developing countries have made major advances. But if expansion is thwarted by foreign restrictions on trade, Colombia will be pushed into developing other subsectors where it is less efficient and where higher rates of protection and subsidy will be needed. The example of textiles is not unique. The objective of full employment will be much more difficult to attain if the present climate in international trade relations persists.

Commodity Producing Sectors: Credit Allocation

Colombian industrialists and bankers maintain that the major obstacle to industrial expansion at the present time is shortage of credit for working capital. This complaint can mean two different things: (a) credit to industry and commerce is more expensive than credit to other sectors; and (b) credit from the organized banking system is simply not available for certain

23. See Chapter 5, *Preinvestment Study Program.*
24. The duty on copper products is 35-40%, on parts for electrical machinery 40% and on parts for mechanical machinery 50%.

classes of industrial borrowers. The statistical evidence confirms (a): credit is regulated in such fashion that industry and commerce pay substantially higher interest rates than other sectors. Lending to industry and commerce for working capital is done mostly by commercial banks at the nominal interest rate of 14%;[25] to this should be added commissions and there is also a frequent practice of requiring compensating balances; the result is an effective interest rate of 17-18%. Lending to agriculture, mostly through the Caja Agraria and the Livestock Bank, occurs predominantly at interest rates ranging from 8-11%(Table 1-12). Similarly, lending for housing carries interest rates of 9-13%.[26] It is maintained that some industrial and commercial borrowers of lower credit standing have to obtain funds in the street market at 2% per month or higher; this market is allegedly fed in part from loans obtained by livestock raisers at low agricultural interest rates.

Table 1-12: PORTFOLIO OF THE BANKING SYSTEM BY INTEREST RATES, 1968
(In thousands of Col$)

Interest Rate	Commercial Banks	Caja Agraria & Banco Ganadero	Mortgage Bank	Financieras[1]
0-6	186,407	173,444	72,287	–
7-8	919,579	1,272,564	44,985	5,746
9-10	1,139,826	949,398	428,800	566,347
11-12	928,522	1,804,788	1,121,822	197,354
13-14	4,800,004	91,615	263,810	596,158
15-16	125,255	1,774	–	306,251
17-18	9,188	–	822,866	586,631
Total	8,108,781	4,293,583	2,754,570	2,271,000

[1]70% of the portfolio is owed by industry and another 25% by construction activities.

Sources: Banco de la Republica, P.I.F. and I.F.I.

There is no direct evidence to confirm (b), inability of certain classes of industrial borrowers to obtain short-term credit. Credit to industry and commerce has risen at a significantly lower rate than the gross product of these two sectors, however, (see Table 1-13) implying a credit shortage which may mean that commercial banks have tightened creditworthiness standards and restricted lending to other than prime customers. This may have affected particularly severely the smaller firms with limited fixed assets: their ability to offer collateral is limited, although their potential to offer employment and thus the need for working capital may be substantial.

Until recently it did not appear that there was a shortage of long-term funds for industrial investment: the industrial portfolio of the *financieras* rose from Col$981 million at the end of 1967 to Col$2,281 million at the end of 1969. Lately, the draw-down on *financiera* resources has accelerated and the applications for loans with the five largest *financieras* are now 35% above the last year's level. At the same time demand for short-term credit, responding to an acceleration of industrial activity, must have risen sharply, bringing to a head the complaints about its shortage. This shortage appears to be felt in the first instance at the level of commerce: the lag in banking accommodation to commerce (the share of commerce in total credit has fallen from 22% in 1960 to 15% in 1969) is apparently offset by industry extending credit to distributors, which then causes a liquidity squeeze in industry itself.

25. The part of the portfolio of commercial banks at interest rates below 14%, shown in Table 1-12 is owed by privileged borrowers, mostly the agricultural sector, to which commercial banks have to lend a stated percentage of their resources.

26. The exception is lending by the mortgage bank for general purposes (30% of its portfolio where the house is collateral); these transactions take place at 17%.

Table 1-13: INDUSTRY AND COMMERCE: LOANS BY COMMERCIAL
AND SPECIALIZED BANKS (OTHER THAN FINANCIERAS)
AND GDP, 1960-69
(In millions of current Col$)

	Credit Outstanding			GDP			Credit outstanding as percentage of GDP
	Industry	Commerce	Total	Industry	Commerce	Total	
1960	756	963	1,719	4,939	4,086	9,025	19
1961	933	1,128	2,061	5,655	4,476	10,131	20
1962	977	1,276	2,253	6,708	4,799	11,507	20
1963	1,372	1,452	2,824	9,050	5,990	15,040	19
1964	1,662	1,397	3,059	10,320	8,033	18,353	17
1965	1,763	1,635	3,398	11,966	9,803	21,769	16
1966	2,088	1,798	3,886	14,213	12,800	27,013	14
1967	2,443	2,146	4,589	15,662	13,879	29,541	16
1968	2,711	2,559	5,270	17,550	16,711	34,261	15
1969	3,112	2,786	5,898	20,095	19,210	39,305	15

Source: Banco de la Republica.

Three conclusions follow from the above. First, if the demand for finance by the commodity producing sectors continues to be high, room for government borrowing from the banking system during the next several years will be narrow. Second, foreign lending agencies should consider allowing their credit lines to be used for lending for working capital. Third, a comprehensive reform of the Colombian credit system is needed. As a result of a series of regulations over the years, there is at present an array of lending windows for different classes of borrowers, each class enjoying different terms; a very large proportion of the resources of the banking system is preassigned to favored borrowers; and the burden of adjustment, in terms of high interest rates and shortage of credit, falls with full force on the residual claimants. Credit management has not been pushed to the point at which there are significant classes of borrowers obtaining credit at negative real rates of interest, but while rates in real terms for industry are as high as 10-11% those for agriculture and housing range from 1-6%. There is a case for low subsidized interest rates for small farmers and also for low-income housing. It is difficult to find a case for such rates either for large commercial farmers or for middle-income and high-income housing. With respect to agriculture, there probably should be a transitional period in order to avoid the risk of disturbances to production. The authorities are aware of the imperfections and complexity of the present system and have been examining its operation and the possibilities of reform. This is an urgent issue requiring priority attention.

Infrastructure: Transport and Power

Considerable progress has been made in assuring improved supplies of transportation services and electric power. In both sectors large investments have been made in the past; public policy in both has faced the problem of integrating separate systems into national networks; both will continue to claim large public resources, although their proportionate shares, particularly that of transport, may decline; and in both there are unresolved issues of administration and of financial policy although in different degrees.

Transport.   Colombia has coastlines on both the Pacific Ocean and the Caribbean Sea; but this transport advantage is offset by the difficulty of movement between the coasts and the interior. The three massive ranges of the Andes present formidable barriers to communication between the main areas of population and production, which until recently developed as separate and almost isolated communities. Transport investment policy over the past twenty years has been aimed at national integration and at overcoming the situation imposed by geography. Within the next few years the task of establishing what might be termed the basic transport network of the country should be completed.

Investment in transport averaged 30% of public investment in the four years 1966-69, two-thirds of which was for highway construction and improvement. The emphasis has been on the main trunk system, and this component of expenditure will continue to loom large in the total during the next several years as projects now under way are completed. The emphasis will be gradually changing, however, with increasing attention being given to the subsidiary network, including feeder roads. It is suggested that planning of the latter be done in the context of specific schemes for agricultural improvement, to the maximum extent possible. This is the case in particular in the southern and south-eastern parts of the country (Narino, Caqueta and Meta) where colonization is taking place, as well as in the north (Cesar and Ariguani Valleys). In constructing feeder roads, the possibility of maximum use of labor should also be examined.

Colombia's railways have been experiencing declining passenger traffic and stagnating freight traffic for a number of years, and they will face further problems of adjustment as the trunk road system is completed. About 260 km of apparently uneconomic lines (out of a total of 3,400 km) are being studied for possible closure. Further rationalization of operations is needed, to reduce the number of derailments, improve the service, and improve the financial position. Needed investments include track rehabilitation, replacement of old rolling stock, and acquisition of additional motive power.

Recent and scheduled investments are expected to provide adequate capacity in the major ports. Cargo handling has presented a problem, particularly in customs clearance, and it is suggested that a management study of port operations be undertaken.[27]

Power.   During the last twelve years, energy demand has been increasing at 11% per annum. This rate will be maintained and probably accelerated in the future. The resource base is excellent: large hydroelectric potential in the extensive central mountain system, oil in the north and southwest, natural gas in the north, and coal in several parts of the cordilleras. A large investment program is under way and additional investments are planned or are proposed for study.[28]

Steps have been taken since 1969 to interconnect the various regional systems in the central and southern parts of the country, which will permit the development of larger and more economical projects and joint planning of power utilization. Similarly, steps are now under way to interconnect individual systems in the north. With these developments Colombia is approaching a fully integrated national power network: it is suggested that a preinvestment study be undertaken to examine alternative programs of transmission and generation projects to achieve such full integration.

Despite large investments in the past shortages of power have been frequent in particular areas, and they were especially noticeable in 1969 when demand accelerated. There have been gaps in both generating and distribution facilities; present investments are expected to fill the deficits in power generation, while studies are under way to develop a comprehensive program of subtransmission and urban distribution projects. The latter have been particularly lagging. The standardization of types and sizes of equipment and materials for distribution facilities, expected from ongoing studies, will facilitate greater use of local manufactures. Domestic industry is able to produce a fairly wide range of equipment: small transformers, cables, insulators, conduits and fittings, poles, steel towers, minor switchgear and control boards, lighting fixtures, etc. Practically all of these local manufactures include foreign components or materials in various degrees, and their prices are usually higher than those of foreign supplies for public utilities which are exempted from import duties. Domestic producers will have to undertake capacity expansion and improve quality control to be able to meet the expected increase of demand, while adjustments in tariffs and in procurement practices of the utilities

27. Chapter 5, *Preinvestment Study Program.*
28. See Chapter 13, *Power.*

are needed to enable the domestic producers to compete with foreign suppliers within a reasonable margin of effective protection.

Rural electrification is in its initial stages in Colombia, and the only systematic program thus far has been carried out in the coffee-growing regions in cooperation with the Coffee Federation. There is an increasing awareness of the need to approach the program on a national scale. Solutions will have to be worked out through close coordination between the electrical agencies and agricultural entities, such as INCORA, the Caja Agraria and the Coffee Bank. Because of the magnitude and complexity of the issue it is suggested that a comprehensive preinvestment study be undertaken to prepare and evaluate alternative programs of rural electrification in priority areas, including preliminary designs, estimates of construction costs, and future financial position, which could then serve as a basis for determining the scope and the rate at which rural electrification can be undertaken.

The power sector suffers from inadequate and poorly structured rates in parts of the system. The establishment of a comprehensive and rational tariff policy has been needed for years; until recently, tariff adjustments have been granted on an *ad hoc* basis, and sometimes they have been too little and too late. In 1968 the Government established the Public Utilities Board (Junta Nacional de Tarifas de Servicios Publicos) as part of the Planning Department to regulate public utility tariffs, including their restructuring and upward adjustments to cover operating expenditures and provide a reasonable return on revalued assets. A comprehensive system of analysis and procedure has been worked out, including national uniformity in accounting, reporting, and valuation techniques. The Planning Department is now considering the revision of the basic structure of tariffs. The problem to be resolved by all these activities is of some significance: the national government's budgetary subsidies to service the debt of the *Instituto Colombiano de Energia Electrica,* a holding company for 28 utilities, have increased from Col$45 million in 1968 to Col$73 million in 1969 and are programmed at Col$120 million for 1970 (US$6.0 million). Only a part of these amounts is channeled to rural electrification systems.

Social Sectors

Education. In the last decade, Colombia has been confronted with the problem of reconciling demands for school places and the need to improve and reorient the education system. Under the pressure of growing social aspirations and the strain of the population explosion, expansion in practice received priority. Overall enrollments between 1960 and 1968 increased on average at a rate of 6.2%, 11% and 14.2% per annum in primary, secondary and higher education respectively with enrollments in 1968 of 2.7 million in primary, 0.6 million in secondary and 64,000 in higher. (Table 1-14)

Traditionally, there have been inequalities in the distribution of educational opportunity, and development of technical skills has been lagging. The overall rate of illiteracy was reduced considerably between 1951 and 1964, but it has remained three times higher in the rural areas

Table 1-14: SCHOOL ENROLLMENTS, 1960 AND 1968

Level	1960		1968	
	Enrollment in '000's	As Percentage of Appropriate School Age Population	Enrollment in '000's	As Percentage of Appropriate School Age Population
Primary	1,690	77%	2,733[1]	94%[1]
Secondary	254	9.8%	587	17%
Higher	22	1.6%	64	3%
Total	1,966	32.9%	3,384	40.6%

[1]Including 737,000 of over-age pupils; of the total 7 through 11 age group 69% were enrolled in 1968, compared with 59% in 1960.

Source: Chapter 22, *Education and Training.*

(41%) than in the urban (15%); the average length of schooling in the former was 1.7 years as compared with 5.1 years for the urban dwellers. A major problem in primary schools, particularly in the rural areas, is a large proportion of over-age students. Capital construction is lagging. Technical education has been insufficient, particularly at the medium level. Funding has not been adequate.

A number of measures have been taken in recent years. They include: development of more modern curricula; reorganization and rehabilitation of school facilities with particular reference to rationalization and consolidation at secondary and higher levels; increased pre-service and upgrading teacher programs; expansion of the multiple-grade schools to improve educational opportunities in the rural areas, combined with expansion of the tested instructional television program; establishment of well-endowed, more centrally situated first-cycle comprehensive schools and provision of text books; more systematic educational research activities. What now appears to be needed is to formulate an overall program of reform and expansion covering the next ten years, within which both a short-term project-oriented plan and the needed preinvestment studies can be determined.[29] The possible objectives of such program could be the following:

(a)   A smoothing of the flow of students through the primary education system. This would make possible achievement of universal primary education in the late 1970s, with special emphasis given to fulfilling needs in the rural areas;

(b)   a phasing out of first-cycle technical schools (which have proved ineffective), but combining this with increased provisions for first-cycle comprehensive secondary education and assumption by SENA (a successful apprentice training system) of increasing responsibility for school leavers and dropouts who have no employment skills;

(c)   a shift in the proportion of students in second-cycle, technical education or technically-oriented education from 30% of total second cycle enrollments in 1968 to about 70% in 1980;

(d)   a shift in the proportion of students in technician level courses in higher education as compared with students in degree courses from 16% of higher education enrollments in 1968 to 30% in 1980;

(e)   a giving of priority in the process of restructuring and rationalization, to conversion and reequipping over new construction, and always first providing improved facilities for the rural and rural-urban areas.

The expansion implicit in such a program would, in addition to achieving universal primary education, raise the enrollments in secondary schools from 17% of the relevant age group in 1968 to 45% in 1980, and those in higher education from 3% to 5.5%. A substantial financial cost would be involved, both in capital and in current expenditures. Total education expenditures would rise from 4% of GDP in 1968 to 4.6% and 5% in 1975 and 1980, respectively, which the country should be able to handle.

The apparent alternatives, expansion or reforms, are mutually exclusive only for so long as expansion remains undirected and uncontrolled. Additional or expanded facilities have been and will be required for implementation of some of the reforms—for example, the IBRD-assisted diversified secondary education project; the UNDP/Unesco agricultural institutes project; the proposed centralization of industrial secondary facilities; expanded and improved facilities in educationally underprivileged areas; facilities for courses to train neglected or new skills.

In judging the desirability of expansion and reform, one more factor has to be taken into account: the impact of education on fertility and on population growth. "The urban pregnancy rate of persons with some primary (and up to three years of secondary) education is some 13%

---

29. For specific suggestions see Chapter 22, *Education and Training.*

lower than for persons with no education, and a further 22% lower among persons with more than eight years of education. Differences of this order exist within both rural and urban areas, even though all the rural rates are higher. These differences are not alone sufficient to justify a program of educational expansion . . . ; but in conjunction with other programs, education can play an important part . . ."[30]

Public Health.   Between 1961 and 1969, public health expenditures rose in real terms at 9.7% per annum. The main beneficiaries of this expansion of the public health system have been the relatively small fraction of the employed population covered by social security and other special programs. Per capita public health expenditures for the preponderant segment of the population outside these programs appear to have fallen in real terms. This has inevitably affected the rural population. It is in these areas that the availability of both health personnel and health facilities is particularly low.

The above situation notwithstanding, substantial advances have been made in the reorganization of the public health system, in the supply of health services and in the institution of a comprehensive National Health Plan, 1968-77. Future advances will be faster and even more substantial than in the past if the priorities established by that Plan are followed and its objectives are met. Almost all specific programs included in the Plan—improved environmental sanitation, mass vaccination against major epidemic diseases, widespread nutrition education and dietary fortification, tuberculosis prevention, malaria eradication, augmented maternal and child health services, and expansion of comprehensive health and medical systems—call for rapid increases in current spending. A family planning program has recently been launched to cope with the urgent and mounting problems of a rapidly increasing population complicated by accelerated mass migrations to urban centers.

In the past, the building of health facilities was almost exclusively a responsibility of local authorities or local philanthropic groups. The absence of national or regional plans, insufficiency of funds to complete construction and install equipment or to initiate and maintain operations, has resulted in a large proportion of unused capital resources. A recent inventory identified 865 partially completed and unequipped hospitals and other health care facilities scattered throughout the country. This compares with 1,800 facilities now in operation. The National Health Plan has attached priority to completion and equipment of some of those unfinished structures, as well as modernization and re-equipment of the majority of existing hospitals, health centers and health posts; and it has for the first time established a rational and systematic approach to future capital investments by creating the National Hospital Plan to set standards, review and approve construction plans and award funds on a competitive basis according to a national plan.

Shortages of all categories of essential health personnel and the maldistribution of the limited health manpower supply comprise the most difficult and demanding problems currently being faced by Colombia's health leaders. These manpower problems require reorientation and augmentation of education and training at all levels, particularly for middle level personnel— auxiliary nurses, technicians of all types, medical and dental assistants, sanitarians, statistical assistants and higher level clerical workers. This will be feasible provided other educational institutions, in addition to the university medical schools, are fully mobilized for this purpose and their health manpower training programs are integrated within the framework of a national health manpower plan. Efforts in this direction are evolving but are handicapped by severe limitations in both capital and operational resources.[31]

Water Supply.   Since the mid-1960s the Colombian authorities have been expanding water supply facilities at an accelerating rate. At present about one-half of the population is

30. ILO, *op. cit.,* p. 191, based on Carlos Agualimpia et al, "Demographic Facts of Colombia," *Milbank Memorial Quarterly,* July 1969.
31. See Chapter 24, *The Present Health Situation,* and Chapter 25, *Resources for Health and the National Health Plan.*

connected to a water system or has access to water services; this compares with 40% five years ago (Table 1-15).

Table 1-15: WATER SUPPLY SERVICES AND POPULATION SERVED, 1965 and 1970

Agency	Estimated Population Under Agency Jurisdiction (millions)			Estimated Population with Water Services (millions)			Percentage of Population Served	
	1965	1970	Increase	1965	1970	Increase	1965	1970
Empresas (larger cities)	5.8	7.2	1.4	4.0	5.9	1.9	69	82
INSFOPAL (medium and smaller cities)	4.6	5.8	1.2	2.0	2.8	0.8	43	48
INPES (cities under 2,500 population and rural areas)	8.0	8.6	0.6	1.5	2.2	0.7	18	25
	18.4[1]	21.6[1]	3.2	7.5	10.9	3.4	41	51

[1]Equals total population of Colombia.

Source: Chapter 23, *Water Supply.*

Faster advance in the larger cities than in the rest of the country is explained by their financial strength and better organization. In smaller cities very low internal cash generation and the absence of long-range investment programs represent major obstacles to expansion. In the rural areas, additional factors are dispersal of population and, until recently, the absence of a national organization responsible for construction of rural water systems. Since 1968 such an organization, the National Institute for Special Health Programs (INPES), has been operating within the Ministry of Health.

Between 1965 and 1969 investment in water supply doubled; it is expected to double again by 1975. The planned expansion should meet 85% to 90% of the demand in the cities and 50% in the rural areas. Substantial advance will also have been made in the supply of sewerage facilities where the lag has been much greater than in water supply.

The achievement of these objectives will call for a major organizational effort, particularly in smaller cities and in their holding company, INSFOPAL, as well as in INPES for the rural systems. It will also call for an improvement in the financial position of the urban water systems. The national government's budget for 1970 includes subsidies to INSFOPAL for operating expenditures and debt service of its subsidiaries in the amount of Col$40 million. The government intends to reduce and eventually to eliminate these subsidies, and to use authorizations for external credits and internal financing to induce the companies to adopt the criteria which govern the operations of the Public Utilities Board. The capacity of the companies to generate funds internally and thus to meet at least a part of local currency expenditures will be a significant factor in the implementation of their plans to attract foreign finance.

Public Investment and Finance

Note: The first two parts of this section review the public investment program and financing plan 1969-72; they were written in mid-1970. The third part, written in mid-1971, summarizes the recent developments.

1970-72 Public Investment Program

Toward the end of 1969 the Government presented to Congress a Development Plan 1969-72. The plan includes a public investment program in low, medium, and high versions.

These versions correspond to different assumptions concerning growth rates of output and exports. For 1970 the government has accepted the high version and it is this version which is discussed below for the period 1970-72. It is associated, according to the plan, with overall growth rates ranging from 6.6% to 7.3% per annum.

For the purposes of the plan the public sector has been defined to exclude departments and municipalities but includes entities which "participate in foreign credit extended through the mechanism of the Consultative Group." Public investment includes debt amortization, administrative expenditures of many decentralized agencies, gross purchases of products by IDEMA (the price support agency), and various current expenditures, mainly in the field of technical assistance, training, extension services and maintenance expenditures, as well as the entire portfolio of some specialized semi-official banks.

For the purposes of the analysis below the public sector has been redefined to agree with available historical statistics as well as to correspond to the more conventional concept of public investment. Table 1-16 shows the redefined public investment program: it consolidates central, departmental, and municipal investments as well as those of decentralized agencies; it includes budgetary transfers to the private sector; but it excludes current expenditures, amortization payments, banks' portfolios, and the like. Table 1-16 also shows the mission's adjustments to the redefined program. They are mainly in electric power, water supply, education, industry, and transport. Power projects firmly planned for the next few years will require larger investments than were foreseen in the program; in water and sewerage, larger investments than those planned would be needed to achieve the objectives stated in the plan; in industry, a rescheduling of expenditures is required in view of known and probable delays in project execution; and in transport, in addition to rescheduling, there is a suggestion for a reduction. In the aggregate, these adjustments of the redefined program call for an expenditure level 4% higher than was programmed, over the three-year period.

In real terms the increase between 1969 and 1972 works out at 12% per annum. This is a deceleration from the 1966-69 period when public investment rose at the extraordinary pace of 21% per annum, but investment was starting then from a depressed level. With a 12% annual increase now projected, public investment will still be rising faster than gross product and total investment.[32]

Most of the planned increase is concentrated in 1970. Although executive capacity has risen substantially in recent years it is doubtful that the 1970 schedule can be met. Slippages which can be clearly foreseen have been taken into account in the mission's adjustments.

Finance in 1970-72

Table 1-17 sets forth the pattern of financing for 1966-69 and the projections for 1970-72. The basic assumptions underlying the projections are:

(a)   In the absence of new revenue measures current income of all levels of government and its decentralized agencies will increase in real terms at 8.5% per annum. The projection is based on specific assumptions concerning individual major sources of revenue and an overall assumption that GDP will grow at 7%. The projected revenue growth rate is lower than recorded in 1966-69 (11.5%), when new income sources were introduced and the system of collection accelerated, but it is much higher than the long-run growth rate of 5% annually.

(b)   Current expenditures will increase in real terms at 9% per annum, a deceleration from the 12% rate of 1966-69, but again much higher than the long-run average of 4.8% per annum. The projection is a composite of a faster growth than in the recent past for the central government and departments and a deceleration for decentralized agencies. The former need more funds, particularly in education and health, while the latter have already undergone a major expansion.

32. This has been the long-run trend in Colombia. In 1950-68 public investment rose at 9.5% annually, total investment 4.1%, and private investment 3.2%. The share of public investment was 11% in 1950; it is now nearly 30%, and this is an understatement.

Table 1-16: PUBLIC INVESTMENT, ACTUAL 1966-69 AND PROJECTED 1970-72
(In millions of current Col $)[1]

	1966	1967	1968	1969[2]	1970 Program	1970 Adjusted Program	1971 Program	1971 Adjusted Program	1972 Program	1972 Adjusted Program
Transport	1,205	1,826	1,957	2,300	3,321	2,974	2,931	2,989	3,076	3,139
Energy	596	776	944	1,180	1,951	2,226	1,671	1,959	1,909	2,473
Communications	144	206	256	335	661	661	474	474	533	533
Water and Sewerage	365	422	591	737	765	888	1,095	1,187	1,335	1,422
Housing	269	385	577	640	724	724	720	720	861	861
Education	180	241	374	365	478	504	567	634	649	690
Health	69	142	148	260	228	228	326	326	303	303
Agriculture	498	784	1,127	1,260	1,884	1,884	2,293	2,293	2,694	2,784
Industry	162	199	392	590	1,166	977	1,141	1,041	1,001	1,018
Tourism	–	–	10	30	55	55	87	87	106	106[3]
Studies and Research	4	13	25	50	101	101	132	132[4]	146	146[4]
Other	229	273	423	465	664	664	661	661	682	682
Total	3,721	5,267	6,824	8,212	11,998	11,886	12,098	12,503	13,295	14,157

[1] For 1970-72, it is assumed that prices will increase at 7% per annum.

[2] Provisional.

[3] An increase likely if studies are accelerated.

[4] An increase likely on account of the Preinvestment Study Program.

(c)   Internal government borrowing does not exceed amortization of internal debt. The latter is quite large for Colombian conditions. The demand for credit by the commodity producing sectors is heavy and will continue so if a 7% growth rate of GDP is attained; under these conditions, net government borrowing could raise interest rates and aggravate the already tight credit position of the manufacturing sector. Furthermore, the government in 1970 will already be engaged in a form of deficit spending by drawing on its cash balances. The assumptions concerning government borrowing should be reexamined if coffee prices go up sharply.

(d)   There will be no delay in utilizing existing project loans, and continuing efforts will be made to resolve all problems faced in contracting new project loans. While a major advance has been made in project preparation and in contracting project loans, there have been occasional difficulties in arriving at satisfactory arrangements concerning availability of matching peso funds and future operating conditions of the projects. This issue is particularly relevant for the projects of enterprises of municipalities and departments, which are now increasingly offered for foreign financing.

The major findings emerging from the projections are:

(a)   Without new revenue measures the current budgetary surplus continues to grow in real terms, but at a rate (4.8% per annum) slower than real income. In 1972 it is expected to account for 5.4% of GDP, compared to 6% in 1967-69.

(b)   A very large proportion of aggregate capital claims (investment and amortization) continues to be met out of internal resources—70% in 1970-72. There is a decline in the proportion from the earlier period, but this is caused by a sharp rise in the amount of claims.

(c)   A financing gap is apparent in 1971 and it continues to grow in the subsequent two years (line (p) in Table 1-17). Its precise magnitude depends on the flow of disbursements on project loans to be contracted in 1970-72. A higher estimate of this flow (line (o), Series B) is based on the preliminary listings of project commitments prepared by the planning authorities and adjusted by the mission to reflect the foreign exchange component of project disbursements; but this listing contains an element of target setting particularly in the years 1970 and 1971 and is therefore on the high side. The lower estimate (line (o), Series A) is derived from the planning authorities' aggregative estimate of disbursements (including a certain element of local cost, on the average of 8% of total project cost) and probably approximates reality more closely.[33] The deficit may exceed Col$1,000 million in 1971 and approach Col$2,500 million in 1972.

The Colombian authorities count on further U.S. program loans to help fill a part of the gap. If new program loans in 1971 and 1972 amount to US$60 million and $50 million, respectively (compared to $85 million in 1969 and $70 million in 1970), peso disbursements would work out at Col$565 million in 1971 and Col$1,100 million in 1972.[34]

The gap which would remain would be moderate in 1971 (Col$500-700 million). It would tend to increase considerably in 1972. These findings are broadly consistent with the projections of the 1969-72 Development Plan that the gap to be filled by additional domestic savings will run at Col$800 million in 1971 and Col$2,000 million in 1972.[35] CIAP in its analysis in early

33. Conceptually, any lower level of disbursements would lead to a reduction in aggregate investments of the size approximately double the lag in disbursements (foreign financing on the average works out at 50% of total project cost). But in reality the relation is not so close, since construction activity goes on even when equipment is delayed.

34. It is assumed that one-half of the loan is disbursed in the year of commitment and the other half in the following year.

35. Development Plan, p. VI, B. The plan used a coffee price projection of 50-52 ¢ per pound compared to the present projection of 55-60 ¢.

Table 1-17:   FINANCING OF PUBLIC INVESTMENT, ACTUAL 1966-69 AND PROJECTED 1970-72
(In millions, of current Col$)[1]

	1966	1967	1968	1969	1970	1971	1972
Claims							
(a) Public Investment	3,721	5,267	6,824	8,212	11,886	12,503	14,157
(b) Debt Amortization							
(1) External	375	615	659	768	870	890	995
(2) Internal	(731)	(146)	(403)	(153)	1,110	1,270	1,450
(c) Financial Investments	40	184	158	750	500	500	600
(d) Total Claims (a + b + c)	4,867	6,212	8,444	9,883	14,366	15,163	17,202
Sources							
(e) Current Budgetary Surplus	3,791	4,474	5,972	6,352	7,665	8,327	8,975
(f) Capital Account Resources							
(Internal)	342	348	559	663	935	800	800
(g) Internal Borrowing	n.a.	n.a.	n.a.	n.a.	1,110	1,270	1,450
(h) Draw-down of cash balances	–	–	–	178	862	–	–
(i) Sub-total, Internal Resources							
(e + f + g + h)	4,133	4,822	6,531	7,193	10,572	10,397	11,225
(j) Disbursements on Existing							
Project Loans	927	818	984	1,347	1,285	1,540	1,670
(k) Disbursements on Existing							
Program Loans	218	605	1,229	1,343	1,500	935	100
(l) Sub-total, Assured External							
Resources	1,145	1,423	2,213	2,690	2,785	2,475	1,770
(m) Total Resources in Hand							
(i + l)	5,278	6,245	8,744	9,883	13,357	12,872	12,995
(n) Gap (d – m)	(411)[2]	(33)[2]	(308)[2]	–	1,009	2,291	4,207
(o) Disbursements on New Project							
Loans							
Series A					845	1,000	1,620
Series B					721	1,542	2,291
(p) Remaining Gap					164-288	749-1,291	1,916-2,587
(q) Possible Sources of Finance							
Program loans					–	565	1,100

[1]For 1970-72, it is assumed that prices will increase at 7% p.a. The following accounting exchange rates for US dollars are used for external resource flows: 1966: 9.0; 1967: 12.75; 1968: 13.7; 1969: 16.3; 1970: 17.6; 1971: 18.8; 1972: 20.1.

[2]Accumulation of cash balances.

Notes:

(a)   From Table 1-16.
(b)   From documents of the Planning Department and from external debt statistics.
(c)   Purchases of bonds by the Social Security System, INCORA, etc.
(e)   Projected by the mission.
(f)   Income from and sales of assets; receipts of loan repayments.
(g)   For 1970-72 projected in the same amounts as amortization.
(h)   From budgetary documents.
(j)   From debt statistics.
(k)   From documents of the Planning Department.
(o)   Series A derived from Planning Department estimates. Series B represents a hypothetical draw-down on the foreign exchange component of public sector projects as listed by the Planning Department.
(q)   Program loans assumed equivalent to commitments of $60 million in 1971 and $50 million in 1972.

1970 placed the gap at Col$200 million in 1971 and Col$1,680 million in 1972[36] (In both projections after program loans).

Two implications follow. First, increases in tax revenue will be needed. It is not desirable to increase the budgetary surplus by curtailing current expenditures: both the functioning of the administration and the needed expansion of social sectors preclude this route. Fortunately, Colombia spends little on either defense or administration (on defense 8.9% of the central government budget in 1970 compared to 10% in 1966; on administration 7.5% in 1970 versus 7.2% in 1966). Tax income, however, is low; despite the recent increase from 12.5% of GDP in 1966 to 13.2% in 1969, it is still much lower than the "norm" at Colombia's level of per capita income.[37] Various ways in which tax revenues could be increased have been discussed in a special study (Musgrave Report).[38] The ILO team has also made fiscal suggestions. It should be further added that there is still a substantial lag between earning of income, self-assessment, and reassessment by the tax authorities: at the end of 1968, unliquidated income tax returns numbered 1.2 million cases and the amount that would be collected from the backlog has been put at Col$1 billion. Considerable amounts of additional income taxes could be obtained if collections due to the move to a current payments system were fully made: recent indications are that at present only one-half of the amounts due are actually collected, i.e. the system has been moved to the current basis of assessments, but actual collections are lagging behind this movement. Finally, there is the issue of subsidies: unification of the petroleum exchange rate with the certificate exchange rate could produce Col$800 million, while the reduction of subsidies to public utilities could also yield significant amounts, judging by past increases in the income of municipalities following rate adjustments.

Secondly, foreign lending agencies should be prepared to finance a part of local currency expenditures in project loans. While Colombia can be expected to continue with efforts to raise tax revenues, it will need foreign assistance to finance local costs while this process is under way. There is now an emphasis in public investment on agriculture, water supply, education, health— sectors where the foreign exchange component is low, 30-40%. If foreign lending were to be restricted to this component the government might have to shift the composition of investment away from these sectors although they now have a prominent place in the scale of priorities of the Colombian society.

While the overall tax ratio is low, Colombia has made a special effort in coffee, a critical sector. In the mid-1960s the effective coffee export tax in Colombia was probably the highest among the producing countries; it now amounts to 40%; and if world market prices go higher present arrangements call for a marginal tax rate of 77%.[39]

Recent Developments

In December 1970, the government published the *Economic and Social Development Plan 1970-73.* (Colombia uses the technique of a rolling plan.) Its target output growth rate is 7.5% per annum, and reduction in unemployment is its major objective. Strict comparisons between the public investment program included in this plan and that for 1969-72 (Table 1-16) are not possible because of substantial definitional changes. A rough comparison is shown in Table 1-18. The new program appears to be 12% higher than the adjusted figure for 1971 and 7% higher for 1972. Sectoral composition is similar, but there is greater emphasis, in the new plan, on industry, housing, and education.

Partly as a result of larger public investment, and partly because of the effect on revenues of weaker coffee prices, the fiscal gap for 1971, initially expected to be moderate, had to be revised upward, to almost Col$1,000 million, and for 1972 to Col$1,850-2,100 million. (At projected volumes, each decrease of U.S. 1¢ per pound in the New York price of Colom-

36. CIAP, *op. cit.,* p. 139. The gap is low in 1971 because program loan disbursements are set at a very high level.

37. See Lutz and Nor, "Measuring Tax Effort of Developing Countries", *IMF Staff Papers,* November 1967; Hollis Chenery, *Targets for Development,* January 1970 (mimeo.).

38. *Bases para La Reforma Tributaria en Colombia,* 1968.

39. See Chapter 15, *Coffee.*

Table 1-18: PUBLIC INVESTMENT PROGRAM: OLD AND NEW PLAN[1]
(In millions of current Col$)

| | 1971 | | 1972 | | 1973 |
	Old Plan	New Plan	Old Plan	New Plan	New Plan
Agriculture	2,293	2,800	2,784	2,597	3,421
Communications	474	582	533	413	435
Education	634	677	690	936	1,105
Housing	720	1,116	861	1,220	1,248
Industry	1,041	1,721	1,018	1,999	1,868
Power	1,959	1,959	2,473	2,019	2,047
Public Health	326	456	303	385	354
Sanitation	1,187	1,050	1,422	1,185	1,312
Transportation	2,989	2,690	3,139	3,274	3,546
Other[2]	880	1,025	934	1,140	1,277
TOTAL	12,503	14,076	14,157	15,168	16,613

[1]Old Plan figures are from Table 1-16 (Adjusted Program). New Plan figures were adjusted to obtain rough comparability, then multiplied by .85 to put them on an estimated cash basis. One should not place excessive faith on the sectoral comparisons or the totals because of problems of comparability.

[2]Natural Resources and Regional Development are included in the "Other" category for purposes of this table.

Source: 1970-73 Plan.

bian coffee cuts budget receipts by Col$27 million in 1971, Col$30 million in 1972, and Col$34 million in 1973.) This widening of the fiscal gap called for urgent revenue action. The situation was aggravated further by the need, in late 1970 and early 1971, to purchase coffee for official stock and thus prevent further weakening of the world market.

Fiscal action was taken in the first half of 1971, on a significant scale. Sales and stamp taxes were raised to finance increased public and private pension payments, generating a gross increment of Col$590 million and a net free increment to the national budget of almost Col$350 million in 1971. The petroleum exchange rate (Col$9 per dollar) was raised to the level of the certificate rate (Col$20 per dollar); this reduced the fuel subsidy and also, by raising the tax base, led to an increase in the yield of the fuel tax; to offset the effect on low-income urban population, a new government subsidy to urban bus companies was introduced; the net effect being an increase in government revenue of Col$370 million in 1971 and Col$855 million in 1972. In addition to these two measures, the government is considering a presumptive tax on agricultural income, and changes are also envisaged for corporate and urban property taxes.

The measures already taken will help substantially in solving the fiscal problem in 1971. These measures, with those under consideration, will make a major contribution in the years 1972 and 1973. Whether they will be sufficient depends on the levels of public investment and of coffee prices. Colombia does not have control over the latter. With respect to investment, one can expect steadily growing requirements as full employment increasingly becomes the dominant objective of public policy.

Growth, Capital Requirements, and Debt

Absorptive Capacity

This section examines the feasibility and the implications of an accelerated growth rate for Colombia, both for the near future 1971-75 and the longer run 1976-85. The analysis and related projections are based on a model described in Chapter 3. The model assumes that Colombia's absorptive capacity is adequate to achieve a high growth target, and that savings and foreign exchange are the principal constraining factors to be evaluated. Such an assumption is supported by the remainder of this economic report. Colombia's absorptive capacity—i.e. ability to absorb capital, combine it with other factors of production, and convert it efficiently into output—is shorthand notation for a broad complex of elements that together produce economic growth: land, natural resources, climate, markets, entrepreneurs, managers, workers, ingenuity and determination.

Colombia has a reasonable supply of land, relative to population. The vast plains beyond the Eastern Cordillera have barely been touched, although there are problems of accessibility and quality. Forests are abundant, marine resources are only beginning to be utilized, and several important minerals are known to exist in commercial quantities. Colombia's hydroelectric potential is enormous, and crude petroleum is produced on a scale sufficient to satisfy national requirements and provide a surplus for export. A variety of soils and climates make it possible to grow virtually any kind of agricultural commodity (and frequently two crops per season).

Colombia's institutional development is well advanced, and there are large numbers of entrepreneurs and managers ready and able to innovate and administer both public and private enterprises. There is also a sizable, relatively well-trained labor force on hand, and the activities of the National Apprentice Service (SENA) and other agencies are devoted to increasing the supply of skilled workers. Industry has been fairly successful in adapting complex technical procedures to Colombian conditions, and the output response to recent agricultural incentives has been impressive. The public sector has made great progress in the work of identifying and preparing high-quality development projects, which bodes well for continued quantitative and qualitative gains in investment. Markets should not be a major constraint: domestic demand for both industrial and agricultural products should rise rapidly in response to accelerated income growth. Income elasticity of demand for food products is high, about 0.6-0.7. In the last several years, there was no difficulty in absorbing increased agricultural output, and prices were well maintained. In industry room for import substitution should be considerable, particularly in engineering goods and in some intermediate products. With respect to the export market, Colombia accounts for only small proportions of total supply for all products other than coffee. Unless restrained by trade barriers, it should not have difficulties in rapidly expanding exports of a variety of agricultural and industrial goods.

All things considered, there are no severe bottlenecks in absorptive capacity to prevent Colombia from sustaining the 7% growth rate recently achieved and aiming even higher. It is important to note, furthermore, that much of the upswing in the growth tempo occurred *before* the sharp improvement of world coffee prices in September 1969. Although the 1950-68 average annual GDP gain was only 4.8%, the 1958-68 average was 5.1% and the 1965-69 average was approximately 5.6%, with 6.1% recorded in 1968 and 6.5% in 1969.

Growth Prospects and Requirements 1970-75.

The assumptions underlying the projections for 1970-75 are set forth in Table 1-19.

Three factors are critical for maintaining an accelerated growth rate: a high rate of savings, a rapid expansion in exports, and a high level of capital inflow.

Prospects for increasing domestic savings are closely related to the solution of the public finance problem. Public savings now account for about one-third of total savings; they have increased faster than private savings over the long run and particularly during the last few years. It is of critical importance that public savings continue to grow rapidly. While it is possible in principle for a slack in public savings to be compensated by an increase in private savings, this is highly uncertain. Furthermore, in view of the increasing role which the government plays in accelerating investment (through public investment and through lending to the private sector) failure to increase public savings would mean failure of the attempts to raise the growth rate.

The relatively low growth rate in the past was closely related to the slow expansion of the capacity to import; and unless this capacity expands much faster it is highly unlikely that accelerated growth in income can be achieved. An inadequate capacity to import could lead to under-utilization of already installed capacity and to the undertaking of high-cost production lines; the result would be lower increase in output from a given investment level. A critical item in assuring satisfactory growth in the capacity to import is a continuing high growth in non-traditional exports. An important assumption underlying this projection, in turn, is that overvaluation of the peso will be avoided, i.e. the exchange rate will move parallel with the movement of domestic prices. The authorities expect the latter not to exceed 7% per annum, in line with the experience of recent years, and the same proportionate change or better is planned in the exchange rate. Should domestic prices increase faster a corresponding acceleration would have to be made in changing the rate. The other critical item is a favorable coffee price.

Table 1-20 sets forth the projected external capital requirements.

Resource inflow from abroad in 1970-75 is projected at 1.5% of GDP and almost 7% of gross investment. This compares with 0.9% and 4.2% respectively, in the past five years. Gross

Table 1-19: 1970-75: SELECTED VARIABLES, RATES OF CHANGE, AND COEFFICIENTS

Historical Trend	Projection, 1970-75
1. GDP Growth Rate	
1950-68 : 4.8% p.a.	
1958-68 : 5.1% p.a.	
1968-69 : 6.3% p.a.	7% p.a.
2. Gross Investment Coefficient	
1950-68 : 17.2% of GDP	
1958-68 : 19.0% of GDP	
1965-68 : 19.4% of GDP	24.0% of GDP
3. Gross Domestic Savings Coefficient	
1950-68 : 18.5% of GDP	
1958-68 : 19.3% of GDP	
1965-68 : 18.2% of GDP	22.2% of GDP
4. Marginal Savings Rate	23.2%
5. Resource Gap	
1965-69 : 0.9% of GDP	1.7% of GDP
4.2% of Investment	7.5% of Investment
6. Incremental Capital-Output Ratio[1]	
1950-68 : 4.3	
1958-68 : 3.7	3.2 (determined by
1963-68 : 3.5	sectoral ratios)
1967-68 : 2.9	
7. Import Growth Rate	
1950-68 : 3.4% p.a.	9.0% (1968-75)
1960-68 : 2.8% p.a.	5.6% (1970-75)
8. Export Growth Rate	
1950-68 : 2.3% p.a.	8.8% (1968-75)
1960-68 : 2.7% p.a.	5.5% (1970-75)[2]

[1] Based on data in constant prices of 1968; excludes inventory investment.
[2] Coffee prices assumed to decline gradually from 57.4 U.S. cents per lb. f.o.b. in 1970-71 to 42.4 cents in 1974-75.

Table 1-20: BALANCE OF PAYMENTS, ACTUAL 1965-69 AND PROJECTED 1970-75
(In millions of US dollars)

	1965	1966	1967	1968	1969	1970	1971	1972	1973	1974	1975
Exports of goods & non-factor services	709	663	712	788	855	1,085	1,165	1,205	1,255	1,305	1,420
Imports of goods & non-factor services	653	867	696	866	980	1,206	1,297	1,348	1,411	1,425	1,585
Resource gap	-56	204	-16	78	125	121	132	143	156	170	165
Factor payments, net	79	86	105	113	123	137	149	162	179	196	214
Interest on public debt[1]	n.a.	n.a.	n.a.	28	33	42	49	57	69	81	94
Others	n.a.	n.a.	n.a.	85	90	95	100	105	110	115	120
Net unrequited transfers	12	10	22	31	25	20	15	10	5	5	5
Current account	-11	-280	-67	-160	-223	-238	-266	-295	-330	-361	-375
Net private capital	-41	193	34	52	90	95	100	105	110	115	120
Net public capital[1]	27	47	44	155	144	151	230	256	285	286	295
Gross inflow, existing loans				228	210	136	127	83	82	52	35
Amortization, existing loans				73	66	83	74	77	74	72	72
Gross inflow, new loans						98	177	253	284	321	356
Amortization, new loans						–	–	3	7	15	24
Net reserve change (- increase)	-42	67	-62	6	-11	-8	-65	-65	-65	-40	-40
Errors and omissions	67	-27	51	-53	–	–	–	–	–	–	–

[1]Long-term public and publicly-guaranteed debt repayable in foreign currency. "Existing" loans refer to contracts signed through 12-31-1969.

Source: Chapter 3, Growth, Capital Requirements, and External Debt, 1970-85.

disbursements on public account (government borrowing plus borrowing guaranteed by the government) are projected to average slightly less than $340 million per annum, compared to the 1968-69 average level of $220 million. Less than one-third of projected gross disbursements consist of draw-down on existing loans; the rest would have to come from loans to be contracted (see Table 1-21).

Table 1-21: COMMITMENTS OF NEW LOANS ON PUBLIC ACCOUNT
ACTUAL 1966-69 AND PROJECTED 1970-75
(In millions of US dollars)

	1966	1967	1968	1969	1970	1971	1972	1973	1974	1975
Project loans[1]	89	86	179	233	299	229	316	286	294	312
Program loans	–	100	78	85	70	60	50	50	50	50
Not identified	45	31	13	–	–	–	–	–	–	–
Total	89	217	270	318	369	289	366	336	344	362

[1]In 1966-69 includes some projects in the private sector not guaranteed by the government.

Source: Chapter 3.

The feasibility of this commitment level has been verified through informal discussions with lending agencies which loom large in the total supply of capital to Colombia. Also, the aggregate of project loan commitments over the six years approximates the cumulative total contained in the preliminary project list of Colombia's Planning Department.

The aggregate level of project commitments in the six-year period 1970-75 amounts to US$1.7 billion. Such commitments would lead to a total disbursement of US$1,185 million during the period, roughly US$195 million per year. Adding these disbursements to the US$430 million expected from commitments made prior to 1970 gives a total gross project loan inflow of US$1.6 billion. Half of this gross inflow will be needed to make interest and amortization payments (stemming largely from debt already contracted), leaving a net effective transfer of US$800 million or US$135 million per year. Thus, external project lenders will have to enter into US$290 million worth of new project commitments each year in order to transfer half that amount to Colombia. It is unlikely that this can be accomplished by financing only the foreign exchange component of projects.

The above projections are of a similar order of magnitude to the subsequently prepared estimates contained in the Colombian *Economic and Social Development Plan, 1970-73,* December 1970. For a 7.5% GDP growth rate, the Plan estimates the required project loan commitments in 1971-73 at US$315 million annually. The Plan envisages program-sector borrowing averaging US$70 million per annum in 1971-73, compared to US$60 million in Table 1-21.

Long Run, 1976-85

The variables stated in Table 1-19 can be extended into the future, so that:

(a)   The gross investment coefficient reaches 24.4% of GDP by 1985;

(b)   the marginal savings rate rises to 27.3% in 1985, pulling up the average savings coefficient to a level equal to the gross investment coefficient by 1985;

(c)   the overall incremental capital-output ratio declines slightly, since sectors with lower ratios expand output faster than those with higher ratios;

(d)   exports rise at 8% per annum, under the impact of growth of non-traditional products; even though the rate of increase of non-traditionals is assumed to decelerate from 20% in 1970-75 to 15% in 1975-80 and 10% in 1980-85, their weight in total exports steadily increases and assures rapid export growth overall;

(e)   imports rise at roughly the same rate as real income, so that the import coefficient remains unchanged at 16.5% of GDP, thus assuring that there are no import capacity bottlenecks.

Under these circumstances, which are believed plausible, a 7% growth rate in aggregate output could be sustained throughout the 1970-85 period.

The needed capital inflow would be determined by the size of the cumulative resource gap resulting from the difference between gross investment and gross domestic savings (and imports and exports) and by the terms of borrowing: the harder the terms the larger the amounts of gross borrowing needed to accomplish any given resource transfer. The terms of existing debt are known. New lending commitments now being made average 5.0% interest, 23.4 years to maturity, and 5.6 years of grace. By 1985 these terms harden considerably, to 6.4% interest, 14.6 years maturity, and 3.7 years of grace. The hardening does not arise from changing terms within each debt category, but rather from changes in the relative importance of future flows. Over the period as a whole, however, the terms assumed are favorable: 22% of gross new borrowing comes as loans repayable in pesos or loans at 3%.

Under these assumptions, public external capital flows and debt service would be of the following magnitudes (Table 1-22):

Table 1-22: PUBLIC BORROWING AND DEBT SERVICE, 1970-85
(In millions of US dollars)

	1970	1975	1980	1985
Total gross disbursements	234	391	536	648
Amortization payments	83	96	204	332
Interest payments	42	94	181	283
Debt service	125	190	385	615
Net disbursements (gross disbursements-debt service)	109	201	151	33
Outstanding disbursed debt, end year	1,212	2,278	3,568	4,914
Outstanding debt, incl. undisbursed, end year	1,738	2,717	4,049	5,440

Disbursed debt which now amounts to 17.5% of GDP would gradually rise to a peak of 26.2% in 1980 and decline to 25.6% in 1985. Since the resource gap would be closed by 1985 outstanding debt would also start declining in absolute terms sometime in the 1990s.

The debt service ratio—the proportion of exports of goods and services absorbed by debt service—in 1968 amounted to 12.8% and is estimated at 11.6% in 1969. Debt service on existing debt declines to 8% of projected exports in 1975 and to 4% in 1980. Aggregate debt service, on both existing and newly contracted debt, stays at 10-12% through 1973 and then climbs to a peak of 19.8% in 1984.

With 7% GDP growth, per capita income would increase from US$300 at present to US$585 in 1985, but it is doubtful that full employment would be reached by that year. The ILO projection, based on a productivity growth assumption of 3.2% annually in 1970-75, labor force growth of 3.5% and an estimated 1970 unemployment equivalent to one-fourth to one-fifth of the total labor force, calls for an 8.1% output growth to reach 95% full employment by 1985. Using the same assumptions concerning productivity, labor force growth, and present unemployment, the 7% GDP growth rate would yield an 84% employment level by 1985. The full employment objective would have to be put off 10-12 years; if one allows for a slight reduction in productivity growth and labor participation rates or for the possibility that the present unemployment level is lower, the objective would be reached 6-8 years beyond the 1985 target.

An 8% growth target would call for larger investment (27% of GDP), larger domestic savings (25% of GDP), and larger external capital inflow than the 7% case. The resource gap should normally be expected to widen, for some years, when the target growth rate is shifted upward. How much additional gross borrowing would be needed to finance this increase in the resource gap critically depends on the terms of borrowing. If provided on private suppliers' terms, additional gross borrowing needed to shift from 7% to 8% growth would be 43% larger during 1970-85, than if provided on development finance agency-type terms. The 1985 debt service ratio would climb, compared to the 7% GDP growth case, by 22.7 percentage points if resources are borrowed on the private market, and by 10.5 percentage points, or less than a half, if they can be borrowed on development finance agency-type terms (see Chapter 3, Growth, Capital Requirements, and External Debt, 1970-85).

If exports were to increase between 1970 and 1985 at a considerably slower rate than assumed above, at 4.4% annually instead of 7.5%, the debt service ratio would climb to a peak of 28.4% in 1984 in the 7% GDP growth variant (and very much higher in the 8% growth variant). More important, the import coefficient would have to be forced down from 17% of GDP to 11% in 1985. The key question in this case is whether the 7% rate of GDP growth (and, of course, the 8% rate) is feasible in the face of such relatively slow growth in the capacity to import.

The limitations of this kind of exercise are formidable. Attempts to project economic activity even one year into the future usually fail, and a 15-year projection based on uncertain statistical foundations is almost bound to go wrong. The projection does help, however, to throw light on some of the key issues. First, an 8% growth rate is more certain to solve the unemployment problem within the visible future than a 7% rate, and the long-run creditworthiness of a borrower, who is more successful in reducing unemployment, is enhanced. On the other hand, the liquidity risk is higher when debt service ratio moves up sharply. One way out of this dilemma would be provision of much of incremental assistance on development finance terms. Second, there is the need to expand exports to the utmost. This calls for strenuous efforts on the part of Colombia to maintain the high growth rate of non-traditional products, for readiness of the importing countries to accept these exports, and for successful international efforts to assure stable and relatively favorable coffee prices. A depressed coffee market would make it very difficult to approach the GDP growth rates of the magnitude discussed in this report.

CHAPTER 2

POPULATION, EMPLOYMENT, AND UNEMPLOYMENT

Salient Features

In recent years increasing attention has been given to the problem of unemployment in the developing countries, and it is by now generally recognized that many popular indicators such as GNP and per capita income tell only part of the story of economic progress. Although a strong positive correlation normally exists between rising output or income and employment levels, even high rates of gain are often accompanied by increasing numbers of unemployed persons. In large measure this results from the rapid population growth experienced by many countries during the postwar period, but it can also be due to the nature of their development processes. Some countries face acute unemployment in spite of achieving substantial growth for several years, while others seem to have a milder problem even though growth has been relatively slow.

The International Labor Organization (ILO), in recognition of the urgency of the unemployment problem for most developing nations, launched the World Employment Program in 1969. As part of this program it was envisaged that qualified teams of experts would visit selected countries to make comprehensive studies of the causes and possible cures of unemployment. At the invitation of the Colombian Government the ILO chose Colombia as the first country to receive such a mission, and its report *Towards Full Employment, A Programme for Colombia,* was prepared in 1970. The Bank mission has drawn heavily on ILO's findings.

An expected growth rate of 3.5% annually in Colombia's labor force over the next 10-15 years will keep the system under constant pressure to provide new jobs. In addition to the existing backlog of more than half a million frustrated job-seekers this growth will raise by nearly 4.4 million the supply of available workers. Thus the economy is somehow going to have to generate jobs for 5 million workers between now and 1985 if urban unemployment is to be eliminated. Many thousands more will be needed if anything is to be done in the rural sector. If one assumes an average labor productivity gain of 3.2% annually it will require a sustained output growth rate of 7% to 8% to meet this need.

After verifying that a continuation of present trends would result in a staggering 30% to 35% level of unemployment by 1985, the ILO mission examined various alternative models to identify plausible growth patterns leading to full (95%) employment. The "basic" model involves a 1.8% annual increase in agricultural employment and a 7.0% increase in non-agricultural employment between 1970 and 1985. With their assumptions of 3.5% and 1.8% annual gains in productivity, output growth rates of 5.4% and 8.9% are implied for agriculture and non-agriculture, respectively.

These assumed growth rates would reduce agriculture's relative importance from 30% to 20% of total output between 1970 and 1985. Within the non-agricultural sector modern manufacturing industry would expand output by 9.2% per year and handicraft industry by 7.9%, with each achieving an average employment growth of 5.8%. Consumer goods would lose importance relative to investment goods as a proportion of modern manufacturing output.

Supply of Labor

Population Estimates

There are two sides to the market for human labor, as for any other commodity or service, supply and demand. The supply side will be considered first, commencing with Colombia's population. At present the total population is estimated at 21.6 million, up 38% from a decade ago. The Economic Development Studies Center (CEDE) of the University of the Andes in Bogota has made projections of this population to 1985, and these estimates are used here without adjustment. CEDE expects a population of 25.3 million in mid-1975, 29.2 million in 1980, and 32.8 million in 1985. Table 2-1 breaks these figures down by age group for each year of the 1970-75 period, 1980, and 1985.

Table 2-1: TOTAL POPULATION PROJECTIONS, BY AGE GROUP, 1970-85
(Mid-year estimates in '000's)

Age Group	1970	1971	1972	1973	1974	1975	1980	1985
0-4	4,012	4,102	4,194	4,288	4,384	4,482	4,757	4,562
5-9	3,110	3,240	3,376	3,517	3,664	3,819	4,299	4,595
10-14	2,948	2,972	2,997	3,022	3,047	3,073	3,780	4,263
15-19	2,304	2,415	2,534	2,653	2,781	2,914	3,043	3,750
20-24	1,835	1,914	1,996	2,083	2,173	2,268	2,874	3,008
25-29	1,467	1,528	1,591	1,658	1,727	2,799	2,230	2,833
30-34	1,204	1,248	1,292	1,340	1,387	1,437	1,767	2,195
35-39	1,062	1,084	1,106	1,129	1,152	1,176	1,407	1,735
40-44	949	964	981	998	1,015	1,033	1,147	1,376
45-49	733	766	801	838	875	915	1,001	1,115
50-54	580	601	625	648	674	700	878	963
55-59	497	505	514	524	533	543	659	830
60-64	307	332	358	387	418	451	496	604
65-69	297	290	283	276	269	263	390	433
70-74	150	163	178	195	213	232	208	312
75 and over	177	175	174	174	173	172	230	244
TOTAL	21,632	22,299	23,000	23,730	24,485	25,278	29,165	32,818

Source: Proyecciones de la Poblacion Colombia, 1965-85, Enrique Perez, C.E.D.E., Bogota, Octubre de 1968.

To reach these conclusions the CEDE demographers had to work through a series of steps which can be summarized as follows. First, it was necessary to correct the 1951 and 1964 census results for error due to underreporting. Second, the corrected census data for 15 July 1964 had to be shifted forward to 30 June 1965, the desired projection base. These two steps led to a 1965 base-year estimate of 18,425,158 Colombians. Third, this base population was extrapolated by means of the component method, wherein separate calculations were made for each sex and age group. The number of survivors from one year to the next was computed for each sex and age group by using specific survival probabilities.

Death rates were deduced by manipulating life expectancy figures. In accordance with historical trends, life expectancy at birth of males was assumed to rise by .4, and of females by .5, of a year per year. This meant that the 1965 expectancies of 50 and 52 years for men and women, respectively, would rise to 58 and 62 by 1985. It was known that between 1951 and 1964 Colombia had a "quasi-stable" population, characterized by constant fertility and declining mortality rates (death rates began to fall around 1949). The 1965 crude birth rate appeared to be about 47.2 per thousand inhabitants. General fertility rates were then projected as follows:

Births per Woman in 15-59 Age Group

	1965-70	1970-75	1975-80	1980-85
Male Births	.10869	.10006	.08855	.07128
Female Births	.10451	.09621	.08515	.06855

On the basis of these fertility rates it was possible to estimate crude birth rates per thousand:

1965-70	1970-75	1975-80	1980-85
47.2	43.4	38.4	30.9

It is interesting to note that Colombia's population is expected to age, in accordance with the fertility assumptions adopted. As a result, children under 15 decline from 46.8% of the 1965 population to 40.9% in 1985. Persons over the age of 59 increase slightly, on the other hand, from 4.82% of the 1965 population to 4.86% in 1985. The two groups combined fall from 51.6% of the population in 1965 to 45.7% in 1985, and the dependency ratio—the number of young and old dependent persons to be supported by persons in the 15 to 59 age group—falls from 1,066 dependents per thousand in 1965 to 843 in 1985. This phenomenon should be favorable to economic development.

Once Colombia's population was projected by sex and age it was possible to tackle the forecast by department. Again it was necessary to adjust 1951 and 1964 census data to eliminate known errors, after which birth rates, death rates, and migratory shifts were analyzed for the 1951-64 period. It was then feasible to project these data to 1985 by assuming that inter-departmental migration would continue at the historical rate.[1]   The departmental projections are shown in Table 2-2.

The Work Force

In addition to their analysis of inter-departmental flows, CEDE's demographers studied the historical 1951-64 rural-urban movement. By assuming a continuation of this trend they were able to break down the 1965-85 projection into rural and urban components. Colombia's population age ten or more is shown by urban and rural residence, sex, and major age group—i.e. 10 to 14, 15 to 64 and 65 and over,—for 1970, 1975, 1980, and 1985 in Table 2-3. Participa-

1. For a full explanation of the methodology used to make these projections see the following CEDE publications: *Analisis Demografico de los Censos Colombianos, 1951 y 1964* (Alvaro Lopez Toro, 1968). *Proyecciones de la Poblacion Colombiana, 1965-85; Proyecciones por Departamento de la Poblacion Colombiana, Resultados Estadistices; Estimacion de Parametros Regionales Demograficos Colombianos, 1965-85* (Enrique Perez S., October 1968, July 1969, and September 1969).

Table 2-2: TOTAL POPULATION PROJECTIONS, BY DEPARTMENT, 1970-85
(Mid-year estimates in '000's)

Department[1]	1970	1971	1972	1973	1974	1975	1980	1985
Antioquia	3,146	3,248	3,356	3,469	3,583	3,706	4,313	4,895
Atlantico	891	919	949	979	1,011	1,044	1,203	1,357
Bolivar	1,971	2,032	2,096	2,165	2,233	2,308	2,650	2,975
Boyaca	1,248	1,278	1,310	1,342	1,377	1,412	1,575	1,712
Caldas	1,772	1,822	1,874	1,929	1,984	2,044	2,336	2,546
Cauca	734	756	779	803	828	854	980	1,095
Cundinamarca	3,675	3,814	3,957	4,107	4,263	4,426	5,283	6,165
Choco	225	231	238	246	254	262	299	333
Huila	500	515	531	545	564	581	664	739
Magdalena	978	1,009	1,041	1,075	1,109	1,146	1,319	1,481
Narino	825	844	865	887	909	932	1,039	1,130
Norte de Santander	656	677	700	723	747	773	899	1,017
Santander	1,219	1,253	1,289	1,326	1,365	1,405	1,597	1,772
Tolima	960	980	1,001	1,022	1,044	1,068	1,165	1,240
Valle	2,146	2,213	2,283	2,357	2,432	2,510	2,916	3,316
Intendencias and Comisarias	686	708	731	755	780	806	930	1,045
TOTAL	21,632	22,299	23,000	23,730	24,485	25,278	29,165	32,818

[1]Administrative divisions existing in 1951.

Source: <u>Proyecciones por Departamento de la Poblacion Colombiana: Resultados Estadisticos</u>, Enrique Perez, C.E.D.E., Bogota, Julio 30 de 1969.

tion rate assumptions specific to age group, location, and sex were then made to derive the economically active population for the same future years. This information is set forth in Table 2-4.[2]

The results of the foregoing discussion are summarized in Table 2-5. There it can be seen that Colombia's global rate of participation,—i.e. economically active population as a percentage of total population, is expected to rise from an estimated 29.9% in 1970 to 33.0% in 1985. The overall population should increase by an average of 3.2% between 1970 and 1975, 2.9% between 1975 and 1980, and 2.4% between 1980 and 1985. Because of the aging demographic structure of this population, however, the labor force will grow at a steady 3.5% per annum throughout the 1970-85 interval.

Two observations are appropriate at this juncture. First, the 29% estimate for the current global participation rate is a low figure, and one should indeed expect it to rise during the next several years if economic growth continues. Second, a 3.5% average annual increase in the work force is high, relative to other countries, and this will definitely aggravate Colombia's unemployment problem. The urban labor force is expected to rise from 3,695,000 in 1970 to 7,944,000 in 1985, an average gain of 5.25% per year. The rural labor force should grow much more slowly, given the assumptions concerning migration, rising from 2,781,000 to 2,897,000 between 1970 and 1985, an average annual gain of only 0.3%.

An average increment of 5.25% means approximately 225,000 new urban workers per year during 1970-75; 275,000 in 1975-80; and 350,000 in 1980-85. Existing open unemployment in the urban sector is estimated at about 550,000. Including only half of the additional 370,000 persons who are now technically unemployed, one gets a total need for 5 million new urban jobs between now and 1985. In the rural sector the apparent requirement totals only 115,000 new

2. See *Proyecciones de la Poblacion Colombiana Economicamente Activa, 1965-85,* CEDE, July 1969.

Table 2-3: PROJECTION OF POPULATION AGE TEN OR MORE YEARS BY URBAN AND RURAL RESIDENCE, SEX, AND MAJOR AGE GROUP, 1970-85 (Mid-year estimates in '000's)

	Age 10-14		Age 15-64		Age 65 and Over	
	Male	Female	Male	Female	Male	Female
1970						
Urban[1]	823	909	2,980	3,455	158	210
Rural	673	543	2,438	2,066	130	125
Total	1,496	1,452	5,418	5,521	288	335
1975						
Urban	929	1,026	3,918	4,517	185	242
Rural	630	488	2,655	2,146	126	114
Total	1,559	1,514	6,573	6,663	311	356
1980						
Urban	1,238	1,369	4,982	5,726	251	323
Rural	679	494	2,730	2,064	137	117
Total	1,917	1,863	7,712	7,790	388	440
1985						
Urban	1,511	1,675	6,426	7,346	318	426
Rural	648	429	2,754	1,883	136	109
Total	2,159	2,104	9,180	9,229	454	535

[1]Urban refers to population centers with more than 1,500 inhabitants.

Source: Proyecciones de la Poblacion Colombiana Economicamente Activa 1965-85: Resultados Estadisticos, C.E.D.E., Bogota, Julio de 1969.

Table 2-4: PROJECTION OF ECONOMICALLY ACTIVE POPULATION BY URBAN AND
RURAL RESIDENCE, SEX, AND MAJOR AGE GROUP, 1970-85
(Mid-year estimates in '000's)

	Age 10-14		Age 15-64		Age 65 and Over	
	Male	Female	Male	Female	Male	Female
1970						
Urban[1]	44	47	2,541	976	71	16
Rural	142	14	2,284	245	86	10
Total	186	61	4,825	1,221	157	26
1975						
Urban	43	52	3,323	1,300	77	17
Rural	116	12	2,455	251	82	9
Total	159	64	5,778	1,551	159	26
1980						
Urban	48	70	4,263	1,679	96	22
Rural	106	11	2,506	237	87	9
Total	154	81	6,769	1,916	183	31
1985						
Urban	48	84	5,496	2,179	111	26
Rural	83	9	2,499	213	85	8
Total	131	93	7,995	2,392	196	34

[1]Urban refers to population centers with more than 1,500 inhabitants.

Source: Proyecciones de la Poblacion Colombiana Economicamente Activa 1965-85: Resultados Estadisticos,
C.E.D.E., Bogota, Julio de 1969.

jobs, but it is obvious that many more are needed to reduce the underemployment so prevalent
in the countryside.

Demand for Labor

Turning to the demand side of the labor market, two dominant factors retarded the creation
of jobs in Colombia in the postwar period: slow economic growth, particularly in the agricultural
sector, and rising labor productivity (output per man-year of labor input). Total output grew
by 4.6% between 1950 and 1960 and 5.1% between 1960 and 1969, while agriculture grew by
3.1% and 3.8%. Labor productivity grew by roughly 2.6% and 2.8% yearly during the two
periods, respectively, while the work force increased by 2.5% and 2.9%. Assuming the same
rates of productivity increase, output would have had to rise by 5.1% annually during 1950-
60 and 5.7% during 1960-69 to absorb the new entrants into the work force. Since
productivity gains normally rise with higher output growth rates, furthermore, one can
justifiably assume that output should have expanded by as much as a full percentage point
faster than it did during the fifties and sixties.

Assuming an average productivity gain of, say, 3.2% yearly, it would take an output
growth of 7% to 8% yearly to remedy Colombia's unemployment situation by 1985. The lower
rate would be sufficient to generate 5 million new jobs, while the higher figure would also permit
considerable improvement in the rural underemployment situation. Although the economy
grew by nearly 7% in 1970, it would be an exceptional performance indeed for this pace to be

Table 2-5: SUMMARY PROJECTION OF TOTAL AND ECONOMICALLY ACTIVE POPULATION, 1970-85
(Mid-year estimates in '000's)

	1970	1975	1980	1985
(1) Total Population	21,632	25,278	29,165	32,818
Age 0-9	7,122	8,301	9,056	9,157
Age 10-14	2,948	3,073	3,780	4,263
Age 15-64	10,939	13,236	15,502	18,409
Age 65 and over	623	667	828	989
(2) Economically Active				
Population	6,476	7,737	9,134	10,841
Age 10-14	247	223	235	224
Age 15-64	6,046	7,329	8,685	10,387
Age 65 and over	183	185	214	230
Urban	3,695	4,812	6,178	7,944
Rural	2,781	2,925	2,956	2,897
Male	5,168	6,096	7,106	8,322
Female	1,308	1,641	2,028	2,519
(3) Percentage, 2/1	29.9	30.6	31.3	33.0
Average Annual Rates				
of Growth:	1970-75	1975-80	1980-85	
Total population	3.2	2.9	2.4	
Active population	3.5	3.5	3.5	

Source: Tables 2-1 and 2-4.

maintained for the next 15 years. It can be done, however, and Colombia should leave no stone unturned in its efforts to achieve this target rate of growth.

The International Labor Organization Model

Accepting, therefore, the obvious desirability of a 7% to 8% growth rate in output between now and 1985, it is useful to explore some of the alternative paths that this growth might take. The ILO report has made some illuminating computations. It breaks Colombia's economy down into two sectors, agriculture and non-agriculture, dividing the latter into three sub-sectors: Alpha, taking in mining, modern manufacturing, public utilities, and transportation; Beta, including construction, handicraft manufacturing, commerce, and personal services; and Gamma, including banking and other services. Alpha is in general both capital-and skill-intensive. Beta is neither, and Gamma is not capital-intensive but does require a fairly high level of skill. Productivity gains are most likely to be high in Alpha.

Stressing the precarious nature of the available data, the ILO report has estimated 1970 output, employment, and productivity for these sectors and sub-sectors as shown in Table 2-6; "Labor productivity" is defined as output divided by labor force minus unemployed, where unemployed contains the full-time equivalent of the estimated number of underemployed workers. Since 1964 was the latest year for which employment by sector was known, 1970 had to be estimated by assuming a continuation of observed 1951-64 productivity trends and then deducing employment from productivity and estimated output.

The 1970-85 perspective is explored by means of four hypothetical sensitivity models. Each of the four was predicated on 95% employment by 1985, but each differed in the rate of growth assumed for agriculture. The first merely extended the 1964-70 experience, the second had an "industrial" pattern, and the third had an "agricultural" pattern, and the fourth had an "intermediate" pattern.[3] The last model was taken as the "basic" or most plausible case. It involves a 1.8% annual growth of agricultural employment, with non-agricultural employment gains arising mostly in low-productivity activities. Tables 2-7 and 2-8 show what would happen if all assumptions were fulfilled. (One should bear in mind that the "rural" definition used earlier is not identical to "agricultural" in the present usage; many city and village dwellers could be employed in agriculture in 1985.) To raise the growth rate of agricultural output from 3.4% to 5.4% would undoubtedly be challenging. The model has this accomplished by boosting productivity from 2.0% to 3.5% and employment from 1.4% to 1.8%[4]. Non-agriculture would bear the brunt of the job-creation effort, raising em-

Table 2-6: OUTPUT, EMPLOYMENT AND PRODUCTIVITY BY SECTOR, 1970

Sector or Sub-Sector	1970 Gross Output at Factor Cost[1]	Average % Change, 1964-1970	1970 Employment, Million Man-Years[2]	Average % Change, 1964-1970	1970 Gross Output per Man-Year[3]	Average % Change 1964-1970
Agriculture	10.8	3.4	255	1.4	4.2	2.0
Non-agriculture	26.1	5.7	250	3.2	10.5	2.5
Alpha	11.9	6.6	59	2.5	20.3	4.0
Beta	9.3	5.1	135	3.6	6.9	1.4
Gamma	5.0	5.1	56	3.1	9.0	2.0
Total	37.0	5.2	504	2.3	7.3	2.9

[1]Output value in billions of 1958 Col $.

[2]"Standardized" figures, which include an adjustment for underemployment.

[3]Output value in thousands of 1958 Col $.

ployment levels by 7.0% yearly. The Alpha sub-sector—mining, modern manufacturing, utilities, and transportation—would increase productivity by only 2.9% annually, as compared with an observed 4.0% rate for 1964-70. Total output per man-year would rise from 2.9% to 3.2%, however, as output growth accelerates from 5.2% to 8.1%.

Agricultural employment would decline from half the total in 1970 to a third in 1985. Within the non-agricultural sector Alpha would lose a few percentage points of relative importance, Beta would remain about the same, and Gamma would rise from 22.4% to 26.8% of the sector total. One can appreciate, therefore, that the move to full (95%) employment in 1985 in the ILO model would be accomplished by a shift to low-productivity activities within the non-agricultural sector, even though overall productivity would rise.

Despite this shift in emphasis an 8.9% increase in non-agricultural output would require a substantial investment effort. Although capital formation data by sector are not available for

3. A continuation of past trends would result in a 30% to 35% level of unemployment by 1985.

4. With total population increasing by an average 2.8% per annum between 1970 and 1985 and income rising 7% to 8% yearly, plus a need for exportable surpluses, an agricultural output growth of 5.4% annually would not appear excessive.

Colombia the ILO mission attempted to estimate incremental capital-output ratios (ICORs) by referring to the experience of other countries:

Sector or Sub-sector	ICOR Projections	
	1970-75	1975-85
Agriculture	5.5-6.0	5.0-5.5
Alpha	4.5-5.0	4.0-4.5
Beta	2.0-2.5	1.8-2.3
Gamma	1.0-1.5	0.9-1.4

Thus, in order to obtain an additional unit of output from agriculture it will be necessary to spend 5.5-6.0 units for capital formation. For the Gamma sub-sector of non-agriculture (banking and other services), however, this investment requirement is only 1.0-1.5 units.

Table 2-7: OUTPUT, EMPLOYMENT AND PRODUCTIVITY BY SECTOR, 1985

Sector or Sub-Sector	1985 Gross Output at Factor Cost[1]	Average % Change, 1970-1985	1985 Employment, '0,000 Man-Years[2]	Average % Change, 1970-1985	1985 Gross Output per Man-Year[2,3]	Average % Change, 1970-1985
Agriculture	23.8	5.4	335	1.8	7.1	3.5
Non-agriculture	94.3	8.9	690	7.0	13.7	1.8
Alpha	43.7	9.1	140	6.0	31.2	2.9
Beta	31.5	8.5	366	6.9	8.6	1.5
Gamma	19.1	9.3	185	8.3	10.5	1.0
Total	118.1	8.1	1,026	4.8	11.5	3.2

[1]Output value in billions of 1958 Col $.

[2]"Standardized" figures, which include an adjustment for underemployment.

[3]Output value in thousands of 1958 Col $.

If one arbitrarily adopts ICORs of 5.5, 4.5, 2.5, and 1.5 for agriculture and the three sub-sectors of non-agriculture during the 1970-85 period as a whole, the following results hold:

Sector and Sub-Sector	Level of Output in 1970[1]	Level of Output in 1985[1]	Average Annual Growth Rate, 1970-85	Total Growth Increment 1970-85[1]	ICOR	Total Investment Required 1970-85[1]
Agriculture	10.8	23.8	5.4	13.0	5.5	71.5
Non-Agriculture	26.1	94.3	8.9	68.2		219.8
Alpha	11.9	43.7	9.1	31.8	4.5	143.1
Beta	9.3	31.5	8.5	22.2	2.5	55.5
Gamma	5.0	19.1	9.3	14.1	1.5	21.2
Total	37.0	118.1	8.1	81.1		291.3

[1]Billions of 1958 Col $.

The overall rate of growth in required investment is a function of each sector's initial weight, output growth rate, and assumed ICOR. With the above assumptions total capital formation would have to rise by about 8.7% yearly, somewhat faster than output.

The ILO mission intended this model to serve primarily as an illustrative device, showing the results of one particular combination of assumptions out of many possibilities. As is to be expected, questions may be raised concerning particular assumptions. A 5.5 ICOR for agriculture, for instance, implies a 30% sectoral investment coefficient at a 5.4% rate of output growth. This high ICOR is related, of course, to the assumed increase of labor productivity from 2.0% to 3.5%. One might also question the postulated reduction of Alpha's productivity gain from 4.0% to 2.9% and Gamma's from 2.0% to 1.0%.

Table 2-8: NON-AGRICULTURAL OUTPUT, EMPLOYMENT AND PRODUCTIVITY PROJECTIONS, 1970-85

Subsector or Activity	Estimated 1970 Output[1]	Targeted 1985 Output[1]	Average % Change	Labor Productivity % Rates, 1964-70/ 1970-85	Estimated 1970 Employment[2]	Targeted 1985 Employment[2]	Average % Change
Alpha	11.9	43.7	9.1	4.0/2.9	.59	1.40	6.0
Mining	1.3	2.5	4.6	2.5/2.5	.07	.10	2.1
Modern manufacturing	7.4	27.6	9.2	4.5/3.2	.31	.72	5.8
Public utilities	0.5	2.8	12.5	8.5/8.5	.01	.02	4.0
Transportation	2.8	10.8	9.5	3.0/2.0	.19	.56	7.4
Beta	9.3	31.5	8.5	1.4/1.5	1.35	3.66	6.9
Construction	1.4	6.4	10.8	2.0/1.8	.26	.94	8.9
Handicraft mfg.	1.0	3.3	7.9	1.6/2.0	.32	.74	5.8
Commerce	4.5	16.1	8.5	1.0/1.0	.40	1.15	7.3
Personal services	2.4	5.7	6.5	1.5/1.0	.37	.83	5.5
Gamma	5.0	19.1	9.3	2.0/1.0	.56	1.85	8.3
Banking	1.2	4.0	8.5	2.5/1.0	.09	.25	7.5
Other services	3.8	15.1	9.5	1.8/1.0	.47	.16	8.5

[1] Output value at factor cost in billions of 1958 Col $.

[2] "Standarized" figures in million man-years.

The general approach of specifying output growth rates, ICORs, and labor productivities by sector in order to achieve full employment by 1985 seems useful. On the other hand, there are substantial uncertainties when dealing with a projection period of 15 years and assuming a sharp departure from past trends. One of these uncertainties concerns the unstable nature of ICORs. It is generally believed that gross ICORs such as those used here tend to decline as growth rates accelerate, because of a diminishing share of capital replacement in total investment. Historical ratios associated with 4% to 5% growth rates would normally be higher, therefore, than those one would anticipate for 7% to 8% growth rates.

The Challenge

While population control measures are desirable for many reasons, including their effect on employment over the long run, they can do little to resolve Colombia's unemployment problem between now and 1985. This problem is inescapable because most of the potential workers have already been born, and the 3.5% growth rate of the labor force is essentially independent of fertility and birth rates in the next decade. The only solution in sight is to maintain output growth rates at the highest level possible, while systematically applying every feasible measure to create new jobs. Without rapid and sustained growth the probabilities of eliminating unemployment are very low. On the other hand, a high growth rate will not by itself create full employment. Labor legislation would have to be adapted, government policies reconsidered, and a persistent, all-out campaign launched, to ensure that the maximum number of work opportunities is created.

Although the main lines of battle will be drawn around Colombia's urban areas it is impossible to ignore the underemployment found in the countryside. In this context one must beware of misleading figures; a 1.8% rate of growth in agricultural employment seems modest enough, but when translated into an absolute figure of 50,000 jobs annually the task appears quite formidable. It is clear, furthermore, that the thorny problem of land redistribution will have to be resolved somehow if these workers are to remain in the countryside.

CHAPTER 3
GROWTH, CAPITAL REQUIREMENTS, AND EXTERNAL DEBT, 1970-85*

Conceptual Framework

This chapter describes a simulation exercise conducted to gain insight into Colombia's growth prospects, balance of payments, and external indebtedness during the next fifteen years. The model employed was originally a "requirements" model, wherein external capital inflow is determined by the needs of the domestic economy. Certain modifications to the original program, however, made it somewhat of a hybrid "requirements/availabilities" model. The meaning of this will be clarified in the following paragraphs.

The exercise is based on an assumption that savings and foreign exchange are the two main constraints on Colombia's economic growth, and that the country's absorptive capacity (ability to absorb capital and convert it efficiently into output) will be adequate at the rates of growth specified. Thus the model is essentially a "two-gap" model, a type that has received a good deal of attention in recent years.

When one posits a relationship, fixed or variable through time, between future capital formation and a given rate of growth in output one also determines the amount of resources that will be needed to finance that investment. Any shortfall of anticipated domestic savings relative to that investment may be called a "domestic resource gap." Any expected excess of a country's imports over its exports (goods and non-factor services) constitutes a second, "external resource gap." Capital resources from abroad can fill these gaps and make desired rates of output growth a reality.

The two gaps are always equal, *ex post facto,* and the economy can grow only at the rate permitted by the "dominant" or more constraining gap. A country that expects to save at a rate sufficient to cover all its investment requirements may still be thwarted in reaching its growth target, for example, if it cannot obtain imported goods or materials essential to the productive process. It can acquire these items only by paying out foreign exchange, exchange that must either be earned or borrowed abroad. The extent to which exports and external borrowing can be increased will determine how rapidly imports can be expanded.

Sometimes the link between imports and output growth can be "stretched" through import substitution. It is true that many countries have succeeded in lowering the import coefficient for selected sectors of their economy, but it is not so common to see a dramatic decline in the ratio of their total imports to total output. Colombia seems likely to continue to achieve selective import substitution during the next 10-15 years, but it is equally likely that the overall ratio of imports to output will not fall drastically.

This import-output relationship is crucial to gap analysis and if assumptions about it are far off the mark most conclusions will be erroneous. Related to this key ratio is the incremental capital-output ratio (ICOR), which relates output growth to investment. If a dominant external gap forces a country to substitute domestically produced capital goods for foreign ones on a massive scale in order to grow at the desired rate, this may raise the cost of the items involved, and thus increase the capital spending needed to achieve a unit increase in output.[1] A rising ICOR in turn means that more savings will be necessary to achieve a target rate of growth, and if this process continues far enough the domestic resource gap will become the dominant constraint.

*Some projections and other figures used in this chapter have not been included in tables, but will be supplied on request.

---

1. Should absorptive capacity turn out to be less than desired, because of shortages of specialized skills or managerial abilities, structural inflexibilities in the system, technological drag, or dozens of other possible reasons, this would also result in a rising ICOR and falling returns to investment. And one can speak of intermediate imports of goods and materials as well as capital goods; shortages of these items normally affect output well before capital goods shortages.

Colombia really has only one way to insure that high rates of growth will be feasible, and that is to raise *both* domestic saving and exports to levels compatible with investment and output targets. Any substantial reduction of the import coefficient and/or the capital-output ratio is not considered likely to occur within the next fifteen years, the period examined in this exercise.

One may correctly point out that adequate provision of foreign resources could permit Colombia to grow rapidly even if domestic savings and exports were not increased. It is here, however, that a third constraint is encountered: external debt service. Unless sizable amounts of the inflow were made as interest-free loans or grants it would not be long before the *gross* inflow required to achieve the desired *net* resource transfer would reach an astronomical level.

There is, in fact, a fourth constraint relevant to this discussion: public-sector revenue. If government revenue is not adequate to meet the demands of growing debt service, current expenses, and the domestic-currency portion of new investment projects, external lenders may be unable to commit resources on the desired scale. This point applies to public and private shares of saving and investment, and may perhaps be ignored for many purposes. It is critical to the present report, however. *In the model* an assumption that the public sector will find suitable ways of financing its spending program—by taxing or borrowing—is embedded in the general absorptive capacity assumption.[2]

The Model

The model used for this exercise is highly aggregative in nature, and is accordingly subject to many criticisms. It has the advantage, nonetheless, of directing attention to basic relationships in the system. The Colombian economy is divided into four productive sectors: (1) Agriculture, Forestry, and Fishing; (2) Modern Manufacturing, Mining, Transport, and Energy; (3) Handicraft Manufacturing, Construction, Commerce, and Personal Services; and (4) Banking and Other Services. This division is identical to that used by the International Labor Organization study group for the analysis of employment prospects in Colombia. A growth rate is specified for each sector, along with an incremental capital-output ratio, which together determine the required fixed investment. Inventory investment is computed separately as a constant 25% of the overall growth increment. Using the notation set forth in Table 3-1:

$$(1) \qquad Y_t = \sum_{i=1}^{4} Y_t^i ; \quad Y_t^i = (1 + r_t^i) \, Y_{t-1}^i ; \quad i = 1...4$$

i.e. total GDP in period t is equal to the sum of the four sectoral GDPs, each of which is equal to one plus the specified rate of output growth times the value of the previous period.

$$(2) \qquad I_t = \sum_{i=1}^{4} K_t^i + V_t ; \quad K_t^i = ICOR_t^i \, (Y_{t+1}^i - Y_t^i) ; \quad i = 1...4$$

$$V_t = .25 \, (Y_t - Y_{t-1})$$

i.e. total gross domestic investment in period t is equal to the sum of the four sectoral fixed investments plus inventory change. Each sector's investment is equal to its specified ICOR times its growth increment. (As indicated, fixed investment in any given year is related to the growth increment of the following year.)

Domestic savings are computed on the basis of marginal saving rates specified for the model:

---

2. It should be noted that in Colombia, as in most other developing countries, levels of imports and exports have a powerful effect on the public finances. Coffee export taxes alone provide a tenth of all central government current receipts, and import duties account for another 20%.

$$(3) \qquad S_t = MSR_t \ (Y_t - Y_{t-1}) \ + \ S_{t-1}$$

Total consumption is computed by applying (1–MSR) to the growth increment:

$$(4) \qquad C_t = (1 - MSR) (Y_t - Y_{t-1}) + C_{t-1}$$

Table 3-1: SYMBOLIC NOTATION FOR MAJOR VARIABLES

Notation	Variable
Y(1)	GDP, Sector 1 (Agriculture, Forestry, Fishing)
Y(2)	GDP, Sector 2 (Modern Mfg., Mining, Transport, Energy)
Y(3)	GDP, Sector 3 (Handicraft Mfg., Construction, Commerce, Personal Services)
Y(4)	GDP, Sector 4 (Banking, Other Services)
Y	Total Gross Domestic Product, all sectors[1]
C	Total Consumption Expenditure
CG	Government Consumption Expenditure
CP	Private Consumption Expenditure
V	Inventory Investment
K(1)	Fixed Investment, Sector 1
K(2)	Fixed Investment, Sector 2
K(3)	Fixed Investment, Sector 3
K(4)	Fixed Investment, Sector 4
I	Total Gross Domestic Investment
ICOR(1)	Incremental Capital - Output Ratio, Sector 1
ICOR(2)	Incremental Capital - Output Ratio, Sector 2
ICOR(3)	Incremental Capital - Output Ratio, Sector 3
ICOR(4)	Incremental Capital - Output Ratio, Sector 4
ICOR	Overall Incremental Capital - Output Ratio (I/ Y)
S	Gross Domestic Savings (Y – C)
MSR	Marginal Savings Rate (S/ Y)
X	Exports of Goods and Non-factor Services
M	Imports of Goods and Non-factor Services
ERT	External Resource Transfer (X – M = C + I – Y = NPT + NOT)
NFP	Net Factor Payments to Foreigners (NII + IPD)
NII	Net Private Investment Income Payments to Foreigners
IPD	Interest Payments on Public External Long-term Debt
NUTR	Net Unrequited Transfers
CAB	Current Account Balance (defined as ERT – NFP + NUTR)
NPRIVC	Net Private Long-Term Capital Movement
NOCM	Net "Other" Capital Movement (private short-term + errors and omissions)
R	Net Change in International Monetary Reserves (total system)
GPUBLC	Gross Public Long-term Capital Movement
A	Amortization Payments on Public External Long-term Debt
NPUBLC	Net Public Long-term Capital Movement (GPUBLC – A)
NPT	Net Public External Resource Transfer (NPUBLC – IPD)
NOT	Net "Other" External Resource Transfer (NPRIVC + NOCM + NUTR + R – NII)
PDC(1)	Public External Debt Category 1 : AID Program /Sector Loans
PDC(2)	2: AID Project Loans
PDC(3)	3: IBRD Loans
PDC(4)	4: IDA Loans
PDC(5)	5: IDB FSO (Fund for Special Operations) Loans
PDC(6)	6: IDB OC (Ordinary Capital) Loans
PDC(7)	7: Other Development Project Loans
PDC(8)	8: U.S. Export-Import Bank Loans
PDC(9)	9: Non-U.S. Official Export Finance
PDC(10)	10: Private Suppliers' and Financial Credits
DS	Debt Service (interest + amortization) on Public External Debt

[1] All GDP values at Market Prices.

Source: IBRD.

Government consumption CG is set to grow at 10% per annum and private consumption is computed as a residual:

(4-a) $CG_t = (1 + .10) CG_{t-1}$

(4-b) $CP_t = C_t - CG_t$

Exports of goods and non-factor services are specified exogenously for each year of the projection period. Imports of goods and non-factor services are determined by the model as equal to exports plus the savings-investment gap:

(5) $M_t = X_t + I_t - S_t$

This of course means that the two gaps are identical, *ex post,* as required by the accounting identity $I-S = M-X$. The gap value determines the extent of any required external resource transfer ERT, which in turn is composed of a net public resource transfer NPT and a net "other" resource transfer NOT. To calculate the gross resource flows required to achieve these net transfers the model requires specification of net private investment income payments NII, net unrequited transfers NUTR, net private capital movements NPRIVC & NOCM, reserve changes R, and terms to be applied to the new external debt. It computes total net factor payments NFP by summing the given NII with the calculated interest on public debt IPD, then determines the overall current account balance CAB.

A novelty of this particular exercise arises from the manner in which debt is treated. Ten public external debt categories (PDCs) are specified, each with its own set of terms and repayment scheme.[3] The file for each PDC contains fully specified disbursement, amortization, interest, and outstanding balance values for all debt contracted prior to January 1, 1970. This "Old Debt" information is furnished to the model for each year of the projection period, along with assumed gross disbursements arising from commitments made after that date ("New Debt"). But these "new" disbursements are stated for only nine of the ten categories; the tenth, referring to private suppliers' and financial credits, is determined by the model as the final residual element needed to close the external gap ERT-NOT.

Although the model works on the basis of disbursements, furthermore, these have been elaborated by applying explicit disbursement patterns for each PDC to assumed commitments in each year. The one case where this link is broken is that of new PDC 10 flows, but since private credits frequently involve a variable relationship between commitments and disbursements one can set the former equal to the latter without introducing excessive bias.

Summing up, the model requires exogenous specification of sectoral growth rates and ICORs, the marginal savings rate, exports, private capital and capital service flows, unrequited transfers, reserve changes, full information on "Old Debt," and disbursement values for nine of the ten "New Debt" categories with terms and payback schemes to be applied to them. It processes this information and computes absolute values and several ratios relating to production, investment, saving, trade and payments, and external indebtedness.

The Assumptions

The year 1968 was chosen as a base year for the exercise, since that is the most recent period for which national accounts data are available. Peso values were converted into U.S. dollars at Col\$15.90 per dollar, the rate implicit in the national accounts treatment of imports and exports. Colombia's accounts do not present capital formation by economic sector, and it was necessary to estimate 1968 investment levels (Table 3-2; these assumed sectoral values for 1968 do not affect investment calculations for subsequent years because investment is determined by the assumed ICORs and stipulated growth rates).

The selection of ICORs for the exercise was made on the basis of the historical record, work

---

3. The greater the number of debt categories the lower is the risk of introducing mathematical bias into service computations because of aggregation. For an example of the error one may create by using "average" terms see *Possible Improvements in Techniques of Lending,* a study done by the IBRD staff for UNCTAD in April 1970 (p. 27).

Table 3-2: ESTIMATES OF SECTORAL INVESTMENT, 1968
(In millions of Col$)

Sector	1967 GDP[1]	1968 GDP	1967-68 GDP Increment	Estimated 1968 Fixed Investment
1	25,784	27,554	1,770	2,910
2	22,740	23,850	1,110	8,585
3	28,185	30,085	1,900	5,650
4	14,115	14,895	780	1,670
Total	90,824	96,384	5,560	18,815

[1]Expressed in millions of constant 1968 Col$.

done by the ILO employment mission, and judgment about the future of the Colombian economy. The postwar experience is summarized in Table 3-3.

The ILO employment mission posited fixed ICORs of 5.5, 4.5, 2.5, and 1.5 for sectors 1 through 4, respectively—see Chapter 2. The ILO's 5.5 agricultural ICOR was believed to be high, however, and a value of 4.0 was substituted. This had the effect of reducing the overall gross total ICOR (which includes inventory accumulation) from approximately 3.7 to 3.4, on the average, for the 1969-85 projection period. In total, four combinations of GDP growth rates and sectoral ICORs were considered:[4]

Sector	Case 1 Rate	Case 1 ICOR	Case 2 Rate	Case 2 ICOR	Case 3 Rate	Case 3 ICOR	Case 4 Rate	Case 4 ICOR
1	.050	4.0	.050	5.5	.054	4.0	.054	5.5
2	.080	4.5	.080	4.5	.091	4.5	.091	4.5
3	.075	2.5	.075	2.5	.085	2.5	.085	2.5
4	.075	1.5	.075	1.5	.093	1.5	.093	1.5
Total[1]	.070	3.4	.070	3.7	.081	3.4	.081	3.7

[1]Total GDP growth rate refers to average for 1969-85 period; total ICOR includes inventory investment.

Case 1 is identified hereafter as the "Base Case". The 3.4 gross total ICOR contains about 0.2 points of inventory accumulation, i.e. the gross fixed ICOR is 3.2. This is nearly 10% below the 3.5 value recorded in the recent 1963-68 five-year period, but 10% higher than the value achieved in 1968. When considering this ICOR value for the 15-year projection the mission relied on its findings about Colombia's economic situation as of 1970. They were that the coffee outlook was generally favorable; combined with the recent impressive growth of non-traditional exports and a strong inflow of foreign resources, this suggested that the chronic foreign exchange constraint on Colombia's development might be less severe in the future. It followed that a better and more continuous supply of imports would permit the economy to function at higher levels of efficiency that hitherto achieved. It was observed that low ICOR-high growth years tended to coincide with high import levels in past years, and the mission concluded that if capital plant and equipment could be more fully utilized in the future this would certainly have a beneficial impact on capital

4. A fifth, "low-export" variation was also considered, using the growth rates and ICORs of Case 1.

productivity (this capacity-utilization improvement was not viewed as a one-shot cyclical phenomenon). The mission also took note of the fact that gross ICORs tend to fall as output growth rates accelerate, because of the diminishing importance of capital replacement in total investment.[5]

The specification of marginal savings rates for the exercise also required judgment. After due consideration of the historical record (savings data for the 1950-68 period are provided in Table 3-11) it was decided that the Base Case MSR should be set so as to maintain average savings at about 22% of GDP for the next 4-5 years, then raised steadily to nearly 25% by 1985. This implies a vigorous and continuous effort to increase savings from the 20% level of 1968, in view of the decline forecast for coffee prices after 1971. The MSR specification was linked very closely with a separate calculation of needed imports, since $M + (I - S) = X$. That is, once investment and exports are known savings must be set so as to generate an appropriate level of imports. Of course the exercise deals with *capacity* to import, and the objective is to obtain a capacity figure equal to or greater than the indicated requirement. An estimating equation based on the 1958-68 experience was used to determine this requirement (cf. Table 3-15), and further verification was then made by means of an ordinary least-squares multiple regression analysis relating imports to GDP and the overall terms of trade.

The export projection was built up from separate estimates for coffee, crude petroleum, "non-traditionals," non-monetary gold, merchandise freight, other transportation, travel, and other service receipts. Most of these estimates are given in Tables 3-12 and 3-13. Apart from the coffee projection, the growth assumption for "non-traditionals" is next in importance. The government's 20% annual growth target has been adopted for the 1970-75 period, with the rate lowered to 15% between 1975 and 1980 and 10% between 1980 and 1985. Overall exports of goods and non-factor services rise by an average annual 8.5% between 1968 and 1985. It should be noted, however, that preliminary estimates have been taken into account for 1969 and 1970, and that the export growth rate for the 1970-85 period is only 7.3%. (The difference is caused by the dramatic coffee price increase dating from September 1969.) A "low" export variant has non-traditionals growing by a constant 10% per annum between 1970 and 1985, pulling the overall export average down to 4.7% annually.

The actual export developments since these projections were made have been less favorable than expected. The price of coffee was projected to stay at 57.5¢ per pound f.o.b. in 1970 and 1971 and to decline gradually in 1972-75; in fact, under the pressure of unexpected stock disposals, it fell abruptly in late 1970 and amounted to 45.5¢ in mid-1971. Non-traditional exports, which rose at 25% annually in 1965-69 and were projected to grow at 20% in 1970-75, showed an actual increase in 1970 of 4% to 8%: the deceleration was caused by shortfalls in production of some items (cotton) and by buoyant demand on the domestic market for others. Aggregate exports in 1970 still rose considerably above 1969, but less than expected (1969 actual, US$662 million; 1970 projected, US$880 million; 1970 actual, US$800 million). While the developments in any one year can be normally expected to diverge from the forecast and do not invalidate a 15-year projection, they do serve as a reminder of the limitations of the exercise, particularly for an economy heavily dependent on a single primary export, call for a revision of the projection if the divergencies persist, and underline the need for considering the alternatives—such as the "low" export variant in the present case.

Private capital and capital service flows were exceedingly difficult to project, and finally were set equal and rising by an arbitrary US$5 million per year. (By setting NII equal to NPRIVC + NOCM one effectively neutralizes the impact of private flows in the exercise.) Net unrequited transfers were lowered in steps of US$5 million per year from US$31 million in 1968 to US$5 million in 1973 and held constant thereafter. This is a conservative specification which may serve to offset somewhat optimistic projections elsewhere. Reserve change is set to reflect reality through 1970, then jumped to US$65 million for each of the three years 1971-73,

---

5. Cf. Jaroslav Vanek, *Estimating Foreign Resource Needs for Economic Development* (McGraw-Hill, New York, 1967); and Vanek and Studenmund, "Towards a Better Understanding of the Incremental Capital-Output Ratio," *Quarterly Journal of Economics,* 82-3 (August 1968).

after which it is held at a constant US$40 million per year. These values are not so arbitrary as they may appear; they are designed to raise Colombia's net reserves to a level equivalent to three months' imports as soon as possible and hold them there.

To obtain the required debt information historical data were examined for each PDC and informal discussions were held with the Washington agencies in order to project new commitments. These commitments were then translated into disbursements for the exercise by the use of standardized percentage patterns. These same patterns were used to disburse the "pipeline" of funds already committed to Colombia prior to 1970. In general they are "longer" than estimates based on contract closing dates, meaning that it requires more time to disburse funds after the date of contract. (These patterns were based on an earlier examination of lending data.) One must admit that the potential margin of error here is enormous, and it should be emphasized that the commitments shown are not "forecasts."[6] It is also important to observe that the terms assigned to these PDC flows for the exercise may harden or soften significantly during the next fifteen years, which could have a profound effect on the debt service outlook.

The Results

The results of the four cases outlined above—differing in projected income growth rates and in ICORs—are set forth in Tables 3-18 to 3-22. Other variants were also processed. The main findings are discussed below.

7% Growth Rate, Low ICOR

Colombia's gross domestic product increased by 6.1% in 1968, 6.4% in 1969 and approximately 7% in 1970—a substantial acceleration from the 4.8% average in 1950-68. If this 7% GDP growth rate were maintained for the next fifteen years Colombia would generate a GDP of US$19,195 million (constant 1968 prices) in 1985, more than three times the US$6,062 million level reached in 1968. With a population rising from approximately 20.3 million in mid-1968 to 32.8 million in mid-1985 this would boost per capita GDP from US$300 in 1968 to US$585 in 1985. Under relatively favorable assumptions about returns to capital and supply of foreign exchange, such a goal would call for an increase in gross domestic investment from 21.2% to 24.4% of GDP and in gross domestic savings from 19.9% to 24.4% of GDP between 1968 and 1985.[7] Exports of goods and non-factor services would have to rise by an average 8.5% per annum between the same two years, 7.3% if measured from the estimated 1970 level. Imports would average 16.5% of GDP for the period as a whole. The productive structure of the economy would change, with agriculture's GDP share dropping from 28.6% in 1968 to 20.7% in 1985. The external resource gap hovers around 1.8% of GDP through 1975, then declines steadily to zero in 1985.

Debt data and projections are shown in Tables 3-20 to 3-22. Projected service on public external debt repayable in convertible currency would fluctuate between 10% and 12% of exports through 1973 (compared to actual 12.2% in 1968-69) then climb to a peak of 19.8% in 1984. Table 3-4 gives a summary of public external capital flows and service projections and Table 3-5 of basic balance of payments entries to 1985.

New lending commitments made in 1970 average 23.4 years to maturity, 5.0% interest, and 5.6 years of grace, with a 41% grant element. By 1985 these terms harden considerably, to 14.6 years maturity, 6.4% interest, 3.7 years of grace, and a 24% grant element. This hardening does not arise from changing terms within each debt category, but rather from changes in the relative importance of future flows. In 1970 bilateral and multilateral lenders account for 76% of total disbursements, whereas in 1985 this percentage declines to 51%.

---

6. A *projection* is merely a conditional statement, one which says that something will happen if certain conditions are met. A *forecast*, on the other hand, represents someone's best judgment as to most likely outcomes. In view of the variables and time periods involved in this exercise it would take great courage to label it a forecast.

7. In 1968 both savings and investment coefficients were a full percentage point above their 1966-68 averages.

Table 3-3: GROSS FIXED ICORS, 1950-68[1]

		1958 Prices	1968 Prices
Unlagged:	1950-68	4.03	4.47
	1958-68	3.52	3.91
	1963-68	3.39	3.77
	1967-68	3.05	3.38
Lagged:	1950-68	3.86	4.29
	1958-68	3.32	3.69
	1963-68	3.16	3.51
	1967-68	2.65	2.94

[1]Unlagged ICORs relate investment in a given year to the GDP gain of that same year; lagged ICORs related investment to GDP increment of the following year. For fuller 1950-68 record see Tables 3-9 to 3-11.

Within the bilateral grouping, moreover, AID lending drops from 83% to 23%. Since AID program and project lending is done on generous terms replacement by other flows cannot help but harden average terms.

If the Base Case sectoral growth rates are combined with the ILO labor productivity estimates set forth in Chapter 2, the following results are obtained for the 1970-85 period:

Sector	Base Case Output Growth	ILO Output per Man-Year Growth	Indicated Employment Growth	1970 Employment Level[1]	1985 Employment Level[1]
1	.050	.035	.015	255	319
2	.080	.029	.051	59	124
3	.075	.015	.060	135	324
4	.075	.010	.065	56	144
			(.040)	(504)	(911)

[1]ILO standardized figures in millions of man-years.

The implication is that at the 7% growth rate full employment is not reached before the mid-1990s. The projected labor supply in 1985 is 10.84 million (see Chapter 2); at a 7% growth rate of the economy, 9.11 million would be employed by 1985, or only 85% of the labor force. Assuming that the work force grows by 3% yearly after 1985, it would take another 10-12 years to reach full (i.e. 95%) employment. Allowing for a possible slight reduction in productivity growth and/or labor participation rates, or for the possibility that the 1970 employment levels estimated by the ILO team may be on the low side (see Chapter 1), one might anticipate full employment sometime in the early nineteen-nineties, 6-8 years beyond the 1985 target year.

7% Growth Rate, High ICOR; 8% Growth Rate, Low and High ICOR

If the assumed exogenous values prove reasonably accurate, the above results indicate that Colombia can sustain an average seven percent GDP growth rate without encountering severe debt service problems during the next fifteen years. These results are entirely dependent, however, on three major elements: (1) a high and rising rate of domestic saving and investment; (2) a fairly low capital-output ratio, relative to the postwar experience through 1968; and (3) a high rate of growth in non-traditional exports. If capital/output ratio turns out higher, however (because of less favorable export growth or for other reasons), savings and investments have to be higher still, and more external help is required. The same holds to an even larger

Table 3-4: PUBLIC EXTERNAL CAPITAL FLOWS AND SERVICE PROJECTIONS
(In millions of US$)

	1970	1975	1980	1985
Total Gross Disbursements	234	391	536	648
Amortization Payments	83	96	204	332
Interest Payments	42	94	181	283
Debt Service	125	190	386	615
Net Disbursements				
(Gross Disb. − D.S.)	109	201	151	33
Debt Service Ratio	11.5	13.4	17.9	19.6
Outstanding and Disbursed				
Debt at End of Year	1,212	2,278	3,568	4,914
Debt as % of GDP	17.5	23.5	26.2	25.1

degree for the 8% target growth rate—the rate preferable from the viewpoint of maximum employment.

In the 7% high ICOR case (Case 2) investment rises to 26% of GDP, and debt service rises to 26% of exports in 1985, compared to 19.6% in the Base Case (Case 1). Of course if some or all of this additional requirement could be obtained on softer terms the debt service ratio might be reduced to a peak of several points less. Since exports are already set to grow at 7.3% annually between 1970 and 1985 (with non-traditionals growing at an average of about 15%) it is perhaps too ambitious to expect still higher rates of increase for that variable.

The eight percent cases look more formidable, with investment coefficients of 27 and 29, respectively, in 1985. Although domestic savings climb to 25% and 26% of GDP the additional external flow required raises outstanding debt to US$10,029 and US$11,506 million, and debt service goes up to 42% and 50% of exports. Is there perhaps room for maneuver in the high growth cases by lowering the import coefficient? Referring to the historical import data shown in Tables 3-14 and 3-15, one can see that imports averaged 16.8% of GDP during the 1958-68 period, when measured in constant prices, and 13.4% when measured in current prices. Real GDP growth averaged 5.1% during this period. It is likely that a 7% growth rate would require a 16.5% import coefficient, at least initially; and an 8% rate would normally exert upward pressure on this coefficient. There is a possibility that exports may increase faster than stipulated: one would normally expect a higher level of exports at a higher rate of output growth, at least after several years. If exports were higher the internal gap would also have to be reduced and, at an unchanged capital-output ratio this would require an increase in domestic savings beyond the projected level of one-fourth of GDP.

Effects of Terms of Borrowing

There are two major types of sensitivity variations that should be conducted in this sort of exercise. The first has to do with basic economic variables: production, investment, savings, exports, and imports. The second covers the amounts and conditions of external assistance. If one admits that the achievement of either a 7% or an 8% rate of growth requires some irreducible minimum level of imports, believes that level to be somewhere near 16%-17% of GDP, and accepts the export projection, then there is only one way to get debt service down: obtain assistance from abroad on more favorable terms. To the extent that more help can be found on such terms, that amount can be deducted from the residual private financial and suppliers' credit category. (This is the category which otherwise expands rapidly to offset any shortfalls in official development finance and in which the terms of borrowing are particularly unfavorable.) The level of gross borrowing, of debt, and of debt service are very sensitive to such shifts in composition.

One way of illuminating the issue is to raise the following query: in shifting from a 7% GDP growth rate to an 8% rate, how much additional assistance would be required and what

Table 3-5: SUMMARY PROJECTION OF BASIC BALANCE OF PAYMENTS ENTRIES

(In millions of US$)

	1970	1975	1980	1985
Exports	1,085	1,420	2,160	3,145
Imports	1,206	1,585	2,275	3,143
Resource Transfer	121	165	115	-2
Net Factor Payments	137	214	326	453
Net Investment Income	95	120	145	170
Interest on Public Debt	42	94	181	283
Net Unrequited Transfers	20	5	5	5
Current Account Balance	-238	-375	-437	-446
Net Private Capital	95	120	145	170
Net Public Capital	151	295	332	316
Change in Reserves				
(- increase)	-8	-40	-40	-40
Cumulative Reserves	105	380	580	780
(as % of Imports)	(8.7)	(24.0)	(25.5)	(24.8)
Resource Transfer as				
Percentage of GDP	(1.7)	(1.7)	(0.8)	(-0.0)

would be the effect of financing this increment on development finance agency-type terms (7% interest, 25 years term of repayment, 5 years principal grace) rather than on suppliers' terms (8% interest, 9 years term, 2 years grace)? Table 3-7 shows the results obtained for (a) the incremental net resource transfer needed to pass from 7% to 8 %; (b) the incremental gross flow (disbursement) required to achieve this transfer if it were made on suppliers' terms, and (c) the incremental gross flow required if it were made on development finance agency-type terms. Also shown in rows (d) and (e) are the incremental debt service ratios for each of the two alternatives.

To transfer an additional US$356 million in 1970-75 requires a gross inflow of US$481

Table 3-6: PROJECTION OF SELECTED VALUES AT 7% AND
8% GROWTH RATES AND DIFFERENT ICORs

	Case 1 7% GR at 3.4 ICOR	Case 2 7% GR at 3.7 ICOR	Case 3 8.1% GR at 3.4 ICOR	Case 4 8.1% GR at 3.7 ICOR
US$ GDP per capita				
1969	310	310	313	313
1985	585	585	691	691
Investment/GDP				
1969	.239	.260	.270	.271
1985	.244	.260	.276	.291
1969-85	.242	.260	.274	.291
Savings/GDP				
1969	.219	.236	.249	.267
1985	.244	.257	.251	.263
1969-85	.232	.246	.249	.262
Debt Service/Exports				
1969	.116	.116	.116	.116
1985	.196	.263	.424	.503

million if financed on suppliers' credit terms versus US$403 million if financed on more generous development agency-type terms. This difference increases with the passage of time. The high debt service associated with suppliers' credits shows up clearly in the incremental ratios: by 1980 it adds 13.5 percentage points to the 7% growth case ratio versus 4.8 points from development agency-type financing. The gross flow needed to achieve any desired net transfer depends on the terms of financing: the more generous the terms the lower is the necessary gross flow.

Low Export Growth Variant

In the Low Export Growth Variant, the values set out in Table 3-8 have been specified for exports of goods and services, compared to the cases so far discussed:

If all other Base Case exogenous values are left unchanged, and since imports are determined by the resource gap plus exports, a decline in the latter results in substantial cuts in imports relative to the basic run. The import coefficient would have to fall from 17.4 in 1970 to 11.3 in 1985, implying a very strong import substitution. The debt service ratio, on the other hand, would rise to a peak of 28.4 in 1984. The key question in this case is whether a high rate of growth is feasible in the face of such relatively slow growth in the capacity to import.

General

One must be careful to treat the results of an exercise such as this with a proper degree of skepticism. Attempts to project economic activity even one year into the future usually fail, and a fifteen year projection is almost bound to go wrong. This exercise, moreover, involves a mixture of positive and normative values that may or may not be appropriate. Also, the results should be viewed as illustrative in nature because the exercise requires a number of strong assumptions any one of which can substantially affect the outcome. If the incremental capital-output ratios (ICORs) assumed here were raised, for example, investment requirements would go up. The assumption reflects a series of judgments concerning the forward course of the Colombian economy, and incorporates a certain amount of "target-setting" with respect to economic efficiency, capital/labor combinations, capacity utilization, and export growth. But one can say that *if* the values chosen are approximately correct Colombia should be able to grow at a rate of 7% without encountering severe debt management problems. If additional domestic efforts can be made and if additional external assistance can be obtained on reasonably favorable terms, Colombia could grow at 8%, as posited by the ILO team, which would permit the attainment of full employment some years sooner. It would be desirable to reexamine the complex of factors referred to earlier as "absorptive capacity" to verify that such a rate of change would be feasible in terms of institutional and skill capabilities. Its achievement would enhance Colombia's creditworthiness over the long run, other things being equal, although over the medium term it would involve a high liquidity risk as evidenced by high debt service ratios—unless, of course, a substantial improvement were to occur in Colombia's terms of borrowing. Very much would depend on the development in the world coffee market which, as amply demonstrated in the last two years, still plays a major role in the growth process of the Colombian economy. A prolonged slump in this market would make it very difficult to approach growth rates of the magnitude discussed in this chapter.

Table 3-7: INCREMENTAL RESOURCE FLOWS NEEDED FOR RAISING 7% TO 8% GROWTH RATE
(In millions of US dollars[1])

	1970	1971	1972	1973	1974	1975	1976	1977
(a) Net resource transfer	22	37	51	63	80	103	134	166
(b) Gross borrowing, suppliers' terms	22	41	61	84	115	158	215	284
(c) Gross borrowing, development finance agency-type terms	22	38	55	71	93	124	164	209
(d) Incremental debt service ratio, suppliers' terms[2]	.000	.003	.008	.016	.027	.039	.053	.071
(e) Incremental debt service ratio, d.f.a.-type terms[2]	.000	.001	.004	.006	.010	.014	.019	.026
	1978	1979	1980	1981	1982	1983	1984	1985
(a) Net resource transfer	195	228	276	325	371	436	494	571
(b) Gross borrowing, suppliers' terms	358	450	569	704	775	931	1,097	1,292
(c) Gross borrowing, development finance agency-type terms	253	307	380	459	542	651	762	902
(d) Incremental debt service ratio, suppliers' terms[2]	.091	.113	.135	.163	.172	.183	.207	.229
(e) Incremental debt service ratio, d.f.a.-type terms[2]	.033	.040	.048	.058	.068	.080	.092	.105

[1]Rows a, b and c only.

[2]Ratios based on unchanged export projection of the 7% growth case.

Table 3-8: EXPORT VALUES SPECIFIED IN LOW EXPORT GROWTH MODEL
(In millions of US$)

Year	Low Export Growth Variant	Base Case and other Variants
1968	788	788
1969	855	855
1970	1,085	1,085
1971	1,140	1,165
1972	1,145	1,205
1973	1,160	1,255
1974	1,150	1,305
1975	1,205	1,420
1976	1,260	1,530
1977	1,320	1,655
1978	1,385	1,795
1979	1,465	1,969
1980	1,560	2,160
1981	1,660	2,320
1982	1,775	2,500
1983	1,900	2,700
1984	2,030	2,910
1985	2,175	3,145

Table 3-9: INCREMENTAL CAPITAL OUTPUT RATIOS, 1950-68
(In millions of Col$)

Year	GDP	GDP Increment	Gross Fixed Investment	Fixed Investment Coefficient	ICOR	Lagged ICOR
1950	7,860.5	...	1,112.7	14.15	...	...
1951	8,940.9	1,080.4	1,189.3	13.30	1.10	1.03
1952	9,650.9	710.0	1,333.2	13.81	1.88	1.68
1953	10,734.7	1,083.8	1,785.6	16.63	1.65	1.23
1954	12,758.8	2,024.1	2,161.8	16.94	1.07	0.88
1955	13,249.8	491.0	2,383.0	17.98	4.85	4.40
1956	14,862.8	1,613.0	2,526.7	17.00	1.57	1.48
1957	17,810.6	2,947.8	2,643.3	14.84	0.90	0.86
1958	20,682.5	2,871.9	3,338.8	16.14	1.16	0.92
1959	23,648.8	2,966.3	3,907.9	16.52	1.32	1.12
1960	26,746.7	3,097.9	4,844.9	18.11	1.56	1.26
1961	30,421.0	3,674.3	5,580.3	18.34	1.52	1.32
1962	34,199.2	3,778.2	6,136.9	17.94	1.62	1.48
1963	43,525.5	9,326.3	7,167.5	16.47	0.77	0.66
1964	53,760.3	10,234.8	8,653.8	16.10	0.85	0.70
1965	60,797.6	7,037.3	9,504.2	15.63	1.35	1.23
1966	73,612.3	12,814.7	12,303.6	16.71	0.96	0.74
1967	83,525.2	9,912.9	14,729.1	17.63	1.48	1.24
1968	96,383.7	12,858.5	18,815.1	19.52	1.46	1.14

Source: Banco de la Republica.

Table 3-10: INCREMENTAL CAPITAL OUTPUT RATIOS, 1950-68
(In millions of 1958 Col$)

Year	GDP	GDP Increment	Gross Fixed Investment	Fixed Investment Coefficient	ICOR	Lagged ICOR
1950	14,688.8	...	2,771.8	18.87	...	...
1951	15,146.6	457.8	2,752.5	18.17	6.01	6.05
1952	16,102.0	955.4	2,965.4	18.42	3.10	2.88
1953	17,081.0	979.0	4,011.7	23.49	4.10	3.03
1954	18,262.3	1,181.3	4,670.0	25.57	3.95	3.40
1955	18,976.1	713.8	4,935.7	26.01	6.91	6.54
1956	19,745.7	769.6	4,683.7	23.72	6.08	6.41
1957	20,186.2	440.5	3,511.6	17.40	7.97	10.63
1958	20,682.5	496.3	3,338.8	16.14	6.73	7.08
1959	22,176.9	1,494.4	3,587.7	16.18	2.40	2.23
1960	23,123.4	946.5	4,225.6	18.27	4.46	3.79
1961	24,300.2	1,176.8	4,584.7	18.87	3.90	3.59
1962	25,615.3	1,315.1	4,602.0	17.96	3.50	3.49
1963	26,457.2	841.9	4,234.0	16.00	5.03	5.47
1964	28,088.8	1,631.6	4,764.2	16.96	2.92	2.59
1965	29,100.0	1,011.2	4,498.9	15.46	4.45	4.71
1966	30,658.2	1,558.2	4,859.7	15.85	3.12	2.89
1967	31,947.0	1,288.8	5,182.6	16.22	4.02	3.77
1968	33,902.2	1,955.2	5,958.0	17.57	3.05	2.65

Source: Banco de la Republica.

Table 3-11: DOMESTIC SAVINGS RATIOS, 1950-68
(In millions of Col$)

Year	GDP	GDS[1]	GDS/GDP (%)	Marginal Domestic Savings Rate[2]		Reference Column: NYC Price for Manizales Coffee[3]
				Annual	Cumulative	
1950	7,860.5	1,382.6	17.59	...	...	53.25
1951	8,940.9	1,463.7	16.37	.0750	.0750	58.70
1952	9,650.9	1,587.1	16.44	.1738	.1142	57.01
1953	10,734.7	1,751.6	16.32	.1518	.1284	59.92
1954	12,758.8	2,191.0	17.17	.2171	.1650	79.93
1955	13,249.8	2,126.8	16.05	-.1308	.1381	64.38
1956	14,862.8	2,671.1	17.97	.3374	.1840	73.97
1957	17,810.6	3,801.1	21.34	.3833	.2431	63.94
1958	20,682.5	4,481.5	21.67	.2369	.2417	52.34
1959	23,648.8	5,081.1	21.48	.2021	.2342	45.22
1960	26,746.7	5,498.1	20.56	.1346	.2179	44.89
1961	30,421.0	5,820.5	19.13	.0877	.1967	43.62
1962	34,199.2	6,143.5	17.96	.0855	.1804	40.77
1963	43,525.5	7,351.7	16.89	.1295	.1674	39.55
1964	53,760.3	8,809.1	16.38	.1424	.1618	48.80
1965	60,797.6	11,361.2	18.69	.3626	.1885	48.49
1966	73,612.3	12,859.3	17.47	.1169	.1745	47.43
1967	83,525.2	15,769.9	18.88	.2936	.1901	41.94
1968	96,383.7	19,146.3	19.86	.2626	.2007	42.60

[1] Gross Domestic Saving equals Gross Domestic Investment plus surplus from trade in goods and non-factor services.

[2] Marginal Savings Rate equals change in GDS divided by change in GDP.

[3] Price in U.S. cents per pound.

Source: IBRD.

Table 3-12:   F.O.B. MERCHANDISE EXPORTS, ACTUAL 1950-68 AND PROJECTED 1969-85[1]
(In millions of US$)

Year	Coffee[2]	Coffee Adjustment[3]	Adjusted Coffee	Crude Petroleum[4]	"Non-traditionals"[5]	Non-traditionals Adjustment[6]	Adjusted Non-traditionals	Non-Monetary Gold	Total Goods Exports
1950	308	0	308	65	23	0	23	12	408
1951	360	0	360	74	26	0	26	14	474
1952	380	0	380	71	22	0	22	14	487
1953	492	0	492	76	40	0	40	14	622
1954	550	0	550	76	31	0	31	13	670
1955	487	-4	483	61	35	0	35	13	592
1956	413	116	529	70	54	0	54	15	668
1957	389	19	408	76	46	60	106	11	601
1958	355	11	366	67	39	55	94	12	539
1959	361	-15	346	73	40	55	95	14	528
1960	332	-30	302	80	53	45	98	15	495
1961	308	3	311	68	58	25	83	14	476
1962	332	-25	307	61	69	25	94	14	476
1963	303	12	315	77	67	15	82	11	485
1964	394	50	444	75	79	25	104	13	636
1965	344	29	373	88	107	12	119	11	591
1966	328	3	331	71	109	13	122	10	534
1967	322	11	333	61	127	28	155	9	558
1968	351	17	368	36	171	28	199	6	609
1969	354	6	360	55	209	31	240	7	662
1970	514	6	520	75	250	30	280	5	880
1971	527	3	530	80	300	30	330	5	945
1972	493	2	495	80	360	30	390	5	970
1973	457	-2	455	80	430	30	460	5	1,000
1974	419	1	420	55	520	30	550	5	1,030
1975	429	1	430	40	620	30	650	5	1,125
1976	433	2	435	30	715	30	745	5	1,215
1977	438	2	440	20	820	30	850	5	1,315
1978	442	-2	440	10	945	30	975	5	1,430
1979	446	-1	445	0	1,085	30	1,115	5	1,565

Year									
1980	451	-1	450	0	1,250	30	1,280	5	1,735
1981	455	0	455	0	1,375	30	1,405	5	1,865
1982	460	0	460	0	1,510	30	1,540	5	2,005
1983	465	0	465	0	1,665	30	1,695	5	2,165
1984	470	0	470	0	1,830	30	1,860	5	2,335
1985	475	0	475	0	2,015	30	2,045	5	2,525

[1] Values in millions of current dollars through 1968, in constant 1968 prices thereafter.

[2] Coffee projection 1976-85 estimates assume constant 45 cents price and one percent annual volume increase.

[3] Coffee adjustment for balance of payments includes valuation, overseas stock changes, and unregistered shipments.

[4] Petroleum projection 1970-75 by the National Planning Department, 1976-78 figures are IBRD estimates.

[5] Non-traditionals increased by 20% annually through 1975, 15% – 1975-80, and 10% – 1980-85.

[6] Non-traditionals adjustment covers unrecorded border trade.

Sources: DANE; Banco de la Republica; IMP *Balance of Payments Yearbook*.

Table 3-13: EXPORTS OF SERVICES, ACTUAL 1950-68 AND PROJECTED 1969-85[1]
(In millions of US$)

Year	Merchandise Freight Receipts[2]	Other Transportation Receipts[3]	Travel Receipts[4]	Other Service Receipts[5]	Total Service Receipts	Total Export Receipts	Service Receipts/ Total Receipts
1950	7	2	7	8	24	432	.055
1951	11	3	8	10	32	506	.063
1952	13	3	9	11	36	523	.069
1953	12	4	11	17	44	666	.066
1954	8	5	13	20	46	716	.064
1955	12	11	14	13	50	642	.084
1956	16	10	9	30	65	733	.089
1957	17	12	11	43	83	684	.121
1958	19	10	17	34	80	619	.129
1959	24	10	17	30	81	609	.133
1960	28	11	23	32	94	589	.160
1961	30	13	23	36	102	578	.176
1962	33	15	13	34	95	571	.166
1963	33	16	19	37	105	590	.178
1964	36	19	25	33	113	749	.151
1965	44	18	28	28	118	709	.166
1966	41	23	33	32	129	663	.195
1967	41	31	46	36	154	712	.216
1968	39	32	45	63	179	788	.227
1969	41	35	50	67	193	855	.225
1970	43	39	54	69	205	1,085	.189
1971	45	43	60	72	220	1,165	.190
1972	47	47	66	75	235	1,205	.196
1973	50	52	72	81	255	1,255	.203
1974	52	57	80	86	275	1,305	.210
1975	55	62	88	90	295	1,420	.207
1976	58	69	96	92	315	1,530	.206
1977	60	75	106	99	340	1,655	.205
1978	63	83	117	102	365	1,795	.204
1979	67	91	128	109	395	1,960	.201
1980	70	100	141	114	425	2,160	.196
1981	73	110	155	117	455	2,320	.197
1982	77	121	171	126	495	2,500	.198
1983	81	134	188	132	535	2,700	.198
1984	85	147	207	136	575	2,910	.198
1985	89	162	227	142	620	3,145	.198

[1]Services exclusive of investment income receipts. Values in millions of current US$ through 1968, in constant 1968 prices thereafter.

[2]Primarily earnings of the Gran Colombiana merchant fleet. Average annual growth rate 1950-68: 10.0%; 1958-68: 7.5%; 1968-85: 5.0%.

[3]Primarily passenger fare receipts and port payments made by foreign carriers. Average annual growth rate 1950-68: 16.7%; 1958-68: 12.3%; 1968-85: 10.0%.

[4]Tourism, student travel, and a sizable "other" category (US$24 million in 1968). Average annual growth rate 1950-68: 10.9%; 1958-68: 10.2%; 1968-85: 10.0%.

[5]Border workers' earnings, copyright and patent royalties, etc. Average annual growth rate 1950-68: 12.2% 1958-68: 6.4%; 1968-85: 5.0%.

Source: *IMF Balance of Payments Yearbook.*

Table 3-14: IMPORTS OF GOODS AND SERVICES, 1950-68[1]
(In millions of US$)

	F.O.B. Merchandise Imports[2]	Freight Charges[3]	Other Transportation[4]	Travel[5]	Government Services[6]	Other Services[7]	Subtotal, Services	Total Goods and Services	Total Imports as % of GDP[8]
1950	336	8	14	13	13	22	70	406	.101
1951	390	15	14	15	29	16	89	479	.127
1952	384	17	17	19	24	12	89	473	.124
1953	524	20	22	20	26	15	103	627	.146
1954	622	27	20	23	23	26	119	741	.146
1955	620	18	36	23	30	19	126	746	.143
1956	599	19	36	22	29	26	132	731	.126
1957	450	28	32	28	14	29	131	581	.137
1958	384	21	30	23	11	29	114	498	.158
1959	402	18	36	22	7	27	110	512	.143
1960	496	21	49	28	9	31	138	634	.156
1961	531	24	49	24	9	33	139	670	.146
1962	537	30	50	23	14	36	153	690	.129
1963	498	26	34	25	8	65	158	656	.130
1964	582	36	60	55	10	76	237	819	.133
1965	430	29	60	50	13	71	223	653	.104
1966	639	54	42	54	12	66	228	867	.151
1967	464	50	49	58	14	61	232	696	.114
1968	615	53	43	60	23	72	251	866	.143

[1]Imports as adjusted and defined for balance of payments, exclusive of investment income payments.

[2]Derived from c.i.f. values given in trade returns.

[3]Estimated freight payments to foreign carriers.

[4]Passenger fares, port disbursements abroad by Gran Colombiana Merchant fleet and other domestic carriers, and time charters.

[5]Tourism, student travel, and a sizable "other" category.

[6]Government services not included elsewhere (Colombian Embassy and consular expenses, etc).

[7]Payments for advertising, film rentals, copyrights and patent royalties, border workers' earnings, and a sizable miscellaneous category.

[8]Imports as recorded in pesos for national accounts divided by GDP. The average for 1950-68 is 0.143 (import coefficient of 14.3%).

In constant 1958 prices, the average for 1950-68 is 0.187, and for 1958-68, 0.168 (import coefficient of 16.8%).

Sources: DANE; Banco de la Republica; IMF *Balance of Payments Yearbook.*

Table 3-15: C.I.F. IMPORTS OF GOODS, 1958-68
(In millions of US$) [1]

	Consumer Goods Imports	Intermediate Goods Imports	Capital Goods Imports	Unclassified Goods Imports	Total C.I.F. Goods Imports [2]	Total Imports Of Goods and Services [3]	C.I.F. Goods as % of Total Imports	Total Imports, in Col$ [4]
1958	21.599	173.056	82.805	122.472	399.932	498	.803	3.271
1959	21.548	163.660	98.887	131.493	415.588	512	.812	3.384
1960	37.850	233.604	169.946	77.185	518.585	634	.818	4.161
1961	59.416	262.480	163.852	71.381	557.129	670	.831	4.435
1962	32.751	260.516	166.232	80.852	540.351	690	.783	4.408
1963	28.075	258.505	157.432	62.011	506.023	656	.771	5.666
1964	26.522	303.915	195.804	60.050	586.291	819	.715	7.169
1965	21.032	182.315	177.164	72.991	453.502	653	.695	6.324
1966	47.359	350.097	207.932	68.758	674.146	867	.777	11.098
1967	34.074	214.673	176.632	71.529	496.908	696	.714	9.521
1968	32.213	231.500	233.723	145.882	643.318	866	.742	13.780

	C.I.F. Goods [5]	Consumption Expenditure [6]	Gross Fixed Investment [6]	Gross Domestic Product [6]	Consumer Goods Imports/ Consumption [7]	Inter. and Unclassified Imports/GDP [7]	Capital Imports/Fixed Investment [7]
1958	2.627	16.201	3.339	20.682	.009	.094	.163
1959	2.748	18.568	3.908	23.649	.008	.082	.167
1960	3.403	21.249	4.845	26.747	.012	.076	.230
1961	3.685	24.600	5.580	30.421	.016	.073	.194
1962	3.451	28.056	6.137	34.199	.007	.064	.173
1963	4.369	36.174	7.168	43.526	.007	.064	.190
1964	5.126	44.951	8.654	53.760	.005	.059	.198
1965	4.396	49.436	9.504	60.798	.004	.041	.181
1966	8.623	60.753	12.304	73.612	.010	.073	.216
1967	6.798	67.755	14.729	83.525	.007	.047	.164
1968	10.224	77.237	18.815	96.384	.007	.062	.197

[1] Except where indicated in millions of current Col$.

[2] All C.I.F. goods import values are from trade returns, and are not adjusted to cover unrecorded border trade, ship purchases by Gran Colombiana Merchant fleet, etc.

[3] Balance-of-payments imports, exclusive of investment income payments.

[4]Total imports of goods and services, exclusive of investment income payments, as recorded in national accounts.

[5]In millions of Col$; obtained by applying preceding dollar percentages to peso total.

[6]In millions of Col$; consumption, investment, and GDP values from national accounts.

[7]Peso values for each category of C.I.F. goods imports obtained by applying known percentages of dollar total c.i.f. imports to peso total. Each computed value was then divided by the appropriate macroeconomic aggregate. Weighted average percentages for the 1958-68 period were .008, .067, and .188, respectively. These values, plus average .766 for c.i.f. Goods/Total Imports during 1958-68 period, provide a basis for the equation M = 1.33 (.01 C + .07 GDP + .20 GFDI). This equation says future imports of goods and non-factor services should equal 1.33 times the sum of 1% of projected consumption, 7% of GDP, and 20% of gross fixed domestic investment (multiplying by a factor of 1.33 is equivalent to dividing by .750). Values obtained by this method were used as a rough check on imports determined by the gap model. It was found that a multiplier of 1.35 (i.e. 100/.743) is required to raise the estimated c.i.f. goods subtotal for the 1970-85 projection period (1969 value checks against provisional figure) to the gap-determined total import value for the period. That is, the projection total coincides with results obtained by use of the estimating equation if one raises the share of "non-c.i.f." services from 23.4 to 25.7% of the total. Such an adjustment is clearly within reasonable limits, in view of the 1958-68 variation, and happens to be equal to the observed 1968 value. Hence the two projections of imports are entirely compatible (with the slightly higher values determined by the gap model further supported by the fact that output grew by an average of only 5.1% per annum between 1958 and 1968, as contrasted with the projected 7.0% rate for the 1968-85 period).

Sources: DANE; IBRD.

Table 3-16:   PROJECTED IMPORTS OF GOODS AND SERVICES, 1969-85[1]
(In millions of Constant 1968 US$)

	(1) Projected GDP	(2) Projected C	(3) Projected GFDI	(4) Imports of Consumption Goods (.01 C)	(5) Imports of Intermediate Goods (.07 GDP)	(6) Imports of Capital Goods (.20 GFDI)	(7) Total C.I.F. Goods Imports (4 + 5 + 6)[3]	(8) Projected Total Imports[4]	(9) Residual, "Non-C.I.F." Services[5]	(10) Total Imports as Percentage of GDP
(1968)[2]	(6,062)	(4,857)	(1,183)	(32)	(377)	(234)	(643)	(866)	(223)	(.143)
1969	6,481	5,059	1,442	51	454	288	793	980	187	.151
1970	6,929	5,394	1,544	54	485	309	848	1,206	358	.174
1971	7,410	5,768	1,653	58	519	331	908	1,297	389	.175
1972	7,925	6,169	1,770	62	555	354	971	1,348	377	.170
1973	8,477	6,599	1,896	66	593	379	1,038	1,411	373	.166
1974	9,069	7,059	2,031	71	635	406	1,112	1,475	363	.163
1975	9,703	7,533	2,177	75	679	435	1,189	1,585	396	.163
1976	10,382	8,039	2,332	80	727	466	1,273	1,689	416	.163
1977	11,111	8,581	2,500	86	778	500	1,364	1,806	442	.163
1978	11,892	9,159	2,679	92	832	536	1,460	1,937	477	.163
1979	12,729	9,778	2,872	98	891	574	1,563	2,090	527	.164
1980	13,628	10,440	3,078	104	954	616	1,674	2,275	601	.167
1981	14,591	11,148	3,300	111	1,021	660	1,792	2,419	627	.166
1982	15,624	11,905	3,539	119	1,094	708	1,921	2,579	658	.165
1983	16,732	12,715	3,795	127	1,171	759	2,057	2,756	699	.165
1984	17,920	13,582	4,070	136	1,254	814	2,204	2,939	735	.164
1985	19,195	14,509	4,366	145	1,344	873	2,362	3,143	781	.164
(1969-85)	(199,798)						(24,529)	(32,935)	(8,406)	(.165)

[1] Imports of goods and services exclusive of investment income payments.

[2] Base year actual values.

[3] Unadjusted for unrecorded border trade, etc; figures from DANE trade returns.

[4] Total imports as determined by gap model.

[5] Includes some goods and related services arising from border trade, ship purchases by Gran Colombiana Merchant fleet, etc. (estimated at US$44 million in 1966, US$33 million in 1967, and US$43 million in 1968).

Source: IBRD.

Table 3-17: BALANCE OF PAYMENTS, ACTUAL 1950-68 AND PROJECTED 1969-85[1]
(In millions of US$)

Year	F.O.B. Merchandise Exports[2]	F.O.B. Merchandise Imports[3]	Service Receipts[4]	Service Payments[5]	Exports Minus Imports	Net Factor Payments[6]	Net Unrequited Transfers	Current Account Balance	Net Private Capital[7]	Net Public Capital[8]	Net Reserve Change[9]	Errors and Omissions
1950	408	336	24	70	26	-39	-1	-14	6		(25)	-17
1951	474	390	32	89	27	-36	14	5	12		(-17)	0
1952	487	384	36	89	50	-19	-2	29	0		(8)	-37
1953	622	524	44	103	39	-23	-1	15	16		(-13)	-18
1954	670	622	46	119	-25	-15	-2	-42	83		(11)	-52
1955	592	620	50	126	-104	-23	3	-124	-16		(145)	-5
1956	668	599	65	132	2	-16	2	-12	8		(77)	-73
1957	601	450	83	131	103	-26	3	80	-84		(29)	-25
1958	539	384	80	114	121	-62	5	64	-64	-2	4	-2
1959	528	402	81	110	97	-36	2	63	61	-9	-89	-26
1960	495	496	94	138	-45	-40	6	-79	40	4	-9	44
1961	476	531	102	139	-92	-50	9	-133	30	34	78	-9
1962	476	537	95	153	-119	-57	14	-162	43	40	46	33
1963	485	498	105	158	-66	-81	18	-129	118	50	33	-72
1964	636	582	113	237	-70	-73	14	-129	227	18	16	-132
1965	591	430	118	223	56	-79	12	-11	-41	27	-42	67
1966	534	639	129	228	-204	-86	10	-280	193	47	67	-27
1967	558	464	154	232	16	-105	22	-67	34	44	-62	51
1968	609	615	179	251	-78	-113	31	-160	52	90	6	12
1969	662	980[3]	193		-125	-123	25	-223	90	144	-11	0
1970	880	1,206	205		-121	-137	20	-238	95	151	-8	0
1971	945	1,297	220		-132	-149	15	-266	100	231	-65	0
1972	970	1,348	235		-143	-162	10	-295	105	255	-65	0
1973	1,000	1,411	255		-156	-179	5	-330	110	285	-65	0
1974	1,030	1,475	275		-170	-196	5	-361	115	286	-40	0
1975	1,125	1,585	295		-165	-214	5	-375	120	295	-40	0
1976	1,215	1,689	315		-159	-232	5	-387	125	302	-40	0
1977	1,315	1,806	340		-151	-254	5	-401	130	311	-40	0
1978	1,430	1,937	365		-142	-278	5	-414	135	319	-40	0
1979	1,565	2,090	395		-130	-302	5	-427	140	327	-40	0
1980	1,735	2,275	425		-115	-326	5	-437	145	332	-40	0
1981	1,865	2,419	455		-99	-351	5	-445	150	335	-40	0
1982	2,005	2,579	495		-79	-377	5	-450	155	335	-40	0
1983	2,165	2,756	535		-56	-402	5	-453	160	333	-40	0
1984	2,335	2,939	575		-29	-428	5	-452	165	327	-40	0
1985	2,525	3,143	620		2	-453	5	-446	170	316	-40	0

[1]Values in millions of current US$ through 1968, in constant 1968 prices thereafter. [2]Table 3-12
[3]Table 3-16. Column refers to merchandise and services together after 1968. [4]Table 3-13. [5]Table 3-14
[6]IMF *Balance of Payments Yearbook* for 1950-68; IBRD projections for 1969-85.
[7]Net Private Capital includes direct investment, short-term and long-term asset and liability changes.
[8]Gross disbursements minus amortization payments, cf. Table 3-22.
[9](-) indicates reserve increase.
Source: IBRD.

Table 3-18: BASE CASE PROJECTION, 1969-85: SELECTED VALUES, RATES, AND COEFFICIENTS

	Projected Mid-year Population[1]	GDP per Capita[2]	Annual Growth in GDP per Capita	Incremental Capital Output Ratio[3]	Annual Growth of Investment	Investment/GDP	Domestic Savings/GDP	Marginal Savings Rate[4]	Growth of Private per capita Consumption[5]	Growth of Exports	Growth of Imports	Imports/GDP	Resource Gap/GDP
(1968)	20.3	299	...	...	...	.212	.199	.235	...	...	...	.143	.013
1969	20.9	310	.038	3.063	.205	.239	.219	.518	.006	.085	.132	.151	.019
1970	21.6	321	.035	3.447	.071	.239	.222	.252	.029	.269	.231	.174	.017
1971	22.3	332	.036	3.445	.071	.239	.222	.222	.033	.074	.075	.175	.018
1972	23.0	345	.037	3.443	.071	.240	.222	.222	.034	.034	.039	.170	.018
1973	23.7	358	.038	3.441	.071	.240	.222	.222	.035	.041	.047	.166	.018
1974	24.5	370	.035	3.439	.071	.240	.224	.252	.032	.040	.045	.163	.019
1975	25.3	384	.036	3.438	.072	.241	.226	.255	.030	.088	.075	.163	.017
1976	26.0	399	.041	3.436	.072	.241	.228	.257	.035	.077	.066	.163	.015
1977	26.8	415	.038	3.434	.072	.241	.230	.259	.032	.082	.069	.163	.014
1978	27.5	432	.043	3.433	.072	.242	.232	.261	.036	.085	.073	.163	.012
1979	28.3	450	.040	3.432	.072	.242	.234	.263	.033	.092	.079	.164	.010
1980	29.2	467	.038	3.430	.072	.242	.236	.265	.031	.102	.089	.167	.008
1981	29.9	488	.046	3.429	.072	.243	.238	.267	.039	.074	.063	.166	.007
1982	30.6	511	.046	3.428	.072	.243	.240	.269	.039	.078	.066	.165	.005
1983	31.3	535	.047	3.427	.072	.243	.242	.271	.040	.080	.069	.165	.003
1984	32.1	558	.044	3.426	.072	.244	.244	.273	.037	.078	.066	.164	.002
1985	32.8	585	.048	3.425	.073	.244	.244	.273	.041	.081	.069	.164	.000
(1968-85)	...	...	(.040)	...	(.079)	...	...	...	(.033)	(.085)[6]	(.079)[7]	...	...

[1] In millions.

[2] Constant 1968 US$ (total GDP increases by 7.0% per annum)

[3] GDP increase divided by gross domestic investment. (This overall ICOR is determined by the sectoral ICORs and rates of output growth, plus rate of inventory accumulation.)

[4] Increase in saving/increase in GDP.

[5] Total consumption is determined by GDP and saving rate; public consumption set to grow by 10% annually; private consumption is residual.

[6] Average annual export growth, 1970-85: .073, slightly above GDP growth.

[7] Average annual import growth, 1970-85: .066, slightly below GDP growth.

Source: IBRD.

Table 3-19: VARIANT PROJECTIONS, 1968-85[1]
(In millions of US dollars)

	Investment, 7% Growth High ICOR	Savings, 7% Growth High ICOR[2]	Debt Service Ratio, 7% Growth, High ICOR	8% Growth GDP	Investment, 8% Growth Base ICOR	Savings, 8% Growth, Base ICOR[3]	Debt Service Ratio, 8% Growth, Base ICOR	Investment, 8% Growth, High ICOR	Savings, 8% Growth, High ICOR[4]	Debt Service Ratio, 8% Growth, High ICOR
(1968)	1,283	1,205	.142	6,062	1,283	1,205	.142	1,283	1,205	.142
1969	1,683	1,531	.116	6,540	1,763	1,630	.116	1,911	1,748	.116
1970	1,799	1,650	.117	7,057	1,906	1,763	.116	2,062	1,888	.118
1971	1,924	1,762	.113	7,617	2,060	1,892	.109	2,225	2,023	.117
1972	2,057	1,883	.127	8,223	2,227	2,034	.123	2,401	2,171	.137
1973	2,200	2,012	.139	8,879	2,409	2,190	.136	2,591	2,335	.157
1974	2,354	2,150	.156	9,590	2,605	2,356	.156	2,798	2,509	.186
1975	2,518	2,318	.167	10,359	2,819	2,550	.173	3,022	2,710	.209
1976	2,694	2,498	.179	11,193	3,050	2,756	.193	3,264	2,926	.238
1977	2,883	2,692	.195	12,096	3,301	2,983	.220	3,526	3,162	.273
1978	3,086	2,902	.215	13,074	3,573	3,236	.255	3,810	3,425	.314
1979	3,303	3,129	.226	14,134	3,868	3,510	.283	4,118	3,708	.348
1980	3,536	3,375	.239	15,283	4,188	3,796	.314	4,452	4,004	.383
1981	3,786	3,639	.256	16,528	4,535	4,111	.353	4,813	4,331	.429
1982	4,054	3,925	.253	17,879	4,912	4,462	.353	5,205	4,694	.424
1983	4,342	4,233	.257	19,343	5,321	4,830	.377	5,630	5,075	.451
1984	4,651	4,565	.264	20,930	5,765	5,242	.405	6,091	5,500	.482
1985	4,983	4,925	.263	22,652	6,248	5,678	.424	6,591	5,951	.503

[1] Selected variables only. Savings shown, when coupled with related investment and (unchanging) exports, coincide with an adequate level of imports.

[2] Average savings coefficient, 1969-85: .246.

[3] Average savings coefficient, 1969-85: .249.

[4] Average savings coefficient, 1969-85: .262.

Table 3-20:　EXTERNAL PUBLIC DEBT INFORMATION, 1968 AND 1969
(In millions of US dollars)

	1 AID PROGRAM/ SECTOR		2 AID PROJECT		3 IBRD		4 IDA		5 IDB F.S.O.[1]		6 IDB O. C.	
	1968	1969	1968	1969	1968	1969	1968	1969	1968	1969	1968	1969
Disbursement	81.695	78.435	4.836	3.048	39.872	38.800	1.401	0.048	5.489	9.077	13.101	12.421
Amortization	3.213	3.407	0.848	0.874	14.259	15.559	0.000	0.000	0.000	0.000	2.690	3.278
Interest	2.071	3.372	1.146	1.124	14.073	15.622	0.139	0.146	0.000	0.000	2.408	2.585
Debt Service	5.284	6.779	1.994	1.998	28.332	31.181	0.139	0.146	0.000	0.000	5.098	5.863
Debt Disbursed and Outstanding at End of Year	291.659	366.687	68.548	70.722	289.858	317.908	19.452	19.500	0.000	0.000	43.852	52.996

	7 OTHER PROJECT		8 U.S. EXIMBANK		9 NON-U.S. OFFICIAL EXPORT FINANCE		10 PRIVATE CREDITS		11 (2 to 7) SUBTOTAL DEV. PROJECT LOANS	
	1968	1969	1968	1969	1968	1969	1968	1969	1968	1969
Disbursement	0.000	0.000	13.070	12.996	4.647	4.685	63.756	45.557	64.699	63.394
Amortization	0.000	0.000	9.950	6.548	2.289	0.444	39.432	35.926	17.797	19.711
Interest	0.000	0.000	2.181	2.575	0.317	0.293	6.152	7.495	17.766	19.477
Debt Service	0.000	0.000	12.131	9.123	2.606	0.737	45.584	43.421	35.563	39.188
Debt Disbursed and Outstanding at End of Year	0.000	0.000	39.296	45.744	30.335	34.576	165.091	174.722	421.710	461.126

	12 (8 & 9) SUBTOTAL OFFICIAL EXPORT FINANCE		13 (1,2 & 8) SUBTOTAL U.S. BILATERAL		14 (1,2,8 & 9) SUBTOTAL BILATERAL		15 (3,4,5 & 6) SUBTOTAL MULTILATERAL		16 TOTAL EXTERNAL FINANCE	
	1968	1969	1968	1969	1968	1969	1968	1969	1968	1969
Disbursement	17.717	17.681	99.601	94.479	104.248	99.164	59.863	60.346	227.867	205.067
Amortization	12.239	6.992	14.011	10.829	16.300	11.273	16.949	18.836	72.681	66.035
Interest	2.498	2.868	5.398	7.071	5.715	7.364	16.620	25.848	28.487	33.212
Debt Service	14.737	9.860	19.409	17.900	22.015	18.637	33.569	44.684	101.168[2]	99.247[2]
Debt Disbursed and Outstanding at End of Year	69.631	80.320	399.503	483.153	429.838	517.729	353.162	390.404	948.091	1,082.855

[1]Disbursements from Inter-American Bank Fund for special operations generate no amortization, interest, or outstanding balance effects because they are repayable in pesos at the option of the borrower.

[2]Debt service ratio in 1968: .128; estimated 1969: .116.

Source:　IBRD.

Table 3-21: TERMS AND REPAYMENT SCHEMES ASSUMED FOR NEW DEBT, 1970-85

Public Debt Category	Rate of Interest	Years to Maturity	Period of Grace	Repayment Scheme
1	.02/.03[1]	40	10	Equal Principal Payments
2	.02/.03[1]	40	10	Equal Principal Payments
3	.07	25	5	Annuity ("Level Payments")
4	.0075	50	10	IDA[2]
5	.04	20	5	Grant[3]
6	.08	15	5	Equal Principal Payments
7	.03	25	5	Equal Principal Payments
8	.06	12	4	Equal Principal Payments
9	.06	12	4	Equal Principal Payments
10[4]	.08	9	2	Equal Principal Payments
10[4]	.08	12	3	Equal Principal Payments

[1]AID charges 2% interest during grace period, 3% thereafter.

[2]IDA: after grace period expires borrower pays 1.0% of principal for 10 years, then 3.0% of principal for final 30 years (.0075 figure refers to service charge on disbursed, outstanding balance).

[3]IDB FSO loans are treated as grants in this exercise, since Colombia has the option of repaying in pesos (i.e., terms are not applied).

[4]PDC(10) has two sets of terms in this exercise, with the second set applying to the 1980-85 period.

Source: IBRD.

Table 3-22: EXTERNAL PUBLIC DEBT SERVICE PROJECTION, 1970-85[1]
(In millions of US dollars)

	1970	1971	1972	1973	1974	1975	1976	1977	1978	1979	1980	1981	1982	1983	1984	1985	Total 1970-85
Old disbursements	136.284	127.293	82.638	81.827	52.293	34.871	0.000	0.000	0.000	0.000	0.000	0.000	0.000	0.000	0.000	0.000	515.206
New disbursements	97.839	177.365	253.348	284.109	320.878	355.849	408.331	432.961	470.384	498.070	536.168	573.545	593.039	613.056	640.004	647.944	6,902.890
Total disbursements	234.123	304.658	335.986	365.936	373.171	390.720	408.331	432.961	470.384	498.070	536.168	573.545	593.039	613.056	640.004	647.944	7,418.096
Old amortization	82.992	73.658	77.065	73.766	71.861	72.182	70.285	68.622	69.965	61.531	59.620	58.119	65.662	53.017	50.765	43.071	1,052.181
New amortization	0.000	0.000	3.441	6.886	15.490	23.980	36.378	53.680	81.118	109.626	144.803	180.559	191.948	227.081	262.642	298.086	1,626.718
Total amortization	82.992	73.658	80.506	80.652	87.351	96.162	106.663	122.302	151.083	171.157	204.423	238.678	257.610	280.098	313.407	332.157	2,678.899
Old interest	42.222	44.867	45.251	45.200	43.960	42.484	40.031	37.139	34.514	32.193	29.171	26.305	23.511	20.191	17.698	15.403	540.140
New interest	0.000	4.555	12.046	24.284	37.342	51.663	67.443	87.207	108.230	130.024	152.100	172.951	198.123	222.083	244.999	267.356	1,782.406
Total interest	42.222	49.422	57.297	69.484	81.302	94.147	107.474	124.346	142.744	162.217	181.271	201.256	221.634	242.274	262.697	282.759	2,322.546
Old debt service	125.214	118.525	122.316	118.966	115.821	114.666	110.316	105.761	104.479	93.724	88.791	84.424	89.173	73.208	68.463	58.474	1,592.321
New debt service	0.000	4.555	15.488	31.170	52.831	75.643	103.821	140.888	189.348	239.650	296.903	355.510	390.071	449.164	507.641	556.442	3,409.125
Total debt service	125.214	123.080	137.804	150.136	168.652	190.309	214.137	246.649	293.827	333.374	385.694	439.934	479.244	522.372	576.104	614.916	5,001.446
Exports of goods and non-factor services	1,085.000	1,165.000	1,205.000	1,255.000	1,305.000	1,420.000	1,530.000	1,655.000	1,795.000	1,960.000	2,160.000	2,320.000	2,500.000	2,700.000	2,910.000	3,145.000	30,110.000
Old debt service ratio	.115	.102	.102	.095	.089	.081	.072	.064	.058	.048	.041	.036	.036	.027	.024	.018	.053
New debt service ratio	.000	.004	.112	.025	.040	.053	.068	.085	.106	.122	.138	.154	.156	.166	.174	.178	.113
Total debt service ratio	.115	.106	.114	.120	.129	.134	.140	.149	.164	.170	.179	.190	.192	.193	.198	.196	.166
Total debt disbursed Old	1,123.192	1,159.553	1,147.852	1,138.642	1,106.118	1,060.170	989.885	921.263	851.298	789.767	730.146	672.027	606.365	553.348	502.583	459.513	
and Outstanding at New	88.839	245.205	462.111	694.334	945.722	1,217.591	1,529.545	1,848.826	2,178.091	2,506.535	2,837.900	3,170.886	3,511.977	3,837.952	4,155.314	4,454.172	
end of year:　　Total	1,212.031	1,404.758	1,609.963	1,832.976	2,051.840	2,277.761	2,519.430	2,770.089	3,029.389	3,296.302	3,568.046	3,842.913	4,118.342	4,391.300	4,657.897	4,913.685	

[1]"Old" refers to disbursements and service on debt contracted prior to January 1, 1970.

Source: IBRD

CHAPTER 4
REGIONAL AND URBAN DEVELOPMENT

The regional distribution of economic activity and population within Colombia and the related problems of national, sectoral and urban planning are likely to rank among the crucial issues in Colombia's future development. The mission was able to assess only a small part of the material made available on these subjects and could not attempt a comprehensive review of all relevant aspects. However, it obtained a general appreciation of the dimensions of Colombia's regional and urban development problems, largely through working in the sectors covered elsewhere in this report, and was able to formulate a basis for the recommended preinvestment studies in urban development.

Table 4-1: POPULATION OF THIRTY LARGEST URBAN CENTERS[1]

	1951	1964	Average Annual Growth Rates %
Bogota, D.E. (+Soacha)[2]	664,506	1,673,370	7.0
Medellin (+Municipalities of Valle de Aburra)[2]	397,738	948,025	6.7
Cali (+Yumbo)[2]	245,568	633,485	7.2
Barranquilla (+Soledad)[2]	296,357	530,651	4.4
Bucaramanga (+Giron and Floridablanca)[2]	107,517	224,876	5.6
Cartagena	111,291	217,910	5.1
Manizales (+Villamaria)[2]	92,030	195,542	5.6
Pereira (+Santa Rosa)[2]	89,675	179,133	5.2
Armenia (+Calarca)[2]	72,805	155,364	5.7
Cucuta	70,375	147,176	5.6
Ibague	54,347	125,233	6.3
Palmira	54,293	106,502	5.1
Santa Marta	37,005	89,161	6.7
Pasto	48,853	82,546	4.0
Neiva	33,040	75,886	6.3
Monteira	23,682	70,531	8.4
Buenaventura	35,087	70,079	5.2
Giradot	35,665	66,584	4.7
Buga	32,016	65,535	5.4
Barrancabermeja	25,046	59,625	6.6
Popayan	31,866	58,500	4.6
Tulua	28,715	56,539	5.1
Cartago	31,051	55,682	4.4
Cienega	24,358	47,719	5.1
Villavicencio	17,126	45,277	7.3
Sincelejo	21,625	44,001	5.4
Valledupar	9,011	43,553	11.9
Tunja	23,008	40,451	4.3
Sogamoso (+Nobsa)[2]	14,122	34,960	6.9
Duitama	1,723	31,865	–
TOTAL:	2,735,501	6,175,761	

[1] From "Planes y Programas de Desarrollo 1969/72," Departamento Nacional de Planeacion p. II-15.

[2] Urban centers including more than one municipality.

75

The first section of this chapter contains a summary of general background information on regional and urban development. The subsequent sections outline three issues that are considered to be of major importance: the need for a national framework for planning at the regional level; problems associated with the growth of large urban centers; and new approaches to the upgrading and development of low-income communities within urban centers and in rural areas.

Background

Cities in Colombia

Nearly half of Colombia's present population, estimated at 21 to 22 million, is now believed to be living in "urban centers" of more than 10,000 inhabitants. In 1964, the last year for which comprehensive census data are available (total population was then 17.5 million), Colombia had 96 centers of more than 10,000 inhabitants, which accounted for 7.2 million (41%) of the country's total population.[1] Over 6.1 million (87%) of this urban population lived in 30 urban centers that had populations of more than 30,000 (see Table 4-1). In 1966, these 30 centers generated 94% of the manufacturing value added and accounted for 92% of industrial employment. The four largest (Bogota, Medellin, Cali and Barranquilla) accounted for approximately three-quarters of these amounts.[2] The data on migration patterns are given in Chapter 2; socio-economic characteristics in the urban and rural populations are discussed in the chapters dealing with public health, education and water supply.

An important feature of urban development in Colombia is the differential in growth rates for towns of different sizes. Between 1938 and 1964, the country's population doubled, while the urban population trebled and the centers having less than 10,000 inhabitants virtually exchanged positions with those having more than 100,000 inhabitants (in terms of proportionate share of urban population), as indicated in the following:

Table 4-2: URBAN POPULATION BY COMMUNITY SIZE

Size of Urban Communities[1]	Percent of Urban Population		
	1938	1951	1964
Less than 10,000 inhabitants	51.8	33.8	21.3
10,000 to 100,000	25.6	28.2	27.5
More than 100,000	22.6	38.0	51.2
	100.0	100.0	100.0
Total population in the above communities (thousands)	2,744	4,468	9,093
Country's total population (thousands)	8,702	11,548	17,485

[1]Administrative municipal centers ("Cabeceras") only. From "Planes y Programs de Desarrollo 1969-72"; p. I-136.

As indicated in Table 4-1, the 30 largest urban centers in Colombia all have had population growth rates which are higher than the 3.3% national rate. Bogota, Medellin and Cali each have growth rates which, if continued, would double their populations in the next ten to twelve years. It should be noted, however, that the growth rate of Bogota, Colombia's "primate city", would probably be substantially higher if it were not for Colombia's relative wealth in other urban centers, compared to other Latin American countries: Medellin, Cali and Barranquilla (and, to a lesser extent, the eight other centers which had populations in excess of 100,000 in 1964), act

1. Documento DNP-335-UDRU "Modelo de Regionalizacion II; Equipos Urbanos" (Tables No. 1, 12 & 12A).
2. "Planes y Programas de Desarrollo 1969/72", Departamento Nacional de Planeacion (pg. 11-1).

as competing "growth poles" that are potentially attractive as locations for industrial and commercial expansion or new development and probably relieve Bogota of some of the pressures to which it would otherwise be exposed. Nevertheless, population pressures on all major urban centers in Colombia are severe and appear to be increasing. To cope with these problems, the government has been considering new methods of regional development planning in a national framework and changes in the governmental structure of urban areas.

Table 4-3: TAX COLLECTION AND OTHER REVENUES OF SELECTED MUNICIPALITIES, 1967[1]

City	Total Municipal Receipts[2]		Municipal Receipts without Telephone & Water Charges	
	Col$ '000's	Per Capita	Col$ '000's	Per Capita
Medellin	519,360	577	372,360	414
Bogota	593,597	290	330,368	161
Cali	173,689	232	93,071	124
Barranquilla	111,789	207	62,506	116
Cucuta	29,833	157	25,037	132
Bucaramanga	28,449	114	27,569	110
Cartagena	44,337	158	23,180	83
Manizales	27,567	110	14,155	57
Cartago	11,440	163	7,072	101
Buenaventura	5,963	57	5,880	56
Santa Marta	8,833	69	5,216	40

[1]From "Planes y Programas de Desarrollo 1969/72," Departamento Nacional de Planeacion p. II-6.

[2]Includes: direct taxation of properties for general services; property assessments for municipal improvements; general taxes on industry, commerce, retail and amusements; revenues from rentals, franchises, fines, interest and dividends; and user charges for telephone service, water supply, market places and other commercial activity.

The financial resources of individual municipalities in Colombia vary widely, as indicated in Table 4-3. Consequently, the quality of municipal and other services also varies, which tends to give the larger urban centers an added attractiveness over smaller ones. This typifies but one of the elements which contribute to regional imbalance, discussed further below.

Regional Imbalance

Colombia has a wide variety of climatic conditions and contains three mountain ranges which traverse the country, forming barriers between regions and imposing heavy transport costs. Furthermore, the regions are known for the diversity in their endowment with mineral and agricultural resources. Given these conditions, it is difficult to conceive of a state of regional "balance." But the contrasts existing within Colombia today in economic activity, levels of social services and general living standards, while based initially on differentials in climate, natural resources or communications, have been exacerbated further in the process of growth. It is therefore understandable that the Government of Colombia is concerned about regional imbalance and considers measures which would reduce or eliminate these conditions where they impair social and economic development.

Typical symptoms of regional imbalance are: (a) variations in wage scales for similar skills (wage scales in clothing manufacture in Medellin are reported to be five times higher than those in the Department of Narino); (b) differences in illiteracy rates (less than 20% in the Departments of Antioquia, Valle, Caldas and Cundinamarca; higher than 50% in the Departments of Cordoba, Choco and Guajira); and (c) difficulties in access to medical and other social services (72% of the physicians in Colombia reside in the four largest cities).

These conditions exist in spite of a relatively wide dispersal of industry throughout Colombia. As discussed in more detail in the chapter on the regional structure of industry, the small size of many industrial installations in Colombia, serving limited regional markets, has contributed to high production costs. From the point of view of industrial efficiency in the abstract, therefore, greater concentrations of industry in the four existing centers—or perhaps only in two—may be desirable. But the benefits of such industrial concentration could be offset by: increased transport costs; the social costs of greater regional imbalance; and aggravation of the problems already existing in large urban centers.

The process of industrialization in Colombia is thus closely linked to the country's key issues of regional development at the national scale and at the metropolitan scale. Solutions which may be optimal for Colombia's competitive position in foreign markets or for increasing domestic production could carry price tags outside the industrial sector, in associated location decisions, which the country could ill afford. The legislation discussed in the next two sections may provide Colombian planning agencies with tools to measure the impact of industrial location decisions on regional development. These should be weighed against their impact on the national economy.

Germane to the problems of regional imbalance are the typical differences between rural and urban living conditions and the migration caused by rural push and urban pull. Related questions of employment in Colombia, agricultural development, public utilities, transportation, educational facilities and health services are discussed elsewhere in this report.[3]

Government Planning for Regional Development

The Regional and Urban Development Unit of the Planning Office (Departamento Nacional de Planeacion) is conducting a series of studies to provide a basis for national policies on industrial location and regional development. The unit has already completed an analysis of the present economic regions of Colombia, which included a ranking of major urban centers according to industrial indicators, demographic data and infrastructure criteria. This analysis, together with studies of migration patterns, geographic barriers and locations of natural resources, has resulted in the tentative definition of eight regions for future planning purposes. The eight planning regions and data on their current population are given in Table 4-4.

The proposed regions will be more consistent with the geographic, economic and social interdependencies of rural and urban areas than existing departmental boundaries, and thus provide a better framework for regional planning. The existing political subdivisions, however, would not be abolished. A law[4] provides that each region would have a "Regional Development Committee", consisting of the governors of the existing departments which comprise the region, representatives of the major municipalities and other local officials. These committees would be responsible for: advising the national government in matters relating to the preparation, coordination and execution of plans and programs for regional development; proposing to the national government plans, programs and projects of regional interest; coordinating and promoting regional action by national and departmental bodies; and reporting periodically to the Ministry of Economic Development and the National Planning Office on economic and social developments in the region.

Colombian government officials hope that the regional development committees, when established, will enable the National Planning Office, the ministries, and other agencies of the national government to engage in constructive and continuous dialogue with local interests. Difficulties in establishing such dialogue in the past are a major reason for support of this law by the Planning Office.

The law would also provide that secretariats be established for the administrative support of each committee. The National Planning Office intends to assign at least one of its own staff to all secretariats, to provide liaison. Eventually, the secretariats are also to contain groups of urban planners and engineers who could assist the smaller municipalities within each region, where municipal planning offices are weak or do not exist; this would be of particular impor-

3. For a general discussion see "Recent Changes in Urban and Rural Settlement Patterns in Latin America," International Social Development Review—No. 1, United Nations, November 1968 (pages 55-62); and "Latin American Urbanization: Plan or Process?" by Lowdon Wingo; Resources for the Future; January 1969.
4. Document DNP-314-UDRU; September 15, 1969.

Table 4-4: PROPOSED PLANNING REGIONS[1]

No.	Region Name	Estimated 1970 Population (Millions)	Annual Rate of Growth (1951-64)	Existing Major Urban Centers Within Region
1	Atlantic Coast[2]	3.8	3.77	Barranquilla
2	Central	5.8	3.17	Bogota
3	South-West	3.4	2.98	Cali
4	North-West	3.3	3.65	Medellin
5	Central-West	1.8	2.20	Manizales/Pereira
6	North-East	1.5	2.13	Bucaramanga
7	Mid-Magdalena	0.7	3.06	
8	South Central	0.7	3.03	
		21.0		

[1] From "Planes y Programs de Desarrollo 1969/72," Departamento Nacional de Planeacion: page II-20 and Map No. 5.

[2] Including Archipelago of San Andres.

tance to cities of 30,000-200,000 inhabitants, which would not qualify as "metropolitan areas" (explained below), but in which the government intends to foster development during the 1970s.

The functions of the proposed regional development committees and their secretariats are intended to supplement but not to replace sectoral planning by the various national agencies. The draft law provides merely that, for planning purposes, each ministry, the administrative departments of the national government, and national development organizations adopt the territorial boundaries of the regions. The boundaries shown on the map in this chapter are tentative and have been proposed by the Planning Office for discussion purposes only; their final locations are to be formally adopted within one year of the date of effectiveness of the law.

In the mission's view this law, or an equivalent mechanism to coordinate subnational and national planning, would fill an urgent need.

However, the effectiveness of the proposed regional development committees would obviously depend on the degree of collaboration that can be achieved among the departments and municipalities within each region and on the quality of support rendered by the committees' secretariats. Adequate budgetary provisions for the operation of these new agencies would be imperative. Also, a clearer definition would seem to be required of the committees' role in the allocation of financial resources, both for proposed new investments and for the operation and administration of services and projects within the regions. Finally, the establishment of a new mechanism for development planning at the regional level would have to be accompanied by substantial strengthening of sectoral development planning at the national level.

Major Urban Centers

The topics discussed in this section apply primarily to the four largest urban centers in Colombia: Bogota, Medellin, Cali and Barranquilla. Other cities, however, already share some of the features and problems of "metropolitan" areas, even though their present populations are below one-half million; among these, Bucaramanga and Cartagena appear to be natural candidates for inclusion in the category of major centers. Depending on industrial location decisions, Pereira and Manizales could soon reach similar status; growth in Venezuelan tourism traffic could have an equivalent effect on the Santa Marta area, at least during the annual vacation season.

Common Problems

Pressures of population growth in the major urban centers are severe: approximately half of the present growth rates of these centers is caused by rural-urban migration. There are indications that such migration is increasingly direct, from agricultural regions to the big cities, bypassing the smaller centers.

The most obvious problem in all the large cities—though perhaps not the most critical for their social and economic development—is transportation. Public intra-urban passenger transport in Colombia is almost exclusively by bus and collective taxi, with limited commuter rail service in Bogota, Cali and Medellin. Traffic congestion in such cities as Bogota is not yet catastrophic as passenger cars are still relatively few—import duties and other restrictions raise consumer costs of vehicle ownership in Colombia to about four times the level in the United States. A major change can be expected when vehicle production of three proposed plants in Colombia reaches full volume. Independent of this change, however, large investments in urban transport facilities will soon be necessary in Bogota, Medellin and Cali.[5]

Water supply and sewerage in the four largest cities are the responsibility of autonomous public enterprises. However, areas under the jurisdiction of these enterprises for the most part coincide with existing municipal boundaries. Water and sewerage services outside these boundaries, where the bulk of future urban expansion is likely to occur, are the responsibility of other agencies. While the quality of water supply in the core municipalities is improving (except in Barranquilla), outlying areas often have poor water services. Sewerage systems are largely rudimentary (except in Bogota) and none of the large cities has installations for the treatment of sewerage effluent. Therefore, large investments should also be anticipated for water, sewerage and other sanitation facilities in most urban areas (see the chapter on water supply).

The massive proportions of these and other needs—in housing,[6] health services, education, police protection, telephone systems, and related administrative functions—will make heavy demands on Colombia's financial resources and on the governments of major urban centers. In most of these centers, there is little doubt that urban growth rates will continue to be high and that the physical features of each region (e.g. total land area occupied by buildings, types of urban land uses, infrastructure and environmental conditions) will undergo major changes in the next decade. The quality of this growth and its impact on economic and social development will depend to a large extent on the effectiveness of governmental action in each region.

In Bogota, where the municipal government has been concerned with urban planning for many years, the first phase of a regional transport and urban development study[7] has just been completed. This phase of the study was designed to assess possible alternative land-use patterns and transport systems for the entire metropolitan area, and to explore development prospects to the year in which the total population of the region will reach 4.5 million (expected to be about 1980). The general outlines of six alternative land-use patterns, most of which will have more than one possible transport system solution, have been submitted to the government; a selection is to be made of one or possibly two of these, which will then be the subject of more detailed definition in the second phase of the study (see Chapter 5, Preinvestment Study Program). These investigations also cover questions of government policy with regard to land-use planning, land-use control, public transport, housing and other public services in the metropolitan area of Bogota.

Preinvestment studies of a similar type are suggested for all major urban centers of Colombia. Preparations for a regional study of the metropolitan area of Medellin are already under way; the scope of this study generally follows the Bogota pattern. Improvements to this approach should be considered after the results of the Bogota study can be assessed. Future urban studies in the regions of Cali, Barranquilla and Bucaramanga would have to be designed to meet the specific conditions and needs of each locality.

The purpose of these proposed studies would be to assist local governments in the preparation of overall plans for physical development, including broad allocations of land-uses for the

5. For discussion of general transportation problems in Colombia, see Chapters 19 and 20.

6. Data obtained by this mission on housing will be incorporated in a separate report on urban development in Colombia, by a future Bank mission; for general information on housing, refer to Report of the 1970 ILO Mission to Colombia (Chapter IX and Appendix IX).

7. "Bogota–Transport and Urban Development Study" 1969-70, financed with assistance of the UNDP, for which the World Bank is acting as Executing and Participating Agency.

entire region, and phased programs of public investments in basic infrastructure and urban services. After review and discussion of the results of such studies, a general plan for each region should be formally adopted and periodically updated, in accordance with the region's programs for economic, fiscal and social development.

The purpose of these studies probably would not be achieved without the following institutional support: (1) a political process to evaluate and to accept or reject recommendations, (2) an agency to continue planning for each region after termination of the studies, and (3) machinery to implement adopted plans and programs. These prerequisites are still lacking in all but one of the big cities in Colombia, a lack perhaps symptomatic of the most serious problem common to those cities.

The Government of Bogota now has the regional authority and the supporting agencies which could deal effectively with the issues outlined above; present conditions throughout the metropolitan area of Bogota reflect this. In Cali, Medellin, and other major centers no significant change has occurred as yet in the now obsolete structure of municipal governments. As these cities have grown by the merging of neighboring communities, the boundaries of old administrative entities have become internal barriers of critical importance: they are today the primary cause of wide variations in urban infrastructure and in the quality and cost of basic municipal services. They thus have a direct impact on the urban economy. Since they affect commercial and industrial location decisions, they also have an indirect impact, by tending to perpetuate inefficient growth patterns. Finally, they result in large numbers of agencies with fragmentary jurisdictions, which constitute powerful deterrents to comprehensive regional planning and to large-scale urban development programs. Government and private interests have been aware of the need for structural reform in the governments of major urban centers and therefore have initiated institutional changes discussed below.

Prospects for Metropolitan Governments

A proposed law[8] permits the establishment of urban regional governments in areas where core municipalities have populations of 250,000 or more (provided the aggregate population of participating municipalities is in excess of 300,000 and their growth rate, between national censuses, averages at least 4.5% per annum). Only Medellin and Cali would qualify under this law at present, but Barranquilla, Cartagena, Manizales and Pereira will probably be included after the 1972 national census. The law would not apply to Bogota, which is already a "special district" under the national constitution, its Mayor being appointed by the President.

Under this law, new metropolitan governments would achieve status as public "legal entities". They would be entitled to levy an "added value" tax and would be responsible for: preparing and executing plans and programs for the physical, economic and social development of the urban region (including but not limited to public works); regulating land use, building construction and other aspects of urban development; and furnishing joint municipal services within the region, and such other services as may be specified in enabling legislation or delegated by the National Government.

The mayor of the core community of each metropolitan region would be the "prefect" of the new regional government and would also serve as chairman of a metropolitan planning board on which all participating municipalities would be represented. As technical secretariats to these boards, metropolitan planning offices would be established, which would take over all functions of existing municipal planning offices, including the preparation of capital budgets. These offices would thus be directly responsible for land-use planning and control and the issuance of permits and licenses for construction of all kinds. Application of the law would require further legal measures to establish each metropolitan regional government. This would involve definition of the boundaries of the regions and specific legislation on administrative regulations and the composition of metropolitan planning boards. A preinvestment study is suggested to provide advisory services in the establishment of metropolitan regional governments following adoption of enabling legislation (see Chapter 5).

8. Document DNP-375-UDRU; November 5, 1969.

The general principles incorporated in the proposed law for metropolitan regional governments in Colombia appear to be sound and such legislation is urgently needed. However, it is advisable that the caveat to the law which specifies a minimum growth rate be reconsidered, as past growth rates may not necessarily be relevant to the need for governmental reform in the urban centers.

While the Special District of Bogota is not now affected by the administrative problems mentioned above, consideration could be given to the need for adjustments to the area under its jurisdiction. (Specific recommendations on the configuration of the metropolitan region are to be developed in the second phase of the Bogota regional study.) This could be achieved by extending the coverage of the proposed law to Bogota or by separate legislation.

It is also suggested that consideration be given to means of insuring continuity in the organization and staffing of the proposed metropolitan planning offices. Certain provisions in the present draft law would encourage each new mayor of the regions' core municipalities (the "prefect") to reorganize and change the entire staff of the planning machinery on which the metropolitan planning boards depend for support. To attract and maintain competent staff in the metropolitan planning offices—and in all other agencies responsible for construction and operation of urban projects and services—will be of primary importance to the successful implementation of the plans and programs which the proposed law would make possible.

Community Upgrading and Development

Both rural and urban populations in Colombia are equally in need of solutions to the pressing problems of low-income communities. In the past decade, developing countries and various international and bilateral assistance agencies have made major advances toward such solutions, but their efforts have been focused primarily on the construction of new low-cost housing, associated where possible with a minimum of street construction, water supply, sanitation and other public services. Predominantly these solutions involved three steps: (a) planning and construction of infrastructure and housing, usually on vacant or cleared land; (b) population moving into the new neighborhood, after or at a stage of partial completion; and, (c) adjustment to the new environment over a period of time, while various social services and community facilities are being started.

In Colombia, a number of developments for low-income communities have been initiated recently using different approaches which appear to be both successful and promising for future application to other low-income areas. The distinctive features are the attention given by the responsible public agencies, from the outset, to *all* basic needs of the communities, the extensive involvement of the community's population in the organization and construction of the projects, and (in some areas) the avoidance of major population relocations, through new methods of upgrading existing settlements.

The Las Colinas settlement in Bogota is an outstanding example of a comprehensive approach to community upgrading. This settlement was formed in November 1960 by an organized "invasion" of vacant land, not far from the center of Bogota. Its present population of about 7,500 occupies 12 hectares of steeply sloping terrain and has constructed some 940 dwelling units. The initial organization of the "invasion" provided reasonable order in the land subdivision (about 90 square meters for most units), but access to the units on higher ground was difficult and the limited services of water supply and electricity, which eventually emerged, were mostly "contrabando" (illegal). The original construction of dwelling units is typical for this kind of settlement.

An elementary school and central police station were built in Las Colinas in the mid-1960s by the municipality. In 1967, the Caja de la Vivienda Popular of Bogota acquired the land on which Las Colinas was built and, in collaboration with various agencies of the Special District of Bogota, the Centro Colombiano de la Construccion, and the community's own citizens' organizations, initiated a redevelopment scheme which comprises the following:

(a)   Acquisition of land ownership by the settlers, in a "package" which includes construction of a minimum sanitary facility for each plot (water and sewer connection with kitchen and toilet), and financing of this construction and of the land purchase;

(b)   Employment referral services for the population and other family assistance by social service agencies and the municipality;

(c)   Financing of construction materials for house improvements or new construction (after land acquisition mentioned in (a) above);

(d)   Construction of two main streets, which also contain water lines and trunk sewers;

(e)   Construction of secondary passages and other improvements (mostly pedestrian walks, steps and associated retaining walls) by the population through "Accion Communal," with materials provided by the Government; and

(f)   Health services, infant day-care, kindergarten, and adult education courses, all to be located in a new community center.

The Las Colinas project will be completed over a period of years. At an appropriate time—perhaps in 1972—it could be beneficial to have an evaluation and report on the experiences gained in this project, and in others serving both rural and urban communities in Colombia, for use in future developments of low income areas. Such evaluation is suggested in the preinvestment study program.

CHAPTER 5
PREINVESTMENT STUDY PROGRAM

Growth in most sectors of Colombia's economy continues to depend on the implementation of major investment projects. The timing and success of such projects, in turn, depend largely on the timing and success of the studies that must precede each decision to invest. These "preinvestment studies," which were a specific concern of the economic mission to Colombia in 1970, cover the range of technical, economic, financial and organizational investigations needed for sectoral development planning and for the preliminary design and analysis of specific projects.

As many developing countries are finding it increasingly important to set priorities and obtain financing for future studies of this type, governments and international agencies (including the World Bank Group) have been discussing the need for a comprehensive approach to all preinvestment work, which would lead to better allocations of resources, based on the specific requirements of each country.

It is now widely agreed that such an approach to preinvestment work calls for country-wide *programs of preinvestment studies* which are prepared systematically, cover all important sectors of the national economy, and are linked to the overall strategies for economic and social development of the countries. These programs should ensure that studies of high priority investment projects are planned and carried out at the appropriate time, that the studies cover all issues relevant to investment decisions, and that the limited human and financial resources available for studies are used efficiently.

In Colombia, there has been a growing awareness of the need for such a comprehensive approach to preinvestment studies. The Fondo Nacional de Projectos de Planeacion (FONADE), supporting the work of the National Planning Department, of ministries responsible for sectoral development and of private firms, has coordinated and financed a large number of studies since 1967 in various sectors. FONADE has also cooperated with the United Nations Development Programme (UNDP) and with other international and bilateral agencies in the financing and preparation of many types of preinvestment activities. Past achievements in this area by FONADE and the UNDP have been significant and have provided a substantial basis for the work of the 1970 Economic Mission.

The recommended program of preinvestment studies outlined in this chapter has been prepared by the Bank Economic Mission in a cooperative effort with the National Planning Department, FONADE, the resident office of the UNDP, and several specialized agencies of the United Nations.[1] The following sections cover: the objectives of the recommended preinvestment study program; types of studies, time span and sectors covered by the program; methods and criteria used in program preparation; an outline of the main features of the program; a list of the proposed studies with an indication of their priority and cost; and two specimen study data sheets from different sectors of the economy.

More detailed information on the sectoral background of the proposed studies is given in the chapters of this report on agriculture, education, public health, industry, power, water supply, transportation, tourism and regional and urban development.

Objectives of the Preinvestment Study Program

The preinvestment study program outlined in this chapter is intended to:

assist the Government of Colombia in defining and scheduling studies which accord with the national development objectives;
provide the UNDP and other agencies with a sound basis for allocating funds for preinvestment assistance to Colombia; and
accelerate and improve the preparation of development projects in Colombia, for possible financing by international and bilateral lending agencies.

1. FAO, PAHO, UNESCO and the World Food Program.

The program provides general recommendations on the priority, timing and scope of the studies which are considered to be necessary for the successful implementation of future development projects. To the extent possible, the mission compiled background information on each of the studies, outlined suggested staffing requirements, and made preliminary estimates of study duration and costs.

No attempt has been made to define all details of the studies proposed in this program. Further elaboration of the study scope and refinement of the cost estimate will be needed before the government can make formal application to the UNDP (or other development assistance agency) for financing of a specific study. This additional work is expected to be done by the government or by agencies interested in sponsoring or assisting the studies, as part of the steps following adoption of the program.[2] Nor have prospective sources of financing for the studies been indicated, except where potential study sponsors were known to have expressed specific interest. It is expected that decisions on sources of financing for the studies will in general be made after the program as a whole has been reviewed by the government.

Types of Studies, Time Span and Sectors Covered by the Program

The preinvestment study program comprises the studies that are considered necessary to establish investment priorities, determine the feasibility of individual projects, and define such changes in governmental operations or institutions as may be required to ensure the successful implementation and functioning of investment projects. The studies therefore cover the full range, from basic resource inventories, sector surveys on a country-wide scale, and studies of alternative development patterns on a regional scale, to the functional design, preliminary engineering and financial or economic analyses required for specific projects. To the extent necessary for the launching of investments, the studies also include analyses of (or advisory services in) project-related organizations, administrative problems, planning machinery, manpower resources and training requirements.

The program does not include work related to final engineering of projects, preparation of contract documents for construction or procurement, and more specialized types of studies such as those required to establish research institutes or to draft legislation that would implement recommended policy and administrative changes. These activities are considered to be in the "investment" rather than the "preinvestment" stage.

An attempt was made to identify and include in the program all important studies required for investment decisions in the next five years. As a minimum goal, however, the recommended program is intended to cover all studies that should be started within the next two years.

In the preparation of this program, studies in the following sectors were considered: agriculture, education and training, health, industry, power, water supply and sanitation, telecommunications, transportation, tourism and regional and urban development.

Methods and Criteria Used in Program Preparation

Before the 1970 economic mission left for Colombia, discussions were held with the Director of FONADE and the resident representative of the UNDP in Colombia on the proposed approach to the preparation of a preinvestment study program. FONADE and the UNDP resident representative's office in Colombia prepared inventories of all completed, current and proposed preinvestment studies known to them. These inventories and supplementary information provided by various ministries and bilateral agencies, were reviewed and evaluated.

Based on the available information about existing studies and a general review of development prospects in the major sectors, additional needs for future studies were identified. In most sectors, the approach to this work was as follows:

---

2. The World Bank Group will not necessarily be associated with the financing or execution of studies recommended or with the financing of the investment projects resulting from the studies.

With a development strategy for the whole sector as a starting point, both the principal investment needs and the policies and institutional changes necessary for development of the sector were identified;

Where deficiencies in the knowledge of sector problems and resources could be observed, an attempt was made to define the areas where further study is needed to provide a proper basis for investment planning;

By working back from prospective investments (in the order of their priority), the studies needed for establishing project feasibility and the best alternative were considered; and

On the basis of a review of government operations and of the administrative framework in each sector, the advisory services or studies needed to improve policies, organization, management and personnel training were identified, as required for the successful execution of projects.

This resulted in a broad outline of the overall needs for preinvestment studies in the sectors. These results were discussed with the National Planning Department, FONADE, other responsible government agencies, the resident representative of the UNDP and the participating specialized UN organizations. The mission's exchanges of views with these agencies formed the basis for selection of the studies to be included in the recommended program.

Outlines were prepared of the scope of the work to be accomplished by the proposed studies. No attempt was made, however, to define their scope accurately enough for actual execution; nor was it usually considered practical to make a thorough analysis of all available data and to evaluate alternative study designs in sufficient depth to ensure that optimum solutions had been found. Within the time available, preliminary judgments were made on these subjects, so as to provide a meaningful basis for the study program. The result at this stage is merely a "preliminary design" of each of the studies. This includes:

(a)   a statement of purpose, containing the main questions to be answered and the development objectives that would be served;
(b)   an indication of the type of detail (or degree of accuracy) expected in the study results;
(c)   an outline of main areas of investigation, with a list of the important study tasks; and
(d)   a general assessment of data availability and of the difficulties likely to be encountered in data collection.

Based on this "preliminary design," estimates were made of the probable duration and approximate cost of most of the studies. For some studies the time available was insufficient for more than an estimate of the broad order of magnitude of study costs. For most of the proposed studies, however, tentative budgets could be prepared by assessing the likely composition of the study team and the approximate number of man-months required in each category of staff.

The recommended program contains a number of studies which are considered to be of high priority, even though their scope could not be defined at this stage. They include three studies for which the scope depends on the results of currently on-going or proposed preinvestment work, and five studies for which it was felt that only specialists not available to the mission could prepare an adequate definition of scope.

Main Features of the Study Program

The recommended program of preinvestment studies for Colombia comprises 49 studies, classified in nine sectors. This includes 41 studies for which it was possible to make preliminary determinations of scope, duration and cost; the total cost of these studies is expected to be in the order of US$23-million equivalent. The total investments which may be initiated on the basis of all the proposed studies could range in the order of US$2-3 billion equivalent. The sectoral classification of studies and their suggested timing are given in Table 5-1.

The sectoral classification of studies in the program is in some instances arbitrary. For example, one of the studies listed in the agriculture sector also has components of equal importance in the industry sector. Similarly, one study in the education sector comprises important elements of telecommunication, one study in the health sector deals largely with education, and studies in both the power and the tourism sectors cover major planning work for water supply projects. The ability to combine important elements of more than one sector in several of the proposed studies is among the obvious benefits which were derived from a comprehensive approach to the preinvestment study program.

An even more significant benefit of this approach, though perhaps not as obvious in the final results, was the general direction received by each group of sector specialists on the country economic mission. The basic sector analyses, which underlie the study recommendations in this report, could thus be related to the overall socio-economic problems of development in Colombia.

The sector analyses, in turn, have resulted in a large part of the recommended program being concerned with institutional problems and with the planning aspects of sectoral or regional development. It is felt that this area of study, of primary importance to the future growth of Colombia's economy as well as to project implementation, tends to be neglected in the project-by-project approach toward preinvestment work which has been predominant in the past.

While all studies in the recommended program are considered to be of high priority, the mission has indicated twenty-five which it believes to be of greatest importance to the future economic and social development of Colombia; these studies are designated by an asterisk in the List of Proposed Preinvestment Studies.

In the course of preparing this program, many study proposals were considered but not included. Judgments made in selecting the studies were based in part on an assessment of the capacity of agencies responsible for administering and financing preinvestment work and on the resources believed to be available for implementing projects. These judgments should be subject to periodic review. If it is found that the recommended program does not fully utilize the capacities of responsible agencies and the available resources, additional preinvestment studies

Table 5-1:   SUMMARY OF RECOMMENDED PREINVESTMENT STUDY PROGRAM

Sector	Number of Studies and Desirable Starting Year			Total Number Proposed Studies
	1970	1971	1972	
Agriculture	2	2	4	8[1]
Education and training	1	6	–	7
Health	2	3	1	6
Industry	1	1	–	2
Power	3	3	1	7
Water supply & sanitation	2	2	1	5
Telecommunications	–	–	–	–
Transportation	2	3	–	5
Tourism	1	–	–	1
Regional and urban development	–	4	4	8
Total:	14	24	11	49

[1]Forestry industry included in one agriculture study.

may be considered for inclusion in the program. If it is found, on the other hand, that these capacities and resources have been overestimated, the size of the study program should be reduced. In the latter case, the studies designated by an asterisk should be the last to be postponed or deleted.

Particular mention should be made of several study proposals presented to the mission in the industry sector. These fall into two categories: one relates to major distribution centers or industrial developments within the large metropolitan areas (e.g., location studies for new central food markets or planning studies for industrial zones in the cities of Bogota, Cali, Medellin, etc.). This category is in fact covered by the scope of urban development studies which are recommended in the program. The other relates to location and/or development decisions for specific manufacturing subsectors. While three studies of this second category (for the steel, forestry and petrochemical industries) have been included in the program, the mission could not evaluate proposals for the others. Further consideration should be given in the near future to additional industry studies of this kind.

A list of the suggested studies follows, with a brief statement of their purpose, the suggested starting year and the estimated study duration and cost. Two specimen data sheets following this list are indicative of the detail given for most of the proposed studies in the program as submitted to the government.

LIST OF PROPOSED PREINVESTMENT STUDIES

Estimated Study
Cost in
US$ millions

Agriculture

1-1*   Rio Meta: Right Bank Agricultural Development Study   3.30

Prepare program for agricultural development, right bank covering 3-4
million hectares; provide feasibility studies for development projects in
livestock, crops, colonization and settlement. 1970 or 1971 (30 months).

1-2   "Tolima V": Irrigation and Drainage Studies.   1.38

Prepare program to improve and extend irrigation project in Tolima
Department including economic, social and financial review of agricultural
situation in project area. 1970 or 1971 (24 months).

1-3   Forestry Inventories.   1.60

Surveys of selected forest resources; prepare forest industries development
plan; establish research and demonstration centers; outline investment
program for forestry industry development. 1971 (30 months).

1-4*   Atlantico Region: Marketing Study.[1]   0.80

Study marketing possibilities for agricultural output from irrigation and
reclamation projects and studies implemented by INCORA in Atlantico
Region; prepare plan for construction of storage and processing facilities;
establish new marketing organization. 1971 (18 months).

1-5   Ariguani River Stage 2, Feasibility Study   1.25

Prepare feasibility study, second stage development project, irrigation
and drainage for some 20,000 hectares, Ariguani River, Magdalena
Department. 1972 or 1973 (12 months).

1-6   Cesar River Stage 2, Feasibility Study.   1.00

Prepare feasibility study, second stage development project, irrigation
and drainage for some 20,000 hectares, Cesar River, Cesar Department.
1972 (12 months).

1-7*   Narino: Putumayo Regional Development Project.

Prepare series of feasibility studies for specific development projects in
forestry, cacao, oil palm, coconut, dairy industry, livestock and colonization. 1972 (54 months).

1-8   Bajo Cauca Stage 2, Feasibility Study   0.80

Prepare feasibility study, second stage development project for 20-25
thousand hectares: flood control, drainage, land reclamation. 1972
(12 months).

Sub-total   10.13

LIST OF PROPOSED PREINVESTMENT STUDIES (Cont.)

		Estimated Study Cost in US$ millions

Education

2-1 *	Information Base for School Facilities Planning.	0.35

Technical survey and analysis, for national and department education planners, of all public education and training establishments; utilization study, school distribution maps. 1971 (12 months).

2-2*	Post-Secondary Technician Training.	0.07

Study of requirements and program for developing post-secondary technician training (polytechnics) 1970-80. Prepare project-oriented program to set up two schools, in 1971-3. 1970 (3 months).

2-3	The Use of New Communications Media.	0.07

Prepare feasibility study, expanded use of new communications media for solving problems of educational and social development; action program if warranted. 1971 (4 months).

2-4*	Manpower Demand and the Education System.	0.10

Information to ensure matching of educational provision and skilled manpower needs for economic and social development. 1971 (12 months).

2-5	Automated Data Processing for Educational Administration.	0.20

Plan and establish automatic data processing for administration of education system, in Ministry of Education. 1971 (18 months).

2-6	Teaching Aids and Textbook Center.	0.03

Define requirements and organization for teaching aids and text book center. 1971 (2 months).

2-7*	Development of Secondary Education Reform.	0.03

Promote implementation of reforms of structure and content of secondary education and rationalization and consolidation, especially for first-cycle comprehensive secondary schools, industrial and agricultural secondary schools and related teacher training. 1971 (1.5 months).

	Sub-total	0.85

Health

3-1*	Action Program for Education and Training in the Health Sector.	0.40

Long-range projections of health care manpower requirements and plans and strategy for education and training in health sector. 1970 (18-24 months).

3-2*	Study of Medical Care Institutions.	0.25

Assess efficiency and minimal requirements of existing medical institutions as a step towards implementing new Hospital Plan. 1970 (15-24 months).

LIST OF PROPOSED PREINVESTMENT STUDIES (Cont.)

Estimated Study
Cost in
US$ millions

Health (Cont.)

3-3   Nutrition Study: Phase III.   0.25

Improve population's nutrition through adapting domestic food sources
and educating public to change dietary patterns. 1972 (30-36 months).

3-4   Health Care under the Social Security System.   0.15

Plan extension of health and medical care to more people, under social
security coverage as part of new 10-year Health Plan. 1971 (12 months).

3-5*   Vital Statistics and Morbidity Data: Registration and Analysis.   0.08

Modernize national system of registration, tabulation and analysis of
vital statistics and morbidity data. 1971 (12 months)

3-6   Sample Studies of the Health Status and Health Resources of Colombia.   0.40

Reappraise major health problems, facilities and manpower, to assess
progress toward national goals since 1965 and establish objective basis
for revising national health programs; to be modeled on national studies
of 1965-66, to facilitate comparisons.

                                                           Sub-total   1.53

Industry

4-1*   Survey of the Iron and Steel Industry of Colombia.[1]   0.25

Evaluate iron and steel industry; forecast steel demand; prepare overall
devlopment plan to increase steel products capacity and improve
efficiency. 1970 (4 months).

4-2   Andean Group Petrochemical Development Survey.   0.20

Promote cooperative petrochemical projects in Andean Group countries;
determine type, optimum size, location and phasing of production units
over 10 years. 1971 (10 months).

                                                           Sub-total   0.45

Power

5-1*   Rural Electrification.   0.20

Evaluate alternative sets of projects and investment plans in rural electrification as basis for decisions on national rural electrification plan.
1970 (12 months).

5-2   Rio Cauca Hydroelectric Potential.   0.74

Evaluate hydroelectric potential of middle Cauca River; determine
feasibility of constructing reservoirs and power plants to use it. 1970
(36 months).

LIST OF PROPOSED PREINVESTMENT STUDIES (Cont.)

		Estimated Study Cost in US$ millions

Power (Cont.)

| 5-3* | Chingaza Water Supply-Bogota River Basin Power Development. | 0.30 |

Evaluate alternative coordinated construction schedules of water supply projects from Chingaza with flow regulation and power generation in Bogota river basin, as basis for joint EAAB/EEEB analysis of most economic construction schedule. 1970 (12 months).

| 5-4 | Rio Patia Hydroelectric Potential. | 0.63 |

Evaluate hydroelectric potential of Patia River, S.W. Colombia; determine feasibility of constructing reservoirs and power plants to use it. 1971 (24 months).

| 5-5 | Rio Saldana Hydroelectric Potential. | 0.20 |

Evaluate hydroelectric potential of Saldana River, S. Tolima Department; determine feasibility of hydroelectric development.

| 5-6 | Rio Guavio Hydroelectric Development. | 0.58 |

Finish evaluation of Guavio River and tributaries' hydroelectric potential; determine most feasible reservoir and power plant development; prepare preliminary dam and plant designs, cost estimates, construction schedules. 1971 (20 months).

| 5-7* | CORELCA System Interconnection to ISA System. | 0.30 |

Evaluate alternative programs of projects to connect ISA and CORELCA systems, as basis for comprehensive ISA/CORELCA analysis of most economic construction schedule for transmission and generation projects to integrate both systems. 1972 (12 months).

| | Sub-total | 2.95 |

Water Supply and Sanitation

| 6-1* | INSFOPAL Organization and Operations Study. | 0.25 |

Prepare phased program to rationalize INSFOPAL's administration, management and techniques. 1970 (17 months).

| 6-2* | Water Supply and Sewerage, Santa Marta: Immediate Measures. | 0.03 |

Determine water supply and sewerage works urgently needed in Santa Marta and Rodadero. 1970 (5 months).

| 6-3 | Ground Water Development in the Atlantic Coast (Phase I). | 0.04 |

Help assess groundwater resources in Guajira, Magdalena, Atlantico, Bolivar, Sucre and Cordoba. 1971 (3 months).

| 6-4 | Water Distribution Systems Performance. | 0.50 |

Evaluate water distribution systems' performance in INSFOPAL's ten largest towns by finding main leaks and measuring water losses. 1971 (16 months).

LIST OF PROPOSED PREINVESTMENT STUDIES (Cont.)

Estimated Study
Cost in
US$ millions

Water Supply and Sanitation (Cont.)

6-5*   Water Supply and Sanitation in North Coast Region.[2]

              Feasibility study of priority water supply and sanitation projects, in
              north coast, to upgrade health and environment for tourism and resi-
              dents. 1972 (length to be determined by tourism study 9-1).

                                                    Sub-total   0.82

Transportation

8-1*   Highway Feasibility Studies   2.00

              Feasibility study of upgrading sections of existing highways and con-
              structing new ones of the national system (about 100 km). 1970
              (24 months).

8-2*   Colombia National Railroads Investment Requirements.[2]

              Ascertain desirable scale of continued railroad rehabilitation program,
              1972-6. 1970 (3 months).

8-3   Medellin Airport: Improvements to Existing Site; Selection of New
              Site.   0.11

              Improve capacity, reliability and safety of Medellin airport; select
              new one and do preliminary design. 1971 (6-8 months).

8-4*   Study of Cargo-Handling Operations at Major Ports.   0.16

              Improve vessel, truck and railcar turnaround time by improved use of
              existing and planned facilities, emphasizing proper use of transit
              storage, cargo handling gear, pallets, etc., improved operating procedure
              including customs practices. 1971 (18 months).

8-5   Inland Waterway Transport Survey (Magdalena River Basin). 0.60

              Assess needed improvements on inland waterways, their ports and
              operations to complement other transport modes for an integrated
              transport system. 1971 (12 months).

                                                    Sub-total   2.87

Tourism

9-1*   Comprehensive Tourism Survey of Colombia.   1.00

              Forecasts of tourism demand in Colombia; development plan for
              San Andres and North Coast — — facilities, infrastructure, health
              and environmental conditions; recommendations for improving
              tourism institutions; feasibility study for some high priority projects.
              1970 (12 months).

LIST OF PROPOSED PREINVESTMENT STUDIES (Cont.)

Estimated Study
Cost in
US$ millions

Regional and Urban Development

10-1* Region of Bogota: Transport and Urban Development Study, Phase II.   2.00

Prepare comprehensive urban development plan (based on phase I) and
public investment projects for Bogota region; indentify high priority transport projects for 1972 feasibility studies. 1971 (20 months).

10-2   Bogota; Transport Projects Feasibility Studies.[2]

Feasibility studies of high priority transport projects or systems in metropolitan Bogota, including determination of best location and design alternatives and organizational and operational services needed. 1972 (length to
be determined by study 10-1).

10-3* Region of Medellin: Development Study.[2]

Help government determine metropolitan planning boundaries and
optimum future development pattern; general programs for urban development; identify specific high priority projects for feasibility studies. 1972
(15-18 months).

10-4   Region of Cali: Development Study.[2]

Help government determine metropolitan planning boundaries and
optimum future development pattern; general programs for urban
development; identify specific high priority projects for feasibility
studies. 1971 (12-15 months).

10-5   Region of Barranquilla: Development Study.[2]

Help government determine metropolitan planning boundaries and
optimum future development pattern; general programs for urban
development; identify specific high priority projects for feasibility
studies. 1972 (15-18 months).

10-6   Region of Bucaramanga: Development Study.[2]

Help government determine metropolitan planning boundaries and
optimum future development pattern; general programs for urban
development; identify specific high priority projects for feasibility
studies. 1972 (15-18 months).

10-7* Action Program for Establishment of Metropolitan Regional Governments.   0.18

Provide action program for each of six largest cities, to help implement
proposed law for establishing metropolitan governments. 1972
(6 months).

LIST OF PROPOSED PREINVESTMENT STUDIES (Cont.)

Estimated Study
Cost in
US$ millions

Regional and Urban Development (Cont.)

10-8	Comprehensive Planning for Community Development in Low Income Areas.	0.15

Analyze results of earlier pilot developments in planning urban and rural low-income communities; prepare guidelines for future application from lessons learned. 1972 (4 months).

Sub-total   2.33

[1] Appended as examples.

[2] Cost of this study could not be estimated by mission.

*Projects of high priority.

PREINVESTMENT PROGRAM – STUDY DATA SHEET   No.:   1-4 (1)

Area: South America	Country: Colombia	Sector(s): Agriculture

1. NAME OF PROPOSED STUDY: Atlantico Region – Marketing Study.

2. PURPOSE: To: (a) ascertain the marketing possibilities for the agricultural production of irrigation and reclamation projects and studies implemented in the Atlantico Region by INCORA;
        b) prepare a plan for the construction of storage and processing facilities, and
        c) establish a marketing organization.

3. SCOPE: The study is to be carried out in the Atlantico Region, including the Departments of Atlantico, Cesar, Cordoba and Magdalena, and in the Caribbean Area, the Andean Pact Area, the United States, Canada and Europe. It shall include, without being limited to, the following steps:
    a) review of Colombia's demand and supply for agricultural products similar to those to be produced in projects of the Atlantico Region;
    b) study of production cost, transportation cost on a project basis for national consumption and for export;
    c) evaluation of existing transportation, storage and processing facilities in the region and proposals for improvement and for additional facilities;

(continued page 2)

4. BACKGROUND: (a) Related Studies   (b) Other Available Data   (c) Expected Data Problems

Atlantico 3 Project Reports
(1965-1970); on-going master
plans and feasibility studies
for Ariguani, Cesar, Sinu, Magdalena
rivers.

                                       – Market outlets abroad
                                       – Price structures
                                       – Transportation costs.

5. TIMING: (a) Duration and Phasing of Study   (b) Desired Starting Date   1971

                1-1/2 year

6. COMMENT ON POTENTIAL STUDY SPONSORS: A specialized consulting firm with wide international experience should be retained. IBRD is considering financing the foreign exchange of the study cost out of the loan proceeds now being studied for the Caqueta land colonization project. INCORA and CECORA would be the government agencies responsible.

7. PROJECT(S) EXPECTED TO RESULT FROM STUDY (if known):
    (a) Description   (b) Estimated Investment (US$ equivalent)
                                         20 million
    – Processing and storage facilities
    – Transportation equipment.   (c) Financing Need and Potential Source
                                         5-8 million.

8. ORDER OF MAGNITUDE OF STUDY COST (US$ equivalent): 500,000 in foreign exchange 300,000 in local currency	Sheet Prepared by: J. Dumoulin Dept. or Agency IBRD-A.P.D. Date: March 26, 1970
9. STAFF'S COMMENT ON PRIORITY RANKING OF STUDY: Because of Colombia's agricultural policy priority to increase its "minor exports", such a marketing study is urgently needed and it is one of the most difficult but imperative pre-investment action to undertake.	Sheet Revised by: Item(s) Revised: Dept. or Agency Date:

PREINVESTMENT PROGRAM – STUDY DATA SUPPLEMENT   No.:   1 – 4 (2)

(to be filled in when possible)

1. TENTATIVE STAFFING	Type of Specialist	Number on Team	Total Man-Months
(a) Foreign Professional Staff:	– Project Manager	1	18
	– Market Analyst	2	36
	– Market Investigator	1	20
	– Sale Executive	1	18
	– Agricultural Economist	1	20
	– Processing Engineer	1	20
	– Agricultural Engineer	1	6
	– Technical Assistant	4	10
	Total:	12	148
(b) Local Professional Staff: various			
(c) Local Supporting Staff: various			80

2. TENTATIVE STUDY BUDGET (US$ equivalent)	Foreign Currency	Local Currency	Total
(a) Professional Staff Costs :			
(b) Equipment :			
(c) Other (Travel, non-prof. staff, etc) :			
(d) Total :	500,000	300,000	800,000

3.   OTHER COMMENTS

(d) determination for each agricultural product of the foreign markets demands in fresh products, processed products;
(e) establishment of quality standards to be applied to both local and overseas markets;
(f) specific recommendations for export contracts provisions and negotiations;
(g) plans for shipping equipment to be used in the proposed marketing systems;
(h) detailed proposals for setting up a machinery for commercialization of the region's production; review of existing marketing organizations and their eventual integration in the proposed machinery will have to be considered. The need for creating a special marketing board should be examined.

Supplement Prepared by: J.P. Dumoulin
Dept. or Agency: IBRD-A.P.D.
Date: March 26, 1970

Supplement Rev. by:	
Item(s) Revised:	
Dept. or Agency:	
Date:	

PREINVESTMENT PROGRAM – STUDY DATA SHEET No.: 4-1 (1)

Area: South America	Country: Colombia	Sector(s): Industry

1. NAME OF PROPOSED STUDY: Survey of the Iron and Steel Industry in Colombia

2. PURPOSE: To evaluate the current status of the iron and steel industry and prepare an industry-wide development plan designed to increase local manufacturing capacity of steel products and reduce their prices on the domestic market.

3. SCOPE: The study is to evaluate the present status of the sector, review the available data on local raw materials, prepare estimates of production costs, prepare a forecast of the demand for steel in Colombia and an assessment of export possibilities, review presently prepared expansion plans and recommend the most economical program of expansion of the sector. The study should highlight any special transport bottlenecks, whose removal would facilitate the distribution of steel to the major consumption centers from one or two large plants.

The study should also include a discussion on the merits of Colombia's
(Cont. on page 2, item 3)

4. BACKGROUND: (a) Related Studies (b) Other Available Data (c) Expected Data Problems

None

(i) Feasibility studies for a cold rolling mill prepared by H. K. Ferguson and Sofresid,
(ii) Market studies for cold mill products prepared by IFI and Paz del Rio and for all types of steel products prepared by IFI,
(iii) Feasibility study for Siderurgica de la Sabana.

5. TIMING: (a) Duration and Phasing of Study   (b) Desired Starting Date   1971

4 months

6. COMMENT ON POTENTIAL STUDY SPONSORS:

Planeacion (DNP) would appear to be the most suitable sponsor of this study, as its scope falls within DNP's field of operation.

7. PROJECT(S) EXPECTED TO RESULT FROM STUDY (if known):

(a) Description
(i) New basic iron and steel complex,
(ii) Better transportation facilities

(b) Estimated Investment (US$ equivalent)
(i) $40 million

(c) Financing Need and Potential Source
(ii) IFI, suppliers credits, IBRD

8. ORDER OF MAGNITUDE OF STUDY COST (US$ equivalent) 250,000, see page (2), item 1.	Sheet Prepared by: John W. P. Jaffe
	Dept. or Agency: IBRD/I.P.D.
	Date: June 22, 1970

9. STAFF'S COMMENT ON PRIORITY RANKING OF STUDY: High priority, because of number of expansion projects currently being planned or in course of implementation.	Sheet Revised by:
	Item(s) Revised:
	Dept. or Agency:
	Date:

PREINVESTMENT PROGRAM – STUDY DATA SUPPLEMENT   No.: 4 – 1 (2)
(to be filled in when possible)

1. TENTATIVE STAFFING	Type of Specialist	Number on Team	Total Man-Months
(a) Foreign Professional Staff:	Marketing Consultant	1	4
	Engineering Consultant	2	7
	Industrial Engineering Consultant	2	7
	Transportation Consultant	1	2
	Financial Consultant	1	4
	Total:	7	24
(b) Local Professional Staff:	Marketing Consultant	1	4
(c) Local Supporting Staff:	Interpreters, drivers, etc.	3	12

2. TENTATIVE STUDY BUDGET (US$ equivalent)	Foreign Currency	Local Currency	Total
(a) Professional Staff Costs :	150,000	50,000	200,000
(b) Equipment :			
(c) Other (Travel, non-prof. staff, etc.) :			50,000
(d) Total :			250,000

3. OTHER COMMENTS   (continued from page (1), item 3)

(i) entering into a joint venture agreement with another LAFTA country for the production of semi-finished steel products in that country, (possibly using Colombian coking coal) and rolling them in Colombia:

(ii) constructing a single direct reduction plant to produce metallized pellets for the existing arc furnace plants.

The study should also make a recommendation for the establishment of a reporting system to be employed by the basic steel producers to improve the quality of the statistical information on the sector which is presently available.

Supplement Prepared by: John W.P. Jaffe	
Dept. or Agency: IBRD/IDP	
Date: June 22, 1970	
Supplement Rev. by:	
Item(s) revised:	
Dept. or Agency:	
Date:	

CHAPTER 6
ROLE AND CHARACTERISTICS OF COLOMBIAN MANUFACTURING

As a result of significant growth during the recent decades, the Colombian manufacturing industries constitute an increasingly important part of the economy. Manufacturing, which includes the factory and handicraft sectors,[1] accounted for 15% of the gross domestic product in 1950 and rose to contribute about 19% of GDP in 1968, the last year for which national accounts data are available.

The Contribution of Manufacturing

Total value-added in manufacturing as shown in the national accounts combines data for the factory sector as collected by the national statistical office (DANE)[2] and estimates by the Bank of the Republic (Banco de la Republica) for the handicraft sector. Growth in the factory sector has been substantially more rapid than in handicraft, as shown by the declining share of handicraft in total manufacturing value added (Table 6-1). The factory sector alone, which represented about 9% of GDP in 1945 had risen to 11% in 1950, 14% in 1960 and about 16% by 1968. For handicraft, the admittedly crude estimate implies that its share of GDP has dropped from about 4% in 1950 to about 3% in 1968.

Another way of looking at the contribution of manufacturing to national output is to express its contribution in dollar equivalents as is done in Table 6-2.

Thus, the contribution of manufacturing to gross domestic product per capita rose in the 18-year period 1950 to 1968 by US$18 or US$21, depending on the exchange rate used for conversion to dollar equivalents. In either event, the increase amounts to a real increase of about US$1 per capita per year.

The above data are based on value-added in manufacturing (eliminating multiple counting of raw materials and intermediate products used at various stages of production). They should not be confused with gross value of output data used appropriately for other comparisons elsewhere in the report. In Colombia gross value of output is about two-and-one-half times gross value-added.

In 1967, total employment in the factory sector was 293,825 or about 5% of the economi-

Table 6-1: VALUE ADDED AT MARKET PRICES
(In millions of 1968 Col$)

	Factory Sector	Handicraft Sector	Total	Handicraft as % of Total
1950	4,542.9	1,472.1	6,015.0	24.5
1953	5,560.2	1,672.1	7,232.4	23.1
1960	9,284.3	2,096.8	11,381.1	18.4
1967	13,902.1	2,623.2	16,525.3	15.9
1968	14,828.1	2,721.9	17,550.0	15.5

Sources: Banco de la Republica, *Cuentas Nacionales, 1950-1967*, and unpublished Banco de la Republica data.

1. The handicraft sector is defined to include firms employing less than five workers.
2. Departamento Administrativo Nacional de Estadistica–DANE.

Table 6-2: MANUFACTURING VALUE ADDED, TOTAL AND PER CAPITA – DOLLAR EQUIVALENTS

	1958 Prices & Exchange Rates US$ Equivalent			1968 Prices & Exchange Rates US$ Equivalent		
	Value Added (Col$ billions)	Total (US dollars millions)	Per Capita (US dollars)	Value Added (Col$ billions)	Total (US dollars millions)	Per Capita (US dollars)
1950	2.2	290	25	6.1	360	31
1960	4.1	550	36	11.3	660	43
1968	6.4	840	43	17.5	1,030	52

Note: Pesos converted to US$ at the following rates:
       1958 at Col$ 7.6 per dollar.
       1968 at Col$ 17 per dollar.

Sources: Banco de la Republica, *Cuentas Nacionales, 1950-1967,* and unpublished Banco de la Republica data.

cally active population in Colombia,[3] or an increase of about 47% since 1953. For the entire post-war period, the increase was almost 159,000 or 118% above the June 1945 level.

Employment in the handicraft sector is not known and cannot be estimated with any degree of accuracy. Sources in Colombia place it at approximately equal to the recorded employment in the factory sector, or about 300,000. This number appears to be highly exaggerated. According to Banco de la Republica estimates, value-added in handicraft in 1967 was approximately 20% of that in the factory sector. This estimate would imply that value-added per person employed was only one-fifth that for all factory employment, where it averaged Col$52,000 per person per year in 1967 prices. DANE data indicate that small firms employing 1 to 4 workers had an average value-added per paid worker of Col$28,000. On the basis of the foregoing estimates, it appears more reasonable to assume that the equivalent full-time employment in handicrafts in 1967 was more of the order of 150,000 to 200,000 persons, implying a value-added per person engaged of between Col$15,000 and Col$20,000 per year.

New fixed investment in manufacturing is a significant portion of total national fixed investment. In 1967, total new fixed investment in the manufacturing industry was Col$2,364 million[4] (equivalent to about US$150 million) or 16% of total fixed investment in Colombia. In that year national and local government fixed investment was about 29% of the total; of the remaining *private* fixed investment, therefore, manufacturing investment was about 23%. Fixed investment in manufacturing has also been highly cyclical (see Table 6-3). The market for manufactured goods is estimated at about US$2,751 million in 1967, the latest year for which detailed data are available. This figure is arrived at by adding the value of net imports (imports minus exports) to the gross value of production in factory industries (DANE figures),[5] as shown in Table 6-4.

The salient features of the Colombian market for manufactures are:

(a)   Neither imports nor exports are significant for non-durable consumer goods; self-

3. Included in the figures shown above, there were in 1967 about 11,000 persons occupied in manufacturing who were not paid employees—probably represented by the owners of the establishments and their immediate families.
4. The total includes net land purchases by the manufacturers which should be excluded in any precise comparison. Absence of data precludes such exclusion, but it is not believed to have affected significantly the year to year fluctuations although it somewhat overstates the level for the whole period.
5. The output of handicraft industry is not included for lack of detail.

Table 6-3: INVESTMENT IN FIXED ASSETS, 1957-1967

	Total investment in fixed assets in the whole economy	Investment in fixed assets in manufacturing industry	Share of investment in manufacturing industry in total investment in the whole economy (%)
	(In millions of current Col$)		
1957	2,643	500	18.9
1958	3,339	373	11.2
1959	3,908	403	10.3
1960	4,845	499	10.3
1961	5,580	623	11.2
1962	6,137	920	15.0
1963	7,168	774	10.8
1964	8,654	1,247	14.4
1965	9,504	1,633	17.2
1966	12,304	2,096	17.0
1967	14,729	2,365	16.1

Source: Banco de la Republica, *Cuentas Nacionales, 1950-1967.*

Table 6-4: MARKET FOR MANUFACTURES, 1967
(In millions of US$ equivalent)

	Production	Imports	Exports	Total Market	Imports as % of Market	Exports as % of Production
Non-durable consumer goods	1,336.5	25.0	3.0	1,358.5	1.8	0.2
Durable consumer goods	144.9	26.3	2.7	168.5	15.6	1.9
Intermediate goods	764.6	165.0	45.9	883.7	18.7	6.0
Capital goods	78.4	205.2	3.4	280.2	73.2	4.3
Other manufactures	48.8	11.8	0.6	60.0	19.7	1.2
Total manufactures	2,373.2	433.3	55.6	2,750.9	15.8	2.3

sufficiency is high, partly because of stringent import controls, including complete import prohibitions.

(b)   At the other extreme, capital goods imports account for over 70% of the market.

(c)   Imports of durable consumer goods and intermediate goods account for less than 20% of the market.

(d)   Overall imports account for over 15% of the market; this proportion has been reduced from over 30% in 1953.

(e)   Exports account for a very small part of Colombian manufacturing output, slightly over 2% in 1967. The absolute volume, though still small, has been rising rapidly, especially in intermediate goods.

The Growth of Manufacturing Since 1953

The growth of Colombian manufacturing industries[6] during the fourteen years from 1953 to 1967—as measured by trends in output, value added and employment—will now be discussed. The detailed analysis of growth will extend only through 1967 because this is the last year for which comparable statistics are available. In the discussion all value figures have been shown in real 1968 prices and all growth rates calculated on the basis of these constant value figures.

General Trends

In the fourteen-year period under discussion, manufacturing has been characterized by a moderate overall growth. Output has expanded considerably faster than employment, reflecting marked increases in productivity.

The value of output of Colombia's manufacturing industries increased from about Col$17 billion in 1953 to some Col$40 billion in 1967. This increase represents a rise of about 138% and an average annual growth rate of 6.4% for the years 1953 to 1967.[7] Growth was not evenly

Table 6-5: AVERAGE ANNUAL GROWTH RATES IN OUTPUT, VALUE-ADDED AND EMPLOYMENT, %.

	1953-67	1953-60	1960-67
	OUTPUT		
Non-durable consumer goods	4.4	4.3	4.6
Durable consumer goods	9.9	10.5	9.4
Intermediate goods	9.8	12.8	6.9
Capital goods	13.0	15.6	10.5
Other	14.3	16.5	12.0
Total	6.4	7.0	5.8
	VALUE ADDED		
Non-durable consumer goods	5.3	5.1	5.5
Durable consumer goods	8.0	7.9	8.1
Intermediate goods	8.7	9.3	8.0
Capital goods	11.5	11.7	11.4
Other	13.3	12.7	13.8
Total	6.7	6.7	6.8
	EMPLOYMENT		
Non-durable consumer goods	1.5	2.1	0.9
Durable consumer goods	5.8	9.8	1.9
Intermediate goods	4.3	5.4	3.2
Capital goods	11.2	17.0	5.7
Other	9.4	12.7	6.2
Total	3.3	4.3	2.1

Sources: 1953, 1958, 1961, 1963-1966: *Boletin Mensual de Estadistica,* Numbers 67, 117, 148, 170, 180, 201 and 207; 1960, 1962 and 1967: Unpublished DANE data.

6. Manufacturing refers to firms employing five or more workers or the factory sector.
7. Preliminary information supplied by the Bank of the Republic indicates that manufacturing output rose about 6.6% in 1968 and 8.5% in 1969. On this basis, the gross value of production of the factory sector in 1969 is estimated at Col$47 billion in constant 1968 prices.

distributed throughout the period. The average annual growth of output declined from 7.0% from 1953 to 1960, to 5.8% from 1960 to 1967 (Table 6-5).

In 1967, firms employing 100 or more workers produced about 63% of output value. The rate of growth of output was markedly higher in the larger firms as can be seen from Table 6-6. While growth in firms employing between 5 and 15 workers was 3.2% from 1960 to 1967, the output of firms employing between 100 and 200 workers grew at the rate of 6.7% and firms employing 200 and more workers grew at the rate of 7%.

In 1967, value added in manufacturing amounted to about Col$17 billion (1968 prices). This represents an absolute increase of about 150% and an average annual growth rate of about 6.7% between 1953 and 1967. For the fourteen-year period under discussion, therefore, value added grew at a slightly higher pace than gross output.

Conceptually, value added data are a better measure of growth than gross value of production because they eliminate double-counting of intermediate goods. Colombian value added data, however, must be used with great care in analysis of the development of the manufacturing sector. The quantitative import restrictions and exchange rate fluctuations that have prevailed in Colombia for the last fifteen years have brought with them sharp changes in manufacturers' inventories of **raw** materials. Value added data reflect inventory accumulations and depletions as well as the valuation of such inventories because value added is derived by deducting material inputs from the total value of production. It is possible that the value added figures are underestimated in years of inventory buildup if the purchase of raw materials for inventory purposes is counted as an input for production. The reverse would happen in years of inventory depletion. A second difficulty in using value added data relates to the choice of deflators. Indices that apply to gross output (wholesale price indices) can be more readily tested than those applicable to value added. Because of the problems of measuring growth in value added, the discussion on output growth will concentrate on the growth of gross value of production.

In 1967, paid employees in the manufacturing industries numbered about 283,000, an absolute rise of about 56% from 1953 when the work force in the manufacturing industries was about 181,000. This represents an average annual growth rate of about 3.3% or one-half the growth rate of output. The slow growth of employment in manufacturing compared to the growth of output and value added reflects the increases in labor productivity that occurred during the period. The growth rate of employment like that of output, declines over the fourteen years between 1953 and 1967. While manufacturing employment rose at the rate of 4.3% in the first half of the period, the rate of increase in the second half was only 2.1%.

The increases in manufacturing output and employment were not evenly distributed among the different industrial branches. These have been classified for purposes of analysis into the four major sub-groupings: non-durable consumer goods such as food, clothing, textiles[8] and pharmaceuticals; durable consumer goods such as furniture, appliances, and automobiles; intermediate goods such as basic chemicals, petroleum products and metal manufactures; and capital goods (heavy machinery and transport equipment). The role of each sub-group in the growth of output and employment can be measured in terms of the percentage contribution of each group to expanded output and employment and in terms of the relative rate of growth of each sub-group and industrial branch.

Production by Industries

As indicated in Table 6-7, of the Col$23 billion increase in output between 1953 and 1967, some 46% was accounted for by the non-durable consumer goods industries; the remainder was made up of some 40% intermediate goods industries, some 8% non-durable consumer goods industries and only about 5% capital goods industries.

8. Data for the textile industry do not permit a clear distinction between textiles for consumer and industrial uses. The mission has estimated that about half the textiles in Colombia are for consumer use (classified under non-durable consumer goods) and half for industrial uses (classified as intermediate goods).

The contributions to increased output are not indicative of the average annual growth rates for these groups because of the disparate output bases from which each group started. While the non-durable consumer goods industries and some intermediate goods were relatively well-developed by 1953, the other industrial branches were only beginning to be established in Colombia. The growth trends, however, point to the development of new industrial sub-sectors and are indicators of the process of diversification of Colombian manufacturing output. For the entire 1953 to 1967 period, the non-durable consumer goods industries grew moderately, 4.4% per year. The intermediate and durable consumer goods industries grew rapidly, each reaching a growth rate of about 10% for the entire period. The relative growth of the capital goods industries was the greatest, averaging 13% annually.

The faster growth of industrial production in the first half than in the second half of the fourteen-year period under discussion can be observed in most industrial sub-groups. Table 6-8 shows the growth of production in selected sub-sectors. The growth of manufacturing between 1953 and 1960 can be attributed to the development of nontraditional branches.

More significant was the dynamic development of industries producing industrial inputs—the intermediate goods industries. These industries had already attained considerable develop-

Table 6-6: GROWTH RATES IN OUTPUT BY SIZE OF FIRMS

Firm Size	Output (In millions of 1968 Col$)		Growth % 1960-1967
	1960	1967	
5 to 15 workers	2,912.0	3,636.4	3.2
15 to 19 workers	8,425.0	11,629.3	4.7
100 to 199 workers	4,299.1	6,749.9	6.7
200 or more workers	11,401.9	18,210.2	7.0
Total	27,038.0	40,225.8	5.8

Source: 1960: DANE *Boletin Mensual de Estadistica* No. 1967:

ment by 1953 and grew at an average annual rate of about 13% in the seven-year period from 1953 to 1960. The development of the intermediate industries was partly spurred by government investments in this group. Thus, the establishment of Paz del Rio, the steel plant, stimulated the development of the basic metal industries which grew at a rate of 42% per year. The chemical industries grew at the rate of about 18%. A few large investments such as the government-financed soda plant near Bogota were instrumental in their expansion.

The start of production of the ESSO petroleum refinery in Cartagena contributed to the accelerated growth of another important industrial input—refined petroleum products—which grew at an average annual rate of 18% between 1953 and 1960. Partly as a by-product of the development of the steel industry, but also as a result of import restrictions, the metal industries grew rapidly at an average annual rate of about 13%.

The paper industry received its first stimulus in the 1950s—expanding at the rate of 18% per year. Large investments throughout the period by Carton de Colombia, one of the two large producers of paper products in Colombia contributed to this development.

The durable consumer goods industries grew at an average annual rate of about 11% in the 1950s. The rapid development of the tire industry and the establishment of several electrical appliance manufacturers contributed to the expansion of this category.

Between 1960 and 1967, the growth of output slowed down in three out of the four major industrial sub-groups, non-durable consumer goods being the exception. The rate of growth of capital goods declined from about 16% in the period from 1953 to 1960 to about 11% from 1960 to 1967; the growth rate of the intermediate goods declined from about 13% in the first

Table 6-7: INCREASES IN OUTPUT, 1953-1967

	Output 1953	Contributions to Increased Output			Output 1967
		1953-60	1960-67	1953-67	
		(In millions of 1968 Col$)			
Non-durable consumer goods	12,321.1	4,218.9	6,114.0	10,332.9	22,654.1
Durable consumer goods	653.8	658.2	1,143.3	1,801.5	2,455.3
Intermediate goods	3,507.9	4,641.4	4,810.5	9,451.9	12,959.7
Capital goods	239.8	421.5	667.5	1,089.0	1,328.8
Other	128.3	247.1	452.5	699.6	827.9
Total	16,850.9	10,187.1	13,187.8	23,374.9	40,225.8
	Output distribution (%)	Distribution of Increases %			Output distribution (%)
Non-durable consumer goods	73.1	41.1	46.3	46.2	56.2
Durable consumer goods	3.9	6.5	8.7	7.7	6.2
Intermediate goods	20.8	45.6	36.5	40.4	32.1
Capital goods	1.4	4.1	5.1	4.7	3.3
Other	0.8	2.4	3.4	3.0	2.1
Total	100.0	100.0	100.0	100.0	100.0

Sources: 1953, 1958, 1961, 1963-1966: *Boletin Mensual de Estadistica,* Numbers 67, 117, 148, 170, 180, 201 and 207; 1960, 1962 and 1967: Unpublished DANE data.

period to about 7% in the second. The rate of growth of consumer durable goods declined least: from 10.5% between 1953 and 1960 to 9.4% between 1960 and 1967.

The main intermediate goods for which the growth rate fell were basic metals and petroleum; but import substitution sustained a high growth rate in two intermediate industries, chemicals and paper, in which new plants were established. Similarly the growth rate of the capital goods sector was sustained by rapid expansion (about 14% per year) of the output of electrical machinery. Among non-durable consumer goods sugar expanded and also processed foods and this maintained the overall growth rate. The chief durable consumer goods with rapid output growth were cars and electrical goods.

Employment and Productivity

As with output, increases in employment varied among the several industrial branches. Of the 102,000 additional workers employed in manufacturing between 1953 and 1967, about 41% were employed in intermediate goods industries and about 24% in the non-durable consumer goods industries. Only slightly more than one fourth of the additional workers employed were involved in the production of capital goods and consumer durables; but the share of these two sectors in the total manufacturing work-force rose by over two-thirds. (Table 6-9).

By comparing rates of growth in production and employment, one can derive implicit figures of production per worker. It should be noted, however, that the production figures are for gross output and consequently are for gross output per employee. The significance of such figures is limited, particularly as regards any specific industry. There are likely to be offsetting errors or biases in the data for the entire manufacturing sector, but it is not feasible to adequately allow for these in each specific industry. With these limitations in mind, the data in Table 6-10 indicate that for manufacturing as a whole, gross value of output per paid worker grew by 3.1% per year between 1953 and 1967. If employment is related to value-added, the rate is 3.4% per year.

Table 6-8: AVERAGE ANNUAL GROWTH OF OUTPUT

	1953-67	1953-60	1960-67
Non-durable consumer goods	4.4	4.3	4.6
Food	3.5	1.7	5.2
Textiles	5.9	8.4	3.5
Pharmaceuticals	12.0	13.5	10.5
Durable consumer goods	9.9	10.5	9.4
Rubber products	10.2	11.2	9.1
Electrical appliances	15.1	18.8	12.5
Motor vehicles	9.7	6.9	12.6
Intermediate goods	9.8	12.8	6.9
Paper and products	16.2	18.1	14.3
Chemicals, other	19.2	17.6	21.0
Petroleum	10.1	17.5	2.8
Non-metallic mineral products	6.9	6.9	6.8
Basic metals	22.5	41.8	3.2
Metal products	10.7	13.3	8.1
Capital goods	13.0	15.6	10.4
Mechanical machinery	9.3	10.8	7.8
Electrical machinery	24.2	34.7	13.8

Sources: 1953, 1958, 1961, 1963-1966: *Boletin Mensual de Estadistica,* Numbers 67, 117, 148, 170, 180, 201 and 207; 1960, 1962 and 1967: Unpublished DANE data.

By broad categories of manufactures, the rates range from 1.6% to 5.3%; figures derived from value-added, however, show differences for the growth rate of each category. Any interpretation as to productivity in specific industries should, therefore, be based on material presented in Chapters 8 to 10 rather than what may be inferred from the data in Table 6-10.

General Characteristics of Colombian Manufacturing

The general characteristics of manufacturing discussed here include scale of operations, type of ownership and industrial financing. The competitive structure of individual industrial branches is discussed in Chapters 8, 9 and 10, while the regional aspects of manufacturing growth are discussed in Chapter 11.

Size of Plants

Most establishments engaged in manufacturing activities are small, employing less than 20 workers. The data indicate that in 1967 there were only slightly over 1,000 factory establishments in Colombia employing 50 or more persons and about 1,300 more employing from 20-49 persons. In addition there were over 8,000 establishments employing less than 20 persons each, as indicated in Table 6-11.

As can be seen from Table 6-6, the growth rate of output was greater in the larger firms.

Table 6-9:   INCREASES IN EMPLOYMENT, 1953-1967

	Employment 1953	Contributions to Increased Employment			Employment 1967
		1953-60	1960-67	1953-67	
Non-durable consumer goods	109,523	16,669	8,207	24,867	134,399
Durable consumer goods	12,469	11,562	3,395	14,957	27,426
Intermediate goods	52,846	23,420	18,473	41,893	94,739
Capital goods	3,857	7,717	5,519	13,236	17,093
Other	2,645	3,469	3,212	6,681	9,326
Total	181,340	62,837	38,806	101,643	282,983
	Employment distribution %	Distribution of Increase %			Employment distribution %
Non-durable consumer goods	60.4	26.5	21.2	24.5	47.5
Durable consumer goods	6.9	18.4	8.7	14.7	9.7
Intermediate goods	29.1	37.3	47.6	41.2	33.5
Capital goods	2.1	12.3	14.2	13.0	6.0
Other	1.5	5.5	8.3	6.6	3.3
Total	100.0	100.0	100.0	100.0	100.0

Sources: 1953, 1958, 1961, 1963-1966: *Boletin Mensual de Estadistica,* Numbers 67, 117, 148, 170, 180, 201 and 207; 1960, 1962 and 1967: Unpublished DANE data.

Table 6-10:   GROSS OUTPUT PER PAID WORKER

	1953	1960	1967	Average Annual Growth % 1953-1967
		(In thousands of 1968 Col$)		
Non-durable consumer goods	112.5	131.1	168.6	2.9
Durable consumer goods	52.4	54.6	89.5	3.9
Intermediate goods	66.4	106.9	136.8	5.3
Capital goods	62.2	57.1	77.7	1.6
Other	48.5	61.5	88.8	4.4
Total	92.9	110.7	142.2	3.1

Sources: 1953, 1958, 1961, 1963-1966: *Boletin Mensual de Estadistica,* Numbers 67, 117, 148, 170, 180, 201 and 207; 1960, 1962 and 1967: Unpublished DANE data.

Further, the 527 establishments employing over 100 persons, while representing less than 5% of the number of establishments, accounted for 57% of the employment, 72% of the wages and social benefits,[9] 62% of the gross output, 71% of the value added, 82% of the net investment, 66% of the increase in inventories and 63% of the horsepower installed in the total manufacturing sector.

It is interesting to note that of these 500-odd large establishments, 55% were in traditional consumer goods,[10] and slightly over one-fourth were engaged in production of intermediate

9. 70% of the wages proper and 81% of the social benefits.
10. The Colombian data have been adapted to the Brazilian classification.

Table 6-11:   AVERAGE SIZE OF ESTABLISHMENTS, 1967

Establishment Size (Paid Employees)	Number of Establishments	%	Paid Employees ('000's)	%
Under 20	8,413	78	45.3	16
20-49	1,338	12	39.8	14
50-99	525	5	36.3	13
Over 100	527	5	161.6	57
	10,803	100	283.0	100

Source: Unpublished DANE data.

goods. Less than 100 establishments in capital or consumer durable goods employed 100 or more persons.

In Brazil, by comparison there were 3,456 establishments employing 100 or more persons which accounted for 69% of the employment, 76% of the wages and 75% of the value added, indicating a slightly greater concentration of large establishments than in Colombia.

Certain branches of industry are highly concentrated in large establishments in both Colombia and Brazil (e.g., textiles, tobacco, rubber, beverages and chemicals). Brazil has a heavy concentration of employment in larger plants in metals and metal products, paper and machinery of all types, while the percentage of such concentration in Colombia is markedly lower. Certain industries such as furniture, food, clothing and wood products have more small plants, and hence less concentration in larger establishments. A comparison of the percentage of employment by industry in plants employing over 100 persons in Colombia and Brazil is given in Table 6-12.

Factory Ownership

In 1966, the latest year for which published data are available 65% of the establishments were owned by individuals, 23% by limited partnerships and only 5% were corporations. The rest had miscellaneous forms of ownership, such as official or semi-official firms, general partnerships, cooperatives, etc. As might be expected, the larger firms were generally corporations, the medium-sized firms limited partnerships and the small establishments were individually owned.

While corporations represented only 5% of the establishments, they accounted for over 40% of the employment and over 50% of the gross output, 59% of the value added and almost the same proportion (58%) of wages and social benefits paid. They also accounted for over half the new investment and three-quarters of the increase in inventories. The few large government firms (including Ecopetrol and Planta de Soda) accounted for less than 3% of the employment but 7% of the value added and 27% of the new fixed investment. These striking differences point to the capital intensive nature of the petroleum and chemical industries.

The limited partnerships, which enjoy a preferential tax position, are a significant factor in industry, and probably also in trade, as outlined in Chapter 7.

Table 6-12: EMPLOYMENT IN ESTABLISHMENTS EMPLOYING 100 OR MORE
PERSONS AS A PERCENTAGE OF TOTAL EMPLOYMENT, BY INDUSTRY

Concentration of Employment	Industry (ranking by Colombian proportion)	Colombia 1967	%	Brazil 1966
Over 80%	Textiles	85		85
	Tobacco	85		84
	Rubber	81		75
65 to 79%	Beverages	78		63
	Chemicals	67		74
50 to 64%	Paper	58		73
	Non-metallic mineral products	57		58
	Leather	56		44
	Electrical machinery	56		81
	Transport machinery	52		90
	Metals and metal products	50		79
Under 50%	Printing and publishing	48		57
	Wood products	46		21
	Mechanical machinery	46		68
	Food	41		61
	Clothing and footwear	37		53
	Miscellaneous	37		60
	Furniture and fixtures	24		27

Sources: IBRD: *Current Economic Position and Prospects of Brazil,* Vol. III, Report No. WH195a, December 1969.

Labor and Employer Organizations

Trade union organizations have an important function in the manufacturing sector. The existing legislation tends to favor a single union within a company as it allows only one union to act as collective bargaining agent. These enterprise unions are frequently affiliated with a national union but bargaining is customarily with a single firm, rather than with an entire industry.

There are two large national trade union federations in Colombia: the CTC (Confederacion de Trabajadores de Colombia) and the UTC (Union de Trabajadores de Colombia). Union ties with the political parties are not close and it is the impression of the mission that trade union influence was more evident in industrial bargaining and in other matters of direct labor interest, such as minimum wage laws, than in broader issues such as taxation and industrial or foreign trade strategy.

There is no evidence that labor organization has been instrumental in initiating major cost changes in manufacturing industries. The limited data available point more in the direction of wage changes following increases in the cost of living, although obviously the repercussions of such wage adjustments in a particular industrial branch have affected industrial costs and prices in that and related branches.

ANDI (Associacion National de Industriales) is the largest employer organization and engages in economic studies, employment services for foreign technicians and other activities. There are also numerous specialized trade associations.

Industrial Financing

New investment in fixed assets in Colombian manufacturing in 1967 was Col$2,365 million (See Table 6-3), or about US$150 million equivalent. It probably rose slightly in real terms in the following two years. In 1966, the last year for which detailed data are available, private corporations (excluding official societies) accounted for about 51% of total manufacturing fixed investment; if official societies are added, this increases to 78%. What is most significant for present purposes is that in that year, privately-owned corporations accounted for about 70% of the private fixed investment in manufacturing.

The data issued by the Superintendency of Corporations (Superintendencia de Sociedades Anonimas) cover only private corporations. At the end of 1968, a sample of the larger corporations[11] had net assets of approximately Col$23.3 billion.[12] It is likely that all corporations in the manufacturing sector had net assets of approximately Col$30 billion and that total net assets in manufacturing (corporate, non-corporate and official societies) were about Col$55 billion to Col$60 billion.

An approximate condensed balance sheet for 298 large manufacturing corporations is reproduced in Table 6-13. The data do not permit a breakdown between current and long-term obligations.

The means by which larger firms handled their financing requirements from 1964 to 1968 is shown in Table 6-14.

For the larger industrial firms, there has been a tendency for marked swings in borrowings in past years, particularly in periods of large price increases, presumably because of fears that import liberalization policies would not be long sustained. For example, borrowings tripled between 1965 and 1966 and then fell by over 80% in 1967. It is significant to note that borrowings in 1966 were primarily from government, foreign sources and other credits (ac-

Table 6-13: COMPOSITE BALANCE SHEET FOR LARGE MANUFACTURING
CORPORATIONS AS OF DECEMBER 31, 1968
(In billions of Col$)

Assets	
Fixed assets (net of depreciation reserves)	4.7
Cash and securities	2.8
Accounts receivable	6.3
Inventories	5.1
Other assets	4.4
Total assets	23.3
Liabilities	
Payable to banks	1.6
Payable to government	1.0
Payable to external creditors	1.2
Labor obligations	0.7
Other accounts payable	4.7
Capital	4.0
Surplus and reserves	10.1
Total liabilities	23.3

Source: Unpublished data, Superintendencia de Sociedades Anonimas.

11. The sample covers 298 of the 586 corporations, but these 298 accounted for about 80% of gross sales and wages and salaries of all corporations.

12. After deducting Col$3 billion in depreciation reserves.

counts payable or borrowings from domestic non-bank lenders). Increases in bank loans were small, reflecting the tight credit policy of the government. In 1967, after devaluation, borrowings shrank sharply, presumably because increases in inventories and accounts receivable were nominal as compared to a combined increase of Col$3 billion in 1966.

The pattern of the large corporations was not duplicated by the smaller corporations. There are some indications that for the smaller firms the rise in borrowings between 1965 and 1966 was less marked and that the issue of new shares also rose less. While the rise in inventories appears equally steep, the increases in accounts receivable were smaller. Presumably in Colombia, as elsewhere, the smaller firms have less success in borrowing in periods of tight money and high interest rates, except from shareholders or affiliates. These inferences on smaller corporations are drawn from a comparison of sources and uses of funds data for all reporting corporations, and similar data for the 315 large corporations, both reported by the same source. Unfortunately, data for all manufacturing corporations were not available for years after 1966. Table 6-14 shows the proportions of the sources of funds in the three years 1964-66 for which comparable data are available for (a) all corporations, (b) 315 identical large manufacturing corporations, and (c) the other manufacturing firms.

The larger corporations financed between 37% and 49% of their needs from internal cash generation (undistributed profits and non-cash reserves, e.g. depreciation) as compared with 12-15% for the smaller corporations. The smaller firms raised 25-29% of their needs by new equity as against 12-19% for the larger corporations. Borrowings by the smaller firms constituted a larger portion of their financing, 57-61% as against 37-51% for the larger firms. In that connection, it should be noted that such borrowings include borrowings from shareholders or affiliates. Unfortunately, no breakdown of borrowings is available to test the hypothesis that a significant part of the borrowings by smaller corporations probably came from such sources. If this is so, the larger proportion of borrowings may be more nominal than real and may merely reflect tax or other advantages of infusing capital in the form of debt rather than in equity form.

Private development finance companies have played an important role in industrial financing in Colombia. There are eleven such in operation but the five leading ones in the four major cities and Manizales have been operating from five to ten years and their combined activity may be considered to represent approximately 90% of the entire group. As of mid-1969, these finance companies accounted for about 20% of the Col$12.5 billion of assets held by development banks (which cover *all* sectors of the economy). Governmental development institutions like IFI (Instituto de Fomento Industrial–Institute for Industrial Development) are more important sources of capital for industry than any individual financiera. Governmental bodies like IFI and the Central Mortgage Bank (Banco Central Hipotecario) offer stiff competition for savings, partly because their obligations are tax-exempt.

As long as IFI and other government-owned finance companies have greater access to funds, more favorable terms or both, private finance companies will find it difficult to reconcile lending on competitive terms with an adequate financial return to attract additional local capital. The proliferation of effort and costs inherent in eleven separate entities, each with its own staff, management and board of directors, while understandable, is not conducive to improving the private companies' competitive position (see Chapter 7 regarding fiscal and monetary policy).

Table 6-14: SOURCES AND USES OF FUNDS FOR LARGE MANUFACTURING CORPORATIONS
(In millions of Col$)

Sources	1964	1965	1966	1967	1968
Internal Sources	829	980	1,494	1,016	1,035
Depreciation	271	295	311	274	358
Contingency reserves	19	27	-13	11	21
Undistributed profits	539	658	1,196	731	656
Borrowings	638	610	1,846	301	1,217
Banks	187	31	173	98	520
Government	-26	73	198	29	119
Foreign sources	-96	267	519	69	-97
Labor obligations	47	34	64	52	136
Other credits	526	205	892	54	538
Capital	214	404	688	109	177
Share issues	149	284	470	164	119
Borrowings from shareholders and affiliates	65	120	218	-55	58
Total Sources	1,680	1,995	4,028	1,426	2,429
Uses					
New fixed capital	472	610	721	804	943
Inventory increases	355	306	1,456	63	323
Cash and securities	112	286	274	442	314
Accounts receivable	709	618	1,598	28	796
Other assets	32	175	-21	87	53
Total Uses	1,680	1,995	4,028	1,426	2,429

Source: Unpublished data, Superintendencia de Sociadades Anonimas.

Table 6-15: SOURCES OF FUNDS BY SIZE OF CORPORATION (%)

Sources of Funds	1964 (a) Total	(b) Large	(c) Small	1965 (a) Total	(b) Large	(c) Small	1966 (a) Total	(b) Large	(c) Small
Internal Generation	38	49	14	37	49	15	31	37	12
Borrowings	47	42	57	45	37	60	54	51	61
Capital	15	19	29	18	14	25	15	12	21
Total	100	100	100	100	100	100	100	100	100

Source: Superintendencia de Sociedad es Anonimas, *La Industria Manufacturera* and *Revista, 1966.*

CHAPTER 7
GOVERNMENT MEASURES AFFECTING INDUSTRIALIZATION

In internal economic policy as it affects manufacturing, Colombia long emphasized fiscal and monetary measures, limiting direct government intervention to exceptional cases like investment in the Paz del Rio steel plant and special measures in exchange crisis situations. The major emphasis was on tax policy, the incidence of which was more progressive than in most South American countries. This is reflected in the fact that direct taxes constitute a larger percentage of tax revenues in that country than in other South American countries. Business taxation policies, with measures ranging from an excess profits tax to tax exemptions to industries for specific performance on use of indigenous materials, had two main aims: (a) to furnish incentives for industrialization as a means of increasing employment opportunities, and (b) to level down by taxation highly visible income disparities. Monetary policies seemed to fluctuate from period to period.

In the last few years, measures intended to spur economic growth and to improve income distribution and resource allocation have tended to become somewhat more direct, e.g. agricultural incentives, export incentives for non-traditional products, greater governmental direction of bank loans and investments toward favored sectors, and a variety of other measures, which are now discussed.

Tax Policy

The discussion in this section relies extensively on the Report of the Musgrave Commission,[1] a committee appointed in 1968 by the President of Colombia, to evaluate the tax structure of the country. In general, the mission is in agreement with the findings and proposals of the Musgrave Commission on the issue of business taxation.

Fiscal measures affecting Colombian manufacturing industries fall under three general headings: direct business taxes, indirect taxes, and tax incentives. Colombian business taxes, as presently constituted, encompass a multiplicity of complicated and uncoordinated measures. In essence, the incidence of taxation varies markedly according to the legal form of business organization; for example, corporations are effectively discriminated against in favor of non-corporate entities of the same size or income. Tax incentives have not always achieved the objectives for which they were designed: since 1960 there have been incentives intended to foster certain "basic" and "complementary" industries, which have been largely ineffective.

Business Tax Structure

Business taxation can affect manufacturing activity in a variety of ways. Cost deductions, asset depreciation, the inclusion or exclusion of various forms of income in taxable income, and tax rates imposed on different legal forms of business, obviously affect the profitability of enterprises and thus the incentive to invest in them.

At present three types of taxes are levied on business enterprises: (a) income taxes on all forms of business enterprise, (b) excess profits taxes levied on corporations only, and (c) special profits taxes on corporations and limited liability companies. Indirect business taxes are of little importance in Colombia, although the municipal industry tax is poorly structured and an irritant.

The incidence of the business income tax in Colombia depends on the legal form of ownership of the business. The Musgrave Report succinctly summarizes its structure:

"Under the present system, corporations, limited liability companies and partnerships are subject to different treatment as follows:

1. Commission on Tax Reform, Richard A. Musgrave, President, *Tax Reform for Colombia–Report by the Commission on Tax Reform* (hereinafter referred to as the *Musgrave Report.*)

115

–corporations now are subject to a three-rate schedule of 12% on taxable income up to Col$100,000, 24% on Col$100,000 to Col$1 million and 36% on the excess over Col$1 million;

–limited liability companies have a three-rate schedule of only 4% on the first Col$100,000 of taxable income, 8% on Col$100,000 to Col$300,000, and 12% on the excess over Col$300,000;

–partnerships are subject to a two-rate schedule of 3% on the first Col$100,000 and 6% on the excess over Col$100,000.

All of the after-tax income of limited liability companies and partnerships is imputed to the owners for tax purposes at the individual level, while corporate stockholders are taxable currently only on dividends. The retained earnings of corporations are not taxable to the shareholders. Nevertheless, this difference in integration does not adequately equalize the burden differential at the entity level."[2]

In addition to the business income tax, corporations are subject to an "excess profits" tax:

".... levied at graduated rates (20% to 56% depending on the rate of return on net worth) on earnings (after deduction of income tax) in excess of 12% of net worth when net worth is over Col$200,000."

The Musgrave Commission gives several reasons for the original establishment of the excess profits tax: First, the government has granted numerous benefits to the manufacturing sector, and the business sector has derived benefits from the protection vis-a-vis foreign competition granted to its products, as well as from monopolistic pricing. It is felt that the government is, in fact, recovering some of its implicit "subsidies to the business sector". Second, "to encourage employers with high earnings to lower prices or raise wages since this could be done largely at the expense of their tax liability".

Whatever the rationale for the establishment of the excess profits tax, its impact has been to further discriminate against the corporate form of ownership. The Musgrave Commission feels that the high and erratic marginal rate of taxation resulting from the incidence of the excess profits tax applies mainly to corporations.

The third form of business taxation is a pair of special taxes: First, the development and special social security tax—3% of taxable income—applies to corporations, individuals, and limited liability companies, but not to partnerships; and second, the housing tax—6% of taxable income—applies to all legal business entities but not to individuals.

The corporate form of ownership is, therefore, penalized under the Colombian business tax structure.

"This discrimination . . . is unfortunate both from equity and economic standpoints. The corporate form is an important means of mobilizing capital and organization talent for the tasks of economic development. In many instances, corporations and limited liability companies are of equal size and resources, and tax differential created by the present structure is unwarranted by their respective economic powers and resources".[3]

Another important tax problem is the definition of taxable income. This includes questions regarding depreciation allowances, loss carry-over and carry-forward, salary allowances and other items such as entertainment expenses, expenses abroad and head-office expense. The Colombian business tax structure does not at present permit either the revaluation of assets—a measure frequently adopted in inflationary economies or carry-over and carry-forward of losses.

On the question of depreciation allowances, the Commission rejects the proposal to allow asset revaluation so as to help the taxpayer maintain his real (as opposed to nominal) capital.

2. *Musgrave Report*, paras. 6.4 and 6.5.
3. *Musgrave Report*, para. 6.8.

It believes that more liberal depreciation allowances based on historical cost can achieve the same end as effectively and with greater administrative simplicity and will be more effective in "rendering assistance to the growing as against the established but static firm". A first step is to increase the total amount of allowable depreciation by eliminating the 10% salvage estimate. The Commission suggests the optional use of double declining balance rates instead of straight line rates on new machinery and equipment (not buildings); and it recommends consideration of increased depreciation rates for plants engaged in multiple shift operations while recognizing that these may be difficult to administer.

The Bank has supported, indeed urged, asset revaluation in public utilities, because without it price regulation based on a rate of return on original cost in local currency would make it impossible to finance growth out of internally generated cash, and would distort resource allocation. In private industry, where pricing is largely unregulated and where varying degrees of competition, both internal and external, are present, the case for asset revaluation is less strong. This is particularly true when price changes are moderate, as in Colombia in the past few years, and where fixed assets are usually less long-lived than in hydroelectric plants, water supply projects etc. For these reasons, provision for manufacturers to revalue assets does not under present circumstances, appear indispensable for profitable industrial investment.

On loss carry-forward and carry-over, the Commission urges adoption of such provisions to improve incentives for new firms to invest in new risky businesses. The limits, for tax purposes, of Col$15,000 (US$833) per month on salaries generally, and of Col$20,000 per month (US$1,111) on the top manager's salary "pose efficiency and equity problems for a relatively small group of business firms and their highest paid employees." The Commission proposes raising these limits and appointing a "salary board" to hear appeals from firms which seek to justify greater deductions.

The Commission recommends repeal of the housing, development, and social security taxes on business, and of the corporate excess profits tax; it suggests raising the equivalent revenue by raising the corporate tax to a level of 44-46%.

It should be noted that the Commission estimated business income tax (including excess profits tax) for 1963-65 at over 12% of national revenues and individual income tax revenues at just under 15%, making a total of 27%, which compares with 23% for Chile, 20% for Peru, 12% for Brazil and 6% for Argentina.

Indirect Taxes

Indirect taxes are generally low and less important in Colombia than they are in other Latin American countries. The Commission estimates indirect taxes in Colombia at 6-7% of GNP as compared to 8% in Chile, 11% in Peru and 13-14% in Brazil and Argentina. The mission estimates that manufacturers pay about 4% of sales in indirect taxes. There are two types of indirect taxes that affect the manufacturing sector: the municipal industry tax and the national sales tax.

The rate of the former, levied at the municipal level, is relatively low and the nuisance to manufacturers is unjustified. The mission agrees with the Musgrave Commission that the:

". . . Municipal Industry and Commerce tax should be abolished. This tax is an inequitable and unworkable anachronism for a country at Colombia's stage of development. Tax liability is determined on the basis of a curious mixture of gross sales, installed horsepower, value of monthly rent, and even square feet of plant space in some municipios. The tax attempts to bring virtually all firms, no matter how small, into its base (although there is a complex maze of exemptions), and the base as well as the exemption structure varies considerably from municipio to municipio. Evasion is estimated to be inordinately high, and the arbitrary method of imposing and collecting the tax gives rise to substantial opportunities for corruption. The tax is considered to be a nuisance by the business community, is regressive in its distributional impact, and has low revenue elasticity. It lacks any theoretical basis and very likely leads to distortions in business location decisions."[4]

The national sales tax, which is levied at the manufacturers level and on all imports, ranges between 3% and 15%, although with most products at 3%. Indirect business taxes are discussed in a later section on protection.

Monetary Policy–Impact on Industry

The government's monetary policies have had the effect of favoring agricultural borrowers over private industrial or trade borrowers in a variety of ways. Direct preferences for agricultural borrowers have been reflected in (a) preferential interest rates and terms, (b) requirements that banks lend a minimum percentage of assets to favored sectors such as agriculture. Furthermore, the loanable funds of banks available for discretionary lending have been reduced by increasing the reserve requirements of commercial banks with the Bank of the Republic and a requirement to buy government bonds, the proceeds of which are earmarked for specific purposes, usually non-industrial.

Recent social legislation has had the effect of channeling certain funds (for pensions and dismissal wages) formerly held and invested by enterprises, to the Social Security Institute, which has then channeled these funds to the Central Mortgage Bank and other institutions for investment in housing and other government-sponsored projects.

Governmental direction of credit is not new. Law 26 of 1959 required commercial banks to reserve a minimum of 15% of their portfolio for livestock loans. Taken by itself, this directed lending initially probably had limited economic effects. However, when for reasons of monetary policy private commercial banks are required to keep larger cash reserves with the Bank of the Republic and when official banks (Caja Agraria, Banco Cafetero and Banco Popular) are given greater access to such directed funds through preferential treatment on rediscounts, the effect is to rechannel banking funds away from industry and urban trade to agriculture, housing and other public projects favored by government policy.

The effect of all these measures was to restrict the supply of loanable funds available from private commercial banks. While interest rates are nominally controlled, some borrowers and lenders have found loopholes which result in increased borrowing costs. Others, finding access to customary lenders restricted, are borrowing in the "street" market at 2% or more per *month,* as compared to the bank rate ceiling of 14% per year. This "street" market is allegedly fed partly by funds obtained by livestock raisers at much lower rates from Caja Agraria. Another influence is the fact that the Central Mortgage Bank, an official institution, is borrowing at 11-1/2% tax-free to the lender. The lender, moreover, has an instant cash option.

The combined effects of these measures and of prior import deposits have caused a substantial squeeze on the availability and cost of working capital for industry and trade. The extremely high *net of tax* rate offered by an official agency, the Central Mortgage Bank for a highly liquid investment, has put other capital suppliers or intermediaries at a considerable disadvantage and contributed to a high nominal cost of capital. Since the rate of overall price increases has been moderate in marked contrast with a number of other South American countries, the real costs of borrowing are and have been positive and rather high in Colombia in the last few years.

Price Controls

Price controls were put into effect in 1961. They reached a peak apparently in 1965, when controls were administered by a total staff of about 50 persons, half professional, and covered about 35% of the economy. Controls have been eliminated or changed so that less than 4% is now under control. Items remaining under control are primarily those that affect the cost of living index directly or indirectly. Examples are beer, cigarettes, rubber tires, gasoline, transport charges, some drugs and packaging materials. There are almost no controls on agricultural

4. *Musgrave Report,* para. 8.33.

products, and agricultural inputs such as insecticides and herbicides were freed of price control early in 1970.

Where industries are not believed to be monopolistic or oligopolistic, controls have been removed. Certain basic products like steel and cement have also been freed, but the producers in such industries are required to furnish one month's advance notice of price increases, so that a judgment may be made as to whether to restore controls, or more often, to provide an opportunity to negotiate a lower increase. The trend is toward freeing items from price control with more reliance on competition, occasional removal of quantitative import restrictions or tariff reduction (e.g. on glass) and at times concessions to the industry such as reduction of prior import deposit rates on imported parts or materials.

Protection and Quantitative Controls

Over the past ten years, Colombia has gradually evolved from pursuing predominantly inward-oriented trade policies to an outward-looking orientation. While many of the present policies of protection and export promotion can be traced back to the early sixties, it was not until 1967 that they were presented cohesively. The present system of non-tariff trade restrictions, foreign exchange regulations and export promotion policies was fully defined in Decree-Law 444 of March 1967. With some modifications to this Law, the system has remained basically unchanged since that time.

Unlike the trade policies of other Latin American countries, the Colombian policies of export promotion and import substitution were primarily designed to change the structure of the balance of payments in a broad sense, rather than assist industrialization in particular. The policies were, therefore, geared to promote exports and substitute for imports of agricultural products as much as of manufactures. The emphasis which has been given to the agricultural sector in other policy fields, such as credit, bears out this conclusion. As an example of the general nature of Colombia's commercial policy, the import of both processed and unprocessed foodstuffs has been curtailed over the past fifteen years in a drive to attain self-sufficiency. This has been one of the few explicit trade policies pursued by the government. The policies, nevertheless, have had an impact on industrialization and have affected import substitution and export promotion in manufactured goods.

The System of Protection

The present system of protection for Colombian manufactures comprises three elements: an *ad valorem* tariff enacted in 1964, but much amended since; a system of quantitative import restrictions embodied in an import licensing system; and a system of prior deposits.

The protective effect of tariffs and quantitative restrictions has varied with the strictness of quantitative restrictions and applies differently to the various classes of goods. Where import prohibitions exist, the level of protection is extremely high. For products which are subject to restrictive licensing the tariff level is, in fact, a minimum level of protection. Prior deposits raise the level of protection but have been used by the government more as an instrument of restriction on credit than as trade policy.

The Level of Protection

Calculating the level of effective protection for Colombia is a difficult task, particularly for consumer goods, because these imports are extremely restricted. Moreover, constantly changing non-tariff restrictions could make any calculation of effective protection outdated almost before it is completed. It is not surprising, therefore, that no adequate study has been carried out.

An attempt has been made in this chapter to assess the level of protection of selected finished manufactured products by taking into account the major inputs that are needed in producing them. The results of this analysis are summarized in Table 7-1.

The benefits to local producers of protecting a given product are eroded if the protection

Table 7-1: LEVEL OF PROTECTION FOR SELECTED MANUFACTURED PRODUCTS

INPUTS INTO CAPITAL GOODS INDUSTRIES

	Tariff %	Prior Deposit
Heavy Machinery		
Special Steels	25	130
Cast iron	8	130
Copper wire	35	130
Copper sheets	40	130
Parts for electrical machinery (transformers, generators, motors)	40	10
Parts for mechanical machinery (compressors)	50	1
Engine parts	5	10
Arithmetic average	29	77
Transport Equipment		
Chassis: trucks	20	30
jeeps	20	30
buses	25	5
Bodies: jeeps	40	70
buses	40	70
Parts	20	38
Spring steel	40	130
Steel sheets	30	30
Arithmetic average	28	37

OUTPUTS OF CAPITAL GOODS INDUSTRIES

	Tariff %	Prior Deposit
Machine tools	19	1
Hand tools	50	30
Electrical machinery (generators, motors, transformers)	50	30
Engines – steam and internal combustion	27	50
Compressors	53	1
Arithmetic average	39	22
Trucks	120	10
Buses	60	30
Jeeps	20	30
Arithmetic average	67	23

Quantitative restrictions: All products subject to prior license.

INPUTS INTO DURABLE CONSUMER GOODS INDUSTRIES

Appliances		
Parts for electrical appliances	50	130
Motors for electrical appliances	55	30
Electric wire	45	130
Aluminum sheets	30	130
Cold rolled steel sheets	30	30
Parts for sewing machines	75	1
Arithmetic average	48	75
Motor Cars		
Chassis for motor cars	180	70
Bodies for motor cars	180	40
Parts	50	30
Spring steel	40	130
Steel sheets	30	30
Arithmetic Average	96	60
Tires		
Tire cases, threads, tubes, tire flaps	50	30
Zinc Oxide	40	30
Plates, sheet, strip, etc. of unhardened, vulcanized rubber	55	30
Carbon black	5	1
Natural rubber	10	1
Arithmetic average	28	16

OUTPUTS OF DURABLE CONSUMER GOODS INDUSTRIES

Electrical appliances	50	130
Sewing machines	90	1
Arithmetic average	70	66
Motor cars	340	130
Arithmetic average	340	130
Tires (except for tractors)	50	30
Arithmetic average	50	30

Quantitative restrictions: All products subject to prior license except zinc oxide (which is on the free list).

Table 7-1 (Cont.): LEVEL OF PROTECTION FOR SELECTED MANUFACTURED PRODUCTS

INPUTS INTO NON-DURABLE CONSUMER GOODS INDUSTRIES	Tariff %	Prior Deposit %
Textiles		
Cotton yarn	30	130
Raw cotton	20	1
Wool yarn	60	130
Raw wool	16	70
Synthetic yarn	35	130
Synthetic fibers	35	130
Arithmetic average	33	99
Clothing		
Wool textiles	100	130
Cotton textiles	43	130
Synthetic textiles	50	130
Ornaments for clothing	230	130
Arithmetic average	106	130
Leather Goods		
Parts for shoes	100	130
Tanning materials	35	130
Cattle leather	40	40
Raw hides	27	30
Arithmetic average	51	83

OUTPUTS OF NON-DURABLE CONSUMER GOODS INDUSTRIES	Tariff %	Prior Deposit %
Cotton textiles	43	130
Wool textiles	100	130
Synthetic textiles	50	130
Arithmetic average	64	130
Clothing	225	130
Arithmetic average	225	130
Footwear	200	130
Handbags & all other leather goods of consumer use	100	130
Arithmetic average	150	130

Quantitative restrictions: With the exception of textile inputs and tanning materials which are subject to prior license, all other products are prohibited.

INPUTS INTO INTERMEDIATE GOODS INDUSTRIES

Refined copper	8	30
Refined zinc	20	130
Refined lead	20	70
Tin	20	1
Arithmetic average	17	57

OUTPUTS OF INTERMEDIATE GOODS INDUSTRIES

Copper wire	35	130
Copper sheets	40	130
Brass	5	130
Batteries	40	130
Tinplate	25	30
Arithmetic average	29	104

Quantitative restrictions: refined zinc and tin are on the free list; all other products are subject to prior license.

Note: Whenever more than one rate applies to a given product, an arithmetic average has been calculated.

Source: Legislacion Economica, Limitada, *Nuevo Agancel de Aduaman de Colombia.*

on the imported inputs required to produce this product in Colombia is also high. This analysis, of course, applies most readily to products which require large quantities of imported inputs such as capital goods and many non-durable consumer goods. Where imported inputs are not required, the level of protection granted to the final product is equal to the actual tariff (nominal rate) for this product.

Table 7-1 indicates that for machinery and some metal manufactures the protection on value added is probably quite low for two reasons: first, the tariff on the final product is relatively low; second, imported inputs are also protected.

At the other extreme, some consumer goods such as clothing have an almost infinite level of protection, because importation of the final product is prohibited. High protection, however, does not necessarily mean high domestic prices if there is effective competition among the producers.

In considering the level of protection given by the government to local producers, any special charges adding to production costs, such as indirect business taxes, should be deducted. This discussion disregards indirect business taxes because in Colombia their incidence on production costs is almost negligible.

Quantitative Restrictions

All imports into Colombia are classified into one of three categories with three corresponding product lists: imports requiring a prior license, imports imported freely, and goods under embargo. All capital goods and most intermediates are subject to prior license; many consumer goods are on the prohibited list while some intermediates not produced domestically are on the free list.

The protective impact of the licensing system has varied with the type of products and with foreign exchange availability. In years of strict quantitative restrictions the level of protection has been higher than in years when quantitative restrictions are relaxed. Also, in years of strict quantitative restrictions, the import of consumer goods has been severely curtailed, whereas capital goods and intermediate goods have been allowed in with more freedom. The level of protection on consumer goods has, therefore, risen more than that on intermediate and capital goods in such years.

Quantitative restrictions have changed considerably from year to year, depending on the availability of foreign exchange. Hence, while in 1966 only about 45% of the products were subject to prior license, in 1967, the proportion was over 95%. In 1968, the figure fell to 88% and in 1969 80% (see Table 7-2). Further additions to the free list are now being considered. The rate of liberalization of quantitative restrictions is apt to be slow because Colombian authorities fear that pressures to accumulate inventories will cause a drain on reserves large enough to defeat the policy. They cite experiences in 1966 and earlier periods. The analysis of the mission (Chapter 6) confirms that widespread inventory speculation occurred in periods of trade liberalization.

In 1967, a year when strict quantitative restrictions were in effect, about 32% of the licenses requested were refused, in 1968 about 19% were refused, and in 1969—a year of trade liberalization—about 22% were refused. In 1969 there was an increased demand for imports resulting in part from the increased income of the coffee boom but also reflecting the importer's knowledge that there had been a liberalization of the restrictive policies. Table 7-3 indicates the relationship between the demand for foreign exchange and the value of licenses approved.

The time taken in processing license applications is another form of protection and of saving foreign exchange. In years of severe quantitative restrictions, the processing of licenses is allowed to take a considerable time, while in years of foreign exchange liberalization, they are processed quite rapidly. The Institute of Foreign Trade (Instituto de Comercio Exterior–INCOMEX), an agency of the Ministry of Development (Ministerio de Desarrollo) in charge of licensing, determines how much time processing applications should take. In 1967, when there were strict import controls and foreign exchange shortages, it would take an average of two months for a license to be approved. In mid-1968, the time allowed to process a license was shortened to one month, although in practice it took a little longer. In February 1970 the period

Table 7-2: SHARE OF IMPORTS REQUIRING PRIOR LICENSE IN TOTAL IMPORTS – 1956-1968
(In millions of US dollars)

| Year | Imports | | | Share of restricted imports to total imports % (2/3) |
	Free	Requiring Prior License	Total	
	1	2	3	4
1956	360.1	102.4	462.6	22.1
1957	289.4	118.7	408.1	29.1
1958	159.7	116.8	276.5	42.2
1959	230.1	147.0	377.1	39.0
1960	266.3	178.2	444.5	40.1
1961	280.3	182.2	462.5	39.4
1962	207.7	186.8	394.5	47.4
1963	177.1	293.7	470.8	62.4
1964	169.6	285.1	454.7	62.7
1965	72.1	405.1	477.2	84.9
1966	360.2	278.9	639.1	43.6
1967	19.8	505.0	524.8	96.2
1968	75.4	555.1	630.5	88.0

Source: Alberto Musalem, *Demanda por Dinero y Balanza de Pagos; La Experiencia de Colombia, 1950-1967*, unpublished document, 1969.

allowed was further reduced to ten days. The administrative reforms of INCOMEX have contributed to the more rapid processing of license applications, although it is to be expected that at times of foreign exchange shortage delays may occur again.

In 1969 there were 130,000 license applications, which in practice meant that the INCOMEX staff and the Council on Foreign Trade had to analyze and approve about 500 per day. No matter how competent and diligent, the staff of INCOMEX thus does not have time to evaluate the license applications thoroughly. The impact of this form of resource allocation on the manufacturing sector has unavoidably been arbitrary.

It has had three effects on the sector: it has contributed to overcapacity; it has been a bottleneck to increased production because of the difficulty in importing parts and raw materials; and by eliminating entirely import of many consumer goods it has probably lowered the quality of some domestically produced products.

The Colombian manufacturing sector depends heavily on imported raw materials and equipment. In order to be sure of having them when they want them, Colombian manufacturers tend to purchase ahead of time, when foreign exchange is available. This leads to premature and excessive investment, high overhead costs and over-capacity. Over-capacity is further accentuated because manufacturers are reluctant to engage in multishift operation, unless assured of the regular and continued availability of raw materials, especially imports.

The need to obtain a license for maintenance materials and spare parts for machinery has also tended to curtail production. This problem is particularly acute in years of strict quantitative restrictions. Indeed it is so severe that it has been estimated that a large part of the fifty-odd million dollars[5] worth of goods smuggled into Colombia each year consist of spare parts. The smuggling of spare parts negates the protective effect of trade barriers on these products.

There has been a virtual embargo on the importation of many consumer goods, such as clothing, leather goods, and electrical appliances. This prohibition, by eliminating foreign competition, has retarded quality improvements and adaptations in such fields as clothing and leather goods which have export potential. Selective imports of competing goods would have been helpful.

5. This figure is an official estimate and is taken into account in preparing the balance of payments.

The Tariff Structure

Tariffs, on the average, are lowest for capital goods and intermediate products not available domestically, and highest for consumer goods. Table 7-4 shows the frequency distribution of the 3,000-odd manufactured goods in six tariff columns representing different ranges. Half the tariff frequencies for non-durable goods fall in the two highest columns, i.e. are over 60%; tariffs on durable consumer goods are lower—three-fifths of them fall in the range 31% to 60%. Intermediate goods have still lower tariffs, the majority being in the 16% to 45% range. Nearly two-thirds of the capital goods have tariffs of 30% or less. Since future industrial growth will call for a substantial expansion of capital goods industries, the structure of tariffs will have to be changed in order to give them higher effective protection.

If quantitative restrictions had not operated, tariffs would be high enough to preclude competition from imports in clothing, leather goods, and in some appliances. On luxury consumer goods such as automobiles, these tariffs in fact act as a luxury tax levied on consumption.

Prior Deposits

An advance deposit in pesos equivalent to a specific percentage of the f.o.b. value of imports must be paid by the importer prior to submitting application for an import registration and, in most cases, an import license. Some types of government bonds may be used for the deposit. The certificate of deposit may not be used as collateral nor for any similar purpose by the depositor.

Prior deposits are now required on all imports except a selected few such as capital goods brought in by official entities and some "basic industries". Imports from countries in the Latin American Free Trade Association and under some of the export promotion programs can also be exempted.

Imports usually fall, according to their tariff classification, into one of five prior deposit lists: 1, 10, 30, 70 and 130%, depending on the essentiality of the product and the extent of local production. Authorization may be obtained in some cases for reduction to a uniform rate of 5% for individual capital goods valued at over Col$100,000. The prior deposit is never returned before the imports arrive, and is usually held for 6 months. An estimate of the average cost of prior deposits is shown in Table 7-5. Prior deposits have been used to tighten credit rather than for protection, but of course they also have a protectionist effect. Their impact on the manufacturing sector has been to further tighten the availability of working capital.

Table 7-3: PERCENTAGE SHARE OF LICENSES DENIED IN
TOTAL DEMAND FOR LICENSES
(In millions of US dollars)

	1967	1968	1969
Demand for licenses (foreign exchange "pressure")		(646.8 (	815.5
Licenses approved	n.a.	(521.3 (	638.5
Licenses denied		(125.5	177.0
Percentage share of licenses denied in total demand	32.0	19.4	21.7

Source: Unpublished INCOMEX data.

Export Promotion

The Colombian Government began a policy of export promotion in the early sixties when a highly regressive export tax was removed, tax incentives were granted to exporters and an import-export scheme was introduced. The export promotion policies now in operation were introduced in 1967 under Decree 444. The government has a fourfold policy for export promotion: a subsidy is granted on exports, two variants of a drawback-type system are available to the exporter, the government has established an export marketing board, and export financing guaranteed by the Bank of the Republic is available to the exporters.

Tax Benefits

When exporters surrender foreign exchange accruing from an export they are given tax credit certificates (Certificado de Abono Tributario–CAT) in an amount equivalent to 15% of the total value of the export. The certificates are granted for all exports other than coffee, petroleum and raw cattle hides. Certificados de Abono Tributario can be redeemed for cash a year after issue. CATs are negotiable and are traded freely at the Bogota Stock Exchange, although at a discount of their face value. Hence, in January 1970, CATs with cash redemptions dated February 1970 were being sold at 98.50% of their nominal value while those with a cash redemption date of January 1971 were sold at 81.96% of their face value. CATs, moreover, are not subject to tax and are accepted at parity for payment of sales and income taxes within a year of the date of issue. The present 15% rate of refund is subject to annual adjustments depending on the competitive position of Colombian exports in foreign markets.

Certificados de Abono Tributario, which were introduced under Decree 444, supersede the system enacted in the early 1960s under which exporting firms could deduct income from exports—which for this purpose was presumed to represent 40% of sales abroad—from the taxable income accruing from their total operations. The tax exemption incentive was, undoubtedly, largely responsible for the increase of industrial exports in the mid-1960s.

The system enacted in the early 1960s favored large producers since large-scale enterprises exported (sometimes at a loss) in order to minimize taxable profits on domestic sales. Producers with limited sales were not encouraged to export. CATs are more broadly applicable and have led to increased diversification of manufactured exports; the benefits can reach a greater number of exporters, including those operating on a small scale, and therefore contribute to increase capacity utilization in smaller plants. Moreover, the possibility of an annual review and adjustment of the refund percentage gives the system flexibility.

Drawbacks and Similar Arrangements

Drawbacks (refunds of duties paid) and temporary admission systems (conditional or total exemption from payment of duties) were already in force under Colombian law before the new foreign trade statute (Decree 444) was passed. Drawbacks authorizing the refund of 85% of the customs duties paid date back to 1931 (Act No. 79, Article 239). This drawback system was never implemented. Under Decree 444 a new system of drawbacks was introduced which has not yet been made operational; it consists of a partial return of customs duties depending on the value added of the products exported. Two types of import-export schemes are now in operation in Colombia: The Plan Vallejo and the Modified Plan Vallejo—both temporary admission systems.

The Plan Vallejo, first introduced in 1959, provides that a manufacturer can import all the inputs needed for the production of exportable goods, free of tariffs and prior deposits and exempted from licensing requirements. Under a contract between the exporter and the government, the exporter provides assurance that he has obtained foreign financing for his imports, enters into an export guarantee, agrees to use special accounting and to submit regular reports to the government on the fulfillment of his contract.

Table 7-4: TARIFF FREQUENCIES FOR MANUFACTURED GOODS
(As of May, 1969)

	Tariff Range (percent)						Total	Percent Distribution
	15% or under	16 to 30	31 to 45	46 to 60	61 to 100	Over 100		
Non-durable consumer goods	27	39	69	73	94	134	429	16.0
Food	5	7	32	34	17	37	132	4.9
Beverages	–	2	1	8	20	2	33	1.2
Tobacco products	–	–	–	–	–	–	–	–
Textiles	1	13	11	20	45	54	144	5.4
Clothing and footwear	–	–	–	–	7	38	45	1.7
Printing and publishing	5	1	–	4	4	3	17	0.6
Pharmaceuticals and related products	16	16	18	7	1	–	58	2.2
Durable consumer goods	1	8	18	31	8	15	81	2.9
Furniture and fixtures	–	–	3	–	1	9	13	0.5
Rubber products	1	3	3	24	5	–	36	1.3
Ceramic products	–	–	–	–	1	3	4	0.1
Non-electrical appliances	–	–	5	–	–	–	5	0.2
Electrical appliances	–	4	7	7	1	–	19	0.7
Motor vehicles	–	1	–	–	–	3	4	0.1
Intermediate goods	92	373	336	233	183	79	1,296	48.1
Textiles	3	16	83	29	14	11	156	5.8
Wood and products	3	4	8	20	7	7	49	1.8
Paper and products	–	24	2	20	16	11	73	2.7
Leather and products	–	6	5	2	19	9	41	1.5
Chemicals other than pharmaceuticals	32	111	56	55	33	8	295	11.0
Petroleum and coal products	23	19	4	1	–	–	47	1.7
Non-metallic mineral products	1	30	31	16	34	19	131	4.9
Basic metals	29	116	82	11	–	–	238	8.8
Metal products	1	47	65	79	60	14	266	9.9

Capital goods	171	242	107	58	55	12	645	23.9
Mechanical machinery	125	145	41	30	23	—	364	13.5
Electrical machinery (except appliances)	10	62	49	13	12	—	146	5.4
Transport equipment (except motor vehicles)	36	35	17	15	20	12	135	5.0
Other	5	53	57	32	44	48	239	8.9
Total	296	715	580	427	384	288	2,690	100.0

Source: Legislacion Economica, Limitada, *Nuevo Arancel de Aduanas de Colombia*

Plan Vallejo has numerous advantages for the manufacturer: the importer does not have to obtain an import license for his imports; the manufacturer can import any inputs that he may need—even if they are goods on the prohibited list; the scheme reduces the cost of imports by releasing funds which would be tied up in prior deposits or used to pay import duties.

The program, however, has difficulties. The system assists mostly those who already have established markets, since it is difficult for a manufacturer who is new in the export field to obtain an export contract; the exporter's contract which the manufacturer has to enter into with the government is very complicated; the complexity of the system makes it unavailable to small and medium industrialists who would have difficulty in handling all the requirements of the present contract. This is confirmed by the fact that of the 225 Plan Vallejo contracts that were valid in mid-March 1970, 51% were made by 12 large companies and another 34% by 83 companies. In the past, a Plan Vallejo contract was difficult to obtain quickly because of government delays in processing the applications. In June 1969, however, both the legal requirements and the administrative procedures were greatly simplified. Before mid-1969 a contract had to be approved both by INCOMEX and by the Ministry of Development; the approval of INCOMEX alone is now sufficient. While a simpler contract could be designed for smaller producers, it would seem that the difficulties of administering such a program would nullify any benefits derived. It may be more practical to further simplify the exporters' contracts for all manufacturers.

The second temporary scheme is what could be called the Modified Plan Vallejo–known to the Colombians as "Plan Vallejo Junior". The Modified Plan Vallejo offers the same benefits as the Plan Vallejo, but only to a manufacturer who exports for a second or subsequent time. In other words, the industrialist must have exported at least once before he can apply for the benefits of the Plan. As with the old Plan Vallejo, the disadvantage of this program is that it does not encourage new firms to enter the export market. Its advantage is that it eliminates many of the administrative requirements involved in the exporters' contracts under the original Plan Vallejo. The more limited administrative requirements will probably encourage small producers to use the Modified Plan Vallejo.

Table 7-5: IMPLICIT COST OF PRIOR DEPOSITS

(% of value of imports)

Year	Yearly average
1956	5.1
1957	6.4
1958	8.2
1959	7.9
1960	9.1
1961	9.4
1962	8.5
1963	19.6
1964	10.9
1965	18.6
1966	11.3
1967	7.2

Note: This represents the imputed opportunity cost resulting from funds being tied up between the time of deposit and repayment. The opportunity cost estimate is based on the rate of interest paid on a selected number of issues in the Bogota Stock Exchange during a period of six months, the length of time usually required for remittance of the prior deposit. This sum is then taken as a percentage of the c.i.f. value of imports.

Source: Alberto Musalem, *Demanda por Dinero y Balanza de Pagos; La Experiencia de Colombia,   1950-1967,* unpublished document, 1969.

Substantial amounts of manufactured goods have been exported under Plan Vallejo. Exports–most of which are manufactured–and imports under Plan Vallejo are summarized in Table 7-6. It is significant that while exports have increased rapidly in the past four years, imports have remained quite stable, indicating a declining import content of exports.

Export Promotion Fund

The Export Promotion Fund (Fondo de Promocion de Exportaciones–PROEXPO) was created in 1967 as a coordinating agency to promote exports. It studies the export potential of selected products, grants technical advice to exporters, interests manufacturers in the possibilities of exporting, is able to finance expenses of storing exportable items, discounts export credits, serves as intermediary to export credits granted by international organizations, and undertakes promotional activities abroad. At the present time the Export Promotion Fund has a staff of about 140 in Bogota and 10 missions abroad.

One of the major roles of the Export Promotion Fund has been to finance activities related

Table 7-6: TRADE UNDER PLAN VALLEJO – REGISTRATIONS
(In thousands of US dollars)

Year	Exports	Imports Total	Imports Machinery	Other Imports	Imports excluding machinery as a percent of exports
1965	26,147	9,829	875	8,954	34.2
1966	45,906	12,055	1,648	10,407	22.7
1967	40,786	17,012	1,514	15,498	38.0
1968	51,954[1]	17,742	4,163	13,579	26.1
1969	61,478[1]	13,653	1,281	12,282	20.0

[1]Includes some banana exports.

Source: Jose Teigeiro, *Promotion of Non-Traditional Exports in Colombia,* unpublished document, 1970.

to export. As of December 1968, about Col$231 million had been lent for these purposes. The terms of such loans are summarized in Table 7-7.

Export Credits

The most important system of export financing available in Colombia is the so-called "advance exchange surrender", (reintegros anticipados). This system operates as if it were an advance against the surrender of foreign exchange: the Banco de la Republica authorizes a commercial bank to lend the exporter a given amount of national currency with the export as the collateral. The loan is repaid with the pesos accruing from the export. Commercial banks can issue loans for a period of 180 days which may be extended up to one year, at a rate of interest of about 9% per annum, which is considerably below the average rate in Colombia. Up to 80% of the value of the export can be financed on these terms. If the exporter wishes to cover the total value of the export, the usual interest rate of 14% is payable on the remaining 20%. This scheme is available for all exports.

The advance exchange surrender system has been available for some time, although it has only recently become widely used. While exchange surrendered on account of non-traditional exports was equivalent to about 35% of these exports in 1966, it rose to 57% in 1967 and was 56% in 1968. It is believed that the reason why the export credit scheme was not more widely used in the past was the manufacturers' lack of awareness of its availability and usefulness. The

Table 7-7:   TERMS OF PROEXPO FINANCING OF PRODUCTION OF EXPORTS AND PROMOTIONAL ACTIVITIES

Purpose	Maximum Term	Maximum percentage of financing	Interest rate — %
1. New Markets			
Increased exports and diversification	5 years	100	3-5
Promotion and advertisement			
i. Travel	6 months	50	10-12
ii. Expositions, fairs, adv.	2 years	80	6-12
iii. Samples	1 year	100	6-8
2. Working Capital			
Financing for national or imported inputs	According to sales contracts	80	10-14
Storage			
i. Abroad	6 months extendible	75	7-12
ii. Local	3 months	75	7-12
Loans with CAT guarantee	1 year	100	8
3. Other			
Discounts			
i. Capital goods exports and similars	5 years	100	7
ii. All others	2 years	100	6-12
Advance on letters of credit	6 months	100	6-8
Financing of bilateral trade operations	1 year	80	12

Source: Jose Teigeiro, *Promotion of Non-Traditional Exports in Colombia,* unpublished document, 1970.

increased use of this financing scheme also reflects the current shortage of working capital for the manufacturing sector. The interest rate is lower than the average rate for short-term loans and considerably lower than the "street" rate. More importantly, the system provides the exporter with credit when he needs it. Given that the manufacturers are frequently unable to obtain short-term credit, the "advance exchange surrender" contributes to the availability of working capital.

The Andean Common Market

Colombia has been instrumental in the creation of the Andean Common Market, a regional grouping within the Latin American Free Trade Association including Chile, Colombia, Ecuador, Peru and Bolivia. The Treaty of Cartagena, creating the Andean Common Market, was signed in May 1969. Venezuela has not signed the Treaty yet but participated in the negotiations and has become a contributing member of the Pact's financial organ, the Andean Development Corporation.

The final version of the Treaty of Cartagena establishes a rapid integration pace, provided that the numerous escape clauses are used with moderation. Freedom for most intra-Andean trade is scheduled for no later than the end of 1980; all barriers to trade, excluding exchange controls and import licensing restrictions should also be eliminated by then. Trade in goods included under sectoral complementation agreements (which usually involve new industries like petrochemicals) will be freed according to the pace specified in such agreements. Trade in goods not produced in any of the Andean Five should be totally freed by February 1971.[6] Duties on the intra-Andean trade commodities other than those already negotiated under LAFTA will be reduced automatically every year. By the end of 1970 duties in the five countries will be brought down for each product, to the lowest duty found in Colombia, Chile or Peru. Annual ten percent cuts from that duty will start at the end of 1971, so that by the end of 1980 the duties for Andean trade would have been virtually eliminated. Contrary to the LAFTA procedures, therefore, trade liberalization in the Andean Group could be automatic, rapid and across-the-board.

The pace of trade liberalization within the Andean Group will, of course, depend on the use which is made of the escape clauses in the Treaty. Each country can present "lists of exceptions". This escape clause is least generous for Chile and Colombia. Moreover, Bolivia and Ecuador, which are potential markets for Colombian manufactures, will not have to start cutting tariffs by ten percent until the end of 1976, thus postponing complete duty elimination until the end of 1985, while for specified lists of goods they are given preferential free access to the other markets starting already in 1971.

Unlike the LAFTA countries, the resource base of the Andean Five is basically non-competitive, which could facilitate the operation of the Common Market. If trade liberalization in the Andean countries does take place, Colombia could derive considerable gains. Colombia needs the metals of the other Andean countries (copper, lead, iron ore, and tin) for the development of its industrial sector. Colombia, moreover, is an efficient producer of many consumer non-durables and intermediates, which have a market in the Andean Group, particularly in Peru, Ecuador, and Bolivia. The considerable border trade in products like textiles, cattle and leather products confirms this argument (see Table 7-8 for a breakdown of Colombian manufactured exports to the Andean and LAFTA countries). Also, Colombia is a substantial exporter of unprocessed foodstuffs, e.g. meats, with excellent prospects for further development.

Policy Alternatives

Any measures taken to improve the protection and export promotion systems will have a limited impact if they are not implemented in conjunction with monetary, fiscal, labor and other necessary policy changes. What is needed in Colombia is high-level coordination of all policies affecting the industrial sector.

An expanded foreign exchange availability, which would result from good coffee prices and sustained growth in non-traditional exports, would provide a good opportunity for a fundamental and lasting modification of the protective system. At the core of any such reform is the coordination of the quantitative restriction system with the tariff schedule. A major effort should be undertaken to gradually diminish the items on the prohibited list and to modify the tariff structure so as to make it the principal mechanism of protection.

Implicit in the liberalization of the quantitative restrictions system is a restructuring of the tariff schedule to make it the main instrument of import regulation in place of quantitative restrictions by legislative or administrative fiat. The mission suggests that a detailed study of the tariff structure of Colombia is necessary. On the basis of its limited investigation, the mission would argue for lower tariffs on some raw materials and consumer goods. However, for some products, they will have to be raised.

---

6. This has been virtually accomplished by Decision 26 of the Commission of the Andean Pact, as of 1st January 1971.

Table 7-8: COLOMBIAN EXPORTS OF MANUFACTURES TO THE ANDEAN GROUP AND LATIN AMERICAN FREE TRADE AREA
(In US dollars)

	Ecuador	Peru	Chile	Bolivia	Venezuela	Paraguay	Mexico	Brazil	Argentina	Uruguay	Total Andean Group	Total LAFTA
Non-durable Consumer Goods	1,830,455	281,901	18,680	32,338	195,147	36,557	76,246	156,441	16,743	815	2,358,521	2,645,323
Food	—	1,426	3,640	1,011	—	—	6,722	12,651	—	—	6,077	25,450
Beverages	—	—	—	—	—	—	—	—	1,709	—	—	1,709
Tobacco products	—	1,525	—	—	—	—	—	—	—	—	1,525	1,525
Textiles	32,812	11,791	2,021	—	12,989	—	—	23,542	—	—	59,613	83,155
Clothing and footwear	3,600	—	—	200	5,744	—	13,660	111,296	—	—	9,544	134,500
Printing and publishing	87,377	259,044	13,019	12,920	165,262	36,557	52,392	1,029	15,034	815	537,622	643,449
Pharmaceuticals and related products	1,706,666	8,115	—	18,207	11,152	—	3,472	7,923	—	—	1,744,140	1,755,535
Durable Consumer Goods	128,870	32,568	7,129	170,336	92,166	39,075	—	17,423	575,288	—	431,069	1,062,855
Furniture and fixtures	135	5,437	—	—	7,394	—	—	17,423	—	—	12,966	30,389
Rubber products	72,598	25,361	7,129	170,336	2,918	39,075	—	—	575,288	—	278,342	892,705
Ceramic products	36,774	—	—	—	2,936	—	—	—	—	—	39,710	39,710
Non-electrical appliances	2,064	—	—	—	—	—	—	—	—	—	2,064	2,064
Electrical appliances	17,299	1,770	—	—	78,918	—	—	—	—	—	97,987	97,987
Motor vehicles	—	—	—	—	—	—	—	—	—	—	—	—
Intermediate Goods	3,831,040	3,127,255	1,198,968	44,638	3,819,896	1,606	989,566	560,166	1,442,322	6,909	12,021,797	15,022,366
Textiles	1,314,271	1,020,215	815,612	20,127	1,894,174	1,606	—	350,344	719,717	368	5,064,399	6,136,434
Wood products	1,076	470	—	—	21,410	—	—	—	—	—	22,956	22,956
Paper and products	558,928	75,578	7,815	111	99,393	—	43,353	5,368	—	345	741,825	790,891
Leather and products	722	10	2,713	—	4,947	—	—	6,462	119,197	—	8,392	134,051
Chemical products	380,479	353,507	263,252	2,123	510,498	—	422,813	183,800	591,759	4,293	1,509,859	2,712,524
Petroleum and coal products	124,814	1,388,427	26,075	—	39,154	—	523,036	—	—	—	1,578,470	2,101,506
Non-metallic mineral products	974,744	53,441	—	8,267	598,370	—	—	—	—	—	1,634,822	1,634,822
Basic metals	115,150	4,680	—	402	5,435	—	—	302	—	—	125,667	125,969
Metal products	360,856	230,927	83,501	13,608	646,515	—	364	13,890	11,649	1,903	1,335,407	1,363,213

Capital Goods	420,491	40,960	448,600	24,473	686,865	—	4,764	69,631	117,523	—	1,621,389	1,743,676
Mechanical machinery	300,575	39,443	270,727	6,822	586,277	—	4,764	—	69,020	—	1,203,844	1,277,628
Electrical machinery (except appliances)	92,478	600	177,873	17,651	20,308	—	—	69,631	48,503	—	308,910	427,044
Transport equipment (except motor vehicles)	27,438	917	—	—	80,280	—	—	—	—	—	108,635	108,635
Other	38,680	28,318	62,639	40	167,462	—	48,227	—	15	—	297,139	345,381
Total	6,249,536	3,511,002	1,736,016	271,825	4,961,536	77,238	1,118,803	803,661	2,151,891	7,724	16,729,915	20,889,232

Source: DANE, *Boletín Mensual de Estadística*, Number 220.

Lowering the tariff on raw materials such as non-ferrous metals would raise the effective protection of capital goods. Lowering it on luxury goods will eliminate the luxury tax element. The mission is, in general, in agreement with the Musgrave Commission that from the standpoint of resource allocation it would be more satisfactory to have a luxury tax on all luxury consumer goods, domestic and imported, since the prohibitive tariffs on luxury items are encouraging inefficient domestic production of such goods. This may be a difficult measure to implement. Increasing the tariffs on selected capital goods would promote their domestic production, provided the tariffs on inputs are not also raised.

Reform of the licensing system is not an easy task but the following steps could be taken to orient the protective system in that direction. First, increase the limit of spare parts for machinery which can be imported without a license. Second, use the concessions on the import of raw materials which Colombia will probably grant to the Andean Group as the first step towards the elimination of licensing of raw materials imports. The liberalization of spare parts and raw materials would make the task of the licensing board a more manageable one. Third, ease the licensing requirements for domestic producers with good price performance. Agreements between the good performance producers and INCOMEX would contribute to liberalizing imports and grant an incentive to efficient producers. Fourth, allow some formerly prohibited imports of consumer goods so as to stimulate domestic producers to raise the quality of their production and possibly lower their prices. This could be done on a selective basis.

Equipment would have to be kept under license to avoid wasteful and misdirected investment by the manufacturing sector. If the licensing system is to continue to be used for resource allocation it would be helpful to increase the staff of INCOMEX, but it would be equally important to revise the implicit criteria now used in license evaluation which favor self-sufficiency irrespective of cost.

As a last step toward a better protective structure, the Colombian government might consider the gradual phasing out of prior deposits and seek more direct means of restricting credit.

The export promotion policies of Colombia have been very effective. The mission recommends the maintenance of the CAT incentive. The administrative and legal requirements of Plan Vallejo could be further simplified to give the smaller exporters easier access to it. The drawback system could also be helpful to small exporters.

Colombian manufacturers are in great need of marketing assistance and organization to increase their exports. The Export Promotion Fund, if expanded, could assist in this marketing effort, and could be particularly useful in organizing smaller producers.

Given the advances made in the export field, this might be an opportune time to mount a more specific drive in addition to the general export promotion campaign now in progress. Three or four lines of industrial products in which Colombia has obvious advantage could be promoted. PROEXPO could have a team of experts in these products. As examples, the possible export sale of cooked meat, wood products, and ready-made men's clothing could be explored in various markets and prospective producers could be encouraged to engage in a sustained export drive.

CHAPTER 8
INDUSTRY SURVEY

This chapter has two purposes: to appraise the competitiveness of Colombian manufacturing, and to suggest areas of potential improvement and means for achieving such improvement. After a brief discussion of the sector as a whole and a comparison of Brazil and Colombia, specific industries are discussed and analyzed, except for three industries on which more detailed studies are given in later chapters, namely iron and steel, paper and chemicals.

Overall Structure

A comparison of Brazilian and Colombian industrial performance gives perspective to the relative level of Colombian industrial development.[1] Per capita income levels in the two countries are similar and their economies rely heavily on the growth and export of coffee. Beyond that, however, differences outweigh similarities. The aggregate market size differs widely.

Table 8-1 shows that Brazil is considerably more industrialized than Colombia, and its manufacturing structure is more widely diversified. While Colombia is still specialized in the production of consumer goods with its capital goods industries undeveloped, Brazil has achieved considerable diversification into capital goods production. To illustrate, gross output in textiles in Colombia is double the value of capital goods output, a situation which is reversed in Brazil. This partly reflects Brazil's larger market and better resource endowment, but also a policy of stressing self-sufficiency more strongly. The widest relative gap is in capital goods.

Table 8-1: COMPARISON OF COLOMBIAN AND BRAZILIAN INDUSTRIAL STRUCTURE
(In US dollars)

	Gross output in Manufacturing per capita		Percent distribution of gross value of output	
	Colombia (in US$)	Brazil	Colombia	Brazil
Traditional consumer goods:	72.4	90.8	56.6	46.8
of which textiles:	15.3	17.4	12.0	9.0
Intermediate goods	45.1	69.8	35.1	35.9
Capital goods	7.8	30.8	6.2	15.9
Other	2.7	2.9	2.1	1.4
Total	128.0	194.3	100.0	100.0

Source: IBRD *Current Economic Position and Prospects of Brazil,* Vol. III. Report No. WH-195a, December 1969.

---

1. Brazilian statistics in the Bank Report on Brazilian industry (WH195a, 1969) cannot be adjusted to fit the analytical classification used elsewhere in this report. It was therefore necessary to arrange Colombian categories and data to fit the Brazilian classification.

Non-Durable Consumer Goods

In 1967, gross value of output of non-durable consumer goods was Col$22.7 billion (1968 prices) equivalent to over US$1.3 billion. Imports were small amounting to less than US$25 million in 1967, and exports even smaller, under US$3 million; because of this, production is about equal to the internal market, and production growth has been about equal to internal market growth, and this constraint will continue unless exports can be greatly increased.

Food Industries

The food industry accounts for about 15% of the employment in manufacturing and a slightly higher percentage of the value added, but over 27% of gross value of output, because in foods the raw material constitutes over 70% of output as against just under 60% for the manufacturing sector as a whole. A very sizable investment boom occurred in 1966 and 1967; in the latter year, the food industry accounted for over 20% of the fixed investment in manufacturing. Of this fixed investment, the sugar refining industry accounted for about 60% in 1966, and 70% in 1967 which contrasts with a 15% share in employment and about 20% in value added.

The growth rate in food processing which had lagged in the 1950s, accelerated in the 1960s. Gross output of processed food rose less than 2% per annum between 1953 and 1960, while employment declined about 1/4% per annum. In the period 1960-1967, gross output increased by over 5% per annum, while employment rose by less than 2% per annum. This implies a rise in productivity in the latter period by over 3% per annum in gross value of output per employee, but this may have been due to changes in product mix (increased production of refined sugar, for example).

There seems to have been no appreciable change in the ratios of wages to value added in the 1960s. Profits in the corporate sector of the industry rose as a percentage of invested capital in the period up to 1967, but declined somewhat in 1968, possibly because of price controls.

Textiles

Textiles in Colombia have been in the vanguard of industrial development. About 17% of manufacturing employment in 1967 was in textiles; but the industry accounted for a smaller percentage of gross production and value added—12% of gross production and about 13% of value added. Because textiles were already well developed, they accounted for only 9% of the fixed investment in manufacturing in 1967 as contrasted with a peak ratio of over 20% in 1957-58. Investment in textiles is highly cyclical: it fell sharply in the period 1959-62, rose briefly in 1963, slumped again in 1964-66 and showed another upturn in 1967. Inventories in this industry are also highly cyclical with upturns in anticipation of devaluation, notably in 1963 and 1966, each followed by a sharp decline in the following year.

Cotton is the most important of the textiles accounting for 42% of the employment, over 53% of the wages and social benefits, 41% of the gross output, and about 51% of the value added in 1967, but only 41% of the new fixed investment. The wool branch accounted for 11% of the employment, 10% of wages and social benefits, slightly under 9% of value added and 7% of the new fixed investment. The "seda" industry which undoubtedly represents the synthetic fabric plants, accounted for about 14% of employment and wages, 13% of value added, and 23% of new fixed investment. The remainder of the industry which accounts for 33% of the employment consists of knit goods (17%), cordage and hard fibers (4%) and miscellaneous textiles (12%). Synthetics clearly generated the most active investment and continue to do so in 1970 as evidenced by recent information from Colombian private finance corporations.

Textile wage rates in Colombia appear to be relatively high. For example, textile wages plus social benefits per paid employee were 105% of the average per paid employee in all Colombian manufacturing. The corresponding figure for Brazil is 72%. The average wage in Colombian textiles was 130% of the Brazilian textiles wage, while in all industries combined Colombia's wage level was only 88% of Brazil's. In most developed countries, also, textile wages are well below the average for manufacturing. The explanation of the Colombian situation is partly the concentration of this industry in Medellin, the first area to become industrialized, and partly strong labor organization. Like other large employers the textiles firms also tend to pay social benefits beyond the legally required minimum.

Wages in the industry rose as a percentage of both gross output and value added in the 10-year period 1957-67. Wages and salaries, including social benefits, increased from 16% of gross output to 21%; wages increased from 35% to 46% of value added. Data indicate that profits in conventional cotton textiles were somewhat depressed in the period 1963-65, but have since recovered; whether the increased profits are due to a rise in profit margins in cotton textiles or because a growing proportion of output of primarily cotton textile firms is represented by the more profitable synthetic fabrics is difficult to determine from the limited data available. Profits have not increased evenly throughout the sector; one of the larger textile firms outside Medellin has not improved its profits at the same rate as other firms.

Encouraged by the CAT export subsidy, the textile industry has been a leader in the export drive, particularly in such intermediate products as yarns and print cloth. The industry's physical efficiency, particularly in cotton textiles, appears up to international standards.

The tariff levels seem to be sufficiently high in cotton textiles (40%), synthetic textiles (50%) and wool textiles (100%) to afford considerable protection. Furthermore, the structure of tariffs provides adequate effective protection for each stage of output. For example, duties on raw materials are raw cotton (15-25%), uncarded or uncombed wool (15-17%) and synthetic fibers (35%). Clothing and footwear, both on the prohibited list, are also subject to tariffs of 200% or more. Reduced protection in these industries which have long since passed the infant stage would increase competition, reduce margins and distribute more widely the benefits derived from efficient production. It could also act as a stimulus to seek further cost economies in other branches of the textile industry (e.g., synthetic fabrics) and bring some pressure to bear on producers of synthetic yarns and fibers to reduce their prices.[2] Lower textile prices would also help producers of clothing seeking export markets.

Clothing and Footwear

The factory sector of the clothing industry has shown a declining trend relative to manufacturing as a whole. While in 1957 clothing accounted for about 12-1/2% of total manufacturing, employment had fallen to below 11% in 1966 and apparently to less than 10% in 1967. Its share in gross output and value added for all manufacturing has dropped from about 6% to 4% in this ten-year period. This labor intensive industry is also a low wage industry, with about 60% female employees.

The 1967 figures for the clothing industry are somewhat suspect since they indicate that the number of establishments had declined substantially (from 2,126 to 1,780) and that employment had fallen by over 10% in the year. Since this is an industry in which small establishments predominate and there is much handicraft (dressmaking, custom shoes, etc.) the apparent decline in factory employment may have been partly offset by a rise in handicrafts although this cannot be confirmed. The available data would seem to indicate that the share of wages in value added had dropped. For example, in the 1957-58 period, wages represented 43-44% of value added but declined to less than 40% in 1966 and 1967, pointing to higher profit margins.

In the manufacture of shoes there are apparently only a few large companies. These produce less than half of the men's shoes and probably no more than 10% of all the women's shoes produced in the country. The great bulk of shoes are produced in handicraft establishments not covered in the census.

It is the opinion of some observers in Colombia, and a view shared by the mission, that with appropriate organizational changes and a more intensive training effort, both the clothing

---

2. For example, polyester fiber is priced in Colombia at 180% of its c.i.f. price (ex duty).

Table 8-2: COMPARISON OF ACTUAL AND HYPOTHETICAL IMPORTS IN 1960
(In millions of US dollars)

	1953			1960			Import Saving	
	Market	Imports	% Imports	Market	Actual Imports	Hypothetical[1] Imports	Hypothetical - Actual Imports	Saving as % of Hypothetical
Textiles	89.7	26.9	30	115.5	4.2	34.6	30.4	88
Wood Products	10.4	1.3	12	18.2	1.5	2.2	0.7	31
Paper & Products	24.7	15.9	64	53.3	25.1	34.1	9.0	26
Leather	22.4	0.9	4	24.4	0.2	1.0	0.8	80
Chemicals	47.0	36.1	77	97.8	64.2	75.3	11.1	15
Petroleum & Coal Products	55.1	31.5	57	80.7	14.1	46.0	31.9	69
Non-metallic Mineral Prods.	42.2	4.9	12	66.0	7.4	7.9	0.5	6
Basic Metals	57.6	51.0	88	123.5	47.4	108.7	61.3	56
Metal Products	54.7	32.0	59	74.8	20.7	44.1	23.4	53
Total	403.8	200.5	50	654.1	184.6	353.9	169.3	48

[1] Percentage imports in 1953 applied to 1960 market.

Table 8-3: COMPARISON OF ACTUAL AND HYPOTHETICAL IMPORTS IN 1967
(In millions of US dollars)

	1960			1967			Import Saving	
	Market	Imports	% Imports	Market	Actual Imports	Hypothetical[1] Imports	Hypothetical - Actual Imports	Saving as % of Hypothetical
Textiles	115.5	4.2	4	141.1	6.2	5.6	-0.6	neg.
Wood products	18.2	1.5	8	18.1	0.2	1.4	1.2	85
Paper & products	53.5	25.1	47	85.8	22.2	40.3	18.1	45
Leather	24.4	0.2	1	24.4	0	0.2	0.2	100
Chemicals	97.8	64.2	66	196.6	71.8	129.8	58.0	45
Petroleum & Coal products	80.7	14.1	17	84.0	7.1	14.3	7.2	50
Non-metallic Mineral prods.	66.0	7.4	11	93.8	3.4	10.3	6.9	67
Basic metals	123.5	47.4	38	137.1	43.3	52.1	8.8	17
Metal products	74.8	20.7	28	102.7	10.8	28.8	18.0	62
Total	654.1	184.6	28	883.7	165.0	282.8	117.8	41

[1] Percentage imports in 1960 applied to 1967 market.

Table 8-4: EXPORTS OF MANUFACTURED PRODUCTS
(In thousands of US dollars)

	1953	1960	1962	1963	1964	1965	1966	1967	1968
Non-durable consumer goods	762	560	1,232	1,347	3,054	3,113	3,045	2,959	6,039
Food	6	12	–	–	128	–	–	–	550
Beverages	–	1	–	–	–	–	–	–	–
Tobacco products	4	22	–	–	–	–	–	–	–
Textiles	76	12	–	–	–	176	166	111	119
Clothing and footwear	431	26	–	–	264	486	416	378	1,256
Printing and publishing	19	22	268	335	596	794	662	653	1,741
Pharmaceuticals and related products	226	465	964	1,012	2,066	1,657	1,801	1,817	2,373
Durable consumer goods	9	123	31	3	1,327	2,785	4,716	2,721	2,963
Furniture and fixtures	6	69	31	3	–	110	–	131	171
Rubber products	–	15	–	–	–	2,440	4,286	1,915	1,344
Ceramic products	3	6	–	–	–	114	199	481	1,241
Non-electrical appliances	–	–	–	–	517	121	177	–	100
Electrical appliances	–	–	–	–	806	–	–	–	107
Motor vehicles	–	33	–	–	–	–	114	194	–
Intermediate goods	3,580	11,288	25,468	18,390	29,706	34,740	41,744	45,878	57,085
Textiles	720	291	9,006	4,627	8,296	10,383	8,120	7,070	9,185
Wood and products	54	46	1,514	2,494	3,770	2,682	2,424	3,263	4,000
Paper and products	1	10	–	–	–	940	6,624	8,568	10,046
Leather and products	1,807	646	1,640	1,820	3,361	3,506	3,322	2,420	3,510
Chemicals other than pharmaceuticals	28	296	1,781	1,425	2,368	4,492	4,785	2,864	6,248
Petroleum and coal products	343	7,755	7,453	4,600	7,871	7,895	9,690	13,453	14,382
Non-metallic mineral products	646	2,016	4,031	3,373	3,574	2,961	4,375	5,724	7,781
Basic metals	12	10	43	51	159	573	895	735	392
Metal products	22	218	–	–	307	1,308	1,509	1,781	1,541

Capital Goods	137	1,956	1,792	349	780	1,979	3,490	3,373	4,059
Mechanical machinery	133	1,855	1,792	143	678	1,809	2,604	2,821	3,064
Electrical machinery (except appliances)	4	63	—	—	—	170	875	552	736
Transport equipment (except motor vehicles)	—	38	—	206	102	—	11	—	259
Other	52	86	298	489	961	1,161	1,110	637	735
Total manufactured exports	4,531	14,013	28,821	20,578	35,828	43,778	54,105	55,568	70,881
Total exports	596,132	464,578	463,403	446,657	548,136	539,144	507,591	509,923	558,278

Note: 1953 figures were converted to US dollars at the rate of Col$ 2.50 per $1.0 for exports.

Source: 1953 and 1960: DANE, *Anuario de Comercio Exterior*, 1953 and 1960; 1962-1967: United Nations, Statistical Office, *Commodity Trade Statistics-Series D*; 1968: unpublished United Nations data.

and footwear industries could make a substantial contribution to Colombia's export earnings. However, the factors militating against changes are: the high profitability of the plants now catering to the assured domestic market as against uncertainties of export earnings; a reluctance to make changes in product design and techniques necessary to gain consumer acceptance in foreign markets, and a probable reluctance in many larger establishments to delegate responsibility to subordinates outside the immediate family; and, uncertainty of cooperation from suppliers such as producers of textiles or leather, in the form of lower prices or better qualities to meet foreign market requirements.

Intermediate Goods

In 1967 the gross value of output of industries producing intermediate goods was about Col$13 billion (1968 prices) equivalent to US$770 million.[3] As indicated in Chapter 6, it was the growth of output in these industries which sparked the growth of Colombian manufacturing in the period 1953-60 and also, to a lesser degree, in the 1960-67 period. The annual average rate of output growth was 9.8% in the entire fourteen-year period, at rates of approximately 13% in the first half and 7% in the second.

Because of massive import substitution in textiles, refined petroleum products and basic metals and metal products, imports of intermediate goods fell slightly between 1953 and 1960 despite a 60% growth in the domestic demand. The new Cartagena refinery helped achieve the savings in petroleum products and the Paz del Rio steel plant produced substitutes for imported steel. Intermediate imports fell further between 1960 and 1967, primarily refined petroleum, basic metals and metal products and also paper and paper products. In both periods, the absolute value of imports of chemicals (other than pharmaceuticals) rose, but by far less than they would have done had imports supplied the same share of the market as in earlier years. Table 8-2 compares actual imports of intermediates in 1960 with the amounts which would have been imported had imports constituted the same share of the internal market as in 1953. A similar comparison for 1967 as against 1960 is then made in Table 8-3.

Intermediate exports have played an important part in the development of manufactured exports (see Table 8-4). In 1953, they were US$3.6 million, 79% of the $4.5 million exports of all manufactures in that year. They rose to US$11.3 million by 1960 and to US$45.9 million by 1967, in both years accounting for over 80% of manufactured goods exports. The trend continued in 1968, when exports of intermediates rose to US$57.1 million. Table 8-5 shows that exports have also constituted a rising share of domestic output of intermediate products. In wood products and petroleum products, exports have risen from a 1% share of output in 1953, to 15% by 1967. In paper products, where exports were negligible, they have risen to represent 12% of output. Textile intermediates have risen from a 1% share to a 5% share of estimated output. In non-metallic mineral manufactures the rise from 2% to 6% was mainly due to rising exports of cement and glass. Chemicals and metals have participated to a limited degree. Even the leather industry, which has had little growth, has more than maintained its exports relative to domestic output.

The main factors in this growth of exports have been the stimulus afforded by the CAT subsidy (see Chapter 7) to industries such as cotton yarn and print cloth mills which had long had some surplus capacity. In paper, petroleum refining and cement industries, where capacity was being expanded, the staging of expansions was such as to create temporary capacity surpluses available for export. Rarely were such expansions primarily export-oriented, rather, they were mainly intended to meet expected expansion of the internal market. However, the managements seized the opportunity to use such temporary surpluses of output over internal demand to export either main products (cement) or co-products (for example, residual fuel oil). Some few industries like glass and paper developed export markets in an imaginative fashion. Colombia's salt resources on the north coast should enable it to enlarge its exports of heavy chemicals (soda ash and caustic soda) and basic salt as well.

3. For statistical purposes, the output in textiles was divided equally between consumer non-durables and intermediates. The exports of textiles are almost entirely intermediate goods, cotton yarns and print cloth. The textile industry was discussed above in the section on non-durable consumer goods.

Table 8-5:   EXPORT ORIENTATION OF OUTPUT OF INTERMEDIATE PRODUCTS

	Exports (Million US$)			Exports as percent of Domestic production		
	1953	1960	1967	1953	1960	1967
Textiles	0.7	0.3	7.1	1	b	5
Wood & products	0.1	a	3.3	1	b	15
Paper & products	a	a	8.6	b	b	12
Leather & products	1.8	0.6	2.4	8	3	9
Chemicals other than pharmaceuticals	a	0.3	2.9	b	1	2
Petroleum & coal products	0.3	7.8	13.5	1	10	15
Non-metallic mineral products	0.6	2.0	5.7	2	3	6
Basic metals	a	a	0.7	b	b	1
Metal products	1	0.2	1.8	b	b	2
Total	3.6	11.3	45.9	0.2	2.3	6.0

Note:
a less than US$50,000
b less than half of 1%

Source: Table 8-4, and DANE *Boletin Mensual de Estadistica* and unpublished DANE data.

Wood Products

This industrial sub-sector comprises establishments producing semi-finished products (sawn wood, planed wood, and wood-based panels) and finished products (doors, window-frames, packing crates and others). The most important products are sawn wood including planed wood and plywood. Available data indicate an increase of over 9% per annum in gross output of this industry between 1953 and 1960. The rate of growth then dropped to about 3% per annum in 1960-67. This industry accounts for about 2% of factory employment, but only about 1% of gross output and value added. Part of the difficulty with the data lies in that it does not cover small operations.

Average wages are about 40% lower in wood processing than the average wage in manufacturing, and the average size of enterprises (about fourteen paid employees per enterprise) is about 45% smaller. Small-scale operation, inadequate maintenance of equipment, and relatively limited investment impeded especially in sawmills the growth of higher quality output and the reduction of waste, which remains comparatively high.

Although Colombia has about 25 million hectares of natural forests which are considered accessible for economic exploitation, logs for processing in saw mills and plymills are frequently in short supply. The main reasons are poor road transport facilities and low water levels which hamper log floating in rivers or channels. These difficulties can probably be reduced by closer cooperation between the logging and the processing interests and between various wood processing enterprises with different raw material requirements.

Leather

This small industry which accounted for about 1.5% of total manufacturing employment in 1967, has shown the lowest rate of output growth of any of the industries—about 1% per annum or less than the rate of population growth. It is not surprising, therefore, that employment in this industry has declined both absolutely and relatively to manufacturing as a whole. This may partly have been due to the variable supply of hides during this period.

Wages per employee reflected the slow growth of the industry since they have apparently risen less than for manufacturing as a whole and constituted a smaller percentage of both value added and gross value of production in 1967 than in 1957.

Along with textiles, leather products have export potential. As with clothing, there are problems of styling and organization for mass export. Unlike cotton textiles, however, finished leather goods may be hampered in meeting foreign quality standards by variations in the quality of the raw material. Inquiries in the shoe trade indicate that the quality of domestic leather varies; imports of tanning materials are restricted and the quality of local tanning materials is frequently poor. It is recommended that the import restrictions on tanning materials, dutiable at 35%, be removed, since this represents a necessary prerequisite to similar treatment for leather which is dutiable at 40%. The increase in potential, if not actual, competition from imports, which would still be subject to adequate import tariffs, should stimulate quality improvements in both tanning materials and leather. If such improvement materializes, the processors of leather, including shoe producers, would be able to produce a better quality product for domestic and export markets.

Petroleum

The Colombian petroleum industry was originally developed by private firms, including such well known international oil firms as Standard of New Jersey, Shell, Texaco, Chevron, Gulf and Mobil, all of which also operate in neighboring Venezuela. Other smaller oil companies also operate concessions such as Cities Service, Sinclair and several lesser-known companies. The term of the original De Mares concession expired in the early 1950s and that property reverted to the State. An arrangement for a 10-year operating contract was entered into between the former operator (a Jersey Standard affiliate) and the State. In 1961, Ecopetrol, a state-owned enterprise, took over formal operations of the De Mares concession and the petroleum refinery at Barrancabermeja. All other oil fields and refineries are privately operated.

Table 8-6 summarizes the main facets of petroleum operations in Colombia showing data separately for Ecopetrol and the private companies. It indicates that Ecopetrol's share of crude oil output has been declining since 1962, when it represented about 20% of the national total. The absolute volume of crude oil produced by Ecopetrol reached a peak of 13.4 million barrels in 1964 and has since fallen below 10 million barrels in 1969. On the other hand, private industry has increased its annual output by 26 million barrels to a total of 67.3 million in 1969. In addition to the very new Orito field, a Texaco Gulf Oil operation in southern Colombia which produced 17.8 million barrels in 1969, the data indicate that private oil output in the older areas of production rose over 7 million barrels between 1962 and 1969. However, oil production by private companies outside Orito has fallen by 10 million barrels since 1965.

Natural gas operations in Colombia have not been of major significance. In most fields there is a low gas-oil ratio. On the demand side, the climate in the major population areas precludes a major demand for heating, and power generation except in the North and West is primarily hydroelectric. The main demands for gas are for energy in the North Coast and for chemical processing; these are provided by short lines from oil fields or refineries to processing plants or power stations.

Ecopetrol has expanded its refining capacity and has steadily raised its output to about double the 1962 level, on the basis of increased crude oil purchases from other producers. Of the 13 million barrel increase in crude treated by Ecopetrol, almost 10 million has been exported. This rise in exports, almost entirely in the form of fuel oil, constituted 87% by volume of Ecopetrol's exports in 1969.

Private refiners, whose output rose more slowly, exported about 25% of their refinery product in 1962 and less than 10 percent in 1969, of which over two-thirds was fuel oil. Domestic sales have increased rather slowly, about one-third in a seven-year period. The rate of growth has quickened in the last few years, which presumably reflects improved highways, a larger automotive fleet, and perhaps improved gas station service. Marketing is all in private hands, except for small sales by Ecopetrol at the Barrancabermeja refinery to other than the leading marketers.

The two major refineries owned by Ecopetrol and Intercol (a Jersey Standard affiliate) account for 90% of the refined products output. The other five small refineries are operated mainly for field purposes. Ecopetrol plans a new refinery in western Colombia of 40,000

Table 8-6: PETROLEUM PRODUCTION AND EXPORTS BY TYPE OF OWNERSHIP
(In millions of barrels)

	1962	1965	1967	1968	1969
Crude Oil Production					
Ecopetrol	10.5	13.0	10.7	10.4	9.5
Private	41.4	59.5	58.2	53.0	67.3[1]
Total	51.9	72.5	68.9	63.4	76.8
Crude Oil Exports					
Ecopetrol	–	2.0	2.0	0.2	–
Private	24.3	38.7	27.9	18.2	29.2[2]
Total	24.3	40.7	29.9	18.4	29.9
Crude Oil Refined Internally					
Ecopetrol	13.2	16.0	20.2	24.8	26.1
Private	14.3	16.9	18.8	20.4	20.5
Total	27.5	32.9	39.0	45.2	46.6
Product Exports					
Ecopetrol	0.4	3.8	5.8	8.5	10.1
Private	3.5	1.6	2.7	2.2	1.7
Total	3.9	5.4	8.5	10.7	11.8
Domestic Sales	24.1	25.9	27.7	30.7	32.0

[1] of which 17.8 million from the Orito field in Southern Colombia. 1969 was the first year of production.

[2] of which 16.6 million from the Orito field.

Source: Direct communication with the Centro de Informacion de la Industria Petrolera.

barrels/day capacity, which would add about 30 percent to existing capacity. This refinery should add an even larger proportion of light products (e.g. gasoline) because it would have a crude (Orito) better suited for such products and it would probably be designed to maximize light products yield. This additional refinery capacity should suffice to meet Colombia's internal growth for at least five years.

Colombia's oil reserves should suffice to gradually increase crude oil output above the 1969 level (76.8 barrels) in the near future. The likely trend is that Orito output will reach 25 million to 35 million barrels per year, but that annual output in the northern fields may fall below the 59 million figure of 1969 as older fields become depleted and more costly to operate. Total Colombian reserves are estimated in trade journals at 1 billion barrels or more. Any substantial increase in reserves would probably result from drilling in new areas, such as the Llanos; some firms believe the discovery prospects are good there and emphasize the need to stimulate such activity.

Refinery location is largely determined by transport considerations from the oil fields and to the markets. In Colombia, a third new refinery designed to minimize marketing transport costs has long appeared desirable. Its location in western Colombia seems appropriate, but the precise location has not yet been made public.

With the substantial additions at the older Ecopetrol plant in recent years, refining facilities are comparatively modern. In view of the complexity of refining operations, and the numerous alternatives available for conversion of crude oil fractions, only a general opinion of efficient operation can be offered.

Non-metallic Mineral Manufactures

This industry has grown at about the same rate as manufacturing as a whole—an average of slightly under 7% per annum for each of the two periods 1953-60 and 1960-67. This branch of industry accounts for about 8-9% of manufacturing employment and about 6% of value added. The decline below 6% in 1967 probably reflects a price squeeze on profits, probably attributable to price controls.

The largest single part of this industry branch is the cement industry, which accounts for about one-third of the value added but a much smaller percentage of the employment. This is because cement production is more highly mechanized than the other building-supply industries such as the production of bricks and roofing materials. The non-metallic minerals industry has experienced cycles in investment as in other countries, so that while fixed investment was relatively high for the period 1957-59, it remained rather low during 1960-62, then rose sharply in the period 1963 through 1966 and has since apparently remained relatively low.

Cement production has exceeded 2 million tons per year since 1964 and exceeded 2.5 million tons in 1969. Production is divided among ten companies operating 13 plants. Cement industry profits have been above average, although uneven. The plants in Cali and north coast areas, for example, appear to have been more profitable than others. In some years the northern plant has exported a substantial part of its output and is considering a plant expansion to augment its export capacity. Expanded production capacities will be needed in the central area in the near future if projections of increased demand are to be realized.

Cement and cement products are already being exported at competitive prices from the Caribbean coast. In the interior of Colombia, notably in the Cali, Medellin and Bogota areas, natural barriers afford considerable inherent protection for cement plants that serve those areas.

Glass products produced by a company with a substantial foreign participation are already being exported competitively. An asbestos project is under consideration that is expected to export fiber at world prices.

Exports in non-metallic mineral manufactures exceeded imports, which consisted mostly of specialty refractories for metal production, abrasives, and special types of flat glass and glassware.

Metal Products

The metal products industry accounts for about 7% of the employment, 6% of the wages, 4% of the gross output and about 4-1/2% of the value added of the total manufacturing sector. The metal products industry had 700 establishments in 1967, with over 100 paid employees each, which accounted for 40% of the employment, but over 55% of the value added. The main products of this industry are non-ferrous metal products, foundry products, tools and cutlery.

It would appear that the gross value of output in metal products rose about 13% per annum in the period 1953-1960 but the growth rate then declined to an average of about 8% in the seven years ending 1967. The statistics, however, are somewhat suspect. Iron and steel plants do not appear to have been allocated consistently between base metals and metal products, and this may have caused minor distortions.

These industries experienced wide variation in inventories. This was particularly notable in the year 1966 when the industry which then accounted for less than 5% of value added accounted for almost 8% of the increase in inventories in the manufacturing sector.

Colombia's known resources in non-ferrous metals other than nickel are very small. In view of the fact that Colombia's Andean partners–Chile, Peru and Bolivia–are leading producers of copper, lead, zinc and tin, it is reasonable to assume that in these products those countries will seek trade concessions from Colombia. Such concessions would be beneficial for the Colombian production of capital goods.

In view of the wide variety of imported finished metal products, it was not possible to make a detailed study of products in this category. There is little reason to believe, however, that a reduction of tariff barriers within the Andean Group would appreciably harm any significant portion of the industry given that most of the supplies are imported from more developed areas.

Durable Consumer Goods

The durable consumer goods industries are still unimportant in Colombia; in 1967 the total value of output was just under Col$2.5 billion (1968 prices) or less than US$150 million. In 1967, these industries accounted for about 6% of the gross output and over 9% of the employment. The composition of output, value added and employment in the durable consumer goods branches is shown in Table 8-7.

Establishments of this sub-group are small. Of the over 1,100 establishments in these branches, only 42 employ 100 or more persons while total employment is about 13,600. Thus, only half of those employed in the durable consumer goods industries are in large establishments. This is a smaller proportion than in non-durable consumer goods, intermediates or capital goods. Conversely, the share of employment in industry in plants employing fifteen or less is greatest in consumer durables. This relationship is more precisely indicated in Table 8-8.

When the anatomy of employment within durable consumer goods industries is dissected (see Table 8-9), it becomes clear that the concentration of small plants is in two branches: furniture and motor vehicles. Small establishments in furniture are common throughout the world but they are uncommon in motor vehicles. The causes for this unusual feature in Colombia are worth analyzing, and are elaborated in the section on road vehicles.

Rubber Products

In 1967, the rubber industry accounted for about 2-1/2% of factory employment, 3-1/2% of wages and social benefits, and 2-1/2% of value added of the manufacturing sector as a whole. This industry has shown a rapid increase in output and employment throughout the period, but the rate of growth appears to have been greater from 1953 to 1960 than from 1960 to 1967 (11% per annum versus 9% per annum). While employment more than doubled between 1953 and

Table 8-7: OUTPUT, VALUE ADDED AND EMPLOYMENT IN THE DURABLE CONSUMER GOODS INDUSTRIES, 1967

	Gross output	Value added	Paid employment	Gross output	Value added
	(In millions of Col$, 1968 prices)			(In thousands of Col$ per paid employee)	
Furniture & fixtures	194.1	98.1	4,759	411	21
Rubber products	972.0	439.4	6,736	145	65
Ceramic products	146.9	60.0	3,669	40	16
Non-electrical appliances	61.2	28.7	962	64	30
Electrical appliances	431.3	166.8	3,210	134	52
Road vehicles	649.8	296.6	8,090	80	37
	2,455.3	1,089.6	27,426	90	40

Sources: 1953, 1958, 1961, 1963-1966: *Boletin Mensual de Estadistica,* Numbers 67, 117, 148, 170, 180, 201 and 207; 1960, 1962 and 1967: Unpublished DANE data.

Table 8-8:   EMPLOYMENT BY SIZE OF FIRMS IN MAJOR INDUSTRIAL SUB-GROUPS, 1967

Firms employing	Non-durable consumer goods		Intermediate goods		Consumer durable goods		Capital goods	
	Employment	% of Industry	Employment	% of Industry	Employment	% of Industry	Employment	% of Indus
100 & over	93,959	60	39,463	55	13,643	50	11,049	6!
50 – 99	18,277	12	9,944	14	3,461	13	2,124	1:
15 – 49	24,661	16	13,396	19	6,104	22	2,458	1₄
Under 15	20,551	13	8,887	12	4,218	15	1,462	₵
Total	157,448		71,690		27,426		17,093	

Source: Unpublished DANE data.

1960, it rose less than 20% between 1960 and 1967, reflecting major increases in output per man. Tire industry expansion between 1958 and 1962 accounts for virtually all the rise in employment in the rubber industry in those years.

At least through 1967, this industry seems to have been profitable despite an increasing share of wages in value added and gross output. The share of wages in gross output rose from 16-17% in 1957/58 to well over 20% by 1964 and subsequent years, whereas its share in value added rose from 40% or less in 1957 to 1959 to about 45% in 1966 and even higher in 1967. The industry is characterized by wide inventory fluctuations; there was a marked rise in 1963, followed by declines in 1964-65 despite rising production and input usage, and then another sharp rise in 1966-67.

The rubber tire segment of this industry consists of three large plants that had a total employment of 3,200 in 1967. These three plants constitute over 80% of the total employment in the rubber tire industry and almost half of the total employment in the entire rubber products industry. All three are either partly or wholly owned by the international rubber giants.

Rubber tires are subject to a 50% duty, with even higher effective protection, since crude rubber is subject to only a 10% duty. Internal prices have been kept low by price controls and seem to be competitive. Exports in 1967 were almost as high as imports. This industry may benefit from any Andean Group concessions for its products.

Appliances

The electrical appliances industry in Colombia grew quite rapidly from 1953 to 1960, but growth has been slower in recent years, as shown in Table 8-10.

These figures indicate a growth rate in gross output of 19% per year between 1953 and 1960 and about 13% between 1960 and 1967. The growth in value added in the latter period appears to have slowed, possibly reflecting higher costs of components (steel sheets, copper wire) which were not as fully reflected in selling prices as in the past. Also new investment in 1964-1965 was very heavy creating large new capacities, more in those two years than in the four previous years combined.

Most electrical appliances are subject to a 50% duty and require prior licensing. Effective protection is probably not much greater than nominal protection since imported metal inputs are dutiable at 30-45% and production requires great quantities of imported inputs. Items such

Table 8-9: EMPLOYMENT BY SIZE OF FIRMS IN DURABLE CONSUMER GOODS INDUSTRIES, 1967

	Employment Firms Employing					Percentage Distribution Firms Employing				
	100 or over	50 to 99	15 to 49	Under 15	Total	100 or over	50 to 99	15 to 49	Under 15	Total
Furniture and fixtures	1,135	525	1,705	1,394	4,759	24	11	36	29	100
Rubber products	5,424	322	817	173	6,736	80	5	12	3	100
Ceramic products	2,990	252	353	74	3,669	81	7	10	2	100
Non-electrical appliances	405	234	275	48	962	42	24	29	5	100
Electrical appliances	1,723	588	552	347	3,210	54	18	17	11	100
Road Vehicles	1,966	1,540	2,402	2,182	8,090	24	19	30	27	100

Source: Unpublished DANE data.

Table 8-10: GROWTH OF THE ELECTRICAL APPLIANCE INDUSTRY

	Gross output	Value added	Employment	Gross output	Value added
	(In millions of 1968 Col$)			(In thousands of 1968 Col$ per paid employee)	
1953	57.5	27.8	839	69	33
1960	191.8	87.6	2,298	83	38
1963	369.2	137.9	2,937	126	47
1964	373.8	122.0	3,265	114	37
1965	412.4	162.1	3,433	120	47
1966	436.3	171.1	3,615	121	47
1967	431.3	157.8	3,210	134	49

Sources: 1953, 1958, 1961, 1963-1966: *Boletin Mensual de Estadistica* Numbers 67, 117, 148, 170, 180, 201 and 207; 1960, 1962 and 1967: Unpublished DANE data.

as refrigerators, television sets, and electric stoves are highly prized and subject to smuggling. Demand, moreover, is highly responsive to changes in prices and incomes.

Mission studies indicate that the industry has ample installed capacity to produce at least 50% and possibly 100% more output than in 1969. Plant visits established that at least one plant is operating at less than one full shift and others only a partial second shift. Improved utilization of existing capacity would effect substantial cost economies in unit labor costs, overhead, and administration costs, and if reflected in ultimate selling prices would substantially raise effective demand.

Present retail prices for refrigerators are estimated at about three times the U.S. level for a strictly comparable model. This is largely due to the low scale of operations, part of which is the result of insufficient utilization of already existing capacity. Some undetermined part of the difference is undoubtedly due to high retail markups—a problem which also calls for some remedial action, but one which was not studied in detail by the mission.

Motor Vehicles

This category includes: production of motor cars and trucks and components; production of bicycles, and repairs to both bicycles and motor vehicles. In 1967, the industry was divided as shown in Table 8-11.

The net output per paid employee in motor vehicle production was almost three times that of an employee in a repair shop and one and one-half times that of an employee in bicycle production. This is to be expected because the material-input/labor ratio in production is greater than in repairs. Between 1958 and 1967, the census statistics indicate that employment in auto repair shops actually fell while employment in production rose about five-fold. However, in 1967, despite such sharp rises in production, employment in repair shops was still greatly in excess of employment in vehicle production. The employment effects expected from future growth of the automobile industry cannot be extrapolated from past aggregate data.

Within the motor vehicle production branch of the industry, value added per employee varies with the size of establishment as indicated in Table 8-12.

Wages and social benefits per employee in bicycle production averaged about Col$14,000 per man/year and about Col$13,000 in repair shops (Col$19,000 in the largest repair shop) as against Col$18,000 in all plants producing motor vehicles and parts. As might be expected, the two largest plants, (assemblers) paid the highest wages.

A program is being implemented to substantially increase the production of motor vehicles, both cars and trucks. The two leading producers, Chrysler and Lara are planning to double the 1969 output by 1971. A third plant is being constructed in which Renault cars and trucks are to be manufactured.

There were no data available which would permit close analysis of the profitability of the industry. Data by the Colombian statistical office are of limited value for this purpose and show

Table 8-11: MOTOR VEHICLE INDUSTRY BREAKDOWN, 1967

	Establishments	Paid employees	Gross output	Value added	Gross output	Value added
			(In millions of current Col$)		(In thousands of current Col$ per employee)	
Motor vehicle production	78	2,816	410.1	171.0	146	61
Bicycle production	12	409	26.9	15.6	67	38
Repair shops	475	4,865	201.1	104.7	41	22
	565	8,090	638.1	291.4	279	36

Source: Unpublished DANE data.

Table 8-12:   MOTOR VEHICLE INDUSTRY PRODUCTIVITY BY SIZE OF ESTABLISHMENT, 1967

Size of establishment (Employees)	Employment	Gross output	Value added	Total wages and social benefits	Per paid employee Value added	Wages and social benefits
		(In millions of Col$)		(In millions of Col$)	(In thousands of Col$)	
200 or more	622	252.7	96.6	19.9	144	29
100-199	588	36.3	18.2	8.7	31	15
50-99	493	54.8	21.4	8.9	43	18
Under 50	1,073	56.3	34.9	14.0	33	13
	2,816	410.1	171.1	51.5	61	18

Source: Unpublished DANE data.

very great variations from year to year. A comparison of 1965, 1966 and 1967 is given in Table 8-13.

The automotive fleet in Colombia at the end of 1967 is estimated at 256,000 (140,000 passenger cars and 116,000 trucks and buses); in 1968 trucks and buses increased to 125,000. On the basis of population per vehicle, Colombia ranks low in Latin America, well below all South American countries except Bolivia, Paraguay and Ecuador and below Central American countries except Guatemala and Honduras. The fleet is comparatively old; a sample of 17,000 vehicles in public carrier service early in 1969 had a median age of 12 to 13 years.

There is no doubt a significant demand for replacement of older vehicles in addition to the growth requirements of the economy, although precise estimates are difficult to make given the erratic behavior of past trends.

The Development Ministry has made an admittedly crude estimate of 1970 requirements, based on: a useful vehicle life of 15 years; the need to replace vehicles older than 15 years over

Table 8-13:   MOTOR VEHICLE INDUSTRY – NON-LABOR VALUE ADDED

	Gross output	Purchased materials	Value added	Wages and social benefits	Gross return available for capital & overhead Total	Percent of sales
	(In millions of current Col$)					%
1965	232.0	158.0	74.0	36.9	37.1	18.0
1966	220.0	156.6	63.4	41.9	21.5	9.8
1967	410.1	239.0	171.1	51.5	119.6	28.1

Source: Unpublished DANE data.

a 5-year period in equal steps; growth of demand annually of 6% per year; and replacement of vehicles which reach a 15-year life.

On this basis, the annual demand is for about 40,000 vehicles compared with about 9,000 assembled in 1969. The foreign exchange quotas for 1970 are calculated to enable an output of 20,000 vehicles. Figures for earlier years are lower than for 1969, probably of the order of 4,000 per year or less. Consequently, the operational data for these earlier years are unrepresentative of the results expected currently and in the projected future.

In Colombia, the truck and bus park is 80% of the size of the passenger car park, a higher figure than for Argentina (57%), Brazil (63%), and Mexico (51%). The fact that the truck park in Colombia is very old and that truck production and assembly is economic everywhere at much lower levels of output than for passenger cars, suggests the desirability of concentrating initial efforts on truck and bus production and assembly.[4]

Tariffs for truck imports range from 70% to 200%, depending on truck size; buses are subject to a 60% duty, while the average duty for passenger cars is 340%. Passenger cars are also subject to a much higher prior import deposit than trucks and buses—130%. The duties on parts, components or materials are far lower than for the finished products.[5] For trucks, the duties on parts and components are 20-40%. For passenger cars, duties for chassis and body are 180% but duties for parts and materials are 50% or less as against an average tariff of 340% on passenger cars. Since imports of cars and trucks are severely restricted, and domestic assembly and construction is being encouraged by various means, including high duties, serious consideration should be given to a refinement of these incentives to assure that they serve the intended purpose rather than creating windfalls to limited groups. For example, luxury taxes or registration fees might be imposed on purchasers, whether they buy a local or imported passenger car, rather than imposing a very high tariff which may benefit a limited number of domestic producers and perhaps some of their suppliers.

Capital Goods

For capital goods industries, output increased in the 1953-60 period by over 15% per annum, but in the following 7-year period ending in 1967, the rate of growth slackened to slightly over 10%.

It should be borne in mind, however, that this group of industries is still very small in Colombia with a total gross output of about Col$1.3 billion (1968 prices) accounting for only about 3% of manufacturing output and 4% of value added. These industries employed 17,000 paid employees, or about 6% of total manufacturing employment. The reasons for the apparent high employment per unit of output will become evident as each branch is examined. Table 8-14 shows the subdivisions of this group of industries.

As indicated earlier, the concentration of output in larger firms is greater in capital goods than in other industries, but the reasons for this will also become more evident as each of the branches of capital goods is analyzed.

Mechanical Machinery

The available statistical data indicate that there were 240 establishments in this branch of industry, of which only 11 employed 100 or more persons; the distribution of establishments by size in 1967 is given in Table 8-15.

It is evident that the concentrations are in farm and industrial machinery and parts for them. Thus, ten enterprises account for about half the employment and well over half the output in this industry. The output of these firms is so unhomogeneous that it is diffucult to make price or cost comparisons to determine competitive ability. This portion of capital goods industries appears least concentrated in large plants which account for only about 50% of

4. Jack Baranson, *Automotive Industries in Developing Countries,* p. 24. World Bank Staff Occasional Paper No. 8.

5. An unusual anomaly is that bodies for jeeps are dutiable at 40% and the jeeps themselves at only 20%.

Table 8-14: OUTPUT AND EMPLOYMENT IN THE CAPITAL GOODS INDUSTRIES

	Gross output	Value added	Paid employment	Gross output per employee
	(In millions of 1968 Col$)			(In thousands of 1968 Col$)
Mechanical machinery	348.1	203.6	5,691	61
Electrical machinery (except appliances)	760.9	379.3	6,119	124
Road equipment (except passenger motors)	219.8	107.0	5,283	41
	1,328.8	689.9	17,093	78

Sources: 1953, 1958, 1961, 1963-1966: *Boletin Mensual de Estadistica*, Numbers 67, 117, 148, 170, 180, 201 and 207; 1960, 1962 and 1967: Unpublished DANE data.

total employment as compared with 57 percent in electrical machinery and over 90 percent in transport equipment.

The tariff level on machinery is about 30% (see Chapter 7). Because tariffs on inputs are not significantly lower and imported inputs are a major cost element, effective protection is probably not greatly different from the nominal rate in most cases (see Table 7-1). By comparison with other Colombian industries, these branches seem to get relatively little protection.

Electrical Machinery

In 1967, this industry (excluding light bulbs and electrical appliances covered earlier under durable consumer goods) comprised 135 plants employing about 6,100 persons. Fifty-seven percent of total employment in the industry was concentrated in 11 plants, each with more than 100 workers. These plants accounted for over 65% of the gross output and 64% of the value added (see Table 8-16). Seven of these are plants producing electrical equipment, including a Siemens plant in Bogota, two large electrical wire and cable manufacturers and two other large plants, which it is inferred, produce miscellaneous items such as electrical signs and displays.

Indications are that the electrical equipment industry is relatively more advanced than the non-electrical equipment industry. For example, the output of Colombian electrical equipment (including appliances) is at a level of about 40% of Brazil on a per capita basis, while in the mechanical and transport equipment industries, Colombia is at about 20% of the Brazilian level. Value added per employee is about 70% of the Brazilian level in electrical equipment as against 40% in transport equipment. Here, as in mechanical machinery, the tariff levels for finished equipment are only 10-15% above components and parts imports, far lower than, for example, in the automotive field.

Table 8-15: DISTRIBUTION OF EMPLOYMENT, GROSS OUTPUT AND
VALUE ADDED IN THE MECHANICAL MACHINERY INDUSTRY, 1967
(firms employing more than 100 workers)

| | Total Industry | | | | Large Establishments | | | |
	Establishments	Employment	Gross output	Value added	Establishments	Employment	Gross output	Value added
			(In millions of current Col$)				(In millions of current Col$)	
Moving machinery	7	185	12.4	4.4	0	0	0	0
Farm machinery	81	1,550	92.6	47.3	2	527	38.8	18.6
Industrial machinery	75	1,947	146.5	78.4	4	1,042	106.4	55.1
Parts for agricultural & industrial	73	1,810	72.9	48.0	4	904	31.6	22.8
Miscellaneous machinery	4	199	5.8	3.7	1	147	3.1	2.1
Mechanical machinery	240	5,691	330.2	181.8	11	2,620	179.9	98.6

Source: Unpublished DANE data.

Table 8-16: DISTRIBUTION OF EMPLOYMENT, GROSS OUTPUT AND VALUE ADDED IN THE ELECTRICAL MACHINERY INDUSTRY, 1967 (firms employing more than 100 workers)

	Total Industry				Large Establishments			
	Establishments	Employment	Gross output	Value added	Establishments	Employment	Gross output	Value added
			(In millions of current Col\$)				(In millions of current Col\$)	
Electrical machinery	60	3,492	298.1	130.9	7	2,506	236.2	103.8
Wire & cable	6	569	157.0	58.0	2	441	100.3	27.2
Miscellaneous electrical manufactures	69	2,058	264.9	145.5	2	541	136.8	83.8
Total	135	6,119	720.0	334.4	11	3,488	473.3	214.8

Source: Unpublished DANE data.

CHAPTER 9

SPECIAL INDUSTRY STUDIES: STEEL; PULP AND PAPER

The Iron and Steel Industry

Existing basic production facilities in iron and steel consist of one integrated plant, Acerias Paz del Rio at Belencito, four arc furnace and rolling mill plants, (including two capable of producing specification carbon and low-alloy steels), one reroller and one electrolytic tinplate line. All the principal producers are expanding or proposing to expand their facilities at the present time. The most important expansion project is for the installation of a cold reduction mill on the part of Paz del Rio. To guide development of the sector along sound lines, an overall study of the iron and steel industry is recommended. A brief survey of the industry follows.

Structure and Growth

Apparent consumption of rolled steel products in Colombia in 1967, the last year for which detailed data are available, was 375,000 tons of which about 59% was produced domestically (see Table 9-1). The apparent per capita consumption, which averaged 21.0, 24.3 and 27.5 kg in ingot equivalent in the 5-year periods 1951-1955, 1956-1960 and 1961-1965 respectively, rose to 36.7 kg in 1966 but fell back to 25.9 kg in 1967. Both figures are well below per capita consumption for the ILAFA countries [1] as a whole, which averaged 53.5 kg in the period 1965-1967. For a comparison of apparent consumption of rolled steel products in the ILAFA countries in 1967 see Table 9-2.

The modern iron and steel industry in Colombia is only about 20 years old as can be seen from Table 9-3, which shows domestic production of finished steel products in the period 1951-1966. It is entirely privately-owned, although Paz del Rio was originally created in the public sector. Like the rest of manufacturing industries, the iron and steel sector has developed along regional lines and its production facilities are fragmented. The largest producer is the integrated plant at Belencito, some 200 km. northeast of Bogota, where the majority of its products are consumed, and close to the mines and quarries from which the iron ore, coal and limestone required for its operation are derived. The four arc furnace plants are located near the market in the principal cities—Bogota, Medellin, Cali and Barranquilla, while the rerolling plant is located between Belencito, from where it obtains its inputs, and Bogota, the center of consumption of its products.

This is a natural structure in the initial stage of development of the iron and steel industries, in which production is confined to merchant products—light sections, bars and rods—that can be fairly economically produced on a small scale. Each arc furnace plant obtains its scrap requirements from the city in which it is located, and also sells the majority of its production there. As production capacity is expanded, however, to meet the growing demand, scrap requirements tend to exceed local scrap generation which then has to be supplemented by the importation of scrap in order to achieve full utilization of the equipment. In Colombia, this generally involves high inland transport costs and drastically alters the economics of the operation.

At the same time, the diversification of steel production into more sophisticated product lines, such as flat rolled products, requires concentration of facilities in order to achieve economies of scale. This is especially true of Colombia, where demand is comparatively small and barely able to sustain a modern flat products facility. In the interest of efficiency, the sector should initially be served by one flat products mill and its location, vis-a-vis the source of its inputs and the geographical distribution of its market, will have an important bearing on the delivered price of its finished products. When the internal market for flat-rolled products grows beyond about 500,000 tons per annum, the question will arise as to whether to expand the capacity of the existing hot strip mill at Belencito or to put down a second strip mill complex in another location. This is unlikely for at least twelve years.

The iron and steel sector in Colombia has now reached the stage at which first, the

---

1. Member countries of the Latin American Iron and Steel Institute (ILAFA).

Table 9-1: APPARENT CONSUMPTION, DOMESTIC PRODUCTION AND IMPORTS
OF FINISHED STEEL PRODUCTS, 1960-1968
(In thousands of tons)

	1960	1961	1962	1963	1964	1965	1966	1967	1968*
APPARENT CONSUMPTION									
Bars, rods and shapes	153.0	164.7	161.2	194.0	256.2	213.9	276.8	284.1	n.a.
Rails and heavy sections	14.7	15.5	11.3	12.2	16.0	7.2	16.0	12.8	
Bars and light sections	83.1	124.5	121.2	108.3	144.5	128.9	113.7	188.5	
Wire rod	55.2	24.7	28.7	73.5	95.7	77.8	147.1	82.8	
Flat rolled products	137.8	129.0	130.5	157.7	204.2	118.6	224.1	90.9	n.a.
Plates and sheets	109.9	103.4	103.0	125.5	169.9	93.1	169.1	69.2	
Tinplate	27.9	25.6	27.5	32.2	34.3	25.5	55.0	21.7	
Total finished products	290.8	293.7	291.7	351.7	460.4	332.5	500.9	375.0	
DOMESTIC PRODUCTION									
Bars, rods and shapes	113.4	139.0	145.1	168.1	184.3	188.7	211.8	199.8	177.9
Rails and heavy sections	13.2	14.5	10.5	6.6	6.4	4.2	3.2	3.2	1.8
Bars and light sections	68.7	107.0	108.3	91.0	105.9	111.7	80.6	121.5	128.1
Wire rod	31.5	17.4	26.3	70.5	72.0	72.8	128.0	75.1	48.0
Flat rolled products	–	–	–	14.3	14.3	18.1	23.7	21.5	27.5
Plates and sheets	–	–	–	14.3	14.3	18.1	23.7	21.5	23.3
Tinplate	–	–	–	–	–	–	–	–	4.2
Total finished products	113.4	139.0	145.1	182.4	198.6	206.8	235.4	221.3	205.4
Domestic production as percentage of apparent consumption	38.9	47.3	49.7	51.8	43.1	62.1	46.9	59.0	

IMPORTS

Bars, rods and shapes	39.6	25.7	16.1	25.9	72.0	25.3	65.0	84.3
Rails and heavy sections	1.5	0.9	0.8	5.5	9.7	3.0	12.8	9.6
Bars and light sections	14.4	17.5	12.9	17.3	38.6	17.2	33.1	67.0
Wire	23.7	7.3	2.4	3.0	23.7	5.0	19.1	7.6	n.a.
Flat rolled products	137.8	129.0	130.5	143.3	189.8	100.5	200.4	69.4
Plates and sheets	109.9	103.4	103.0	111.1	155.6	75.0	145.4	47.7
Tinplate	27.9	25.6	27.5	32.2	34.3	25.5	55.0	21.7
Total finished products	177.4	154.7	146.6	169.2	261.8	125.8	265.4	153.7

Notes:

*Preliminary figures
n.a. – not available
Totals may not add up because of rounding

Sources: ILAFA – *Anuario Estadistico 1967, 1968 and 1969.*

Table 9-2: APPARENT CONSUMPTION OF ROLLED STEEL
PRODUCTS IN THE ILAFA COUNTRIES IN 1967
(In thousands of tons and kg per capita, ingot equivalents)

	Total	Per Capita
		Consumption
Argentina	1,719	100.3
Bolivia	44	15.7
Brazil	2,916	45.8
Central America	234	21.2
Chile	418	61.9
Colombia	375	25.9
Ecuador	85	20.6
Mexico	2,497	73.8
Paraguay	25	15.7
Peru	291	31.8
Uruguay	59	28.4
Venezuela	755	108.6
TOTAL	9,419	54.3

Source: ILAFA – Anuario Estadistico 1969.

theoretical scrap requirements of the existing electric arc furnaces of about 150,000 tons per annum exceed by approximately 100,000 tons per annum domestic scrap generation; and second, the newly completed Steckel mill at Belencito requires the installation of a complementary cold reduction mill to process the hot rolled coil into cold rolled coil and sheets and tinplate stock for sale to domestic flat steel consuming industries.

Tables 9-3 and 9-1 show domestic production of finished steel products in the periods 1951 through 1966 and 1960 through 1968 respectively. It will be seen that before 1955, when Acerias Paz del Rio was started up, production was confined to Empresa Siderurgica de Medellin and was quite small. Subsequently there was a marked increase in domestic production, especially of merchant products, which in 1967 amounted to approximately 72% of apparent consumption. This probably approached the maximum practical extent of import substitution of this product group, as certain sizes and qualities consumed in Colombia were outside the product range manufactured by the local steel producers. On the other hand domestic production of flat rolled products represented only a small proportion of apparent consumption and points up the need for additional domestic production capacity in this field.

Preliminary figures for 1968 indicate that domestic finished steel production amounted to 205,400 tons of which Paz del Rio's share may have been as high as 80%. Because of its dominant position, Paz del Rio is the price leader for the industry, with which the other producers align their prices.

Consumption and Trade

Table 9-1 shows the apparent consumption of finished steel products in the period 1960-67. While domestic production increased at a fairly steady rate, apparent consumption varied extensively with the availability of foreign exchange for imports.

There is no industry-wide planning of the sector—neither a unified market forecast nor a master program of expansion aimed at the most economical production of the country's requirements. Demand projections are the work of the individual steel producers with Paz del Rio, which because of its dominant position, generally takes the lead. Paz del Rio's demand forecast for finished steel products for 1975 is shown in Table 9-4, where it is compared with the actual demand in 1967.

Demand in the past two years is thought to have increased more rapidly than was expected

Table 9-3: DOMESTIC PRODUCTION OF FINISHED STEEL PRODUCTS, 1951-1966
(In thousands of tons)

	1951	1952	1953	1954	1955	1956	1957	1958	1959	1960	1961	1962	1963	1964	1965	1966
Bars, rods and shapes	4.3	5.3	4.7	6.9	31.7	65.2	69.3	55.3	90.6	101.6	103.3	132.3	140.5	161.2	161.9	134.6
Paz del Rio	–	–	–	–	23.7	54.4	56.5	42.3	74.9	84.0	85.0	110.0	105.1	118.1	114.3	86.4
Empresa Siderurgica	4.3	5.3	4.7	6.9	8.0	10.8	12.8	12.7	13.0	13.4	13.8	16.9	18.9	18.3	19.0	16.3
Sidelpa	–	–	–	–	–	–	–	–	–	–	–	–	3.8	9.0	12.2	13.8
Sid. Muna	–	–	–	–	–	–	–	0.3	2.7	4.2	4.5	5.4	5.5	5.6	5.0	3.7
Sid. Boyaca	–	–	–	–	–	–	–	–	–	–	–	–	7.2	10.2	11.4	14.4
Flat rolled products	–	–	–	–	–	–	–	–	–	–	–	–	3.9	5.9	9.3	9.9
Paz del Rio	–	–	–	–	–	–	–	–	–	–	–	–	3.9	5.9	9.3	9.9
Wire products	–	–	–	–	–	–	8.0	8.4	17.2	19.7	18.7	26.3	32.0	34.6	36.3	33.8
Paz del Rio	–	–	–	–	–	–	7.8	8.0	16.3	19.3	17.9	22.5	22.6	22.9	23.2	20.3
Others	–	–	–	–	–	–	0.2	0.4	0.9	0.4	0.8	3.8	9.4	11.7	13.1	13.5
Total Finished Products	4.3	5.3	4.7	6.9	31.7	65.2	77.3	63.7	107.8	121.3	122.0	158.6	176.4	201.7	207.5	178.3

Source: Estudio sobre Acerias Paz del Rio, 1968.

Table 9-4: DEMAND FORECAST FOR 1975[1]

	1967 Actual	1975 Projected	Growth Rate
	(In tons)		%
Bars, Rods and Shapes	201,300	332,900	6.5
Bars and rods		233,400	
Shapes		99,500	
Flat Rolled Products	90,900	286,600	15.4
Hot rolled products		143,300	
Cold rolled products		97,100	
Tinplate		46,200	
Wire Products	82,800	70,310	
Bright wire		19,540	
Special wire		8,930	
Galvanized wire		14,420	
Barbed wire		27,420	
Total Finished Products	375,000	689,810	7.9

[1]Excluding rails and alloy steels.

Source: Estudio Sobre Acerias Paz del Rio, S.A., January 1968.

when this forecast was prepared. According to Paz del Rio's market survey dated December 1969, the demand for cold rolled coil and sheets in 1976 is expected to be 215,000 tons and that for tinplate stock 48,000 tons. This suggests that total demand for finished products in 1975 will probably be not less than 800,000 tons or over 1 million tons in ingot equivalent.

Paz del Rio's forecast appears to be based on more recent information than that prepared for IFI in October 1969, which uses the projections made by Paz del Rio in January 1968 shown in Table 9-4. The large discrepancy between these two forecasts, both prepared at the same time, points to the importance of a unified market analysis to permit a rational development of the sector.

Colombia is a net importer of finished steel products. Statistics of the commercial trade balance for steel products are shown in Table 9-5. The principal import items are flat rolled products and tubes in that order, while tubes constitute practically the entire export of steel products.

The data show that there has been no sustained increase in the value of net imports in the period 1960 to 1968. This is borne out by Table 9-1 from which it can be seen that the volume of steel imports in this period averaged around 180,000 tons per annum.

Competitiveness and Price

In quality domestically produced steel products are generally comparable with imports. The principal exceptions are the hot and cold rolled sheets produced by Paz del Rio which, because they are rolled on a hand mill, are not up to the standard of imported hot and cold rolled products. This tends to limit the use of Paz del Rio sheets to applications where finish is not of prime importance.

Imported iron and steel products generally are subject to an *ad valorem* tariff ranging from

5% to 65% and prior deposits ranging from 30% to 130%. For the products manufactured in Colombia the specific rates of duty and prior deposit are shown in Table 9-6.

Table 9-5: TRADE IN SEMI-FINISHED AND FINISHED STEEL PRODUCTS
(In millions of US dollars)

Year	Imports c.i.f.	Exports f.o.b.	Net Imports
1960	34.88	(a)	34.88
1961	34.66	0.01	34.65
1962	32.56	0.01	32.55
1963	32.38	(a)	32.38
1964	42.66	0.08	42.58
1965	29.34	0.39	28.95
1966	51.78	0.43	51.35
1967	31.42	0.47	30.95
1968	35.64	0.25	35.39

(a) less than 0.01

Source: *External Trade of Minerals and Mineral Products,* 1960-1968. Ministry of Mines and Petroleum, September 1969.

In addition imports of steel products are subject to prior license, the issuance of which requires the prospective importer to produce proof that the local mills are unable to supply his requirements as to quality and delivery. At the present time domestically produced steel products are considerably cheaper than equivalent imports after duty, and license applications are therefore readily approved.

There is no longer any price control on steel products, but the producers—essentially Paz del Rio—are required to furnish one month's advance notice of intended price increases, so that a judgment may be made whether the increase is reasonable and, if not, to provide an opportunity to negotiate a lower increase. Thus, the list prices represent a compromise between the desire of Paz del Rio to maximize its profits and that of the authorities to hold down the prices of basic inputs.

Table 9-7 shows the movement of prices of some typical steel products, f.o.b. Belencito, for the period November 1963-November 1969.

It will be seen that during 1969, there was a marked increase in prices in line with the increase in export prices of the major steel producing countries. Consequently Paz del Rio achieved its best results in the year ended December 1969, when it made a profit of approximately Col$81.1 million, equivalent to a margin of Col$425 per ton of finished product. These figures compare with the previous year's profit of Col$54.5 million and a margin of Col$330 per ton and the profit for 1967 of Col$21.0 million and a margin of Col$130 per ton. In the same period SIDELPA's profit went up from Col$7.3 million in 1967 to Col$13.7 million in 1968 and an estimated Col$20.5 million in 1969. The corresponding margins per ton of finished product were approximately Col$440, 635 and 705 respectively, reflecting to some extent the higher profitability of special manufacturing as compared with common steel.

Table 9-8 shows a comparison between recent European f.o.b. export prices, c.i.f. prices and delivered prices of imported steel products, before duty and taxes, in some of the major centers of consumption, on the one hand, and the ex-works prices of Paz del Rio and Empresa Siderurgica and the delivered prices of their products in Medellin and Bogota on the other. It is apparent from this table that the 1970 delivered prices of domestically produced bars and rods in Bogota and Medellin were equal to or less than the prices, before duty, of equivalent imports while those of bright wire and hot rolled sheet were less than those of equivalent imports in Bogota, but on account of inland transport slightly higher (8-10%) in Medellin. In Bogota the excess cost of the domestic product over the equivalent import (protection requirement) for

Table 9-6: RATES OF DUTY AND PRIOR DEPOSITS ON IMPORTS
OF SELECTED STEEL PRODUCTS
(Applicable as of May 14, 1970)

Description	Rate of Duty	Prior Deposit
	(%)	
Wire rod	25	70
Bars and rods	25	1
Shapes and sections	25	70
Wire products		
bright	50	70
galvanized	55	70
barbed wire	65	130
Flat rolled products		
hot rolled plates and sheets	28	70
cold rolled sheets	30	30
tinplate	25	30

Source: Acerias Paz del Rio

Table 9-7: MOVEMENT OF PRICES OF REPRESENTATIVE STEEL PRODUCTS
IN THE PERIOD NOVEMBER 1963-NOVEMBER 1969
(In current Col$ per ton, f.o.b. Belencito)

	3/8" dia. bars	3/4" dia. bars	5/16" dia. wire rod	Hot rolled sheets	Angles
November 1963	1,740	1,555	1,930	1,950	2,070
November 1964	1,645	1,420	1,995	1,985	1,965
November 1965	1,645	1,420	1,995	1,985	1,965
November 1966	2,040	1,935	2,245	2,190	2,260
November 1967	2,040	1,935	2,245	2,190	3,000
November 1968	2,504	2,405	2,705	2,975	2,805
November 1969	3,240	3,100	3,480	3,760	3,960

Sources: Prices for 1963-1968 — *ILAFA, Anuario Estadistico 1967, 1968 and 1969.*

Prices for 1969 — *Paz del Rio, Price List dated November 15, 1969.*

the remaining products ranges from 5.5% for barbed wire to 7.4% for tinplate, 7.6% for channels and beams and 10.9% for galvanized wire. In Medellin the protection requirement is somewhat greater and ranges from 5.7% for tinplate to 9.3% for barbed wire, 11.9% for galvanized wire and 16.0% for channels and beams. Thus on the basis of the recent high price levels, the protection requirement of domestically produced steel products in Bogota and Medellin is low. In Barranquilla the protection requirement ranges from zero for ⅜" diameter bars to 24.5% for channels and beams.

Steel is a low-value product which enjoys natural protection in the interior of the country because of the incidence of high inland transport costs on the price of imported steel. In fact, ocean freight and inland transport add approximately 40% to the current f.o.b. export price of steel products. The leading producer, Paz del Rio, is handicapped by the low quality of its iron ore and coal which results in a high pig iron cost. With better inputs and a high standard of operation and maintenance the direct operating costs of Thomas ingots could probably be reduced by some Col$200 per ton (15%) with proportionate reductions for the finished products. An expansion of Paz del Rio's iron and steel making capacity to meet the entire demand

Table 9-8: PRICE COMPARISON BETWEEN DOMESTICALLY PRODUCED AND IMPORTED STEEL PRODUCTS
(US$1 = Col$18.30)

	Imported Steel					Domestic Steel			
	FOB Antwerp US$/ton	CIF Barranquilla	Delivered Barranquilla	Delivered Medellin	Delivered Bogota	FOB Belencito	FOB Medellin	Delivered Medellin	Delivered Bogota
			Col$/ton (before duty and tax)				Col$/ton (before tax)		
1/4" dia. wire rod	151.50	3,149	3,648	3,848	3,908	3,480		3,660	3,545
3/8" dia. bars	153.00	3,176	3,679	3,879	3,939	3,240		3,420	3,305
3/4" dia. bars	128.00	2,719	3,050	3,250	3,310	3,100		3,280	3,165
Channels and beams	138.00	2,902	3,370	3,570	3,630	3,960	n.a.	4,140	4,025
9 gauge bright wire	148.00	3,085	3,577	3,777	3,837	3,740		3,920	3,805
8 gauge galvanized wire	167.20	3,436	3,973	4,173	4,233	4,490		4,670	4,555
Galvanized barbed wire	186.80	3,795	4,521	4,721	4,781	4,980		5,160	5,045
16 gauge hot rolled sheet	152.00	3,158	3,659	3,859	3,919	3,760		3,940	3,825
Electrolytic tinplate (107 lb.)	220.00	4,400	4,900	5,100	5,160	–	5,390	5,390	5,540

Source: Acerias Paz del Rio, Current Price List.

Empresa Siderurgica de Medellin, Recent (but possibly not the latest) Price List.

Continental Iron and Steel Trade Reports, April 21, 1970, Export Prices.

La Superintendencia de Regulacion Economica, Resolucion No. 0334, September 6, 1963.

for bars, rods and wire products in the interior of Colombia would reduce the capital cost per annual ton of installed capacity and thus the capital charges—amortization and interest—per ton of finished product.

The challenge facing the industry is how to develop and expand its production facilities so that the price of finished steel products to the consumer will gradually approach the level prevailing in the industrialized countries. This question will be discussed in the section dealing with recommendations.

Future Development Plans

With total demand for finished steel products expected to approach 1 million tons by 1975, all the principal producers are expanding their production facilities or have reasonably firm expansion plans. In the absence of a master development plan for the industry, these expansion projects have not been coordinated. If implemented, they would accentuate the present short-fall of domestic scrap generation and result in further fragmentation of production facilities.

As already stated, Paz del Rio's next expansion phase consists of the installation of a cold rolling mill at Belencito to complement the recently completed reversing hot strip mill. This mill which would have a rated capacity of some 250,000 tons of cold rolled coil and sheet and tinplate stock per annum, is scheduled to be in operation by the beginning of 1973. A cold mill is certainly needed in Colombia; the demand for hot mill products as such is too small to justify the operation of Paz del Rio's Steckel mill, which should not have been installed without a cold mill to process the hot rolled coil into cold rolled products—coil, sheet and tinplate stock. The cold mill should, therefore, be viewed as the second integral part of the flat rolled products facility, of which the Steckel mill forms the first part. However, Thomas steel, which constitutes about 85% of the ingot steel produced by Paz del Rio, is unsuitable for cold rolling. The serious choice facing Paz del Rio is, therefore, whether in the long term to run its hot and cold mills on imported strip mill slabs or convert the Thomas plant to a BOF plant, capable of producing ingots of the required quality. The relative economics of these alternatives have not been examined.

An associated question is whether, having regard to the low quality of Paz del Rio's iron ore and coal, basic iron and steel-making capacity in Colombia should be expanded by the installation of a second blast furnace at Belencito or alternatively by putting down a semi-finished products plant at a coastal location based on the use of high grade imported ore and coal from the Cerrejon deposit in Guajira. It is understood that this question will be studied jointly by Paz del Rio and IFI. Paz del Rio's decision to install the cold rolling mill at Belencito is based on the belief that any attempt at this stage to investigate the economics of a coastal location, in conjunction with the proposed blast furnace study, would result in such delays as to vitiate any potential savings due to lower inland transportation costs.

Of the smaller steel producers Empresa Siderurgica, Medellin, is currently expanding its steel-making capacity to approximately 100,000 tons per annum by the installation of a 30-ton arc furnace and construction of a new 5-stand merchant mill for light sections, bars and rods. SIDELPA, Cali, expects to install a second 12-ton electric arc furnace thereby increasing to about 50,000 tons per annum its steel-making capacity, principally for specification carbon and low alloy steel. CORPACERO, Barranquilla, is contemplating the installation of a third electric arc furnace and additional rolling equipment to raise its capacity to 20,000 tons per annum. Metalurgica Boyaca, Tunja, has ambitious expansion plans, which envision the installation of an 8 to 10-ton arc furnace in stage 1 and of a 40,000 tons per annum blast furnace and LD-steel making plant, with a continuous casting machine, in stage 2. In addition the recently created Siderurgica de la Sabana (SIDESA), in which IFI has an interest, is believed to be on the point of placing orders for a 30,000 tons per annum pig iron plant at Tipito, on the Altiplano some 100 km northwest of Bogota. It proposes to use the local iron ore, coking coal and limestone deposits and expects to be able to sell its pig iron mainly to the foundry industry at the price of equivalent imports.

Conclusions

The industry is now at the point where scrap requirements exceed domestic scrap generation by about 100,000 tons per annum and the manufacture of flat-rolled and possibly other sophisticated steel products requires concentration of production facilities to achieve minimum economies of scale. It follows that a proliferation of new arc furnace capacity would merely aggravate the present shortfall of domestic scrap and result in an increasing proportion of high-cost imported scrap and at best maintain present selling prices for finished products.

Agreement in principle between Paz del Rio and IFI has already been reached on a joint industry-wide study to select the optimum location for the next blast furnace to be put down in Colombia. This shows an awareness of the importance of planning the growth of the iron and steel sector on a country-wide basis, especially since the high freight costs in Colombia may invalidate some of the solutions found in other countries. It would require one more step to extend the scope of this study to its logical conclusion and make it an all-embracing survey of the iron and steel sector in Colombia, coupled with an evaluation of the various possibilities for expansion of capacity and diversification of product lines. It is therefore recommended that the Government of Colombia commission a comprehensive study of the iron and steel industry which should broadly cover the following points:

(a)   carry out a technical audit of present production capacity,
(b)   review the availability of raw materials, both domestic and imported, determine realistic freight costs and estimate the availability and present and probable future costs of services, particularly of power and water,
(c)   prepare estimates of production costs for the larger plants,
(d)   review and evaluate the recent estimates of the demand for steel prepared by IFI and Paz del Rio, including a long-range forecast for the year 1980, having regard to the likely impact of the Andean Group and LAFTA integration of the pattern of demand and the availability of semi-finished products,
(e)   prepare on a yearly basis, estimates of the differences between projected demand and capacity for groups of products,
(f)   review and evaluate both the existing proposal for installing a cold rolling mill at Belencito and the study now being prepared by Sofresid for installing a cold mill on the Atlantic coast,
(g)   review and evaluate other defined proposals for expansion in the industry,
(h)   after making allowance for importation of items that cannot be economically produced in Colombia, recommend the most economical program of expansion of the industry which would produce the required range and tonnage of products, and indicate likely selling prices in the major consumption centers,
(i)   identify any special transportation bottlenecks whose removal would facilitate the importation of raw materials and/or semi-finished products to and the distribution of finished products from the plants recommended in (h) above.

Since the results of the study will be influenced by the cost of foreign exchange and of transport, it is suggested that a sensitivity analysis be carried out for the plausible range of values of these two variables.

Once the study has been completed it is expected to form the basis of the Planning Department's (DNP) evaluation of expansion and diversification projects in the sector and of INCOMEX's issuance of import licenses. In this way the growth of the industry would be guided along lines aimed at increasing its efficiency and bringing about an all-round reduction in the selling prices of finished steel products. This, in turn, would benefit the entire economy, because the steel consuming industries should be able to pass on to their customers a proportion of these price reductions and at the same time improve their export potential.

The Pulp and Paper Industry[2]

The pulp and paper industry in Colombia has undergone substantial growth and now supplies virtually all internal demand (except mainly for newsprint). As the industry appears to be competitive on an international basis, there may be scope for enlarging its exports in the future. Another area of future interest is the possible development of local raw materials to replace imports, particularly of long fiber pulp.

History and Development

The foundation for modern paper making was laid in 1944, when the Container Corporation of America formed "Carton de Colombia." This company initially established a paper converting unit to produce boxes from imported kraft board; and then integrated backwards, as the volume of business warranted. By 1953, it had installed its first kraft paper machine at Cali, based on imported pulp. Subsequently, it installed three more paper machines, a pulp plant based on local hardwood, and four converting plants, at Barranquilla, Bogota, Medellin and Turbo.

In 1961, writing and printing papers were produced for the first time, using bagasse for raw material, by Productora de Papel (Propal). This company was established by W. R. Grace and the International Paper Corporation, both of the United States. The plant was built at Cali, near the Carton de Colombia facility; and is conveniently located in relation to the sugar-growing area of the Cauca Valley. Two other small companies, which may be regarded as integrated producers have a combined output about one-tenth of that of the two major companies. Today Colombia is practically self-sufficient in writing and printing papers, with the exception of newsprint, all of which is still imported.

Present Structure of the Industry

The total installed capacity of paper factories in Colombia is about 240,000 tons per year. Production, at 203,000 tons in 1969, showed 85% utilization. For pulp manufacture installed capacity is about 133,000 tons; actual production in 1968 was about 85,000 tons, showing 64% utilization.

Carton de Colombia S.A. is owned 60% by Container Corporation of America and 40% by about 350 Colombian shareholders. The largest local shareholder (3%) is an insurance company. The management of the company is largely in Colombian hands, the U.S. interest being represented by two members on a board of five directors.

Its principal plants are located at Yumbo, 15 km from Cali. The location was chosen for its proximity to the major forests, from which hardwood is extracted for pulping, and to an adequate supply of water. The company owns no forests but has cutting rights in several, and operates a reforestation program. The pulp plant is actually owned by a separate company, Celulosa y Papel de Colombia S.A. (Pulpapel), which was originally a joint enterprise of Carton de Colombia and IFI. After it was working at a profit, IFI sold its shares to Carton de Colombia. This plant is perhaps the only one of its kind in the world, producing pulp for papers from tropical hardwoods.

The company operates 4 paper machines and converting and printing machines for production of cartons and has a capacity of 130,000 tons per year of paper products. In 1969 it produced 115,000 tons of various paper items, including box boards, container boards, wrapping, and kraft papers, liners, grocery bags, and clay coated, white patent coated and solid fiber papers. About 50% of the output (by weight) consisted of mill products, i.e. rolls of paper and

---

2. This review is based primarily on interviews with, and plant visits to, the two major producers of paper in Colombia. This information was supplemented by desk study of a report published in November 1969 by the Universidad del Valle on "Production, Apparent Demand, and Projection of Consumption of Paper and Paperboard in Colombia." This report was prepared for the Instituto de Fomento Industrial (IFI), the Cali Financiera, and El Ingenio Riopaila (a sugar milling concern).

standard size boards, and the other half consisted of fabricated products, e.g. printed containers, bags, tubes, etc. The company supplied about 40 customers with mill products, and 1,800 with fabricated products. Total employment in the company amounts to 1,800 persons, of whom about 400 are salaried staff, 1,000 skilled workers, and 400 unskilled workers. The company also employs about 5,000 workers on contract for forestry operations.

Productora de Papel S.A. (Propal), the second largest paper producer, is owned entirely by U.S. interests, 50% by International Paper Corporation and 50% by W. R. Grace and Company. Management is largely Colombian; but there are some Americans in top management positions, including the financial director. The company employs about 700 people, 150 of them salaried employees. Propal's plant also is located at Yumbo. This is an integrated facility using sugar-cane bagasse purchased from 10 nearby mills to produce rolled and cut writing and printing paper products. In 1969 it consumed about 300,000 tons of bagasse, yielding approximately 57,000 tons of paper. This output is achieved from 3 paper-making machines with a capacity of 70,000 tons a year of paper. A fourth machine is to be added, to raise capacity to 100,000 tons per year. The principal products of the company are bond, offset, ledger, duplicator, manifold, manila, wrapping, and bag papers, and napkin, toilet and sulfite tissues.

Both companies rely almost entirely on road transport to draw their raw material supplies to the plants and to deliver their products. The total incoming load is about 700,000 tons, and the outgoing load about 175,000 tons per year. Both companies depend on Planta de Soda, Bogota, for supplies of caustic soda and chlorine.

Compared with the two main producers with a combined production of 172,000 tons per year, eleven small producers in 1969 had a total production of about 31,000 tons, the largest Fabrica Nacional de Carton Ltd., in Cali producing about 7,000 tons per year, the second, Papeles Nacionales S.A., in Pereira, about 4,600; and the smallest less than 400.

Supply and Demand

Pulp. Colombian pulp mills have to depend upon hardwood forests and sugar-cane bagasse for their fiber requirements. No significant softwood resources have yet been located or developed. Waste paper, both domestic and imported, is used to supplement fresh pulp for paper making, on a considerable scale. In 1968 the total quantity of raw materials—pulp and waste paper—used in Colombia for paper making amounted to about 192,000 tons. This figure is broken down by varieties and sources, as indicated in Table 9-9.

Table 9-9: RAW MATERIAL USED IN PAPER MAKING

	Chemical and semi-chemical pulp		Pulp from bagasse		Waste Paper		Total	
	'000 metric tons	% of total	'000 metric tons	% of total	'000 metric tons	% of total	'000 metric tons	% of total
Domestic	39.8	(20.8)	45.1	(23.5)	62.4	(32.1)	147.3	(76.4)
Imported	37.6[1]	(19.6)	1.9[2]	(1.0)	5.9	(3.0)	45.4	(23.6)
Total	77.4	(40.4)	47.0	(24.5)	68.3	(35.1)	192.7	(100.0)

[1]Long-fiber.

[2]Mechanical pulp.

Turning to the local pulp supply—which is all short fiber pulp—the Universidad del Valle study projected the pattern for the future growth of installed capacity and demand as shown in Table 9-10. It concluded that the surplus of local pulp capacity shown to exist through 1975 precludes any immediate prospect for promoting a new pulp project based on local pulping species. On the other hand, with its present surplus Colombia should be in a favorable position to supply other Andean countries. The prime customers would be the smaller non-integrated paper mills.

Paper. Local paper supply meets most of the demand but imports of the higher quality papers are still required. In 1968 imports amounted to some 28,000 tons, but in quantity these were more than balanced by exports of 42,000 tons. The balance of the value of this trade is not known.

The above import figures do not include newsprint, of which Colombia consumed 52,000 tons in 1966, and this is expected to increase to 65,000 tons in 1970 and 87,000 tons in 1975. As all newsprint is imported this large potential demand should provide an added incentive for examining projects to produce in Colombia long fiber pulp, the necessary raw material for newsprint.

The Universidad del Valle study examined the demand for each of the other main categories of paper and compared this with expansion plans of the suppliers for the period 1970-1979. This showed that there would be a short-fall of printing papers and cardboard and a surplus of kraft paper, which would about balance the overall supply and demand. This points to the

Table 9-10: SUPPLY AND DEMAND FOR SHORT FIBER PULP IN COLOMBIA

Year	1970	1971	1972	1973	1974	1975
Installed Capacity	133	185.1[1]	185.1	190.0	197.1	197.1
Demand	103.3	116.8	130.3	146.8	160.6	175.4
Surplus	30	68.3	54.8	43.2	36.5	21.7
Demand as % of Capacity	79	63	70	77	81	94

[1]The increase of capacity between 1970 and 1971 will be caused by a number of smaller bagasse mills coming on stream.

Table 9-11: PERCENTAGE OF SHORT FIBER CONTENT TOLERABLE IN VARIOUS GRADES OF PAPER

Type	%
Cultural Papers	
Newsprint	0
Paper for journals and first class books	60
Paper for 2nd class books	70
Fine paper, 1st class	70
Fine paper, 2nd class	70-85
Industrial Papers	
Packaging paper, 1st class	0
Packaging paper, 2nd class	20-50
Packaging paper, 3rd ciass	70
Cardboard for food packages	0
Liner board	0
Corrugating medium	80-95
Ordinary cardboard	0
Waxed paper	50
Sanitary paper − bleached	90-100
− unbleached and undyed	15

Sources: CEPAL/FAO/UN Forestry Study; data from paper makers.

need for rationalizing the expansion plans of the industry to try to insure that all needs are met adequately without unnecessary surpluses.

Prices and Costs

The principal manufacturers of pulp, papers and boards in Colombia claim cost competitiveness within South America, and a reasonably competitive position vis-a-vis imports from elsewhere. The two largest manufacturers supplied data regarding average prices of their own products and comparable imports in 1969: Carton de Colombia's average selling price[3] per ton for papers was Col$4,020 or US$230 and Propal's was Col$5,000 or US$285, against comparable import prices of US$250.

The average prices have limited significance because they combine a multitude of varieties, and specifications. It appears, however, that Colombia is certainly competitive in specific products in relation to some other Latin American producers. The Universidad del Valle study indicates that in 1965 prices of kraft liner, kraft paper for bags, and printing paper were lower in Colombia than in Chile by 20-90%; and they were lower than in Peru by 40-90%. Subsequently the position changed further in Colombia's favor, because of the considerable inflation in Chile and Peru.

There is only a very small market for domestic pulp in Colombia as the bulk of output is used within the integrated manufacturing facilities. However, Propal indicated sales of about 2,500 tons in 1968 at a price of Col$2,640 per metric ton (= US$150.85). Comparable grades of pulp were not imported in Colombia, but long fiber pulps were imported at the following c.i.f. prices per metric ton: bleached kraft US$165, semi-bleached kraft US$166, unbleached kraft US$134. These reported prices are in line with prices for similar varieties quoted in trade journals.

Two major companies gave the following breakdown of their production costs in 1969:

Item		Company 1	Company 2
Production cost including depreciation per metric ton[1]	) Col$	3,750[3]	3,250
	) US$[2]	214	186
% of cost attributable to raw materials		50%	30%
% of raw material imported		50%	25-30%

[1]Total cost divided by total tonnage of output.
[2]Conversion rate 1 US$ = Col$ 17.5.
[3]Includes taxes.

A large profit margin exists on the "cultural" paper, but there is not much profit margin for the industrial papers (7%). One company stated that 80% of their corporate profit is generated in the pulp production of a subsidiary company. It is claimed that production costs are not out of line with international costs.

Outlook for the Future

Long Fiber Production. There is a demand in Colombia for quality papers which can tolerate only minimum amounts of short fiber content. For instance, newsprint, high-quality cardboard,

3. The average selling price is the total sales value divided by the total tonnage of papers of all types for each company.

liner board and first-class packaging paper cannot have any short fiber components. On the other hand, paper for journals and books can tolerate up to 60% of short fiber.Table 9-11 shows the tolerance of short fiber in various papers.

Colombia is deficient in long fiber pulp and therefore imports all its newsprint and much of its liner board requirements, as well as long fiber pulp and long fiber waste paper. These imports are currently costing Colombia US$16 million per year, a figure expected to reach $24 million by 1975.

The lack of long fiber in Colombia has been known for many years and although many studies have been made to investigate means of supplying it, nothing specific has developed. Half of these studies have concentrated on producing long fiber pulp from local tropical wood species of which the so-called cecropia tree appears to offer the most promise; the other half have been aimed at developing commercial forests of northern hemisphere pine species in Colombia. Both types of studies have been mostly general. They have not been followed through, for example, by pilot plant pulp tests of local species or by attempts to commercialize the existing stands of pine, such as those in Antioquia, at present exploited by smallholders as building material, for which the timber is sold at a high price.

Since long fiber pulp is readily available from international sources, there is no commercial pressure to push forward such studies. However, the broader implications for the economy justify government initiative. IFI has recognized these problems and has recently signed a contract with a Canadian and a local engineering company for a practical study of the feasibility of an integrated pulp and paper plant utilizing the cecropia timber of Colombia. This will also involve planting an experimental stand of trees and pilot plant tests to determine the suitability of using this timber in conjunction with the local pine timber for the production of paper. It is envisaged that it will take one year to set up the study and a further five years for the planting and experimental work.

This study merits attention as its significance goes well beyond Colombia. It will investigate not only the development of a presently untapped forest resource in Colombia and possibly in other tropical countries, but also the economic use of imported tree species which can be grown on land not at present usable.

Development of Magdalena Valley Forests.   IFI and INDERENA (Instituto de Desarrollo de los Recursos Naturales Renovables) are making a major effort with the assistance of FAO, to study—and to invite foreign interest in—the development of the forest resources of the Magdalena and Sinu Valleys. This effort started in 1967 when one of the studies of local production of kraft and newsprint pointed to the advantages of Barrancabermeja as a plant location. This town has a nucleus of skilled labor because of its extensive oil activities. It is also in the center of the Magdalena forest resources and would seem to be ideal for locating a timber processing plant. A study has therefore been in progress under IFI/INDERENA/FAO auspices by the Finnish firm, Jaakko Poyry. Following encouraging results of the first part of the study, the promoting committee appointed by IFI and INDERENA has now written to some 100 concerns around the world to invite their participation in the further development of this large project. The first step would be to develop the necessary infrastructure (roads, power, water) to support logging operations and then begin producing sawn wood and plywood and also pulp based on the by-products and on otherwise unusable forest species.

CHAPTER 10

SPECIAL INDUSTRY STUDIES: CHEMICALS

Present Structure of the Industry

The chemical industry as it has now developed in Colombia produces a variety of products ranging from matches, inedible oils, paints and pigments to such new products as synthetic fibers, fertilizers, petrochemicals and pharmaceuticals. In 1967, there were over 500 establishments employing over 23,000 persons or over 8% of manufacturing employment. Over 350 establishments employing almost 14,000 were in pharmaceuticals and soaps and related products which are discussed separately under non-durable consumer goods. The more narrowly defined chemical industry discussed here accounts for employment of about 10,000 persons and a gross value of output of Col$2.2 billion (US$130 million) in 1967.

The present structure of the industry consists mainly of three basic sub-sectors: a basic chemicals industry, producing mostly the inorganic materials such as soda ash, caustic soda, acids; a fertilizer industry based primarily on conversion of petroleum derivatives but also incorporating conversion of imported phosphate rock and potash; and a petrochemical industry involving the conversion of petroleum to intermediate and finished products which are then converted to consumer goods. This chapter deals with all these sub-sectors except for a part of petrochemicals, synthetic fibers.

Large enterprises predominate in basic chemicals. Fourteen such establishments employ over 5,200 people or 75% of the total employment in basic chemicals. There are about 20 additional establishments employing 100 or more persons each in other segments of the chemical industry, excluding pharmaceuticals and related products. The companies in Colombian ownership are small and none show any signs of expanding to play a major role in the industry.

There is a heavy predominance of both foreign and government ownership in the chemical industry. The foreign companies are involved mostly through their earlier positions in the petroleum business and through subsequent backward integration steps, but also because this industry is heavily dependent on foreign know-how. Many of the foreign companies have minor share-holdings in exchange for their know-how and management contribution.

The government has become involved in the petrochemical industry as an outgrowth of its takeover of the oil companies' operations after the lapse of concessions. Also, it initiated the basic inorganic chemical industry when it decided to exploit its salt deposits for chemical use. No doubt it did this not only to keep this industry under its control, but also because the low profitability and heavy investment required discouraged private investment.

The growth of chemical production in Colombia has been rapid, well above the average for manufacturing as a whole. It averaged 19% per annum in the period 1953-67. The plants producing chemical products are shown in detail in Table 10-1 where they are listed by company, product, annual capacity, location, initial year of production, number of employees, value of production, and local and imported raw materials. The table has been divided to indicate the plants which are producing predominantly basic chemicals, those producing fertilizers and those in the petrochemical sector. Table 10-2 shows the expansion projects which are firmly committed.

Basic Chemicals

This industry is dominated by the two large government-owned enterprises, Planta de Soda and Concesion de Salinas, which are interdependent in that the Concesion de Salinas supplies the salt and raw material to the Planta de Soda for production of the basic soda alkali chemicals.

Concesion de Salinas has production facilities at Zipaquira, about 35 miles north of Bogota where it extracts salt by underground mining. The salt is dissolved at the pit head and transported as a brine to the Planta de Soda facilities 5 km. away. This salt mine has a production capacity

175

Table 10-1: MAJOR CHEMICAL PLANTS

Company	Product	Annual Capacity 1969 (metric tons)	Location	Initial Year of Production	Employees	Value of Production 1969 in million $[1]	Raw Materials Imported	Local
1. Basic Chemical								
Planta Colombiana de Soda	Soda Ash	89,600[2]	Betania and	1953 (Betania)	925 (Betania)	3.2	(	Salt
	Caustic Soda	43,400	Cartagena[1]	1964 (Cartagena)	1,397 (Cartagena)	4.8	(	Limestone
	Chlorine	12,000				0.5	(	
	Sodium Bicarbonate	2,900			61 Bogota	0.2	(	
	Refined Salt	193,000	Betania			4.03	(	
Concesion de Salinas	Rock Salt	250,000	Zipaquira	Colonial Times	400	n. a.	(	
	Solar Salt	350,000	Manaure	1940	400	n. a.	(	
	Refined Salt	193,000	Betania		(260 elsewhere)	7.2		
2. Fertilizer								
Amocar	Ammonia	100,000	Cartagena	1963	40	n. a.		Natural Gas
Abonos Colombianos	Urea	75,000	Cartagena	1963	350	12.5		Ammonia
	Mixed Fertilizer	125,000					Phosphate Rock	
Caja Agraria	Mixed Fertilizer	300,000	3 Plants		600	9.2	Potash	Various Fertilizers
Sulfacidos	Mixed Fertilizer and Sulphuric Acid	100,000		n. a.	n. a.	n. a.	Phosphate Rock	Sulphur
Paz del Rio	Thomas Rock	50,000	Belencito	n. a.	60	n. a.	(By product of blast furnace)	
Quia SA	Mixed Fertilizer	25,000		n. a.	n. a.	n. a.		Sulphur
Fertilizantes Colombiana	Urea	16,000	Barranca	1954	300	n. a.		Natural Gas
	Ammonium Nitrate	42,000						
Other Mixers	Mixed Fertilizer	60,000	Various	n. a.	n. a.	n. a.		Various Fertilizers
3. Petrochemicals								
Cia Quimica Borden	(	(	Cali				(	
Cyanamid de Colombia	(Formaldehyde	(15,800	Cartagena	n. a.	n. a.	n. a.	(Methanol	
Quimica Proco	(	(	Medellin				(	

Company	Product	Capacity	Location	Year			Raw Material	Raw Material
Cia Quimica Borden	Phenol-Formaldehyde Resins	4,000[4]	Cali		n. a.	n. a.	Phenol	Formaldehyde
Quimica Proco			Medellin					
Cia Quimica Borden	Urea-Formaldehyde Resins	5,300[5]	Cali		n. a.	n. a.		Urea and Formaldehyde
Quimica Proco			Medellin					
Cynamid	Malamin-Formaldehyde Resins	800[6]	Cartagena				Melamine	Formaldehyde
Colcarburos	Vinyl Chloride Monomer	8,000	Cajica	1967	n. a.	n. a.		Acetylene and Hydrochloric Acid
Colcarburos	PVC	7,500	Cajica	1967	n. a.	n. a.		Vinyl Chloride Monomer
Petroquimica Colombiana	PVC	5,500	Cartagena	1965	100	2.6	Vinyl Chloride	
Dow Chemical	Polystyrene	3,700	Cartagena	1965	40	n. a.	Styrene	
Carboquimica	Phthallic Anhydride	2,500	Bogota	1962	n. a.	n. a.	Naphthalene and Orthoxylene	Naphthalene[8]
Andercol	Phthallic Anhydride	1,800	Medellin	1968	n. a.	n. a.	Orthoxylene	
Phillips Negro de Humo	Carbon Black	10,000	Cali	1968	50	1.0[9]		Aromatic Oil
Cabot Colombiana	Carbon Black	10,000	Cartagena	1965	77	2.0		Aromatic Oil
Several	Detergents	55,000	Several	–	n. a.	n. a.	DDB and TDB	
Ecopetrol	Sulphur	10,000	Barranca	1967	n. a.	n. a.		Refinery Gases
Intercol	Sulphur	4,000	Cartagena	1965	n. a.	n. a.		Refinery Gases

Note: See Table 10-2 for footnotes.

Table 10-2: CHEMICAL EXPANSION PROJECTS

Company	Product	Annual Capacity (metric tons)	Location	Year Expansion Complete	New Employees	Additional value of Production (US$ million)	Raw materials Imported	Raw materials Local
1. Basic Chemicals								
Planta Colombiana de Soda	Soda Ash	278,800[11]	Cartagena and	1972	1,400	6.0		Salt
	Caustic Soda	109,000[11]	Betania	1972		6.9		Limestone
	Chlorine	49,720[11]		1972		1.0		
	Sodium Bicarbonate	33,600[11]		1972		2.1		
	Sodium Sulfate	2,800[11]		1971		0.5		
	Refined Salt	360,000[11]		1975		2.9[3]		
	Solar Salt	350,000	Manaure	1971		n.a.		
Concesion de Salinas	Solar Salt	1.4-1.8 million	Bahia Honda	1974	100-200	4.0 (average)		
2. Fertilizers								
Monomeros Colombo Ven.	Mixed fertilizer	200,000	B'Quilla	1971	375 [7]	17.6 [7]	Ammonia, potash phosphate rock	Cyclohexane
3. Petrochemicals								
Ecopetrol	Ethylene	20,000	Barranca	1969	n.a.	n.a.	Refinery gases	
Ecopetrol	Propylene	10,000	Barranca	1969	n.a.	n.a.	Refinery gases	
Ecopetrol	Benzene	40,000	Barranca	1970	n.a.	n.a.	Virgin Naptha	
Ecopetrol	Orthoxylene	8,000	Barranca	1970	n.a.	n.a.	Virgin Naptha	
Ecopetrol	Paraxylene	17,000	Barranca	1972	n.a.	n.a.	Virgin Naptha	
Ecopetrol	Mixed Iylenes	16,000	Barranca	1970	n.a.	n.a.	Virgin Naptha	
Policolsa	Polyethylene	15,000	Barranca	1969	n.a.	8.3	Ethylene	
Not defined	Polypropylene	10,000	Barranca	–	–	–	Propylene	

Company	Product	Capacity	Location	Year			Raw material
Ecopetrol	Cyclohexane	20,000	Barranca	1970	n.a.	n.a.	Benzene
Ecopetrol	Tetramer	16,000	Barranca	1970	n.a.	n.a.	Propylene
Ecopetrol	Detergent Alkylate	15,000	Barranca	1972	n.a.	n.a.	Tetramer & Benzene
Monomeros Colombo Venezolanos	Caprolactam	16,500	B'Quilla	1970	375	17.6	Cyclohexane, sulphuric acid (and imported Ammonia)
Not defined	DMT	24,000	Not defined	1972	145	14.0	Paraxylene (and imported Methand)
Carboquimica	Phthallic Anhydride	4,000	B'Quilla	1971	n.a.	n.a.	Orthoxylene
Andercol	Phthallic Anhydride	2,500	B'Quilla	1972	n.a.	n.a.	Orthoxylene

[1]Conversion rate used, 18 pesos = $1.

[2]Some 47,200 tons of soda ash are consumed by Planta de Soda itself to produce caustic soda and sodium bicarbonate.

[3]This represents the "fee" charged by Planta de Soda for refining salt to nutritional standard for sale by Concesion de Salinas.

[4]The capacity consists of 2,000 tons liquid and 2,000 tons of molding powders.

[5]The capacity consists of 4,000 tons of liquid resin and 1,300 tons of powder.

[6]The capacity consists of 400 tons liquids and 400 tons solids.

[7]Figures are total for plant including fertilizers and caprolactam.

[8]Part of the naphthalene is imported.

[9]Although the same capacity as the Cabot plant, Phillips produced at only 50% of capacity in 1969.

[10]Indicates value of production when new capacity is fully utilized.

[11]Indicates total capacity when expansion is complete.

n. a. = not available

of 250,000 tons per year. It reached this capacity within the last five years and has been in operation since colonial times. Because of the high cost of extracting salt by mining methods and the relatively large amount of impurities, it is unlikely that this facility will be expanded in the future.

Concesion de Salinas also produces salt by solar evaporation on the dry north coast of Colombia at Manaure, some 300 km northeast of Cartagena. Its present production is 350,000 tons per year but it is just completing an expansion program which will raise the production to 705,000 tons per year. This area of Colombia is remarkable for the hot dry winds and long hours of sunshine that prevail most of the year. It is a semi-desert area and because of its low-lying coast line, ideally suited to the production of salt by solar evaporation.

The salt is presently harvested half by mechanical means and half by some 2,000 to 3,000 workers. The expanded capacity will be worked entirely by mechanical harvesting. A 700 meter wharf has been built at Manaure to load the three 1,600 ton ships owned by Planta de Soda which carry salt down to the latter's Cartagena plant. The ships return under ballast and make the round trip in about ten days. Planta de Soda has ordered another three 2,000 ton vessels to handle the expanded salt supply.

Planta de Soda built its first plant at Betania, about 30 km north of Bogota, to use the salt from the Zipaquira deposit. The plant steadily expanded as the demands of the country increased. In 1964 a new plant was built in Cartagena as it was realized that the cost of the solar salt would be much lower than that of the mined salt. The Cartagena plant has also expanded as demand increased and is currently undergoing a major construction program which will be completed in 1971.

Both chemical production facilities are characterized by a large number of small capacity production units. This defeats any possibility of their achieving economies of scale, although their total capacity is well in line with the capacities of plants in industrial countries. Expansion by bigger, less frequent steps would have been better but this policy was deliberately avoided partly to maximize the number of jobs that could be provided.

Table 10-3 shows the present production configuration of the two plants and of the Cartagena plant as it will be in 1971.

The plants provide their own power and water. Table 10-4 indicates the large installed capacity of electric power as well as the raw material requirements. Water supply for the Cartagena plant will require a new facility, which will form the basis for expanding the water supplies for the Cartagena region in general.

Until recently both companies were nominally under the direction of the Banco de la Republica. They have now been transferred to IFI, which will be responsible for their management and operation in the future. There are indications that IFI will try to run the two

Table 10-3: DAILY PRODUCTION OF PLANTA DE SODA'S
PLANTS AT BETANIA AND CARTAGENA

Product	Daily Production (Metric Tons)		
	Betania	Cartagena	
	1969	1969	1971
Soda Ash	100	250	750
Caustic Soda	32	70	140
Caustic Soda (Rayon grade)	38	–	120
Chlorine	35	–	108
Sodium Bicarbonate	10	–	80
Hydrochloric Acid	11	–	20
Iodized Salt	500	–	250
Sodium Sulfate	14	–	–

Table 10-4: PRESENT AND ANTICIPATED DAILY REQUIREMENTS
OF PLANTA DE SODA'S PLANTS

Raw Materials and Services	Daily Requirements (Metric tons)		
	Betania	Cartagena	
	1969	1969	1971
Salt	730	500	1,500
Limestone	250	600	1,300
Fresh Water	4,800	10,000	19,000
Steam (installed capacity)	3,000	2,880	5,520
Electric Power (KW of installed capacity)	10,000	7,000	37,000

enterprises on modern business lines and already a modern financial management system has been introduced in Planta de Soda. It is to be hoped that the operation of these two companies can be modernized and streamlined as they both are important factors in the chemical industry of Colombia.

Fertilizers

Of the three basic materials produced by the fertilizer industry: nitrogen (N), phosphate (P_2O_5), and potash (K_2O), Colombia has no resources of potash. A phosphate deposit is being investigated with a view to its economic exploitation. There is a modern ammonia/urea complex (the Amocar/Abocol facility) supplying a good portion of the nitrogen requirements, and with the completion of the Monomeros plant Colombia should be self-sufficient for its nitrogen requirements.

For the immediate future phosphates and potash will continue to be imported. These are presently imported either as raw materials, such as phosphate rock and straight potash, or as constituents of fertilizers ready-mixed—either chemically or physically—such as triple super-phosphate, diammonium phosphate, or even combined NPK fertilizers.

A comparison has been made of the demand for fertilizer in Colombia with the capacity for production in 1971 when the Monomeros plant will be complete. Unfortunately, this has been made on the basis of the number of gross tons of mixed fertilizer rather than the number of tons of nutrient (it is obvious that if the percentage of nutrient in a mixed fertilizer is increased, less gross tons are required to supply the same amount of nutrient). The comparison shows the potential for over-capacity in the industry. On the basis of the 8% growth rate that has prevailed from 1963 to 1968 for mixed fertilizer, it can be predicted that 450,000 tons would be demanded in 1971. In that year the total installed capacity for producing mixed fertilizer either from local finishing (imported phosphate rock and potash and local nitrogen) or from finished imported fertilizers (eg. DAP, TSP, etc.,) will be 950,000 tons. The capacity for producing mixed fertilizer only from local or imported raw materials would be about 500,000 tons. The over-capacity of 450,000 tons arises because the Caja Agraria and the other mixing companies have mixing, bagging and distribution equipment with which they presently process imported finished fertilizers. These companies are already showing a tendency to use locally produced fertilizer for further mixing, bagging, and distribution. It is not clear whether an extension of this step or a continuance of importing mixed fertilizer is the most economical way of meeting Colombia's future requirements. This is one of the reasons why a preinvestment study has been recommended for Colombia's fertilizer industry.

The *Amocar/Abocol* facilities located at Cartagena are an operation of the Standard Oil Company (Esso). The ammonia plant is located on the site of the Esso refinery and it pipes the ammonia to the Abocol facilities about 2 km away. The Abocol plant consists of a urea, a nitric acid, and a mixed fertilizer plant. The phosphate and potash raw materials are imported. The facilities were built in 1963 and are as modern as were obtainable at that time. They have been well maintained and modernized where possible and the management appears extremely efficient and capable.

In addition to its well run production facilities, Abocol also is developing a modern marketing department. It has relied on the distribution facilities of the Caja Agraria and the other mixers, but because of their lack of aggressive marketing, it has decided to develop its own marketing department. It has therefore hired 18 agronomists to provide extension services and recommend fertilizer use to the farmers.

The *Monomeros* facility is primarily a producer of caprolactam—a nylon intermediate. Its fertilizer production is a result of having to dispose of the ammonium sulfate by-product from the caprolactam process. Using the Dutch State Mines process, this can be accomplished with the production of high analysis complex fertilizers. Imports of phosphate rock and potash will be necessary for this process.

The Monomeros plant is expected to be in production in mid-1971. The company has all the elements to be a successful and competitive producer of fertilizer with its young modern management staff, its modern production facilities, and technical backup from Dutch State Mines which has a 10% equity in the company.

The *Caja Agraria* is not a producer of nutrients, but merely mixes, blends, and distributes imported and domestically produced fertilizer materials. It has three mixing plants, the largest of which is near Bogota. It distributes the fertilizer through 12 regional warehouses and approximately 400 retail stores. These stores also supply other farm inputs such as seed, tools, fuel, clothing, etc., and are ideally suited to become centers for extension services.

Petrochemicals

There are two centers of petrochemical production in Colombia which have developed naturally around the two oil refineries in Cartagena and Barrancabermeja.

The *Cartagena* area, known as Mamonal, is located about 10 km south of the city along the shore of the Cartagena bay. This is protected water and relatively deep so that Mamonal is ideally suited to export-oriented industries. At present there are three petrochemical plants in this area receiving feed stocks from the Intercol refinery. There are also three plants which at present depend on imported raw materials and which are really conversion plants, most of

Table 10-5: CHEMICAL PLANTS IN THE MAMONAL AREA, INVESTMENT AND LABOR FORCE

Company	Product	Investment US dollars million	People Employed
Planta de Soda	Soda Alkali	100	1,450
Intercol	Refinery	78	660
Abocol	Fertilizer	12.5	350
Petroquimica	PVC	8	100
Cabot	Carbon Black	3	77
Dow	Polystyrene	2	40
Cyanamid	Formaldehyde Resins	3	50
		207	2,727

them producing polymers from imported monomer. Table 10-5 lists these plants with the invested capital and people employed.

The Intercol refinery, built in 1958 when Esso had to give up its Barranca refinery, has a capacity for 48,000 barrels per day (b/d) crude oil with a catalytic cracking unit of 25,000 barrels per day. It is currently producing the following products:

LPG	350 b/d
Jet fuel	1,000 b/d
Kerosene	4,500 b/d
Diesel oil	7,000 b/d
Regular gasoline	12,000 b/d
Premium gasoline	3,000 b/d
Fuel oil	13,000–18,000 b/d
Sulfur	4.5 tons per day

In addition to its refining activities, it is also a terminal for crude oil lines from the oil fields and has extensive bunkering and loading facilities. (Ecopetrol also has a terminal in this area.)

The facilities of Petroquimica Colombiana were originally established to receive imported vinyl chloride monomer from which polyvinyl chloride (PVC) was produced. In a typical backward integration step this plant will now take naphtha from the Intercol refinery and chlorine from the Planta de Soda to produce monomer from these local materials. Although its capacity is small—at present 17 million pounds per year PVC—the company will use a new process which is reputed to be adaptable to these small capacities. This so-called "Dianor" process produces small amounts of ethylene by cracking naphtha and immediately converting it to ethylene dichloride (EDC), without the need for purifying the ethylene which is normally done in large capacity processes. The EDC is then converted to monomer and then to PVC.

Petroquimica expects to be able to expand to 35 million pounds per year PVC and has also been able to conclude a 5-year export contract with Japan for 50 million pounds of EDC. This is a remarkable export breakthrough. In exporting EDC the company will produce hydrochloric acid as a by-product. Only because Planta de Soda is able to accept the hydrochloric acid has the deal been possible. Petroquimica is also helping to develop export sales for both vinyl chloride and polymer.

The Dow plant produces polystyrene from imported styrene monomer. It has a capacity of 3,700 tons per year and is presently being expanded to 6,000 tons per year. The imported raw material is from a Dow plant on the U.S. Gulf Coast. Although the original plant took five years to reach its capacity, Dow has now developed export sales and feels justified in making its expansion. However, the future of styrene production is somewhat uncertain as styrene has been allocated to Peru under the Andean Pact.

The Cabot carbon black paint receives its aromatic tar feed stock from the refinery and was the only producer of carbon black in Colombia, until the new Phillips plant at Cali was opened. The other resin producer in Mamonal—Cyanamid—is a small plant relying on imported raw materials. The combined capacity of the three small formaldehyde plants is clearly well below the typical size—30,000 to 100,000 tons per year—of modern formaldehyde plants.

Barrancabermeja.   Although the Mamonal area is now the most developed center for petro-chemicals, it will soon be overtaken by the construction of plants around the Ecopetrol refinery in Barrancabermeja. These facilities are all being developed by Ecopetrol either alone or in association with other companies and are forward integration steps rather than backward integration. In other words, the plant which has been predominantly a fuel supplier will be expanded to convert the fuels to petrochemical intermediates (and in some cases finished products) which will be shipped to other parts of the country for further processing.

The refinery has a capacity of 85,000 barrels per day of crude but a current expansion will increase this to 100,000 b/d. It started operations in 1930 as a plant of Intercol. In 1951 the operating concession expired, and Intercol continued running the refinery under a management contract until 1961. At that time Ecopetrol took over the complete operation. The plant consists of a number of production units which have resulted from the continual expansion of the facilities. The main units in the plant are crude distillation, catalytic cracking plants, an alkylation unit and an aviation gasoline plant. When the current round of expansion is completed, there will also be a lubricating oil plant, an aromatics unit, a paraffin wax plant, and a polyethylene plant. The most significant petrochemical items are mentioned below.

The aromatics plant which is currently being completed will produce the following products.

	tons per annum
Benzene	21,000
Cyclohexane	21,000
Orthoxylene	6,000
Ethylbenzene	9,500
Meta and paraxylene	29,000

These products are all destined for conversion in Colombia to caprolactam, dodecylbenzene (for detergent), phthallic anhydride, styrene, and DMT. Benzene will also be exported and will find other minor applications. The investment cost for the plant is US$15 million.

The polyethylene plant is being built in collaboration with Dow Chemical and will have a capacity of 15,000 tons per year of low density polyethylene. It will be based on ethylene produced from cracked gas streams in the refinery. This is an extremely small capacity (modern plants produce as much as 60,000 tons polyethylene and up to 500,000 tons ethylene). However, it will convert into a more useful product a gas stream which would otherwise be used as a fuel.

The paraffin wax plant is designed to produce 122 million pounds per year of different melting point waxes. Of the production, 45% will be for 125-129° Fahrenheit wax and 35% will be 133-135° Fahrenheit wax. It will also produce lube oil base materials which will enable Colombia to produce high grade lubricating oils. The plant cost will be about US$15 million and is expected to save US$6.8 million of present imports and generate $10 million per year of exports. About 65% of paraffin and 50% of the lube basis will be exported.

Other Petrochemical Plants: Cali.   The Phillips plant producing carbon black is owned

100% by Phillips Petroleum Corporation of the United States and was completed in 1967. The plant has built up its production slowly as it has had to have its product accepted by the tire producers, who—as is normal—have taken about two years to thoroughly test and prove a new supply before they will accept it. The Phillips plant is therefore only now beginning to operate at its capacity. It has also started export sales and it expects in 1970 to export as much as 50% of its production. This will be mostly to Peru and Chile, which are both currently using about 8 million pounds per year.

One of the biggest problems of the Phillips plant is the transportation of its raw material from the Ecopetrol refinery some 400 miles to the north. At present the aromatic tar is barged to Cartagena, then shipped by tanker via the Panama Canal to Buenaventura, and then delivered by rail tank car to Cali. This results in an increase in the price of Col$38.50 per barrel at the refinery to Col$78.50 per barrel by the time it is delivered. Phillips hopes that when the new west coast refinery is completed they will be supplied from it, thus doing away with transportation problems.

Comparison of Colombian and International Chemical Prices

A comparison of prices in the chemical industry is quite difficult. Throughout the world it has many prices for the identical product, probably because there has been less elaboration of the middle-man institutions than in other industries. In chemicals, the production chain from primary raw materials to consumer goods started with integrated companies which control their own internal transfer prices to suit their own business. Participation of other companies at various points in the production chain is a phenomenon of the last 10-15 years in this industry, which itself is very new. The merchant prices for intermediate goods usually result from special deals. Only recently has the point been reached in a few items where sellers and buyers are numerous enough to make competition a major price-determining factor.

This pricing problem, already complicated within any one country, becomes even more so when exports are considered. Traditionally, exports of intermediate chemicals have been unplanned surplus production which could not be disposed of in the domestic market and which was sold on a basis of marginal costing. This has resulted in virtually dumping prices in international trade, and exports are sold at much lower prices than those in the domestic markets of the exporting countries.

These factors should be borne in mind in evaluating the specific prices shown below. (Colombian prices in pesos are converted to dollars at a rate of 18 to 1. All tons are metric tons).

Basic Chemicals.   The following price comparison is based on the Planta de Soda price list and listed prices shown in chemical trade journals (U.S. cents per pound).

Product	Colombia Domestic	Colombia Export	USA	Germany	UK	France
Caustic soda (45%)	2.4	–	–	–	–	–
Caustic soda (50%)	2.7	–	3.3	–	–	–
Caustic soda (73%)	4.3	–	3.4	–	–	–
Caustic soda (98%)	5.7	–	–	4.6	4.3	3.1
Caustic soda – flakes	9.8	–	5.8	–	–	–
Soda ash, dense, bulk	2.9	1.8	1.7	2.5	1.5	1.7
Soda ash, dense, in bags	3.0	2.2	2.2	–	–	–
Soda ash, light	3.0	2.6	2.2	–	–	–
Sodium bicarbonate	3.2	3.1	3.4-4.0	–	–	–
Chlorine water treatment	2.1	–	–	–	–	–
Chlorine, liquid	2.9	–	3.8-7.6	3.5	3.5	3.4
Hydrochloric acid, carboys	2.0	–	–	–	–	–
Hydrochloric acid, tanks	1.8	–	1.0-1.8	1.6	1.5	1.1
Sodium sulfide (62%)	12.9	7.5	7.0	–	–	7.9

Polyethylene   The current selling price for imported polyethylene in Colombia is 10 pesos/kg (US ¢ 25 per lb.), and the polyethylene project in Ecopetrol and Dow will sell its product at this price; average selling prices in the United States and Europe are 12 ¢ to 17 ¢ per lb. depending on the grade. The film grades are the cheaper quality, and price for any one grade would vary between 1¢ and 1.5 ¢ per lb. among different manufacturers. Adding 25% to this price for freight and handling one arrives at an average c.i.f. price (without duty) of 15¢ to 21 ¢ per lb.

The feed stock of the ethylene plant is essentially fuel gas from the refinery which Ecopetrol values at Col$3 per million BTU. This is equivalent to 16.5 US ¢ per million BTU which is considerably lower than the 20 ¢ to 40 ¢ paid by US Gulf Coast ethylene producers for their natural gas feed stocks. It is indicative of the uneconomic size of the polyethylene plant that despite these low cost inputs (50% of cost), it has to sell its product up to 40% over the c.i.f. cost of the product from overseas. Ecopetrol stated that the biggest factor in the production cost of ethylene is the amortization of the capital cost of the plant.

Naphtha.   The Ecopetrol aromatics plant has not yet started up and no price policy for the products has yet been announced. They expect to sell at about the c.i.f. price of imported equivalents, and as the plant is of a reasonable size, this should be possible. In addition the feed stock—virgin naphtha—has a transfer price of 4 ¢ to 4.5 ¢ per US gallon. This would average US$15.6 per metric ton which is low in comparison with the $19 to $24 per metric ton paid in the industrialized countries for naphtha used for petrochemical feed stock.

PVC.   The selling price for PVC in Colombia is claimed to be the lowest in Latin America at 20¢ per lb., compared with prices in Argentina, Peru and Mexico of 40 ¢ per lb. The US selling price is between 13 ¢ and 15¢ per lb. and adding 25% for freight and handling would give a c.i.f. value without duty of 17.5 ¢ per lb., only moderately lower than the Colombian selling price.

Carbon Black.   A domestic producer gave these prices for carbon black in US cents per lb. on a c.i.f. basis:

Colombian customer	14.5
Chile, Peru	10−14
Ecuador	9−13

Freight costs in US cents per pound were given as:

Cali − Peru	1.25
Cali − Chile	1.75
Cali − Costa Rica	2.5
Cali − Buenaventura	0.3
Cali − Bogota	1.0

On the basis of the above information, and taking into account trade discounts, it can be calculated that the average price f.o.b. the plant is about 10.2 ¢ per lb.

Carbon black prices in the United States are quoted over a range from 5.75 ¢ to 10.75 ¢ per lb. depending on grade and whether the delivery is in bulk or in bags. These prices are on an f.o.b. plant basis in car lot quantities. (Adding 25% for freight and handling would make the equivalent c.i.f. value of US carbon black in Colombia 7.2 ¢ to 13.4 ¢ per lb., as compared to the Colombian price of 10.2¢ per lb.)

Fertilizer   Abocol stated that they are selling fertilizer at domestic prices equivalent to prices in the USA. On the basis of annual sales and annual production in 1968 their average selling price was Col$1,460 per metric ton of product. This would be equal to US$81 per ton. Abocol produces high analysis complex fertilizer grades.

Monomeros are planning to sell their complex fertilizer domestically at Col$1,150 (US$61 per ton) and export initially about half of it at Col$1,000 (US$55). Their grades will vary from 20:20:0 to 14:14:14, i.e., high analysis fertilizers.

The Abocol and Monomeros prices compare well with the manufacturing cost for equivalents based on international prices for N, P and K. Thus, urea is selling f.o.b. Europe and USA for $50 per ton (range $45-$60). A 20:20:0 blend would cost $58 per ton to produce, and a 14:14:14 blend $46 per ton. Freight costs to Colombia for these products would be $10-20 per ton. These prices may be summarized:

	Landed Price Imports	($/ton)	Colombian Prices
Urea	55-80	Abocol average	81
20:20:0	68-78	Monomeros average	61 domestic
14:14:14	56-66		55 export

The Caja Agraria sells fertilizer at the import cost plus duty, transportation and blending costs with a surcharge of 10% for administration and overhead costs. According to the AID study of the fertilizer industry, the principal grade produced by the Caja is 5:20:12 which was selling in Bogota in 1969 for Col$1,480 per ton, a high price for a relatively low-grade fertilizer. The Caja as the price setter in the Colombian fertilizer industry, thus, has distorted the selling prices of the other grades. A corresponding US price in pesos for this grade of fertilizer varied from 1,330 in 1958 to 1,280 in 1967 and 1,000 in 1969.

In terms of current pesos, fertilizer prices have increased almost 50% since 1964, the year domestic production of fertilizer first became important. Using the wholesale price index as a deflator, the 1969 prices would be at about the same level as the 1964 prices. The deflated prices reached a peak in 1965 and have decreased since then, probably as a result of the increasing efficiency of the major Colombian producers, and the decrease in price of imports.

Future Prospects

The chemical industry appears to have run out of obvious opportunities for import substitution in the near future. The major exception is the fertilizer industry. There are good prospects for development of export-oriented industries. Their realization depends to a significant extent on future cooperation in the Andean Common Market.

Basic Chemicals.   When the current construction program of Planta de Soda is completed, Colombia will be well supplied with basic inorganic chemicals and will need to export considerable tonnages of soda ash (25,000 tons), chlorine (1,000 tons), sodium bicarbonate (25,000 tons), and sodium sulfate (800 tons). These exports would be made in the face of stiff international competition and would probably be profitable only on a marginal basis.

A most important future development is the large solar salt project being developed by Concesion de Salinas, for export. This would be located at Bahia Honda, which is practically the most northern point of Colombia. It would initially produce 1.4 to 1.8 million tons per year of salt. It could be expanded later to somewhere between 2 to 4 million tons per year. In the first stage the production cost is expected to be US$2.20-$2.50 per ton f.o.b., and after expansion this could fall to something below US$2.00 per ton.

The construction cost for the first stage is expected to be about US$20 million including civil works, storage facilities, mechanical harvesting equipment, power plant, housing, and a wharf suitable for ships from 40,000 to 100,000 tons, all adapted to later expansion. As the project is necessarily export-oriented, Concesion de Salinas is holding preliminary discussions with potential buyers in an attempt to work out long-term purchase contracts.

The French firm Saline du Midi is preparing an engineering preinvestment study of the salt facility and a local engineering company has prepared a study on the port. This would be followed by a one-year field trial to test evaporation and seepage rates for the proposed evaporation ponds. It would then be possible for a complete appraisal to be made and, if the project is approved, initial construction could be completed in one more year. Allowing a further year for the initial evaporation, the first products could be available in 3 to 4 years.

Fertilizer Industry   Although consumption of fertilizers has grown at 7.5% annually during 1955-69, the level of fertilizer use is still low. In 1968, about 22% of the land in annual crops received fertilizer, and 16% of that in perennial crops. Apparently, Colombia has not kept up with the rest of South America in the use of fertilizer: between 1964 and 1968 its percentage share of South American fertilizer use fell from 15% to 7% according to an FAO study.

From discussions with industry leaders it appears that the main reason for low fertilizer use is insufficient reliable data on past crop response to fertilizer use, the best types of fertilizer to use or the optimum price levels.

A long-term, preinvestment study has therefore been proposed to make a country-wide review of the fertilizer industry. Its initial focus would be on the existing practice and results of fertilizer use. It would also examine the current distribution chain and the price-cost structure of getting fertilizer to the farmer. Then by determining cost-output ratios for farm production it would attempt to develop use projections for the future. This, together with a look at sources of raw materials and existing plants would be a basis for proposing projects to supply additional fertilizer. These projects would hopefully be integrated schemes including production, distribution and transportation facilities. The study would also recommend needed institutional changes.

Petrochemical Industry   The future of the petrochemical industry in Colombia beyond the present expansion plans appears to be intimately connected with the development of the industry in the Andean Group. The negotiations for the establishment of this common market have reached the point where the first tariff reductions have been implemented and there are hopeful prospects that it will continue. In petrochemicals in particular there have been considerable discussions and agreement in principle has been reached among the nations and their national oil companies. Although the general directions are clear and even some allocations of specific products can be made now, there is no comprehensive basis currently available for rationally deciding how much and where the petrochemical products should be produced. For this reason a preinvestment study is proposed. It would cover marketing projections, feed stock sources, existing production units, freight rates, and financial requirements. Its point of immediate focus could be the location of a petrochemical complex to be based on a large (100,000-200,000 tons per year) ethylene plant.

CHAPTER 11

REGIONAL STRUCTURE OF INDUSTRY

Unlike other Latin American countries where the bulk of industrial production is concentrated in one city, in Colombia it is distributed among four major urban centers and several smaller industrial cities. The process of industrialization has developed along the lines of the country's four distinct regions: the Atlantic Coast, centered in Barranquilla; the southwest in Cali; the northwest in Medellin; and the center in Bogota. All cities except Barranquilla, which grew as a trading center, have developed as centers for regions rich in agricultural or mining resources. Two of the characteristics of Colombian industry, therefore—fragmentation of a small market for industrial goods, and a tendency towards small and frequently unutilized capacities—are closely related to industrial location. At the same time, the country has avoided the disadvantages of extremely large urban agglomerations typical of many developing countries.

Location of Industry

Geographic and political considerations have been important in bringing about the existing pattern of industrial location in Colombia. First, the mountainous topography of the country has made transportation difficult and costly. Second, rural unrest during the 1940s and 1950s caused regional markets to become even more inaccessible to the products of other areas and resulted in regional concentration of large industrial investments. Third, industrial location decisions have been determined almost entirely by the private sector. The relative isolation of the cities has caused each region to develop a local entrepreneurial class, which has invested in the regional center surplus capital available from regional primary activities.

Table 11-1 shows the distribution of manufacturing output and employment by major departments and cities. In 1967, the last year for which comprehensive data are available, about 79% of value-added in manufacturing and approximately 82% of employment in manufacturing originated in the departments where the four main industrial cities are located. Sixty-seven per cent of manufacturing value-added and 71% of manufacturing employment was generated in the four cities themselves. Since data for satellite cities, which surround industrial cities, are not included in city data, departmental figures are generally more meaningful. The difference between figures for the city of Cali and the corresponding Department of Valle, however, derives from the importance of the sugar industry in that department's figures. While Barranquilla contributes only 8% of national industrial value-added and 9% of Colombian industrial employment, its importance derives from the fact that the city is the industrial center for the entire northern coast. Within the city of Barranquilla, the manufacturing sector accounts for 50% of total employment.

Industry in Colombia has thus been concentrated near the several major markets for manufactured goods. In 1964, 45% of the population lived in the four above-mentioned departments where the main industrial centers are located. Together, these departments generated about 50% of the gross domestic product of the country. Figures are even higher if neighboring departments are taken into account.In the sixties, industry has become more concentrated in the four major departments. While national industrial production grew at an average annual rate of 5.8% from 1960 to 1967, the four major departments as a group grew at the rate of 6.5%. Cundinamarca and Valle, where the new capital and intermediate goods industries have been located, grew at more rapid rates, as indicated in the summary table (Table 11-2). (Growth has been calculated on the basis of gross value of output data because of the difficulties associated with measuring changes in valued-added. In the static discussions of the regional structure of industry, however, value-added data were used.)

In addition to Bogota, Medellin, Cali, and Barranquilla, Colombia has several other industrial centers of significance. The cities of Bucaramanga, Cartagena, Manizales, and Pereira are the largest. The Department of Boyaca has some industrial production partly based on Acerias Paz del Rio, the only integrated steel mill in the country, but otherwise Boyaca has not developed a significant industrial center.

Table 11-1: VALUE-ADDED AND EMPLOYMENT IN MANUFACTURING BY MAJOR DEPARTMENTS AND CITIES, 1967

	Value Added Col$ millions	% of national value added in manufacturing	Manufacturing employment	% of national employment in manufacturing	Population '000's
Cundinamarca of which:	4,172.9	27.1	88,861	30.2	3,234
Bogota	3,537.1	23.0	74,442	25.3	
Antioquia of which:	3,590.8	23.3	74,259	25.2	2,793
Medellin	3,372.2	21.9	67,109	22.8	
Valle of which:	3,076.1	20.0	50,597	17.2	1,940
Cali	2,462.6	15.9	41,479	14.1	
Atlantico of which:	1,285.4	8.2	26,809	9.1	804
Barranquilla	1,173.0	7.6	24,274	8.3	
Sub-total (four major Departments)	12,098.2	78.6	240,526	81.7	8,771
Other	3,308.6	21.4	53,299	18.3	10,829
National Total	14,406.8	100.0	293,825	100.0	19,600

Note: City figures include production in the main industrial suburbs. The figures for Cali include industrial production in Palmira.

Source: Unpublished DANE data.

Structure of Manufacturing Industries in the Major Industrial Centers

The structure of industrial production in the major departments is generally similar, as can be seen in Table 11-3, indicating no dominant industrial specialization among Colombia's several regions.

However, certain industries are more heavily concentrated in some departments than in others, as shown in Table 11-4. The department with the greatest degree of specialization is Antioquia (center: Medellin) where 70% of Colombian textiles are produced. Textiles, moreover, account for 34% of industrial production in the department and 13% of national industrial production.

Processed chemical industries which have in the past been concentrated in Bogota, have in recent years grown fastest in Cali, which in 1967 produced about 28% of all chemicals in Colombia. Value-added in the Cali chemical industry grew at the rate of about 18% between 1958 and 1966.

Cali is also the country's major producer of paper products; about 62% of the national value-added in paper originates in that city, which is supplied by the wood industry in the Departments of Cauca and Narino, South of Cali.

The electrical machinery industry has been marked by a tendency toward concentration in Bogota. In 1967, Bogota produced about 51% (in terms of value) of all electrical equipment in Colombia. A large proportion of the automotive industry—consisting of two assembly plants—is also located in the capital. However, the trend toward concentration of the automotive industry in Bogota will probably be reversed with completion of the new Renault plant in Medellin and the start of production in 1971. Electrical machinery production represents 5% of industrial value-added in Bogota, and the automotive industry close to 6%.

There are two types of medium-industrialized centers in Colombia. Cities, such as Bucaramanga, Cartagena and Barrancabermeja, are highly specialized, in that industrial production

Table 11-2: GROWTH OF GROSS VALUE OF OUTPUT IN MAJOR DEPARTMENTS

	1960	1967	Average Annual growth
	(In millions of 1968 Col $)		(%)
Cundinamarca (Bogota)	6,772.4	10,935.0	7.1
Antioquia (Medellin)	5,471.4	8,210.0	6.0
Valle (Cali)	5,115.2	7,880.8	6.4
Atlantico (Barranquilla)	2,073.2	3,102.8	5.9
Sub-total (four major departments)	19,432.2	30,128.6	6.5
National Total	27,038.0	40,225.8	5.8

Source: *Boletin Mensual de Estadistica* nos. 137 and 143, and unpublished DANE data.

Table 11-3: STRUCTURE OF MANUFACTURING INDUSTRIES IN MAJOR DEPARTMENTS, 1967
(% Distribution of Value-Added)

	National Average	Cundinamarca (Bogota)	Antioquia (Medellin)	Valle (Cali)	Atlantico (Barranquilla)
Non-Durable consumer goods	54.7	47.3	53.9	57.7	53.1
Durable consumer goods	6.5	11.5	2.5	8.2	5.1
Intermediate goods	32.6	30.0	35.8	29.0	36.6
Capital goods	3.5	6.4	3.8	3.8	3.7
Other	2.7	4.8	4.0	1.3	1.5
Total	100.0	100.0	100.0	100.0	100.0

is concentrated in one or two plants. Others, like Manizales and Pereira produce a wider range of products. The major characteristics of the industrial structure of the departments where these cities are located are summarized in Table 11-5.

About 67% of manufacturing value-added in Cartagena derives from the petroleum and chemical industries. Unlike the chemical industries in Bogota and Cali, Cartagena has specialized its production in basic industrial chemicals. Industrial production in Barrancabermeja is almost exclusively related to petroleum refining. Bucaramanga, which used to be an important tobacco center, is heavily dependent on metal industries because of the location there of Forjas de Colombia, a steel forging plant.

More representative of the structure of the manufacturing industry in smaller industrial centers are Manizales and Pereira, in the heart of the coffee-growing region. Industrial capital in each of these cities originally came from coffee, and the industrial structure is heavily concentrated in the production of traditional consumer goods (food, clothing, etc.). While some food and beverage (i.e. perishable goods) industries are commonly located near the market, the concentration in consumer goods which are either capital-intensive (i.e. beverages, food canning), or require female labor (i.e. clothing), has not contributed to relieve the unemployment problem in these cities. For example, Pereira, where 18% of industrial value-added is in clothing, has a high unemployment rate for men.

Table 11-4: PERCENT DISTRIBUTION OF VALUE-ADDED IN
SELECTED INDUSTRIES BY DEPARTMENTS

	Textiles	Chemicals including pharmaceuticals	Paper and Products	Electrical Machinery	Mechanical Machinery	Transport
Cundinamarca (Bogota)	14.4	36.6	14.9	51.2	19.8	55.8
Antioquia (Medellin)	70.6	12.6	12.3	10.6	48.4	10.7
Valle (Cali)	5.8	27.8	62.8	28.6	11.6	12.1
Atlantico (Barranquilla)	3.6	10.9	5.5	6.2	5.7	14.0
Sub-total (four Departments)	94.4	87.9	95.5	96.6	85.5	92.5
National Total	100.0	100.0	100.0	100.0	100.0	100.0
Weight	(13.0)	(13.3)	(2.5)	(3.2)	(1.2)	(0.7)

Note: The weight represents the percent contribution of that industry in national value-added.

Source: Unpublished DANE data.

Table 11-5: STRUCTURE OF MANUFACTURING IN MEDIUM INDUSTRIALIZED DEPARTMENTS, 1967
(% distribution of value-added)

	Santander (Bucaramanga) (Barrancabermeja)	Bolivar (Cartagena)	Caldas (Manizales)	Risaralda (Pereira)	Boyaca
Non-Durable Consumer Goods	44.1	52.9	66.2	82.2	40.9
of which:					
Beverages	14.4	8.7	24.7	19.0	36.2
Tobacco products	15.3	7.6	—	—	—
Clothing	4.1	1.4	8.1	17.8	0.5
Pharmaceuticals & related products	0.3	23.9	3.3	0.5	0.4
Durable Consumer Goods	1.8	1.0	2.0	2.3	0.5
Intermediate Goods	51.4	44.6	28.5	14.6	58.4
of which:					
Chemicals other than pharmaceuticals	0.3	17.6	2.5	0.3	0.3
Petroleum	43.8	25.2	0.9	—	7.7
Basic metals	1.0	—	0.2	—	44.6
Capital Goods	2.3	0.9	3.1	0.8	0.1
Other	0.4	0.6	0.2	0.1	0.1
Total	100.0	100.0	100.0	100.0	100.0

Source: Unpublished DANE data.

The Setting for Industrialization in the Major Centers

Capital Availability, Labor and Wages

Investment for fixed capital by government agencies has been concentrated in the three largest cities (Bogota, Medellin and Cali). About 63% of total loans to industry from the Private Investment Funds of the Bank of the Republic, for example, have been lent in these three cities—27% in Cali alone.

The absence of corporations with widespread ownership in Cali and Barranquilla makes the shortage of working capital more acute there than in Bogota and Medellin. Because of the prevalence of family-owned corporations in the first two cities, some of the surplus capital generated there tends to be channeled to well-established firms (Bavaria and Coltejer, for example) located in Bogota and Medellin.

While foreign firms have invested in all major cities, there is a heavier concentration in Cali than in any of the other cities. The bulk of industrial investment in Medellin, on the other hand, is Colombian. The concentration of foreign investment in Cali is attributed in part to the business outlook of that city which happens to view foreign investment favorably. Cali, moreover, has a pleasant climate and is near the market for manufactures.

With high unemployment rates in all industrial cities, there is an ample supply of unskilled labor. Training possibilities are considered adequate through government programs to which most enterprises have to contribute. Labor unrest was a serious problem in Cali in the early sixties, but labor-management relations have improved since. The migration of professionals to Bogota has contributed to the shortage of professional managers in Barranquilla and other small centers. Cali, on the other hand, has an adequate supply of managerial staff. The Advanced School of Business Administration of the University of Valle has contributed to the supply of managers in Cali and other large cities.

The entrepreneurial classes in the four main cities are dynamic and well organized. While Bogota industrialists tend to have an inward orientation, producing mainly for the home market, the entrepreneurial class of Barranquilla is outward-oriented and interested in exporting.

Cali industrialists are becoming more interested in exporting as improved transportation facilities make foreign markets more accessible. The construction of the Palmaseca Airport and of the road to Buenaventura, the closest port, have been instrumental in this development. Cali industrialists have created an organization (Foundation for Industrial Development-Fundacion para el Desarrollo Industrial) with the purpose of encouraging industrialization and of dissipating the frequently held view that investment in Cali is a bad risk because of past labor unrest. The Foundation is encouraging the establishment of a free trade zone for Cali.

The recent trends in average annual wages for the manufacturing sector in the major industrial centers are shown in Table 11-6 below. In 1967, average industrial wages were highest in Cali and lowest in Barranquilla. Average annual wages in Bogota, Cali and Barranquilla have grown faster than in Medellin. The rapid increase in average wages in Cali reflects the large and capital-intensive investments and rapid industrialization of the city in the past few years. The moderate increase of average wages in Medellin partly reflects the relatively slow growth of the textile industry.

Wages are considerably higher in the new industrial suburbs of the three largest cities than in the cities themselves. In Bogota and Cali this reflects the development of very capital-intensive intermediate and capital goods industries outside the city proper; these industries usually pay high wages. In Yumbo, the largest industrial suburb of Cali and the center for some of the new paper industries, industrial wages average about Col$23,000 in 1967 (in 1968 prices). For the same year, average wages in Soacha, the major industrial suburb of Bogota (where some rubber and construction material industries are located), were about Col$19,000 (in 1968 prices).

In Medellin average wages were considerably higher than the national average in the early sixties, primarily as a result of the high wages paid by the textile industry. The high wages in

Table 11-6: AVERAGE ANNUAL WAGES FOR MANUFACTURING INDUSTRIES IN MAJOR INDUSTRIAL CENTERS (in '000 1968 Col$)

	City 1964	1967	City, including industrial suburbs 1967	1967 Index for city 1964 = 100
Bogota	13.7	14.9	15.2	108.7
Medellin	13.9	14.4	15.0	103.4
Cali	14.0	15.3	17.0	109.4
Barranquilla	13.0	14.2	–	108.9
National Average	13.7	14.7	14.7	107.2

Source: Unpublished DANE data.

the city itself led to the rapid development of numerous industrial suburbs; the textile industry was, in fact, one of the first to move to the suburbs. Coltejer, the textile giant, has moved to Rio Negro, one of the industrial towns near Medellin, the Fabricato, the second largest textile producer in the country, has already bought land there and plans to build a plant in the near future.

Average industrial wages were considerably lower in the smaller industrial centers. Barrancabermeja and Cartegena are exceptions in that they depend heavily on the capital-intensive petroleum and chemical industries which are notably high-wage. While average wages were between Col$11,000 and Col$12,000 per year in Bucaramanga, Manizales and Pereira, average wages in Cartagena were about Col$19,000 and Col$30,000 in Barrancabermeja (all wages are in 1968 prices).

Transport

Topography and transportation have, to a large extent, patterned the development of industry in Colombia. Colombia has made notable advances in improving its transportation network and this will unquestionably have an impact on the future pattern of industrialization, although much still has to be done.

There are now good road links between Cali and Medellin and it is expected that by the end of 1972 a good connection will exist between Medellin and the Atlantic coast. For the purpose of moving industrial products, the route between Bogota and the Atlantic coast seems to be less than adequate. Moreover, the low carrying capacity of the bridges limits the weight of loads that can be moved on this road. Certainly the bridge over the Magdalena river that will connect Barranquilla with Santa Marta, the terminal for both the Atlantic railroad and the north highway, will improve transportation between Barranquilla and the center of the country. The road from Buenaventura to Cali should help to connect the interior with the Pacific coast and possibly affect future industrial location decisions.

From the point of view of developing external markets, of particular interest for Cali and Barranquilla, the improvement of port handling and speeding up of customs procedures in Buenventura, Cartagena, Barranquilla and Santa Marta are important.

Urban Infrastructure and Taxation

There is adequate water supply and power for manufacturing in most major industrial cities. At the present time there is a shortage of power for the steel mill in Boyaca and it is anticipated that there will be temporary power shortages in Barrancabermeja where the petroleum refinery is located and in Barranquilla until the plant now under construction is installed. Of the four major industrial cities, electric power rates are highest in Cali and lowest in Bogota. In Cartagena industrial water supply is a bottleneck for the growing petrochemical industry.

Urban transportation could be a bottleneck to industrialization. Transportation in the cities is inadequate partly because of the restrictions on the importation of automotive equipment, but also because of lack of access to the new industrial suburbs and the insecurity of nighttime travel. These problems are most serious in the three largest cities which have developed satellite industrial towns. The difficulties of transportation at night have contributed to capacity underutilization by making second and third shift staffing difficult and costly.

Land for industrial uses is readily available in or near most of the industrial cities; Manizales, however, is an exception.

Departmental and city taxation of industry (primarily a property tax) is not very heavy in Colombia. Medellin, however, charges from two to three times more in taxes than all the other major cities.

Future Directions of Growth

If Colombia's mountainous topography did not entail such heavy transport costs, the size of the Colombian market for manufactured goods would justify the development of only one or two large industrial centers. Many of the geographical considerations which led to the original development of four industrial centers are still valid today, and even with greatly improved means of transportation, transport costs are almost certain to remain so high as to justify the continued pre-eminence of the four main industrial centers. Moreover, low-value, high-bulk industrial goods such as cement will probably have to continue to be supplied locally. At the same time, the present fragmentation of capacity, the underutilization of already existing capacities, the resulting high costs for many industrial projects, and the poor organization of marketing, set a limit on the policy of creating new industrial centers unless founded on inherent resource advantages. The tendency to locate factories near the market has led to the fragmentation of capacity in many industries. Private entrepreneurs, lacking knowledge of government transport investment planning, have located industries irrespective of prospective reduction in internal transport costs and therefore their locational decisions have turned out to be less than optimal. The scale of plants and the related question of location will be more important in the future since Colombia, having already developed the traditional industries, may go into more capital-intensive industries such as basic chemicals, where size and transport costs are a crucial factor in pricing. Some examples of fragmented capacities follow.

By the end of 1971, there will be three automotive assembly plants in Colombia; two in Bogota and one in Medellin. The decision to locate the Renault plant in Medellin will reduce the unemployment in that city that has arisen from the relatively slow growth of the textile sector. However, locating the new plant in Medellin will cut it off from external economies—such as the sharing of equipment and urgently needed inputs—which it might have enjoyed had it been in Bogota, where the other two plants are.

There are steel-making plants not only in Belencito, Boyaca where Paz del Rio is located, but also in Medellin, Barranquilla and Cali. There is also a re-roller in Tunja, Boyaca, halfway between Bogota and Belencito which is planning an expansion program involving backward integration into steel-making.

There are five major electrical appliance manufacturers in Colombia: three in Bogota, one in Medellin, and one in Manizales. All these plants have unutilized capacities, and their prices are substantially higher than the world market price.

There are traditional consumer goods industries throughout the country. Economies of scale which can be derived from large capacities in the clothing, leather products, or footwear industries are more limited than elsewhere. However, large plants or alternatively concentration in one city, would greatly facilitate the redirection of entrepreneurial skills, improved marketing procedures, product design, and industrial services which are essential if an export market is to be opened up for these products. Therefore, while it is possible to develop mass consumption industries anywhere in the country provided that they are located near the market and that there is sufficient labor available, it would be advantageous to concentrate the export sector of these industries in one city so that they will derive the benefits mentioned above.

It would therefore seem advisable, in future investment decisions in Colombian manufacturing to give more attention to location. This is particularly important in this country since the industrial centers have—because of their location—a comparative advantage in some products. Careful study of location issues, such as the following, is therefore advisable as a part of any government policies for the industrial sector.

Advantage could be taken of Barranquilla's position and the outward-orientation of its entrepreneurs to develop an export center there. Barranquilla's coastal location makes it an ideal site for labor-intensive export industries requiring substantial imported raw materials. This is particularly important because the distance between Barranquilla and the main centers of consumption would make it difficult for this city to supply the domestic market in many of the intermediate and capital goods industries which are already established in the southern cities. Barranquilla, with its cheap labor has potential for developing an export-oriented garment industry. This will become more important when there are adequate transport facilities between Medellin and Barranquilla. Average wages for clothing are given in Table 11-7 below. Barranquilla should also promote the development of the meat, fish and wood industries, for which inputs are locally available.

Economic advantages will probably lead to the continued concentration of textile production in Medellin. The efficiency and dynamism of the textile industry of Medellin is a good example of the advantages of concentration in one city.

There has been an increasing concentration of electrical equipment goods in Bogota and of the metal industries in Medellin. Since the market for these products is primarily in the Medellin-Bogota-Cali triangle, the location of these industries seems appropriate. Petrochemicals will probably be developed in Cali if the planned petroleum refinery is located in that city.

The paper industry seems logically located in Cali. The paper industry could consider some of the Andean or Caribbean markets for export. It is important that good transportation facilities be made available between Medellin and Bogota, and Cali and Bogota, if each one of these cities is to specialize in heavy industrial goods.

The possibilities of industrialization for the smaller industrial centers seem more limited. The Manizales area might be able to process some of its coffee locally. Pereira is closer (in time) to Medellin and could continue as a clothing center with the textiles being supplied from Medellin. Pereira could be associated with the growing metal-mechanical industry of Medellin by becoming a supplier of parts for this industry.

As indicated earlier, Cartagena is an obvious choice for chemical production including petrochemicals, based on salt and refinery products. The good harbor, moreover, could facilitate chemical exports. There is a certain conflict between the development of Cartagena as a tourist center and as a major industrial city. It may be possible to minimize this conflict through careful land use planning and strict zoning regulations. A study of this problem is recommended in the proposed comprehensive study on tourism.

Table 11-7:   AVERAGE ANNUAL WAGE IN THE CLOTHING AND FOOTWEAR INDUSTRIES (in '000 1968 Col$)

	Clothing and Footwear
Bogota	9.21
Medellin	9.50
Barranquilla	8.37

Regional Industrial Planning

Pressure has been mounting in Colombia for government regional incentives to industry, and it seems likely that in the near future the President will be given the legal power to grant such incentives. The Regional and Urban Development Unit of the Planning Office in Colombia is undertaking a series of studies designed to assess the present structure of industry in the various regions, and to determine which policies are best suited to encourage optimal regional industrial growth.[1] These studies are part of a program designed to give guidelines for the general development of the regions. As background, the planning group has elaborated a general model of regionalization, which defines the present economic regions of Colombia by ranking the major urban centers according to economic[2] demographic and infrastructure criteria and by determining migration patterns, geographical barriers and political subdivisions. The model has defined four main economic regions and their regional urban centers: the Atlantic Coast (center: Barranquilla), the Central Region (center: Bogota), the Southwest (center: Cali), and the Northwest (center: Medellin).

The model then seeks to redefine the regions of the country for planning purposes, defining eight planning regions for Colombia and identifying development poles for them. All regions except the Putumayo (where petroleum has been discovered) and the Magdalena Region, already have industrial centers (development poles) of some importance, although the model does not presume rapid industrialization in all regions. Bogota, Medellin, Cali, Barranquilla, Manizales/Pereira and Bucaramanga are the "development poles" for six of the regions.

The model also sets general regional sectoral policies. On industry, it assumes that regional industrial strategy and policies must be in agreement with the national strategy and policies for the industrial sector. Incentives to industry in each region will be granted as part of the program of regional development. As a first step in formulating such incentives, the Regional and Urban Development Unit has developed a strategy for regional industrialization and is preparing a series of related studies. The strategy under discussion is two-sided. First, it seeks to rationalize industry at the national level by promoting specialization in the main cities: Bogota, Medellin, Cali and Barranquilla, and in selected smaller industrial centers (all defined as "development poles" by the Planning Office) by encouraging the development of "dynamic" and related industries. "Dynamic" industries will be identified primarily on the basis of past performance according to statistical indicators. Second, labor-intensive industries will be promoted in small cities to absorb the unemployed and reverse the present pattern of migration to the larger cities.

The specific policies designed to carry out the strategy will be based on the results of an investigation, now under way, by the Unit. The investigation will be undertaken for all planning regions and will be carried out in four stages: first a survey of the existing industry in each of the major centers to identify the "dynamic" and related industries, with an attempt to identify possible growth industries in the smaller centers in the region; second, a questionnaire asking private entrepreneurs to assist the Planning Office, in (a) identifying specific industrial projects which could be promoted, (b) determining major production bottlenecks, (c) assessing the availability of capital, (d) establishing intra-regional and extra-regional relationships, and (e) determining proper incentives. Third, on the basis of the survey and the questionnaire, the Planning Office will decide which industrial sectors and subsectors should be promoted in each city or region and develop a program of localized incentives for each area. The last stage will be the preparation of pre-feasibility or feasibility studies for the selected industrial subsectors in each major city. The analysis of existing regional industry and the questionnaire to industrialists could usefully be supplemented with information regarding transport costs, urban infrastructure and demand data.

These attempts to approach the locational problem systematically are useful, but would be even more useful if combined with an overall national strategy for the industrial sector deciding which industries should be stimulated at different stages of development.

1. See chapter 4, *Regional and Urban Development.*
2. Using industrial indicators.

CHAPTER 12
MINING

Colombia has the largest known coal reserves in Latin America, is the world's only important producer of emeralds, the leading producer in South America and the eighth largest in the world of gold and the only producer in South America and the fourth largest in the world of platinum. However, known resources of metallic minerals are not imposing and, given the present incomplete stage of geological investigation, the extent to which Columbia is endowed with mineral resources cannot be fully determined.

In the past, mining has played a comparatively minor role in the economy of Columbia. This is evident from its contribution to gross domestic product in 1968, which was 0.6% or Col$568.3 million.[1]

Mining is not a major source of employment. The most recent census, taken in 1964, registered only 73,000 workers engaged in mining, or slightly more than one percent of the economically active population of the country. This number probably includes the 8,000 workers engaged in the production of petroleum. An indication of the activity of the industry is given in the data on mining concessions. As of mid-1969 there were only about 150 active concession contracts in all branches of mineral development, and only 47 were in exploitation. This number includes captive mines, such as iron ore, coal and limestone supplying Acerias Paz del Rio and limestone quarries exploited by cement companies, but excludes a few generally small-scale mining operations on private properties, for which national concession contracts are not required.

Although Colombia has in the past been a net importer of minerals and mineral products (Table 12-4), the mining industry has obvious export potential. In the medium term the implementation of the Cerro Matoso nickel, Cerrejon coal and Campamento asbestos projects (see section on Mining Potential) would increase foreign exchange revenue by an estimated US$63 million per year. In the longer term the discovery of sizable lead, zinc, copper or bauxite deposits may lead to projects based on their exploitation. However, as in other forms of industrial activity in Colombia, the mountainous topography and the resultant high cost of inland transport make it difficult for low-value materials, such as non-metallic minerals and coal, to reach the ports of export at internationally competitive prices. The granting of a 15% tax credit certificate (CAT) on some mineral exports since January 1, 1969 may promote a greater export orientation by the mining industry.

The growth of the mining sector as a whole has been sluggish over the past decade. In fact, while the gross value of mine production in current pesos increased from Col$499.4 million in 1962 to Col$842.7 million in 1969 (see Table 12-1), production in constant pesos increased by only about 4% in this period. This was recognized by the administration, which progressively enacted legislation designed to stimulate exploration and development of the country's mineral resources and their subsequent exploitation. It is too early to assess the extent to which the proper incentives have now been provided.

Present Production

A brief review of present mining operations by mineral groups follows:

Mineral fuels.   Colombia has an estimated 18 billion tons of known coal reserves, the largest in Latin America. Production used to be entirely geared to the needs of the domestic market, with Acerias Paz del Rio producing about 750,000 tons of coking coal per annum for consumption in its blast furnace at Belencito. However, the new mine at Landazuri, Santander Department, to produce 300,000 to 400,000 tons of anthracite intended for export to Europe, may be the forerunner of a number of other export oriented coal mining operations.

Precious metals and precious stones.   A major portion of Colombia's gold output is accounted

---

1. This figure will not coincide with that given in the National Accounts, because it excludes petroleum.

Table 12-1: BREAK-DOWN OF MINE PRODUCTION IN 1962 AND 1969
(excluding emeralds)

	1962			1969		
	Value		Quantity	Value		Quantity
	Current Col$ millions	%	'000 tons	Current Col$ millions	%	'000 tons
Mineral Fuels						
Coal	165.0	33.0	3,000	248.8	29.5	3,317
Coke	50.4	10.1	360	65.2	7.7	465
Sub-total	215.4	43.1		314.0	37.2	
Precious Metals (thousand troy oz.)						
Gold	125.0	25.0	397	133.8	15.9	218.9
Platinum	6.8	1.4	17	78.4	9.3	27.8
Sub-total	131.8	26.4		212.2	25.2	
Non-Metallic Minerals						
Limestone	16.0	3.2	3,200	127.7	15.2	4,258
Salt	29.4	5.9	305	87.4	10.4	678
Clays and felspar	39.5	7.9	541	39.8	4.7	681
Gypsum	9.1	1.8	83	18.2	2.2	151
Sulfur	4.1	0.8	10	5.8[1]	0.7	12
Sub-total	98.1	19.6		278.9	33.2	
Metallic Minerals						
Iron Ore	37.4	7.5	680	16.2	1.9	352.3
Lead, zinc and mercury	1.4	0.3	1	4.1	0.5	1
Sub-total	38.8	7.8		20.3	2.4	
Others	15.3	3.1		17.3	2.0	
TOTAL	499.4	100.0		842.7	100.0	

[1]Mission estimate.

Sources: 1962: U.S. Department of the Interior, *Minerals Yearbook* 1963;
1969: U.S. Department of State, *Embassy Report* No. A-196 dated April 28, 1970.

for by a consortium of five companies owned or controlled by the International Mining Corporation of the United States. The production of these companies derives from dredging operations and the Frontino underground mine in Antioquia Department which in 1967 produced 25% of the Colombian total.

As can be seen from Table 12-2, the output of gold and silver declined steadily during the period 1960 through 1969, while that of platinum remained practically unchanged, except for a marked increase in 1969. These production totals are only rough estimates as significant quantities of gold, as well as platinum and silver, enter the contraband trade.

The progressive decline in precious metals output stems partly from depletion of the better grade deposits and partly, in the view of the government, from a lack of vigorous development effort by the principal producers, who have large tracts of territory tied up under perpetuity mining titles. In an attempt to reverse this trend, legislation was introduced by the government and approved by Congress in December 1969. The intent of this legislation is discussed in the section dealing with government policies.

Colombia is the world's leading producer of emeralds. The major part of production has in the past been smuggled out of the country. Registered emerald exports for the period 1960 through 1968 are shown in Table 12-3. The sharp increase in registered exports in 1968 is attributed to government efforts to improve controls and provide incentives for legitimate trade. At the beginning of 1969 the responsibility for the production of emeralds was transferred from the Bank of the Republic to the Colombian Mining Enterprises (Empresa Colombiana de Minas, ECOMINAS), the newly created operating arm of the Ministry of Mines and Petroleum.

The Ministry estimates that the annual value of emerald production in Colombia may exceed US$10 million, nearly all of which is exported through legitimate or contraband channels. This would make emeralds a more important mineral product by value than gold and on a par with coal.

Non-metallic minerals.   Colombia is well endowed with non-metallic minerals for the construction industry, such as limestone and gypsum (for cement), clay (for bricks), silica sand (for glass) and marble, and also salt for the chemical industry.

Metallic Minerals.   Iron ore is the only metallic mineral mined in quantity. This is discussed in Chapter 9. Aside from iron ore, less than 10 tons per year of mercury are extracted, while minor quantities of lead and zinc concentrates are produced, essentially as by-products from gold mining operations.

Table 12-2: PRODUCTION OF PRECIOUS METALS, 1960 TO 1969

Year	Gold	Platinum	Silver
	('000 troy ounces)		
1960	434	16.9	134
1961	401	20.2	128
1962	397	14.1	132
1963	325	23.0	106
1964	365	20.6	131
1965	319	11.1	116
1966	381	15.7	107
1967	258	12.4	110
1968	240	15.1	100
1969	219	27.8	77

Sources: *Minerals Yearbook*, 1963 and 1968, U.S. Department of Interior.
Embassy Report dated April 28, 1970, Department of State.

Table 12-3:   REGISTERED EMERALD EXPORTS, 1960 TO 1968

Year	'000's US$
1960	0.1
1961	172.4
1962	118.3
1963	38.5
1964	290.7
1965	221.8
1966	75.2
1967	141.2
1968	1,412.7

Source: Ministry of Mines and Petroleum External Trade of Mineral and Mineral Products, 1960-68, September 1969.

Mineral Trade.   Colombia is a net importer of minerals and mineral products. Statistics of the commercial trade balance for minerals and mineral products for the years 1960 to 1968 are shown in Table 12-4. The mineral trade figures exclude imports and exports of finished and semi-finished metal products, finished non-metallic mineral products (e.g. cement and glass) and petroleum and petroleum derivatives. Sales of gold to the Bank of the Republic constitute the major portion of exports, except in 1968 when they were almost matched by platinum. Indirect exports of minerals in finished products amounted to over US$6 million in 1968. Inorganic chemical products rather than minerals are the leading import item.

Table 12-4: TRADE IN MINERALS AND MINERAL PRODUCTS
(excluding petroleum and petroleum products)

Year	Imports c.i.f.	Exports[1] f.o.b.	Net Imports
	(In millions of US dollars)		
1960	13.3	9.6	3.7
1961	14.4	11.7	2.7
1962	17.7	13.0	4.7
1963	22.1	9.0	13.1
1964	23.1	14.0	9.1
1965	20.0	14.8	5.2
1966	34.3	11.3	23.0
1967	18.9	9.8	9.1
1968	22.9	13.8	9.1

[1]Including sales of gold to the Bank of the Republic.

Source: Ministry of Mines and Petroleum, External Trade of Minerals and Mineral Products, 1960-1968, September 1969.

Mining Potential

The Ministry of Mines and Petroleum estimates that only about 20% of the possible mineralized area in Colombia has been investigated. Sufficient exploration and development work has, however, already been done on a number of deposits to show that they could be economically exploited.

Phosphates.   Indicated reserves of approximately 460 million tons of phosphate rock have been discovered in various locations along the Eastern Cordillera, ranging in grade from 15% to 30% phosphate (P_2O_5). Certain of these deposits may be sufficiently extensive and high grade to supply the fertilizer demands of the country. Table 12-5 shows the location and grade of these reserves.

Considerable surface exploration has been carried out on the Sardinata deposits which are regarded as being the best in both location and quality for future development. Reserves are estimated at 62 million tons, including nearly 11 million tons probably suitable for open-pit mining. The remainder could be extracted by underground methods. A diamond drilling program is being initiated to determine in about two years the overall chemical characteristics of this deposit. The grade of the surface samples is close to 30% P_2O_5, but weathering may have dissolved associated calcite to result in surface enrichment. The deposit is situated within reasonable distance of the Maracaibo district of western Venezuela, where desulfurizing plants of crude oil are projected which could be an economic source of sulphur for acidulation.

A feasibility study for a phosphoric acid and triple superphosphate facility, based on processing Sardinata phosphate, shows that the production costs of a plant with a capacity of 33,000 tons of P_2O_5 per annum would be fully competitive with those of a plant located on the Atlantic coast based on imported phosphate rock.

A diamond drilling program is also being initiated on the Iza-Tota deposit where, in contrast to the Sardinata ore, weathering has probably resulted in a lower grade in the outcrop.

Lateritic Nickel.   A nickel deposit at Cerro Matoso, Cordoba Department, was first discovered by the Chevron Petroleum Company in drilling for oil. Chevron subsequently brought in the Hanna Mining Company which carried out pilot scale tests on the ore and prepared a

Table 12-5: INDICATED PHOSPHATE RESERVES

Location	Reserves (million tons)	Grade % P_2O_5
Azufrada, Santander	168.3	15-20
San Vicente, Santander	18.75	23
Sardinata, North Santander	62.1	30
Oru, North Santander	140.0	25
Gramalote, North Santander	10.0	15-20
San Andres, Santander	7.0	25
Turmeque, Boyaca	4.8	20
Iza-Tota, Boyaca	43.75	25
Tesalia, Hulia	9.0	14-18
TOTAL	463.7	

Source: Memorandum from the Ministry of Mines and Petroleum to Congress, 1968.

feasibility study for its extraction and smelting to ferro-nickel. This project as presently conceived, is to extract the lateritic nickel ore and treat it in an electric smelter to produce 37.5 million lb. per annum of nickel contained in ferro-nickel. This would be the largest mining operation in Colombia and its cost, including the associated infrastructure, is estimated at around US$100 million equivalent. The construction period would be about 3 years. It would contribute about US$37.5 million of exports.

Coal.   A drilling program is in progress on a coal deposit at Cerrejon, close to the Caribbean Coast, in Guajira Department. About 8,000 feet of drilling has been accomplished to date with indicated reserves estimated at 30 million tons and good evidence that they can be extended considerably. Probably a third to a half of the present reserves can be extracted by open pit methods and the balance by underground mining. The coal is reported to be quite gassy, with a low sulfur content. If blended with a suitable hard coal, it is expected to be of metallurgical quality.

The present proposal is to initiate an export-oriented project of some 3 million tons per annum at an investment cost of about US$40 million. IFI is undertaking the drilling and studies; implementation of the project is expected to require parallel investments in road and port facilities.

Two potential coking coal operations are also in view for the more distant future. Carbones del Carare is understood to have the concessions to exploit deposits near Cucuta in North Santander Department, containing an estimated 500 millions tons of coking coal. Samples have been analyzed in the United States and Germany with satisfactory results and a trial shipment of 2,000 tons has recently been sent to Japan. The major obstacle standing in the way of the exploitation of this deposit is its location, which is some 300 km by road from the Magdalena River port of Gamarra, from where the coal would be transported by barge to the company's loading terminal in Cartagena Bay. Unconfirmed reports also indicate the existence of a large coking coal deposit which has attracted Japanese and Venezuelan interests, near Zipaquira in Cundinamarca Department.

Asbestos.   A deposit at Campamento in Antioquia Department has been thoroughly investigated by the Nicolet Asbestos Company. Some 10 million tons of reserves, containing approximately 4% fiber, have been drilled out and exploration for additional reserves continues. A project has been prepared for the extraction of 25,000 tons per annum of short chrysotile fiber, about 45% of which will be used domestically and the balance exported.

Limestone.   The recently published report on "The Mineral Resources of the Sierra Nevada de Santa Marta" has pointed out the existence of a large, good quality limestone deposit near Durania in Cesar Department. A local group is considering the installation of a sizable cement plant there to supply the lower Magdalena and Cesar Valley areas, and to export cement into the Caribbean basin. The site is excellent, with railroad, road and barge transport available, as well as ample water and crude oil supplies. Another large deposit of limestone has been discovered in Meta Department near Villavicencio, close to the Llanos, where the soil is generally acidic. Equipment to produce 500 tons per day of limestone for agriculture is expected to be ordered soon.

Gypsum.   The reserves in a gypsum deposit at Mesa de los Santos in Santander Department are estimated at 10 million tons and could exceed 50 million tons. Diamond drilling to a depth of 1,000 to 1,500 feet is required to develop the reserves. The cost of opening up the mine, including the provision of the associated infrastructure, is estimated at about US$1 million.

Bauxite.   Drilling for bauxite in the Popayan area, Cauca Department, in which Kaiser Aluminum Company holds several claims, has been going on for some time. Indications are that a large deposit has been discovered, but that a number of technical problems will have to be resolved before exploitation can be contemplated. A deposit which indicated reserves of upward of 100 millions tons of 48% bauxite has reportedly also been discovered in the Llanos; but at first sight the remote location of this deposit makes it doubtful if it can be exploited economically.

Other Mining Possibilities

Sulphur.   The domestic production of superphosphate fertilizer would sharply increase the demand for sulfur. The gas fields of Colombia do not contain significant amounts of sulfur. The most likely source for increased reserves and production of sulfur are the volcanic rocks in the southern part of the country. Although known reserves are small, a prospecting program in this region might prove valuable.

Iron Sands.   A deposit of titaniferous iron sand has been discovered between Barranquilla and Cartagena. Insufficient work has been done, however, to determine either the extent or grade of this deposit or whether it could be economically exploited.

Government Policies Toward the Mining Sector

According to the Ministry of Mines and Petroleum there have been several causes for the slow development of the industry in the past: there were no institutions responsible for the planning of the industry and for the development of programs of investigation and investment; the information available on mineral resources was quite limited; there was a shortage of technically qualified personnel for the development of mining; an anachronistic, inadequate and in many instances contradictory mining code governed the relationship between the State and private mining companies; and there was neither a policy for domestic financing nor a clearly defined code for foreign investment in the industry.

In an attempt to correct these weaknesses, stimulate the development of mining and promote the exploitation of mineral resources by domestic and foreign mining companies, the government has evolved a policy with the following declared aims: first, the Ministry of Mines and Petroleum is charged with the formulation of an official policy on exploration, exploitation, refining, transportation and distribution of minerals. Actions on mining concession applications will be speeded up; operations in the public sector are henceforth to be conducted through four organizations, viz the National Institute of Geological and Mining Surveys (INGEOMINAS), Colombian Mining Enterprise (ECOMINAS), Institute of Nuclear Affairs (IAN), and the Colombian Petroleum Enterprise (ECOPETROL). Second, a systematic survey of exploitable mineral deposits will be undertaken on a regional basis. Third, economic information will be gathered to provide basic data for the planning of the industry and the identification of technically and economically feasible projects. Fourth, the government will provide financial assistance for the training of qualified personnel required for the growth of mining. Fifth, the government has created a legal framework which permits the State to be associated in the exploitation of the country's mineral deposits, and to cancel the mining rights held by private concerns if they fail to explore, exploit and continue exploitation of the mineral deposits within stipulated periods. Sixth, the government will facilitate the raising of external funds for the implementation of mining projects by permitting the repatriation of capital and remittance of reasonable profits, and by exempting from duty imported mining machinery and equipment and spare parts.

The degree of success the government has had in speeding up the exploration and development of the country's mineral resources, excluding uranium and petroleum, is apparent from the record of INGEOMINAS. The extent to which recent decrees and legislation have stimulated exploitation of these mineral deposits can be inferred from the progress made on three types of mining projects—large projects requiring the participation of international mining companies; projects based on the exploitation of non-metallic minerals and mineral fuels, such as phosphate rock, asbestos, limestone and coal; and traditional gold, platinum and emerald mining operations.

The best example of a large mining project is the Cerro Matoso nickel project. Compared with Hanna's earlier proposal, the project has been increased in capacity and now includes a smelter. It has thus been made to comply with Mining Law 60 of 1967, which requires mining companies to process their output within the country to the extent that this is technically and economically justified.

In the field of non-metallic minerals and mineral fuels, the start-up in March 1970 of the Landazuri anthracite mine and the proposed construction, during the second half of this year, of the Campamento asbestos project indicate that recent **government** measures have been successful in stimulating exploitation of the country's mineral deposits. On the other hand, the refusal by the **government** to grant the 15% tax credit for exports of asbestos fibers from the Campamento project may seriously delay its implementation. There also appears to be some avoidable delay in establishing the mining title to the Sardinata phosphate deposits as between Chevron and IFI.

In the mining of precious metals and emeralds, the government's primary aims are to stimulate production and reduce the amounts entering the contraband trade. While it is too early to draw conclusions, the effect of Mining Law 20 of 1969, which requires exploitation at an economic rate, and the introduction of improved controls on production and export incentives are judged to be steps in the right direction.

CHAPTER 13
POWER

Present Supply

The electric sector is located in the northern, central and western regions of the country, which are endowed with remarkable complementary resources for power generation: important hydroelectric potential in the extensive central mountain system, with different hydraulic regimes in the Amazonas-Orinoco, Atlantic and Pacific river basins; oil in the north and southwest; natural gas in the north; and coal in several parts of the cordilleras.

In 1969 the public utilities generated a total of 7,100 GWh and at the end of the year had a total installed generating capacity of 1,870 MW; about 75% of the generation was of hydro origin, 15% was generated in steam thermal plants and 10% in gas-turbine and diesel plants. In addition to the public service, 250 MW were installed in industrial facilities which generated 1,000 GWh. The average per capita annual consumption in 1969 was about 400 kWh, below the Latin American average in 1968 of approximately 474 kWh.

The levels of electric development and consumption are substantially different between regions, and even more so between urban and rural areas. The average per capita annual consumption in some departments is of the order of 500 kWh, but in others does not reach 100 kWh. While in the 30 cities of more than 30,000 inhabitants the average consumption in 1969 was about 600 kWh, about 30% of the country's population (70% of the rural population) did not have any electricity service at all. Table 13-1 illustrates the differences between regions and the percentage shares of each electric region in the country's total generation and installed capacity in 1968, as compared with the respective percentage shares in the area and population.

The principal cities, particularly Bogota and Medellin, have enjoyed the benefits of sophisticated planning by the utilities serving them, whereas the development of other parts of the country has at times been haphazard and uncoordinated. Although in the past the planning and efforts for the development of the sector have been concentrated much more in generation and transmission than in distribution, the expansion has not been sufficient to meet the demand in some important areas of the country, which at times have experienced power shortages. In many areas the distribution systems present serious deficiencies, and rural electrification is indeed scarce. This situation of the public sector in the past underlies the comparatively extended practice by industrial consumers of electricity of installing their generating facilities.

Table 13-1: PERCENTAGE SHARES OF ELECTRIC POWER
COMPARED WITH AREA AND POPULATION

Electric Region	Area %	Population %	Generation %	Installed Capacity %
Antioquia (Medellin)	7.9	15.3	28.9	28.3
Central (Bogota)	10.6	30.4	28.3	33.2
Occidental (Cali)	8.8	17.3	18.1	17.5
Norte (Cartagena, Barranquilla)	10.5	18.8	13.3	12.1
Caldas (Manizales)	0.9	8.2	7.3	5.0
Nordeste (Barrancabermeja-Bucaramanga)	6.2	8.7	3.8	3.6
Rest of the Country: Los Llanos and San Andres	55.1	1.3	0.3	0.3

The public service is practically wholly supplied at present by the following four entities:

(a)   Empresa de Energia Electrica de Bogota (EEEB), a municipal utility for electrical
      service only, which supplies energy to Bogota and the Departamento de Cun-
      dinamarca directly and by bulk supply to departmental rural distributing agencies
      and subsidiaries of ICEL. At the end of 1969, the total installed capacity of EEEB's
      own plants was 440 MW, of which 85 MW were thermal and the rest hydroelectric.

(b)   Empresas Publicas de Medellin (EPM), a municipal utility providing electricity,
      water-sewerage and telecommunication services, which supplies electric energy to
      Medellin and the Departamento de Antioquia, directly and by bulk supply to the
      rural distributing subsidiary of ICEL. The total installed capacity in EPM's plants at
      the end of 1969 was 450 MW, all of them hydro.

(c)   Corporacion Autonoma Regional del Valle del Cauca (CVC), a multipurpose, autono-
      mous, nationally-chartered regional entity for the development of the Cauca Valley,
      which supplies energy to the Departamento de Valle, mainly by bulk supply to Empre-
      sas Municipales de Cali (EMCALI) and to other rural distributing agencies, subsidiar-
      ies of ICEL and CVC. CVC is the major owner of Central Hidroelectrica del Rio Anchi-
      caya Limitada (CHIDRAL), a local agency for generation only, which is also owned by
      EMCALI. At the end of 1969, the total installed capacity in CVC-CHIDRAL's plants
      was 270 MW, of which 76 were thermal and the rest hydro.

(d)   Instituto Colombiano de Energia Electrica (ICEL), a National Government In-
      stitute, formerly called Electraguas, which through 15 departmental and 13 minor
      subsidiaries supplies electric energy to the rest of the northern, central and western
      regions of the country. At the end of 1969, the total installed capacity in ICEL's
      subsidiaries was 684 MW, 330 MW in thermal plants and the rest hydroelectric.
      One of the major subsidiaries of ICEL is Central Hidroelectrica de Caldas (CHEC),
      which serves an area of the departments Caldas, Quindio and Risaralda around
      Manizales, in Central Colombia, and has at present a total installed capacity of 200
      MW in hydro plants.

The considerable distances within the country and its rugged mountain chains have isolated
the various regional centers, which traditionally have developed separately their regional institutions and economic resources, and also their own electric systems. One of the results has been
the jurisdictional fragmentation of the electric service. The many entities which provide it are
usually too small; the areas they service are uneconomic and they suffer financial difficulties;
they are not sufficiently connected with other areas; as a result they are unable to provide
satisfactory service. ICEL now has the specific responsibility of carrying out a plan to restruc-
ture the electric service by integration within the different regions. Work has started on this,
but very much remains to be done.

Integration of the System

According to the studies of the National Planning Board (Planeacion), the new structure
is to be based on the grouping of the regional and local electric systems into six zones covering
all the departments. The regional zones were tentatively defined on the basis that each one
should have appropriate geographic limits and be large enough to permit its integrated electric
development and achievement of financial self-sufficiency. The responsibility for coordination
of supply within each zone will rest with a basic zonal system, to which the local distribution
systems will be connected by regional transmission lines. The basic zonal systems will be
interconnected by high voltage transmission lines to form a national network, which will permit
the realization of economies of scale through the planning, construction and operation of large
generating plants. The advantages of integration and joint planning of the sector have become
particularly noticeable in recent years when the demand for power has risen rapidly and in large
amounts.

The six regional electric zones presently contemplated and their respective basic systems
(in parentheses) are: Central (EEEB), Caldas (CHEC), Occidental (CVC/CHIDRAL), Antioq-

MAP 13-I

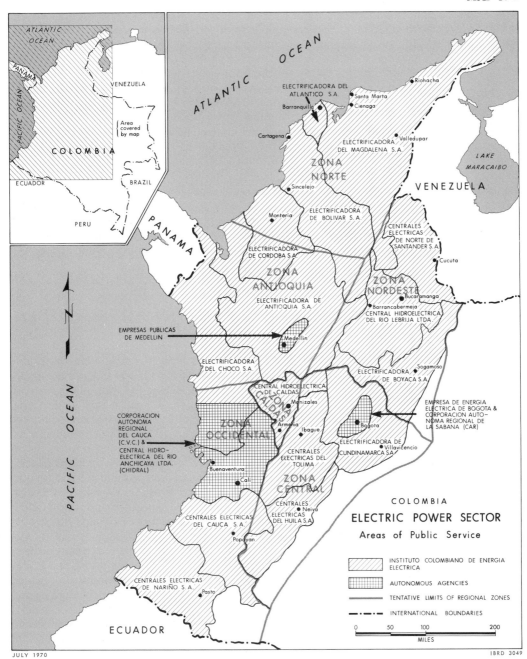

CENTRALES ELECTRICAS
DE NARIÑO S.A.

COLOMBIA

ELECTRIC POWER SECTOR

Areas of Public Service

	INSTITUTO COLOMBIANO DE ENERGIA ELECTRICA
	AUTONOMOUS AGENCIES
	TENTATIVE LIMITS OF REGIONAL ZONES
	INTERNATIONAL BOUNDARIES

0   50   100   200

MILES

IBRD 3049

uia (EPM), Norte (CORELCA) and Nordeste (basic system not established yet). The areas covered by these zones are shown on Map 13-I. Four of the basic systems will be interconnected which will form the foundation for the development of the national network. It is expected that ISA's network will after 1973 be expanded to connect with the basic system now being developed in the northeast. The planned link with the system of CORELCA (Corporacion Electrica de la Costa Atlantica) in the north is further in the future because of distances involved.

ISA, a stock corporation sponsored and owned in four equal parts by EEEB, EPM, CVC/CHIDRAL and ICEL/CHEC, was formed in September 1967 for the interconnection of the sponsors' electric systems and for the planning, construction, ownership and operation of new power generating plants in the interconnected system. In 1968, ISA undertook its first project, a 535 km 230 kV transmission network to interconnect the systems of EEEB, CHEC, EPM and CVC/CHIDRAL, with financing from the IBRD and several equipment suppliers' countries. ISA's interconnection network has made possible the first joint planning in Colombia of a long-range, large-size power generation program at supra-regional scale. ISA and Planeacion carried out several studies, using computer models, to determine the most suitable and economic schedule of new generating plant construction in the interconnected system to meet its forecast demand up to 1980. In accordance with the results of the studies, ISA and its sponsors agreed to the construction of two major hydroelectric generating plants, as follows:

(a)   Alto Anchicaya (340 MW) in the area of Cali, to be built by CVC/CHIDRAL to start operation in 1974; and

(b)   Chivor (first stage, of 500 MW) in the area of Bogota, the first generating plant to be built, owned and operated by ISA, to start operation in mid-1975.

Both projects are now under construction, Alto Anchicaya with financing from the Inter-American Development Bank (IDB) and Canada, and Chivor from IBRD financing complemented by IADB. Map 13-II shows the location of these projects, together with other principal projects, existing, in the construction and planned stage and under investigation. ISA, its sponsors and Planeacion will be continuing and updating the studies to schedule new additions to generating capacity. Various possibilities are being considered, particularly thermal units for short-term construction, and the second stage (280 MW) of Guatape Project in the area of Medellin for longer-term operation, not before 1977/78. At the same time, two studies are under way dealing with the expansion and interconnection of the Nordeste system: (a) a study for ICEL, which includes analysis of the electric market and projections of power demand in the northeast region, and identification and evaluation of prospective generation and transmission projects and alternative construction programs to meet the demand up to 1977; and (b) a study for ISA to determine the technical and economic feasibility of the 230 kV interconnection line Guatape-Barrancabermeja. These studies are expected to provide the bases for a comprehensive analysis of the Nordeste and ISA systems, to be jointly performed by Planeacion, ISA and ICEL to determine the schedule of projects to carry out the integration of the systems and at the same time meet the forecast demands in both systems and in the integrated ISA-Nordeste system. Preliminary conclusions of these studies indicate that additional thermal generation capacity and transmission lines will be required. The new projects would include three 66 MW steam units—two of them in Paipa and Barrancabermeja, ICEL/Nordeste, and the third one in Zipaquira, EEEB—to start operations in 1973/74, and 230 kV transmission lines, Barrancabermeja-Bucaramanga-Cucuta (ICEL/Nordeste, for 1972) Guatape-Barrancabermeja (ISA, for 1973) and Chivor-Paipa (ISA, for 1974). A longer-run aim is interconnection with Venezuela (230 KV lines Bucaramanga-Cucuta-Zulia-Venezuela).

CORELCA, an autonomous regional agency, was established in December 1967 for the planning, construction and operation of new power generating plants and transmission lines in the northern region, which includes seven departments, from Cordoba to La Guajira. COREL-CA is in the process of being organized to assume its responsibilities, which in the interim have been assigned to ICEL. There is urgent need to install additional generating capacity and interconnect individual systems in the Atlantic coast area. A program towards this end has been undertaken, which includes initially the construction by CORELCA of a 132 MW thermal plant in Barranquilla (Termonorte I) and the transmission lines Barranquilla-Sabanalarga-Cartagena (230 kV) and Barranquilla-Santa Marta (115 kV); the construction of these projects, which are

MAP 13-II

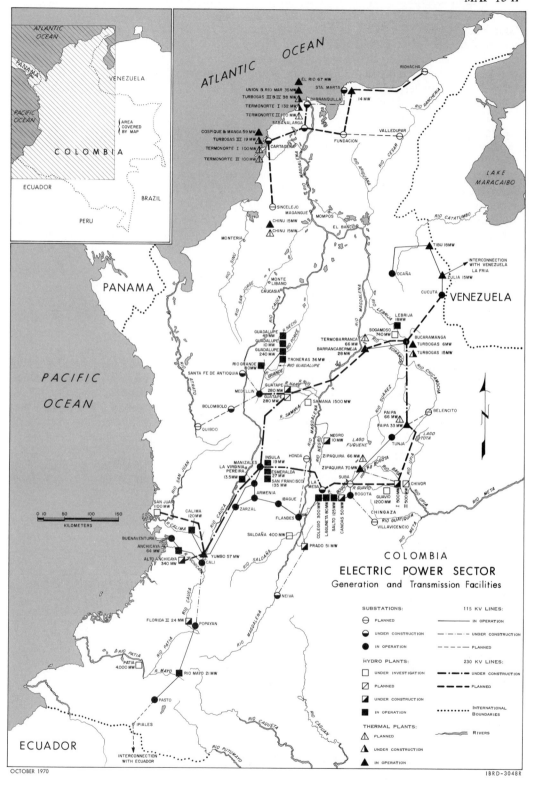

COLOMBIA
ELECTRIC POWER SECTOR
Generation and Transmission Facilities

SUBSTATIONS:		115 KV LINES:	
⊖	PLANNED		IN OPERATION
◐	UNDER CONSTRUCTION		UNDER CONSTRUCTION
●	IN OPERATION		PLANNED
HYDRO PLANTS:		230 KV LINES:	
□	UNDER INVESTIGATION		UNDER CONSTRUCTION
◺	PLANNED		PLANNED
◿	UNDER CONSTRUCTION		
■	IN OPERATION		INTERNATIONAL BOUNDARIES
THERMAL PLANTS:			RIVERS
△	PLANNED		
◭	UNDER CONSTRUCTION		
▲	IN OPERATION		

OCTOBER 1970

IBRD-3048R

scheduled for completion by early 1972, was started in early 1970 with financing from supplier countries. More recently, in order to supply industrial consumers, particularly the expanding Soda Plant, CORELCA-ICEL undertook the emergency construction of a 19 MW gas-turbine unit in Cartagena to start operation by mid-1971. CORELCA's longer-term plan includes the construction of three 100 MW thermal units—two of them in Cartagena (1974 and 1978) and the other one in Barranquilla (1976)—and of the transmission lines Cartagena-Sincelejo (230 kV, 1972), Sabanalarga-Fundacion-Santa Marta (230 kV, 1975), Fundacion-Valledupar (115 kV, 1975) and Santa Marta-Riohacha (230 kV, 1976).

The eventual interconnection of the CORELCA system with the ISA/ Northeast system would complete the integration of the power sector. This interconnection will have to be planned in coordination with the developments taking place in both systems in the next few years, including the need for large new supplies of power to large industrial consumers now in prospect. It is expected that by 1972 many of the developments presently planned and foreseen in both systems will have been defined; it will then be possible to undertake a technical and economic feasibility study of prospective alternative projects for the interconnection of ISA and CORELCA systems. This preinvestment study would provide the bases for a subsequent comprehensive analysis by CORELCA/ISA to determine the optimum schedule of construction of transmission and generation projects which would complete the national integration of the power system.

Demand Growth and Capacity Expansion

Past Rates

The evolution in the last 25 years of the total installed generating capacity and annual generation by the country's public utilities are shown in Charts 13-I and 13-II. The development of the Colombian electric sector has been remarkable: energy demand has increased at an average rate of about 12% per year. Growth has not been steady, however. There have been considerable short-run fluctuations, reflecting economic problems of the country, which depressed market growth in some years and brought about financial difficulties in the sector, which interfered with the expansion of capacity.

The annual peak loads and gross generations in the period 1965-69 for the three major electric systems in the country are shown in Table 13-2. The overall annual rates of growth

Table 13-2: ANNUAL PEAK LOADS AND GROSS GENERATION, 1965-69

System	1965	1966	1967	1968	1969
EEEB					
Peak Load (MW)	243.4	267.7	315.1	350.1	422.8
Gross Generation (GWh)	1,085.2	1,218.6	1,383.6	1,629.7	1,920.6
EPM					
Peak Load (MW)	267.0	289.0	309.8	327.0	349.5
Gross Generation (GWh)	1,373.3	1,478.4	1,579.0	1,698.4	1,829.1
CVC/CHIDRAL					
Peak Load (MW)	164.3	n.a.	196.0	211.0	n.a.
Gross Generation (GWh)	825.4	n.a.	n.a.	1,033.9	911.3[1]

[1]In addition, about 170 GWh were supplied in 1969 to CVC/CHIDRAL system from EEEB (43 GWh) and other systems.

CHART 13-I

COLOMBIA
INSTALLED GENERATION CAPACITY
IN THE PUBLIC SECTOR 1945-1969

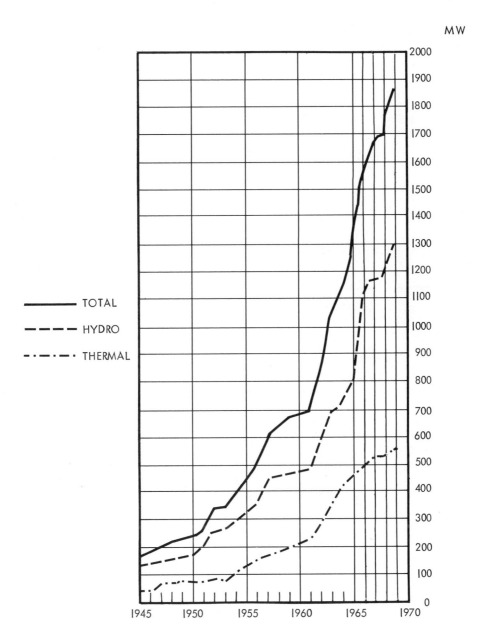

IBRD - 5038

CHART 13-II

COLOMBIA – POWER GENERATION
BY THE PUBLIC SECTOR 1945-1969

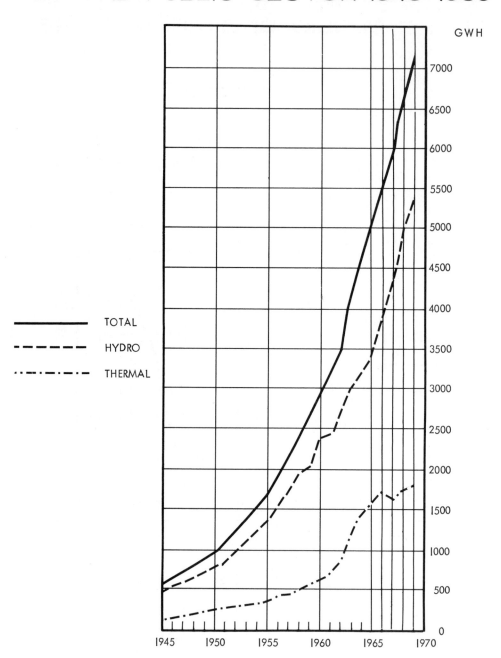

IBRD - 5037

experienced by the three systems in the last decade have been approximately 12% in generation and peak load for EEEB and CVC/CHIDRAL systems, and 10% in generation and 9.3% in peak load for the EPM system.

Recent Shortages

In 1969 and 1970, demand growth accelerated, in response to the accelerating rate of general economic activity. This was accompanied by serious shortages of power in four areas of the country. Some emergency actions have been taken to correct them temporarily, until long-range solutions can be achieved.

Cali and Cauca Valley: the CVC system presented important generation deficits aggravated by unfavorable hydraulic conditions, and the help received from CHEC was not sufficient to prevent serious power shortages. The 115 kV line Ibague-Zarzal (see Map 13-II), in operation since September 1969, is being intensively used to supply surplus energy from EEEB to CVC, thus helping to solve the problem temporarily. The situation will remain critical until ISA's interconnection network, scheduled for mid-1971, is operating, with sufficient capacity for the necessary transfers from EEEB, EPM and CHEC. The CVC system itself will present generation deficits until the operation of Alto Anchicaya, scheduled for 1974.

Atlantic coast: This area has experienced chronic deficits of generation and corresponding power shortages in recent years. An emergency program of installation of gas-turbine units in Barranquilla, Cartagena and Chinu presently under way will help to solve the problem temporarily. The situation will not be definitely improved until the completion, scheduled for 1972, of the 132 MW steam plant in Barranquilla and the transmission lines Barranquilla-Cartagena and Barranquilla-Santa Marta. Additional thermal units and transmission lines are planned to meet the demand in the area from 1974.

Northeast: A delay in the start-up of a new 25 MW steam plant in Barrancabermeja (Termobarranca), initially scheduled for September 1969, caused power shortages in the area of Bucaramanga. This illustrates the deficiency of electric service in the Departments of Santander, Norte de Santander and Boyaca, where lack of coordination between their small and isolated electric systems has caused inadequate development. It is expected that the operation since early 1970 of Termobarranca, together with an additional 15 MW gas-turbine plant in Bucaramanga, under construction for operation by mid-1970, will suffice to meet the demand in Santander until about 1972, when the 230 kV lines Paipa-Bucaramanga and Bucaramanga-Cucuta are scheduled to start operation (see Map 13-II). These lines are the first development toward the much-needed electric integration of the Northeast's power systems, which are later to be linked by 230kV lines Guatape-Barrancabermeja and Chivor-Paipa to ISA's system, if the studies now under way confirm the preliminary conclusion that integration appears the most feasible and economic long-term solution to assure satisfactory electric service in the region.

Narino (south): Delay of about one year in starting up Rio Mayo Hydro Plant (21 MW) caused serious power shortages during 1969 in the Pasto area until early 1970. A new 24 MW hydro plant (Florida II) under construction near Popayan and the 115 kV line Popayan-Cali are scheduled to start operation by end 1972 and 1971, respectively. No serious problems are foreseen in meeting the demand in the Narino system during the next few years.

Industrial Consumption

Timely expansion of capacity by the public utilities and the integration of the system are particularly important for assuring reliable power supply for industry. At present, industrial consumption served by the utilities is about 34% of the total public service consumption (see Table 13-3), and it has stayed at this level for the last five years. The relatively low level has been supplemented by the extended practice of large industrial consumers installing their own generating facilities, particularly in areas not served by EEEB, EPM and CVC.

The progress being achieved by the public service, particularly in ISA's interconnected system, underlies the present intention of important industrial consumers of electricity to rely on public supply in the future. Such are the cases of Acerias Paz del Rio in Belencito and ECOPETROL Refinery in Barrancabermeja, both in the Nordeste, which plan important

Table 13-3: COMPOSITION OF ENERGY SALES, 1969

System	Total Sales GWh	Composition (%)			
		Residential	Industrial	Commercial	Other
EEEB	1,600	32	32	17	19
EPM	1,330	48	31	8	13
CVC	912	36	42	12	10

expansions in coming years, with corresponding increases in power demand to be served by the public sector. The power consumption in Paz del Rio and ECOPETROL will increase, according to their forecasts, from about 200 GWh (peak load 31 MW) and 260 GWh (peak load 42 MW) consumed in 1969, to about 360 GWh (peak load 75 MW) and 440 GWh (peak load 70 MW) in 1973, respectively. An expansion of Siderurgica del Pacifico in Cali will increase by 2 GWh/month the demand from EMCALI in 1971. EPM is entering into an agreement with Hanna Mining Company to supply electric power to the Cerro-Matoso Nickel Plant, planned to be built in Monte Libano (Cordoba), with a peak demand of 65 MW, 90% load factor and strict requirements for very high reliability of supply. This new approach of the industry will be very beneficial for the public utilities, because of the base-load nature of industrial demand, and for the industries themselves, which will thus be freed from the complexities and higher costs usually associated with the small, isolated plants. The benefits of course, will materialize only if the public sector is able to comply economically with its commitments, and for this a continuing process of planning and expansion is required. There is no doubt that this can be accomplished in the systems integrated in ISA, which is already applying long-term, updated planning on a large scale for those commitments. All this emphasizes the need and urgency of carrying out the integration of the Nordeste and its interconnection with the ISA system.

Local Distribution and Rural Electrification

Priority has been given in the past to the development of generation and transmission facilities, and until recently, only isolated, non-coordinated efforts were devoted to the development of local distribution and rural electrification, which in many areas are acutely deficient, to the point that about six million people in the country do not have electric service. ICEL undertook in 1969 a plan to improve and expand, in a first stage, subtransmission (facilities at 13.2 kV and 33kV) and urban distribution (service to cities and population centers of more than 1,500 inhabitants); and in a second stage, rural electrification, practically non-existent at present except in coffee-growing areas, where some successful developments have been carried out in cooperation with the Federacion Nacional de Cafeteros (FEDECAFE).

In mid-1969, ICEL with Planeacion's support and FONADE's financing, retained consultants to prepare a comprehensive national plan which will identify subtransmission and urban distribution projects, establish priorities, estimate financial requirements, etc. The program they are preparing for construction of subtransmission and urban distribution projects is based on a planned investment of US$40 million equivalent in the period 1971-74; the government intends to request the IDB to participate in financing the program. It is expected to include, among others, projects to improve the service in Cartagena, Santa Marta, Sincelejo, Monteria, Valledupar, Riohacha, Bucaramanga, Villavicencio, Pie de Monte (Meta), Quibdo, Ibague, Neiva, Popayan and Pasto.

Rural electrification in Colombia presents special difficulties, because of the difficult topography of the country and the wide dispersion of its rural population (centers of up to 1,500 inhabitants). It seems that the solution to the problem would have to be worked out through close coordination between the electric agencies, particularly ICEL, and agricultural entities

Table 13-4: SUMMARY OF COSTS OF MAJOR POWER PROJECTS, 1970-76

	Cost Estimate		External Financing US$ millions	
	Total Col$ millions	Foreign Exchange US dollars millions	Obtained	Additional Required[2]
Generating Plants:				
under construction	6,096	232.0	204.7	28.1
planned	2,070	77.1	–	77.1
Transmission Lines:				
under construction	913	37.2	26.3	10.9
planned	619	26.9	–	26.9
Sub-transmission and Urban Distribution Program: (planned)[1]	800	not determined	–	25.0
TOTAL	10,498	373.2, plus amount not determined	231.0	168.0

[1]ICEL's program, not included in Tables 13-7 and 13-8.

[2]Status as of mid-1970.

such as INCORA, FEDECAFE, Banco Cafetero, Caja Agraria, Banco Ganadero,etc. Because of the magnitude and complexity of the problem, it is recommended that a comprehensive preinvestment study on rural electrification on a national scale be undertaken as soon as possible. This study would identify areas with potential demand and prepare demand forecasts; identify rural electrification projects for selected priority areas and prepare preliminary designs and estimate construction costs; and evaluate alternative project schedules for prospective investment plans. ICEL is the natural agency to assume the primary responsibility for the rural electrification study.

Domestic Manufacture of Electrical Equipment

ICEL's consultants preparing the plan for subtransmission and urban distribution projects are also engaged in drawing up codes and standards for distribution systems, facilities and equipment. These two studies are inter-related: it is planned to apply the codes and standards to the projects in the program. The standardization of types and sizes of equipment and materials, in conjunction with the schedule of procurement for the construction program, will facilitate greater participation in the supplies by local manufacturers. They may need some adjustments in their present capacities and programs of production to be able to participate substantially in the program, as is desirable and expected. The Colombian manufacturing industry is qualified to supply to the electric sector equipment and materials for subtransmission and distribution, in particular transformers up to 33 kV, cables, insulators, conduits and fittings, poles, steel towers, minor switchgear and control boards, lighting fixtures, etc. Practically all of these local manufactures include foreign components or materials in various degrees, and their prices are usually higher than those of foreign supplies for public utilities, which are exempt from import duties. The quality of local manufactures has not always been satisfactory; there has generally been a lack of appropriate quality control of fabrication. The work in progress to establish quality standards of fabrication should be intensified and accelerated, in order to assure the reliability of national supplies to the subtransmission and distribution program.

Finance

At present, only EEEB and EPM are financially self-sufficient to carry out their operations and to finance the local cost of construction investments; external financing for foreign exchange costs of their main projects has been available to them. CVC/CHIDRAL, ICEL and its subsidiaries, on the other hand, have needed in the past, and still do, substantial budgetary contributions and credits to cover part of their expenditures and investments, as well as to service external credits and loans. These agencies have in the past perennially experienced financial difficulties partly because of delays in applications for tariff increases, and subsequent delays by the government in granting them. ISA has obtained external financing for the foreign exchange cost of its two projects. It is dependent on its sponsors for domestic financing of its operating expenses and of the local cost of construction investments.

The establishment and implementation of a comprehensive, rational public utility tariff policy in Colombia has been needed for many years. Until recently, tariff adjustments have been granted on an *ad hoc* basis, and sometimes they have been too small and too late. In December 1968, the government instituted the Junta Nacional de Tarifas de Servicios Publicos (Junta), as part of Planeacion, to regulate public utility tariffs, appropriately structuring and adjusting them to cover operating expenditures and provide a reasonable return on revalued assets to permit orderly financing of expansion. The preparation by the utilities and the study and processing by the Junta of tariff adjustment applications have been organized by the use of comprehensive data forms and computer programs which permit fast and complete evaluation of alternative structures and levels of adjustment. The Junta thereby has been able to process a good part of the backlog of applications by power agencies. Much work is at the same time being done by Planeacion and ICEL, in close coordination, to bring about national uniformity in accounting, reporting, valuation techniques, etc. Since the beginning of 1970, a new accounting plan prepared by ICEL is being used by all its subsidiaries and affiliates. The plan is coordinated with the data forms used by the Junta for the processing of tariff adjustment applications. Planeacion and ICEL have been helping those utilities to initiate the use of the new techniques, particularly with regard to the collection of statistical data and the preparation of tariff adjustment applications. Planeacion is at present considering the revision of the basic structure of tariffs. The problem to be resolved by all these activities is important. The National Government's budgetary subsidies to service ICEL's debt have increased from Col$45 million in 1968 to Col$73 million in 1969 and were programmed at Col$120 million (equivalent to more than US$6 million) for 1970. These subsidies represent a drain on resources, which curtails the government's capacity to finance new investments.

Investment

An impressive process of expansion of power generation and transmission facilities is under way throughout the country. In 1969, six new generating plants, aggregating a total of 200 MW, and 270 km of 115 kV lines were put in service. Presently under construction are 14 new generating plants or extensions aggregating 1,624 MW, to be completed in 1970-75: this is almost equal to the total generating capacity existing in the country at the end of 1969. Also under way is construction of 1,545 km of 230 kV and 115 kV lines, for completion in 1970-75. Additionally, seven plants—aggregating 778 MW—and 1,160 km of 230 kV and 115 kV lines are planned for start of construction during 1970-76. The size, schedule, cost estimate and status of financing of the generating plants and major transmission lines presently under construction and planned, are shown in Tables 13-5, 13-6, 13-7 and 13-8. This information is summarized in Table 13-4.

The program of total investments in the public power sector for the period 1970-72 and the forecast investments for 1973-75 are indicated in Table 13-9. The expected sources of funds to finance the 1970-72 program are also given. This program includes both the investments to

Table 13-5: GENERATING PLANTS UNDER CONSTRUCTION

| | Installed Capacity MW | Scheduled Initial Operation | Cost Estimate | | Foreign Financing | | Additional Requirement[1] US dollars millions |
| | | | Foreign Exchange US dollars millions | Total Col$ millions | Obtained | | |
					US dollars millions	Source	
Colegio II – Hydro (EEEB)	150	1970	7.5	159	7.5	IBRD & Suppliers	–
Bucaramanga-Turbogas III (ICEL-CORELCA)	15	1970	1.6	30	1.4	Suppliers	0.2
Barranquilla-Turbogas IV (ICEL-CORELCA)	15	1970	1.6	30	1.4	Suppliers	0.2
Chinu-Turbogas III (ICEL-CORELCA)	15	1970	1.6	30	1.4	Suppliers	0.2
Barranquilla-Turbogas III (ICEL-CORELCA)	23	1970	2.5	49	2.4	Suppliers	0.1
Guatape I-Hydro (EPM)	280	1971	42.0	680	42.0	IBRD	–
Canoas-Hydro (EEEB)	50	1971	5.8	200	5.8	IBRD & Suppliers	–
Cartagena-Turbogas III (ICEL-CORELCA)	19	1971	1.7	35	1.5	Suppliers	0.2
Rio Prado – Hydro (ICEL)	51	1972	13.0	400	13.8	IDB & Suppliers	–
Florida II – Hydro (ICEL)	24	1972	2.4	78	0.9	Suppliers	1.5
Barranquilla-Termonorte I (ICEL-CORELCA)	132	1972	16.1	340	13.2	Suppliers	2.9
Rio Negro – Hydro (ICEL)	10	1973	–	75	–		–
Alto Anchicaya – Hydro (CVC/CHIDRAL)	340	1974	61.1	1,609	61.1	IDB & Canada	–
Chivor I – Hydro (ISA)	500	1975	75.1	2,381	52.3	IBRD	22.8
TOTAL	1,624		232.0	6,096	204.7		28.1

[1] As of mid-1970.

Table 13-6: GENERATING PLANTS PLANNED

	Installed Capacity MW	Estimated Schedule		Cost Estimate	
		Initiation	Completion	Foreign Exchange US$ million	Total Col$ million
Paipa – Thermal (ICEL/Nordeste)	66	) 1971/72	) 1973/74	7.4	190
Zipaquira – Thermal (EEEB)	66	)	)	7.4	190
Barrancabermeja – Thermal (ICEL/Nordeste)	66	)	)	7.6	200
Guatape II – Hydro (EPM)	280	1973	1978	26.0	740
Cartagena – Termonorte (ICEL-CORELCA)	100	1972	1974	10.5	270
Barranquilla – Termonorte II (ICEL-CORELCA)	100	1974	1976	9.1	240
Cartagena – Termonorte II (ICEL-CORELCA)	100	1976	1978	9.1	240
TOTAL	778	–	–	77.1	2,070

Table 13-7: MAJOR TRANSMISSION LINES UNDER CONSTRUCTION

	Voltage kV	Length km	Scheduled Completion	Cost Estimate		Foreign Financing		
				Foreign Exchange US dollars millions	Total Col$ millions	Obtained[1] US dollars millions	Source	Requirements[1] US dollars millions
Guatape – Medellin (EPM)	230	64	1970	1.0	23	1.0	Suppliers	–
Interconnection Network (ISA) Bogota-Manizales Manizales-Guatape								
Manizales-Cali	230	535	1971	21.0	503	14.6	IBRD & Suppliers	6.4
Paipa-Bucaramanga (ICEL)	230	165	1971	1.0	44	0.9	Suppliers	0.1
Barranquilla-Sabanalarga-Cartagena (ICEL-CORELCA)	230	120	1972	5.5	121	5.5	Suppliers	–
Flandes-Prado-Neiva (ICEL)	115	170	1970	2.0	50	2.0	IDB & Suppliers	–
Bogota-Villavicencio (EEEB)	115	75	1970	0.3	9	0.3	Suppliers	–
Medellin-Bolombolo (ICEL)	115	45	1971	0.4	13	0.4	Suppliers	–
Medellin-Santa Fe de Antioquia (ICEL)	115	45	1971	0.2	8	0.2	Suppliers	–
Zipaquira-Chivor (EEEB)	115	96	1971	0.4	10	–		0.4
Popayan-Cali (ICEL)	115	120	1971	1.0	37	0.2	Suppliers	0.8
Barranquilla-Santa Marta (ICEL-CORELCA)	115	110	1972	4.4	95	1.2	Suppliers	3.2
TOTAL	–	1,545		37.2	913	26.3		10.9

[1] As of mid-1970.

Table 13-8: MAJOR TRANSMISSION LINES PLANNED

	Voltage kV	Length km	Estimated Schedule		Cost Estimate	
			Initiation	Completion	Foreign Exchange US dollars millions	Total Col$ millions
Bucaramanga – Cucuta (ICEL)	230	120	1970	1972	1.0	35
Bucaramanga – Barrancabermeja (ICEL)	230	100	1970	1972	2.3	50
Guatape – Barrancabermeja (ISA)	230	200	1971	1973	3.4	76
Cartagena – Sincelejo (CORELCA)	230	150	1971	1973	7.5	165
Chivor – Suba – La Mesa (ISA)	230	180	1971	1974	Part of Chivor I – Hydro Proj.	
Chivor – Paipa (ISA)	230	110	1972	1974	3.2	73
Sabanalarga – Fundacion – Santa Marta (CORELCA)	230	170	1973	1975	9.0	200
Fundacion – Valledupar (CORELCA)	115	130	1973	1975	0.5	20
TOTAL	–	1,160	–	–	26.9	619

Table 13-9: PUBLIC POWER SECTOR INVESTMENT PROGRAM, 1970-72
(In millions of Col$)

	1970			1971			1972			Forecast Total Investments		
	Total Investment	Expected Financing		Total Investment	Expected Financing		Total Investment	Expected Financing		1973	1974	1975
		Local	External		Local	External		Local	External			
ICEL Subsidiaries and CORELCA	840	301	539	576	327	249	532	394	138	651	662	801
ISA, EEEB, EPM and CVC/CHIDRAL	1,314	470	844	1,300	739	561	1,844	1,114	730	1,855	2,205	1,795
Others (Municipalities)	72	69	3	83	83	—	97	97	—	120	135	204
TOTAL	2,226	840	1,386	1,959	1,149	810	2,473	1,605	868	2,626	3,002	2,800

[1] Incomplete; will be revised upwards.

carry out the projects listed in Tables 13-4 through 13-8 and all other investments by the public power entities in the country. The forecasts are based on the plans as of mid-1970. The revisions will be upwards as new projects are formulated.

The present and forecast finances of EEEB and EPM appear adequate to carry out, without need for budgetary contributions, their operations and investment programs and also to make the necessary contributions to ISA's investment program. CVC/CHIDRAL will need considerable national assistance to meet its investment program and its obligations to ISA; this is due mainly to the need to make substantial investments in Alto Anchicaya. ICEL/CHEC will fulfill its obligations to ISA with appropriations from the national budget. During 1970-72, ICEL subsidiaries and CORELCA will continue to rely heavily on national budgetary contributions and credits to finance their investment programs, as their internal generation of funds is expected to cover not more than half of the planned local financing. It is expected that this situation will be gradually improving as a result of progress achieved in the organization and development of the sector and in the implementation of appropriate tariff policies.

Planning

The active participation of Planeacion in the industry's recent planning and consolidation of ISA's role in planning long-range generation and transmission projects have helped to promote the development of a remarkable enthusiasm among the country's major power agencies to organize and expand their planning activities. Some of them have recently formed new planning departments. Planeacion and ISA have promoted the use of modern analytical techniques which allow simulation, for each alternative program of construction, of the operation of reservoirs, plants and transmission lines of the system under study, and appropriate calculation of the costs of each solution. To undertake such analyses, it is necessary that appropriate feasibility and other preinvestment studies be available; the use of local and foreign consultants by power agencies to carry out these basic studies is also being extended. It is notable that FONADE's financing of preinvestment studies in the power sector has recently absorbed about 50% of FONADE's total financing.

Although a good number of studies have been performed and are presently under way in the power sector, the process of continuing evolution and development that the sector is undergoing implies the need for additional preinvestment studies and also for a careful programming and definition of their priorities and scopes. Throughout the review of the industry presented in preceding sections, attention has been drawn to the need to undertake preinvestment studies on the interconnection of ISA and CORELCA systems and on rural electrification on a national scale. On the other hand, planning of power generation programs requires that appropriate plant feasibility studies be available to permit the consideration of sufficient alternative construction schedules. In Colombia, which has important hydroelectric resources, the availability of studies of prospective hydro developments is important, especially as the rate of growth of power demand in coming years is likely to be high. These studies require long-term surveys and investigations and considerable corresponding expenditures. It is therefore advisable that a good number of hydroelectric studies be undertaken in addition to those already under way. Five such studies, considered of high priority, have been included in the suggested preinvestment study program.

CHAPTER 14
STRUCTURE AND PROBLEMS OF COLOMBIAN AGRICULTURE

Introduction

The annual rate of agricultural growth in Colombia has increased from approximating 3% over many years to an average of 5.2% since 1966. This reflects an increase in production of basic food crops to keep pace with a population growth of approximately 3.2% plus additional growth in production of crops and livestock for export and import substitution.

It is quite possible that Colombia is ready to enter into a period of accelerated growth. With the help of the international coffee agreement, which Colombia is supporting to the maximum, there are possibilites that world coffee stocks can be maintained at reasonably low levels for some years to come. In the meantime, government policy to expand minor exports appears to be succeeding. The principal measures taken by the government have been a 15% export subsidy, a heavy infusion of credit for export crops, especially cotton, and direct intervention of the government marketing agency, IDEMA, in the purchase and foreign sales of farm products, principally rice and cattle.

The main products involved in recent growth and their annual growth rates over the past years are: seed cotton 16.0%, soybeans 16.3%, sorghum 22.2%, sugar 7.8%, sesame 7.8% and rice 5.5% (see Table 14-1). If these overall growth rates are to continue and if output of the other crops is to expand, Colombia faces several major problems the most serious of which is the generally high cost per unit of production. In part this is a result of high cost systems for producing and distributing modern inputs—a fairly typical situation in developing countries. More than this, however, it is the inefficient combining of inputs and husbandry resulting in low yield levels for most crops. Several measures are now being taken to correct this shortcoming. The main ones are a tripling of the agricultural research budget and an immunization program aimed at eventually eliminating aftosa from the cattle. Added investments are also scheduled for agricultural extension.

The problems of distribution of wealth in agriculture are serious because of the large number of very small holders. Of the approximately 1.5 million farm families, more than 50% have under three hectares of land which, with the exception of certain labor intensive crops, is not sufficient to provide an adequate level of income. Many of these families supplement their incomes with jobs other than agriculture or by working as laborers on larger farms, particularly in the older settled areas where traditional systems of large extensive livestock holdings still remain in the face of a rapidly growing population. In the newer lowland areas where land availability is not a severe constraint, the problems of coping with wet tropical conditions by traditional hand methods limit the area which family labor alone can handle. Typically the pattern which develops is a shifting agriculture which provides only a low subsistence level of living.

To transform this mass of part-time laborers and subsistence farmers into productive family farm units requires the injection of considerable technical assistance and capital. The experience to date of the Colombian Agrarian Reform Institute (INCORA) and other agencies shows the relatively high cost per family aided and the relatively small number of farmers who are effectively reached.

The government has taken several measures which have simultaneously increased production and helped the smallholder sector, but so far only a small number of farmers has benefited from these measures. The operations of the Coffee Federation are one notable example of progress achieved by providing an assured market for smallholder production. Another example is the work of the Caja Agraria in providing credit and modern inputs for small potato producers. Additional work opportunities have also been provided by the government decision not to allow the importation of mechanical cotton pickers. Some progress has also been made by reallocating land resources and colonizing new lands. The income and employment problems which remain are very large, however, and sustained efforts on a substantial scale are needed to solve them. The rural population, most of it poor, accounts for almost one-half of the total. Further, it is estimated that a 1.8% annual increase in agricultural employment is needed during

TABLE 14-1: AREA UNDER CULTIVATION AND OUTPUT, SELECTED CROPS, WITH GROWTH RATES,
1950-1969

(Area in thousands of hectares — Output in thousands of tons)
(Output in parentheses)

Crops	1950-54 Av.	1965	1966	1967	1968	1969	Growth Rate[1]
Coffee	739	812	811	811	816	813	0.6
	(366)	(474)	(492)	(468)	(480)	(474)	(1.5)
Cereals:	1,131	1,446	1,394	1,279	1,271	1,320	0.9
Maize	729	869	846	790	775	825	0.7
	(783)	(871)	(850)	(850)	(880)	(900)	(0.8)
Wheat	176	118	115	105	120	140	
	(133)	(106)	(94)	(107)	(120)	(170)	(1.5)
Rice	151	375	350	291	277	262	3.3
	(287)	(672)	(680)	(662)	(786)	(720)	(5.5)
Barley	52	54	53	53	54	54	0.2
	(62)	(65)	(62)	(63)	(63)	(68)	(0.6)
Sorghum	23[2]	30	30	40	45	39	11.1
		(70)	(60)	(90)	(100)	(90)	(22.2)
Potatoes	55	66	67	79	85	95	3.3
	(554)	(762)	(760)	(800)	(900)	(950)	(3.2)
Sesame	16	85	85	72	21	36	4.9
	(7)	(59)	(58)	(35)	(15)	(25)	(7.8)
Soybeans	12[3]	30	35	48	47	46	16.1
		(50)	(52)	(80)	(87)	(75)	(16.3)
Oil Palm	n.a.	14	17	21	21	21	9.4
(Palm oil)		(2)	(3)	(9)	(14)	(25)	(29.9)
Cotton	56	134	165	175	199	236	9.4
(Seed cotton)	(27)	(158)	(200)	(255)	(321)	(339)	(16.0)
Sugar	50	81	92	90	100	n.a.	1.1
	(196)	(485)	(537)	(597)	(663)	(709)	(7.8)
(Sugar for Panela)[4]	217	246	235	234	241	n.a.	0.7
	(620)	(560)	(650)	(680)	(700)	(650)	(0.3)
Bananas	n.a.	29	32	22	24	24	−4.6
		(338)	(392)	(366)	(353)	(330)	(−)
Cacao	32	37	37	37	39	40	1.3
		(17)	(18)	(17)	(18)	(19)	(3.4)
Tobacco	19	25	27	23	22	24	1.4
	(22)	(40)	(44)	(42)	(43)	(44)	(4.2)
Beans	94	76	64	69	70	54	−3.2
	(47)	(40)	(35)	(38)	(40)	(48)	(−1.2)

[1] Percent annual cumulative using as end points the data for the earliest and the latest years available.

[2] 1962-66 average, earliest figures available.

[3] 1958-1962 average, earliest figures available.

[4] Non-centrifugal sugar.

Source: Based on tables which appear in the crop section of this report, principally from data of the Office of Planning, Ministry of Agriculture.

the next fifteen years. It is in this perspective that future agricultural policies, as well as overall policies, must be viewed.

Salient Features

In 1969, the agricultural sector—crops, livestock, forestry and fisheries—contributed 30% of GDP. This proportion has been gradually declining over time as industrialization has proceeded. At the same time, there has occurred a significant diversification within agriculture itself. The overwhelming reliance on coffee has been reduced. While coffee has remained the country's major export, as a proportion of all agriculture it has declined from over 90% prior to 1965 to 75% in 1969. The recent acceleration of agricultural growth has occurred in the face of unchanged coffee output and is therefore so much more remarkable. In the meantime, the world coffee picture has improved, as a result of measures taken during the 1960's by the major producing countries to control production and of the frost in Brazil in 1969.

Colombia's wide range of environmental conditions provides good natural pastures for cattle grazing, and gives scope for great diversity of basic food and cash crops. Breakdowns of the growth by crop (area, output and yield) over the past two decades are provided in Tables 14-1 and 14-2. The data show that most of the increase in production may be attributed to an expansion in area rather than to greater productivity. The important exceptions are cotton, sugar, rice and tobacco which have shown notable increases in yields over the past decade. The yields of the basic food crops—corn, yucca, plantains and potatoes—have remained relatively static.

Agricultural Exports

Coffee exports amounted to US$353 million in 1969. The various "minor" agricultural exports have steadily increased their combined earnings from US$24.5 million in 1960 to US$119.7 million in 1969, accounting now for 25% of the agricultural export earnings (Table 14-3).

Import Substitution

Table 14-4 shows the changes in principal agricultural imports during the 1960-67 period. The main achievement here has been to avoid any notable growth in overall agricultural imports. The need to import vegetable oils and oil seeds has been almost eliminated. Rice too was occasionally imported in quantity in the past and is now in plentiful supply. However, wheat imports continue to grow and could become an important drain of foreign exchange if adequate measures are not taken to increase national production. Cocoa still represents several million dollars annually of exchange loss and Colombia has ideal natural conditions to become self-sufficient. Natural rubber and paper pulp fit in the same category. Possibilities also exist for replacing the imports of wool but it appears that little progress is being made. For the future the oil seed picture looks especially promising with annual growth rates in soybeans and cotton seed of over 19% during the past decade and with an even higher growth rate in palm oil, which started from a much lower base. Although import substitution alone, in general, does not offer the same field for expansion as exports, in certain products, especially those produced in the tropics, it is feasible that Colombia could go from an importing situation to one of important exports.

TABLE 14-2: YIELD PER HECTARE, SELECTED CROPS, 1950-1969

(Kilograms per Hectare)

Crops	1950-54 Av.	1965	1966	1967	1968	1969	Growth Rate[1]
Coffee	499	584	606	577	588	590	1.0
Cereals:							
Maize	1,071	1,002	1,005	1,076	1,135	1,090	0.1
Wheat	754	898	823	1,013	1,000	1,214	2.8
Rice	1,903	1,790	1,940	2,275	2,835	2,750	2.2
Barley	1,205	1,181	1,158	1,200	1,167	1,259	0.3
Sorghum	(2,122)[2]	2,330	2,000	2,250	2,290	2,300	1.6
Potatoes	9,978	11,463	11,343	10,127	10,588	10,500	0.3
Sesame	489	690	680	490	710	700	2.1
Soybeans	1,441	1,690	1,490	1,700	1,800	1,650	0.8
Oil Palm[3]	N.A.	160	160	410	670	1,170	64.4
Seed Cotton	435	740	760	905	1,005	905	4.4
Sugar (White)	3,951	6,026	5,864	6,658	7,057	7,385	3.8
Panela	2,863	2,279	2,763	2,909	2,909	N.A.	0.1
Bananas	N.A.	N.A.	N.A.	17,000	15,000	14,000	−9.3
Cacao	314	460	480	460	460	470	2.4
Tobacco	1,169	1,580	1,640	1,850	1,910	1,845	2.7
Beans	505	526	547	550	700	700	1.9

[1]Percent annual cumulative using as end points the data for the earliest and the latest years available.

[2]1962-1966 average, earliest figures available.

[3]Growth rate reflects trees maturing and coming into full production.

Source: Based on tables which appear in the crop section of this report, principally from data of the Office of Planning, Ministry of Agriculture.

TABLE 14-3: AGRICULTURAL EXPORTS BY VALUE OF EXCHANGE SURRENDER, 1960-69

(In Thousands of U.S. Dollars)

	1960	1961	1962	1963	1964	1965	1966	1967	1968	1969
Bananas	5,031	5,564	4,195	4,957	17,548	25,384	23,729	19,173	15,571	18,559
Tobacco	2,212	3,069	5,111	8,609	10,904	5,332	4,441	5,072	7,072	9,145
Meat and Livestock	—	21	169	179	362	8,780	7,404	2,922	3,159	12,211
Skins, Leather, Glands, Horns, etc.	—	331	1,102	1,067	1,652	2,403	2,806	1,711	1,724	2,000[1]
Sugar and Honey	—	5,233	7,451	5,038	3,282	7,696	10,043	15,947	22,035	17,495
Shrimp, Lobsters and Seafood	1,691	1,420	1,527	1,406	1,012	1,466	1,092	1,635	2,874	4,560
Timber	2,279	2,195	2,508	3,861	4,145	3,688	3,877	4,526	5,647	7,204
Cotton	13,293	10,770	20,230	6,212	9,296	6,662	4,954	19,607	33,695	36,413
Cotton Cake	—	—	—	395	910	2,313	2,705	1,114	5,026	7,275
Other Agricultural Products	—	570	637	964	469	1,449	1,043	172	922	4,840
Subtotal	24,506	29,173	42,930	32,688	49,580	65,173	62,094	71,879	97,725	119,702
Coffee	332,200	307,700	332,000	303,000	394,200	343,900	382,300	322,400	351,400	353,100
Total	356,706	336,973	374,930	335,668	443,780	409,073	390,394	394,279	449,125	482,802

[1] Preliminary estimate.

Source: Banco de la Republica and DANE (Central Statistical Office).

TABLE 14-4: PRINCIPAL IMPORTS OF AGRICULTURAL PRODUCTS, 1960-1967

('000 U.S. $) c.i.f.

	1960	1961	1962	1963	1964	1965	1966	1967
Dairy products and eggs	–	–	–	–	3,499	112	85	119
Wheat	7,496	11,289	13,041	8,337	12,849	12,852	19,958	12,757
Barley	–	–	–	–	203	0	4,276	529
Maize	0	2,985	0	0	1,206	0	0	0
Other cereals (mainly rice)	24	5,526	575	8	2,259	937	1,223	814
Cereal preparations (including malt)	2,516	2,702	71	52	1,658	268	957	252
Fruit and vegetables (including dry pulses)	2,217	3,528	1,377	1,222	3,069	1,496	2,091	1,273
Cocoa, tea, coffee and spices (mainly cocoa)	2,454	3,707	4,576	3,551	6,758	7,317	10,551	6,766
Fodder (including oil seedcake)	–	–	–	–	896	985	1,337	582
Beverages and tobacco	3,045	2,727	2,494	1,966	1,479	1,375	4,078	1,542
Oil seeds, nuts and kernels (mainly copra)	8,157	5,891	5,119	2,723	3,598	1,243	2,512	207
Natural rubber and rubber-like gums	5,869	3,303	4,476	4,597	3,356	3,944	5,793	3,641

Pulp and waste paper (mainly pulp)	4,847	5,922	6,301	7,358	7,280	8,149	10,997	5,795
Wool and other animal hair	10,140	12,853	9,867	10,057	11,104	8,298	10,835	5,253
Raw cotton, other than linters	730	322	504	1,190	2,061	5,593	4,204	458
Crude animal and vegetables materials	—	—	—	—	1,815	1,375	2,260	1,678
Animal and Vegetable oils and fats	9,586	4,938	10,897	7,018	12,678	10,369	24,119	10,653
Total Agricultural Imports	57,081	65,693	59,298	48,079	75,768	65,313	105,276	52,320
Total Imports	518,585	556,807	540,351	506,022	586,291	453,501	674,146	496,862

Note: Dashes indicate that an item was either zero or less than 1/2% of total imports.

Source: *United Nations Yearbooks of International Trade Statistics.*

Livestock

Poultry and hog production have been growing very slowly in Colombia, in comparison with the growth in other countries which have reached a similar stage of development. Apparently the biggest hindrance to expansion is the high cost of feed grains. The present growth rate in sorghum production suggests that it might play an important role in solving this problem. Sorghum is of approximately equal food value to corn and present yields are running almost double those of corn. During the period between 1960-64 and 1969, the area in sorghum and total sorghum production have quadrupled. It is very possible that the next decade may see the development of a strong poultry and hog industry in Colombia based on low cost sorghum; the expansion of oil seed production should yield as a by-product high protein cake for protein supplementation of livestock rations. If this happens, higher internal meat consumption plus the freeing of additional beef for export can be expected.

Policies Related to Minor Exports and Import Substitution

Table 14-5 compares the growth of exports and imports showing a growth rate of 19.3% in minor agricultural exports against 1.4% in agricultural imports. It must be acknowledged that export products started out from a very small base. Of special importance, however, have been government incentives for encouraging exports, especially the 15% direct fiscal subsidy. During this time there has been an important change in government policy away from exclusive import substitution to export promotion.

Recently price support policy has played an important part in stimulating production of certain crops, especially rice. The best grade of paddy has had a support price of Col$2,000 to Col$2,050 during each of the past three years. At the 1969 exchange rate this was roughly equivalent to US$115 per metric ton, above the world price. A surplus has now accumulated and it has been necessary to dispose of part of it at a loss to the price support agency (IDEMA). This was handled in two ways. Rice was sold to Chile and Peru under bilateral agreements above the international market price. In addition IDEMA imports certain foodstuffs which are sold at high prices in the domestic market and the profits are used to balance the losses in export operations.

Exchange rate policy and export subsidies are going to be major determinants of the level of minor exports in the years ahead. However, the comparative advantage of Colombian producers depends equally heavily on efficiency of production. Their cost of production depends on the level of prices for inputs and the cost of credit to purchase these inputs as well as labor costs and the productivity of labor. Interestingly enough, Colombia has built its major export agricultural sector—coffee—on small producers. The new minor exports, on the other hand, hither-

TABLE 14-5: AGRICULTURAL EXPORT-IMPORT BALANCE, WITHOUT COFFEE, 1961-1969
(In millions of US$)

	1960	1961	1962	1963	1964	1965	1966	1967	1968	1969	Growth Rate[1]
Exports	24.5	29.2	42.9	32.7	49.6	65.2	62.1	71.9	97.7	119.7	19.3
Imports	57.1	65.7	59.3	48.1	75.8	65.3	105.3	52.3	60.0	65.0	1.4
Balance	-32.6	-36.5	-16.4	-15.4	-26.2	-0.1	-43.2	+19.4	+37.7	+54.7	

[1] Percent annual cumulative through 1969 on base of 1960.

Source: Tables 14-3 and 14-4.

to have been based largely on capital-intensive enterprises rather than the labor-intensive enterprises involved in coffee production.

Reorganization of the Ministry of Agriculture

Before 1968, public investment in the agricultural sector was channeled through a multitude of separate organizations, many responsible for only one particular crop or function, such as livestock credit, crop credit, agrarian reform, research, extension and the like. Because of the weak position of the Ministry, the successful growth of a program usually required its separating from the Ministry. The 1968 reorganization, has dramatically changed this situation.

By two new decrees, the Ministry was made not only fully responsible for the country's agricultural and livestock planning, for drawing up and implementing a comprehensive development policy, but for the control, regulation and coordination of the programs of the different organizations which function within the agricultural and livestock field. As a member of the National Social and Economic Council, made up of the President's Cabinet, the Minister of Agriculture also has an important role in price policy, import restrictions, and measures to encourage or restrict the production of certain commodities.

In formulating policy, the Minister is advised by a National Agricultural Council and there is also an Executive Committee made up of the director or general manager of the seven major organizations within the agricultural sector:

Livestock Bank (Banco Ganadero)
Farm Credit Bank (Caja Agraria)
National Coffee Growers Federation (Federacion Nacional
    de Cafeteros)
Agricultural Research and Extension Institute (ICA)
Agrarian Reform Institute (INCORA)
Institute for Crop and Livestock Marketing (IDEMA)
Institute for Renewable Natural Resources (INDERENA)

The function of this Executive Committee which meets at least once a month is to analyze all development plans and budgets, advise on credit and marketing policies, review the research program, and generally assist the Minister in the execution of his various functions.

The Minister's office includes a Vice-Minister, and a Secretary General, supervising sections dealing with planning, judicial matters, technical supervision, and national peasant organization. The planning office of the Ministry is intended to play a key part in formulating agricultural policy. Its role is to coordinate the efforts of the planning sections within each of the agencies associated with the Ministry and serve as their contact point in relations with the agricultural section of the National Planning Department. In practice there are still problems in making this functional, but it would appear that the basis has been laid for effective agricultural planning at the national level.

In addition to the seven agencies, there are attached to, or form a part of, the Ministry of Agriculture: (i) public agencies: the Weather and Water Resources Service, the Fund for Diversification in the coffee zones and the regional autonomous development authorities for the Cauca Valley, Quindio, Choco, and Sabena of Bogota; (ii) semi-official business agencies: INAGRARIO (storage program operated jointly by IDEMA and Caja Agraria), VECOL (veterinary products company), and the Coffee Producers' Bank; (iii) joint public-commercial corporation, COFIAGRO (Financial Corporation to promote crops and cattle exports).

Problems and Potential of Agriculture

Despite the output growth attained in certain commodities, and the reorganization of the Ministry of Agriculture, the agricultural sector has several serious problems. The main problems shared by the majority of Colombian farmers are: uneconomically small farms and difficulty of access to additional land; lack of locally tested information on optimal use of modern inputs;

difficulty of access to credit and modern inputs; and inadequate markets and unattractive relationships between cost of inputs and prices of farm products. Low yields of most crops are one result of this combination of factors.

Access of Farmers to Land

Total land resources in Colombia amount to 113.8 million hectares. The available indication of land use is the 1960 agricultural census which covered 46.7% of the national territory— an area which contained an estimated 97.5% of the population. A total of 1,209,663 farm units were enumerated, with a total of 27,372,000 hectares, or just 24% of Colombia's total area and 51% of the area included in the census. The land use is analyzed in Table 14-6.

The pattern of land distribution by size of farm from 1960 census data is shown in Table 14-7. The inequality is striking. This census was carried out just before the passing of the agrarian reform law of 1961 and consequently does not reflect any changes during the past decade. However, the DANE (Central Statistical Office) sample survey for 1968 shows a growth of 300,000 in number of farms and an increase of 2 million hectares in total farm area. The new farm area comes principally from colonization and to a minor extent from redistribution of large holdings. Consequently, the majority of new farms should be in the 10 to 50 hectare range. The fact that the average additional holding is only 6.7 hectares (2 million hectares divided by

TABLE 14-6: LAND USE ON FARMS ENUMERATED IN 1960 CENSUS

	Hectares ('000)	%
Perennial Crops	1,458	5.3
Annual Crops	2,015	7.3
Land under fallow	1,581	5.8
Grazing Land	14,626	53.6
Forests	6,396	23.4
Other types	1,296	4.6
Total	27,372	100.0

TABLE 14-7: PATTERN OF LAND DISTRIBUTION BY FARM SIZE, 1960

Farm Size (hectares)	Number of Farms	%	Total Area (hectares)	% of total area
Less than 1.0	298,971	24.7	131,993	.5
1-3	308,352	25.5	545,964	2.0
3-5	150,182	12.4	561,019	2.0
5-10	169,145	14.0	1,164,749	4.3
10-20	114,231	9.4	1,572,076	5.8
20-30	44,049	3.6	1,043,554	3.8
30-50	42,740	3.6	1,595,147	5.8
50-100	39,990	3.3	2,680,471	9.8
100-500	36,010	3.0	6,990,471	25.6
500-1000	4,141	.3	2,730,764	10.0
over 1000	2,761	.2	8,321,619	30.4
TOTAL:	1,209,672	100.0	27,337,287	100.0

Source: 1960 Agricultural Census.

300,000 farms) probably reflects the fact that established farmers have continued to subdivide smallholdings.

There is a strong correlation between size of farm and percentage of the farm in grazing land (see Table 14-8). Only 4% of the smallest farms are in pasture, whereas the corresponding figure for the largest farms is 78%. Certain crops tend to be concentrated on small holdings and others on large holdings. Even on the large holdings, only small areas of certain crops are grown. For example, the average area in yucca on holdings of 200 hectares or more is only 3 hectares; the average area in plantains is under 4 hectares. In contrast the average area of corn grown on these larger holdings is over 12 hectares, the average rice area is nearly 25 hectares, barley is 44 hectares and cotton is 83. The yucca and plantains are grown as food crops for farm labor, whereas these farmers grow the other crops as commercial enterprises. Table 14-9 shows crop distribution by farm size. Although there is no particular technical reason why yields should be higher on large farms, this commercial orientation of production, along with easier access to credit and modern chemical inputs results in a positive correlation between size of farm and yield in certain crops (see Table 14-10). This is inconsistent with a finding quoted in the ILO study *Towards Full Employment,* pp. 64-65 that crop value of output per hectare in the sub-family farms is much higher than on the very large farms. This may happen because the very large farms normally use a large proportion of land for livestock grazing which has low output value per hectare (or even leave parts of the land unworked) while sub-family farms use all the land for growing the highest value crop that is technically possible.

Colombian policy on land distribution is carried out by a large public investment through the Colombian Institute for Agrarian Reform (INCORA) which became operative in 1962. The major results achieved by INCORA from 1962 to 1970 may be summed up as follows:

Land Titles.   INCORA has issued a total of about 90,000 titles for 2.7 million hectares of farm land. Most of the titles issued have been for small and medium-sized farms, the average size being about 30 hectares. Such titles are important in increasing productivity as they can be used as collateral in obtaining credit for agricultural production and other purposes.

TABLE 14-8: PERCENTAGE OF LAND DECLARED TO VARIOUS USES BY SIZE OF FARM

Hectares	Total	Arable Land Temporary Crops	Fallow	Permanent Crops	Pasture (Temporary & Permanent)	Mountains & Forests	Other Types of Land
Less than ½	39.08	30.29	8.78	23.33	4.44	.45	32.78
½-1	51.89	40.54	11.35	25.74	8.78	1.21	11.64
1-2	51.03	39.94	11.09	25.34	13.54	2.25	7.86
2-3	49.36	38.36	11.00	23.20	17.04	3.51	6.68
3-4	43.50	32.98	10.52	23.86	21.36	4.79	6.34
4-5	41.92	31.40	10.52	22.43	23.37	6.08	6.18
5-10	34.57	24.57	10.00	21.35	28.68	9.30	6.15
10-20	27.10	17.57	9.53	17.23	34.78	14.78	6.10
20-30	22.65	13.09	9.56	12.76	38.52	20.16	5.88
30-40	19.54	10.47	9.08	10.23	40.85	23.44	5.63
40-50	18.07	9.23	8.85	8.16	41.51	26.59	5.09
50-100	15.35	7.27	8.09	5.54	43.46	30.80	4.82
100-200	12.41	5.34	7.07	3.30	48.26	31.66	4.45
200-500	9.41	3.76	5.65	1.97	53.37	30.89	4.22
500-1000	7.24	2.61	4.63	1.34	58.90	28.21	4.26
1000-2500	5.26	1.74	3.52	0.85	63.64	26.12	4.10
2500 and over	1.46	0.45	1.01	0.56	77.89	15.88	4.00
TOTAL	12.89	7.13	5.76	5.53	53.31	23.31	4.74

Source: Agricultural Census 1960

TABLE 14-9: AREA PLANTED TO DIFFERENT CROPS ACCORDING TO FARM SIZE

(No. of farms in thousands, farm size in hectares, area in thousands of hectares, and percentage of total area)

Crop	0 – 5			5 – 50			50 – 200			200 and over			Total		
	No.	Area	%	No.	Area	%	No.	Area	%	No.	Area	%	No.	Area	%
Cotton[1]	3.3	3.5	3.9	2.6	16.8	18.8	0.9	25.5	28.6	0.5	43.5	48.7	7.3	89.3	100
Sesame	8.1	11.3	22.2	4.9	21.1	41.5	1.4	10.4	20.6	0.5	8.0	15.7	14.9	50.7	100
Peas	18.2	9.9	31.3	13.1	18.0	56.8	0.9	2.8	8.8	0.2	1.0	3.1	32.3	31.6	100
Rice	15.6	16.1	7.1	23.3	59.4	26.2	10.6	63.9	28.2	3.7	87.4	38.5	53.3	226.8	100
Sugar Cane	113.2	63.4	18.4	95.6	143.1	41.6	11.4	54.3	15.8	2.8	83.4	24.2	223.1	334.1	100
Barley	21.2	12.3	21.2	11.1	23.2	39.8	0.9	13.2	22.6	0.2	9.6	16.4	33.4	58.3	100
Beans	43.2	28.1	24.2	37.2	53.9	46.5	5.1	22.2	19.2	1.1	11.7	10.1	86.7	115.9	100
Corn	301.6	231.3	26.2	196.2	368.4	42.3	32.5	156.9	18.0	9.1	114.5	13.1	539.2	871.2	100
Potatoes	68.8	39.3	31.8	36.1	59.7	48.3	2.9	16.1	13.0	0.6	8.6	6.9	108.4	123.7	100
Sorghum & Millet	4.9	3.1	35.3	2.8	3.6	41.3	0.4	1.2	14.3	0.1	0.8	9.1	8.2	8.7	100
Tobacco	11.7	9.6	41.0	7.0	11.4	48.8	0.6	1.3	5.5	0.2	1.1	4.7	19.5	23.3	100
Tomatoes	3.3	1.5	45.5	1.2	1.4	41.7	0.1	0.3	8.4	0.04	0.1	3.3	4.7	3.3	100
Wheat	31.1	39.7	30.6	28.2	68.0	52.5	1.4	16.0	12.3	0.2	6.0	4.6	60.9	129.7	100
Yucca	112.7	53.6	24.6	115.4	111.1	51.1	21.1	35.2	16.2	6.0	17.5	8.1	255.2	217.3	100
Bananas	30.6	7.7	13.9	27.2	23.7	42.6	4.7	15.0	27.0	1.2	9.2	16.5	63.6	55.7	100
Cocoa	21.1	8.8	17.1	22.2	27.7	53.8	4.9	9.6	18.6	1.4	5.4	10.5	49.6	51.5	100
Coffee	238.9	209.6	21.6	169.1	557.7	57.6	17.8	145.5	15.0	3.3	55.9	5.8	429.0	968.6	100
Platanos	227.7	90.1	22.0	182.0	220.9	53.8	29.2	66.2	16.1	9.2	33.0	8.1	448.2	410.2	100

[1] Data supplied by Cotton Development Institute

Source: CIDA op. cit. p. 426, originally from Agricultural Census of 1960

TABLE 14-10: CROP YIELDS IN KILOGRAMS PER HECTARE BY SIZE OF FARM AND FOR INCORA PROJECTS

	Size of farm (hectares)								INCORA Projects
	0 to 2	2 to 5	5 to 10	10 to 20	20 to 50	50 to 200	200 to 500	500 to 2,500	
Sesame	474	454	378	413	530	432	1,005	653	525
Barley	806	794	987	778	837	1,460	1,790	1,996	1,802
Grain Sorghum	758	1,010	1,023	1,674	1,889	2,145	1,310	2,194	2,875
Coffee	433	447	468	502	435	497	549	591	
Bananas	735	693	724	750	725	726	668	825	
Cacao	356	271	257	250	240	226	231	342	
Yucca	7,371	6,618	6,114	5,955	6,693	9,056	9,802	9,953	8,274
Beans	255	284	271	288	291	297	360	469	739
Plantains	715	757	794	733	708	892	710	771	
Corn	786	791	774	819	830	1,013	1,231	1,136	1,967
Potatoes	4,090	4,578	4,459	6,904	4,780	7,174	6,682	11,421	15,550
Wheat	704	620	639	694	642	1,142	1,742	1,858	1,592
Tobacco	957	1,093	932	907	964	785	970	1,523	1,762
Lima Beans (Arveja)	322	350	268	347	344	434	387	965	1,158
Cotton	1,167	1,253	1,793	1,158	1,201	1,619	1,708	2,090	1,777
Rice	1,635	1,767	1,517	1,693	1,595	1,781	1,899	2,367	2,847
Sugar Cane	26,668	31,364	28,422	28,595	32,369	42,656	72,424	68,771	

Sources: The data by size of farm are from L. Jay Atkinson, *Agricultural Productivity in Colombia*, 1969, and consist of special tabulations made by the Central Statistical Agency of Colombia (DANE) of a sample survey covering the first semester of 1966. The INCORA data are from the DANE publication of *La Reforma Agraria en Cifras*, p. 131, January 1970 and the data are full year averages for 1968, thus the two sets of data are not fully comparable but nevertheless suggestive.

Colonization of Government Lands.   INCORA estimates suggest that it has participated in one way or another in opening up nearly 1 million hectares for colonization.

Flood Control, Drainage and Irrigation Projects.   INCORA has made infrastructure investments in some 0.6 million hectares. About 0.3 million hectares have been fully developed and are in production. In addition, INCORA and regional corporations are involved in pre-investment studies of about 1 million hectares of land for drainage and irrigation projects. These projects may call for over US$1 billion equivalent in investments if proved technically, economically and financially feasible.

Agricultural Credit.   This has absorbed more than one-third of INCORA's total investment (Table 14-11) and the majority of the agency's personnel is involved in this activity. Supervised credit provides the capital and technical assistance for establishing and developing farms, for settlement or colonization and for parceling as well.

In general it can be said that the INCORA projects are having a positive effect on crop yields and farm income for the affected families. However, the number of farmers helped directly is still very small. Out of some 40 million hectares of cultivable land, settled and unsettled, INCORA has acquired 3.8 million, most of it relinquished or annulled ownership.[1] Out of these 3.8 million hectares, only 190,000 have been distributed to 20,000 farmer families (Table 14-12). Against this, it is estimated that there are about 500,000 landless families, and their number is increasing at 10% per year. On the other hand, INCORA has granted 90,000 titles for 2.7 million hectares for unoccupied land (see above) acquired by INCORA for colonization and settlement purposes.

It should be clearly stated that the basic goals of more efficient allocation of land resources as specified in the agrarian reform law are still not being achieved. More than half of the farm families of Colombia still have less than 3 hectares of land and nearly two-thirds have less than 5 hectares (See Table 14-7). For most families and most crops 5 hectares can be considered the minimum of crop land needed to earn enough to support some minimum level of living. No matter how ambitious a man or his family may be, they must have some basic elements of production with which to begin—some land first and then access to modern inputs and credit— in order to produce efficiently. To efficiently farm more than 2 or 3 hectares under wet tropical conditions, a farmer must have more than a hoe and machete—at least the use of draft animals or tractor services.

The reasons for the lack of success in providing more adequate land for the landless and the very small holders are fairly clear. Although Colombia has a relatively good endowment of agricultural land, historically Colombia's abundant rainfall caused serious drainage problems in the valleys and lowlands. As a result, human diseases—especially malaria and yellow fever— caused serious difficulties and the population tended to concentrate in the Andean highlands. Eventually cattle grazing on an extensive scale spread into the river valleys and northern plains. This enterprise yields a profit with a minimum of supervision and therefore remains popular with absentee landowners. However, the rationale for this type of holding has changed. In the past few decades medical science has succeeded in bringing malaria and yellow fever under control. The chemical industries are producing insecticides, fungicides and herbicides to control the main limitations to crop production. Civil engineers have learned how to drain the lowland areas and thereby convert second-class grazing land into first-class crop land.

In spite of these changes, for political reasons, the land allocation which took place in past centuries has been difficult to change. Consequently the majority of the farming population continues to be concentrated on tiny mountain farms where the small size of their holdings also limits their access to credit and modern inputs. One reason for moving slowly in reallocating land resources has been a fear that reallocation would reduce production per unit area. In fact it is true that efficient commercial crop farms in Colombia produce higher yields than present small holdings. On the other hand, the yields on small holdings in the INCORA projects, where adequate technical assistance and credit are provided, compare very favorably with those on large commercial holdings (Table 14-10), pointing up the fact that efficient modern agricultural

1. Through expropriation 70,000 hectares were acquired in 1962-69.

TABLE 14-11: INCORA USE OF FUNDS BY MAJOR ACTIVITIES, 1962-1969
(in millions of Col$)

Activity	1962-1966	1967	1968	1969	Total	%
Land acquisition	112	51	68	81	312	8.8
Land reclamation	189	99	207	220	715	20.0
Roads	66	22	31	36	155	4.4
Farm credit	313	270	373	336	1,292	36.2
Other direct costs	55[1]	49[2]	105[2]	156[2]	365	10.2
Indirect costs[3]	252	147	178	150	727	20.4
Total	987	638	962	979	3,566	100.0

[1] Includes regional administration, reforestation, and community development.

[2] Includes regional administration, reforestation, and community development, titling, district maintenance, hydrology, building construction, topography, legal consulting, tenant and sharecropper administration (arrendatarios y aparceros).

[3] Includes central administration, debt service, and transfers.

TABLE 14-12: LAND ACQUIRED BY INCORA ACCORDING TO THE MANNER OF ACQUISITION AND USE, 1962-1969.
('000 Hectares)

Kind of Use	Manner of Acquisition					
	Voluntary Sale and Expropriation	Annulment of ownership (or relinquished)	Reversion	Cession	Total	Percent
Provisional allotment	58.9	6.7	—	0.4	66.0	34.7
Final allotment	19.7	—	—	43.1	62.8	33.0
Cooperative and communal exploitation	7.7	—	—	—	7.7	4.1
Housing centers	0.1	—	—	0.1	0.2	0.1
Experimental farms	0.1	—	—	—	0.1	—
Forest reserve	9.6	1.9	—	—	11.5	6.1
Land reclamation	27.9	—	—	—	27.9	14.7
Unusable land	1.7	2.0	—	5.3	9.0	4.7
Other uses	1.4	3.5	—	—	4.9	2.6
Total hectares distributed by INCORA	127.1	14.1	—	48.9	190.1	100.0
Total hectares acquired by INCORA	251.4[1]	3,197.4	24.3	276.1	3,749.2	
Remaining hectares	124.3	3,183.3	24.3	227.2	3,559.1	

[1] Of which voluntary sale 180,000 hectares and expropriations 70,000 hectares.

Source: INCORA.

production tends to consist more in achieving yield increments through the use of improved seed, chemical fertilizers, insecticides, herbicides and fungicides, than in labor substitution. Good management is essential for this.

Agricultural research in Colombia has been lagging as regards tropical crops and cultivation under irrigation. This has been mentioned in the past but the situation is now improving. Much closer cooperation in the field and at headquarters should be established between ICA and INCORA.

In part, too, adequate land utilization is being hindered by land speculation, which is in turn facilitated by inadequate land taxation. Colombian authorities are cognizant of this problem and have begun to take corrective measures through combined efforts of the National[2] Cadastral Institute "Agustin Codazzi" and INCORA.

The need for this kind of measure is suggested in Table 14-13 which shows a strong negative correlation between farm size and assessed value per hectare. Although one interpretation of these figures may be that the quality of land in the large holdings is extremely poor, it appears that in fact the soil and climate endowment of much of this land is good and that what is needed is well-directed pressure to bring the land into greater productivity.

INCORA still faces serious problems in carrying out its broad charter. The land resources which it has manipulated up to now are largely those which, for one reason or another, have been ceded by previous holders because it would be unprofitable for them to make the necessary investments to bring the land into production. Consequently, much of the land held by INCORA is marginal, whereas extensive good land resources continue to be under-utilized. The reasons for this are found in the interpretation of the agrarian code. Only irrigation projects make it possible for INCORA successfully to reallocate land. In all intended expropriations based on under-utilization, the legal action must first be settled in the courts. Such actions take years, so INCORA has made little attempt to prove under-utilization. Hence instead of looking at the entire land resources of Colombia and attempting to arrive at rational development plans, INCORA has been unduly limited in its reallocation of land resources. Consequently, decisions have sometimes had to be made in terms of choosing the least expensive of several high-cost alternatives. Colombian authorities are now seriously discussing possible changes in the agrarian laws to rectify this and other limitations.

In supporting development projects it appears that in some cases external lending agencies may also have had to decide among high cost projects, rather than choose among the best alternatives for improving production and productivity. One example of a promising area for development which appears not to have been considered is the extremely fertile 300,000 hectare Cauca Valley in the midst of the heavily populated central area of Colombia, which still has approximately half its area under extensive livestock production. The explanation given is that drainage on many of these lands is inadequate; they must therefore be kept in extensive livestock production. The next logical step would be a feasibility study to determine what it would cost to put in a drainage system for the Cauca Valley. If reclamation can be shown to be economically justified, a drainage project, combined, if appropriate with irrigation, could be established and land reallocation could then proceed under relevant provisions of the agrarian reform law.

The Problem of Low Yields

Average yield levels for most crops in Colombia are fairly low. Yet the potential for high yields clearly exists. Table 14-14 sets out the range in national average yields for the more important crops and for comparison also gives yields achieved under good management.

There are a variety of reasons for the relative lack of success in raising average yields. First, a large proportion of crop land is under traditional crops, produced for subsistence rather than for market, and the level of husbandry has been low. On these crops there has been little use of improved varieties, chemical fertilizers, herbicides, pesticides and fungicides. Most grazing lands still do not benefit from introduction of improved species or fertilization and thus their carrying capacity is low. However, beginnings have been made in the use of advanced technology, particularly in the production of crops to be marketed, either internally or abroad.

---

2. Central Government.

TABLE 14-13: NUMBER, AREA AND ASSESSED VALUE OF THE ASSESSED PLOTS BY SIZE GROUPS

	Assessed Plots		Assessed Area		Assessed Value Total		Averages	
	Number	%	Hectares	%	Thousands of Col$	%	Per Plot (in Col$)	Per Hectare (in Col$)
Less than 0.5	292,679	20.40	51,894	0.24	435,855	3.35	1,500	8,400
0.5- 1	186,513	13.00	120,405	0.55	317,083	2.44	1,700	2,600
1- 2	254,935	17.73	324,338	1.48	610,938	4.70	2,400	1,900
2- 3	135,327	9.40	297,811	1.34	460,791	3.55	3,400	1,500
3- 4	93,291	6.50	299,555	1.36	428,186	3.30	4,600	1,400
4- 5	57,828	4.00	239,030	1.10	294,782	2.27	5,100	1,200
5- 10	148,312	10.30	976,876	4.46	1,140,877	8.78	7,700	1,200
10- 20	101,831	7.08	1,350,382	6.16	1,277,025	9.83	12,500	950
20- 30	43,545	3.03	1,001,089	4.57	769,804	5.92	17,700	800
30- 40	26,439	1.84	867,662	3.96	579,427	4.46	21,900	700
40- 50	17,245	1.20	734,425	3.35	470,509	3.62	27,300	650
50- 100	39,598	2.75	2,623,309	12.00	1,426,106	10.98	36,000	550
100- 200	21,670	1.50	2,860,004	13.05	1,382,581	10.64	63,800	500
200- 300	7,665	0.53	1,777,606	8.11	777,461	6.00	101,400	450
300- 400	3,582	0.25	1,173,325	5.36	530,536	4.10	148,100	450
400- 500	2,009	0.14	854,896	3.90	348,652	2.67	173,500	400
500-1,000	3,217	0.22	2,155,092	9.84	899,932	6.92	279,700	400
1,000-2,500	1,322	0.10	1,859,999	8.50	552,184	4.25	417,700	300
2,500-5,000	334	0.02	1,677,715	7.65	273,197	2.10	817,900	160
more than 5,000	68	0.005	662,562	3.02	15,891	0.12	233,700	20
Total	1,437,410	100.00	21,907,975	100.00	12,991,817	100.00	9,040	600

Source: INCORA, based on data from the Institute Geografico, "Agustin Codazzi", February 1963. Data for 723 municipios out of a total of 837 in the departments.

TABLE 14-14: CURRENT RANGE IN CROP YIELDS AND POTENTIAL PRODUCTIVITY UNDER IMPROVED MANAGEMENT

	Yield Range National Average 1965-1969	Range in Yields achieved under proper management [1]	
	(kgs/Ha)	(kgs/Ha)	
ANNUAL CROPS		Commercial	Experimental
Cotton-fiber	440- 600	1,100	
Cotton - seed	760- 1,000	2,700	
Tobacco	1,600- 1,900		
Corn	1,000- 1,100	3,500	7,000
Wheat	900- 1,300	2,800	4,500
Barley	1,560- 1,950	3,000	5,900
Rice (irrigated paddy)	2,900- 4,200	4,500	6,000
Soybeans	1,500- 1,800	2,000	2,500
Sesame	650- 800		
Beans	520- 570	1,500	2,200
Potatoes	10,100-11,500[2]	40,000	60,000
Yuca	5,600- 5,900		
PERENNIAL CROPS			
Coffee	˙550- 600	5,000	
Sugar (Centrifugal)	6,000- 7,380	10,000	40,000
Sugar (Panela)	2,300- 2,900		
Cacao	450- 470	800	1,000
Bananas	11,200-13,300		
Plantain	6,300- 8,100		
Palm oil		3,000	6,000

[1] Data from "La Brecha en la Productividad Agricola en Colombia" ICA 1969

[2] The Ministry of Agriculture - IDEMA series are used here. However, it should be mentioned that Caja Agraria data show a range of 6,900 to 7,300 kgs/ha and the DANE sample shows 6,200 to 7,100 for the same period. The IDEMA series may be somewhat biased in favor of commercial sales.

The knowledge problem related to yields is twofold: (1) to determine the optimum combination and level of inputs for specific soils and climates, and (2) to gain general acceptance of these sets of practices among farmers. Knowledge, however, is not enough in itself to raise productivity. The inputs needed to achieve this, the mechanical equipment, the fertilizers, the improved seed, the pest control materials, all require finance, and without credit cannot be purchased.

Another constraint that still hinders the full application of inputs is price in relation to the returns they yield, and the availability of the inputs at the right time and place and in sufficient quantities. There is inadequate information at present on whether supplies of fertilizer and plant protection products are always readily available at the various distribution centers.

Finally there is the incentive that prices can give to increasing output. Price supports have been used for some time to induce investment and obtain technical change and this aspect will be dealt with in more detail in a later section.

Availability and Use of Modern Inputs

There are six principal inputs that may serve as indicators of the degree of modernization that Colombian agriculture has achieved: farm machinery, improved seeds, herbicides, fungicides, insecticides, and fertilizers.

Farm Machinery.   To move from a traditional low income subsistence agriculture to a more productive level requires some form of mechanization to enable the farmer to handle sufficient land to produce a reasonable income. As a minimum, draft animals or tractor services will be required. The imports of farm tractors have varied considerably from year to year as can be seen in the following data:

Year	Number
1954	2,374
1955	2,493
1956	2,239
1957	852
1958	1,565
1959	1,844
1960	2,428
1961	1,930
1962	1,905
1963	1,137
1964	2,000
1965	1,540
1966	1,756
1967	1,764
1968	2,989

Colombia is expanding domestic production of a considerable range of farm implements. One company now appears ready to initiate production of a 12 hp tractor developed in cooperation with ICA for use on small holdings. At present only 3.6% of the farms are mechanized although the percentage of the area operated with tractor power is much higher.

Improved Seeds.   The importance of quality is well recognized and the agencies responsible for developing, testing and distributing better seed have greatly expanded output during the past decade (see Table 14-15). The basic research work for developing new varieties or introducing them from abroad has been done by the research institutes. The early work in corn and wheat was assisted by scientists of the Rockefeller Foundation. In 1953, the Caja Agraria took on the task of multiplying and distributing the first improved seed of wheat and corn. Beans were added in 1956 and the use of these locally developed improved seeds has slowly expanded. When local rice breeding work resulted in improved varieties adapted to irrigated production, acceptance grew from 2.5% in 1961 to 55% in 1967.

Good foreign varieties of soybeans, grain sorghum and cotton were found to be well adapted in Colombia. Subsequently, local seed production was begun and now accounts for most of the seed planted.

Seed distribution presents a gradually improving picture. Future success will depend in large part on the success of the Colombian Agricultural Research Institute (ICA) and the new International Agricultural Center for Tropical Research (CIAT) in developing more productive seeds which can be multiplied and distributed by public and private agencies.

Herbicides and Pesticides.   Not one of the modern inputs is essential for all crops or all areas and this is reflected in the state-by-state breakdown in Table 14-16. Herbicide use is heaviest in the wheat and barley areas of the highlands and in some of the new lowland cropping areas of Bolivar, Cordoba, Magdalena and Meta. Insecticides and fungicides are heavily used in potato production in Boyaca, Cundinamarca and Narino.

TABLE 14-15: PERCENTAGE OF LAND AREA PLANTED TO IMPROVED SEEDS BY CROPS IN COLOMBIA, 1953-67 [1]

Year	Wheat	Corn	Beans	Irrigated rice	Barley	Cacao	Soybeans	Grain Sorghum	Cotton	Tobacco	Potatoes
1953	0.7	0.5									
1954	4.4	1.4									
1955	0.5	2.6									
1956	3.1	4.2	0.04								
1957	2.8	7.0	0.3								
1958	8.4	4.5	–								
1959	15.3	5.6	0.3								
1960	11.2	6.2	1.2		88.8		100.0				1.9
1061	14.7	6.5	0.7	2.5	89.3		100.0				0.4
1962	13.7	10.4	1.9	18.9	75.5		100.0				0.2
1963	15.5	9.8	3.3	25.1	89.0		100.0	100.0	98.7	100.0	0.1
1964	15.6	14.3	2.1	38.5	71.2		100.0	100.0	99.3	100.0	
1965	19.3	14.1	9.4	50.8	79.2		100.0	100.0	90.7	100.0	
1966	23.6	15.1	7.4	54.4	84.7		100.0	68.6	100.0	100.0	
1967	45.1	22.8	12.2	54.9	72.1	29.3	86.7	83.6	94.2	100.0	0.4

[1] In 1967 these were all locally produced seeds with exception of the following importations: rice, 2.4%, sorghum, 35%, and cotton 5.6%.

Source: Boletin Mensual de Estadistica, DANE, January 1970.

TABLE 14-16: FARM MECHANIZATION, IRRIGATION AND USE OF HERBICIDES, INSECTICIDES AND FUNGICIDES FOR THE MAIN AGRICULTURAL CROPS BY DEPARTMENTS, 1968
(Percent of farms using modern inputs)

Departments	Total No. of Farms	Machinery		Irrigation		Herbicides		Insecticides		Fungicides	
		Number	%	Number	%	Number	%	Number	%	Number	%
Antioquia	197,789	436	0.2	135	0.1	1,042	0.5	8,477	4.3	7,639	3.9
Atlantico	6,254	235	3.8	15	0.2	74	1.2	108	1.7	18	0.3
Bolivar	75,00	1,017	1.4	126	0.2	10,772	14.4	5,806	7.7	1,824	2.4
Boyaca	230,820	5,871	2.5	23,164	10.0	13,238	5.7	60,030	26.0	62.715	27.2
Caldas	91,541	104	0.1	5	0.0	591	0.6	10,586	11.6	883	1.0
Cauca	89,941	1,131	1.3	432	0.5	704	0.8	1,943	2.2	1,082	1.2
Cordoba	76,854	1,771	2.3	120	0.2	4,036	5.3	1,529	2.0	671	0.9
Cundinamarca	166,916	11,212	6.7	5,519	3.3	11,746	7.0	29,342	17.6	23,310	14.0
Huila	48,747	637	1.3	766	1.6	637	1.3	2,652	5.4	2,098	4.3
Magdalena	73,284	2,053	2.8	344	0.5	5,197	7.1	960	1.3	411	0.6
Meta	29,707	4,147	14.0	350	1.2	2,923	9.8	2,622	8.8	1,519	5.1
Narino	107,958	1,909	1.8	1,379	1.3	15,266	14.1	17,817	16.5	16,606	15.4
Norte de Santander	43,690	47	0.1	345	0.8	556	1.3	1,620	3.7	1,610	3.7
Santander	105,524	91	0.1	662	0.6	2,407	2.3	9,867	9.4	6,122	5.8
Tolima	89,307	15,196	17.0	463	0.5	1,292	1.4	8,225	9.2	9,851	11.0
Valle	71,130	8,042	11.3	1,434	2.0	1,476	2.1	9,106	12.8	3,834	5.4
TOTAL	1,504,462	53,897	3.6	35,259	2.3	71,957	4.8	170,690	11.3	140,193	9.3

Source: DANE Sample Survey.

Trends in Fertilizer Use

The soils in the arable areas of Colombia are largely acid Latosols that have been depleted of much of the nutrient necessary for plant growth by natural leaching coupled with many years of intensive farming. Fertilizer use, expressed in nutrient terms, grew at an annual rate of 7.6% from 1955 through 1969. During the 1960-64 to 1965-69 period, the growth rate declined slightly to 5.8%. However, nitrogen use continued to increase at an average annual rate above 15% during the full period. (See Table 14-17).

Table 14-18 shows sample survey data on fertilizer use by crops. Several significant facts stand out. It is not only the export crops that receive fertilizers; the most important consumer of fertilizers in terms of total area fertilized is a crop produced mostly by small holders principally for the internal market—potatoes—with more than 90% of the producing area fertilized. Next in line are barley and wheat, crops also produced mostly by small holders in the highlands. Tobacco is next, then cotton. Cotton is an interesting case in that there are two important planting periods each year. Only 17% of the main planting is fertilized, yielding an average of 1,500 kilos per hectare; whereas 59% of the other crop is fertilized, and yields close

TABLE 14-17: APPARENT CONSUMPTION OF FERTILIZERS
EXPRESSED IN THOUSANDS OF TONS OF NUTRIENTS 1955-69

Year	N (Nitrogen)	P_2O_5 (Phosphorus)	K (Potassium)	Total Nutrients	Percentage with respect to 1955
1955	7.3	26.2	15.8	49.3	100
1956	7.7	31.4	10.1	49.2	100
1957	10.8	49.9	10.2	70.9	144
1958	10.1	36.7	20.2	67.0	136
1959	7.2	26.7	11.4	45.3	92
1960	10.9	36.5	13.9	61.3	124
1961	15.0	47.4	18.6	81.0	164
1962	15.3	43.6	20.1	79.0	160
1963	22.5	45.3	24.6	92.4	188
1964	42.4	55.0	34.9	132.3	269
1965	29.3	33.8	21.8	84.9	172
1966	45.3	45.4	31.8	122.5	248
1967	47.9	48.0	29.9	125.8	255
1968	44.9	45.7	31.5	122.1	248
1969	54.0	49.1	33.4	136.5	277
Percent 1969 with respect to 1955	740	187	211	277	
Annual growth rate 1955-1969	15.4%	4.6%	5.5%	7.6%	

Sources: Data for 1955-65 from 1970 CIAP report on Columbia. Data for 1966 and 1967 "Informe Sobre La Produccion y Consumo de Fertilizantes en Colombia", National Planning Department Data for 1968 and 1969 calculated from unpublished manuscript of W. Gregory.

TABLE 14-18: AREA PLANTED, PERCENTAGE OF AREA FERTILIZED
AND AVERAGE YIELDS OF SELECTED CROPS, 1967-68[1]

Crop	Area Planted in Hectares	Area Fertilized	Percentage of Planted Area	Average Yield Kg/Ha
(Second Half 1967)				
Annual Crops				
Sesame	91,109	1,938	2.1	497
Cotton	127,408	21,672	17.0	1,507
Broad Beans	41,905	4,295	10.2	382
Rice	118,634	43,011	36.2	2,255
Barley	24,953	16,015	64.2	1,062
Beans	71,023	2,503	3.5	362
Corn	629,162	34,851	5.5	918
Sorghum	27,389	10,554	38.5	1,805
Potatoes	63,989	59,917	93.6	6,648
Tobacco	11,047	6,949	62.9	1,110
Wheat	25,419	10,478	41.2	1,005
Yuca	121,656	6,178	5.1	6.575
TOTAL	1,353,694	218,361	16.1	
(First Half 1968)				
Sesame	21,184	542	2.1	601
Cotton	75,935	45.161	59.4	1,970
Broad Beans	31,687	3,944	12.4	403
Rice	277,838	58,392	21.0	2,050
Barley	36,167	24,324	67.2	1,211
Beans	83,474	2,439	2.9	346
Corn	691,023	41,466	6.0	984
Sorghum	16,274	4,059	24.9	1,307
Potatoes	98,170	86,302	87.9	6,218
Tobacco	26,326	15,370	58.3	1,020
Wheat	97,556	69,768	71.5	988
Yuca	175,127	4,958	2.8	8,960
Subtotals	1,630,761	356,725	21.8	
Perennial Crops				
Bananas	82,080	5,389	6.6	825 Stems
Cacao	49,441	2,420	4.9	300
Coffee	946,332	109.912	11.6	442
Sugar Cane	408,872	60,624	14.8	48,332
Platano	374,983	3,798	1.0	810 Stems
Subtotals	1,861,708	182,143	9.8	
TOTAL	3,492,469	538,868	15.4	

[1] One full crop year consisting of second half of 1967 and first half of 1968. This is the most recent full year available. Data are presented separately here for the two semesters to point up the differences in rates of fertilization and yields for the two seasons. The data for perennial crops are given on a yearly basis and published in the first semester report.

Source: DANE National Agricultural Sample.

to two tons. In rice and sorghum too, there are notable differences in yields. Yuca, beans and corn—traditional food crops—receive very little fertilizer, although they cover a vast land area. The lowest percentage of area fertilized is for an oil seed crop—sesame—that has been grown in Colombia for many years but for which genetic material with high yielding potential has been lacking.

Crude approximations of total fertilizer needs for the nation have been made by ICA, using as a basis average recommended rates for the principal crops. These are expressed in terms of elemental nitrogen, P_2O_5 and K_2O. Summed up on a national basis, the following estimates are obtained:

Nitrogen:		222,500 tons
P_2O_5	:	135,000 tons
K_2O	:	132,700 tons

These must be considered conservative estimates. According to these figures, in 1969 Colombian farmers were consuming as much as 25% of the nitrogen, 35% of the phosphorous and 20% of the potash indicated as minimum national requirements. On the other hand, only 20% of the land in annual crops received fertilizer and about 16% of that in perennial crops. If pasture land is also included, then the fertilized area is only about 4% of the total. Obviously there remains a large area which may require fertilization.

Response to Fertilizer.   There is a serious knowledge gap in regard to crop response to the various fertilizer elements. The ICA soil testing laboratory has begun to calibrate its procedures by carrying out soil fertility trials in certain parts of the country. However, progress has been slow and in the meantime fertilizer recommendations are at best approximate. In addition much of the soil fertility work has been conducted with inadequate experimental designs; consequently, it has not been possible to make economic interpretations of the data. In the absence of response curves, general recommendations are made for use of mixed fertilizer, including all three of the major elements to insure against a deficiency of any one. This has two important cost implications: first, the additional cost of unneeded elements, and second, the additional cost of mixing and transporting a bulkier product because mechanical mixes also include a certain amount of sand filler.

Fertilizer Costs Related to Produce Prices.   There are two main difficulties in making this comparison: inadequate data on product prices received by farmers, and lack of information on fertilizer prices at the farm level. However, this is a crucial relationship for determining the changing profitability of fertilizer use.

During recent years prices of fertilizers have increased in a series of jumps and on the average have risen more rapidly than farm produce prices. The relationship has varied considerably from year to year, but in general has deteriorated as can be seen in Table 14-19.

Farm level prices are not available for international comparisons; however, a comparison of retail prices at Bogota with those in the Washington, D.C. area shows Colombian prices 10% higher on urea (US$117 vs US$106) and about 21% higher (US$88 vs US$73) on mixtures such as 5-20-12. These relative prices place Colombian farmers at somewhat of a disadvantage. However, Colombian peso price increases should be less in the next few years as nitrogen production facilites begin to produce more nearly to full capacity.

In the case of phosphorus, reductions in world market prices are of direct benefit to Colombia as 85% of needs are imported.

Transportation of Fertilizer.   The costs of moving fertilizer accounts for more than 20% of the cost for many farmers. This is due in part to imports of phosphorus and in part to the location of the main nitrogen plants. About 40% of all mixed fertilizer is also made on the north coast of Colombia. Shipping is costly and in the past has frequently caused serious delays in

TABLE 14-19: COMPARISON OF PRICES FOR FERTILIZERS AND FARM
PRODUCTS 1958-67

Years	Fertilizer Prices[1] Col$	Index of Fertilizer Prices	Index of Prices of Farm Products[2]	Farm Products Fertilizer Index
1958	526	100	100	100
1959	577	110	106	96
1960	576	110	107	97
1961	580	110	126	115
1962	629	120	123	103
1063	1,086	207	172	83
1964	1 268	241	234	97
1965	1,302	243	224	90
1966	1,484	282	255	90
1967	1,669	318	267	84

[1] Average price of a metric ton of an average formula of 10-22-11.

[2] Without coffee.

Source: National Planning Department of Colombia, "Informe Sobre la Produccion y Consumo de
Fertilizantes en Colombia", 1968.

delivery. Hopefully recent purchases of new rolling stock will correct this problem for future plantings.

Research and Dissemination of Knowledge

In attempting to attain high productivity in agriculture, Colombian authorities are fully cognizant of the key importance of public services for research and dissemination of knowledge. However, in Colombia, the development and testing of modern technology is complicated by the ecology—the vast number of soil and climates in the producing areas—and by the large number of crops grown in each ecological zone. As a result, plant breeding and varietal testing must be done with many different crops and at many locations. Soil fertility work must take into account various crops in attempting to determine the optimal fertilizer application for a given soil. And disease and insect protection programs must discover the optimum methods for controlling insects and diseases on many soils and climates, as must also the research on weed control. To accelerate progress in this most important field, Colombia has reorganized the Instituto Colombiano Agropecuario (ICA) to give it the major research responsibility in agriculture. Among other responsibilities it was given the work of the previous Animal Disease Prevention Institute, the Cotton Development Institute and the Tobacco Development Institute. Equally important, the major extension responsibility has been transferred to ICA, thus assuring close ties between research and extension programs.

The sharp increase in ICA's budget from 1968 to 1969 is in large part a reflection of this added staff and responsibilities. The technical staff on research totaled 524 at the beginning of 1970, which is more than double the number employed in 1968. The annual budget for 1970 is Col$137.6 million, a fourfold increase on the 1968 budget. Many new experimental stations have been established and the earlier criticism that too much attention was being given to temperate crops has been heeded and the emphasis now is more towards tropical crops. For example, 60% of the technical staff as well as 60% of the 1970 budget is now allocated to the lowlands and warmer regions. Tables 14-20 and 14-21 give the allocation of technical staff to the temperate and tropical experimental stations over the past five years, as well as the increasing financial provisions that have been made over this period.

ICA's program of investigations covers breeding and selection of all the major crops as well

TABLE 14-20: DISTRIBUTION OF ICA EXPENDITURES BY LOCALITY, 1965-70

(In '000 of Col$)

Year and Type of Expenditure: A=Operative B=Investment

	1965 A	1965 B	1966 A	1966 B	1967 A	1967 B	1968 A	1968 B	1969 A	1969 B	1970 A	1970 B
Cold Climate												
Tibaitata	1,918	9,015	2,552	8,133	3,101	12,274	3,443	2,073	6,573	14,563	5,325	20,242
Surbata	203	458	252	409	282	516	288	620	2,629	4,623	1,197	6,747
San Jorge	263	285	156	539	178	718	194	862	1,753	3,930	1,819	5,735
Obonuco	454	899	545	1,024	759	1,856	759	2,227	2,018	5,657	1,197	7,022
La Selva									222	757	306	997
El Arsenal									230	395	835	2,526
Tinaga									114	237	573	1,636
Total	2,838	10,657	3,505	10,105	4,320	20,364	4,684	5,782	13,539	30,162	11,252	44,905
Hot Climate												
Palmira	1,134	4,504	1,606	4,214	1,813	8,013	2,031	9,616	3,364	9,429	3,591	11,703
Turipana	1,340	1,322	1,336	1,760	1,881	2,839	2,420	3,407	2,334	6,330	2,409	7,248
La Libertad	325	492	393	515	1,048	1,336	1,290	1,603	1,106	2,156	1,173	3,855
Nataima	331	531	432	481	906	1,152	1,173	1,382	1,680	3,190	1,243	5,285
Cesar	294								294	3,471	1,310	6,919
El Carmen									1,245	3,376	1,204	3,624
Tulio Ospina									1,335	4,541	1,668	5,440
Carimagua									284	554	302	991
La Caldera									71	126	384	1,180
Llano Grande									269	632	1,361	3,563
Iraca									190	370	201	661
Mira									1,009	2,829	898	3,511
La Esperanza									117	317	201	603
San Joaquin									194	528	201	603
Maranones									187	354	138	587
El Nus									178	605	250	816
La Pepilla									46	546	150	850
Libano									42	496	241	1,150
Balboa									336	943	299	1,170
Uraba									489	1,665	556	1,813
Marconia									38	447	170	870
Caqueta												1,012
Total	3,130	6,849	3,767	6,970	5,648	13,340	6,914	16,008	14,808	42,905	17,950	63,554
Grand Total	5,968	17,506	7,272	17,075	9,968	33,704	11,598	21,790	28,347	73,067	29,202	108,459
Hot Climate as % of Total	52	39	52	41	57	40	60	74	52	59	61	59

Note a: Investment expenditures for 1969 and 1970 were calculated according to government budget categories.

    b: The large differences in investment expenditures for 1969 and 1960 compared to 1970 are due to the reorganizing of government agencies in agriculture which gave new responsibilities to ICA including those which had been carried out previously by the Tobacco Institute, the Cotton Promotion Institute and the Institute for Prevention of Livestock Diseases.

Source: ICA.

TABLE 14-21: DISTRIBUTION OF TECHNICAL PERSONNEL BY LOCALITY I.C.A. 1963-70

Locality	1963	1965	1967	1968	1969	1970
Number						
Cold Climate						
Tibaitata	62	75	90	104	135	144
Surbata	1	2	2	4	9	10
San Jorge	3	2	2	4	6	6
Obonuco	6	6	7	11	11	15
La Caldera	–	–	–	–	–	32
Sub-total	72	85	101	123	161	207
Hot Climate						
Palmira	34	41	46	50	53	61
Turipana	9	12	14	17	34	38
La Libertad	2	6	8	10	16	17
Nataima	4	5	6	9	20	21
Tulio Ospina	–	–	–	–	19	23
San Jose del Nus	–	–	–	–	5	9
Uraba	–	–	–	–	–	1
Clarconia	–	–	–	–	–	17
Est. La Pepilla	–	–	–	–	–	5
Est. El Libano	–	–	–	–	–	15
Granja Valledupar	–	–	–	–	–	4
Est. El Mira	–	–	–	–	6	7
Est. Balboa	–	–	–	–	3	3
Carimagua	–	–	–	–	–	4
Llano Grande	–	–	–	–	–	71
Saravena-Tinaga El-Arsenal	–	–	–	–	–	21
Sub-total	49	64	74	86	156	317
total	121	149	175	209	317	524
Hot Climate as % of Total	40.5	43.0	42.3	41.1	49.2	60.2

Source: ICA

as studies of disease, pest and weed control measures. More attention is being given to irrigation, agricultural engineering, animal husbandry and farm management practices.

Although soil fertility requirements are being studied for the main crops at most stations, there is insufficient experimentation at the farm level to test the results thus obtained. Consequently there is as yet insufficient knowledge about the fertilizer needs of the main groups of soils in the country and consequently it is not possible to make precise recommendations on optimum fertilizer use. A pre-investment study on this problem seems appropriate and if carried out should yield much needed basic information on the optimum combination of elements, levels of application, desirable plant population, etc., for the major ecological conditions and crops of Colombia. This could then provide a sound economic basis for greatly expanded investment in fertilizer use.

In addition to ICA, two private organizations undertake some agricultural research. The National Coffee Federation has for a long time provided funds for work on coffee, and on some crops or enterprises which could be used for diversification away from coffee. The Institute of Technological Research also has projects related to agriculture. One recent study has been on the possibilities of using surplus rice for making flour to mix with wheat in the baking industry.

The range of areas and crops covered by research would appear to be reasonable in view of past budget limitations. The total investment in research is still small and should be enlarged as rapidly as competent personnel can be trained to tackle the most promising leads for improving the efficiency of production.

ICA's extension activities started in 1967 when it took over the Ministry of Agriculture's 16 extension agencies. This number was expanded to 42 and recently has been increased to 58. Each agency comprises a basic establishment of either two agronomists, or one agronomist and one livestock specialist or veterinary officer, or in areas largely devoted to livestock, of two livestock specialists. In addition, each agency has a home economics adviser. Attached to this nucleus of three professional staff is a team of 5 "practicos" or technicians with a technical high school education, though some of these may also be graduates.

In addition to ICA other organizations carry out technical assistance, usually in conjunction with the supervised credit made available through INCORA, the Caja Agraria and CO-FIAGRO. Their extension staff may either be their own permanent employees or independent agricultural consultants engaged to provide technical assistance, registered with and supervised by ICA. The Federacion Nacional de Cafeteros also has its extension service organization, with over 500 agronomists and "practicos"; and regional development organizations such as the CVC have between 40 and 50 extension workers. Extension-type services are also provided by the national federations of cotton, rice and cocoa growers and by various firms selling agricultural inputs such as plant protection products and fertilizers.

It is estimated that altogether the professional and non-professional extension staff and technical assistance personnel now total nearly 2,000 though accurate figures are not available. These provide a variable type of service, from fairly cursory and generalized advice at one extreme, to a detailed examination of farm resources and potentialities for drawing up farm budgets and cropping programs at the other.

If the cadre of extension workers in the field is assumed to be 1,500 and the number of farms in the country 1.5 million,[3] there would only be one extension worker available for every 1,000 farms. Since it would be physically impossible to visit this number of farms in the course of a year, it is obvious that an adequate density of extension workers has not yet been achieved. Despite the considerable expansion that has taken place recently this service will need to be further strengthened, particularly if the example of the Coffee Federation and of INCORA is to be followed. The Federation's 512 extension workers have visited 88,000 families in 1965, an average of 172 per worker.[4] INCORA's loan supervisors on the other hand expect to make about 50 calls each month in the course of supervising outstanding loans. Whereas loan supervision and the special needs of the coffee grower demand such an intensive service, the more general requirements of an advisory service could be met with a higher ratio of farmers to advisory staff, say of the order of 300 farms for each extension worker.

Price Policy

The Colombian Government takes an active role in coordinating price policy with other agricultural policies. The formulation of agricultural price policy is carried out jointly by the National Superintendency for Prices, the National Planning Department, the Ministry of Agriculture and the Institute for Crop and Livestock Marketing (IDEMA). The National Superintendency regulates prices of the agricultural products (a) for which the government has "compulsory absorption quotas" (e.g. cotton, oil cake, rubber), or (b) where there are producer associations that control a significant part of the market. The markets for these products are considered to have characteristics of monopoly in production and/or distribution (e.g. sugar and cotton). For those products where there are a large number of unorganized producers but the distribution is controlled by monopolies, the Superintendency fixes processing margins leaving producer prices to move freely (e.g. milk and meat). The Superintendency does not intervene in regulating market prices for unprocessed products where IDEMA is carrying out an adequate role of stabilizing prices through strategic stocks. This is the main objective of IDEMA.

3. DANE sample survey, 1968.
4. IICA-CIRA. Organization Administrativa del Sector Agropecuario de Colombia, -1966.

Since the restructuring of the agricultural agencies in September, 1968 IDEMA has become the principal instrument for carrying out price policy for agricultural produce. It has the responsibility for integrating price policy with overall agricultural policy. Its present functions are: to promote greater agricultural production of basic food crops; to guarantee minimum prices to farmers for all food crops; to assure adequate supplies for the national market; to buy and sell basic food products in order to regulate prices and markets; and to sell surplus production abroad.

In setting minimum support prices, the IDEMA applies criteria established at the Cabinet level by the National Council for Economic and Social Policy, taking into account three principal groups of products: (a) those in which the country is not self-sufficient (e.g. wheat, oil crops and barley) but where the policy is to promote production and carry out necessary imports; (b) products in which the country is generally self-sufficient (e.g. corn, beans and rice) but where the policy is to promote production only to the level that will cover national requirements without generating large surpluses that would cause losses when exported; and (c) products in which the country generally exports notable quantities (e.g. cotton and bananas) that do not have support prices at present. In carrying out this price policy, IDEMA is prepared, if necessary, to absorb occasional losses in fixing producer and consumer prices in order not to affect disadvantageously certain areas of production and consumption. A compensation fund permits IDEMA to absorb temporary losses, due for example to a decrease in price on the external market.

Without adequate storage IDEMA could not purchase a sufficient proportion of a particular crop to sustain its prices. At present it is carrying out an ambitious grain silo construction program with the help of IDB and EXIMBANK loans in order to have a total storage capacity of 338,000 tons completed by 1973.

TABLE 14-22: IDEMA PURCHASES OF COLOMBIA PRODUCED BASIC FOOD PRODUCTS, 1965-69

	Rice (Unhulled)	Beans	Corn	Potatoes	Wheat	Total
1965						
Metric Tons	13,916	8,201	46,723	3,543	11	72,394
Col $'000	43,343	27,183	42,145	2,439	15	115,125
% of Purchases	37.6	23.6	36.6	2.1	0.1	100.0
1966						
Metric Tons	16,426	2,616	11,029	1,339	2,613	34,023
Col $'000	22,886	9,256	10,756	1,648	4,359	48,905
% of Purchases	46.8	18.9	22.0	3.4	8.9	100.0
1967						
Metric Tons	11,971	35	21,234	1,403	750	35,393
Col $'000	24,823	167	22,505	1,329	1,379	50,203
% of Purchases	49.5	0.3	44.9	2.6	2.7	100.0
1968						
Metric Tons	69,789	7,182	54,611	7,650	17,637	156,869
Col $'000	125,965	41,199	67,886	6,363	35,695	277,108
% of Purchases	45.4	14.9	24.5	2.3	12.9	100.0
1969						
Metric Tons	143,360	6,778	65,354	2,463	31,710	249,665
Col $'000	240,887	36,894	85,521	4,059	64,074	431,435
% of Purchases	55.8	8.6	19.8	0.9	14.9	100.0

Source: IDEMA.

At the time of its creation in 1968, IDEMA also took over the cotton promotion, marketing and processing functions of the former Instituto de Fomento Algodonero (IFA). IDEMA now operates 60 of the 64 existing ginneries. These 60 ginneries have a daily throughput capacity of 7,050 tons of seed cotton, a capacity which is more than adequate for even the present record cotton crops. Its storage capacity is also substantial: total warehouse capacity for over 410,000 bales (84,000 tons of lint). IDEMA's export activities in 1969 included the disposal of 19,720 tons of rice to Peru, Ecuador and Tanzania, as well as small quantities totaling 820 tons to various Caribbean ports. It also exported 16,186 tons of potatoes, 30,000 tons of maize and 21,000 head of cattle, the latter mainly to Peru. The rice and maize exports had to be subsidized to the extent of 32.5 million pesos, for which a direct budgetary subsidy was obtained.

When the grain purchases are compared to total production it can be seen that IDEMA, in 1970, plans to purchase about 17.3% of the rice, 12.5% of the wheat and only 7.8% of the corn production. In fact, total purchases have been up sharply in the past two years (Table 14-22). In 1969, wheat purchases were triple the Col$22.5 million shown in the original appropriation. However, the major increase has been in rice which in 1969 accounted for 55.8% of all purchases of Colombian produce. In view of the upward trend in rice production, and the fact that domestic support prices are well above world levels, it is very likely that IDEMA will again be called upon to purchase rice, especially because so much of the rice is produced within project areas of other agricultural agencies.

Corn is perhaps the weakest point in the IDEMA program at present. The total corn area covers nearly a million hectares in both hot and cold climates throughout the country. An effective price support program would require a large number of purchase points to avoid local price declines at harvet. Farmers apparently encounter sharp seasonal price fluctuations but good data do not exist on farm gate prices for commodities such as corn.

The influence of support prices on farmers' production decisions depends basically on: (1) the level of the support price; (2) the amount of confidence in the declared prices which the farmer develops over time; and (3) the farmers' access to the support price. This third point depends largely on (a) the number of purchasing points; (b) the timeliness of purchases at these points; and (c) varying quality specifications of the purchasing agent. The real test of a price support program comes when a combination of favorable production factors results in a heavy surplus and it becomes crucial to maintain the price level. If at this point the program does not maintain the declared price, farmers then conclude that they cannot rely on the support price and subsequently are reluctant to make purchases of inputs such as fertilizer to increase production and productivity. This is precisely what happened when a corn promotion program was conducted by the extension service a few years ago. With growing needs for corn, it remains to be seen whether IDEMA is now ready to handle an effective support program for this grain, although this is not an immediate problem in view of the high present market price.

On wheat there appears to be general agreement among the millers, IDEMA, and others involved in agricultural policy to give minimum emphasis to import substitution. The millers prefer to import wheat even though the price is approximately equivalent to the cost of local purchases when transportation, carrying charges, and the 30% import duty are paid. It is said that the quality grades on the external market are consistent and convenient for milling. On the government side, the favorable provisions of U.S. law PL480, make it attractive to continue to import wheat and, if possible, increase the local production of crops, such as barley, that compete for land use on cold climate soils.

Credit

Lending to agriculture is relatively high in Colombia and has been growing faster than credit to the other sectors of the economy. In 1968, outstanding loans to agriculture accounted for 35% of the total portfolio of the banking system (excluding the Banco de la Republica). This compares with the share of agriculture in GDP of 29%. Between 1958 and 1968, in real terms (deflated values), the agriculture portfolio rose by 6.6% p.a. compared to 5.3% p.a. for non-agricultural portfolios (see Table 14-23).

TABLE 14-23: DISTRIBUTION OF THE BANKING PORTFOLIO[1] – BY ACTIVITY IN ACTUAL AND DEFLATED (REAL) PRICES 1958-68
(In Millions of Col $)

	Total Portfolio		Non-Agricultural Portfolio[2]		Agricultural Portfolio		Livestock Portfolio		Other Agricultural Portfolio	
	Current	Deflated	Current	Deflated	Current	Deflated	Current	Deflated	Current	Deflated
1958	3,258	1,807	2,214	1,228	1,044	579	601	334	443	246
1959	3,760	1,903	2,432	1,231	1,328	672	700	354	627	317
1960	4,444	2,159	2,979	1,447	1,465	712	831	404	635	308
1961	5,370	2,447	3,516	1,602	1,854	845	1,091	497	763	348
1962	6,109	2,713	3,960	1,758	2,149	955	1,288	572	862	383
1963	7,670	2,697	4,827	1,697	2,843	1,000	1,662	584	1,181	415
1964	8,386	2,510	5,263	1,575	3,123	935	1,772	530	1,351	405
1965	9,294	2,570	6,022	1,665	3,272	905	1,740	481	1,531	423
1966	10,623	2,502	6,771	1,595	3,852	907	1,916	451	1,937	456
1967	12,626	2,784	8,140	1,795	4,486	989	2,283	503	2,202	486
1968	15,168	3,147	9,869	2,047	5,299	1,100				

1 Excluding the Banco de la Republica.

2 This includes commercial, industrial, construction and other activities.

Note: The price deflator was the general price index with base 1952 = 100.

Source: Banco de la Republica and Banco Ganadero.

The growing share of agriculture in total credit absorption is partly a result of priority accorded the sector by the government in general credit allocations. Commercial banks must lend to agriculture 15% of total deposits; in addition, they must invest 6 percent of their total loan portfolio in subscription to six-month bills of the Fondo Financiero Agrario (FFA) whose proceeds are used to rediscount agricultural loans; and they must also invest 5% of their sight deposits in the bonds of the Caja Agraria (agricultural bank). Ample rediscounting facilities are available for agricultural loans, both short-term and long-term. Special agricultural lending institutions are very active; in addition to FFA and Caja, they include Banco Ganadero (livestock bank), while Banco Popular has its lending program to agriculture. INCORA, the agrarian reform agency, also lends to agriculture, mainly through Caja and through Banco Ganadero; in addition, it disburses credits obtained abroad. Interest rates on agricultural loans are generally lower than interest rates on lending to other sectors.[5]

Within agriculture, loans for crops have expanded much faster than lending for livestock. The outstanding portfolio of livestock loans ten years ago was 50% above the portfolio of other agriculture. At present, the portfolios of these two sub-sectors are equal. It is the crops whose output has expanded rapidly in recent years giving rise to increased demand for credit; and sufficient supply of funds has been available to meet this demand.

Among crops, cotton and rice have absorbed most of the funds. These are crops grown mostly in commercial agriculture, and have enjoyed particular government support, cotton as a major export product absorbing much labor, and rice as a major domestic staple stimulated by high support prices and benefiting from irrigation investment. These two crops absorbed as much as 75% of total FFA rediscounts in 1969 (Table 14-24).   The proportion absorbed by corn and wheat, the major minifundia crops was below 10%.

The distribution of loans by size is skewed. In Caja lending during 1967/68, the loans below Col$5,000 (US$250) accounted for three-fourths of the number of loans; but their aggregate value was one-fourth of the total. In Banco Ganadero lending during 1968, loans below Col$30,000 (US$1,500) accounted for 53% of the number of loans, but their aggregate value was 16% of total amount lent.

Only about 25% of bank credits are advanced as a result of a detailed technical appraisal of requests.[7]   Creditworthiness of the applicant, not the expected return on the proposed investment, is the only consideration in much bank lending in Colombia. This, unfortunately, excludes many farmers capable of executing sound investment programs and is partly responsible for the skewed size distribution of loans. Greater emphasis on credit coupled with technical services would help introduce modern production practices into much of Colombian agriculture, where lack of technical know-how is the greatest factor limiting rapid expansion of output. The agricultural sector cannot reasonably expect to increase further its share of total lending, so if agricultural output growth is to be accelerated, technology and credit will have to be regarded as mutually dependent inputs. Harnessing credit as the instrument to induce modernization of Colombian agriculture is the great challenge facing the government and banking system.

5. See chapter 1, The Overall View.
6. FFA generally rediscounts up to 65% of loan value.
7. Ministry of Agriculture, "Aspects of Institutional Agrarian Credit in Colombia", Bogota, January 1968.

TABLE 14-24: NUMBER, VALUE AND AREA COVERED, FOR CREDITS APPROVED BY FONDO FINANCIERO AGRARIO IN 1969 BY CROPS AND PRINCIPAL DEPARTMENTS

	Barley	Beans	Cotton	Maize	Potatoes	Peanuts	Dry-land Rice	Irri-gated Rice	Sesame	Sorg-hum	Soy-beans	Wheat	Total	% Distri-bution
No. of Credits														
Cesar	—	—	1,049	72	—	—	7	160	4	ʼ13	—	—	1,305	15.0
Tolima	—	—	611	84	—	8	—	775	122	131	—	—	1,731	19.8
Valle	—	73	165	582	—	—	—	113	—	178	966	—	2,077	23.8
Cordoba	—	—	472	100	—	—	78	—	10	1	—	—	661	7.6
All others	223	10	883	366	85	0	107	799	79	210	74	169	2,955	43.8
Total	223	83	3,180	1,154	85	8	192	1,847	215	533	1,040	169	8,729	100.0
% Distribution	2.6	1.0	36.4	13.2	1.0	0.1	2.2	21.2	2.5	6.1	11.9	1.9	100.0	
Value of Credits ('000 Col$)														
Cesar	—	—	239,206	7,640	—	—	321	33,438	91	1,163	—	—	281,859	27.1
Tolima	—	—	46,039	4,176	—	456	—	123,931	3,886	7,267	—	—	185,755	17.9
Valle	—	3,356	21,294	49,764	—	—	—	12,527	—	11,101	72,630	—	170,672	16.4
Cordoba	—	—	37,857	6,212	—	—	5,766	—	408	55	—	—	50,298	4.8
All others	16,028	525	111,607	24,930	7,396	—	6,350	151,479	3,912	65,131	5,086	7,558	349,732	33.8
Total	16,028	3,881	456,003	92,722	7,396	456	12,437	321,375	8,027	34,717	77,716	7,558	1,038,316	100.0
% Distribution	1.5	0.4	43.9	8.9	0.7	0.0	1.2	31.0	0.8	3.3	7.5	0.7	100.0	
Hectares Covered														
Cesar	—	—	112,461	5,226	—	—	181	10,007	76	926	—	—	128,877	26.3
Tolima	—	—	20,237	2,931	—	326	—	36,970	3,238	5,848	—	—	69,550	14.2
Valle	—	2,160	9,360	33,967	—	—	—	6,099	—	8,799	51,051	—	111,436	22.8
Cordoba	—	—	17,799	4,174	—	—	3,273	—	340	45	—	—	25,631	5.2
All others	10,020	350	51,738	17,030	2,113	—	3,593	45,309	3,035	12,136	3,596	4,741	153,661	31.5
Total	10,020	2,510	211,595	63,328	2,113	326	7,047	98,385	6,689	27,754	54,647	4,741	489,155	100.0
% Distribution	2.0	0.5	43.3	12.9	0.4	0.1	1.4	20.1	1.4	5.7	11.2	1.0	100.0	

Source: Banco de la Republica.

This chapter describes Colombia's coffee economy and the financial arrangements that facilitate its operation. The material presented is highly selective, and those desiring fuller detail are referred to *The Coffee Economy of Colombia,* a study arising from a 1967 IBRD mission as a part of the World Coffee Study sponsored by the IBRD, FAO and the International Coffee Organization (ICO), and to the *Plan Nacional de Politica Cafetera,* a document prepared by the Government of Colombia in December 1969 and submitted to ICO.

The least reliable information presented here concerns tree population, yields, production costs, and returns to the grower. The National Coffee Growers Federation conducted a complete coffee census in 1970, fortunately, and it should furnish better data on these topics. Existing data on production, consumption, and exports are considered satisfactory.

Despite its recent decline, coffee is still vitally important to the Colombian economy in at least four ways: it accounts for at least a third of the value of agricultural crop and livestock production and a tenth of total gross domestic product[1] ; it generates two-thirds of the foreign exchange earned by merchandise exports; it provides employment for an estimated two million persons, nearly a tenth of the population, and it brings in approximately a tenth of all central government current revenues.

Colombia's major coffee growing areas are located in the Central and Western Cordilleras, where three-fourths of the total crop is raised.[2] The range of these areas, from one to eleven degrees north latitude, coincides with a pattern of rainfall distribution that results in two coffee harvests per year. When the weather is unfavorable in one area it is generally favorable in another, and total output varies relatively little from year to year.[3]

The Production Process

Colombian coffee is of the *arabica* species, varieties *typica* and *bourbon.* After the tree-ripened berries are picked they are depulped and left to ferment for 12-24 hours. Following fermentation they are washed to remove the remaining fleshy coating, then dried. The product at this stage of processing is known as parchment (*pergamino*) coffee, and almost all coffee grown in Colombia is marketed in this form. It takes about four pounds of ripe berries to yield one pound of dry parchment coffee. Final processing is called threshing or cleaning, wherein the parchment skin is removed to expose the green coffee underneath. Green coffee is coffee ready for export, and represents about 80% of the parchment coffee, by weight. Coffees judged unsuitable for export are called *pasilla* coffees.[4]

Number and Size of Coffee Farms

Colombia has more than 300,000 coffee growing farms, the average size of which decreased from 3.6 to 2.7 hectares between 1955 and 1965[5] as a result of a 40% increase in

1. The relative importance of agriculture to GDP declined from 36.7% in 1958 to 31.3% in 1968, as measured in constant 1958 prices. Coffee's share in agriculture dropped from 43.5% to 30.4% between the same two years, and coffee's GDP share fell from 16.0% in 1958 to 9.5% in 1968. While there is no doubt about the declining role of coffee in the economy, the percentage shares quoted underestimate the importance of coffee since the tax system operates to reduce the internal price of coffee and therefore the value of its output in relation to other goods.

2. The seven most important coffee-growing departments in Colombia are Antioquia, Caldas, Cundinamarca, Quindio, Risaralda, Tolima and Valle, which together account for 85% of production in recent years.

3. The main harvests come during the fourth calendar quarter in Antioquia and Caldas, during the second quarter in Quindio, Tolima, and Valle. Secondary harvests occur in the second and fourth quarters, respectively.

4. Pasilla beans are small, and may contain up to 20% of dark or black beans. Pasilla circulates internally in partially roasted form to distinguish it from export grades.

5. The National Coffee Growers Federation estimates size and number as follows:

Year	Size in Hectares			Total No.	Total Area in coffee ('000 Ha.)	Average size of coffee farm (Ha.)
	Less than 1	1 - 50	More than 50			
1955/56	77,245	135,148	577	212,970	777	3.65
1965/66	109,670	191,017	843	301,530	811	2.69

the number of farms. Table 15-1 gives greater detail for the departments of Caldas, Quindio, and Risaralda in 1965. Of the 59,291 farms enumerated 50% averaged 3.5 hectares or less, with another 41% averaging between 4.5 and 15.0 hectares. These figures confirm that coffee cultivation takes place on thousands of tiny farms, the average size of which is shrinking because of population pressure. The table also reveals that the smallest units dedicate two-thirds of their available land to coffee cultivation, whereas farms in the 4.5-15.0 hectare range use only 51% for coffee, those in the 25.0-45.0 range 30%, and the largest units 15% .

TABLE 15-1: NUMBER AND SIZE OF COFFEE FARMS IN THE DEPARTMENTS OF
CALDAS, QUINDIO AND RISARALDA, 1965

Average Farm Size in Hectares	Number of Farms	% of No.	Total Farm Area in Hectares	% of Area	Area Planted to Coffee	Average Coffee Area in Hectares	% Average Coffee Area/ Average Farm Size	% Total Coffee Area
0.25	2,640	4.4	660	0.1	458	0.17	68	0.2
0.75	3,660	6.2	2,745	0.4	1,759	0.48	64	0.7
1.50	7,920	13.4	11,880	1.8	7,672	0.97	65	3.2
2.50	8,400	14.2	21,000	3.1	13,374	1.60	64	5.7
3.50	6,961	11.7	24,364	3.7	17,358	2.49	71	7.3
Subtotal	29,581	49.9	60,649	9.1	40,621	1.37	67	17.1
4.50	5,221	8.8	23,495	3.5	13,340	2.56	57	5.7
7.50	12,422	20.9	93,165	14.0	50,863	4.09	55	21.5
15.00	6,879	11.6	103,185	15.5	47,221	6.86	46	20.0
Subtotal	24,522	41.3	219,845	33.0	111,424	4.54	51	47.2
25.0	2,081	3.5	52,025	7.8	18,856	9.06	36	8.0
35.00	1,172	2.0	41,020	6.1	18,511	15.80	43	7.8
45.00	259	0.4	11,655	1.8	3,898	15.05	33	1.7
Subtotal	3,512	5.9	104,700	15.7	41,265	11.75	39	17.5
65.00	942	1.6	7,650	10.5	23,806	25.27	34	10.1
150.00	392	0.7	58,800	8.9	9,166	23.38	16	3.9
350.00	301	0.5	105,350	15.9	7,385	24.54	7	3.1
750.00	30	0.1	22,500	3.4	2,074	69.13	9	0.9
1,750.00	6		10,500	1.6	215	35.83	2	0.1
2,500.00	5		12,500	1.9	200	40.00	2	0.1
Subtotal	1,676	2.9	280,300	42.2	42,846	25.56	15	18.2
TOTAL	59,291	100.0	665,494	100.0	236,156	3.98	35	100.0

Source: Coffee Zones Development and Diversification Fund.

Yield Estimates

Table 15-2 shows output and yield by farm size in these three departments in 1965. By rough interpolation one can deduce that the small plots produced an average of 360 kilograms of green coffee per hectare planted, medium-sized plots 450 kilograms, and the large plots about 335 kilograms. Applying these yield estimates to the data of Table 15-2, it appears that the three size groups accounted for 20%, 65%, and 15%, respectively, of the green coffee produced in this area in 1965. That is, nearly three-fifths of the farms produced only one-fifth of the coffee. These relative shares result primarily from the different total acreages devoted to coffee, but the higher yields of farms in the 15-40 hectare range are worth noting.

The apparent yield, for Colombia as a whole, per hectare planted has risen from 532 kilograms in 1958/59 to 605 kilograms in 1966/67.[6] Total area planted to coffee has declined

TABLE 15-2: ESTIMATED OUTPUT AND YIELD BY FARM SIZE IN THE DEPARTMENTS OF CALDAS, QUINDIO, AND RISARALDA, 1965

	Average Farm Size in Hectares						
	1.0-1.9	2.0-3.9	4.0-7.9	8.0-14.9	15.0-29.9	30.0-39.9	40.0 Over
Average area in coffee, hectares	1.0	2.0	4.1	7.6	17.0	28.0	15.0
Kilograms of green coffee per hectare	344	355	365	413	506	550	336
Apparent average production of coffee in kilograms	344	710	1,496	3,139	8,602	15,400	5,040

Source: Coffee Zones Development and Diversification Fund.

6. The National Coffee Growers Federation has estimated the implicit yields from area and output series as follows:

	1958/9	1959/60	1960/1	1961/2	1962/3	1963/4	1964/5	1965/6	1966/7
Total area planted to coffee '000 Ha.	840.0	836.0	831.5	824.1	810.0	813.1	812.0	811.4	810.6
Green coffee output '000 kg. bags	7,422	7,648	7,500	8,035	7,500	7,800	7,900	8,200	8,178
Apparent yield kg. per Ha.	532	549	541	585	556	576	584	606	605

Table 15-2 suggests that the Caldas-Quindio-Risaralda area has average yield lower than elsewhere, yet with less than 30% of total acreage it usually produces over a third of national output. The yield estimates used in Table 15-2 are therefore probably too low.

slowly since 1958, while output has risen slightly. The most recent estimate of coffee tree population refers to 1962/63, when there were just over two billion trees. At that time 60% of the trees were older than 15 years, and replanting rates appeared to be very low. On the basis of the fragmentary data available it is not possible to identify a clear relationship between aggregate tree population and the level of output.

Production and Consumption

Colombia's production, domestic consumption, and exportation of green coffee are shown in Table 15-3 for the 1958/59-1968/69 period. The stability of the output series is remarkable, and reflects the success of efforts to limit new plantings. Domestic consumption has risen slowly, while exports have fluctuated between 5.6 and 6.6 million bags. Colombia accounted for 11.7% of world production and 12.8% of recorded world exports in this period.

The Export Record

Coffee exports dominate Colombia's trade returns. On the average in 1958-68 coffee accounted for 69% of total merchandise exports. This proportion has fallen to 63% in recent years, however, as a result of soft coffee prices and encouraging growth in non-coffee exports, though volume has declined little. Colombia earned US$4,085 million from coffee exports during the 12-year period, an average of US$340 million per year. The geographic distribution of exports is shown in Table 15-4 for the 1968/69 coffee year. The United States took 40% of the total, Europe another 40%, bilateral agreement countries 14%, and various others the remainder. The European market has gained enormously in relative importance during the past decade: in 1958/59 it received only 18% of Colombia's exports versus 78% for the United States.

TABLE 15-3: SUPPLY AND DISTRIBUTION OF GREEN COFFEE, 1958/59-1968/69[1]
(In thousands of 60-kilogram bags)

Coffee Year (Oct-Sept)	Stocks Carry-In	Pro-duct-ion	Domestic Consump-tion[2]	Exports			Stocks Carry-Out
				Quota Markets	Annex B Markets	Total	
1958/59	11	7,442	908	6,372	59	6,431	114
1959/60	114	7,648	1,197	5,597	74	5,671	894
1960/61	894	7,500	1,270	5,990	53	6,043	1,081
1961/62	1,081	8,035	1,526	5,536	58	5,594	1,996
1962/63	1,996	7,500	1,416	5,952	104	6,056	2,024
1963/64	2,024	7,800	1,375	6,229	81	6,310	2,139
1964/65	2,139	7,900	1,354	5,612	131	5,743	2,942
1965/66	2,942	8,200	1,202	5,669	196	5,865	4,075
1966/67	4,075	8,178	1,250	5,421	213	5,634	5,369
1967/68	5,369	7,995	1,270	6,344	251	6,595	5,499
1968/69	5,499	7,900	1,290	6,204	330	6,534	5,575

[1] Revised figures provided by the National Coffee Growers Federation.

[2] Domestic consumption includes Federation sales, roaster purchases from other domestic sources, and estimated on-farm consumption.

Source: National Coffee Growers Federation.

TABLE 15-4: COFFEE EXPORTS BY COUNTRY OF DESTINATION, COFFEE YEAR 1968/69[1]

Country of Destination	Number of 60-kilogram Bags Shipped	Percentage of Total
Americas	2,834,771	43.4
Argentina	108,242	1.7
Canada	99,623	1.5
United States	2,623,355	40.2
Other	3,551	- - - -
Europe	2,668,790	40.9
Belgium	149,815	2.3
Czechoslovakia	42,187	0.6
Denmark	67,014	1.0
Finland	232,222	3.6
France	68,769	1.1
Germany, W.	1,217,915	18.6
Greece	1,495	- - - -
Italy	55,915	0.9
Netherlands	385,236	5.9
Norway	48,504	0.8
Sweden	329,385	5.0
Switzerland	25,153	0.4
United Kingdom	45,180	0.7
Other Countries	126,722	1.9
Israel	5,862	0.1
Japan	116,823	1.8
Other	4,037	- - - -
Subtotal, Free Convertibility Countries	(5,630,283)	(86.2)
Bilateral Agreement Countries	903,733	13.8
Bulgaria	7,916	0.1
Germany, E.	138,593	2.1
Hungary	9,166	0.1
Poland	83,413	1.3
Russia	118,335	1.8
Spain	458,805	7.0
Yugoslavia	87,505	1.4
Total, All Countries	6,534,016	100.0

[1] October 1968 through September 1969.
Source: National Coffee Growers Federation.

Prices and Price Control

New York prices for Colombian coffee have shown very wide fluctuations. Following a high of 80 cents per pound in 1954, Colombian Manizales fell steadily to less than 40 cents in 1963, but spurted to nearly 49 cents in 1964. A new decline then ensued, with the price falling to 42 cents and below in 1967-68 and the first eight months of 1969. Price increases occurring in September-December 1969 pulled the yearly average up to 45 cents, however, and the average for the first quarter of 1970 was 58 cents per pound. The price weakened in late 1970 and early 1971.

Table 15-5 provides price series for the 1948-70 postwar period, both New York and domestic support prices, with each series deflated to constant 1948 values. The final entry of 58 cents amounts to less than 45 cents when expressed in base period prices; this is slightly above 1964-65 prices but considerably below those recorded for most of the nineteen-fifties. Domestic support prices also show the 1970 first-quarter average barely restoring the grower to his 1951 level.

ICO Membership

Colombia is a charter member of the International Coffee Organization (ICO), and has a basic quota fixed at 12.7% of the world export total. All ICO members exporting more than 100,000 bags to quota markets are subject to compulsory participation in the Coffee Diversification Program. A levy of 60 U.S. cents per 60-kilogram bag is collected on annual quota shipments in excess of the first 100,000 bags, beginning with the 1968/69 year and continuing through 1972/73. The levy has three components: an "A" portion, 78% of total, payable in the contributing member's currency, to be used only in the contributing member country; a "B" portion, 2% of total, payable in convertible currency, to be used for Diversification Fund Administration; and a "C" portion, 20% of total, payable in convertible currency, to be used in any contributing member nation. Colombia's contribution to the Coffee Diversification Fund can be estimated as follows. The quota in the ICO year 1968/69 was 6.1 million bags,[7] and the equivalent of US$2.85 million was contributed as the "A" portion and US$0.8 million as the "B" and "C" portions; the quota for 1969/70 was 6.35 million bags, the contributions as the "A" portion US$3.0 million and as the "B" and "C" portions US$0.85 million.

Diversification Efforts

Colombia has had a coffee diversification scheme, the Five-Year Program for the Development and Diversification of Coffee Zones, since 1963. This program was launched with the aid of technicians from the Inter-American Committee for Agricultural Development. A Coffee Zones Development and Diversification Fund was created to coordinate activities of the various agencies involved (Coffee Federation, Banco Cafetero, Caja Agraria, INCORA, Corporacion Financiera de Caldas, Manuel Mejia Foundation, and others). The five-year "pilot" program was designed to diversify agricultural production in a traditional coffee area encompassing the departments of Caldas, Quindio, Risaralda, and the northern portions of Tolima and Valle del Cauca. Stated objectives included reduction of the relative importance of coffee, increased incomes for small farmers, regularization of employment throughout the year, and the development of foodstuff production and livestock raising in the area covered. Receipts and expenditures for the pilot program are shown below.

A program recently submitted to the ICO represents a continuation of this pilot scheme. The area covered would be extended to include the coffee zones of Antioquia and Cundinamarca, thereby reaching an area that accounts for 85% of national coffee production. The Develop-

---

7. Adjusted to include first 100,000 bags.

TABLE 15-5: FOREIGN AND DOMESTIC PRICES FOR COLOMBIAN COFFEE, 1948-70

Year	New York Price in Cents per Pound of Manizales Coffee	U.S. Wholesale Price In- dex, 1948 Equals 100 [1]	New York Price in Constant 1948 Prices	Peso Price per Arroba of Mani- zales Cof- fee in the Interior	Colombian Wholesale Price In- dex, 1948 Equals 100 [2]	Interior Price in Constant 1948 Prices
1948	32.57	100.0	32.57	10.62	100.0	10.62
1949	37.61	94.3	39.88	13.87	107.6	12.89
1950	53.25	97.7	54.50	19.88	121.0	16.42
1951	58.70	109.1	53.80	24.02	130.6	18.39
1952	57.01	106.8	53.38	25.99	129.0	20.14
1953	59.92	104.5	57.33	27.80	136.5	20.36
1954	79.93	105.7	75.61	37.90	146.1	25.94
1955	64.38	105.7	60.90	31.98	147.2	21.72
1956	73.97	109.1	67.80	41.61	159.6	26.07
1957	63.94	112.5	56.83	48.76	198.3	24.58
1958	52.34	113.6	46.07	46.74	232.6	20.09
1959	45.22	113.6	39.80	38.75	255.0	15.19
1960	44.89	113.6	39.51	42.93	265.7	16.15
1961	43.62	113.6	38.39	47.13	283.1	16.64
1962	40.77	113.6	35.88	47.79	290.6	16.44
1963	39.55	113.6	34.81	55.55	367.0	15.13
1964	48.80	113.6	42.95	71.81	431.1	16.65
1965	48.49	115.9	41.83	71.70	466.7	15.36
1966	47.43	120.4	39.39	75.63	547.9	13.80
1967	41.94	120.4	34.83	75.92	585.3	12.97
1968	42.60	122.7	34.71	88.91	621.9	14.29
1969	44.93	127.3	35.29	98.22	660.6	14.86
1970 [3]	58.00	130.0	44.62	126.00	675.0	18.67

[1] Shifted from original 1958 base.

[2] Shifted from original 1952 base.

[3] Figures for 1970 are first quarter estimates.

Sources: Banco de la Republica; International Financial Statistics.

TABLE 15-6: FINANCE OF DIVERSIFICATION PROGRAM, 1963-69

Investment	Source of Funds. Millions of US $		
	National	Foreign	Total
Rural Credit	4.30	7.00[1]	11.30
Food Assistance	0.41	0.50[2]	0.91
Penetration Roads	1.34	....	1.34
Industrial Development	20.94	....	20.94
Total	26.99	7.50	34.49
(%)	(78.2)	(21.8)	(100.0)

[1] Loan from Inter-American Development Bank.

[2] Donation from World Food Program.

ment and Diversification Fund has sponsored a systematic investigation of climate, soils, topography, demographic concentration, land distribution, and infra-structure facilities in order to identify optimal coffee-growing zones and areas suitable for other crops. The program envisages increased production of cocoa, platanos, yucca, sugar-cane for panela, fruits, vegetables, ramie, fique, poultry, hogs, and cattle, plus the planting of some 20,000 hectares of eucalyptus and conifers.

Total expenditure under the proposed program is expected to reach US$10.6 million per year for five years. Table 15-7 reveals that 62% of these outlays will be for agricultural credit, and another 23% for marketing investments. The ICO would put up 45% of the funds, as computed in the table, 52% of the total if one excludes "reinvestments." Since Colombia's "A" contribution to the ICO fund is estimated at US$15 million over the five-year period, US$8.6 million of the ICO portion would have to be in convertible currencies. The program is subject to modifications as ICO and Colombian authorities move toward more detailed estimates. The program as it now stands includes very little directly for industry.

Organization and Policies

The Coffee Federation

The National Coffee Growers Federation, a private organization with semi-official status, is the key entity in Colombia for making and carrying out coffee policy. It determines quality standards, buys coffee from farmers, stores surplus production, and controls marketing for domestic consumption.[8] The Federation is responsible for the administration of the National Coffee Fund, an account on the books of the National Treasury. This fund is nourished from the proceeds of Federation exports, sales to private exporters and domestic buyers, a retention tax discussed below, and a special tax of 1.5% on the c.i.f. value of all Colombian imports.

The Federation buys about three-fifths of Colombia's coffee output each year.[9] It then either exports, sells to private exporters, sells to local dealers, or adds to its stockpile. For several years the Federation sold relatively more coffee to private exporters than it shipped abroad on its own account. In 1965 and 1966, for example, private traders exported two-thirds of all coffee shipped. The Federation's share jumped to 50% in 1967 and 1968, however, and at present is

8. An eleven-member National Committee sets policy. It is composed of the Ministers of Finance, Development, Foreign Affairs, and Agriculture; the Manager of the Caja Agraria (a government-owned agricultural credit bank); and six representatives from the private sector. Twelve departmental committees assist with marketing, extension services, and investment operations in rural areas.

9. Another fifth is purchased by cooperatives acting in large measure as agents for the Federation, and the remaining fifth is purchased by private dealers.

TABLE 15-7: SOURCES AND APPLICATION OF FUNDS FOR PROPOSED COFFEE
DIVERSIFICATION PROGRAM
(In thousands of U.S. dollars)[1]

	Sources of Funds	%
External	25,555	(48.3)
ICO	23,611	(44.6)
IDB	1,944	(3.7)
National	19,656[2]	(37.2)
"Reinvestments"	7,661	(14.5)
Total	52,872	(100.0)

Application of Funds by Year and Purpose

Purpose	Year 1	Year 2	Year 3	Year 4	Year 5	Total	(%)
Agricultural Credit	4,078	5,000	6,922	8,261	8,394	32,655	(61.8)
Direct Investment	389	278	556	556	556	2,335	(4.4)
Marketing	4,417	3,300	2,944	839	839	12,339	(23.4)
Debt Service and Banking Fees[3]	683	689	694	705	717	3,488	(6.6)
Experimentation	111	111	111	55	55	443	(0.8)
Integration of Minifundies	......	167	333	556	556	1,612	(3.0)
Unspecified							
Total	9,678	9,545	11,560	10,972	11,117	52,872	(100.0)
(%)	(18.3)	(18.0)	(21.9)	(20.8)	(21.0)	(100.0)	

[1] Dollar estimates converted from peso figures at Col $18 per dollar.

[2] US$15,872,220 "contributions" plus US$3,783,330 "yield from subloans."

[3] Amortization of IDB US $7.9 million loan, central bank fees for guarantees of maintenance of value of IDB loan, and administrative charges of national banks.

Source: Coffee Zones Development and Diversification Fund.

between 40% and 50%. While shipments to the United States are made chiefly by private dealers the Federation takes care of most European trades. It also has a monopoly on exports to non-traditional markets, bilateral agreement countries, and transactions in aged coffees.

Policy Objectives

The main policy objectives of the Colombian government with respect to coffee are to: maximize the country's foreign exchange earnings; realize sufficient peso income to finance the accumulation and storage of surplus production, in addition to making a substantial contribution to the national budget; and insulate the coffee sector and the overall economy from short-term fluctuations in world prices, without at the same time generating undesirable incentives to invest in new coffee capacity. The policy instruments used to achieve these objectives include the Federation Support Price, Exchange Surrender Requirement, Coffee Export Tax, Coffee Retention Quota, and the Pasilla Tax.

Policy Instruments

The Federation Support Price is set to guarantee an acceptable economic return to growers, as well as to control production incentives. It is adjusted fairly often to keep up with changes in external coffee prices and the domestic price level. On September 4, 1969, it was raised from Col$880 to Col$942.50 per *carga* (a 125-kilogram lot) of parchment coffee.[10] It was raised five more times in September and October, reaching Col$1,230 per carga on the 29th of October. This represented a 40% increase in two months, prompted by an equivalent percentage increase in world prices during the period.

The Exchange Surrender Requirement determined by the Monetary Board sets the amount of foreign exchange per bag that exporters are required to surrender to the central bank. It is sometimes set slightly above the prevailing FOB market price, which forces exporters to purchase additional exchange to meet the requirement.

The Coffee Export Tax was introduced as part of the March 1967 exchange reform. The special coffee exchange rate then in force was abolished, with foreign exchange surrender from coffee exports becoming subject to the flexible certificate market rate and a 26% tax. This tax was lowered in steps of one-fourth of one percent per month until it reached a level of 20% in December 1968. Four points of the tax go to the National Coffee Fund and sixteen to the government's Special Exchange Account on the books of the central bank. These special account receipts constitute a major source of income to the government.

The Coffee Retention Quota is paid by producers to the Federation. It was raised from 19% to 20% in September 1968, to 23% in April 1969, and to 25% in October 1969. It is levied on the quantity of green coffee sold, payable in the equivalent volume or cash value of parchment.[11] The proceeds of this tax are normally used to finance the acquisition and storage of surplus coffee. The price sharing arrangement discussed below alters the role of the Retention Quota, however, and will also require more frequent adjustments to it. The sharing threshold was crossed on March 25, 1970, when the Support Price was set to exceed Col$1,300 per carga, and at that time the Retention Quota was raised to 25.5%.

A Pasilla Tax of 6% is also paid by producers to the Federation. It is computed on the volume of green coffee sold, as in the above case, but is payable in the same quantity of low-grade pasilla coffee. It is designed to remove inferior coffee from the export market. Whenever possible the Federation sells pasilla to domestic dealers and gives the peso proceeds to departmental coffee committees to finance rural investments.

The Sharing Agreement

Late in 1969 an agreement was reached between the government and the coffee growers concerning future prices. It was agreed that when the Federation Support Price reached Col$1,300 per carga—at that time a level equivalent to about 57 cents per pound in New York—a novel sharing mechanism would be activated. All price gains beyond the limit would be apportioned 35% to producers via adjustments in the Support Price, 30% to the National Coffee Fund, and 35% to departmental coffee committees and a Rotating Fund administered by the Banco Cafetero.[12]

Table 15-8 presents a step-by-step calculation of the Support Price with and without the sharing agreement. If the agreement were implemented in strict conformity to technical consid-

---

10. One often encounters domestic coffee data expressed in *arrobas* rather than cargas. An arroba in Colombia equals 12.5 kilograms, one-tenth of a carga.

11. If a producer were to pay in kind he would have to deliver 31.25 bags of parchment for every 100 bags of green coffee that he sells (25 = .8 x 31.25). It is more common, however, for this payment to be made in cash. (The Retention Quota is computed on the value of coffee at interior collection points, i.e., after deducting ocean transportation charges, the export tax, and domestic handling and transport costs.)

12. The Rotating Fund, not to be confused with the National Coffee Fund, is a revolving source of credit to the coffee sector.

TABLE 15-8: PRODUCER RECEIPTS WITH AND WITHOUT COFFEE PRICE SHARING AGREEMENT[1]

		New York Price in Cents per Pound						
		57¢	58¢	59¢	60¢	65¢	70¢	75¢
(1)	New York Price, US$	87.96	89.50	91.05	92.59	100.31	108.03	115.74
(2)	Ocean Transport, US$	4.00	4.00	4.00	4.00	4.00	4.00	4.00
(3)	Colombian FOB Price, US$	83.96	85.50	87.05	88.59	96.31	104.33	111.74
(4)	Colombian FOB Price, Col$[2]	1,511	1,539	1,567	1,595	1,734	1,873	2,011
(5)	Export Tax, Col$[3]	302	308	313	319	347	375	402
(6)	After-tax Value, Col$	1,209	1,231	1,254	1,276	1,387	1,498	1,609
(7)	Domestic Costs and Charges[4]	45	45	45	45	45	45	45
(8)	Value at Interior Collection Points, Col$	1,164	1,186	1,209	1,231	1,342	1,453	1,564
(9a)	Indicated Support Price per Carga, Col$[5]	1,330	1,355	1,380	1,405	1,535	1,660	1,790
(9b)	Indicated Support Price per 70-kg. Equivalent[6]	930	950	965	985	1,075	1,160	1,250
(10a)	Adjusted Support Price per Carga, Col$[7]	1,330	1,340	1,350	1,355	1,400	1,445	1,490
(10b)	Adjusted Support Price per 70-kg. Equivalent[7]	930	940	945	950	980	1,010	1,045
(11)	Effective Retention Quota as % of (10b)[8]	25.0	26.4	27.9	29.6	36.8	43.6	50.0
(12)	Effective Retention Quota as % of (8)[8]	20.0	20.9	21.8	22.8	26.9	30.4	33.3
(13a)	Indicated Producer Receipts as % of Pre-tax FOB Value	61.6	61.6	61.6	61.7	61.9	62.0	62.2
(13b)	Adjusted Producer Receipts as % of Pre-tax FOB Value	61.6	60.9	60.3	59.6	56.6	54.0	51.9

[1] Approximate values, all per 70-kg. bag unless otherwise indicated.

[2] Exchange rate Col $18.00 per U.S. dollar.

[3] Export tax rate 20% of FOB value.

[4] Milling, handling, transport, and pasilla tax levy.

[5] Computed as follows: 87.5 kgs. parchment yield 70.0 kgs. green coffee, and 25% (Retention Quota) of 87.5 equals 21.875. Producer must deliver 87.5 + 21.875 = 109.375 kgs. parchment for each 70 kgs. of green shipped. Dividing (8) by 109.375 gives value per kg. of parchment, and multiplying by 125 gives value per carga.

[6] Computed as follows (example): Col $1,330 per 125-kg. carga is same as Col $1,330 per 100 kgs. of green coffee or Col $13.30 per kg. of green; Col $13.30 multiplied by 70 equals Col $931 equivalent value.

[7] Adjusted to pass only 35% of increase to producer (threshold set here at Col $1,330 for purpose of illustration).

[8] Computed from adjusted support prices.

Source: IBRD.

erations these figures would be correct, but of course in actual practice variation may occur. One should bear in mind that the illustration is computed at a constant Col$18 exchange rate: It can be appreciated that if the New York price were to reach 75 cents per pound the burden of coffee taxation in Colombia would approach 50% of FOB value, in contrast to a present burden of about 40%. The *Retention Quota* would have to rise substantially to bring this about.

This sharing arrangement is an extraordinary measure, and it reflects the sophistication that Colombia's coffee policy has acquired over the years. When prices strengthened in 1969 as the world coffee situation improved, Colombia's leaders took this step to prevent excessive stimulus to new plantings and replantings.

Key Issues

The coffee policy issues confronting Colombia's leaders are fairly easy to identify but difficult to resolve. One fundamental problem is that there are thousands of farmers working plots too small to provide a decent level of living, even when coffee prices are relatively favorable. At a yield rate of 500 kilograms per hectare a one-hectare farm planted two-thirds to coffee can produce 335 kilograms of parchment coffee. At the 1970 support price of Col$132 per arroba this generates a gross revenue of about Col$3,540. Allowing Col$75 per arroba[13] to meet current costs of production, this leaves a return of only Col$1,530 (US$85) to the farmer, before deductions for capital depreciation, interest charges, administrative expenses, or taxes. Even if the entire series of planting, weeding, pruning, harvesting, and processing steps is accomplished by members of the farmer's family the gross return of US$195 seems pathetically low when it is recognized that there are some 6.5 persons per family, on the average.

Unless the situation has changed substantially since 1965 there are at least 110,000 farm families raising coffee on plots of one hectare or less. This number understates the magnitude of the problem, however, because the desirable cut-off size for an agricultural unit is certainly higher than one hectare. The agrarian reform legislation of Colombia prohibits the subdivision of farms of less than three hectares, and if that is taken as an acceptable minimum size roughly 40% of Colombia's coffee farms would be excluded.

One obvious solution to this problem is to transfer people off the minifundia into alternative employment, assembling their properties into economically-sized parcels and utilizing modern techniques of production to raise yields (experimental plots have recorded yields of 8,000 to 10,000 kilograms per hectare). Through productivity increases the demand for Colombian coffee could easily be satisfied at the same time that land was shifted to other uses.[14]

The same solution seems appropriate to nearly all of Colombia's agricultural sector, however, and the principal obstacle to its implementation is that to date the economy has been unable to generate alternative employment for persons transfering from the rural areas. Hence the Coffee Federation's program to upgrade the small farmer and to help him to diversify into hog- and poultry-raising, small-scale dairying, and planting other crops. Until the system can offer meaningful jobs elsewhere many country folk have no choice other than to remain on the land, no matter how poor an existence it provides. It is in this context that the need for accelerated industrial development in the coffee producing areas has to be considered.

13. One arroba = 12.5 kilograms. Costs per arroba have been estimated as follows:

Year	1960	1961	1962	1963	1964	1965	1966	1967	1968	1969
Cost Col$	36.63	38.63	39.66	45.05	46.66	46.86	55.14	55.95	64.51	72.78

Cost is estimated for zones yielding 500 kilograms of parchment coffee per hectare planted. Cultivation and harvest labor account for 95% of cost, the remainder being fertilizers, insecticides, fungicides and tools.
Source: National Coffee Growers Federation for 1960-1966; IBRD for 1967-1979.

14. The outlook for significant gains in coffee yields from the minifundia in the near future is not promising, since these gains require knowledge and capital that the small farmers do not possess and are not likely to acquire quickly.

Another major coffee problem remains: the difficulty of maintaining reasonable balance between supply and demand in world markets. If other producing countries permit massive new plantings to take place a wave of overproduction and surpluses will inevitably follow, and Colombia will suffer in spite of its own enlightened efforts to hold production on a flat trend line. Officials from Colombia have labored diligently to launch and improve the International Coffee Organization precisely to avoid recurring boom-or-bust cycles; Colombia has pursued a most austere coffee-tax policy; but only if other member nations of ICO apply similar measures can stability be maintained in the world coffee market at prices satisfactory to producers.

Realistic production controls and international regulation of coffee stocks would appear to be essential to the stabilization of world prices. Production control calls for consistent tax policies in all producing countries, whereby price increases beyond agreed limits are taxed away in large part—as under Colombia's sharing arrangement. This would prevent the creation of undesirable incentives causing producers to rush into new plantings. International management of stocks could obviate much of the problem caused by producers and importers as they withhold coffee from the market and hoard inventories in search of short-term profits, or dump them on a weak market when downward price expectations prevail.

Colombia has exhibited a high degree of economic maturity through its coffee policies of the postwar period. The Federation has worked continuously to preserve the country's share of the market and to wring the maximum benefit from the share. A stated policy objective is to hold output levels to modest increases during the next few years, thereby permitting some reduction of the stocks accumulated in the last decade (5.5 million bags at present). Although ample credit will continue to be made available for improvements in cultivation, harvesting, and processing the present prohibition on lending for new plantings will be maintained.

CHAPTER 16
GROWTH POTENTIAL: CROPS OTHER THAN COFFEE

Expansion of production will depend first of all on the existence of a market and second on consistent and adequate prices. It is highly probable that the traditional starchy food crops, yuca and plantains, which in the past have expanded at approximately the same rate as population growth, could expand much more rapidly if market outlets could be found either as human food or as animal feed. Corn, another traditional food crop, now has an expanding outlet as a basic ingredient in feed concentrates for hogs, poultry and dairy cattle. For export crops, potential markets will largely depend on decisions in other countries, on international or bilateral marketing agreements, and sometimes on natural calamities such as frost or drought in important producing areas elsewhere.

Ample physical production possibilities do exist: Colombia has extensive areas of good land which could be brought into intensive crop production rather quickly. The following paragraphs set out crop by crop the more promising expansion possibilities.

Cotton

There has been an impressive upward trend in cotton production over the past five years. The area under this crop has nearly doubled, yields have improved by approximately 25%, and output has more than doubled, giving a record crop in 1969 of 125,000 tons of lint. A further rise in area to 240,500 hectares should ensure a crop of approximately 140,000 tons of lint for 1970. Prior to 1958 the national average yield never reached 1,000 kg. per hectare of seed cotton, but by 1968 the average had risen to 1,679 kg., with the lint component just above 600 kg. per hectare. This increase reflects the improvements in management that have been achieved as a result of more widespread extension efforts and the greater use of inputs such as fertilizers and pest control. The expansion in the area under cotton has also been stimulated by the higher price offered for seed cotton over the past three years and by the special credit facilities made available to cotton growers. Some 11,000 farmers now grow cotton.

As the internal demand for cotton over the past few years has remained relatively static at slightly more than three kilograms per capita, the bulk of the increased production has been available for export. Thus in four years exports have risen from 5,000 tons to over 63,000 tons in 1969, the latter valued at US$35 million.

The National Federation of Cotton Growers are confident that a growth rate of 7.4% for the area under cotton will be maintained over the next five years; but even if a more conservative rate of 4.5% is accepted and yields continue to rise at the present rate of 3%, the annual output should reach 514,000 tons of seed cotton by 1975. In fact, yields per unit area should rise more rapidly with the growing strength and experience of the extension service. However, there is still much to be done to attain adequate land leveling, weed control, correct sowing dates and optimum plant densities. For these reasons, a 3% growth rate appears to be a more prudent estimate for the period until 1975. After that, a more modest 2% has been calculated largely because of uncertainties about the world market, where cotton is slowly being replaced by synthetic fibers. Accepting also a lower growth rate of 2% for the expansion in area under cotton during the decade 1975-1985, the projected outputs for 1985 are 762,500 tons of seed cotton or 274,500 tons of cotton lint. Whether these expansion rates are realized will depend largely on general policy decisions on exchange rates and export subsidies as well as on measures to slow down the rise of the main production costs—fertilizers, insecticides and labor.

Sugar

Sugar cane is grown in order to produce two types of sugar, the white centrifugal sugar produced from cane grown on large plantations almost all in the Cauca Valley; and the brown sugar, or panela, produced from cane grown on small holdings throughout the warmer parts

273

TABLE 16-1: COTTON, STATISTICS AND FORECASTS

	Area (Hectares)	Seed Cotton Yield (Kg/Ha)	Lint Production (Tons)	Seed Production (Tons)	Lint Exports[2] (Tons)	Value of Line Exports[1] (US$ Million)
Mean 1960-64	156,000	750	42,480	73,000	18,100	n.a.
1965	134,200	1,203	58,300	99,300	16,097	8.0
1966	164,900	1,264	75,400	125,000	5,100	2.2
1967	174,538	1,519	96,580	158,195	35,782	20.0
1968	198,879	1,679	120,135	200,725	58,222	33.7
1969	236,060	1,512	125,240	213,490	63,612	36.4
1975	294,000	1,750	185,200	329,200	n.a.	n.a.
1985	358,000	2,130	274,500	488,000	n.a.	n.a.

[1] United Nations *Yearbook of International Trade Statistics* up to 1967; Banco de la Republica exchange surrender data for 1968 and 1969.

[2] Annual growth-rate assumptions %: actual 1965-69, area 15.2, yield 5.9; projected 1970-75, area 4.5, yield 3.0; projected 1975-85, area 2.0, yield 2.0.

of Colombia. Production of the centrifugal sugar in the Cauca Valley totaled 708,850 tons in 1969, the fifth record crop in succession (Table 16-2). In addition to this, some 7,000 tons of white sugar were produced in the Atlantic coast area, and a small estate near Cucuta exported about 35,000 tons of cane across the border to Venezuela. The production of panela sugar for 1969 was estimated at 650,000 tons.

The steady increase in the production of centrifugal sugar has not been due to any marked increase in the area under cane, but is the result of the wider use of high-yielding varieties, better cultural methods, higher applications of fertilizers, and of some improvement in extraction rates. Thus over the past four years the yield of sugar has increased from 5.9 to 7.4 tons per hectare. Further increases in yields are planned and to this end the government has made credit available

TABLE 16-2: SUGAR (WHITE), STATISTICS AND FORECASTS[1]

	Area (Hectares)	Yield (Kg/Ha)	Production (Tons)	Apparent and Projected Internal Consumption (Tons)	Raw Sugar Exports (Tons)[2]	Value of Exports (US$ Million)[2]
Mean 1960-64	n.a.	n.a.	n.a.	n.a.	36,760	4.3
1965	80,510	6,026	485,190	383,543	101,647	7.6
1966	91,633	5,864	537,365	423,435	113,930	8.3
1967	89,600	6,658	596,575	420,105	176,470	11.3
1968	94,000	7,057	663,365	425,054	238,311	22.0
1969	96,000	7,385	709,000[3]	535,505	173,495	17.5
1975	107,400	8,125	873,000	663,000	210,000	n.a.
1980	128,000	8,250	1,057,750	846,000	210,000	n.a.
1985	151,770	8,500	1,290,000	1,080,000	210,000	n.a.

[1] Annual growth-rate assumptions %; actual 1965-69, area 4.5, yield 5.2, production 9.9; projected 1971-75, area 3.1, yield 2.4, production 5.7, 1975-85, area 3.1, yield 0.5, production 3.7.

[2] Data from United Nations *Yearbook of International Trade Statistics* up to 1967; Banco de la Republica exchange surrender data for 1968 and 1969.

[3] Including 10,000 tons of white sugar produced in the Atlantic Coast Region.

to finance changes in the system of growing cane as advocated by advisers from Hawaii. It is hoped that these changes will bring about a further rise of 10% in productivity over the next five years.

Sugar exports are controlled by quotas and prices ruling in the United States and the world markets. The value of sugar exports, though starting from a small base has increased nearly four-fold during the past decade. In addition to the United States, sugar is sold under the International Sugar Agreement to Japan, New Zealand, Canada and a small amount to Ecuador.

Domestic demand for white sugar is expected to grow at about 5% per year. While improved productivity may be able to meet both internal demands and a reasonable allocation for exports for another few years, an expansion in the area under cane must be considered soon to meet future export quotas and maintain the present levels of foreign exchange earnings from sugar. There is an important policy question here as to whether to reclaim poorly drained grazing land in the Cauca Valley to expand sugar production in the present major producing area, or expand into the north, in areas such as **Codazzi** or Cartagena where two small enterprises are already located. If domestic demand for white sugar increases at 5% a year— **because of population growth and changeover from use of brown "panela" sugar to white which tends to occur as the population shifts from rural to urban—the projections for 1975, 1980 and 1985 indicate requirements for 663,000, 846,000 and 1,080,000 tons, respectively. To these amounts must be added an allocation for exports. At present this would total 210,000 tons for both the U.S. and Sugar Agreement quotas; but with an assumed expansion in U.S. and world consumption of about 1.8% per annum, the quotas will increase and failure to meet them could result in forfeiting some of the allocation. The total production in the next decade and a half would then require some 56,000 hectares of additional land under sugar cane to produce the amounts projected.**

Bananas

Bananas have in the past made an important contribution to export earnings; this ranged from US$19 million to US$25 million a year between 1965 and 1967, but declined to US$15 million in 1967 and about US$18.6 million in 1969 when the impact of the virtual abandonment of the Santa Marta production area was taking effect.

The present main banana-producing area continues to be Uraba; its production in 1969 of 271,000 tons, all Gros Michel type, represented 37% of the country's production for export. Of this nearly nine-tenths is produced by the Compania Frutera de Sevilla (United Fruit Company) while the Union de Bananeros de Uraba produces the remainder.

Much of the decline in banana exports over the last three years has been a result of disease problems with plantings of the established Gros Michel variety. Large areas of bananas south of Santa Marta have gone out of production since the Compania Frutera de Sevilla left its long-established enterprise in this region. Recently INCORA has undertaken to rehabilitate this area with the help of Caja Agraria credit by remodeling the irrigation and drainage system and by removing all Gros Michel bananas and substituting the better adapted and higher yielding Cavendish type. This rehabilitation started in 1969 with the intention of establishing a total of 5,000 hectares under Cavendish. The expectations for 1970 are that the initial plantings of Cavendish should produce at least 17,500 tons of fruit. The overall average yield is expected to rise from the present 15 tons per hectare to 20 tons because of the Cavendish plantings which should be yielding at least 30 tons per hectare when fully productive.

Since little further expansion will take place in the Uraba area, and with the Santa Marta plantings to be restricted to 5,000 hectares because any further move north would mean returning to an area subject to hurricane damage, output in the future is not expected to reach more than 550,000 tons per annum. Because production of such a highly perishable product as bananas has to be tied to an assured market, any further expansion will depend in part on long range agreements which might be worked out with market outlets. Recent expansion in other tropical countries may limit further near term growth in Colombia.

TABLE 16-3: BANANAS, STATISTICS AND FORECAST

	Area (Hectares)	Yield (Kg/Ha)	Production (Tons)	Exports[1] (Tons)	Value[1] (US$ Million)
1965	29,000	11,600	338,000	10,892[2]	18.6
1966	32,000	12,200	392,000	13,148[2]	19.9
1967	21,500	17,000	365,500	325,582	25.0
1968	23,500	15,000	352,500	310,440	15.6
1969	23,600	14,000	330,400	309,090	18.6
1975	27,600	18,000	496,800	490,000	24.5
1980	28,000	20,000	560,000	550,000	27.5
1985	28,000	20,000	560,000	550,000	27.5

[1] United Nations *Yearbook of International Trade Statistics* up to 1967; Banco de la Republica exchange surrender data for 1968 and 1969.

[2] Exports as thousands of stems.

Cacao

Before 1918 cacao was exported from Colombia, but plant diseases and other factors resulted in local demand outstripping production and from that date the country has had to rely on imports to meet the growing internal requirements. Thus in the period 1960-64 production averaged 15,000 tons per annum but this had to be supplemented by imports of approximately 7,500 tons per annum (see Table 16-4). The internal demand continued to grow and is now in the region of 33,000 to 34,000 tons. While production had increased to an estimated 18,500 tons in 1969, the shortfall of some 14,500 tons represented, at 1969 world market prices, more than US$12 million in foreign exchange.

The need to increase the production of cacao to offset this drain on foreign exchange is fully appreciated and a number of programs to raise output are already being implemented. These include the coffee diversification program, mainly in the Caldas region, where the plan is to plant to cacao some 10,000 hectares, and a similar program to establish 10,000 hectares in Uraba under a Cofiagro scheme. These schemes are now proceeding and some 1,200 hectares of new cacao will be planted in Uraba and 1,300 hectares in Caldas. The shortage of planting material which is now all hybrid stock being raised by ICA at Palmira and by the Chocolateria Luker S.A. is restricting the pace of this development, but it is planned to have sufficient material available by 1971 to plant up a further 2,800 hectares in Uraba and 2,000 hectares in Caldas as the next stage in these programs.

The importance of credit in expanding the area under a perennial crop such as cacao has been recognized and sufficient funds were made available in 1968 and 1969 to finance the establishment and rehabilitation of 15,000 hectares. Under this credit scheme loans of up to US$1,000 per hectare were granted for planting new units of 15 hectares or more, and smaller loans for the rejuvenation of existing plantings. Technical assistance is provided with the loans and a market is guaranteed for ten years.

Assuming that an additional 20,000 hectares of cacao can be established in the next decade,

TABLE 16-4: CACAO, STATISTICS AND FORECASTS

	Area (Hectares)	Yield (Kg./Ha)	Production (Tons)	Consumption (Tons)	Imports (Tons)	Value (US$ Million)
Mean 1960-64	34,000	440	15,000	22,460	7,460	4.0
1965	37,000	460	17,000	30,720	13,720[1]	7.0
1966	37,000	480	17,800	35,480	17,680[1]	9.4
1967	37,000	460	17,000	32,325	15,325[2]	14.3
1968	39,200	460	18,000	32,000	14,000[2]	n.a.
1969	39,500	470	18,600	n.a.	n.a.	n.a.
1975	50,000	650	32,500	n.a.	n.a.	n.a.
1980	60,000	750	45,000	n.a.	n.a.	n.a.
1985	60,000	800	48,000	n.a.	n.a.	n.a.

[1] United Nations *Yearbook of International Trade Statistics.*

[2] U.S. Embassy with total including 4,000 tons contraband from Ecuador.

Source: Cacao Federation and Ministry of Agriculture for production data.

and higher yields achieved by the use of disease-resistant hybrid planting material and improved management (including better sanitation, disease control and the use of fertilizers), production by 1985 should be 48,000 tons. If the present rate of consumption of 1.55 kilograms per capita is maintained, the 1985 expanded population will require 50,860 tons. Some imports will therefore still be necessary and Colombia will not have fulfilled the hope of once more becoming an exporter of cacao. It would appear advisable to speed up as much as possible the present cacao development program, and to extend it by further stages after the success of the first stages has been confirmed.

Tobacco

The production of tobacco appears to remain relatively static, although there was a small increase in acreage in 1969 and output reached an estimated 43,990 tons, an increase of 3% on the previous two years. Almost 98% of this production comprises dark air-cured varieties, the types exported mainly to Germany and the United States for filler or binder use in cigars. Exports in the last four years have been fluctuating from a high of US$9.1 million in 1969 to a low of US$4.4 million in 1967. The quantities involved have been in the range of 10,000 to 13,000 thousand tons and unit prices also have varied widely.

The remainder of the annual production is used in the manufacture of cigarettes and cigars for local consumption. Although there is a strong demand for the lighter leaf tobacco, local production of Virginia and Burley types continues to remain at about 1,000 tons a year, so that considerable imports of cigarettes have to be permitted each year. In 1968 about 30 million packs, valued at US$5 million, were imported, mostly under PL 480 through IDEMA. The apparent reluctance to increase the area under light leaf tobacco needs thorough investigation in order to establish whether there are serious difficulties involved in attaining a greater measure of import substitution.

On the assumption that the recent improvements in tobacco yields continue through 1985, though at lower rates of growth, and that not only will the area under tobacco by 1975 recover to the level achieved in 1965, but will increase at a rate of 1.9% per annum to 1985, production in that year could reach a total of 67,500 tons (Table 16-5).

TABLE 16-5: TOBACCO STATISTICS AND FORECASTS[1]

	Area (Hectares)	Yield (Kg./Ha.)	Production (Tons)	Exports[2] (Tons)	Value[2] (US$ Million)
Mean 1960-64	n.a.	n.a.	n.a.	n.a.	n.a.
1965	25,450	1,580	40,190	10,890	7.2
1966	27,000	1,640	44,250	13,150	5.5
1967	23,000	1,850	42,500	11,945	4.4
1968	22,000	1,910	42,500	n.a.	7.1
1969	23,850	1,845	43,880	n.a.	9.1
1975	25,000	2,035	50,875	n.a.	n.a.
1980	27,500	2,140	58,850	n.a.	n.a.
1985	30,000	2,250	67,500	n.a.	n.a.

[1] Annual growth rate assumptions %: actual 1965-69, area -1.6, yield 3.9, production 2.5; projected 1970-75, area 1.9, yield 2.0, projection 2.0; projected 1975-85, area 1.9, yield 1.0, production 1.7.

[2] United Nations *Yearbook of International Trade Statistics* up to 1967.

TABLE 16-6: VEGETABLE OIL AND FATS – PRODUCTION, IMPORTS AND PROBABLE CONSUMPTION
(In thousands of tons)

	Production		Imports of Edible Oils and fats	Total Supply	Probable Consumption (Least Squares Trend)
	Vegetable Oils	Lard and Edible Tallow (Estimated)			
1960-64	35.1	n.a.	n.a.	n.a.	n.a.
1965	51.7	22.0	20.7	94.4	103.1
1966	56.3	22.0	59.1	137.4	107.9
1967	65.4	21.0	24.3	110.7	112.8
1968	65.6	22.0	21.7	109.3	117.6
1969	86.2 (est.)	22.0	14.3	122.5	122.4

Fats and Oils

The consumption of edible fats and oils in Colombia cannot be assessed from any official statistics but has to be estimated from production and imports. Estimates for the decade 1960-69 are given in Table 16-6:

The production of vegetable oils increased at a rate of nearly 17% annually between 1960 and 1969. Self-sufficiency, although at a low consumption rate of just under 6 kg per head, is thus steadily being achieved and the need for importing edible oils and fats had decreased from a high 59,000 tons in 1966 to only 14,300 tons in 1969.

The main crops used for vegetable oils and tonnages of edible oil produced by each in 1969 are as follows:

Cotton seed	—31,500	Oil palm	—24,600
Soybeans	—11,600	Copra	— 300
Sesame	—11,000	Maize	— 3,000

Of the annual crops the most spectacular increase in production has been in soybeans which had an annual growth rate of 19.6% between 1960-64 and 1969. Cotton seed increased by 19.2% per annum over the same period, while sesame had an annual growth rate of 16% between 1960-64 and 1966, but a serious epidemic of *Fusarium* wilt ("marchitez") in 1967 caused wide-scale loss of crop and reduced production from 57,500 tons to 35,000 tons. This was followed by a switch from sesame to other crops in 1968 resulting in a further fall in production to 15,000 tons of seeds. The introduction and local development of resistant varieties has reversed this trend and the area under sesame expanded again in 1969.

The African oil palm is the newest oil crop in Colombia. The planted area has grown from less than 1,000 hectares in 1960 to an estimated 21,000 hectares in 1969. At present about half these plantings have come into production and the output of palm oil in 1969 was estimated to be 24,600 tons. The anticipated average yield for mature plantings is expected to be 3 tons per hectare so that production by 1975 should reach 63,000 tons even if no further plantings are achieved. At present no further credit is being given to implement an ambitious plan for planting up to a total of 115,000 hectares which should have produced at maturity over half a million tons of palm oil per annum. Such a plan had, in 1967, been based on faulty assumptions on costs and future trends in world prices, and in view of the substantial decline in the world price from US$238 in 1967, to its 1970 price of US$170 (Col$2,910), a review of the plan is to be undertaken.

The production of vegetable oils brings a valuable by-product in oilseed cake, and the output of this commodity has grown from 67,300 tons in 1960 to an estimated 174,000 tons in 1969. Cotton seed cake and soybean cake represented 58% and 36% of the 1969 total. Oil cake is in strong demand both by Colombian manufacturers of concentrates and abroad. In 1968 the home market absorbed 105,000 tons of cake and an estimated 48,000 tons valued at US$4 million was exported, of which about 40% went to Latin American countries and 60% to Europe.

The expansion in the production of vegetable oils over the past ten years has reduced earlier dependence on the import of these commodities. Although the recent rate of increase in consumption will soon level off, it is reasonable to expect expansion from the present per capita consumption of 5.93 kg per annum to surpass the minimum of 9 kg recommended by the Colombian National Institute of Nutrition. On this basis, the projected population of 32.8 million for 1985 could require 354,000 tons of edible oils and fats (i.e. assuming 10.8 kg per capita consumption).

The consumption and production of butter and lard is not included in these estimates. Tallow production, however, is estimated to be approximately 35,000 tons a year. Of this, about 25,000 tons is manufactured into margarines and cooking fats for human consumption. The remaining 10,000 is used for soap manufacture but has to be supplemented by about 24,000 tons of imported tallow.

To produce all of the projected 354,000 tons required by 1985 without reliance on imports or on edible tallow and fats, would require a substantial increase in productivity and a great expansion in the area under soybeans and sesame. Table 16-7 shows how this total may be achieved by 1985 on the assumptions that there will be no further increase in the area under palm oil, but that palm kernel oil will contribute a small additional supply; that cotton seed production will increase as indicated in the section under cotton; and that maize oil and coconut will contribute 12,300 tons. This will leave the balance of 200,000 tons to be met by soybeans and sesame. If present sesame acreage can be doubled and yields can be increased to 800 kilograms per hectare, the balance to come from soybeans would be 140,000 tons of oil. This would involve expanding the area at least tenfold to 450,000 hectares and raising yields from the present 1,700-1,800 kilograms to 2 tons per hectare. Such expansion might take place in the Cauca Valley[1] where most of the present production is located as well as in the northern lowlands.

Of course it is not assured that consumption of edible oils and fats will increase at the rate indicated. If consumption by 1985 is assumed to be only 8 kilograms per capita, the reduced

1. Although corn yields are somewhat higher than soybean yields in the Cauca Valley, the higher price of soybeans make them competitive.

TABLE 16-7: OIL SEEDS AND OIL, STATISTICS AND FORECASTS

	Soybean	Sesame	Cotton Seed	Coconut Oil	Palm Oil	Maize Oil	Total Oils
1960-64							
Area (ha)	16,700	46,900	156,000				
Yield (kg ha)	1,580	600	470				
Seed							
Production (tons)	26,200	28,140	73,000				
Oil							
Production (tons)	3,700	13,100	10,220	500	400		27,920
1965-67							
Area (ha)	36,900	80,700	157,870		17,400		
Yield (kg ha)	1,627	620	800		243		
Seed							
Production (tons)	60,700	50,370	127,530				
Oil							
Production (tons)	8,870	23,600	18,200	270	4,530	2,300	57,300
1968							
Area (ha)	47,000	21,000	198,900		21,000		
Yield (kg)	1,800	710	1,005		670		
Seed							
Production (tons)	87,000	15,000	200,700				
Oil							
Production (tons)	11,800	7,000	29,400	300	14,100	3,000	65,600
1969							
Area (ha)	45,500	35,500	236,000		21,000		
Yield (kg)	1,650	700	905		1,170		
Seed							
Production (tons)	75,000	25,000	213,490				
Oil							
Production (tons)	11,600	11,000	31,500	300	24,600	3,000	82,000
1985 (Assumption A)[2]							
Area (ha)	450,000	170,000	358,000				
Yield (kg)	2,000	800	1,363				
Seed							
Production (tons)	900,000	136,000	488,000				
Oil							
Production (tons)	139,500	60,000	72,000	300	63,000 7,500[1]	12,000	354,300
1985 (Assumption B)[2]							
Area ha)	225,000	110,000	358,000				
Yield (kg)	2,000	800	1,363				
Seed							
Production (tons)	450,000	88,000	488,000				
Oil							
Production (tons)	69,750	38,720	72,000	300	63,000	12,000	263,270
Growth rates for 1960-64 to 1969							
Area (ha)	15.4%	-4.1%	6.1%				
Yield (kg)	0.6%	2.2%	9.8%				
Seed							
Production (tons)	19.6%	-1.7%	19.2%				

[1] Palm kernel oil.

[2] Per capita consumption of oils and fats 10.8 Kg (A) or 8 Kg (B).

Source: Planning Department, Ministry of Agriculture and Mission estimates.

total requirement—262,400 tons—could then be met by five times the present area under soybeans, namely from 225,000 hectares of this crop, and from 110,000 hectares of sesame, an increase of 30% on the maximum area previously achieved, in addition to the contributions made by the other oil seed crops.

The world price of vegetable oils is expected to take a downward trend but the price of the protein residue, oil seed cake, is expected to continue firm. For this reason, much of future production should be derived from soybeans, the oilseed crop with the highest ratio of protein cake to oil, so that exports of it could be used to offset any imports of oils which may still be necessary. In total the amount of oilcake which can be expected from the projected increased production of soybeans, sesame and cotton seed in 1985 should provide enough surplus for export to earn at least some US$10 million in foreign exchange.

Rubber

Imports of natural rubber average over 8,000 tons annually, valued at more than US$4 million. Colombia, on the other hand, possesses natural rubber and appears to have the climatic conditions which favor rubber production. In order to examine the possibilities of Colombia becoming self-sufficient in rubber, INCORA undertook to establish an initial 2,000 hectares of rubber as part of the Caqueta colonization project, and followed up the investigations started in this area in 1964 with improved clonal material imported from Guatemala grafted on to local seedlings. Field plantings were started in 1966 but after 420 hectares had been established, it was decided to defer further plantings until production had started and results justified continuation of the program. At this stage the 1966 plantings are reputed to be growing well and, provided there are no disease setbacks and that the settlers can be persuaded to accept the long delays involved in obtaining any return, this venture could be expanded into a full program for achieving self-sufficiency in rubber.

Rice

The 1969 paddy crops of 720,000 tons reversed the steady upward trend in production which has continued since 1960, and which culminated in the record crop of 786,300 tons in 1968. Consumption of rice has apparently risen at an average annual rate slightly above the rate of population growth. However, during this period Colombia has moved from occasional imports of rice to a heavily stocked position. Stocks began to accumulate after 1965, and reportedly reached nearly 200,000 tons of unhulled rice in early 1969. At this stage it was possible to dispose of 25,000 tons to Peru, Ecuador and Curacao, but at some financial loss because of the disparity between internal and export prices.

Since 1966 the area under rice has been shrinking, from the peak of 375,000 hectares in 1965 to 277,000 in 1968. Of this 1968 area, 46% represented irrigated paddy, a ratio which has been growing since 1966 when interest in rain-grown rice began to decline following the fall in the real price of paddy which occurred in 1965. Not only has there been an increase in the area under irrigated paddy, but average yields for irrigated paddy have also been rising from under 3,000 kg per hectare prior to 1964 to well over 4,000 kg in recent years[2] This is a reflection of the better management given to irrigated paddy, increased use of inputs, and the introduction of higher yielding varieties. The switch to irrigated rice is likely to continue, as INCORA's reclamation program will bring considerable land under irrigation that is more suited to rice than to other crops.

2. The Ministry of Agriculture and INCORA give the following figures for average yields of paddy (kg/ha):

	1964	1965	1966	1967	1968
Irrigated paddy	3,100	3,049	2,994	3,468	4,220
Rain grown paddy	1,206	1,126	1,436	1,551	1,668

As to pricing, the IDEMA support price was held for the past three years at Col$2,000 per ton of type 1, grade A, paddy. In 1970, it has been raised to Col$2,250. However, IDEMA's capacity to purchase a significant proportion of the national crop has been limited by lack of funds and storage. In 1968 it could purchase only 8.9% of the year's crop. The true market price has therefore been less than the support price, probably in the region of Col$1,600, or less, for the bulk of the crop, most of it of lower quality than type 1, grade A. Taken in terms of 1958 prices, there has been no actual improvement in the real price and, in fact, a downward trend. In consequence, growing rice under rainfall has become less remunerative, which in turn has either forced many dryland farmers out of business or has induced those who already irrigate, or could turn to irrigation, to offset the fall in prices by achieving higher productivity and better net returns.

Assuming that no further increase in the per capita consumption occurs over the next 15 years, the rise in population will nevertheless increase the internal requirement for rice to 728,000 tons by 1985. This amount could be obtained from 305,000 hectares if yields continue to rise at the rates projected in Table 16-8. This area would still be 70,000 hectares less than the area under rice in 1965, but with the difficulties which face Colombia in exporting surplus rice, careful study must be given before proposing a greater rate of expansion than can be absorbed internally. World market prices have recently dropped and many of the South and Central American countries are becoming self-sufficient in rice. However, there may be prospective markets in Ecuador, Peru and Chile. Study should be made of further possibilities for reducing production costs, possibly through measures for lowering fertilizer prices.

It should also be noted that preliminary results of studies carried out by the Instituto de Investigaciones Tecnologicas have shown that up to 30% rice flour can be mixed with imported wheat flour to make acceptable bread. Larger scale acceptability tests will have to be conducted before determining whether the process can be adopted commercially. If the product proves acceptable, internal demand for rice could be substantially increased and in turn wheat imports could be reduced by equivalent amounts.

Corn and Sorghum

The area under corn, the most widely produced subsistence crop in Colombia, appears to have grown slower than the population during the 1960-64 period, averaging 2.7% annually. During the same period average yields appear to have fallen at an annual rate of 1.5% so that annual production has perhaps increased at 1.2%. The inability to achieve any significant

TABLE 16-8: RICE, STATISTICS AND FORECASTS[1]

	Area (Hectares)	Yield (Kg paddy/ Ha) (Raingrown, Irrigated)	Production (Tons Paddy)	Production (Tons Rice)
Mean 1960-64	260,000	2,046	532,000	341,000
1965	375,000	1,790	672,000	414,100
1966	350,000	1,940	680,000	416,000
1967	291,000	2,275	661,500	414,400
1968	277,000	2,835	786,300	511,000
1969	262,000	2,750	720,000	469,000
1975	274,900	3,190	877,000	570,000
1980	284,900	3,510	1,000,000	650,000
1985	305,100	3,680	1,123,000	730,000

[1] Annual growth-rate assumptions %: actual 1965-69, area -7.4, yield 11.3; projected 1970-75, area 1.1, yield 3.0, 1975-80, area 1.1, yield 2.0, 1980-85, area 1.1, yield 1.0.

Source: Ministry of Agriculture and INCORA.

improvements in the overall average yields, despite the introduction of better seed and improved technology, must be ascribed to the preponderance of small producers and the lack of attention credit and extension programs pay to introducing new technology to this large body of producers, particularly those growing corn at the higher altitudes. Under commercial farming, however, and particularly in regions such as the Cauca Valley, yields average 2-3 tons per hectare, and exceptional cases reach 6 tons and more. With corn production remaining relatively static and the population growing at 3.2% per annum, the per capita consumption is apparently declining. This decline in apparent consumption (from 57 kilograms per head in 1960 to 45 kilograms in 1969), is partly influenced by the steady move of the population from rural to urban areas and the resulting changes in diet.

Sorghum is discussed in conjunction with corn since almost all the sorghum produced is used for the manufacture of concentrates and as such is interchangeable with corn. Significant sorghum production started in 1962. The estimated area sown in that year was 3,250 hectares and this rapidly increased to 45,000 hectares in 1969, producing a total of some 90,000 tons of grain. The reason for this rapid expansion is that considerably higher yields than corn, approximately 2.25 tons per hectare, are obtained at no extra cost of production. Under improved management well over three tons are achieved.

The concentrates industry has had a remarkable growth over the past decade and now produces 500,000 to 600,000 tons of feed. With an estimated grain content of about 45% the production of 550,000 tons of concentrates would require about 250,000 tons of coarse grains. If it is assumed that all the 90,000 tons of sorghum produced in 1969 was in fact used for concentrates, corn's contribution would have had to be 160,000 tons. The market for corn and sorghum as feed grains is expected to expand rapidly with sorghum making a major contribution because of its proven yielding abilities and ease of mechanization, which is a major attraction for large producers.

The internal price for corn is well above world prices, so that if production were to increase, the possibilities for export would not be promising, except at a considerable loss. In fact, over the past three years a certain amount of corn has been exported. In 1969, 30,000 tons were shipped to Puerto Rico and Tanzania. As the IDEMA support price in 1969 was Col$1,300 per ton for yellow maize, while the export price ranged between Col$780 and Col$1,070 f.o.b. (normal world prices and the special price paid by Puerto Rico respectively), the subsidy element in the consignments exported was considerable. However, because of the limited number of purchase points, most farmers cannot make production plans based on the IDEMA price.

Production policy for corn should be focused on increasing yields and lowering per unit costs, largely through better fertilization and other improved practices. The goal should be to lower the support price in order to provide low-cost feed material for livestock and to compete with a minimum of subsidy on the world market. Table 16-9 estimates area, yield and production of the two crops during the next fifteen years.

Wheat and Barley

Wheat and barley have been successfully grown in Colombia only in the highlands. For this reason they compete for the same soil resources and are considered as alternative crops by many farmers. Both are grown largely on small holdings. In 1966 a total of 80,000 farmers grew about 110,000 hectares of wheat and 33,000 farmers grew about 55,000 hectares of barley. Table 16-10 gives production figures for 1948-69, including two series for the past six years to illustrate the wide divergence in estimates from two government sources. The disparity is especially important in barley yields and production where it is possible that the higher yield series of the Ministry of Agriculture reflect commercial yields obtained through IDEMA sources and the lower DANE series is the result of a general sample. Whichever series most nearly reflects the true situation, there has apparently been substantial yield improvement in wheat and little change or a substantial decrease in barley. It should be pointed out that the DANE sampling procedures have markedly improved in recent years and recent figures may accurately reflect both level and trend.

TABLE 16-9: CORN AND SORGHUM, STATISTICS AND FORECASTS[1]

	Corn Est. 1	Corn Est. 2	Sorghum
1960-64			
Area ('000 ha)	719.5	1,261[2]	10.9[3]
Yield (kg/ha)	1,145	912	2,300
Production ('000 tons)	823	1,150	25.1
1965-67			
Area ('000 ha)	835	1,062	33
Yield (kg/ha)	1,028	920	2,193
Production ('000 tons)	857	977	73
1968			
Area ('000 ha)	775		45
Yield (kg/ha)	1,135		2,290
Production ('000 tons)	880		103
1969			
Area ('000 ha)	825		39
Yield (kg/ha)	1,090		2,300
Production ('000 tons)	900		90
1975			
Area ('000 ha)	850		69
Yield (kg/ha)	1,300		2,400
Production ('000 tons)	1,105		16
1980			
Area ('000 ha)	900		111
Yield (kg/ha)	1,400		2,500
Production ('000 tons)	1,260		277
1985			
Area ('000 ha)	900		178
Yield (kg/ha)	1,500		2,500
Production ('000 tons)	1,350		445

[1] Annual growth rate assumption for sorghum 10% for area and production; no change in yield.

[2] 1964 only.

[3] For sorghum mean of 3 years 1962-64.

Source: Estimate 1: Planning Office, Ministry of Agriculture
Estimate 2: Departmente Administrative Nacional de Estadistica, DANE.
Full year statistics are not yet available for 1968 and 1969.

TABLE 16-10: AREA, PRODUCTION AND YIELD OF WHEAT AND BARLEY, 1948-1969

Year	WHEAT Area '000 Ha		WHEAT Production '000 Metric Tons		WHEAT Yield Kg/Ha		BARLEY Area '000 Ha		BARLEY Production '000 Metric Tons		BARLEY Yield Kg/Ha	
	A		A		A		A		A		A	
1948	177.3		118.7		668		24.4		29.2		1,199	
1949	180.7		128.3		710		45.2		51.1		1,129	
1950	145.4		102.0		702		43.9		50.5		1,149	
1951	174.2		130.0		746		47.0		56.2		1,196	
1952	188.0		140.0		745		51.0		61.0		1,196	
1953	175.0		145.0		829		62.9		79.0		1,256	
1954	195.0		146.0		749		53.0		65.0		1,226	
1955	182.0		147.0		808		43.0		52.0		1,209	
1956	170.0		140.0		824		50.0		70.0		1,400	
1957	178.0		110.0		618		48.0		60.0		1,250	
1958	160.0		140.0		875		43.3		75.0		1,734	
1959	166.0		145.0		873		60.5		101.0		1,669	
1960	159.9		142.0		888		56.3		106.0		1,883	
1961	160.0		142.1		888		48.1		99.4		2,065	
1962	150.0	B	162.0	B	1,080	B	49.0	B	108.0	B	2,204	B
1963	113.0		90.0		796		58.0		117.6		2,027	
1964	100.0	131.1	85.0	126.0	850	962	58.0	61.0	113.6	73.5	1,959	1,195
1965	120.0	118.2	110.0	106.0	917	898	46.1	54.0	90.0	64.8	1,953	1,181
1966	110.0	114.6	125.0	94.0	1,136	823	55.0	53.0	95.0	61.9	1,727	1,158
1967	68.0	105.4	80.0	107.0	1,176	1,013	61.0	53.0	95.2	63.3	1,561	1,200
1968(P)	93.0	120.0	125.0	120.0	1,344	1,000	46.8	54.0	74.8	63.0	1,600	1,200
1069(P)	58.0	140.0	68.0	170.0	1,200	1,214	47.0	54.0	76.0	68.0	1,600	1,259

(P) Preliminary

Sources: Complete 1948-69 columns, A, are data compiled from Colombian Ministry of Agriculture and other
government sources by L. Jay Atkinson and brought up-to-date by the Planning Office of the Ministry
of Agriculture; the short 1964-69 columns B are from the National Statistics Department (DANE).

There are sharp differences between the wheat estimates for 1969 and some support is found
for the higher DANE figures in the fact that wheat imports were down.

Our best indication of the wheat market situation comes from the import data which appear
in Table 16-11. A comparison of the 1960-64 period with 1955-59, shows that wheat imports
grew at an average rate of 8.2% annually. By 1965-69 the annual growth, comparing the 1965-69
average with 1960-64, had increased to 10.5%. If this present growth trend continues without
further increase, annual imports by 1980 will total more than 630,000 tons. In terms of present
costs of wheat f.o.b. (US$59.79) plus maritime freight ($6.56), this will mean a balance of
payments loss of US$42 million. When credit costs and internal shipping are included, this
wheat placed in Bogota costs US$108.71 (not including the 30% import tax).

This would appear to cancel out many of the gains being obtained through increasing minor
exports. However, to the extent that a sizable portion of this wheat can continue to be imported

TABLE 16-11: WHEAT IMPORTS IN METRIC TONS
AND VALUE, 1955-69

Years	Metric Tons	Value (US$)
1955	51,873	4,073,069
1956	90,221	6,793,007
1957	101,827	7,611,026
1958	91,488	7,275,677
1959	97,000	7,482,240
1960	92,490	6,880,587
1961	137,194	10,352,949
1962	124,857	10,015,024
1963	102,885	8,281,147
1964	183,801	12,719,738
1965	187,821	12,058,382
1966	220,824	14,112,283
1967	185,924	12,069,711
1968	267,939	17,373,173
1969	192,723	11,074,680

Source: Office of Planning, IDEMA.

under the favorable provisions of PL 480, these imports may entail little problem. In view of PL 480, Colombian authorities have decided to reduce emphasis on wheat research and production programs. In contrast, increased emphasis is planned for barley in order to avoid imports (US$1.5 million in 1969) and if possible begin to export malting barley to neighboring Venezuela.

This decision was based in part on the statistical series showing barley yields more than double those of wheat. It appears likely, however, that the barley series was based heavily on yields of commercial farms selling to the malting industry, whereas the wheat series reflected a more general level of productivity. The recent DANE series, based on generally accepted sampling procedures, indicates similar yields for both crops and similar fertilization practices.[3]

Potatoes

Potato production is an important cash crop in Colombia as well as providing a subsistence food for many families in the highlands. Yearly production approximates one million tons. About one-third is grown for the January-February harvest and two-thirds for the June-August harvest, the bulk of the crop being produced in Boyaca and Cundinamarca and Narino. Potato farms are usually small with over 70% having less than one hectare. Average yields per hectare appear to have changed very little over the past decade and currently are somewhere between 7 and 11 tons, depending on the estimate accepted (see Table 16-12). However, efficient prod-

3. DANE figures are as follows (crop year 1967/68):

	Total Planted Area (Ha)	Fertilized Area (Ha)	% Fertilized	Average Yield
Barley	61,120	40,339	66.0	1,043
Wheat	122,975	80,246	65.2	977

Source: DANE.

TABLE 16-12: POTATO PRODUCTION, 1960-85

	IDEMA-Atkinson Estimate[1]			Caja Agraria Estimate[2]		
	'000 Hectares	Yield Tons/Ha	Production (Tons)	'000 Hectares	Yield Kg/Ha	Production[3]
Mean 1960-64	65	10.9	703	169	7.1	1,200
1965	67	11.5	762	171	7.2	1,225
1966	67	11.3	760	159	7.2	1,144
1967	79	10.1	800	154	6.2	857
1968	85	10.6	900	160	7.5	1,200
1969	95	10.5	950	n.a.	n.a.	n.a.
1975	100	13.0	1,300	n.a.	n.a.	n.a.
1980	110	14.0	1,540	n.a.	n.a.	n.a.
1985	120	15.0	1,800	n.a.	n.a.	n.a.

[1] From USDA *Changes in Agricultural Production and Technology in Colombia* and brought up-to-date by Planning Office, Ministry of Agriculture. Based on IDEMA estimates.

[2] This estimate is taken from "Improving Performance of the Production Distribution System for Potatoes in Colombia," ICA, 1969.

[3] In thousands of metric tons.

ucers with top quality land obtain up to 40 tons. The main production problems are disease control and, in some cases, inadequate fertilization and low seed rates. On the other hand, most potato growers use some fertilizer and many also spray their crops. With regard to seed, ICA has recently developed five new varieties and supplies are now being made available through the Caja Agraria. These varieties have better fungus and virus resistance characteristics which should help to increase yields in the future.

Urban consumption absorbs about 43% of the total production, rural consumption takes another 20% and the remainder is used as seed or represents harvest or storage losses. At the present rate of consumption of 56 kilograms per capita, by 1985 production will have to double to provide for consumption needs of approximately 1,800,000 tons. This could be attained with a combination of yield increase and expansion of area under potatoes. As there is usually a wide variation in prices over the seasons, there is no great incentive to increase production. Price stabilization measures will have to be considered (including the encouragement of on-farm storage through easier credit), as well as the provision of additional credit to enable producers to obtain the required inputs of improved seed fungicides and fertilizers. The projections in Table 16-12 indicate that at least another 25,000 hectares should be under potatoes by 1985 and that greater extension efforts should be directed to raising the average yield of at least 15 tons per hectare through technological improvements.

Traditional Crops

Basic food crops such as beans, yuca, yam, and plantains have been classified as traditional because they have been least affected by modern technology and are grown by small farmers using hand cultivation. Except for beans they are subsistence crops.

The area and yield estimates on these crops are the weakest of all and it is hoped that the 1970 census will provide a new base for initiating a better series. Disparities such as those shown in Table 16-13 make meaningful comments difficult.

Production has probably increased somewhat more slowly than total population but perhaps slightly faster than rural population.

Undoubtedly yields could be raised more rapidly with the addition of modern inputs and by using better management practices. In general this would have little impact on the standard of living of farm families because only beans are cash crops. But the land thus freed could be

TABLE 16-13: TWO ESTIMATES OF AREA AND YIELD OF THREE TRADITIONAL CROPS, 1967

	'000 Ha	Estimate [1] Production '000 Tons	Yield Kg/Ha	'000 Ha	Estimate [2] Production '000 Tons	Yield Kg/Ha
Yuca	259	2,005	7,740	144	850	5,903
Beans	145	49	342	69	38	551
Plantains	315	n.a.	n.a.	230	n.a.	n.a.

[1] National Statistics Department of Colombia (DANE).

[2] Office of Planning, Ministry of Agriculture.

used for producing other crops and thus might contribute to new employment opportunities and better labor utilization for the individual smallholder.

CHAPTER 17

GROWTH POTENTIAL: LIVESTOCK, FISHERIES AND FORESTRY

Livestock

Livestock production accounts for about one-third of agricultural output, or approximately 10% of GDP, and is growing at an annual rate of approximately 4%. Until 1961 the exports of livestock products were negligible but since then a sizable export value has been attained by beef and live cattle, and in 1969 these exports reached over US$12 million.[1] In 1970 livestock exports are expected to reach between US$25 and US$30 million, mostly in live cattle and beef to Peru. Practically no livestock products are imported for food purposes but small amounts do enter under special food programs. Substantial quantities are imported for industrial uses especially in the form of wool and tallow. In general, livestock production is not a labor-intensive enterprise. In Colombia, the input of labor is unlikely to be appreciably affected by wage rates or expansion of output. Employment creation potential over the next five year period, apart from INCORA colonization schemes, is probably close to zero or negative. In Colombia, there are 167,000 farms listed as livestock but only about 50,000 have units larger than 40 hectares.

Colombia with an area of 1.14 million km[2] is the fifth largest country in Latin America. Although falling wholly within the tropics (latitude 13°N to 4°S), three prongs of the Andes running approximately south-north, cause a veritable mosaic pattern of ecological zones in the western third of the country where land surface ranges in altitude and contour from low-lying flat plains to mountains, which rise steeply to more than 5,000 meters above sea level. The eastern two-thirds of the country, beyond the Andean Mountains, consists of savanna to the north and tropical rain forests to the south. In consequence, there are wide variations in temperature, rainfall, vegetation; and conditions suitable for all the common farm animals can be found in Colombia, though, of course, in varying proportions.

Of the 114 million hectares in Colombia only about 40 million hectares are suitable for crop and livestock production; the remainder are under forest or else wasteland. Cropland occupies approximately 5 million hectares which leaves 35 million hectares under livestock. Even if crop acreage increases at 7% per annum during this decade, which would be very rapid growth, there would still be 30 million hectares in 1980 with no practical alternative use but grazing. The nation has the choice of producing cattle on this land or letting it go idle. Credit and managerial manpower are the only scarce inputs used by the livestock industry.

Beef Cattle

Although statistical data are derived largely from estimates subject to errors of unknown magnitude, it is likely that Colombia supports about 20 million head of cattle (Table 17-1). Of these slightly more than 17 million are beef animals. About 8 million head are carried in La Costa zone (Departments of Atlantico, Bolivar, Cordoba, and Magdalena), about 3 million in Los Llanos (Departments of Boyaca, Meta and the Intendencia of Arauca) and the remainder in the rest of the country, especially in the Departments of Antioquia, Caldas and Cauca. Over the period 1950 to 1969 the rate of increase in cattle numbers has been in the region of 2% per annum; however, since 1956 the rate of increase has been close to 3% per annum. Due to the violence in the early fifties, cattle numbers in 1956 were identical to those in 1950. In recent years the rate of increase has accelerated, and over the period 1965-1969 herd numbers increased at about 4% per annum.

Total slaughterings indicate an annual extraction rate[2] of approximately 12% over the past three years. Although this figure is as good as or better than, in most tropical areas, it is still relatively low and leaves much room for improvement. The production rate[3] has been about

---

1. Except where otherwise stated, beef and live cattle exports are exclusive of illegal live cattle exports to Venezuela.
2. Number of cattle slaughtered and exported live annually as percentage of total cattle population.
3. Number of cattle slaughtered and exported live annually, plus inventory change expressed as percentage of total cattle population.

TABLE 17-1: CATTLE NUMBERS IN THE NATIONAL HERD, SLAUGHTER AND EXPORT OF LIVE ANIMALS, EXTRACTION[1] AND PRODUCTION[2] RATES, 1950-1969

Year	No. of Cattle	Change in Inventory	Registered Slaughter	Unregistered Slaughter	Total Slaughter	Registered Exports	Unregistered Exports	Total Exports	Total Exports and Slaughter	Total Production	Extraction Rate - %	Production Rate — %
1950[3]	13,900	300	1,397	140	1,537	12	—	12	1,549	1,849	11.1	13.3
1951[3]	13,750	- 150	1,431	143	1,574	10	—	10	1,584	1,434	11.5	10.4
1952[3]	13,600	- 150	1,414	141	1,555	10	—	10	1,565	1,415	11.5	10.4
1053[3]	13,450	- 150	1,336	134	1,470	6	—	6	1,476	1,326	11.0	9.9
1954[3]	13,300	-150	1,313	131	1,444	—	15	15	1,459	1,309	11.0	9.8
1955[3]	13,600	300	1,354	135	1,489	—	15	15	1,504	1,804	11.1	13.3
1956[3]	13,900	300	1,550	155	1,705	—	49	49	1,754	2,054	12.6	14.8
1957[3]	14,200	300	1,677	168	1,845	—	60	60	1,905	2,205	13.4	15.5
1958[3]	14,500	300	1,651	165	1,816	—	120	120	1,936	2,236	13.4	15.4
1959[3]	14,800	300	1,523	152	1,675	—	200	200	1,875	2,175	12.7	14.7
1960[3]	15,329	529	1,530	153	1,683	—	200	200	1,883	2,412	12.3	15.7
1961[4]	15,679	350	1,703	170	1,874	0	100	100	1,974	2,324	12.6	14.8
1962[4]	15,979	300	1,876	188	2,063	0	120	120	2,183	2,483	13.7	15.5
1963[4]	16,279	300	1,948	195	2,143	—	100	100	2,243	2,543	13.8	15.6
1964[4]	16,584	305	2,025	202	2,228	3	114	117	2,345	2,650	14.1	16.0
1965[4]	16,882	298	2,038	204	2,242	56	101	157	2,339	2,697	14.2	16.0
1966[4]	17,372	490	1,884	188	2,072	46	81	127	2,199	2,689	12.7	15.5
1967[4]	18,082	710	1,866	186	2,052	8	96	104	2,156	2,886	11.9	15.9
1968[4]	18,830[5]	748	1,956	195	2,152	10	100	110	2,262	3,010	12.0	16.0
1969[5]	19,576	746	2,024	202	2,226	406	100	140	2,366	3,112	12.1	15.9

1 Extraction rate is defined as the total number of cattle slaughtered and exported live annually expressed as a percentage of total cattle population.

2 Production rate is defined as the total number of cattle slaughtered and exported live annually, plus the change in inventory, expressed as a percentage of total cattle population.

3 USDA, *Foreign Agricultural Economic Report No. 52,* "Changes in Agricultural Production and Technology in Colombia", June 1969.

4 DANE.

5 US Agricultural Attache.

6 IDEMA.

Note: Unregistered slaughter is estimated at 10% of registered slaughter.

Sources: U.S. Department of Agriculture, DANE and IDEMA.

16% per annum in recent years, indicating large build-ups in the national herd. Both these measures of productivity of the national herd have increased slowly over the past twenty years. The wide gap between extraction rate and production rate indicates that should ranches stop herd build-up, quite dramatic increases in slaughterings and live exports could occur. In a stable cattle population both these indices are, of course, equal.

Techniques.   The majority of beef cattle are maintained in tropical zones where they are bred and fattened on natural grassland or artificial pastures. Breeding is concentrated on poorer quality native pastures, on areas subject to seasonal drought, and on the rougher and more hilly country. The savanna of Los Llanos is devoted mostly to breeding with some good fattening land in the vicinity of Villavicencio, where many of these mature animals are taken for fattening. In Los Llanos, which has 20 million hectares and 3 million animals, a breeding cow and her calf are carried on from one to ten hectares according to region and species of grass grown. In La Costa and the Magdalena Valley from one to three animals per hectare are fattened annually. La Costa (breeding and fattening) and the Magdalena Valley (mostly fattening) have much more intensive livestock systems than Los Llanos.

The national beef herd has been derived from "Criollo" breeds which still account for approximately 20% of the total. The remainder have been upgraded from "Criollo" by Zebu (mostly U.S. type Brahman) especially in La Costa and the Magdalena Valley for up to three or four generations.

Accurate statistics on herd size distribution do not exist but estimates for La Costa indicate that the majority of cattle are in herds of about 400 head. Only a small percentage of herds exceed 1,500 head. Management is on an extensive pattern so that care and attention for the individual animal are minimal. This applies throughout the country but especially in Los Llanos.

In La Costa, extensive methods are reflected by calving percentages[4] of 60% to 70%, calf mortality of about 10%, and the consequent low effective calving percentage of under 60%. In Los Llanos, the comparable figures are 50% to 60%; 20% and 40% respectively. Poor feeding results in slow growth during the growing phase so that slaughter age is about 4 years. Steers from La Costa are slaughtered at about 450 kg liveweight while Los Llanos steers average 390 kg.

Mortality and performance at all stages of growth are affected materially by inadequate health control measures. Major diseases or parasites causing mortality or loss of thrift are endemic: foot-and-mouth (types A and O), rabies, anthrax, brucellosis, septicemia, ticks and tick-borne fevers, black leg, screw worm, and a great variety of internal parasites. It is important, however, to realize that effective control measures exist for most of these diseases and that they could be applied in Colombia.

Incentives for beef cattle production in Colombia are crucially affected by government policy. Raising cattle is attractive financially because of the favorable tax treatment accorded to income from the sale of cattle. The essential feature of this tax policy relates to the cost basis on which profits are calculated. For tax purposes, the cost of livestock sold is the purchase price only if acquired during the tax year, otherwise the approximate market value at the end of the previous year. The difference between the purchase price and the assessed end of the year market value is treated as an increase in capital and is not subject to income tax. Tax policy is also designed to encourage ranchers to hold females rather than males in inventory in order to build up the national cattle herd. There are two taxes which support this policy. The first is a slaughter tax which differentiates between the sexes: Col$50 per head for males and Col$100 per head for females. The second is a selective inventory tax which applies only to males over two years of age. The amount of this tax varies from year to year. In 1966 it was Col$18 per head. A final element in government taxation of the livestock industry is a general inventory tax. Any individual or corporation whose investment in livestock exceeds Col$15,000 at the close of any year from 1959 through 1970 is subject to a levy of one percent on the net investment. Taxpayers who elect to subscribe for shares of the Banco Ganadero and the Fondo Ganadero at par, in

---

4. Calving percentage is the number of calves born alive in any year expressed as a percentage of the number of females let to the bull in the previous year.

an amount equal to the total tax due, are exempt from payment of the tax in cash. This is in fact the customary form of payment, and it provides an important part of the capital of these credit institutions.

Beef Consumption.   Beef consumption per capita in South America ranges from 8 kg in Bolivia to 80 kg in Argentina. In Colombia it was about 21 kg in 1969, and price elasticity of demand has been estimated at -0.7 which is quite inelastic for this commodity. Prices of cattle at the ranch, on a liveweight basis, were approximately Col$5.17 per kg in early 1970, equivalent to US$0.28 per kg liveweight (Table 17-2). Deflated consumer beef prices have increased by 18% since 1964, while prices at the ranch increased only by 13%.

Beef Markets and Marketing.   In 1969 approximately 97.5% of beef production was consumed domestically and 2.5% exported (Table 17-1). Cattle are slaughtered under very unhygienic conditions by comparison with developed country standards, which are the relevant ones for an exporting country like Colombia. The value of live cattle exports in 1969 was US$7.4 million, with Peru the most important market. Other destinations were Dutch Antilles, French Guiana, Venezuela and Argentina (Table 17-3). Illegal exports of live animals, predominant to Venezuela, were estimated at 100,000 head in 1969. Spain imported 5,651 metric tons of frozen

TABLE 17-2: AVERAGE PRICES PER KG. OF LIVE CATTLE, 1964-1969

Year	Half of Year	Current Prices		Deflated Prices		Index of Deflated Price of Beef to Consumer	National Index of Consumer Prices [1]
		Col$ Per Kg.	Index	Col$ Per Kg.	Index		
1964	1	2.94	100	2.94	100	100	100.0
,,	2	3.32	113	3.23	110	104	102.8
1965	1	3.63	123	3.42	116	112	106.0
,,	2	3.95	134	3.50	119	113	112.8
1966	1	4.61	157	4.00	136	130	124.7
,,	2	5.20	177	3.98	135	129	130.7
1967	1	5.37	183	3.95	134	129	136.1
,,	2	5.22	178	3.70	126	125	140.9
1968	1	5.29	180	3.61	123	122	146.6
,,	2	5.18	176	3.43	117	118	151.1
1969	1	5.16	176	3.31	113		156.1
	2	5.17	176				

[1] This was the deflator used in all cases.
Source: Banco Ganadero; DANE.

TABLE 17-3: EXPORTS OF ANIMALS, MEAT AND MEAT PRODUCTS BY DESTINATION, 1969[1]

Type of Product	UNIT Number	UNIT Metric Tons	Total Value ('000 US$)	Country of Destination
Steers	9,281		1,632	Dutch Antilles
Steers	1,690		274	French Guiana
Steers	20,794		4,117	Peru
Steers	2,050		142	Venezuela
Steers of "bullfighting" breed	30		14	Venezuela
Pure-bred bulls	85		45	Venezuela
Bulls	9		13	Argentina
Bulls for bullfighting	34		41	Venezuela
Breeding bulls of "bullfight-ing" breed	9		36	Venezuela
Cows of "bullfighting" breed	120		82	Venezuela
Cows	300		65	Venezuela
Heifers	5,144		825	Venezuela
Heifers	218		77	Argentina
Total	39,764		7,363	
Pigs	100		3	French Guiana
Sheep	100		1	French Guiana
Horses	711		5	Dutch Antilles
Horses	25		1	French Guiana
Total			10	
Special Cuts		20	12	Dutch Antilles
Frozen Beef		5,651	3,102	Spain
Refrigerated beef		881	540	French Antilles
Refrigerated beef		102	66	French Guiana
Chilled beef		988	649	French Antilles
Chilled beef		359	224	Peru
Chilled beef		257	166	French Guiana
Total of Beef		8,258	4,759	
Frozen lamb		1	1	Venezuela
By-products		24	10	French Antilles
Viscera		96	39	French Antilles
Viscera		6	2	France
Viscera		50	15	Spain
Viscera		16	12	French Guiana
Total of Viscera		168	68	
Grand Total			12,211	

[1] Official exports only.

Source: Instituto de Mercadeo Agropecuario, Comision de Mercadeo Exterior de Ganado Y Carne.

beef in 1969, valued at US$3.1 million. Lesser markets were French Antilles and French Guiana, each importing both refrigerated and chilled beef. Offals valued at US$68,000 were exported to French Antilles, France, Spain and French Guiana.

Dairying

Milk production increased at a rate fractionally above that of population during the period 1950 to 1967. Production increased more rapidly for a few years between 1955 and 1959 and then was nearly stationary through 1962. Since then production has kept pace with population growth (Table 17-4). Since 1964 fluid milk production has expanded more rapidly than total milk production. In recent years a little more than half of the estimated milk production has been used for fluid purposes, about one-third of which is pasteurized. About 5% of total milk production is used in commercial production of butter and cheese, and approximately 40% is used on farms, some to make homemade butter and cheese, a part of which is marketed.

Near the large cities there are some large modern dairy farms. Only a few use modern production methods either in handling the animals or in feeding them. European dairy breeds, mainly Holstein, are the rule in the Sabana de Bogota and Narino. Most of the milk in Colombia, however, comes from milking the beef cows once a day in La Costa in the early months after calving. At the present time milk is transported daily from Monteria to Medellin. Beef cows are also milked in Los Llanos, though mostly for local consumption.

The most common channel of milk marketing in Colombia involves a number of intermediaries: collectors, processors, wholesalers and retailers. Handling margins are controlled by government regulations in cities larger than 70,000 inhabitants. With the increasing demand for milk in the larger urban centers the extension of production areas introduces transport problems in some regions. Colombia faces a basic policy decision on milk production. No country in the world has an efficient tropical dairy industry. Temperate regions have highly efficient systems such as are found in New Zealand, Holland, United Kingdom, Ireland, and Wisconsin, U.S.A. Colombia has plenty of temperate areas to produce milk using already known methods; or Colombia can pioneer in tropical dairy production. One is a sure and proven method, the other highly risky. This decision, however, has not been made, yet Colombia must make it because demand for milk is outstripping supply at the present controlled price levels and there is no agreed national policy to increase production.

The price of milk to the farmer is Col$1.40 to Col$1.80 per liter, depending on distance to market. This is equivalent to US$7.6 per hectoliter, which is low by international standards. No allowance is made in the government price control program for higher costs of production in the dry period. Consequently, production fluctuates widely throughout the year. Annual per capita consumption in Bogota, Medellin, Cali and Barranquilla is of the order of 100 liters whereas in rural areas it is as low as possibly 50 liters. On a countrywide per capita basis, consumption has increased by approximately 35% since 1954. National average per capita consumption figures remain low because the majority of the population cannot afford to buy milk.

Sheep, Hogs and Poultry

Lamb and mutton account for no more than 1% of the total meat consumption in Colombia. Most sheep in Colombia are of the native or "Criollo" breeds. Wool produced is coarse and generally unsuitable for use by the textile industry which relies on imports. About 85% of Colombian wool production is consumed by the spinning and weaving cottage industry. The major wool producing areas are Boyaca, Cundinamarca, Narino, Santander, and Caldas. Mutton and lamb production are not increasing.

Production of pork and bacon is rather small in Colombia and shows little or no expansion. Hog slaughter increased moderately during the fifties, reaching a peak in 1961. After that, slaughter declined through 1965, but was higher in 1966 and 1967, although still below that attained in 1961 (Table 17-4). Output of poultry and eggs was stationary in the fifties. Since 1958 production has expanded each year, not quite doubling in the nine years up to 1967. As

TABLE 17-4: OUTPUT OF SELECTED LIVESTOCK PRODUCTS, 1950-1967

	Milk ('000 Tons)	Wool Tons	Poultry (million)	Eggs (million)	Hog Slaughter ('000Head)	Sheep Slaughter ('000Head)
1950	1,160	900	22.5	900	863	150
1951	1,194	938	20.6	825	749	156
1952	1,228	900	20.8	833	797	165
1953	1.263	863	21.3	853	910	188
1954	1,300	836	21.3	853	1,018	184
1955	1,333	777	21.5	860	1,084	177
1956	1,489	718	20.0	799	1,026	189
1957	1,587	659	22.0	879	945	197
1958	1,681	600	22.5	900	1,036	190
1959	1,753	600	25.0	1,000	1,118	178
1960	1,753	600	26.2	1,048	1,154	170
1961	1,762	645	27.4	1,096	1,284	184
1962	1,785	686	30.0	1,178	1,235	198
1963	1,833	761	35.0	1,400	1,226	180
1964	1,860	855	36.5	1,460	1,124	180
1965	1,973	906	38.0	1,521	1,100	183
1966	2,020	951	39.5	1,580	1,112	173
1967	2,080	996	41.0	1,643	1,245	150

[1] Source: USDA, Foreign Agricultural Economic Report 52, *Changes in Agricultural Production and Technology in Colombia,* June 1969.

TABLE 17-5: BEEF: SELECTED INDICATORS OF MARKET PRICES, 1955-1969

	(US$ per metric ton)		
	United Kingdom	Australia	Argentina
1955	441.9	365.2	–
1956	367.2	330.0	–
1957	378.7	299.0	–
1958	451.8	315.8	–
1959	512.7	421.8	321.1
1960	525.3	475.3	340.1
1961	486.2	475.5	328.7
1962	491.4	439.5	292.6
1963	457.0	459.3	338.2
1964	620.7	467.4	562.4
1965	661.6	486.4	575.7
1966	660.1	535.3	499.7
1967	633.4	570.4	397.1
1968	637.8	591.5	n.a.
1969	638.0	628.0	n.a.

[1] U.K. weighted average of import unit values for boneless beef and chilled and frozen quarter beef.

[2] Average Australian export unit value (carcass weight basis).

[3] Fat steers, special, for export; assuming killing out percentage of approximately 52.

n.a. = not available

Source: 1955-1967 — FAO, *Review of Characteristics, Trends and Major Problems of the World Meat Economy;* and *Production Yearbook.*
1968-1969 — Official national trade statistics.

might be expected, there is a strong dualism between the traditional small flocks of poultry, often of 15 to 20 hens, and the modern broiler and egg installations of several thousand birds.

Consumption of poultry meat was 1.062 kg per capita in 1969, which indicates a one percent per annum growth in per capita consumption in recent years. The per capita consumption of eggs reached 57.4 in 1969, up from 55.6 in 1966.

Future of the Livestock Industry

The expansion in poultry and eggs is very gratifying, but if the present price structure is maintained, the expansion possibilities are limited relative to the potential. The same holds for hog production. The cause of this is the present high price of feed grains, which is running at least 50% above the world market price. Since feed costs account for at least 60% of the costs of poultry and hog production, the problem is clear. At the present time poultry meat in Colombia is priced higher than beef, whereas in Western Europe and the United States the reverse is true. If the price of feed grains in Colombia can be reduced to reasonable levels, then the expansion in poultry production could be quite dramatic because production units capable of rapid expansion already exist. In Colombia poultry meat is a luxury food, with an income elasticity of over one. As incomes grow, poultry has the potential to satisfy much of the growth in demand for meat. Due to lack of refrigeration, broilers there have not yet reached the mass market. The conversion rate of feed to broiler meat in Colombia is estimated at 3:1 which is one-third higher than that achieved in the United States. This is a management problem, because the rations and breeds are as good as in the United States. Losses, either through mortality or "disappearance" of birds and feed, are mainly responsible for this high conversion rate. Expansion in hogs is also limited by high feed costs, but a nucleus of commercial producers already exists which will be capable of expansion if given the proper incentives. Essentially, poultry and hogs have few problems that a cheap feed supply would not solve—high feed cost is the problem.

Colombia has good potential for sheep production, but the managerial and technical skills required to realize this potential are lacking. In the area around Medellin the ability to run a modern sheep farm has been demonstrated. Dissemination of this information to laborers, technicians, and managers is the priority task. Colombia can acquire this knowledge while concentrating on expanding mutton and lamb supply from "Criollo", and "Criollo" crossed with imported rams in commercial size flocks. This would entail purchasing the "Criollo" breeding females locally, and establishing the commercial units which are almost non-existent at present. This is a much cheaper method of modernizing the industry than attempting high grade wool production in the early years. Increased mutton production would help satisfy domestic demand for meat, thus releasing beef for export. Consequently, it could be just as beneficial to the balance of payments as substituting for wool imports, which is a more expensive and hazardous task since it involves importing large numbers of female parent stock.

In cattle, considerable expansion of exports is now under way. Frigorifico Guadalupe has a contract to deliver 400 tons of chilled beef per month from February 1970 through February 1971. The beef is flown from Bogota to Lima, and the price is US$740 c.i.f. per metric ton, Lima. Some frozen beef is being sold to Spain for US$545 per metric ton, f.o.b. Barranquilla. Chilled beef for the Caribbean Islands at present is selling for US$650 per metric ton f.o.b. Barranquilla and Santa Marta. Under the recent French agreement, the Colombians will import Charollais semen and cross with Zebu. France will give technical assistance without cost. Concentration on the Atlantic coast is planned. It is planned to export the resulting feeder cattle to France at one year. Present thinking is in terms of a target of 100,000 head per year after three or four years. This is probably over-optimistic. IDEMA and the Government of Peru have a contract for Colombia to deliver 72,000 head of cattle to Peru in one year. The price is US$690 per metric ton carcass weight at Lima. It costs US$15.45 per head to transport the animals from Buenaventura to Lima. Only steers are exported. They weigh 480-510 kg liveweight at the farm. They lose about 80 kg per head in transit to Peru. They are killed in Lima and it is only then that ownership changes hands.

The above implies an export level of US$30 million per annum. This is more than double the actual exports in 1969 (US$12 million) and a five-fold increase over the exports in 1965-68

(US$5.5 million per annum). Is the contemplated expansion within the capacity of the country, or will prices increase drastically? Is Colombia sufficiently competitive in the world market to sustain this expansion?

Colombian f.o.b. prices are just low enough to enable exports to take place (Table 17-5). The 15% tax rebate is crucial and is just sufficient to move beef into export markets. Export of frozen beef to Europe is not very attractive to Colombia and she is probably not able to compete with Argentina for this market except in marginal cases (Table 17-6). The Caribbean market for chilled beef and the Peruvian market, however, are profitable for Colombia at present. Slaughter of females in 1969 declined to 35% of the total from a high of 41% in 1965.[5] This would indicate that herd building is still in progress, and augurs well for Colombia's ability to maintain cattle exports at around US$20 million over the next few years. La Costa and the lower Magdalena Valley, which at present are the most developed beef cattle areas of the country, are the areas of greatest potential for beef cattle production and should be given priority in any program to expand Colombia's beef output.

The problems of Colombia's cattle industry are production problems. The marketing system is relatively efficient and exporters have shown their ability to market the product when it is available at competitive prices. Ranching methods leave tremendous room for improvement. The introduction of better grasses and tropical legumes, better utilization of pasture by grazing animals, combined with improved livestock management are still the areas of greatest potential improvement. ICA needs to carry out some adaptive research in these areas, which calls for new initiatives. Tropical legume research is just getting started at Turipana in the heart of La Costa, while research on animals that would aid the rancher is almost non-existent. ICA, however, appears to be realizing this great gap in their basic supportive role to Colombia's livestock industry.

Fisheries

Fisheries have in the past contributed less than 1% to the national economy. This is despite 1,170 miles of ocean front—510 on the Pacific and 660 on the Atlantic—and considerable freshwater fishery potential. The situation is changing rapidly and special attention has been given by INDERENA and the Instituto de Fomento Industrial (IFI) to developing the relatively untapped ocean fishing resources.

Particular attention has been focused on the lucrative shrimp export market. Until the last few years almost all the Colombian shrimp catch has been from the Pacific grounds. Investigation into the shrimp potential, however, has shown that while the Pacific offers the most promising prospects for future expansion of Colombian shrimping, there are also plentiful supplies of high quality, good-sized shrimp along the country's Atlantic coast. These banks are deeper than those off the Pacific coast but the higher costs of catching shrimp are more than offset by the quality and size of the shrimp. Given these favorable resources, shrimp exports can be expected to continue their rapid growth. With the development of the ocean fisheries more and more edible fish caught in the shrimping operations are sold on the local market.

In late 1968 and in 1969 extensive test fishing off the Atlantic coast by the U.S. fishing vessel Oregon II under the supervision of Colombian marine biologists, FAO personnel and U.S. Bureau of Commercial Fisheries representatives proved the value of resource research and has been responsible for much of the increased development interest along the Atlantic coast. A

5. Registered cattle extractions by sex in 1961-69, were as follows:

'000 Head	1961	1962	1963	1964	1965	1966	1967	1968	1969
Steers	1,079	1,161	1,185	1,211	1,230	1,213	1,221	1,281	1,342
Heifers	624	715	763	818	865	719	652	686	722
Total	1,703	1,876	1,948	2,028	2,095	1,932	1,873	1,966	2,064
Heifers as % of Total	36.6	38.1	39.2	40.3	41.3	37.3	34.8	34.9	35.0

Source: DANE.

TABLE 17-6: DISTRIBUTION OF THE FOB VALUE PER METRIC TON OF BEEF

	%	Refrigerated Quarters Col$ Per MT	US$ Per MT	Col$ Per kg. l.w.	Port	%	Frozen Quarters Col$ Per MT	US$ Per MT	Col$ Per kg l.w.	Port
FOB Price	100.0	12,352	597		Bogota	100.0	10,036	485		Barranquilla
Price at the Slaughterhouse		10,655		5.90			9,391		5.20	
Slaughterhouse Margin	13.7	1,697				6.4	645			
Transportation & Marketing	5.0	619				6.2	619			
Taxes	1.7	215				2.1	215			
Price at the Ranch	79.6	9,821		5.08		85.3	8,557		4.42	

[1] Calculations based on the following assumptions:
  (a) Col $18 = US$1.00 (March 1970) + 15% export subsidy, gives Col$20.70 = US$1.00
  (b) 4.3 steers make 1 M.T., i.e. they weigh 425 Kg at slaughter, and kill out at 55%;
  (c) Costs of slaughter, chilling, freezing and transport to port covered by viscera and other by-products;
  (d) Steers leave the ranch weighing 450 Kg and arrive at slaughterhouse weighing 425 Kg;
  (e) Transport and marketing include transport cost of Col$0.15 per Kg and middleman's profit and
    losses of Col$0.17 per Kg.

Source: USAID Bogota.

TABLE 17-7: SHRIMP EXPORTS: VOLUME AND VALUE

Year	'000 lb	US$ '000
1965	1,997.6	1,558.1
1966	2,164.9	1,796.8
1967	2,296.5	2,089.7
1968	2,289.0	2,295.3
1969[1]	n.a.	4,560.0

[1] For 1969, exchange surrender, all other years export registrations.
Source: INDERENA.

UNDP project—development of marine fisheries—with the FAO as the executing agency is also under way. In addition to resource evaluation the project provides technical assistance to INDERENA to evaluate fishery regulation, to decide appropriate means of commercial exploitation of the resources and assistance in the necessary investigations. The National Apprentice Service (SENA) is constructing a National Fishing Center in Buenaventura where up to 150 persons per course will be trained in modern fishing techniques and vessel operation and maintenance.

Oysters are becoming a significant export item and in 1969 over US$2 million worth were processed and exported, principally to the United States. Oysters are harvested primarily in the Cienega de Santa Marta but can also be found in many other estuarine areas which are not yet commercially developed. Provided the oyster bed areas can pass the U.S. health regulations, considerably greater export earnings could be achieved from the same volume of exports by marketing fresh, rather than processed, oysters. INDERENA should examine the possibilities of meeting U.S. import requirements for fresh oysters.

Other minor exports include lobster, which are plentiful at the eastern extremity of the Atlantic coast and exported as frozen tails. Prospects for continued expansion of these exports appear to be good. Possibilities also exist for a tuna as well as a local crab industry, and investigations are under way to prove their feasibility. A fishmeal processing plant is under construction in the Pacific port of Tumaco, near the Ecuadorian border, which is expected to eliminate the need for importing all fishmeal products.

A substantial percentage of domestic fish consumption comes from catches made in the fresh water lakes and streams, particularly near the population centers in the Andean highlands. The principal fresh water fish consumed is the *bocachico*. INDERENA is actively carrying out research to select and propagate *bocachico* so that their fry can be released in suitable areas. Trout have also been successfully bred and released, mainly in the lakes where, as tourism increases, sport fishing is becoming more popular. Commercial trout fishing is expanding also as there is a good local demand.

Recently, IFI and private interests have formed the Colombian Fishing Consortium to accelerate the expansion of the Colombian fishing industry. The Consortium is introducing modern technology in fishing vessel construction with the help of Spanish engineers and technicians. It has already fifteen modern fishing boats and another ten are under construction. Thus, the potential for a rapid expansion in production and exports of fisheries' products is excellent.

Forestry

Colombia's indigenous forests are widely dispersed. Exploitation has normally been undertaken by small operators who dispose of timber to sawmills and other forest industries. These industries, including 10 sawmills producing annually more than 10,000 m^3, five plywood mills, two board plants and one pulp mill, have developed independently and there is little integration of harvesting, manufacturing or marketing. Timber exports have increased rapidly in recent years, from US$3.7 million in 1965 to US$7.2 million in 1969.[6]

The systems of harvesting used are primitive; 50% of the lumber cut for conversion by sawmills is still hand-sawn into squared balks and shipped to the sawmills or exported. Power saws and tractors have only recently been introduced. The mixed tropical hardwood forests are rich in species (some 258 tropical hardwood species have been identified), but exploitation has concentrated on a few of the more valuable. Waste, both in the forest and at the mill sites, has been excessive and there is considerable scope for technical development and the control of exploitation.

INDERENA is responsible for the administration of the country's forest resources. Timber harvesting is controlled by permit (Permiso de Aprovechamiento) which requires the concessionaire to prepare a plan of forest management which will establish the volume of timber to be harvested. The permit also requires that information on the location of operations, cutting

6. Exchange surrender. Source: Banco de la Republica.

systems used, silvicultural treatment adopted, technical supervision of operations, log volumes and the destination of logs be provided.

On receipt of the "harvesting permit" the concessionaire is charged Col$2 per hectare, and during exploitation a stumpage fee of 5% of log value in the forest is levied, plus a further Col$5 per cubic meter. These charges are very low. Unfortunately, the INDERENA field staff is not adequate in numbers to insure the collection of charges and to control the export of logs, a high proportion of which are exported to the veneer trade.

It is essential that a number of investigations and studies be undertaken. These should include the compilation of inventories for the major forest areas, the calculation of growth rates, timber quality studies of secondary species, an examination of silvicultural systems of forest regeneration and investigations of modern logging methods suitable for local conditions. It is the government's intention to invite overseas contractors to participate in the development of the forest industry and it is essential that effective contracting procedures are produced as soon as possible.

Recently, INDERENA, with the aid of UNDP, commenced a forest inventory in the Magdalena and Sinu River valleys and an investment proposal has been prepared for an industrial forest complex to exploit the timber in the two valleys. The development would include a sawmill producing 55,000 m³ per annum, a veneer plywood mill of 35,200 m³ capacity, a short fiber pulp mill producing 50,000 tons annually and a board mill manufacturing annually 30,000 tons of kraft liner board and 42,000 tons of fluting. To manufacture the kraft paper 25,000 tons of long fiber pulp will be imported. The government is anxious to attract the necessary investment for the establishment of the manufacturing complex, based on the resources of the area.

Colombia is a heavy importer of long fiber pulp and products in the value of US$16 million per annum, expected to reach US$24 million in five years unless import substitution takes place. **It is estimated that 120,000 hectares of softwood plantations are needed to replace long fiber pulp imports by 1975.**

In the Medellin area some 20 private concerns are planting cypress and pine at an annual rate of between 3,000 and 4,000 hectares. There is said to be adequate land within 100 km of the city—estimates as high as 367,000 hectares have been mentioned. With current costs, the estimated internal rate of return on this investment on a 15-year cycle is 20%, due largely to the high prices paid for pulpwood per cubic meter (between Col$200 and Col$250). This is four times as much as is paid in Brazil and more than twice the price paid in Chile and Canada. To achieve self-sufficiency (120,000 hectares of softwood plantations by 1975) the annual cost at current prices would be in excess of US$10 million.

The potential for development of Colombia's indigenous forest resources is considerable, but much requires to be done if progress is to be in accordance with good forest management. Prospects for investment in fast growing conifer plantations for the production of timber and pulpwood are excellent and should receive encouragement, and possibilities of increasing exports of tropical hardwood should be explored further.

CHAPTER 18
UNEMPLOYMENT, LABOR ABSORPTION AND FUTURE POSSIBILITIES IN AGRICULTURE

The Problem

Colombia's population is currently growing at a rate of 3.2% annually. In spite of heavy migration to urban areas, rural population continues to grow, and it is estimated that agriculture will need to provide employment for an additional 1.8% annually[1] for the next fifteen years. The total size of the labor force for the next fifteen years is, of course, determined by children already born.

Present employment in agriculture is estimated at roughly 2.5 million. The 1.8% growth rate means that employment will be needed for 760,000 additional persons by 1985, an average of about 50,000 persons per year. At the present ratio of approximately two economically active rural people per farm family, this indicates a need for new farms or wage employment in agriculture for about 25,000 additional rural families per year. This will be a strain on projected settlement and colonization projects, because of the large number of underemployed in the present rural population. On the other hand, employment expansion in urban areas cannot be relied upon to absorb these persons so that agriculture must continue to play an important role in labor absorption.[2]

Closing the gap in relative incomes between the sectors by raising agricultural incomes is basic for reducing employment problems in both sectors. However, Table 18-1 shows that this gap has been widening over the past decade. Compared to 1960, industrial workers were earning

TABLE 18-1: INDICES OF REAL WAGES AND SALARIES IN INDUSTRY AND AGRICULTURE, 1960 TO 1968

(1960 = 100)

	Industry				Agriculture Workers only	
	Employees		Workers			
	Salaries[1]	Cost to the Employer[2]	Wage[3]	Cost to the Employer[2]	Wage[4]	Cost to the Employer[5]
1960	100.0	100.0	100.0	100.0	100.0	100.0
1961	123.0	126.7	120.9	125.2	103.3	106.5
1962	129.2	134.2	133.2	137.4	113.1	118.5
1963	127.7	132.3	145.4	153.0	112.3	117.3
1964	125.7	138.1	140.6	159.8	115.0	114.1
1965	129.8	140.0	145.7	160.0	115.8	114.0
1966	127.2	135.0	142.0	153.4	114.3	114.3
1967	130.8	138.7	145.0	155.3	111.3	116.1
1968	134.9	145.7	148.9	162.0	n.a.	n.a.

[1] Deflator: National living cost index for employees.

[2] Deflator: Wholesale price index, excluding food.

[3] Deflator: National living cost index for workers.

[4] These wages have been calculated as the average of hot and cold climate wages, for a man over 18 years of age, who does not receive part of his salary in the form of food. As a deflator, the living cost index for workers in the city of Pasto has been chosen, Pasto being the city most representative of rural conditions, for which such an index is available.

[5] Deflator: Wholesale price index for food.

Source: Banco de la Republica and DANE.

1. Figure based on CEDE projection.
2. See International Labor Organization *Towards Full Employment,* Bogota, 1970

45% more in 1967, rural workers only 11%. Probably this trend is one of the major factors accelerating rural-urban migration. Only rapid improvement of rural conditions could relieve the pressure on the cities.

Proposed Measures for Increasing Employment in Agriculture

Colombia's excellent land and climate resources suggest the following possibilities for raising productivity, incomes and labor absorption in agriculture:

(a)   Search systematically for new external and internal markets for agricultural products. Production should be expanded in the particular export crops that Colombia appears to have now, or can develop, at a comparative advantage. Colombia's geographical location and its natural endowment of climate and soil place it in a favorable competitive position as a low-cost producer of tropical crops such as oil seeds, cocoa and sugar. On the internal market there will be a sharply growing demand for milk, eggs and pork as well as for the feed grains and oilcake to produce them.

(b)   Carry out wherever possible the initial processing of agricultural products instead of exporting the primary product.

(c)   Invest in producing modern technology which will give higher yields per unit area on small and intermediate sized holdings and does not depend on large-scale mechanization. This means developing and adequately testing new seeds as well as determining optimum application rates for herbicides, fertilizer, fungicides and insecticides. Although certain of the chemicals, especially the herbicides, substitute to some extent for labor, this is usually balanced out by increased labor requirements at harvest.

(d)   Increase farm incomes by improving cost-return relationships. This can be effected in large part through: price reductions on the most expensive inputs especially fertilizer, reduction of farm production costs through research on how to obtain optimum yields for the main crops, soils and climates of the country, and more adequate attention to the distribution of information and inputs to raise yields nearer to the optimum.

(e)   Expand the farming area through family-sized holdings wherever possible and if feasible with labor-intensive rather than labor-substitution techniques. For cotton, Colombian authorities have taken successful measures by prohibiting the importation of mechanical pickers. This measure has reduced the need for foreign exchange, absorbed considerable labor on a seasonal basis and, as an additional benefit, made it possible to obtain a higher price on the world market for the better quality hand-picked cotton. Sugar cane, too, is cut by hand and tractors are used only for hauling. It should be added, that among large holders there is strong pressure for mechanization. In some cases workers have formed unions and have succeeded in raising salary levels for their members, which may have stimulated mechanization by plantation operators. This would appear to be an additional reason for directing expansion into new agricultural areas on the basis of family-sized farms rather than plantation holdings. This will require some degree of mechanization—either in the form of draft animals or tractor services to enable the farmer to bring sufficient land into production to effectively utilize his family labor.

(f)   Continue with reallocation of land resources to assure the maximum productive use of good land. For historical reasons which have been discussed, much of the best agricultural land is concentrated in large holdings and used for extensive grazing. In contrast, the small holdings are found for the most part in extremely rough terrain and more than half are too small to provide an opportunity for a family to use all its labor effectively in crop production. Land redistribution must be accompanied by sufficient technical advice and credit to enable smallholders to develop viable productive units.

(g)   Invest more public funds in rural social services to approach on a per capita basis those for urban areas.

In Chapter 16 which covered individual crops, estimates were made of the increased area, yields and production which might be reached by 1985. Special attention was given to export and import substitution. The additional areas were estimated on the basis of various assumptions about yields and output and suggest an increased area of 744,150 hectares by 1985 allocated as shown in Table 18-2. This table does not include yuca and plantains as expansion of these crops is expected to be largely for home consumption on the farm.

To deduce information from this table on the amount of employment opportunity that will be created, certain assumptions need to be specified: first, that in general at least half (and for cacao, tobacco and potatoes nearly all), the new area coming into production will be on family size farms; next, that on these family-size crop holdings, the family will produce yuca, plantains and other subsistence food, and in addition an average of three hectares of some combination of the above crops; finally, that on the remaining farms, with more mechanization, among farm owners, managers and employed labor, each family unit will on the average operate 7 hectares of the crops shown in the table. On these assumptions, the increased area of 744,150 hectares will provide employment for 148,830 families (744,150/5). As these new farms will be more intensively worked than the average existing farm, the number of economically active persons per farm might be put at 3 to 4. Thus, these farms might provide employment for 450,000 to 600,000 persons, or 60% of the employment absorption which agriculture should provide.

What other possibilities exist? While livestock production is not a labor-intensive enterprise, it is sure to feature prominently in the development of the grasslands in the Orinoco region and in the forest areas of the Amazon and southern Pacific Coast, where INCORA colonization projects will be based largely on cattle production. In colonizing new areas of the tropics, family size cattle farms offer possibilities for productive employment for an undefined number of families. The possibilities for expanding beef exports appear to be excellent and this enterprise could provide cash income for a large number of farm families interested in colonizing new lands.

Finally, increasing the number of farms should create some additional non-farm employment opportunities in rural areas. Whether expansion of livestock farming and this non-farm employment will be large enough to absorb the remaining 20% to 40% of persons to be employed in rural areas by 1985 is difficult to say, but the remaining gap in employment opportunities implies an unemployment rate of 5% to 10%, probably a vast improvement on the present situation.

TABLE 18-2: ESTIMATED LAND REQUIRED FOR PRODUCTION[1]

	1969 (actual) Hectares	1985 (projected) Hectares	Required Increase by 1985 Hectares
Cotton	236,000	358,000	122,000
Sugar cane	96,000	151,000	55,000
Cacao	39,500	60,000	20,500
Tobacco	23,850	30,000	6,150
Soybeans	45,500	225,000	129,500
Sesame	35,500	110,000	74,500
Bananas	23,600	28,000	4,400
Rice	262,000	305,100	43,100
Corn	825,000	900,000	75,000
Sorghum	39,000	178,000	139,000
Potatoes	95,000	120,000	25,000
Total			744,150

[1] Based on tables in Chapter 16.

Future Possibilities and Priorities

In spite of impressive advances in recent years, the development of Colombia's agricultural sector can still be considered in its initial stage. In judging the chances of agriculture to contribute to the export drive, it is therefore not so much a comparison of present Colombian prices for individual agricultural products with world market prices that would indicate the range of products in which Colombia might have a comparative advantage, but rather a comparison of world market prices with the potential price in Colombia if the development effort were to concentrate on that particular product.

The latter is difficult to quantify, but basically Colombia's chance to become competitive in the production of any agricultural product depends on two factors:

(1) The quality of the purely technical factor endowment—quality and availability of required soil type, climate and weather, and the chance to develop the required seed or type of plant (disease resistant, high yielding, etc.)

(2) The cost of bringing technical standards of production up to world market levels and the time required to do this.

As has been pointed out elsewhere in the report, Colombia has an unusual variety of soils and climates and therefore would appear to be suited—technically—to produce almost any crop or type of livestock. To a certain degree this can be substantiated by comparing yields obtained by the most efficient farm size groups in Colombia with yields in other developing countries which have specialized in particular crops. The following list gives such yields of selected crops in developing countries with low, medium and high average yields; for Colombia, average yields for the two farm-size-groups obtaining the lowest yields, and average yields for the two farm-size-groups obtaining the highest yields.[3]

(Yields in hundreds of kilograms per hectare)

Corn		Potatoes	
Botswana	5.4	Malta	84.0
Congo (B)	8.6	Chile	91.0
Guinea	12.2	Cyprus	157.7
Argentina	18.8	Ireland	229.0
Colombia	7.8-16.0	Colombia	42.7-134.0

Wheat		Barley	
Algeria	4.9	Algeria	4.8
Turkey	11.1	Spain	14.3
Yugoslavia	21.1	Korea	18.3
Mexico	24.4	Colombia	7.9-19.0
Colombia	6.3-17.3		

Grain Sorghum		Rice (Paddy)	
Botswana	7.3	Panama	10.9
Sudan	7.7	Thailand	16.3
Ethiopia	6.4	Burma	16.3
Colombia	8.8-25.3	Taiwan	37.3
		Colombia	15.6-26.1

Sugarcane		Cotton (Lint only)	
India	432.0	Uganda	0.9
Panama	433.0	Sudan	3.1
Venezuela	709.0	U. A. R.	6.6
Uganda	916.3	Guatemala	11.9
Colombia	275.5-706.0	Colombia	4.4-7.3

3. Sources: Table 14-10 and "Agricultural and Nutritional Indicators," Comparative Data Unit, IBRD, Economics Department, April 1969.

For all crops listed, yields in the more efficient farm size groups in Colombia indicate that the country certainly does not have a natural disadvantage in producing any of these crops, i.e. sufficiently high yields can be attained to compare favorably with high yields obtained in some other developing countries. Thus, the fact that Colombia's agriculture today is not competitive for many crops does not in itself preclude the possibility that these crops could be grown competitively if techniques and management were sufficiently improved.[4]

The decisive question then is in which crops Colombia could achieve competitiveness with the lowest cost and in the shortest time possible. Obviously, this is a very difficult question to answer in a precise fashion since the cost and time spans involved cannot be estimated across the board, and also, since many non-economic factors enter the analysis, for instance the adaptability of farmers to new techniques, the probability of developing a new, suitable seed in a reasonable time, the political possibilities of changing land distribution in certain areas suitable for certain crops, etc. In addition, prospects for successful promotion differ greatly as between the great mass of farmers using traditional production methods as against the limited number of farmers using modern methods. Prospects also differ substantially between applying modern methods to traditional or subsistence crops or to commercial and/or entirely new crops.

Some rough generalizations of the complex situation can nevertheless be made. Clearly, improving average yields in Colombian agriculture is a crucial problem, and the expansion of area under crop is equally important. The majority of Colombian farmers today are still growing subsistence crops on small farms using traditional methods. They are very poor and lack education—often even functional literacy—which is an important requirement for any attempt to introduce modern methods. Only limited research has been done to develop new seeds for traditional crops like yuca, panela sugar cane, plantain and beans and little is known about how these crops would react to various fertilizers, pesticides, and other modern inputs. More is known about the semi-traditional crops like corn, potatoes, wheat, tobacco, as well as cattle, hog and poultry raising, which are also found on smaller, traditional farms. But the application of modern methods to these requires substantial amounts of capital, sometimes a larger scale of operations than is possible for the traditional farmer, as well as a certain level of technical knowledge.

On the other hand, the as yet small but dynamic "new" sector of Colombian agriculture has concentrated on commercial crops, like cotton, rice, sugarcane for centrifugal sugar, sesame, grain sorghum and barley. Farms growing these crops are usually much larger, and the area planted to the crops is usually much larger too. Modern inputs are more widely used. It is from this group that the majority of non-coffee agricultural exports come.

As the capacity for agricultural research and development in Colombia is limited, as is the capacity to provide extension services, the dilemma arises in what proportion these scarce resources should be allocated to the two sectors. Colombia's economic future undoubtedly rests largely on the country's ability to break out of the foreign exchange constraint through rapid growth of non-coffee exports. Much of this growth will have to come from agriculture. On the other hand, the poverty of the majority of traditional farmers represents one of the major economic and social problems in the country and only if their lot can be improved substantially can one hope to keep the tide of migration to urban centers in manageable proportions.

In view of this dilemma it is clear that the answer cannot be a decision to concentrate the effort in agriculture entirely on the new or the traditional sector. Both are too important to permit neglect of their problems. It is also clear that prime priority—at least in the short and medium term—should be given to the most rapid expansion possible of both agricultural research and extension services. Principally this means an expansion of ICA's activities and to some extent of INCORA's technical assistance work.

---

4. The implicit assumption being that the improvement can be obtained at reasonable cost. As hundreds or thousands of farms are involved in the higher of the two Colombian figures, this assumption seems warranted.

It is important to devote enough of the available research and extension service capacity to maintaining a high rate of expansion in new agricultural exports. Services to agricultural non-coffee exports well established by now (cotton, sugar and bananas) should be continued, and new exports should be stimulated, paying particular attention to those produced by small farmers.

Possibilities to develop new agricultural exports are difficult to predict without further detailed study. However, on the basis of the analysis in Chapter 16 and from the comparison of yields given above, a few products can be identified where an intensive development effort is likely to lead to future exports. Among these are soya beans, produced mostly on large farms, with an IDEMA support price in 1970 of US$109 compared to a Rotterdam Grain Market quotation for US No. 2 Yellow of US$128 c.i.f. Another promising product is cocoa, produced on medium-sized and small farms. Various areas of the country are well suited for cocoa growing and if the present cocoa development program could be stepped up beyond what is suggested in Chapter 16 it might be possible eventually to go from present import substitution to exports, particularly since cocoa prices already today—at the beginning of the development program— are comparable with world market prices.

Judging from yield data, Colombia should be in a position to develop sorghum exports as a feed grain if yields can be improved somewhat. Sorghum is produced mostly on small and medium-sized farms. At present the IDEMA support price is still some 20% over the world market price but the growth rate of sorghum production (20% annually from 1963 to 1969) suggests that the support price provides a strong incentive to expand acreage.

A controversial product is rice. Yields differ widely, but even in the lower range are not far below those obtained in main exporting countries, such as Burma and Thailand. Nevertheless, the IDEMA support price in 1970 was set at about US$122 per ton for type 1, grade A unhulled rice which compares with an average of US$187 per ton for all milled rice exported from the United States in 1969 and a quoted price of US$151 for Thailand.[5] A major reason for IDEMA's high support price is the fact that there is a fairly large number of small dry land farmers growing rice under rainfall. Yields on these farms are 1.5 to 1.6 tons of paddy per hectare, while the average yield on irrigated—usually larger—farms in 1968 was 4.2 tons. It is unlikely that the latter would be unable to compete on the world market. Rather, the problem may be what other crops might be suitable for low-yield farms, a problem encountered in price support policy for many other crops. Alternatively, they should be given access to better land.

Another important sector from which additional exports might come in the future is livestock. Conditions suitable for all types of common farm animals can be found in Colombia. The most important immediate problem is the high cost of feed grains, mainly due to the high cost of corn production, which in turn is due to the fact that roughly three quarters of total output is grown on plots of 3 hectares and less, and therefore can be assumed to be grown largely by traditional, inefficient methods. However, at least some 260 thousand farms of under 5 hectares and a further 70 thousand under 10 hectares are among those planting no more than 3 hectares to corn. If the average farm population is assumed to be six persons, this means that some 1.5 to 2.0 million people are involved, most of whom are living close to the subsistence level. Clearly, any measures designed to improve the productivity of these farms should receive high priority, particularly in view of the crucial importance of the cost of corn as a feed grain for the livestock sector. The success of INCORA projects in increasing yields on small holdings indicates that the required improvements are technically feasible. The heart of the problem is the very large number of people involved, and therefore the very large amount of extension service required.

This problem is not easy to solve. For instance, of the total area planted to corn in 1967 only 22% was planted with improved seed, and as large plantings amount to somewhat over 20% of total area it is possible that it was mainly large growers who used improved seed. Beyond the development of an improved seed not much appears to have been done for the small holder's sector and the constraint is likely to have been the limited capacity of extension services and research rather than a lack of funds. The rapid expansion of the modern sector of Colombian agriculture required more skilled personnel than could be quickly trained. Consequently, the

5. 5% broken Bangkok, milled. Roughly, the US$122 for unhulled rice imply a price of around US$190 for milled rice.

traditional smallholder sector has received comparatively little technical assistance. In the future, as more skilled personnel become available higher priority than hitherto should be given to the smallholder sector.

After export crops and help to the traditional smallholder, the next problem that should be immediately tackled is the high price of modern inputs, especially of fertilizers. As production costs do not seem to be unreasonably high, the problem is likely to be in transport cost and in the distribution system. In view of the importance of this question, a preinvestment study on fertilizer has been included in the suggested preinvestment study program.

If cheaper modern inputs and adequate extension services could be provided to the small-holders, a large step in the direction of solving the key problems of Colombia's agriculture would have been taken. Improved yields, lower production cost, cheaper feed to support expanding hog and poultry production, probably could substantially improve the lot of the majority of the small holders. However, a large number of small holders will not be able to improve their situation since their holdings simply are too small. Added to these are the large numbers of landless workers, for whom the solution may lie in improving their productivity and working conditions, and this calls for colonization, land redistribution or finding employment in other sectors.

In the long run, Colombia's food and fiber requirements can be produced by a much smaller number of farmers. However, in the medium term agriculture will have to continue to provide productive employment for a large share of the increasing labor force. Consequently high priority should be given to bringing new land into production as well as intensifying production on existing farmland. Studies to devise more effective methods of land distribution and colonization should be continued. In the meantime INCORA should continue its programs for land redistribution and colonization, and efforts should also be directed toward reducing unit costs of settlement and development. At the same time government should continue with its efforts to provide incentives for commerical agricultural producers through its pricing and credit policies.

The System

General

Colombia has coastlines on both the Pacific Ocean and the Caribbean Sea, but this advantage of having two coastlines is offset by the difficulty of movement between the coasts and the interior. The three massive ranges of the Andes Mountains which run from south to north present formidable barriers to communication between the main areas of population, which until recently developed as separate and almost isolated communities. Transport investment policy over the past twenty years has been aimed at national integration and at overcoming the situation imposed by geography. Within the next year or two the task of establishing what might be termed the basic transport network of the country should be completed.

Highways

Colombia has some 45,000 km of roads, of which about 5,000 km are paved. The total number of road vehicles—260,000 in 1968—has been increasing by about 6% per annum in recent years, and trucks by about 4% per annum. This is a fairly slow rate of growth compared with that in other countries at a similar stage of development. However, since there has been a slight trend towards larger vehicles, total trucking capacity has been expanding at a somewhat faster rate. Now that the government is exercising control over the importation of heavy vehicles to protect the highway system from excessive loads, this trend may not continue. On the main trunk highways, truck traffic predominates.

About two-thirds of public investment in transport is being devoted to highway construction and reconstruction. To a certain extent the development of the highway network has been complementary to the railway system rather than competing with it. Transport between Bogota-Medellin and Santa Marta, for example, is essentially the province of the railway; on the other hand, the large rural areas in the northwest between Medellin and Cartagena depend almost entirely on the trunk highway between these two cities as their main artery. The provision of modern highways has nevertheless resulted in considerable diversions of traffic from rail to road in some areas. In some cases this is due to the present rundown condition of parts of the railway system; where good services can be provided with adequate equipment, the railway is under much less competitive pressure. On the Paz del Rio-Bogota route, for example, it seems likely that most of the steel traffic is returning to rail now that a reasonable service can be offered. In other cases, particularly the routes Bogota-Espinal-Ibague, Cali-Medellin and, in future, Cali-Buenaventura, road transport is likely—primarily because of the difficult operating conditions imposed by the terrain—to offer many types of traffic sufficient advantages to attract it away from the railway. Development of communications in Southern and Eastern Colombia will be in the form of highways and the government has prepared an ambitious feeder road system as a complement to the primary and secondary highway program now under way.

Railways

The Colombian National Railways (CNR) operate a unified network of lines totaling 3,436 route km. The system has access to the Pacific at Buenaventura and to the Atlantic at Santa Marta. Traffic from the other Atlantic ports of Cartagena and Barranquilla is transferred to the railway through road and water routes. The Atlantic line is the most important.

Traffic on the main trunk lines averages about 500,000 ton-km per route km per annum, and in 1969, total traffic achieved a record 1,159 million ton-km. However, completion of some major highway projects, particularly the new Buenaventura-Cali highway in 1970, is expected to result in substantial diversion of traffic from some routes. Passenger travel has been declining at 6% per annum for several years, and in 1969 the CNR carried one million (or 28%) fewer passengers than in 1968. About 260 km of apparently uneconomic line are being studied for possible closure. Consultants (SOFRERAIL of France) have been assisting the CNR since 1967 in advising on and implementing a track rehabilitation and maintenance program and training technical personnel.

Ports

Most foreign trade dry cargo is handled by four ports, Buenaventura on the Pacific and the Caribbean ports of Barranquilla, Santa Marta, and Cartagena. Total exports grew at a rate of 5.4% per annum during 1956-68 while imports have in recent years been less than in the mid-1950's, reflecting both foreign exchange difficulties and import substitution effects. When the expansions being made at Buenaventura and Santa Marta are completed and in use, the country as a whole will probably have adequate port capacity for the next ten years. There are problems in operation of the ports arising from low labor productivity, poor timing of arrival of bulk imports, and poor coordination with railway and highway operators and consequent difficulties of access.

River Transport

There are several navigable rivers in Colombia, but 96% of the inland shipping takes place on the Magdalena and most of the rest operates on the Cauca. River shipping is possible in all seasons on the lower regions of the Magdalena. Upriver from Gamarra, 473 km from the mouth, however, the river is not navigable on a 24-hour basis and travel becomes extremely hazardous and unreliable in the dry season. In favorable seasons, the river is navigable for 930 km to La Dorada; at other times only 600 km. The volume of traffic varies from year to year according to the condition of the river, and in recent years there has been competition from the Atlantic line of the railroad over the whole length but especially in the northern reaches of the river. Yet, the absolute level of cargo traffic on it has been continuing to grow; a record 2.8 million tons or 1.3 billion ton-km of traffic was transported on the river in 1968. Passenger traffic has suffered much more from the improvement of road and rail services in the Magdalena Valley. In 1956, 363,000 passengers were carried on the river; in 1966, the last year of record, only 6,979 traveled by this mode.

Air Services

Colombia's very difficult terrain encouraged the early development of air services for internal as well as international transportation. There are about 700 aircraft landing facilities in the country. There are seven with jet services. Internal passenger traffic has increased by 4.6% per annum between 1964 and 1968 and internal air freight movement is more or less static. In 1968, only about 103,000 tons of traffic, generating 72 million ton-km, were handled. There are evidences of recent overexpansion of investment in airport facilities. In 1967, Avianca canceled its Bogota-Popayan jet flight and the new airport at Popayan is almost unused as a good road now connects Popayan to Cali. Other recent improvements in surface transport facilities have led to a decline in traffic on certain routes.

Pipelines

Petroleum products, Colombia's second largest foreign exchange earner after coffee, are mainly transported by pipeline. Crude oil pipelines supply five refineries, including one at Cartagena, which ships refined products via the Panama Canal to Buenaventura for distribution to western Colombia. Another line supplies crude to Santa Marta for export. Refined products are also moved by pipeline from refineries in the north to Bogota, Medellin and the Cauca Valley, and from Buenaventura to the Cauca Valley.

Investment Plans

During the period 1970-72 the government intends to increase public investment in most sectors, including transport, substantially. The best estimate of current plans for investment in the transport sector is given in Table 19-1, together with a tentative extrapolation for 1973-75. In spite of increased absorptive capacity, the investment targets are unlikely to be fully realized, particularly if final investment decisions are based on careful appraisal of economic merit.

Highways

Highway Network

Of a road network totaling about 45,000 km in length, about 19,000 km form the national highway system, a further 19,000 km are departmental, and the balance are municipal (linking towns with outlying communities and farms) and private (such as to oil concessions). The **departmental** system includes about 3,000 km of "caminos vecinales", which are low-standard feeder roads built under a national program established in 1960; materials and labor for these are furnished by the local communities. Agricultural produce boards and departmental and central authorities all contribute to this program. About 20% of the national system is paved, but less than 5% of the departmental roads are paved (Tables 19-2 and 19-3). The national highway network over the years 1962 to 1969 increased from 16,500 km to about 19,000 km.

The difficult terrain (which leads to high construction costs) was a major factor in the isolation and traditional independence of the various regional centers. Only in the last two decades has there been any real effort to link the main population and economic centers of the country by good roads.

The national highway system includes the basic trunk network which connects the main centers of population and a number of secondary roads linking the smaller towns to the primary network, as well as some minor roads which at present have purely local importance, but which may in future form part of new long-distance routes (Map 19-I, see Map Annex).

TABLE 19-1: ANTICIPATED PUBLIC SECTOR INVESTMENT IN TRANSPORT – 1970-1975

	1970	1971	1972	1973	1974	1975
Roads	2494	2429	2722	2800	2900	3070
Railways	240	289	235	120	140	160
River Transport	40	47	95	100	107	114
Seaports	126	174	82	83	20	35
Civil Aviation	284	122	125	119	128	126
Total	3184	3061	3259	3222	3295	3505

Notes:

1. In current Col $ with an assumed 7% per annum price increase included.

2. Some of these figures, particularly roads, include maintenance estimates.

3. These figures differ from the sub-sector totals discussed in the various chapters because they include estimates for local government and a small element of private investment.

TABLE 19-2: THE NATIONAL HIGHWAY NETWORK

| District H.Q. | Length in 1959 by District and Type (kilometers) | | |
	Paved	Gravel	Total
Medellin	320	1,345	1,665
Cartagena	396	309	705
Tunja	261	1,720	1,981
Manizales	530	606	1,136
Popayan	116	891	1,007
Monteria	168	329	497
Bogota	513	518	1,031
Quibdo		225	225
Riohacha		435	435
Neiva	226	803	1,029
Valledupar	319	957	1,276
Villavicencio	58	878	936
Pasto	20	1,316	1,336
Bucaramanga	345	1,150	1,495
Cucuta	188	1,666	1,854
Ibague	352	909	1,261
Palmira	413	414	827
Forencia	66	198	264
San Andres	12	48	60
Total	4,303	14,717	19,020

Historic Composition, 1962-69

Year	Length (Km)	% Paved
1962	16,512	11.5
1963	16,692	13.7
1964	17,054	14.6
1965	17,479	15.0
1966	17,564	15.4
1967	17,997	16.6
1968	18,842	22.5
1969	19,020	22.6

Source: MOP, Planning Office, December 1969.

Highway Administration

The Ministry of Public Works (MOP) is responsible for planning, constructing and maintaining the national highway network, which accounts for about 90% of MOP's activities. Efforts to create a modern transport system started in the early 1950's but limitations were imposed by lack of funds and by organizational difficulties. In 1966, the government engaged management consultants to make recommendations for improvement and subsequently to help implement these recommendations. The implementation phase is still in progress. Progress has been achieved in almost all the ministry's activities, and particularly in maintenance, but not at the pace which the government had foreseen.

In the past, highway projects were numerous and ambitious, but many were never completed; the policy of the last three years has been to concentrate more on completing projects already begun than on starting new projects. There is, however, evidence of a tendency to go back to working on a large number of fronts. One of the main causes of poor performance on earlier highway projects was the inadequate provision of local funds. This not only forced construction contractors to gear their output to known availability of funds, but led directly to the financial failure of some firms. The establishment of the National Highway Fund at the end of 1966 provided a more assured source of financing for highway works. Table 19-4 shows recent and projected expenditures on the national highway system. A considerable increase over past levels of spending is planned, but the execution is likely to fall short of the target.

Currently under way is an inventory of the national highway system. About 7,000 km have so far been covered. It will facilitate future highway planning and operations and help to establish the basis for classifying roads. The first comprehensive national traffic census was conducted in 1968; the results were used, together with the inventory and field inspections and some additional counts, to plan the 1970-73 highway paving program. The analysis of similar traffic counts for 1969 has recently been completed and these counts will be continued on an annual basis.

TABLE 19-3: DEPARTMENTAL ROADS

Department	Paved	Length in 1969 by District and Type (kilometer) Gravel	Earth	Total
Antiquia		2,481.0		2,481.0
Atlantico	338.2	180.0	34.2	552.4
Bolivar		95.1	109.0	204.1
Boyaca		552.0	308.0	860.0
Caldas		862.0	18.0	880.0
Cauca		264.9	162.0	426.9
Cesar				
Cordoba		155.0	112.0	267.0
Cundinamarca	95.1	2,499.6	387.0	2,981.7
Choco				
Guajira		30.0	312.2	342.2
Huila		350.5	267.0	617.5
Magdalena		28.0	153.0	181.0
Meta		352.0	435.0	787.0
Narino		643.0	128.0	771.0
Norte de Santander		68.0	111.0	179.0
Quindio		344.0	82.0	426.0
Risaralda		497.0	10.0	507.0
Santander		837.4	1,024.1	1,861.5
Sucre		76.0	88.0	164.0
Tolima		707.0	646.0	1,353.0
Valle	79.0	2,929.7	267.9	3,276.6
Total	512.3	13,952.2	4,654.4	19,118.9

Source: MOP, December 1969.

Highway Engineering, Construction and Maintenance

In Colombia, pavements have frequently been overdesigned to overcome deficiencies in drainage. The MOP is now being assisted by an expert from the Road Research Laboratory (UK), whose main task is to review and advise on pavement design in the country.

Although its personnel are competent, the ministry has limited design capacity and uses consultants for this purpose. While reorganization of the ministry could increase its engineering capability and thus enable some design to be undertaken directly, it will continue to be necessary to use consultants for most design work.

The consulting profession is now well established in Colombia. There are a number of large and capable Colombian engineering firms, some of which have developed as a result of their participation in foreign-financed projects in highways, power supply and other fields. For most road projects in future there will be no need for foreign experts. For large projects, such as Barranquilla Bridge and El Pailon-Buenaventura Road, the government intends to continue to utilize associations of Colombian and foreign consultants. Consultants are frequently engaged by government on open-ended contracts activated by work orders. This type of arrangement can result in high engineering costs and the government is considering changes which, it is hoped, will simplify administration, improve control of consultants and keep costs at reasonable levels.

Modern methods of highway construction were first introduced in Colombia in the early 1950s. Mountainous terrain and corresponding heavy earthmoving led to intensive use of heavy equipment which had not previously been operated to any extent in Colombia. There are now several local firms capable of undertaking contracts worth US$5 million equivalent or more.

Major highway construction is now almost invariably carried out under unit price contracts let after competitive bidding. Delays formerly experienced in legalizing contracts have been overcome and this is now done within thirty days of award.

The quality of maintenance work on the national highway system has been uneven. The activity of the maintenance division was mainly geared to the reconstruction of pavements which had deteriorated because of deferred maintenance; the introduction of extensive routing maintenance has taken place only recently. A pilot program in one of the maintenance districts has already yielded considerable benefits. During 1970 the results of this program will be extended to other districts.

Most districts have now been staffed with mechanical engineers who are in charge of equipment. Workshop facilities have been improved, and maintenance operations are now planned centrally rather than being dependent on the interest of individual district engineers. The ministry is using the proceeds of United States and British credits to procure highway equipment worth US$21 million equivalent, which should more than meet the ministry's needs for maintenance.

Characteristics and Growth of Road Traffic

The road vehicle fleet grew at an average annual rate of 5.6% per annum between 1958 and 1967 (Table 19-5). The number of trucks increased at a lower rate of about 4%, with trucks of less than 3-ton capacity increasing at 8% and heavier trucks at 3.2% per annum. The motor fuel consumption statistics show somewhat higher growth than do vehicle registrations; 6.6% for gasoline and 7.2% for diesel (Table 19-6). The increased motor fuel taxes introduced in 1966 have had no discernible effect on fuel consumption. Although in 1967 there was a sharp drop in the growth in consumption of gasoline and a drop in diesel sales, there was a recovery in the following year. The restrictive factor in fleet growth has been import policy for balance of payments reasons. The motor industry is limited to assembly of cars, buses and trucks at present, but plans for manufacture are being discussed with foreign interests.

About 95% of trucks are still single axle vehicles and overloading is common. The government has banned the import of trucks whose dimensions and axle load capacities do not

TABLE 19-4: PAST AND PROJECTED NATIONAL HIGHWAY EXPENDITURE
(In millions of Col$)

	Construction	Maintenance	Total
1963	n.a.	n.a.	557.6
1964	n.a.	n.a.	616.3
1965	n.a.	n.a.	711.4
1966	n.a.	n.a.	643.7
1967	n.a.	n.a.	873.9
1968	n.a.	n.a.	1088.3
1969	711.0	388.0	1099.0
1970	1178.9	744.0	1922.0
1971	1326.3	432.5	1758.8
1972	1427.0	604.8	2031.8

Sources: National Planning Department and MOP, National Road Fund, Budget 1970.

Note: The maintenance estimates include provision for equipment in the year acquired.
The construction expenditure forecasts are based on very tentative timing of
projects. Planned expenditure on feeder roads is not included. Expenditure is
shown in current prices and therefore actual historical growth is overstated.

TABLE 19-5: VEHICLE REGISTRATIONS — 1958-1967

	Passenger vehicles	Buses	Jeeps	Panels and Pickups	Light Trucks	Trucks	Others	Total
1958	67,761	12,283	11,414	25,092	4,991	36,949	895	159,385
1959	68,808	13,358	12,375	27,578	5,155	39,275	927	167,476
1960	72,353	15,030	14,539	30,601	5,336	43,061	998	181,918
1961	84,605	15,850	17,225	31,043	5,696	44,145	1,037	199,601
1962	n.a.	n.a.	n.a.	n.a.	n.a.	n.a.	n.a.	n.a.
1963	85,273	17,911	23,315	41,980	7,270	39,381	2,210	217,340
1964	86,423	18,341	24,936	40,673	8,049	43,880	2,450	224,752
1965	87,977	19,345	27,037	41,994	8,724	45,171	2,643	232,891
1966	95,654	20,719	29,831	44,991	9,830	47,286	2,786	251,107
1967	98,216	n.a.	n.a.	n.a.	n.a.	n.a.	n.a.	259,608

Source: Departamento Administrativo Nacional de Estadistica. (DANE) December 1969.

comply with legal requirements and has indicated that it will not license replacement of engines
for such trucks imported during a period of lax enforcement of loading standards. INTRA (the
National Transport Institute) has recently introduced highway patrols to enforce compliance
with the law. A new draft law on vehicle weights and dimensions has just been prepared to
replace Law No. 0102 of 1955. The same maximum loads will be prescribed as before, i.e. 8.2
tons for single axles and 14.5 tons for tandem axles but maximum permitted lengths have been
extended somewhat. All trucks will be required to carry a certificate issued by INTRA de-
scribing their dimensions. The problem, as with the existing law, will be enforcement. To comply
with vehicle weight regulations, the permissible maximum load of a two-axled truck would vary,
according to type, between six and eight tons.

In 1968 the average age of vehicles in the truck fleet was 12 years. About 88% of the fleet
is of American origin and 12% is European. Although there are 48 makes in use in the country,
Ford trucks constitutes 53% of the total. Over 90% of vehicle owners have one truck and over
99% have less than four vehicles. The average age of the passenger car fleet is also high; in 1967
over 40% of total cars were more than 10 years old.

Taxes on Vehicle Ownership and Use

The revenue from taxes on vehicle ownership and use is not known precisely. Planeacion is currently collecting data on the subject. The most important tax affecting vehicle operation is the import duty on vehicles and spare parts. There are a large number of rates and exceptions, but the main rates are shown below:

Vehicle Type	Rate of Duty (on c.i.f. value)
Jeep	20%
Car (0-US$1,850) assembled)	230%
Car (0-US$1,850-3,00) (assembled)	350%
Car (over US$3,300) (assembled)	450%
Bus	60%
Truck (Chassis, no body)	
(0-5,000 lb)	180%
(5,000-9,999 lb)	70%
(Others)	30%
Trucks, Pickups, etc.	
(0-5,000 lb)	200%
(5,000-9,999 lb)	100%
(Others)	70%
Unassembled Trucks	
(0-5,000 lb)	10%
(5,000-9,999 lb)	50%
(Others)	140%

Annual license fees are collected by municipalities. These fees are based on the weight of the vehicle and the following are rough average rates:

	US $ Equivalent
Passenger vehicles	2.8
Trucks	1.4
Buses	0.9

These fees probably do not cover the cost of collection. However, there is a national stamp tax on the municipal license. This is based on the age of the vehicle. Following are the annual rates:

Age of vehicle	Tax US $ Equivalent
Before 1950	0
1950-55	18.50
1956-59	25.80
1960-63	36.80
1964-date	58.80

There is in addition a 20% surcharge on all vehicles weighing more than 1,400 kilograms.

Ad valorem taxes are levied on motor fuels. Until 1964 there was only a minor tax, Col$0.004 per gallon, collected by the municipalities. In 1964, a 10% *ad valorem* tax equivalent to less than Col$0.1 per gallon was introduced. In 1967, an additional tax of one Col$1 per gallon was introduced. This was converted to an *ad valorem* tax in 1968 at the rate of 114% of the refinery price, the equivalent of Col$1 per gallon at that time. A 55.5% *ad valorem* tax on diesel fuel, equivalent to Col$0.48 per gallon, was also introduced in 1968. Consumers of motor fuel in general received, for a long time, a subsidy as a result of the artificial ex-refinery price for motor spirit and the low effective tax. The price was raised in mid-1971 and the subsidy reduced. A subsequent step would be to review the rationale for and structure of all taxes on vehicle ownership and use with the object of devising a coherent policy in this regard. Distortions in the choice of fuels are likely to be caused by the tax differential between diesel and gasoline.

TABLE 19-6: MOTOR FUEL CONSUMPTION – 1958-1968[1]

(In millions of U.S. gallons)

	1958	1959	1960	1961	1962	1963	1964	1965	1966	1967	1968
Gasoline	303.5	317.7	354.7	399.6	434.5	442.0	460.5	491.3	527.6	535.0	583.8
Annual Increase %		4.6	11.6	12.6	8.7	1.7	4.1	6.6	7.3	1.4	9.1
Diesel	95.0	99.0	113.5	124.5	134.9	135.5	151.5	166.0	176.9	166.9	190.7
Annual Increase %		4.2	14.6	9.6	8.3	0.4	11.8	9.6	6.6	-5.7	14.2

Average 1958-1968   Gasoline 6.6%   Diesel 7.2%

[1] Converted at 1 barrel = 42 U.S. gal.

Source: Colombian Petroleum Information Center, December 1969.

Tolls on National Highways

Tolls were first imposed on some Colombian roads in 1954 with a view to raising all or a substantial part of maintenance costs of the corresponding road. Rates have never been changed and they now barely cover the cost of collection. Total revenues from 25 stations on 10 roads totaling about 1,200 km were Col$8 million in 1968. The costs of administration were about 30% and as much as 50% in the Cartagena area where the level of tolls is lowest. The rates vary between US$0.04 and US$0.16 per km for a car and US$0.18 and US$0.36 per km for heavy vehicles. Ten percent of toll receipts are given to the Ministry of Education and the remainder, varying from US$50 to US$500 per km, is spent on highway maintenance.

The government is authorized under existing law to impose tolls. In turn the government has vested this responsibility in the Ministry of Public Works. Under present regulations, the proceeds of tolls must be kept in a special account of the highway fund (Fondo Vial) and used, after paying the cost of collection, for: a) maintenance of toll roads and b) the construction of additional toll roads.

The ministry intends to levy tolls on certain new facilities when: they constitute a distinct improvement over previous facilities; the use of the new facilities will provide substantial savings to the users; the tolls envisaged are less than these savings; and alternative, toll-free facilities are available.

Tolls are viewed as a revenue-producing measure, justified by the provision of an improved alternative to an existing facility. In order to be politically acceptable, the new tolls will be levied in accordance with a general policy applicable to similar facilities throughout the country.

Records of Highway Traffic

The mission studied the Ministry of Public Works traffic census data and information on traffic volumes recorded at highway toll stations. Data were available for 7-day, 24-hour counts taken at about 600 stations in 1968 and for similar counts made in 1969. Roads on which traffic in excess of 250 vehicles per day (the level at which it is frequently economic to pave roads in Colombia) has been recorded and which are not paved or planned for paving in the near future are shown in green on Map 19-I. [1] Changes between the 1968 and 1969 counts, however—and other evidence—suggest that these counts are not a safe guide. This can be remedied by more frequent checks. Since only about 40 sections are involved, the task should be an easy one and should be undertaken before the inclusion of these roads in a future highway improvement program. More generally, traffic counts need to be taken frequently during the year wherever investment decisions are involved.

1. See Map Annex. The circled green figures refer to an analysis of traffic counts which has been omitted from the published version of the report.

Foreign Assistance to Highways

The World Bank has been closely involved with the improvement of Colombia's transport facilities since 1951 when it made its first loan. It has since made five other loans and IDA has given one credit for highways. Altogether $136 million has been provided for this purpose up to 1970. Other international and national lending agencies have also contributed substantially to highway improvement in Colombia. USAID provided funds and equipment for the government's feeder road program in its early stages and in 1968. The Inter-American Development Bank (IDB) made a loan for the construction of the Cienaga-Santa Marta-Paraguachon Road which will link Colombia and northern Venezuela. The IDB has recently agreed to finance a four-year feeder road program with a loan of US$17 million and is also providing some $31 million to finance the foreign exchange costs of the Popayan-Pasto Highway and the Santuario-Puerto Triunfo highway. Recently the Bank of London and South America has opened a sterling line of credit for £4 million for the purchase by the Ministry of Public Works of British road maintenance equipment and the Export-Import Bank and two New York commercial banks have made loans totaling US$10 million for the purchase of road maintenance equipment in the United States.

The sixth World Bank highway loan, signed in June 1970, is to finance the foreign exchange costs, amounting to US$32 million equivalent, of a project costing a total of US$62 million. The project includes the paving of 1,618 km. of national highways, the construction of a major highway bridge over the Magdalena River at Barranquilla, the construction of 9.5 km. of multi-lane highway at the entry to the port of Buenaventura and consulting services for the supervision of the above work.

Highway Feasibility Studies

A number of highway feasibility studies are under way or proposed. They are identified in Map 19-II[2] and their status is shown below (as of mid-1970):

A.	Cali-Buga Highway	Study recently completed; proposed for revision.
B.	Fundacion-Le Ye (Santa Marta)	Study under way.
C.	Tres Puertas-Irra-La Felisa and La Virginia-Irra	Updating of earlier studies.
D.	Guadelupe-Florencia	Study completed.
E.	Cucta-Ocana	Study Proposed.
F.	Villavicencio-Puerto Lopez- Puerto Carreno	Study proposed.
G.	Carretera Troncal de Los Llanos	Study proposed.
H.	Honda-Bogota	Study proposed.
I.	New route between Tolima and Valle	Study proposed.
J.	Puerto Araujo-Barrancabermeja/ Bucaramanga road	Study proposed.
K.	Barbosa-Puerto Olaya road	Study proposed.
L.	El Carmen-Zambrano-Boscoma	Study proposed.

Some of the above roads are improvements and upgrading justified by current traffic volume (e.g., A, B, C, H, K, and perhaps F—Villavicencio-Puerto Lopez). Some would be completely new roads. The studies should indicate the degree of probability of new traffic generation on these development roads.

2. See Map Annex

Feeder Roads

The Fondo Nacional de Caminos Vecinales (FNCV) began its activities in 1961 and since then has constructed 2,446 km of feeder roads. Another 7,837 km have been identified for future construction. The program for 1970-73 includes 45 roads totaling 1,550 km., with widely varying traffic volumes. One 90 km section (Puerto Lleras-San Jose del Guaviare) currently has traffic in excess of 100 vehicles per day. Most of the sections, 1,075 km, have traffic in the 50-100 vehicles per day range and there are 383.5 km with daily traffic of less than 50 vehicles.

The roads in the FNCV program, at an average cost of over US$20,000 per km, are expensive in relation to the traffic which they are initially expected to carry. Their main justification must therefore come from the increased production which their construction is expected to stimulate. About ten of the roads are in the south and southeast part of the country in Narino, Caqueta and the Meta where colonization is taking place. In general, these are likely to prove beneficial and worthwhile, in particular the connection to San Vicente del Caguan from Algecira and the Puerto Lleras-San Jose del Guaviare road. Many of the other roads appear to have been selected to form part of future trunk roads or to provide some form of geographical balance in the distribution of feeder road funds. This system may lead to a dispersal of funds and the question arises whether it would not be possible to relate more closely the construction of feeder roads to the expected economic benefits. There is a need for improved transportation in many areas as part of a program of agricultural improvement, particularly in the south (already mentioned) and in the Cesar and Ariguani valleys in the north between Valledupar and the Magdalena river. Feeder roads in the latter area would be an essential part of the development of irrigated agriculture. The probable form of road development would be the preparation of networks of simple roads designed as an integral part of the agricultural investment programs rather than the simple connection of an isolated community to the main road system.

A recent ILO study of the Colombian employment problem recommends a "reexamination of the existing network of feeder roads and its rapid extension where most useful (cost-benefit analysis), partly within the framework of a public works program, partly through Accion Comunal." Where the opportunity cost of labor used for road construction is low this may provide possibilities of lowering transport costs between the small farmer and the market and increasing the competitiveness of his prices while at the same time lowering the cost of his inputs and consumption goods.

Railways

The Railway System

Railroads in Colombia were first built to provide access from the interior cities to water transport through either river or ocean ports from which goods could be imported or exported. In the early stages, rail and river transport tended to complement one another. Because the highway system was undeveloped and other modes of transport apart from the river did not exist, the railroads had virtually no competition until the 1950s. The railroads themselves were not well-integrated and operated as independent regional railroads until 1954 when Colombian National Railroads (CNR) was incorporated.

With the completion of the Atlantic railroad down the Magdalena Valley to the Caribbean at Santa Marta in 1961, the overall rail system was integrated into a single operating system. It also continued to offer service to many areas which had no other means of access and in the lower Magdalena provided transport to areas which had formerly been inaccessible. The faster and more reliable rail service proved more attractive than the river for many commodities, in particular highly valued imports.

The CNR is organized in five divisions as follows:

	km
Central	1,368
Pacific	903
Santander	400
Magdalena	425
Antioquia	340
	3,436

MAP 19-III

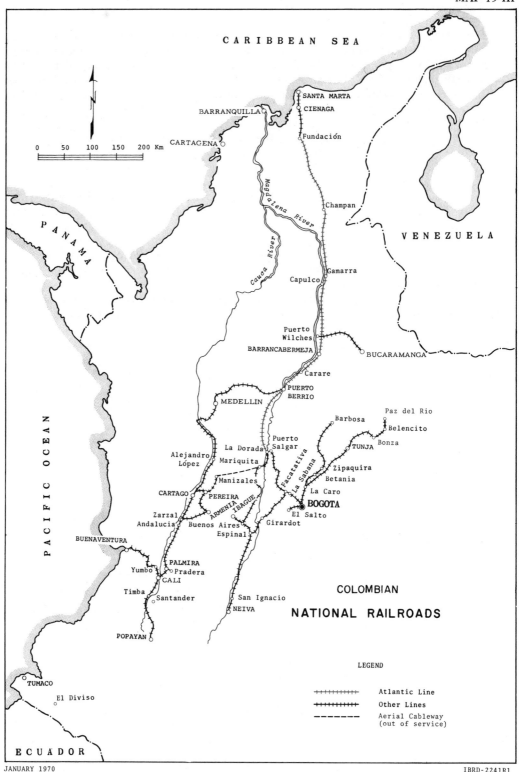

COLOMBIAN

NATIONAL RAILROADS

LEGEND

+++++++++++	Atlantic Line
+++++++++++	Other Lines
- - - - - -	Aerial Cableway (out of service)

A full description is contained in Map 19-III. The railway gauge is standardized at 914 mm, or 36 in.

The tremendous expansion in the highway network in the past ten years has greatly improved the quality of service which can be offered by truckers. As a result, the railroads have been forced to compete more actively than was formerly necessary. The first stage of a program of rehabilitation of track which had been neglected for many years during the construction of the Atlantic railroad is currently under way and should be completed in 1973. Improved management and operating practices have also been initiated. Rail pricing policy was reviewed and revised in 1966. This change has increased revenues and resulted in larger rail shipments and longer hauls which have improved efficiency and net revenues.

From time to time, new rail projects have been proposed with the object of improving the railroad's competitive position. These projects, because they parallel existing highway facilities which are being improved, would duplicate highway capacity which will shortly be provided. Consequently, any proposal for extension of the existing rail network must be examined carefully before any financial commitment is made.

The railroad network serves many cities in the country. In fact, the only principal cities not served by it are Barranquilla and Cartagena on the Caribbean coast. There was formerly a railway from Cartagena to the Magdalena river port of Calamar but it was abandoned some years ago. The areas of the country which at present have no rail service include the Llanos, the upper Magdalena river valley, the Guajira, the Choco and much of the north coast area.

The Colombian topography presents the national railroad system with geographical obstacles more severe than those confronting railroads in most other parts of the world. Gradient is probably the most important single feature of the system. The topographical characteristics of the rail network are briefly discussed below.

The heavily traveled line from Buenaventura to Cali is one of the more rugged on the Colombian railroad system and is the most difficult section in the Pacific division. For its 174 km length it has an average grade of over 2.5% and a maximum of 4.2%. In some places the hillsides traversed are too steep to permit even short radius turns, so switchbacks are used, requiring trains to reverse direction to proceed up the hill. Location of some track on the steep wall of a river canyon requires heavy annual maintenance expenditure to repair damage caused by landslides. Maintenance of way investments on this line over the last few years have greatly improved its condition. However, severe landslides caused by river erosion closed the Buenaventura-Cali line for six weeks in late 1969 and adversely affected the company's financial operating results.

From Cali northward up the Cauca Valley as far as Alejandro Lopez, the grades are less than 1% and curvature is minimum. Beyond this point, however, grades increase and the final ascent to Medellin is again quite circuitous, involving a ruling gradient of about 3%. The railroad from Medellin eastward to Puerto Berrio on the Magdalena river includes severe grades of up 4.4% and curves of very short radius, requiring low operating speeds and short trains.

The conditions encountered on the central division are also quite varied. Within the Magdalena Valley, the line from Neiva to La Dorada has small curvature and occasional moderate grades of up to 2.5%. Operating conditions there are generally good. From Ibague down to the Magdalena Valley, severe grades are encountered once more and the maximum grade is 3.5%. The line from Girardot up to Bogota is in a mountainous section which has a ruling grade of 4.6% and an average grade of 2%, thereby limiting train length to 6 cars or less. The ascent from Puerto Salgar to Bogota is similarly difficult.

The main line of the Atlantic Division from La Dorada north to Santa Marta is quite level and very straight, permitting lower operating costs than anywhere else on the national system. However, the very old branch line from Puerto Wilches up to Bucaramanga is winding and has a ruling grade of 2.5%.

On lines where the rehabilitation program has been vigorously pursued, these efforts have been rewarded by improved operating conditions. However, in 1969 only 116 km out of a

TABLE 19-7: COLOMBIAN NATIONAL RAILROADS: DERAILMENTS

Division	Central		Pacific		Santander		Magdalena		Antioquia		Total	
Length of Main Line	1,362		904		393		416		339		3414	
	Accidents	Hours	Accidents	Hours	Accidents	Hours	Accidents	Hours	Accidents	Hours	Accidents	Hours
1967	1,005	3,828	637	3,410	509	1,340	110	396	298	855	2,555	9,829
1968	1,063	5,053	480	2,752	1,139	2,477	64	367	1,201	4,434	3,947	15,033
1969	1,444	4,426	583	3,979	1,098	2,493	43	195	1,526	4,931	4,694	16,024

Source: FCN, *Los Ferrocarriles en Cifras, Boletin Anual.*

planned 192 km of track were relaid. In the mid-1960's there was a reduction in derailments on the Buenaventura to Cali line following a major rehabilitation of the road bed, ballast and track there. Much of the system, however, still does not rest upon satisfactory ballast or adequate ties or employ rail of sufficient weight to allow efficient operation of the railroad. The number of derailments has been increasing (Table 19-7), causing time losses and cost increases.

Vehicle Fleet

In recent years, the CNR has not been able to carry all traffic offered because of lack of rolling stock in good condition. This situation has improved considerably during the past two years with the acquisition of 60 new diesel locomotives and will improve further when 1,200 new rail cars and wagons which are currently being assembled are put into service. Dieselization has been taking place since 1959 and now more than half the system's locomotives are diesel powered. About 84% of train kilometers are by diesel and steam engines are confined for the most part to switching and repair duties.

While the 1969 Boletin Anual of the CNR gives the number of steam engines in service as 146, 74.6% of the time of these was spent in the workshops either being repaired or awaiting repair. In fact, many of these locomotives will never be used again and the productivity figures such as amount of time spent on trips (3.2%) and average kilometrage per engine (12,500) are misleading.

The average capacity of rail wagons is about 30 tons. The appropriate size of wagons is governed partly by the narrow gauge and sharp curves of the railroad. Small average shipments also make these wagons more appropriate than the larger vehicles used on most other systems.

Characteristics of Train Traffic

Total train traffic in 1969 decreased by 400,000 train-km by comparison with the previous year when commercial trains traveled 9.9 million km. The reduction, which took place in spite of increased ton-kilometrage, is related to the increased use of multiple engine trains which permit increased train size. The average commercial speed of freight trains was 22.3 km per hour with an average train of 6.8 loaded cars and a load of 162.8 net tons per train. Passenger trains traveled 1.98 million km with an average speed of 21 km per hour and an average train length of 8 coaches. In 1969 the average load of a loaded car was 24 tons. The average capacity of a car was 30 tons and therefore the average utilization is 80%. The average haul was 380 km (Table 19-8).

The daily average freight traffic on the Colombian railroad network is shown on Map 19-IV. On only a few sections of the system does traffic exceed 1,000 tons per day. Of the five divisions of the CNR, only the Magdalena Division averages more than 1,000 tons of cargo per day for the entire division.

Between 1962 and 1969, total freight loaded on the railroad dropped from 3.6 to 3.0 million tons (Table 19-8). In the same period the number of ton kilometers increased from 918 to 1,159 million. The fact that while the total tonnage loaded has been decreasing, the average length of haul has been increasing has been interpreted as a healthy sign because the longer the haul the more profitable the traffic. Part of the reason for the increasing length of haul has been the chronic shortage of equipment on the network, which has meant that the railway has been in a position to choose and has naturally selected the most attractive traffic. The recent substantial increase in locomotive capacity and prospective increase in rolling stock will make a great difference in this situation. It remains to be seen whether the high costs of terminal operations will permit the shorter hauls to be handled economically.

Freight carried by the railroad is concentrated on particular parts of the network, especially those which traverse zones of industrial and agricultural production, as can be seen in Map 19-IV. On the Atlantic line between Puerto Salgar and Santa Marta, the flow of traffic is dense in both directions, but in general terms the volume tends to be greater near producing and consuming centers. The density is particularly high in the main industrial zone of the country

MAP 19-IV

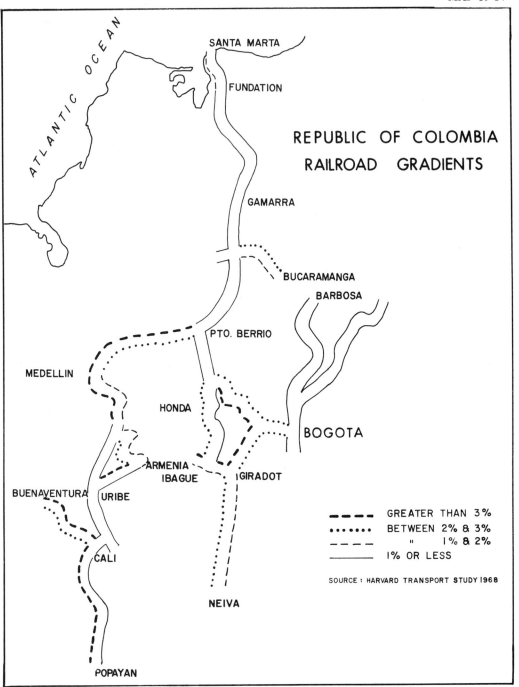

TABLE 19-8: COLOMBIAN NATIONAL RAILROADS: LENGTH OF HAUL AND REVENUE, FREIGHT AND PASSENGERS' 1962-68

	1962	1963	1964	1965	1966	1967	1968	1969
Freight								
Tons (mn.)	3.6	3.7	3.3	3.1	3.3	3.2	3.2	3.0
Ton − km. (mn.)	918	891	952	890	1,114	996	1,125	1,158
Average haul (km.)	248	241	288	287	338	311	352	380
Revenue (Col$ mn.)	119	179	194	181	253	252	296	350
Average revenue per ton - km. (Col¢)	13.0	20.0	20.4	20.4	22.7	25.3	26.3	30.1
Passenger								
Passengers (mn.)	8.2	8.6	7.4	6.5	4.8	4.8	3.7	2.6
Pass. - km. (mn.)	571	627	546	513	491	418	351	273
Average journey (km.)	70	73	74	79	85	87	95	103
Revenue (Col$ mn.)	22	30	28	28	31	33	35	34
Average revenue per passenger (Col¢)	3.8	4.7	5.1	5.5	6.2	8.0	9.9	12.3

Source: F.C.N., February 1970.

located in and around Bogota, a logical consequence of the consumption requirements of the population and the supply requirements for local industries.

Thirteen products constitute 69% of the CNR's freight and contribute 65% of its freight revenues.

Coffee is the most important commodity to the railroad because of the tonnage and long average haul (540 km in 1969). It moves from the coffee growing area between Manizales and Medellin, north to Santa Marta, a distance of almost 1,000 km or from this same growing area southward toward Buenaventura, a distance of over 400 km. Although coffee dominates both total freight and contribution to revenue, it contributes far less to revenue than its share of traffic would imply that it should.

Fertilizer is an increasingly important commodity for the railroad. In 1969 approximately 207,000 tons were carried for 93 million ton-kilometers or 8% of the railroad traffic. A large portion of this fertilizer moves southward, entering the rail system at the river transfer terminal at Capulco and then traveling to either Medellin and the Cauca Valley or up to Bogota. This

	Tonnage %	Position	Ton-Km %	Position	Revenue %	Position
Coffee	4.8	5	12.6	1	9.3	1
Wheat	6.7	3	8.7	2	8.2	2
Fertilizer	6.7	3	8.0	3	7.8	3
Petroleum Products	14.7	1	7.5	4	7.6	4
Iron and Steel	3.9	8	6.9	5	6.6	5
Sugar	7.1	2	6.9	6	5.7	6
Salt	3.5	10	3.3	7	3.1	9
Newsprint	1.3	12	3.2	8	3.2	8
Barley	1.2	13	3.0	9	2.8	11
Cattle	4.8	5	2.5	10	3.7	7
Coal	4.3	7	2.3	11	2.0	12
Cotton	1.4	11	2.1	12	2.9	10
Cement	3.9	8	1.7	13	1.9	13

is a bulk commodity not requiring particularly good service and is profitable for the railroad because of the long distances involved (450 km average haul).

Sugar has become an important commodity for the railroad as exports have climbed rapidly in the past ten years. It is produced primarily in the Cauca Valley and all exports are through Buenaventura. Domestic refined sugar finds markets northward in Medellin and up to the north coast cities. The tonnage of sugar carried on the railroad has risen from 74,000 tons in 1964 to 217,000 tons in 1969, at which time it constituted 74 million ton-km or approximately 6% of total rail traffic. The average haul was 350 km.

Imports, mainly wheat, have historically played an important role in rail traffic in Colombia. A large percentage of the imports coming through Buenaventura move inland by rail at least as far as Cali, although relatively little continues by railroad past that city. Of the imports entering the country through Santa Marta, almost all move inland by railroad. The Santa Marta import flow is particularly profitable to the railroads because most of it is destined for Medellin and Bogota and thereby provides one of the longest hauls on the railroad system (500 km).

The increase in the highway passenger fleet and the expansion and marked improvements of the national highway network in recent years have been significant factors in the rapid decline of rail passenger traffic. Passenger travel by rail declined from 8.2 million to 2.6 million between 1962 and 1969. The average journey has increased from 70 km to 103 km. Passenger kilometrage also declined substantially, though less severely, from 571 to 273 million passenger-km, in the same period. In 1969 alone, the railway lost one million passengers, the equivalent of 23% of its traffic.

Passenger traffic is offered on all lines of the railroad system, although the journey is generally very short and the revenue does not even cover direct costs of providing the service such as crew salaries, fuel and the repair of equipment. The railways are offering a purely social service, with the possible exception of some express services between Bogota and the Caribbean coast which have increased in popularity in the past few years.

Outlook for Future Traffic

The quality of future rail service will be an important factor in the retention and attraction of traffic. At present, the railway suffers both from natural characteristics related to the country's terrain and from track and rolling stock in very poor condition. It is thought that perhaps 1,500 km of the 3,400 km of main line may be seriously defective. The wheels of much of the rolling stock are in poor condition and responsible for many of the accidents. In 1970 a program was introduced of screening wagons for defects and withdrawing them from service until corrected.

It is highly desirable that the CNR make an inventory of the current condition of track, rolling stock and maintenance facilities. A review of the effects of defective state of repair on the quality of railroad service, on costs of operation and on life of equipment should be used as the basis for a phased program of economically feasible rehabilitation which could be undertaken during the period 1972-76. The study would ensure adequate lead time for arranging financing and placing orders for imported materials.

It is essential that any track rehabilitation take place only on economic lines. The railroad will face increasing competition from the improving highway system. The railroad enjoys a competitive advantage over highway transport on long hauls with easy grades along the Magdalena River Valley from Neiva north to Santa Marta. But this line, to serve main centers of production and consumption, is joined to lines which have to negotiate very severe terrain. Completion of the Buenaventura-Buga highway in 1970 will have a substantial impact on the Pacific division of the railroad. The heaviest traffic on that division is carried between Buenaventura and Cali. When the present narrow, steep, partly unpaved highway is replaced in 1971 by the much more direct and better graded and wider paved highway now under construction, the highway capacity between the Cauca Valley and Buenaventura will be greatly increased and the cost of operating trucks will be reduced markedly. The distance from Buga to Buenaventura will become 121 km compared with 216 km at present. This will certainly confront the railroad with much more severe competition than that which presently exists, although no efforts to forecast the effect seem to have been made. It has been pointed out, however that just over 200 trucks per day could carry all the railway's present traffic, which at 1,800 tons per day utilizes virtually the full capacity of the rail line between Cali and Buenaventura.

The other important impact of the new Buenaventura highway will be to shift some imports and exports presently using the north coast ports to the port of Buenaventura as inland surface transport to and from this port improves. Thus, the Atlantic division of the railroad as well as the Pacific division, may feel some impact from this new highway. Increased sugar production in the Cauca Valley should lead to larger rail shipments of this commodity. If exports increase as they have in the last few years, the potential traffic between Cali and Buenaventura will increase and may compensate for some of the loss of rail traffic expected when the Buga-Buenaventura highway opens.

On the other hand, construction of the San Roque-Las Pavas Highway, which will take place by 1973, may have relatively moderate potential diversion effect on Atlantic rail flow in spite of the substantial improvement that completion of this highway link will make in the eastern and central trunk systems. However, completion of a highway from Medellin to Puerto Berrio, together with a new highway from Puerto Berrio down to Barrancabermeja and Capulco, could have a very serious competitive effect upon the railroad. The authorities are anxious to complete highway improvements along this route and it is desirable that before doing so they should study the implications of improved road and/or rail service from Medellin to Puerto Berrio, Barrancabermeja and Bucaramanga and the costs to the economy of alternative investment decisions.

Much of the railroad system is already paralleled by highways of relatively high design standard. These sections of the railroad should not be seriously affected by future highway improvements, except as long-distance highway trips suddenly become more feasible.

The introduction of the Caldas refined product pipeline may have slightly diminished rail traffic in refined products. No other pipeline construction is anticipated in the area of the country served by the railroads, so the remaining gasoline and kerosene traffic is not likely to be seriously affected.

Uneconomic Lines

Following earlier arrangements with the World Bank, the government engaged consultants (SOFRERAIL) to study uneconomic lines. Their 1969 draft report recommended closure of the following lines:

Armenia	-	Pereira (60km)
Guacheta	-	Barbosa (100 km approx.)
Palmira	-	Pradera (14 km)
Manizales	-	Mariquita (72 km)

Traffic on Manizales-Mariquita has in fact been suppressed for some years. Palmira-Pradera has also been closed. By closing the Armenia-Pereira line, the CNR would save about Col$1.5 million per annum and would in addition be able to recover some capital from the sale of the line, buildings and warehouses in good condition. Suitable highway connections already exist between the two towns. The closure of the line from Guacheta to Barbosa would save about Col$2.4 million per annum. No decision has yet been made on the closure of these two lines.

The study also examined the possibility of reconnecting Manizales to Pereira (78 km). The line was cut in 1959 for eight km north of Pereira. Subsequently, service was withdrawn from Santa Rosa and then Chinchina, and finally the whole line was closed to traffic in September 1968. The consultants felt that the line could be reopened with some major realignment for an investment of some Col$25 million and that it could compete effectively for traffic with the road system between Manizales and Buenaventura. The mission considers however that a far more comprehensive study of the road and rail network in the upper Cauca Valley would be required before such an investment decision was made.

A 1968 study prepared by the Harvard University staff suggested that the Barbosa-Bogota, Cartago-Pereira, Cali-Popayan, and Facatativa-Girardot lines be abandoned because of low traffic. The government in its 1969/72 development plan drew attention to the low traffic, less than 100 tons a day, on the 31 km Bogota-Soacha (El Salto) line, but it has taken no action to close the line, apparently because it provides rail access to some large industries. It appears that, rather than face the political problems of closing these lines outright, the railroads have adopted a policy of progressive neglect, keeping services and expenditures to a minimum. This may well be the least costly solution to the problem. But in instances where passenger traffic has declined to negligible proportions and adequate alternative highway transport already exists, it may be desirable to pursue the rapid abandonment of rail services. On the Bogota-El Salto line, for example, valuable right-of-way is being withheld from alternative use.

Possible Extensions

Frequently over the past ten years, proposals have been made for the construction of extensions to the rail network. The current status of proposals which are made from time to time is given below.

A study of three alternative proposals for an extension from the Magdalena line to Barranquilla and Cartagena was made by consultants in 1965. The proposed routes were:

(a)   *North*—from Cienaga along the coast parallel to the highway on the island of Salamanca to Barranquilla and then to Cartagena.

(b)   *South*—from Algarrobo, 41 km south of Fundacion on the Atlantic line, crossing the Magdalena near Calamar and then branching, one line down the west bank of the Magdalena to Barranquilla and the other going to Cartagena with a crossing of the Canal del Dique.

(c)   *Central*—from Fundacion, crossing the river at Santa Rita. A branch would follow the west bank of the Magdalena to Barranquilla and another would go to Cartagena and Mamonal, via Sabanalarga.

The consultants preferred the Central alternative because it would be 80 km shorter to Cartagena than by the northern alternative and only 17 km longer to Barranquilla. It would require fewer large river crossings and avoid the congested banana traffic between Cienaga and Fundacion. The Southern route would involve much more expenditure and would not be suitable for a connection to Barranquilla.

The forecast of traffic which would be generated by the advent of the railway is out of date and other improvements have been made to highways both on the parallel Medellin-Caribbean coast and Bogota-Caribbean coast routes and on the Bogota-Cali/Buga-Buenaventura route. The CNR is currently preparing an updated traffic forecast. The 1965 study did not make a comprehensive economic analysis of the project. No incremental comparison was made of the yield on the proposed investment resulting from the difference between truck/river and rail *costs*. In fact, the only comparison made in the report is between point to point *prices* by different modes. Average 1965 ton-km CNR revenues multiplied by the projected traffic volumes were used to ascertain whether the yield would cover the investment.

Presently there is substantial excess capacity in the river fleet. Furthermore, the crude oil pipelines have large amounts of unused capacity which could divert oil traffic from the river, leaving even greater excess river capacity. From a capacity standpoint there is no need for the rail extensions for carrying bulk cargoes.

The Harvard Report entitled *An Analysis of Investment Alternatives in the Colombian Transport System* (1968) came to the conclusion that, if any extension was warranted, it was probably a line from Cienaga to the east bank of the Magdalena opposite Barranquilla, but that this should be studied more carefully before any investment decision was made. Recent investigations have led the U.N. industrial consultant to the government to a similar conclusion. It is hoped that the CNR study will when it is completed later this year indicate whether in the light of current traffic prospects there is a case for any extension in the area.

From time to time in the past, the possibility of constructing a line across the central Cordillera from Ibague to Armenia has been raised. At present, rail traffic is transshipped by truck between the two points under contract to the CNR. In 1969, it averaged 116 tons per route km per day, and the justification for the considerable investment involved in tunnelling through the Cordillera would have to be based on calculations of potential diversion of regular truck traffic using this route and of traffic now using other rail routes. The SOFRERAIL study recommended further investigation.

In 1969, a firm of American consultants (Madigan-Hyland de la Cruz, Ltda.) made an engineering study of a proposed new section between Loboguerro and Yumbo on the Cali-Buenaventura line which would maintain a 2% grade and still avoid construction of the tunnel which had been proposed in earlier projects. The line would however have been 26 km longer than the other proposals. The study found that, at present, there was no economic justification for any major engineering work between Cali and Buenaventura.

Railroad Costs and Pricing

In general, rail line-haul operations are characterized by very low unit costs due to the small crew required per ton of cargo and the small number of units required. Efficiency also depends heavily upon the ability to run long distances at relatively constant speeds utilizing a low power to weight ratio. This means, however, that a train which is efficient for operation in level or nearly level conditions will be able to ascend only very slight grades. Therefore, trains must usually be divided into numerous smaller trains at the base of a mountain or additional power must be added to the train. The latter solution is limited by the strength of the couplers or the cars themselves and their tendency to derail or capsize when negotiating sharp turns under heavy drawbar pull. This constraint applies to many of the older cars in Colombia. In addition, the tortuous terrain encountered in the mountains of Colombia creates many sharp turns which cause hazardous conditions for the operation of long heavy trains. Thus, the sections of the system which involve steep gradients and sharp curves would probably require the use of very short trains even with the best of rolling stock. Still shorter trains are now required because the equipment is not in ideal condition.

The division of a train into several smaller ones is essentially a yard operation and therefore adds significant costs to any line-haul movement where it is required. Thus, rail operating costs rise much more rapidly in mountainous territory than do the costs of truck operations because trucks can adapt to steep grades simply by shifting gears, as traction and derailment are no problem for a truck. For example, Harvard found that, even ignoring the greater deterioration of roadbed in mountainous terrain, rail operating costs in the flat areas of the Magdalena Valley were only one-half the magnitude of comparable costs in the mountainous areas.

Railroad transportation usually involves very substantial terminal costs for loading and unloading cargo and also for yard operation, where cars are stored for assembly into trains or trains separated into individual cars for delivery to the consignee. Yard costs are not incurred in trucking operations since a loaded truck can depart directly for its destination without waiting for others. Railroads, therefore, do not begin to reap the benefits of their low-cost line-haul operations until the length of the haul ensures that the fixed terminal and yard costs are offset by line-haul savings.

In 1969, the average revenue per ton-km on the entire Colombian railroad system was 30.2 centavos. The range except for coffee at 22.2 centavos, was between 26.5 centavos and 156.8 centavos. Only 5,000 tons of packages were carried at the latter price. These revenues reflect the railway's short run marginal costs. Truck costs in 1969 were estimated to range from 25 to 60 centavos per ton-km. Although truck costs are lower in flat than in hilly terrain, they are probably somewhat lower than rail in mountainous regions and much higher in the flat regions. However, investment or abandonment decisions should be based on much more disaggregated information than is available from national averages.

Comparison of rail operating costs with those of the river fleet is more difficult because accurate cost figures are simply not available for barge operation. River tariffs have generally been approximately two-thirds the magnitude of rail tariffs on a ton-km basis. This has occurred despite the persistent excess capacity of the river fleet which raises their cost somewhat above the most efficient level.

Prior to 1966, the railroad tariffs had consisted of a fixed part and a variable part. These two tariff components were computed separately for almost every line on the railroad; that is, traffic between Ibague and Facatativa would pay a different fixed portion from that paid for traffic between Barbosa and Bogota in addition to having a different variable charge per ton-km. In addition, there were three classes of commodities: class A, class B, and class C. Finally, there were a number of special rates for commodities which were exempted from these general categories. The special tariffs had their own fixed and variable parts which were different for different lines on the railroads and included such important commodities as fertilizer, combustible goods, cattle, coffee, and bananas.

In 1966, introduction of a new tariff system based on the recommendations of consultants (SOFRERAIL) considerably simplified the rate structure. This reform was designed to help the railroad specialize in longer-haul and bulk traffic and is consistent with the aim of exploiting the natural comparative advantages of rail transport. Under the new system, cargo is classified as either class A or class B. Tariffs are computed using a table entitled "Tarifas Especiales por Cupes Completos y Generales de Cargo y Ganada" which gives the total tariff charged for class A and class B goods for any distance traveled. For cargo which does not fill a complete car, another rate is available based on the percentage of the car which is occupied. A shipper has a choice between paying the class A or class B rate, whichever is applicable to his commodity, or instead paying the percentage occupancy rate which does not depend upon commodity classification. For class B commodities the percentage occupancy rate will be cheaper for a shipper who has less than 75% of a carload. For class A commodities the percentage occupancy rate is cheaper for shippers who have less than 67% of full carload.

The rate given is based on distance but the unit of distance is not a kilometer. Rather it is called "unidad ferrera de liquidacion." These "units" are roughly proportional to distance between points but they have been adjusted to account for competition or costs and other factors thought to be relevant by the railroads. Published tables specify the number of units between each terminal and other stations along the route. Thus, to determine the rate, the shipper simply classifies his cargo as class A or class B. He then decides whether to pay the appropriate class rate or to pay the rate based on percentage occupancy. He then looks up in a table the number of units between the relevant origin and destination and computes the tariff he will have to pay.

In the new rate structure, special rates have been retained for a few selected commodities. Coffee, for example, has a separate rate table independent of the unit concept. As indicated above, this may warrant review. Refined petroleum, kerosene in tank cars and cattle are also charged special rates.

General

Although there are sections of line and quantities of traffic which it would be more economic to dispense with, it is possible to say that in the past few years the policy has been changing in the correct direction. The restructuring of rates and drastic simplification of the tariffs, the rationalization of passenger and less-than-carload freight traffic, the replacement of old rolling stock and the acquisition of additional motive power, together with the rehabilitation program are all highly commendable and have secured for the railways a much greater share of the nation's freight traffic than could otherwise have been secured. The concentration of traffic in large shipments has been particularly successful (Table 19-9) and the reduction of the labor force from 14,900 in 1963 to just over 11,000 in 1969 is impressive.

Table 19-10 gives the summary income accounts for 1962-1969. While operating revenues for 1969 were 15% higher than in 1968 and better than forecast, operating costs have also risen sharply, mainly because wage awards increased labor costs by 10% in 1969, with a further 10% in 1970, so that net operating revenues are less than expected. Interest charges, because of slower disbursement of foreign loans than earlier anticipated, are somewhat lower than forecast, but revenues are still insufficient to cover them. An operating ratio of just under 100 was achieved in 1969 for the second time in the history of the CNR. However, CNR's working capital position

TABLE 19-9: COLOMBIAN NATIONAL RAILROADS DISTRIBUTION OF
RAIL FREIGHT BY SIZE OF SHIPMENT – 1969

Size (kilos)	Revenue Col $'000	%	Kilos millions Car	%	Ton-km millions	%	No. of Ship-ments	%	Kilos per Car	Revenue per ton-km Col $
35.0 and over	124,702.9	35.6	1,105.8	36.2	471.5	40.7	30,971	8.1	35.7	0.265
31.5 - 34.99	56,459.9	16.1	388.5	12.7	200.1	17.3	11,622	3.0	33.4	0.282
28.0 - 31.49	24,854.4	7.1	226.9	7.4	84.1	7.2	7,604	2.0	29.8	0.296
24.5 - 27.99	24,363.8	7.0	222.4	7.3	81.0	7.0	8,670	2.3	25.7	0.301
21.0 - 24.49	24,745.6	7.1	255.0	8.4	80.8	7.0	12,200	2.9	20.9	0.306
17.5 - 20.99	24,673.7	7.0	194.4	6.4	73.9	6.4	10,187	2.7	19.1	0.334
14.0 - 17.49	23,848.5	6.8	262.8	8.6	78.4	6.7	16,086	4.2	16.3	0.304
10.5 - 13.99	9,113.2	2.6	69.7	2.3	25.3	2.2	5,816	1.5	12.0	0.360
7.0 - 10.49	13,505.8	3.9	106.5	3.5	31.0	2.7	11,715	3.0	9.1	0.436
3.5 - 6.99	6,185.9	1.8	38.7	1.3	10.9	0.9	7,641	2.0	5.1	0.569
1.0 - 3.49	7,026.0	2.0	52.0	1.7	10.0	0.9	28,133	7.3	1.8	0.700
.1 - .99	5,922.4	1.7	43.3	1.4	6.7	0.6	128,849	33.5	.3	0.887
.01- .09	1,805.7	0.5	5.2	0.2	1.2	0.1	105,834	27.5	.05	1.568
Sub-total	347,207.9	99.2	2,971.3	97.4	1,154.8	99.7	384,328	100	–	0.301
Bananas	2,724.9	0.8	78.6	2.6	4.0	0.3	–	–	–	0.687
Total	349,932.8	100.0	3,049.9	100	1,158.7	100		100	–	0.302

Source: FCN, *Boletin Anual.*

TABLE 19-10: COLOMBIAN NATIONAL RAILROADS SUMMARY
INCOME ACCOUNTS – 1962-1969

(In millions of Col $)

	1962	1963	1964	1965	1966	1967	1968	1969
Operating revenues								
Freight	119	179	194	180	263	265	311	370
Passenger	22	30	29	29	31	34	35	34
Other	4	6	6	8	11	13	19	16
Total operating revenue	145	215	229	217	305	312	365	420
Operating expenses (excluding depreciation)	161	238	233	247	266	316	345	364
Depreciation	14	24	30	34	36	43	42	53
Total operating expenses	175	262	263	281	302	359	387	417
Net operating revenues (deficits)	(30)	(47)	(34)	(64)	3	(47)	(22)	2
Interest charges	13	22	26	31	29	40	45	53
Net loss	(43)	(69)	(60)	(95)	(26)	(87)	(67)	(50)
Non-operating income (net)	5	21	17	7	13	16	12	31
Net deficiency	(38)	(48)	(43)	(88)	(13)	(71)	(55)	(19)
Operating ratio (%)	121	122	115	129	99	115	106	99

has deteriorated; this was due to lower than expected net earnings and to the failure of government to provide the full amount of local currency funds required for the rehabilitation program. In respect of the latter, there was a net shortfall in 1969 of Col$24 million. The effect of this has been that the railway has had to resort to high interest borrowing from local banks.

While it should be official policy to continue to rationalize the railway's operations in keeping with current and prospective demand for its services, economically justified rehabilitation should not be hampered by shortage of local funds at a time when this shortage is not being experienced by other agencies responsible for transport investment. It also becomes difficult for the CNR to function as a commercial enterprise when additional costs, such as the pension increases, are imposed on the corporation.

CHAPTER 20
OTHER TRANSPORT AND TELECOMMUNICATIONS

Inland Waterways

The Magdalena River provides an important complement to the highway, railway and pipelines for transportation of goods between the Atlantic coast and the interior. The river is navigable from its mouth near Barranquilla about 930 km southward to the Honda rapids. Depths in the river limit operations to vessels of about five feet in the lower reaches up to Gamarra (473 km upstream) and it becomes progressively more difficult to navigate further upstream, with limitations on drafts to as little as three feet during periods of low water and restrictions on night operations.

The port of Cartagena is connected with the river at Calamar, 91 km from Barranquilla, by the Canal del Dique, which has a controlling depth of about seven feet. Typical river operations consist of a tugboat pushing several barges, with an average capacity of about 350 tons each.

Total traffic on the river has exhibited a steady growth of about 5% per year over the last decade and in 1968 amounted to 1.3 billion ton-km, of which almost 1.0 billion consisted of petroleum traffic. Since 1964 general cargo traffic has declined from 430 million ton-km to 350 million ton-km in 1968, while petroleum traffic increased from 700 million ton-kms to about 970 million ton-km over the same period. Petroleum traffic consists mainly of crude oil shipments from Barrancabermeja down to a refinery at Cartagena. General cargo traffic is about 2/3 upstream and 1/3 downstream. The average haul of cargo transported on the river is about 500 km, with an average of 580 km for general cargo and 470 km for petroleum.

Crude oil is also moved to the refinery at Cartagena by pipeline. In 1968 this pipeline carried about three times as much crude as the river. The pipeline and the river barge fleet have a combined capacity far in excess of the present crude oil traffic. The tariffs for moving crude by pipeline and river transport are regulated by the government in a complicated manner, resulting in practice in similar prices for transport by either mode and an apportionment of the traffic over the two modes. Crude oil traffic from Barrancabermeja to Cartagena is not expected to rise in the near future and no investments in either river fleet or pipelines are contemplated. It is not clear why it would not be more economical to use the pipeline to its capacity and move the remainder of the crude, if any, by river. The incremental cost of moving additional oil via a pipeline not used to capacity would presumably be much lower than transport by the river.

For certain cargoes, especially bulk cargo, the river will continue to be the most economical means of transport. This requires that the navigability of the river and the Canal del Dique is maintained, river ports have sufficient capacity and are adequately equipped and the river fleet itself is efficiently operated.

Before embarking on an investment program in port facilities and river works, the government intends to undertake a comprehensive study of the prospects for river transport in the context of other modes which compete with or supplement the waterways. The objective should be to bring about an efficient integrated transport system.

Air Services

In 1968, significant changes were made in the management of civil aviation in the public sector in Colombia and it is still too soon to assess the full impact of these changes. The Department of Civil Aviation commissioned a comprehensive study by consultants[1] to review the aviation needs of the country and to prepare an investment program. This study has been completed and presented to the Department which will use it to develop a national Aviation Plan. Much of the material used and presented hereunder was obtained from the consultants' study.

---

1. *National Airports Plan,* Cia. de Estudios y Interventorias, Restrepo y Uribe Ltda; and R. Dixon Speas Associates, February 1970.

Passenger Traffic

In contrast to the trend in most countries, Colombia's domestic passenger traffic declined in several of the recent years. The statistics relating to passenger traffic in Colombia show several trends: good growth in passenger-km (8.5% per annum 1956-68), substantial increases in average trip length, and little growth in numbers of passengers (4% per annum 1956-68 but static for the last five years of this period).

The development of total domestic passengers and passenger-km has been affected by the development or improvement of alternative travel modes; air fare changes; air service changes; and general economic factors.

Improved highways have had a significant impact on air traffic. In 1964, before the road between Bogota and Neiva was opened, air traffic had dropped to 49,000 passenger trips. Demand for air traffic at Popayan was significantly affected by the new highway from Cali. In 1966, the total passengers at Popayan were 21,000 while in 1968, after completion of the highway, the number dropped to 3,500. It is now recognized that the recent investment in an airport at Popayan was the result of inadequate planning and forecasting.

Air Cargo

The rate of growth of air cargo traffic has been moderate (see Table 20-2); service has been inadequate and unreliable.

The fluctuations in air cargo traffic flow are a problem in Colombia and may account for some of the apparent lack of interest of the carriers in air cargo. However, such fluctuations are not peculiar to Colombia. Although there has been a decline in actual terms of air cargo carried, the number of ton-km has increased slightly. This reflects the longer average haul. In addition, the domestic portion of traffic has been declining and the international portion has been increasing. The consultants believe that only if a vigorous marketing effort were made would the current growth rates be exceeded.

TABLE 20-1: AIR PASSENGER DEMAND

Year	Number of Enplaned Passengers ('000)	Number of Passenger-Kilometers ('000)	Average Kilometers per Trip
1956	1,389	562,490	405
1957	1,490	615,163	413
1958	1,436	631,821	440
1959	1,484	680,591	459
1960	1,515	745,265	492
1961	1,685	822,749	488
1962	2,074	993,442	479
1963	2,316	1,219,727	527
1964	2,571	1,343,747	523
1965	2,519	1,336,903	531
1966	2,511	1,429,772	569
1967	2,432	1,525,699	627
1968	2,462	1,610,846	654

TABLE 20-2: GROWTH OF AIR CARGO, 1953-68

Year 1953-1968	Thousands of Ton-Kilometers		
	Domestic	International	Total
1953	59,135		59,135
1954	64,469		64,469
1955	61,222		61,222
1956	63,349		63,349
1957	56,269		56,269
1958	51,614		51,614
1959	52,751		52,751
1960	39,748	5,301	45,049
1961	41,279	6,867	48,146
1962	45,931	7,620	53,551
1963	56,602	10,496	67,098
1964	56,513	14,181	70,094
1965	47,552	16,307	63,859
1966	54,060	20,114	74,174
1967	49,185	19,497	68,682
1968	48,625	23,349	71,974
Average Compound Growth rate 1960-68	2.5%	18.5%	7.3%

Long-Range Aviation Needs

There should be a strong market for aviation services in Colombia. The size of the country, the nature of the terrain and the improved services provided, all contribute to the demand for modern air services, both in the high density routes and in the remote areas of the country. The greatest long-range needs for aviation are good technical planning of services and facilities, a sound plan of investment, an accurate and comprehensive statistical data base and realistic forecasting of demand.

The consultants have forecast that domestic passenger traffic will increase by 4.5% per annum and international passenger traffic will increase by 14% per annum. Revenue passenger kilometers (RPK) will increase from 1,700,000 in 1968 to 3,500,000 in 1978. Cargo traffic also, will increase but the most significant increase in the air industry will be in general aviation, i.e. in activities other than scheduled carrier work.

Major improvements are recommended for Bogota, Barranquilla, Medellin and Cartagena airports. Lesser improvements are recommended for 27 airports, and it is recommended that some airports be operated on a reduced scale and some abandoned. Improvements in navigational aids are recommended, including: the installation of 20 additional Very High Frequency Omni-Directional Ranges; radar systems at Bogota, Barranquilla, Cali, Medellin and Bucaramanga; Instrument Landing Systems at Barranquilla, Cali and Bucaramanga.

The financial program recommended by consultants indicates the estimated capital costs for 1970-79 of Col$798 million for airports and Col$175 million for navigational aids. This is less than the existing rate of expenditure. The estimated operating and maintenance costs of the recommended airports system for the same period is Col$415 million. Estimated revenue is Col$921 million. The economic analysis indicates a rate of return of the order of 17%. However, this excludes the acquisition of Pereira airport, the construction of the new Medellin airport and the new parallel runway at Bogota on which insufficient information was available.

Air Services Provided

The percentage of international traffic handled at Colombian airports, although relatively small, is very significant as it is concentrated at only five airports; it accounts for nearly all of the larger jet operations at Colombian airports and requires special facilities and services.

There are three major and three minor routes within the Americas and to or from Colombia. There is only one major route pattern outside the Americas; the middle Atlantic route to Europe, with flights offered by five carriers under a pool arrangement. All such flights originate in or pass through Bogota. There is no air service from Colombia to Asia or Africa.

Domestic Routes

Nearly all the intra-regional services are provided by piston engine aircraft ranging from single engine Beavers to DC4's. There are no jet or turboprop intra-regional operations except for flights between Cartagena, Barranquilla and Santa Marta.

The inter-regional routes can be designated as *trunk* routes in contrast to the intra-regional *feeder* routes. Inter-regional non-stop services are limited in number. Nearly all of the city pairs are made up of major Colombian centers, and nearly all services are operated by the national carrier, AVIANCA, two of its subsidiaries SAM and Aerotaxi, or the third trunk carrier, Aerocondor. The services out of Villavicencio show this town's importance not only as the intra-regional Llanos center, but also as the focus of all longer routes to fringe settlements at Leticia, Inirida, and in the Yari. Many linkages exist between the Antioquia region (Cauca North) and both the Atlantic Coast (Costa) and Santander. Bogota is included in more inter-regional city pairs (20) than any other city; Medellin is second with 12. San Andres has linkages with diverse areas of the country, which is an indication of its unique status in the Colombian interaction pattern.

The National Airports System

Air activity in Colombia is performed in a relatively extensive airports system. There are 685 airports registered with the Civil Aeronautics Department. However, the majority (520) are in flat terrain, generally with grass surface, for operation—almost exclusively in the dry season—of single-engine private aircraft or single-engine aircraft for spraying crops. These landing strips are mainly situated in flat zones, such as the Llanos Orientales (Eastern Plains) and the Valle del Rio Magdalena (Magdalena River Valley). They are generally owned by private individuals or by the municipalities in which they are located.

Of the remaining 165 airports, 70 are owned by the Fondo Aeronautico Nacional (FAN), 5 are military and the rest are privately owned or belong to a municipality. Among the most important privately owned is the present Cali Airport (Calipuerto). The airport of Pereira, which is also one of the main commercial airports in the country, belongs to the city of Pereira.

The main airports of the country are those which at present have runways for jet operation, domestic or international. The ten major commercial airports, listed in rank order by activity, are as follows: Bogota; Medellin; Cali; Barranquilla; Cucuta; Bucaramanga; Cartagena; San Andres; Pereira and Santa Marta. Of the preceding airports, Bogota, Barranquilla, Cali, Medellin and San Andres have regular international flights of foreign and domestic airlines. Cartagena has regular international flights of only domestic airlines. The ten airports listed above account for 80% of the country's air activity, based on the total enplaned and deplaned passengers at each airport. Bogota, the center of activity in Colombia, accounts for 28% of total domestic passengers and for 70% of international passengers.

At present, the Civil Aeronautics Administrative Department through the Fondo Aeronautico Nacional is constructing three new airports at Cali, Bucaramanga and Ocana and is improving seven additional airports at Cartagena, San Andres, Pasto, Corozal, Mangangue,

MAP 20-I

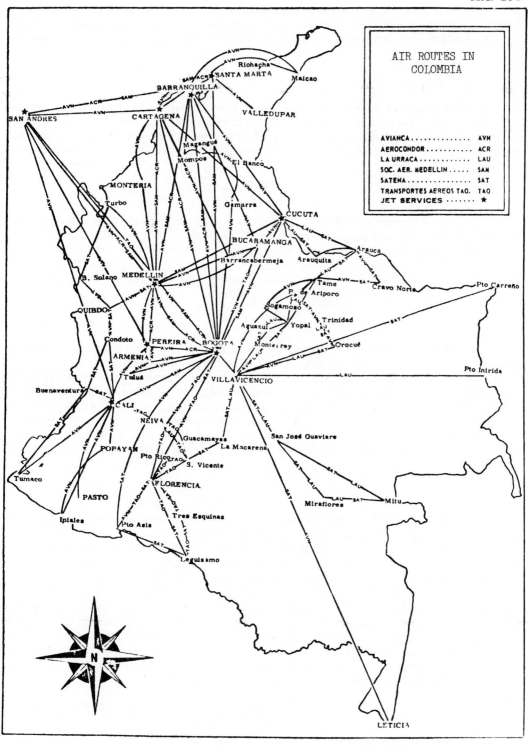

AIR ROUTES IN
COLOMBIA

AVIANCA.............. AVN
AEROCONDOR.......... ACR
LA URRACA............ LAU
SOC. AER. MEDELLIN..... SAM
SATENA.............. SAT
TRANSPORTES AEREOS TAO. TAO
JET SERVICES ...... ★

Tumaco and Guapi. In the airways system, improved navigation coverage is required. This will most likely be done by expanding the existing system which uses Very High Frequency Omni Directional Ranges (VOR's). The consultants have recommended that radar coverage and ILS systems should be provided in the terminal areas of Bogota, Barranquilla, Cali and Bucaramanga.

Pricing, Tariffs and User Charges

The present level of domestic aviation fares is low compared with international fares in Central and South America. In the past, the domestic operations were subsidized by the international operations. With the relatively high load factors on the domestic jet routes, this is now coming more into balance and AVIANCA believe that each part of their system is viable.

Ports

The principal seaports of Colombia are Cartagena, Barranquilla and Santa Marta on the Atlantic or north coast, and Buenaventura on the Pacific coast. These ports, as well as the much smaller Pacific coast port of Tumaco, are administered by a national port authority, Empresa Puertos de Colombia, a semi-autonomous agency of the National Government. The Port Authority is financially independent of the National Government; port charges are designed and periodically adjusted to cover the cost of port operations.

Port Charges

The tariff of port charges applies uniformly to all five ports administered by the Port Authority. Port charges in the aggregate cover the overall cost of the Port Authority's operations, but specific charges are not directly related to the cost of rendering the service. Charges for the handling of imported cargo are significantly higher than those for the handling of exports. In fixing charges no distinction is made between the costs of handling different types of goods and the same charge per ton applies to solid bulk, liquid bulk or general cargo. It would seem desirable to revise this policy and bring charges more in line with actual handling costs. Average cargo-handling costs to the shipper are of the order of US$10.80 per ton for imports and US$3.15 for exports.

Port Capacity

The capacity of a port is usually expressed as the number of metric tons of cargo that can be handled annually. Port capacity depends not only on the physical facilities provided but on many other factors such as the type of cargo (liquid bulk, solid bulk, uniform or miscellaneous), the regularity of vessel calls and the number of tons transferred per call, working hours, efficiency of operations, etc. Considering that the four principal Colombian ports are general-cargo terminals which handle a mixture of uniform bagged or baled cargo (about 30%), miscellaneous cargo (about 50%), and solid bulk cargo (about 20%), and have a reasonably steady flow of cargo throughout the year, the number of berths at each port can be used as a rough measure of their capacity. The 1968 Harvard Transport Study made an evaluation of "effective" port capacities on the basis of port facilities in place in 1967 and actual tonnages handled using a somewhat arbitrary, but not unreasonable, assumed berth occupancy factor of 70%, with the following results:

Port	Capacity (tons per year)	No. of Berths (1967)
Pacific: Buenaventura	1,300,000	8
Atlantic: Cartagena	430,000	4
Barranquilla	560,000	4
Santa Marta	600,000	3
Total Atlantic	1,590,000	

On the basis of tons per berth per year, the figures indicate a capacity range from just over 100,000 tons per berth in Cartagena to approximately 160,000 tons per berth in Buenaventura and 200,000 in Santa Marta with Barranquilla at about 140,000 tons per berth. The range of these figures reasonably reflects and is consistent with known conditions at the ports. The capacity of Buenaventura and Santa Marta (the only ports with direct rail access to the interior) is favorably influenced by the fact that they handle most of the country's dry bulk cargo. In addition, one of Santa Marta's berths has a length of 240 m and can accommodate two small vessels. On the other hand, Cartagena's capacity is adversely affected by the operationally awkward configuration of its port facilities. In contrast to the marginal wharves at the other ports which make possible an efficient use of berthing space, Cartagena has four berths alongside two finger piers, which afford no flexibility in berthing. In addition, these berths have the disadvantage of very limited working space and are at a considerable distance from cargo storage areas.

Since 1967, the year on which these capacity estimates were based, improvements and expansion of port facilities have taken place and more are under way or planned. The number of berths now available in the ports and the number expected to be available by 1973 on completion of present expansion plans, are as follows:

Port	No. of Berths Available		
	1967	1970	1973
Buenaventura	8	13	13
Cartagena	4	4	5
Barranquilla	4	4	5
Santa Marta	3	4	5
Total	19	25	28

Substantial improvements of the transit storage and cargo handling areas and facilities are under way and planned, particularly in the north coast ports. An average capacity figure of 150,000 tons per berth per year would be reasonable as a measure of the overall capacity of the Colombian ports in 1973. The capacity per berth in Cartagena would probably fall considerably below this (probably in the order of 120,000 tons) but other ports would probably exceed it, particularly Santa Marta and Buenaventura, once efficient bulk handling facilities for wheat and sugar, now under construction in these ports, become operational. With 15 berths at the north coast and 13 at Buenaventura, Colombia should be able to handle more than 2,000,000 tons per year at each coast.

Port Operations

The capacity of the ports depends on the efficiency of port operations. The capacity figures computed in the Harvard Study are based on observed handling rates in the ports and therefore reflect the actual level of efficiency. A higher level of efficiency in the Colombian ports can be achieved by providing better transit storage and cargo handling facilities and by improving cargo handling operations. The current and proposed investment programs focus primarily on providing the transit storage and cargo handling facilities necessary to keep the cargo handling capacity between vessel and berth in balance with that between berth and inland transport system. With one relatively minor exception, the investment program is properly conceived to achieve this purpose. Substantial improvement, however, can be achieved in the operation of the facilities. Such operational improvements should reduce both vessel and truck or railcar turnaround time and reduce the time cargo remains in storage in the port. This is an important issue calling for urgent study.

Traffic

Practically all of Colombia's foreign trade moves through its ocean ports on the Atlantic and Pacific coasts. The four principal seaports administered by the National Port Authority together moved about 2.4 million metric tons of general cargo in 1969, of which one million tons were exports. In addition, petroleum, bananas, cement, and timber are exported through other port facilities.

About 52% of the 2.4 million tons moved via the Pacific coast port of Buenaventura and the remainder via the three North coast ports. Buenaventura accounted for about two-thirds of the total exports and about 40% of the total imports through the four ports. The distribution of import and export traffic over the four ports, for 1960 and 1969, is set out in Tables 20-3 and 20-4.

Since 1960 total traffic has increased by some 50%. Exports grew by some 125% and imports by about 28%. North coast traffic has grown faster than traffic through Buenaventura (by 62% and 41% respectively over the period). The north coast's share of both imports and exports has increased, but the increase in its share of exports has been particularly significant, growing from 22% to 32% of the total. Its share of imports grew from 53% to 59% over the same period. The biggest factor in this shift has been the completion of the connection of the Atlantic Railroad to the port of Santa Marta in 1962. Before that time, virtually the only traffic through Santa Marta consisted of banana exports via a special banana wharf.

These shifts of traffic between the four ports are possible because important parts of the

TABLE 20-3: PORT TRAFFIC, TONNAGES

(in thousands of metric tons)

	1960			1969		
	Imports	Exports	Total	Imports	Exports	Total
Buenaventura	539	333	872	575	655	1,230
Cartagena	302	56	358	168	85	253
Barranquilla	296	39	355	326	98	424
Santa Marta	16	—[1]	16	341	132[1]	473
Total	1,153	428	1,581	1,410	970	2,380

[1] Excluding bananas handled by a special facility.

TABLE 20-4: PORT TRAFFIC, PERCENTAGE COMPOSITION

	Imports				Exports				Total			
	1960 '000 tons	%	1969 '000 tons	%	1960 '000 tons	%	1969 '000 tons	%	1960 '000 tons	%	1969 '000 tons	%
Buenaventura	539	47	575	41	333	78	655	68	872	55	1,230	52
North Coast	614	53	835	59	95	22	315	32	709	45	1,150	48
	1,153		1,410		428		970		1,581		2,380	
		(100)		(100)		(100)		(100)		(100)		(100)

hinterland such as the Medellin and Bogota areas are served by all four ports. It is considered that the effect of the construction of the Atlantic Railroad on this pattern has by now fully developed and that no further shift of traffic to the Atlantic coast will take place because of it. Improvements in road connections such as Cartagena-Medellin and Buenaventura-Medellin-Bogota may affect future traffic distribution.

Investment Program

The Port Authority proposes to spend Col$325 million over the period 1971-73 for port works and equipment as follows:

	1971	1972	1973
Port Works	95.0	82.0	68.0
Equipment	80.0	–	–

Of the total about Col$170 million is to be spent for civil works at the Atlantic coast ports and Col$75 million for works at Buenaventura. The remainder of Col$80 million is allocated for equipment, the largest item (Col$65 million) being for new dredging equipment for Buenaventura.

Although the economic evaluation presented by the consultants in support of the program does not constitute a full justification, the mission believes that the program is basically sound and that a convincing economic case could probably be made. The only doubtful investment is that for a new passenger vessel berth in Cartagena to serve cruise ships. The mission feels that if such a berth is to be constructed, it should be designed with shore facilities that will serve general cargo as well as passenger vessels to make the best use of the berth. This can be accomplished by the construction of a cargo transit shed which incorporates passenger facilities. The passenger facilities can be designed to keep passenger movement completely separate from the cargo handling operations.

IDEMA is constructing bulk grain silos, including ship loading and unloading facilities in Santa Marta and Buenaventura. These installations should considerably increase the capacity of the two ports.

Telecommunications

Present Facilities

The number of automatic telephone lines in Colombia has about doubled—from 270,000 in 1960 to 560,000 in 1969. All but 17,200 lines are automatic; i.e. they do not require an operator when local calls are placed. The telephone density in the country has increased from 1.75 in 1960 to about 2.75 telephones per hundred population in 1969. This compares with approximate figures of 4.2 for Panama, 3.8 for Venezuela, and a range of 30 to 54 for the developed countries.

Automatic telephone services are available in 109 cities and towns. In an additional 360 towns there are a total of 17,200 manual lines. Table 20-5 gives an approximate classification of the population centers with telephone services. It shows that only about half of Colombia's approximately 21 million people live in areas with telephone services. There are about 19 areas with populations greater than 20,000 that have no local telephone service. Less than half of the towns between 10,000 and 20,000 population and very few of the remaining 775 centers have

TABLE 20-5: DISTRIBUTION OF TELEPHONE SERVICES ACCORDING TO POPULATION

Centers in Population Range	Total Population (million)	Number of Centers	Number with Telephones
Greater than 20,000	9.5	79	60
10,000 - 20,000	1	62	27
5,000 - 10,000	1	136	12
100 - 5,000	1.5	639	10
Rural	8	–	–
Total	21	916	109

Source: Population estimates by government Census Department.

local service; in these areas there are only a long-distance office, a telegraph office, and a small number of manual lines. Some commercial enterprises, however, maintain private radio systems with circuits to the nearest telephone exchange. For example, in the area around Barrancabermeja in the northeast corner of Antioquia and Santander Departments, 25 private companies, mostly in the petrochemical industry, are licensed by the Ministry of Communications to operate 250 circuits to Bogota because local services are insufficient.

Local Telephone Services.   Data on local services are detailed in Tables 20-6 and 20-7, which list the 61 entities and give data on telephone density and exchange size in the 109 centers they serve. These 61 entities have been licensed by the government to provide local services; they include TELECOM (Empresa Nacional de Telecomunicaciones) whose main operations are international and national long-distance telephone, telegraph and telex services. In some of the larger cities such as Bogota (190,000 lines at present) and Barranquilla (30,500 lines), the municipality has created a separate telephone entity to administer and operate the local telephone service, whereas in the smaller cities and towns the telephone service is often operated in conjunction with such other public services as water supply and electric power. The eight largest entities, ranging from Bogota to Cartagena (9,000 lines), are large enough to be financially viable and are providing good service at reasonable tariffs. The same can be said for TELECOM's local telephone services—5,400 automatic lines in 12 towns and another 6,009 lines of manual exchanges in some 210 small localities throughout the country. However, about half of the 61 entities, each of which operates 1,000 lines or less, are in financial and technical difficulties because of the small scale of their operations.

Table 20-8 lists the local telephone tariffs of 14 cities and the TELECOM tariffs that apply to its automatic exchanges. Without a detailed study it is difficult to comment on the adequacy

TABLE 20-6: AUTOMATIC EXCHANGES, LOCAL TELEPHONE SERVICE

Name of Entity	Number of Lines (as of December 1968)
Empresa de Telefonos de Bogota	185,000
Empresas Publicas de Medellin	112,600
Empresas Municipales de Cali	54,800
Empresa Municipal de Telefonos - Barranquilla	30,500
Empresa Municipal de Telefonos - B/manga	15,600
Empresas Publicas de Manizales	15,400
Empresas Publicas de Pereira	11,050
Compania Telefonica de Cartagena S.A.	9,000
Empresa de Telefonos Dptales. N/Santander	6,800
Empresas Publicas Municipales - Palmira	6,250
Empresas Publicas de Armenia	6,000
Empresa Departamental de Telefonos Boyaca	5,800
Empresas Publicas Municipales de Ibague	5,000
Telefonica Municipal de Santa Marta	5,000
Empresa Nacional de Telecommunicaciones	4,600
Compania Telefonica del Huila S.A.	4,000
Empresas Municipales de Cartago	3,900
Empresas Municipales de Girardot	3,600
Empresa Dptal. de Telefonos de Narino	2,800
Telefonica Municipal de Popayan	2,800
Empresa Municipal de Telefonos B/bermeja	2,100
Empresas Municipales de Buga	2,000
Empresas Municipales de Tulua	2,000
Empresas Departamentales de Antioquia	1,500
Empresas Municipales de Calarca	1,500
Planta Telefonica Departamental - Meta	1,500
Empresa Telefonica de Bolivar	1,200
Empresa Municipal de Telefonos de Armero	1,000
Telefonica Municipal de Caicedonia	1,000
Empresa Telefonica de Fusagasuga	1,000
Empresa Municipal de Telefonos de Ipiales	1,000
Empresa Municipal de Telefonos de Rio Sucio	1,000
Compania Telefonica de San Gil S.A.	1,000
Empresa Municipal de Telefonos del Socorro	1,000
Empresas Publicas Municipales - Sta. Rosa Cabal	980
Telefonica Municipal de Yarumal	980
Empresas Publicas Municipales de Sevilla	900
Telefonica Municipal - Espinal	800
Telefonica Municipal de Zarzal	800
Empresas Publicas Municipales de Honda	700
Empresa Municipal de Telefonos de La Dorada	700
Empresa Telefonica Municipal de Salamina	700
Empresa Municipal de Telefonos - Garzon	600
Planta Telefonica de Valledupar	560
Telefonica Municipal de Aguadas	500
Planta Telefonica de Cionaga	500
Telefonica Municipal de Mariquita	500
Telefonica Municipal de Zipaquira	500
Telefonica Municipal de Jerico	450
Telefonica Municipal de Florencia	420
Telefonica Municipal de Chia	400
Empresa Municipal de Telefonos de Riohacha	400
Telefonica Municipal de Boldanillo	400

Telefonica Municipal de El Cerrito	300
Empresa Municipal de Telefonos de Fundacion	300
Telefonica Municipal de Cajica	200
Telefonica Municipal de Guacari	200
Telefonica Municipal de Tumaco	200
Telefonica Municipal de Urrao	200
Telefonica Municipal de Ginebra	130
Telefonica Municipal de Yotoco	50
Total Lines	522,670
Total Entities	61

In addition, the following manual lines are in service:

Operated by TELECOM	6,009
Operated by departmentals (regional governments)	1,569
	7,578

TABLE 20-7: NUMBER OF CENTERS, LINES PER CENTER, AND POPULATIONS SERVED AT DIFFERENT TELEPHONE DENSITIES,[1] 1969 AND PLANNED FOR 1975

(Number of lines per hundred population)

1969	Over 6.5	5.5-6.5	4.5-5.5	3.5-4.5	2.5-3.5	1.5-2.5	Under 1.5
Number of Centers	5	3	14	15	20	30	22
Populations Served (thousands)	4,042.0	519.5	1,336.6	695.5	1,152.0	623.0	606.9
Planned 1975							
Number of Centers	9	9	11	16	28	25	11
Populations Served (thousands)	6,593.2	1,924.5	575.2	1,424.5	1,431.3	617.0	91.8

(Number of lines per center)

	Over 50,000	10,000 to 50,000	5,000 to 10,000	1,000 to 5,000	500 to 1,000	100 to 500	Under 100
Number of centers 1969	3	4	7	22	23	35	15
Number of centers planned, 1975	3	10	3	38	21	24	10

[1] Number of lines per hundred population.

Source: PLANEACION.

TABLE 20-8: LOCAL TARIFFS IN SELECTED CITIES

(In Col $)

	Present Capacity in Lines	Monthly Rental	Number of Free Calls	Cost per Subscriber Call	Connection Charge	Subscriber Deposit	Capital Contribution
Bogota	190,000	10 - 30	nil.	.10	300	900	500 - 2,400
Medellin	115,600	5 - 30	nil.	.20	300	250	nil.
Cali	64,800	6 - 35	100 - 210	.05	150	500	nil.
Barranquilla	30,500	5 - 30	200	.10	25 - 50	250	nil.
Bucaramanga	15,600	12 - 32	150	.05	150	500	nil.
Manizales	15,500	10 - 30	nil.	.10	300	900	nil.
Pereira	11,050	15 - 28	nil.	.10	300	900	nil.
Cartagena	9,000	10 - 30	nil.	.05	300	900	nil.
Armenia	6,000	10 - 20	nil.	.10	300	900	nil.
Ibague	5,000	15 - 20	150	.05	70	250	nil.
Girardot	5,000	10 - 15	nil.	.10	300	900	nil.
Neiva	4,000	8 - 20	150	.05	100	250	nil.
Pasto	2,800	10 - 20	nil.	.10	300	900	nil.
Honda	700	10 - 15	nil.	.10	300	900	nil.
TELECOM	4,600	25 - 30	nil.	.10	350	800	1,000 - 1,200

Source: PLANEACION.

of tariffs in these local areas. Up to now no such study has been made, although PLANEACION is reviewing these tariffs to propose some reforms of the rate structure and to systematize the method for setting the rates. Some of the special features to be noted in the table are:

Bogota requires a capital contribution from its new subscribers that varies depending on whether they are residential (Col$500) or business (Col$2,400). The amount that residential subscribers are required to pay in Bogota also varies in relation to the value of their homes. TELECOM's tariffs also provide for a capital contribution.

The deposit, which all the cities require, is ostensibly to protect the entities in the event of unpaid bills.

Only five cities provide free calls as part of the rental charges, the numbers are shown in parentheses—Cali (100-210), Barranquilla (200), Bucaramanga (150), Ibague (150) and Neiva (150). (The tendency is to discontinue these free calls.)

Cali and Barranquilla provide good telephone services at very low tariffs. In those cities a rental of about US30 cents per month can bring up to 210 free calls. They are able to provide such good service without subsidies because of their operating efficiency.

As in most countries, developed as well as less developed, the installation of new subscriber lines in Colombia has not kept pace with demand for telephone connections. In Bogota 70,000 applicants await connections, and the average waiting time is four years.

Long Distance Services.   Responsibility for international and national long-distance telephone, telegraph, and telex services lies with TELECOM. Created in 1945, this government-owned public entity began operations two years later with the purchase of Compania Telefonica Central, a government-owned company that provided international and national long-distance services. In 1958, with the end of a concession to an expatriate company (All America Cables C.L.), all international telephone and telegraph services were brought under TELECOM. In 1964, all the national telegraph services together with 3,500 telegraphic staff were placed under TELECOM. TELECOM maintains seven large regional offices to coordinate its long-lines network, and also hundreds of small offices throughout the country to handle its long-distance telephone, telegraph, and telex connections. The head office in Bogota does all the major planning. Development programs have been financed by an IBRD loan, supplier credits, and internal cash generation.

An IBRD loan to TELECOM in 1967 provided for the expansion of national long-distance communications by means of microwave radio links with automatic switching equipment, and the expansion of international links by high-frequency equipment. The loan included equipment for a few local telephone exchanges (4,500 lines). An Earth Satellite Station, financed by supplier credits, was completed in March 1970, making for quick and high-quality international connections. Subscriber trunk-dialing (STD) is available in Colombia, although many subscribers prefer to place their calls manually through the operator because the periodic pulse-metering system does not provide details of the long-distance calls.

Future Expansion Plans

Local Services.   As part of their ongoing operations the larger entities such as Bogota (ETB), Medellin, and TELECOM have been drawing up plans for expanding local telephone services. Figures compiled by PLANEACION show that from each entity's expansion plan the total number of automatic telephone lines in Colombia is projected to increase from the present 556,000 to 988,000—a growth of 78% over the next five years. A few known features with respect to financing are:

(a)   Bogota (ETB) has recently placed a contract for 92,000 new lines to be installed over the next three years. ETB now has 190,000 lines and by 1975 expects to have 375,000. This expansion will be financed out of supplier credits and internal cash generation.
(b)   EMCALI expects to increase the number of lines from the present 64,800 to 116,200 by 1975, with financing provided by supplier credits.
(c)   TELECOM has applied to IBRD for a second loan, about a third of which would be for installing over the 1971-74 period some 270 local exchanges with a total capacity of 30,000 lines in various parts of the country.
(d)   Corporacion Autonoma Regional de la Sabana de Bogota (CAR) will be installing over the 1971-73 period about 40 exchanges, with a capacity of about 8,000 lines, in the Bogota Plain area. There already are 2,500 lines in operation in that area. CAR's development program is proposed to be financed out of supplier credits.

Long Distance Services.   TELECOM has applied for a second IBRD loan to cover the foreign exchange costs of additional long-distance channeling and switching equipment, toll-ticketing equipment and television links, besides the equipment for local exchanges mentioned above. The additional circuits will relieve the present congestion and thus enable TELECOM to provide good long-distance telephone service to its subscribers for the next five years. Toll-ticketing equipment is being installed in Barranquilla under the first loan and would be installed under the proposed second loan in nine other cities. This will overcome the billing problems and thereby encourage more subscribers to use the subscriber trunk-dialing (STD).

Reorganization of the Service

The major problem to be dealt with in Colombia's telecommunications is fragmentation. The proliferation of small telephone entities makes for duplication of planning efforts, and complicates the technical integration and interconnection of the sector. The smaller entities are not financially viable, nor are they able to employ experienced engineers to do their planning since most of the engineers are working in the large entities. It is most important that the technical skills needed in planning and developing the service should be available to all the entities regardless of size.

Another major weakness is that there is no clearly defined decision as to who is responsible for undertaking the development of services to the unserved areas. At present TELECOM is the only entity whose license permits it to develop those areas throughout the country. In the 1971-75 period TELECOM proposes to extend local telephone services amounting to 270 exchanges with a capacity of 30,000 lines. Some of these exchanges will be for sizable towns; 19 have more than 20,000 population with no local telephone service.

What kind of structure is necessary in Colombia's telecommunications service—one national entity, a few regional entities, or continued operation by some 60 entities? In most other countries there is a single national entity that operates all local and long-distance telephone services. This is because of the administrative, technical, and economic difficulties that are encountered whenever there is such fragmentation as exists in Colombia: non-viable entities and a lack of unified policy and procedures, no economies of scale in bidding and procurement, and substantial technical problems in integrating circuits and switches, made for different systems, into a national network.

Although a single national entity for the whole sector should be the long-term objective for Colombia, several factors inhibiting such reorganization have to be taken into account. For example, the larger and financially viable entities are reluctant to merge with the smaller ones and any form of merger is likely to be resisted since local and regional interests foster the desire to maintain autonomy.

There are two possible approaches to rationalization: TELECOM could grow toward a national monopoly in telecommunications by installing new exchanges in the unserved areas, and by absorbing those small entities that are in financial difficulties and are amenable to the idea of merging with others. Larger entities such as the ETB may remain independent or may merge later if they agree; about eight of the largest centers could expand progressively by developing unserved areas and absorbing the entities around them, until eventually the country is practically covered by eight regional authorities.

Evolution of the sector in the next ten years will probably follow both lines. In the short run, the important aspect of reorganization is not that there should be only one national entity, but that the entities should be large enough to be technically and financially viable.

The Ministry of Communications and PLANEACION are making studies to determine what structural changes could be made. PLANEACION has been working on a study to come up with proposals and procedures for merging the small local telephone entities. The Urban and Regional Development Division of PLANEACION proposed eight regional authorities.[2] Similarly, the Communications Division has been studying the possibility of establishing metropolitan areas first and regional areas later. For the short term, PLANEACION has been studying a proposal to set up a National Development Fund for local telephone entities, which would channel funds to the small entities and plan and control their expansion. The objectives are to improve national and regional planning, to facilitate investment where necessary and to avoid unnecessary investment.

It is desirable and urgent that the 52 entities which now have 80,000 lines, outside of the eight largest entities and TELECOM, be merged at an early date. This would not be difficult

2. PLANEACION—"Planes y Programas de Desarrolo, 1969-72."

from the technical or financial point of view. Estimated value of the total assets of the 52 entities is US$32 million, and appropriate compensation could be paid to them. With the expansion of TELECOM's operations to cover additional areas and with the expansion of the metropolitan areas around the big cities, the sector fragmentation will tend to become less of a problem within a few years. But it is essential that all future action be directed toward achieving a reasonable degree of consolidation, leading in the long run to a single national entity serving all of Colombia.

CHAPTER 21
TOURISM

Colombia's Caribbean and Other Assets

Tourist Assets for Short-Term Development

Colombia is a Caribbean, a Pacific and a South American country.[1] At present, international tourists visit Colombia and almost exclusively Bogota, as one stop of perhaps three nights duration, on a South American package tour. Buenaventura on the Pacific coast is a port of call of a few hours by cruise ships but the beaches south of this port are barren of tourist facilities and are difficult to reach; therefore their potential must remain for medium-term to long-term development. Colombia's main tourism potential for development in the short-term is its 1,000 miles of Caribbean coast from Venezuela in the east to Panama in the west. Tourist assets are centered in Cartagena and Santa Marta and include the Colombian islands of San Andres and Providencia in the Caribbean sea off the coast of Nicaragua. The area most feasible for short-term development is specifically then from southwest of Riohacha (between Santa Marta and the Venezuelan border) to southwest of Cartagena, (including the nearby islands: Islas del Rosario and Baru) and the island of San Andres.

The delimitation of this area does not exhaust the medium-term or long-term tourist assets with development potential along this coast or in the rest of Colombia.[2] To the west, land surveys will identify those beaches from the Cartagena area to the Panamanian border with development potential. To the east, the coast from Buritica to Riohacha is reported to have potential for beach tourism. Discussions have already been held in Colombia under UNDP auspices, about the possibilities of a regional development plan for the peninsula of La Guajira, north of Riohacha, which is bisected by the Troncal del Caribe (the international highway that will connect Santa Marta with Maracaibo in Venezuela). The construction of tourist facilities would be feasible in La Guajira within an overall development plan that provided basic infrastructure and particularly water supply. These areas however, should be considered for medium-term to long-term development. The Caribbean island of San Andres, Santa Marta and Cartagena are presently the established destinations for domestic tourism and—with Bogota—for incipient international tourism.

The Caribbean Coast

The Colombian north coast shares the Caribbean area characteristics of average temperatures between 75° and 83° and warm water temperatures. Trade winds—the "never failing air conditioner"—keep the coastal temperatures within reasonable bounds even in summer. The intermittent rainy season is over the period April-November, but rain is not constant and in Santa Marta particularly, falls for one to two hours mainly at night. Table 21-1 shows average temperatures and average rainfall in these areas. As in other Caribbean resorts, deep sea fishing, water-skiing, skin diving, sailing, boating and all other water sports are practiced. The Colombian coast shares with its neighbors the advantage of easy accessibility from the U.S. tourist supplier market and its two-hours' flying time from Miami brings it closer even than Curacao or Barbados. The new group fares recently introduced now make Colombia competitive in air fares with its Caribbean neighbors (see the next section). In terms of tourist supplier markets, the proximity of high-income Venezuela, is an additional asset. Most importantly, as part of the Caribbean tourist market, the Colombian north coast has the comparative advantage of price relative to the rest of the area, as is shown in Table 21-2. Colombia's present price structure makes feasible a holiday in a Caribbean atmosphere at from half to two-thirds the cost elsewhere in the area in season.

The definition of Colombia as a Caribbean tourist country, though automatic in the better

---

1. See Map 21-I in the Map Annex.
2. See Map 21-II in the Map Annex.

349

TABLE 21-1: ALTITUDE, AVERAGE TEMPERATURES AND RAINFALL, SELECTED CENTERS

	Altitude Above Sea Level		Average Temperature Degrees		Average Annual Rainfall	
	Meters	Feet	Centigrade	Fahrenheit	m.m.	Inches
Barranquilla	4	13	28	82	808	31
Santa Marta	4	13	29	83	573	23
Cartagena	5	16	28	82	881	35
San Andres	5	16	29	83	n.a.	n.a.
Bogota	2,630	8,629	14	57	1,013	40
Cali	1,003	3,291	25	77	1,153	45
Medellin	1,474	4,836	21	70	1,440	57
Cucuta	215	705	28	82	763	30

Note: Appendix 6 of the recent Tourism Report for Venezuela shows average rainfall in Maiqueta, Venezuela at 24.4 inches; in Willemstad, Curacao at 23.1 inches, San Juan, Puerto Rico at 60.8 inches and Port of Spain, Trinidad at 54.5 inches. Average temperatures in fahrenheit are: Maiqueta 81°, Willemstad 82°, San Juan 78°, and Port of Spain 78°.

Source: Corporacion Nacional de Turismo.

guide books to the area,[3] surprises even Colombians who are used to considering themselves a South American country. Yet Colombia's natural assets are comparable to those of its established Caribbean neighbors. Land use surveys are only at the planning stage for the coastal area with the exception of the Parque Tayrona east of Santa Marta. However mission estimates of the total beach mileage, along that part of the coast identified for short-term development, suggest that Cartagena has some 12 miles in the immediate vicinity, plus the beaches on the cluster of small coral reef islands, the Islas del Rosario, southwest of the city which can be reached in about one hour by launch. Santa Marta, called the "Pearl of the Americas", because of the half-moon bay on which the city fronts, has some 12 miles of beaches to the west; within the national park to the east, beach inlets of some 7 miles in length; and further east still, some 12 miles facing the open sea to Riohacha. Imposingly poised above these tropical beaches in the Santa Marta area, is the Sierra Nevada mountain range which culminates at 19,000 feet in snow capped peaks, below which river streams meet the sea. The availability of some 45 miles of beaches becomes a serious development possibility when the surprising comparison is made with Barbados whose total coastal perimeter is only 55 miles. The famous "platinum coast" from Speightstown to Bridgetown in Barbados is a mere 14 miles long, so that the beach area is considerably less; and the Montego Bay area in Jamaica extends for no more than 20 miles.

The Caribbean Islands

At some one hour's distance north by jet, off the coast of Nicaragua, are the Colombian islands of San Andres and Providencia, which were discovered by Christopher Colombus on his first voyage. Only San Andres has a jet airport and connections with Providencia are poor. Because of the importance of tourism in the economic development of the island, San Andres has been given free port status in order to induce tourist traffic. Colombians must stay five days to benefit from customs clearance for their purchases on re-entry to the mainland. Tourist traffic to the island has varied in direct relationship to the imposition of customs controls on the free port purchases. The islands do however have beautiful white beaches, though in San Andres not very extensive, rolling surf and Caribbean climate. Their lack of infrastructure is discussed in a later section.

3. See Fodor's Caribbean 1970: *"Colombia-Emerald of the Spanish Main"*.

TABLE 21-2: COMPARATIVE PRICE LEVELS: COLOMBIA vis-a-vis REST OF CARIBBEAN
(In US dollars)

Country	Per Diem Allowances[1]		Hotel Price Ranges[2] Single room, in season	
	UN	U.S. State Department	EP	MAP
COLOMBIA				
Bogota	20	17	4-15	7-20
Elsewhere	18		3-18	6-24
MEXICO				
Acapulco	18	19-24	3-50	6-65
Elsewhere	16	17	2-22	5-35
GAUDELOUPE	18-22	n.a.	12-25	20-47
MARTINIQUE	20	n.a.	10-30	18-55
TRINIDAD and	21		8-32	12-42
TOBAGO	21-28	23	12-25	16-35
BARBADOS	18-23	20-30	10-45	15-75
JAMAICA	20-23	23-27	10-45	18-75[3]
VENEZUELA				
Caracas	25	25	12-30	18-40
Elsewhere	21			
U.S. VIRGIN ISLANDS	20	34-46	15-42	32-62
ARUBA	26-32	30-36	10-36	15-55
CURACAO	26-32	30-36	10-28	13-40
PUERTO RICO	23-26	24-47	15-55	38-85
BERMUDA	25-30	25-30	5-45	18-62
BAHAMAS	23-33	25-41	12-52	18-70
ANTIGUA	18-25	n.a.	15-30	25-55
ST. LUCIA	18-26	n.a.	12-27	25-42

[1] Where two estimates are shown, the lower figure is for 'out of season' visits and the higher is for the tourist season — generally December 15 to April 15. These allowances are allocated by the UN and the U.S. State Department to employees traveling to these countries.

[2] MAP: Modified American Plan includes breakfast and dinner; EP - European plan is hotel only. Generally resort hotels tend to offer MAP. A wide range tends to indicate highly developed facilities catering to different tourist income groups. The lower range generally refers to 'boarding-house-type' accommodation, the higher range luxury and first-class accommodation tends to be approximately in the upper third of the price range.

[3] Jamaica has several hotels in this upper price range in Montego Bay where the maximum for a single room, American Plan is US$115 per day. In Ocho Rios the maximum MAP rate is US$65 per day.

Sources: Per Diem Allowances: UN and State Department documents.
         Hotel Price Ranges: Table 21-9; Caribbean Vacation Planner, BWIA, Fodor's Caribbean, 1970;
                                Mexico: Guia de Hotels, Departamento de Turismo.

Historic Assets

The north coast of Colombia has the advantage over most of its Caribbean neighbors of important historic assets. Cartagena's beach resources are of secondary importance to its historic and cultural ones which make it one of the most interesting cities in the Western Hemisphere and of international importance culturally. The old city is virtually a series of enormous fortresses, the biggest of which took one hundred years to construct. In the colonial period Cartagena was the main port for shipment of New World wealth to Spain and as such, was sacked on several occasions by, among others, Henry Morgan and Sir Francis Drake. Cartagena impresses because of its grandeur and history, but its sea setting has a natural beauty that reminds the visitor of Mallorca. The old city is in an unfortunate state of lack of preservation. Some useful studies by the University of the Andes and UNESCO have been begun and local residents are beginning a campaign to restore and preserve individual houses. However, a major restoration program is urgently required if Cartagena is to realize its international tourist potential.

Santa Marta, principally a resort area, was the first city to be settled in the New World in 1525 and, most importantly for international tourism, was where Simon Bolivar, the Liberator of five South American republics died. Although his remains are now in Caracas, the Quinta de San Pedro Alejandrino where Bolivar died in Santa Marta is a national monument and place of pilgrimage in South America. Local groups are presently trying to improve and preserve this estate as well as the house in which the autopsy was performed. Although as yet relatively inaccessible, the substantially intact archaeological remains of the Tayronas, possibly the most developed of pre-colonial cultures in the region, are being excavated in the Santa Marta area. At present all examples of this culture are to be found in Bogota, since Santa Marta has no museum.

Bogota and Other Contrasts

Bogota in the heart of Colombia contrasts with the Caribbean north coast. One of Colombia's tourist fascinations is the existence of every type of climate within its borders. The range from tropics to temperate to snow, is a result of the varying altitudes caused by the different mountain ranges that divide the country lengthwise. Table 21-1 illustrates these wide ranges in altitude and temperature. Despite Bogota's altitude of 8,660 feet and chilly climate, the city has attractions for international tourists, though its colonial architecture is inferior to Quito or Lima for example. Visitors from the tropics such as Venezuela are even attracted to the experience of a cold climate. Most tourists visit the Gold Museum, which exhibits examples of pre-colonial gold and silver art which are of world importance; the immense cathedral of Zipaquira carved out of a salt mine; Monserrate, the monastery reached by cable car and perched high on a mountain overlooking Bogota and sometimes surrounding areas (such as Boyaca) with the subsequent change of scenery and climate at a different altitude. Some tourists visit a bullfight during the season and many visit an emerald mine. Almost all tourists are interested in seeing—and many even in buying—the emeralds of the non-industrial variety of which Colombia is the world's largest producer.

Secondary Tourist Circuits

Colombia has many other areas such as Manizales, Popayan-Cali and the Medellin area that could be developed as secondary circuits of interest to general tourists. In addition, Colombia also offers big and minor game hunting, fishing and exploration of the Amazon river in Leticia on the borders of Colombia, Peru and Brazil; and mountain lake and river fishing, as well as deep sea fishing all year round in various centers, with international competitions held in Barranquilla twice annually. Pre-colonial archaeological remains particularly those in San Agustin, are of interest to specialized groups and UNESCO recently financed a study of those in Peru, Ecuador and Colombia as a means of exploring the possibility of a cultural tourist circuit between these countries. The variety of Colombia's physical features is a dual tourist asset because of the variety and excellence of locally produced food for the tourist's diet.

External and Internal Transport

Chapters on transport deal extensively with this sector; this section discusses only its tourism aspects.

External Transport

Colombia, which is well served by international air traffic (see Table 21-3), is a dispersion center for traffic southwards whether east or west and similarly can serve either the east or west coast of the U.S.A. Critics of Colombia's air traffic policies consider that Bogota in particular could be even better served by international air traffic had the international reciprocity principle with the local airline, AVIANCA, not been applied so severely and exclusively. These critics feel that air communication with Europe in particular would be more varied and more frequent had an 'open skies' policy been adopted in Colombia. A very recent measure which should stimulate air traffic to Colombia is the agreement by IATA that Group Fares be instituted for travel from New York and Miami to Barranquilla with the possibility of extending the Colombian destinations directly to Santa Marta and Cartagena (see Table 21-4). These fares make Colombia competitive in group travel for the first time with other Caribbean areas. Lack of cargo, inefficient port services and facilities as well as lack of strictly tourist facilities prevent more frequent docking by cruise ships at the north coast ports. Notwithstanding, cruise ships visit Cartagena and to a lesser extent Buenaventura on a regular basis (see Table 21-5). With the opening of the Troncal de Caribe in 1971, Colombia will have two good road entry points on the borders with Venezuela, i.e. at Paraguachon and at the present entry point at Cucuta.

TABLE 21-3: AIRLINES SERVING COLOMBIA

	Port of Arrival	Weekly Frequency
Foreign Airline		
Braniff	Bogota	Daily
	Cali	5 flights weekly
Pan American	Barranquilla	6 flights weekly
ALM	Barranquilla	3 flights weekly
	Medellin	2 flights weekly
VIASA	Bogota	4 flights weekly
VARIG	Bogota	1 flight weekly
BOAC	Bogota	1 flight weekly
AIR FRANCE	Bogota	6 flights weekly
ECUATORLANA	Cali	4 flights weekly
LAN CHILE	Cali	4 flights weekly
IBERIA	Bogota	6 flights weekly
APSA	Bogota	8 flights weekly
AEROLINEAS ARGENTINAS	Bogota	6 flights weekly
LUFTHANSA	Bogota	4 flights weekly
SAHSA	San Andres	
LADECA	San Andres	
Colombian Airlines	Destination	
AVIANCA	U.S.A.	
	Mexico	
	Central America	
	South America	
	Europe	
AEROCONDOR	Miami	
	Curacao	
	Aruba	
SAM	Costa Rica	

TABLE 21-4: AIR FARES: COMPETITIVENESS OF COLOMBIA WITH OTHER NEARBY TOURIST AREAS AND EUROPE
(Fares in US Dollars)

Between	Group Inclusive Tour Fares[1]		Excursion Fares[2] Mid-week, Economy		Normal Round Trip Fares Economy
	New York	Miami	New York	Miami	New York
Kingston/Montego Bay (Jamaica)	135		155	64	232
Antigua	145	115	161	133	236
Dominica	152	125	173	145	264
Pointe a Pitre (Guadeloupe)	145	120	161	138	254
Fort de France (Martinique)	155	130	175	149	278
St. Lucia	159	134	181	153	288
St. Vincent	175	144	199	165	300
Barbados	165	135	189	161	300
Grenada	180	145	204	168	314
Port of Spain (Trinidad)	180	145	209	170	320
Tobago	180	145	209	170	320
Georgetown (Guyana)	210	180	247	210	356
Paramaribo (Surinam)	235	200	270	245	400
Aruba	150	120	165	135	265
Curacao	150	120	165	135	265
Colombia					
Barranquilla)					
Cartagena)	190	115	255	135	314
Santa Marta)					
Bogota	–	–	270	160	346
Puerto Rico	–	–	–	112	156
U.S. Virgin Islands			152	126	186
Mexico					
Acapulco	–	–	259	–	286
Mexico City	–	–	227	–	254
London	175	–	265-300		420
Madrid	170	–	290-331		464
Paris	184	–	290-331		464
Rome	220	–	315-409		573

[1] GIT Fares are also permissible under IATA for Santo Domingo, Port-au-Prince, St. Martin, St. Kit's, Cayenne and Bonaire in the Caribbean. The application of the GIT system is subject to many restrictions including the time of year in which it is applicable. For Colombia the seasons are:

January 1 - March 31
April 26 - June 30
September 15 - November 30

For all other points in the Caribbean the seasons are April 26 to June 30 and Sept. 15 to Nov. 30. The peak season for tourist traffic to Europe is May 22 to Sept. 18.

[2] These excursion fares require the passenger to travel for a specific minimum period ranging from 17 to 45 days. The European fares shown above refer to excursions of 45 and 28 days respectively. The minimum travel time for applicability of the excursion fare to Colombia is 30 days.

Source: British West India Airways; other airlines.

Table 21-5: CRUISE AND PASSENGER BOATS SERVING COLOMBIA

I. Passenger Boats

A. Grace Line

Ship	Ports		Frequency
	Embarkation	Disembarkation	
S.Mariana	New York	Cartagena Buenaventura	Every 4 weeks
S. Maria	New York (Friday)	Cartagena (Alternate Thursday)	Weekly
S. Mercedes	New York (Friday)	Buenaventura (every Sunday)	
S. Magdalena			

B. Italian Line

Ship	Ports		Frequency
	Embarkation	Disembarkation	
Donizetti	Genoa	Cartagena	Every 3 weeks
Rossini		Buenaventura (2 days later)	
Verdi			

II. Cruise Boats

Company	Ship	Colombian Port of Call[3]	Other Port of Call
Grace Line[2] Embarkation in New York	S. Magdalena	Cartagena-Buenaventura	Bermuda
	S. Mercedes	Cartagena-Buenaventura	Santo Domingo, Dominican Rep.
	S. Maria	Cartagena-Buenaventura	Port au Prince, Haita
	Stella Oceanis	S. Marta-Cartagena-S. Andres	Kingston, Jamaica Panama Canal Zone Guayaquil, Ecuador
Italian Line	Princess Italia	Cartagena	San Juan
	Leonardo Da Vinci	Cartagena	Port Everglade, Nassau
	Princess Carla	Cartagena	
Lineas C	Federico C	Cartagena	San Juan Nassau
French Line (Paquet Line)	Rennaissance	Cartagena-S. Andres	St. Thomas Port Everglade

FOOTNOTES

Notes: The frequency of the cruise boats varies greatly.

Fares are all First Class and from New York to Cartagena one-way range from US$325.-US$590.00 in the regular season (mid-December to mid-April and mid-June to end of August); US$290-US$530.00 in the off-season. The range from New York to Buenaventura in the on-season is US$470.-US$845.00.

The average voyage takes 6 days from New York to Cartagena and 8 days from New York to Buenaventura.

TABLE 21-6: VARIOUS OFFICIAL ESTIMATES OF BASIC TOURISM DATA

| | Tourist Arrivals | | | | Average Length of Stay | | | Tourist Nights | | |
	CNT	Bco Rep. Number	DANE	IUOTO	CNT	Bco Rep. Days[1]	IUOTO	CNT	Bco Rep. Number	IUOTO
1960	42,735	47,872		48,384	4	5.8		170,940	284,640	
1961	54,329	51,772		52,864	4	5.8		217,316	298,414	
1962	70,218	36,878		38,117	4	5.8	(17)	280,872	206,364	633,640
1963	78,936	45,462		45,462	4	5.8	(16)	315,744	261,940	715,900
1964	77,337	44,841		95,017	5	5.8	(10)	386,685	258,983	956,500
1965	79,196	53,437		53,437	5	5.8	6	395,980	312,503	(320,622)
1966	93,744	65,468	70,161	70,258	5	5.8	4	468,720	382,678	(281,032)
1967	106,095	71,555	74,235	86,608	7	5.8	4	742,665	415,591	(346,432)
1968	139,429		77,913		7	5.8		976,003	550,371	
1969	142,585				7	5.8		998,095		

| | Average Daily Expenditures | | | Receipts from Tourist Expenditures | | |
	CNT	Bco Rep. US$[1]	IUOTO	CNT US$ '000	Bco Rep.	IUOTO US$m
1960	20	28.1		3,419	7,985	
1961	20	28.8		4,346	8,580	22.6
1962	20	29.4	(20)	5,617	6,064	12.6
1963	20	28.8	(22)	6,315	7,546	16.0
1964	25	28.7	(25)	9,667	7,436	23.8
1965	25	28.4	(23)	9,900	8,889	6.4
1966	25	28.5	25	11,718	10,890	7.0
1967	30	28.6	25	22,280	11,882	8.7
1968	30	28.6		29,280	15,736	
1969	30			29,943		

Notes:

CNT = Corporation Nacional de Turismo.

Bco Rep. = Banco de la Republica de Colombia.

DANE = Departamento Administrativo Nacional de Estadistica.

IUOTO = International Union of Official Travel Organizations.

The local source for the IUOTO data is given as the Empresa Colombiana de Turismo S.A. the predecessor of the CNT and the Banco de la Republica.

Estimates in ( ) are derived implicitly from other data shown.

1 Weighted average of individual area estimates.

To increase road traffic from Venezuela it will be necessary to modify the documentary and customs requirements that the Colombian officials impose on their Venezuelan and other foreign visitors. At present the red tape irritations even long after the frontier has been passed, act as a disincentive to road traffic to Colombia. Except for border traffic confined to its specific area no major entry points to the interior exist on other frontiers.

Internal Transport

Colombia's mountainous terrain hinders the development of long-distance road travel as a major transport mode in internal tourism. A cheap and efficient way of travel particularly from Bogota and Medellin to Santa Marta, is by rail. Air services within Colombia are reasonable both in price and variety of destination (although better connecting services would be desirable) since they provide the only feasible solution to the transport problems that Colombia's various mountain ranges create. AVIANCA presently offers a US$50 all inclusive ticket that provides travel within Colombia to any destination within a period of 90 days provided no one city is visited more than once. The availability of reasonable internal air travel connections makes feasible the development of secondary tourist circuits within Colombia as well as frequent traffic between the north coast and Bogota. Air taxi services are also available to more distant and less frequently visited tourist centers. The improvement of internal road transport will contribute to the development of tourism. The development of the Santa Marta area will increase tourist traffic to Cartagena: the road-time distance between Santa Marta and Cartagena is now only five hours, and the bridge over the river Magdalena at Barranquilla will reduce that time by at least one hour.

The Present Pattern of Tourist Demand

Caribbean and South American Traffic

Currently total foreign visitor traffic to the Caribbean amounts to some 2.5 million and has averaged a growth of 13% over the past few years. Foreign visitor traffic to South America currently amounts to about one million tourists with an annual average increase of about 15%. Colombia, with 140,000 foreign visitors per year, attracts about 4% of the total tourist traffic in surrounding areas. Foreign exchange revenues from tourism are variously estimated at either US$16 million or US$30 million as shown on Table 21-6, and represent between 3% and 6% of total commodity exports depending on the estimate used. The lower estimate is more probable.

The characteristics of Caribbean tourism are: short-distance from the US supplier market and therefore relatively cheap air fares, reverse climatic conditions and exceptional beach assets. All these, with the recent introduction of cheap group inclusive tour fares from New York and Miami, are characteristic of the Colombian North Coast and islands. Miami is only two hours flying distance from Barranquilla, the main North Coast airport. However, while Bermuda and Jamaica are able to attract over 280,000 tourists plus some 90,000 cruise passengers, and US$65 million respectively in tourism foreign exchange earnings, Colombia in 1969 received 140,000 visitors and only about US$16 million in foreign exchange earnings. Another nearby example is Mexico, which in 1945 had about the same level of tourist arrivals as Colombia now has, but in 1969 received 1.8 million visitors and over US$400 million in foreign exchange (excluding nearly US$800 million additional income from border traffic). Furthermore, while visitors to the Caribbean tend to be long-stay, resort-type tourists, a majority of those to Colombia are probably business travelers, many must be visitors from neighboring countries, and tourists are mainly short-stay visitors combining Colombia with other stops on a package tour.

Until 1968, Colombia's tourism potential was neglected in economic development plans. There are various explanations, but the main reasons seem to be: public sector skepticism and apathy about the net economic benefits of tourism, particularly because of fear of the infrastructure costs involved in tourism development; lack of knowledge of market demand for tourism;

and the availability of alternative development opportunities in other sectors. Recently, growing concern with the high unemployment rates in potential tourist areas, greater realization of the net foreign exchange benefits of tourism and concrete investment proposals from the private sector have aroused public sector interest in tourism development.

Statistics

The statistical base for planning for the tourism sector in Colombia is inadequate. Three institutions engage in the processing of data collected by one of them and each produces different estimates. Statistical data in the tourism sector are required for an analysis of demand: size of traffic, country of origin, length of stay, average and total expenditures; for an estimation of supply; and for an analysis of the economic benefits from tourism development. Only with an accurate estimate of the size, distribution and potential of demand, can maximum benefits be obtained from promotion expenditures; an equilibrium supply of facilities be provided; and rates of return on specific projects be determined. The present inadequacy of tourism data suggests strongly that present collection and collation methods be improved and that a wider variety of data be collected on a regular basis from hotel records for example and that a sample survey be a priority in the pre-investment study program.

Characteristics of Tourists

This report defines as a foreign visitor using tourism facilities both business travelers and tourists on vacation. At present foreign business travel to Colombia is significant and, in terms of numbers, is probably greater than tourist travel. These travelers tend to use the same facilities as tourists in Bogota but also frequently visit for business reasons other cities which are only secondary tourists circuits, principally Cali, Medellin, Barranquilla and to a lesser extent Manizales. Business travel originates mainly from the United States, to a lesser extent from Venezuela and appears to be growing from Europe and other areas. However European tourists to Colombia are often residents of nearby countries. A statistical problem with substantive ramifications consists specifically in the danger of inclusion of excursionists (whether for business or tourism) at integrated border areas with neighboring countries.

Entry and Destination Points

About 90% of tourists to Colombia travel by air and although there are fifteen air, road, sea and river entry points, about 60% of tourists enter through Bogota, although international air traffic also directly serves Cali, Medellin, Barranquilla and San Andres (Table 21-3). Both Cartagena and Santa Marta have airports that take small jets and connecting international flights are frequent, so that the dispersion of tourists after arrival becomes difficult to estimate. Cruise and passenger ships visit Colombia on a regular and an irregular basis as is shown on Table 21-5. The port visited with most frequency is Cartagena, the second is Buenaventura and, infrequently Santa Marta. Cartagena's historic grandeur and its proximity to the Panama Canal makes the city an attractive stop on Caribbean and Pacific north coast cruises. Buenaventura is often a port of call mainly for reasons of cargo but tourist interest is provided with a short inland river trip. Cruise and sea traffic is small and its impact on tourist facilities is limited to use of internal transport, guides, probably some food and drink consumption and some purchases. Road traffic is also on a small scale because of difficult terrain caused by the sequence of mountain ranges in Colombia and is generally limited to specific areas in isolation from each other e.g. Bogota and surroundings and the North Coast area. A recent innovation, however, facilitated by road improvements is the introduction of one-way seven day bus tours with return by plane, between Caracas and Bogota, following the so-called 'Liberator's' route.
    Three patterns of tourist demand are evident:

(a)   International tourist and business traffic to Bogota, which is sometimes a destination

per se from which secondary international tourist circuits are visited; or more frequent-
ly, where United States visitors are concerned, Bogota forms part of a package tour of
South America organized by United States wholesalers. In the latter case, the average
length of stay is some 2-3 nights and this traffic is estimated by travel agents in
Colombia to be growing by at least 30% per annum. These tend to be middle income
United States tourists and in the upper age groups.

(b)   Colombia is a destination for Venezuelan business and tourist traffic. Ethnic and
        cultural relations between the two have always been strong, particularly between resi-
        dents of the coast. This tourist traffic is expected to grow when the opening of the
        Caribbean trunk road (Troncal del Caribe) brings the high-income area of Maracaibo
        in Venezuela within five hours driving time of Santa Marta in the north. However,
        Colombia's regional historic assets and different climate away from the coast, also
        attracts the Venezuelans to the interior. Continuing road improvement programs in
        Colombia and increasing incomes in Venezuela are likely to stimulate traffic even
        further. The Venezuelans tend to be middle income and often travel in a family group.
(c)   International air and cruise traffic (excluding the Venezuelan) has begun to the Caribbe-
        an north coast and is likely to be stimulated by public sector development plans for the
        region and by private sector investment and promotion as described in the following
        chapters. Tentative estimates of the present size of that traffic are shown on Table 21-7.
        Air and road traffic to this coast would tend to be for resort-type tourism, in which
        Colombia's comparative price advantage in relation to both Venezuela and the Caribbe-
        an (Table 21-2) is likely to be a major asset for stimulating the demand and for
        extending the average length of stay.

Seasonal Patterns

Since no data on monthly tourist arrivals are available, identification of seasonal patterns
can only be qualitative. The peak tourist months for domestic tourism are end-December to
end-January, Holy Week and the school-holiday period in June-July. Venezuelan traffic is
year-round but to the coast is principally in August—the time for school holidays in that
country. Tourist arrivals from the United States and from most other areas though year-round,
reach their peak in January and February and again in the mid-June to end-August period.
Bogota's climate is much the same all the year round. The rainy season on the coast is principally

TABLE 21-7: ESTIMATES OF FOREIGN ARRIVALS AT COLOMBIAN CARIBBEAN TOURISM CENTERS

Year	Barranquilla	Cartagena	Santa Marta	San Andres	Total
1960	15,413	5,622	4,760	4,062	29,857
1961	14,381	7,219	5,111	4,813	31,524
1962	11,778	9,227	4,213	6,694	31,912
1963	9,001	8,557	4,188	7,582	29,328
1964	7,861	8,537	4,483	7,973	28,854
1965	9,187	9,611	5,354	6,594	30,746
1966	10,806	10,044	6,082	8,184	35,116
1967	12,708	10,839	6,747	9,024	39,318
1968	12,995	11,537	7,164	11,215	42,911

Note: The addition of the individual totals implies that a total of some 40,000 tourists out of a total traffic of
      140,000 to Colombia visited the north coast and San Andres in 1968, i.e. approximately one foreign
      tourist in three visited the area. The mission believes that the individual resort totals could be correct but
      that the probabilities are that the same tourist visited two or more cities, so that an incorrect impression
      of the size of the traffic is given if the totals are added into one grand total.

Source: Corporacion Nacional de Turismo (CNT).

May-June and October-November, but is not a severe handicap to year-round tourism. There is little inherent reason why tourism in Colombia should be seasonal. Caribbean neighbors with similar coastal climates raise numbers of visitor arrivals in trough periods by offering incentive prices both for accommodation and for air fares. These are among the many techniques of successful administration of tourism development that Colombia is only beginning to utilize.

The Supply of Tourist Facilities

The main constraint on growth of international tourist traffic to Colombia is the poor quality of accommodation and hotel service and the lack of related tourist services. Colombia has too few centers to which tour organizers would be prepared to send clients given the quality of present facilities. Since, currently, some new first-class accommodation is under construction or at the planning stage, an increase in group tours could eventually stimulate demand for even more first class accommodation.

Availability of Accommodation and Expansion Plans

A statistical inventory of Colombia's hotel plant is contained in Table 21-8, and an analysis of hotel data for the major tourist centers is shown in Table 21-9. The main conclusion to be drawn is that 72% of hotel rooms are distributed among the following seven centers, in declining order of importance: Bogota, Barranquilla, Cartagena, Medellin, Santa Marta, Cali and San Andres. Nearly 30% of the total is concentrated in Bogota. The pre-eminence of the commercial and industrial centers of Barranquilla, Medellin and Cali illustrates the importance of business visitors in the utilization of hotel accommodation. Cartagena, Santa Marta and San Andres are clearly identified as the main tourist centers in Colombia. While bed-per-room estimates are flexible, the number per room tends to indicate the lower quality of the accommodation. Data on average number of rooms per hotel indicate the limited number of sizable hotels—i.e.,with a minimum of 100 rooms. An excellent promotional plan by Avianca to encourage domestic tourism in the off season by reduced air fares and incentive rates at the best hotels in Colombia,[4] lists only nine hotels in eight centers (two in Medellin), which gives an indication of the limited number of major hotels. The price data while illustrating cheapness also indicate that most accommodation is third rate, with first-class accommodation scarce and luxury accomodation unavailable. At present, some 1,350 rooms can just barely be classified as first class, though none as luxury, and some 1,762 as second class out of a total of 6,310 rooms available in these tourist centers. (As pointed out in the footnotes to Table 21-9, these are generous classifications by international standards). Prices for accommodation undoubtedly reflect lack of quality but also reflect relative cheapness compared with price levels in nearby tourist areas as is shown in Table 21-2.

Accommodation in Bogota.   The only big first-class hotel in Bogota, with convention facilities and all services is the Tequendama under Inter-Continental Hotels management. A 400-room hotel was built by the Military Forces pension fund, just over twenty years ago and another 400 rooms have been added since 1968. The average room occupancy rate is about 90% and there is virtually no seasonal problem. Some 60% of the clientele are foreigners (mainly from the United States), of these only perhaps 10% are tourists rather than business travelers. In addition to the 200 rooms to complete the Tequendama, first class hotel capacity in Bogota will be increased by the 444-room new hotel which is being built by the Police Pension Fund and planned to be managed by Hilton. Tariffs are expected to be competitive with those of the Tequendama, i.e. between US$13-US$15 per single room European Plan even though the impression given by the yet incomplete decor, planned convention and other facilities and public rooms is that this hotel is more truly a 'luxury' rather than first-class hotel. The addition of 644 rooms will more than double first-class capacity in Bogota. With respect to the second-class accommodation, interviews with hotel managers indicate that several of the hotels with room

4. AVIANCA Plan H.A. 25/1970.

for expansion are likely to add to their capacity during the next three years, since present occupancy rates, despite the additions to capacity in the last three years, are very high and average about 80% with few off-weeks. Some fifty percent approximately of second-class hotel occupants tend to be foreigners and a maximum of 20% are tourists as opposed to business visitors.

First Class Accommodation in the Rest of Colombia. A new Inter-Continental hotel opened in Medellin in April 1970 and another is due to open in 1971 in Cali. These hotels will give both cities their first international class hotels. The Pan-American Games, due to be held in Cali in 1971, were a big incentive for the construction of a new hotel. In both centers existing first-class hotels have high occupancy rates of about 85% average per annum mainly because of business travel. The two most important hotels in Barranquilla and Cartagena have been and are in the process of remodeling and improvement: both the El Prado in Barranquilla and the Hotel del Caribe in Cartagena are old, spaciously aristocratic hotels, presently very much in need of maintenance and improvement. Both hotels are frequently used for conventions, though not major international ones. The Hotel del Caribe increased its capacity by 40 rooms in 1968/69.

Accommodation in Cartagena. Data are not available on the age of construction of second-class hotels in Cartagena, but interviews with hotel managers suggest that most were built about 1960 as family ventures. Staff numbers are limited and occupancy rates around 100% during the on-season permit profits, even though the rate falls for most of the year to uneconomic levels. Hotels are maintained open throughout the year. Quality nears third-class rather than second-class by international standards but prices are very cheap: from US$3-US$8 per single room. Some slight difference in price levels is made in most hotels between the off and on season. Cartagena's best hotel is the del Caribe as described above. This is not a luxury hotel, nor are any good resort hotels available. Vacation homes used by wealthy Colombians on weekends throughout the year, are not rented commercially when not in use by their owners.

Accommodation in Santa Marta. Several of the international hotel chains have visited Colombia in the past year, but as yet the only certain expansion plans in the main tourist centers are those that are under way in Santa Marta. The Rodadero area to the west of Santa Marta is the main center for domestic tourism because of the quality of the beaches. During the past ten years this area has seen the construction of seven small high-rise, second-class to third-class hotels (with from 14 to 46 rooms each) and a series of high-rise condominiums, generally owned by Colombians living in other cities. At each of the three peak tourist seasons (end-December to mid-February; Holy Week; and mid-June to mid-July) some 30,000 domestic tourists spend 15-20 days in the Santa Marta area and occupancy rates soar to 100% of room capacity. The apartments are generally vacant most of the rest of the year. Hotel accommodation in the city of Santa Marta is both second-class and relatively old. The only major recent hotel construction, though to the west of Santa Marta and the Rodadero, is a resort-type hotel (with only very limited facilities however) consisting of 50 bungalows and some 200 beds, and classified as a first-class hotel within Colombia. United States visitors comprise most of the guests but many are residents of Colombia; however the Hirotama is presently the only destination for United States tourists to the Santa Marta area. A major new project is the 112-room Carib Inn. This will be a luxury resort type hotel to the east of Santa Marta catering mainly for the sportsman and offering every kind of related sports facility. The project has a second-stage expansion plan which would increase the hotel capacity to 232 rooms and which foresees the construction of villas on a condominium basis. The investor is South American Sportsman's Development Corporation (SASCO), which with an affiliate TISA, invests in tourism projects in South America; but because of its belief in Colombia's tourism potential, SASCO concentrates on Colombia. SASCO is registered in Panama and has close relations with Braniff. The investors have also acquired the Tamaca Hotel on the Rodadero and intend to remodel and add thirty new rooms, which would raise the then 100-room hotel to international second-class category. Tariffs are expected to be raised only slightly above the present US$8 per single room, in order to retain comparative price advantage with other resort areas outside Colombia. Another project

TABLE 21-8: AVAILABLE HOTEL ACCOMMODATION 1969: ANALYSIS BY REGIONS

City and Region	Population 1970 '000	Number of Hotels in Main Centers	Number of Rooms per City and Region	Average Number of Rooms per Hotel in Main Centers	Estimated Number of Beds per City and Region	Average Number of Beds per Room in Main Centers	Percentage Distribution of Rooms	Estimated Distribution of Beds %	Number of Rooms per '000 Inhabitants	Estimated Number of Beds per '000 Inhabitants
	(1)	(2)	(3)	(4)	(5)	(6)	(7)	(8)	(9)	(10)
NORTH COAST AREA										
Barranquilla	650	10	851	85	1,626	1.9	10.0	8.1	1.3	2.5
Santa Marta	133	16	505	32	1,259	2.5	6.0	6.3	3.7	9.4
Riohacha	16	1	14	14	35	2.5	0.2	0.2	0.8	2.1
Valledupar	89	1	56	56	140	2.5	0.7	0.7	0.6	1.5
Cartagena	196	11	651	59	1,627	2.5	7.7	8.1	2.1	5.4
Sincejo	61	1	35	35	87	2.5	0.4	0.4	0.5	1.4
Tolu	9	2	83	42	207	2.5	1.0	1.0	8.7	21.8
Monteria	116	2	124	62	310	2.5	1.5	1.5	1.0	2.6
Total	1,371	44	2,319	53	5,291	2.3	27.4	26.3	1.7	3.9
San Andres	17	12	470	39	1,192	2.5	5.6	5.9	26.9	68.3
BOGOTA AND SURROUNDINGS										
Bogota	2,571	15	2,518	168	6,290	2.5	29.7	31.3	0.9	2.4
Girardot	89	4	65	16	162	2.5	0.8	0.8	0.7	1.8
Melgar	6	1	60	60	150	2.5	0.7	0.8	10.4	26.1
Ibague	183		141		282		1.7	1.4	0.7	1.5
Espinal	34		17		42		0.2	0.2	0.4	1.2
Guano	4		28		70		0.3	0.4	7.4	18.5
Honda	22		40		100		0.5	0.5	1.8	4.5
La Dorado	34		36		90		0.4	0.5	1.0	2.6
Villavicencio	71		119		297		1.4	0.5	1.6	4.2
Tunja	52	1	30	30	50	1.7	0.4	0.3	0.5	0.9
Sogamoso	48		15		37		0.2	0.2	0.3	0.7
Villa de Leiva	3		16		39		0.2	0.2	5.8	14.3
Pueblo Viejo	1		17		42		0.2	0.2	30.5	75.5
Paipa	5	1	60	60	135	2.3	0.7	0.7	12.9	29.1
Puente Nacional	4		45		112		0.5	0.6	12.4	30.9

Neiva	111	1	124	124	280	2.3	1.5	1.4	1.1	2.5
San Agustin	4		18		40		0.2	0.2	4.9	10.9
Silvia	4		27		63		0.3	0.3	7.6	17.7
Purace	1		22		50		0.3	0.3	21.0	47.8
Total	3,244		3,398		8,331	2.5	40.1	41.4	1.0	2.6
BUCARAMANGA AND SURROUNDINGS										
Bucaramanga	305		174		435		2.1	2.2	0.5	1.4
San Gil	24		35		87		0.4	0.4	1.4	3.5
Cucuta	206	3	176	59	415	2.4	2.1	2.1	0.8	2.0
Pamplona	31		48		120		0.6	0.6	1.5	3.8
Barrancabermeja	89		63		147		0.7	0.7	0.7	1.6
Total	655		496		1,204	2.4	5.9	6.0	0.8	1.8
CAUCA VALLEY										
Pasto	105	2	38	25	75	2.5	0.5	0.4	0.3	0.7
Popayan	77	3	50	164	125	2.4	0.6	0.6	0.6	1.6
Cali	950		491		1,170		5.8	5.8	0.5	1.2
Buga	91		64		150		0.8	0.8	0.7	1.6
Buenaventura	96	1	16	16	35	2.2	0.2	0.2	0.1	0.3
Total	1,319		659		1,555	2.4	7.8	7.7	0.5	1.2
ANTIOQUIA										
Medellin	1,026	11	642	58	1,455	2.3	7.6	7.2	0.6	1.4
Santa Fe de Antioquia	7		30		70		0.4	0.4	4.1	9.6
Quibdo	29		23		50		0.3	0.3	0.8	1.7
Total	1,062		695		1,575	2.3	8.2	7.8	0.7	1.5

Continued

CALDAS										
Manizales	269	3	112	37	240	2.1	1.3	1.2	0.4	0.8
Armenia	179		127		280		1.5	1.4	0.7	1.5
Pereira	199		160		355		1.9	1.8	0.8	1.7
Mariquita	78		30		75		0.4	0.4	2.5	6.3
Total	725		429		950	2.2	5.1	4.7	0.6	1.3
AMAZONAS										
Leticia	6	1	6	6	24	4.0	0.1	0.1	1.0	4.2
Total above centers	8,398	136[1]	8,472	62	20,122	2.4	100.0	100.0	1.0	2.4

[1] It has not been possible to distribute throughout Column 2 all the hotels shown in the total.

Source: Planeacion Nacional and mission estimates.

TABLE 21-9: ANALYSIS BY CATEGORY, PRICE AND OCCUPANCY OF HOTEL ACCOMMODATION – SELECTED CENTERS

Main Tourist Centers	Total Rooms Number	Number of First Class Rooms	Price Range Single Rooms EP - US$	Number of Second Class[2] Rooms	Price Range Single Rooms EP - US$	Percent[1][2] of Total First or Second Class	Price Range of Remaining Accommodation EP - US$	Expected Additions First and Second Class	On Season	Type of Traveller	Tentative Average Annual Occupancy Rates for all Classes of Accommodation[7] Percent
Barranquilla	851	200	9-18	270	7	55	3-7	–	Year round Peak: Carnival	Business Tourist	60
Santa Marta	505	74	9	111	6-8	37	3-7	1426	1. End-Dec.-mid-Feb. 2. Holy Week 3. Mid-June-Mid-July	Tourist	58
Cartagena	651	176	10	220	7-8	61	3-4	–	1. Dec. 15-Jan. 15 2. Holy Week 3. Mid-June-Mid-July 4. November 3-4	Tourist Business	70
San Andres	470	–	–	79	9-12	17	4-9	–	Year round	Tourist	65
Bogota	2,518	600	13-15	722	8-10	53	4-7	6445	Year round	Business Perhaps 10% Tourist	85
Leticia	6	–	–	6	8	100	–	50	Year round	Tourist	–
Cali	491	–	–	154	10	31	5-6	(231)[3]	Year round	Business	56
Medellin	642	300	10-15	100	6	62	3-6	336[4]	Year round	Business	57
Cucuta	176	–	–	100	7-10	57	–	–	Year round	Business Tourist	60

1 By international comparative standards most of this accommodation is second-class; only by Colombian internal standards can all but the new Intercontinental in Medellin and the Tequendama in Bogota and El Prado in Barranquilla (in terms of size and facilities, though not of quality of service or rooms) be classified as First Class.

2 Given the comment under 1 above, it follows that Second Class accommodation is comparatively nearer third class by international standards.

3 New 231 room hotel with IHC management to be constructed for completion in 1971.

4 In fact new Medellin Intercontinental opened in April 1970.

5 Comprising a 200 room addition to the Hotel Tequendama (IHC); and the new Bogota Hilton (444 rooms made up of 1-3 bedroom suites) and due to open in October 1970.

6 Comprising the new 112 room Carib Inn due to open in November 1970 and 30 rooms of additions to a renovated Tamaca, which is expected to be re-opened in December 1970.

7 These are average rates for all accommodation: occupancy rates for first and second class accommodation are generally higher.

EP = European Plan, room only without meals.

Source: Table 21-8 and basic data provided by the Corporacion Nacional de Turismo.

in the Santa Marta area which was at the letter-of-intent stage in 1970, is that the Club Mediterranee would administer an initial 600-bed resort complex, with a possibility of a second larger complex, and with 30% participation in equity: feasibility studies were to be undertaken.

Expansion Plans in Other Areas.   Hotel expansion plans in the rest of Colombia are limited and are of significance for tourism in San Andres where there is no first-class hotel and where 127 rooms may be added to present capacity, and in Leticia where verbal agreement has been reached with the Carib Inn investors for the construction of 50 rooms of sports-lodge-type facilities. These investors are also constructing a small 26-bed fishing lodge in the Llanos area, which will receive the same international publicity as their other projects.

The Effect of Expansion Plans.   The overall effect of new construction and extension, will be to increase present first-class and second-class capacity from just over 3,000 rooms in the main tourist centers (see Table 21-9 for their distribution) by some 1,400 rooms during the next two years (plus another 600 beds if the Club Mediterranee project is undertaken). Both Cali and Medellin will benefit from the world-wide publicity of the IHC-Pan-Am group and the Carib Inn from their investors' direct relationship to Braniff. The same wide promotion for Colombia is likely to result from the Hilton Management of the New Bogota Hotel. For the first time, the quality of accommodation in Colombia is being substantially raised and for the first time hotels that enter the 'luxury' category form part of the supply of facilities. Despite the improvement in quality, prices where known remain competitive with first-class luxury prices offered elsewhere. The new Carib Inn, which is the most luxurious project of its type in Colombia would expect to charge between US$34 and US$45 for a single person, with two meals per day and use of many of the Club's sporting facilities, during the winter (December 16-April 30), with summer rates some 30% lower. By international standards these tariffs are on the low side compared with rates for similar facilities elsewhere. These new projects will also inject a much-needed competitive spirit into the hotel industry, particularly in the first-class category, where high occupancy rates because of lack of alternative supply had led to inefficient management, poor service and little maintenance. The major operational difficulties likely to face the new hotels are described below.

Domestic Inputs

The Construction Industry and Imported Components.   The imported content of first-class hotels is a minor element in the capital cost; also current expenditures in foreign exchange are minimal and consist only of payments for liquors, wines and special items such as caviar. All construction materials are produced in Colombia and the only items of imported equipment are: central air conditioning units (individual units have some imported parts), dry cleaning equipment, elevators, bath tubs, and telephone switchboards. Most hoteliers considered that among locally produced items for hotel use, only cutlery and china were inferior to the imported goods. A less than first-class category hotel can have 100% locally produced equipment, as well as construction materials. Most constructors or architects interviewed stated that shortages or bottlenecks in availability of construction materials were temporary and generally due to distribution rather than production problems. The big construction companies are generally all-Colombian owned and staffed. The quality of architectural design and actual construction is high and generally better than the quality of internal finishing.

Employment Generation.   While the construction industry is still relatively labor-intensive the proportion of capital to labor inputs is becoming continually greater. As an example of the income generating possibilities of the industry, a tentative scheme for a new Bogota Hotel which is being proposed for financing by HOTURISMO, would employ 560 workers for a period of three years: a total of 510,000 man days. The present average wage is Col$5.75 per hour which was expected to increase to Col$6.50 in the last year, so that total income generated would be approximately Col$25 million or US$1.2 million in wages alone by the new construction. The average wage rate of approximately US$0.30 per hour is one indication of Colombia's relatively low construction costs.

Construction Costs.   Information on these is not readily available. However, the proposed new HOTURISMO hotel for Bogota, consisting of 622 rooms, with all the facilities of a first-class international hotel, and with over 40% of public space out of the total 38,512 square meters would have an average construction cost per room of just over US$21,100. By international standards, these costs are acceptable and on the low side. In other areas of the Caribbean these costs could be one-third higher. However, the type of construction more suitable for resorts and therefore for the north coast area, is likely to cost between US$5,000 and US$10,000 per room depending on the number of facilities. Tentative estimates of the construction costs of good second-class hotels in Bogota (first-class by present Colombian standards) are between US$7,000 and US$10,000. With heavy unemployment on the coast and no scarcity of construction materials and equipment, most of which would be locally produced, there are no reasons inherent to the construction industry why the cost structure should change in case of a construction boom provoked by the tourist sector.

Financing and Incentives

Availability of Public Sector Funds.   Until 1968 sources of financing for hotel construction were limited. The legislation decreed in that year authorized the five Financieras, the Instituto de Fomento Industrial (IFI), the Banco Central Hipotecario (BCH), the Fondo de Inversiones Privadas (FIP) and the commercial banks with public sector funds, to finance tourism projects and provide the tourist industry with all the financial incentives given to priority industries. The Corporacion Nacional de Turismo was also equipped with capital resources for direct investment and for loans for hotel construction and other tourism projects.

Incentives.   Law 60 of 1969 introduced tax incentive certificates which are issued once only and on termination of the work, for 15% of the capital cost of new hotel investment. These certificates will be issued to the bearer and will be freely negotiable and serve at their nominal value to pay all types of national taxes. A related incentive permits those who manage new or greatly improved hotels or hostels to receive tax certificates for up to 40% of taxable net income annually and for a period of not more than 10 years. In effect, the government is financing a part of the capital cost of hotel investment and is reducing taxes on net income from hotel management. These certificates are an undoubted incentive for private sector investment. Many investors would prefer a clear-cut tax holiday for a stated period of time, since the tax certificates are liable to depreciate in current values as well as in terms of foreign exchange. As yet, these certificates have not been issued but their estimated discount if sold on the market would be 20%. The incentive value of these certificates is proved by the formation of HOTURISMO and other private sector investment that is taking place or is planned since the introduction of the certificates.

Actual Public Sector Financing.   As yet public sector financing for hotels or other tourism projects has been limited. Each institution operates independently so that collection of data on a comprehensive basis is not easy. The direct financing known to the mission by mid-1970 has been by:

(a)   the Banco Hipotecario: an unknown amount for the financing of high-rise condominiums in the Rodadero area of Santa Marta;

(b)   the Corporacion Nacional de Turismo (CNT): a Col$3.5 million loan to the Hotel del Caribe in Cartagena for remodeling; and two other credits totaling Col$11.5 million for two hotels in Pasto and Paipa; in 1969 the CNT also spent some Col$6.8 million of its investment budget in minor construction throughout Colombia, in restaurants, small hostels and camping places, etc. The biggest individual item was Col$1.5 million in infrastructure works for San Andres;

(c)   three institutions for the Carib Inn resort project complex in the Santa Marta area, as follows: Col$500,000 from the Corporacion Financiera del Norte; an unknown amount for a five-year period and at 10% interest from the First National City Bank; a loan from the Institute de Fomento Industrial (IFI);

(d)   in 1969 the Compania de Desarrollo de Hoteles y Turismo (HOTURISMO) was formed to provide Colombia with a major hotel in, initially, the principal cities of Medellin, Cali, Santa Marta, Cartagena, San Andres and Bogota. The members of the group are: IFI, CNT, Avianca, four of the five Financieras (Colombiana, Nacional, del Norte and del Valle); the Compania Colombiana de Seguros and the Compania de Seguros Bolivar; three private firms (two breweries: the Bavaria and the Cerveceria Andina; one of the largest construction companies Cuellar Serrano Gomez); the Inter-Continental Hotels Corporation (IHC), the chief hotel chain operating in Colombia; and the World Bank affiliate, the International Finance Corporation (IFC). HOTURISMO, without IFC direct investment, has already financed the construction of the new Medellin Inter-Continental—which however received participation in equity by ADELA[5] —and is financing the one being built in Cali. On the drawing board is a new major hotel for Bogota and as stated above, a letter of intent has been signed with the Club Mediterranee for a 600-bed resort complex in the Santa Marta area. A site for the Cartagena hotel has been tentatively selected and the hotel will shortly be on the drawing boards. No firm plans as yet exist for San Andres, although the Club Mediterranee was rumored to be considering a 1,000-bed resort complex for the island;

(e)   an important source of hotel financing in Colombia has been pension funds, in that the Military Forces Fund financed the construction of the Tequendama and the Police Funds are financing the proposed Bogota Hilton. These are the only two cases known to the mission. The Military stated that their object was to diversify their portfolio and that they therefore were now interested in livestock rather than real estate. The Police Pension Fund however has plans for a second stage to the Bogota Hilton.

The Private Sector.   In general most hotel construction has been financed by the private sector with assistance to a limited extent from the commercial banks' own funds and at commercial rates of interest. The incentives offered are attracting investment from the private sector and from foreign private investment. With respect to the latter, by Decree Law No. 444 of March 1967 remittance of profits is limited to an annual 10% of the net value of the foreign exchange invested in the project. Difficulties and delays have been reported in obtaining the incentives. Most likely they are temporary and with greater experience in both the public and private sector, the incentive will be authorized, where applicable, with speed and efficiency.

Management and Labor

Availability of Staff.   Management for the four Inter-Continental Hotels (Bogota, Barranquilla, Medellin and, in the future, Cali) as well as for the Hilton, is provided from the chains' international resources, as are generally a few of the key staff. Management for the other main new projects as well as that for the Hirotama, will be or already has been imported from abroad. Although some of the traditional hotels are managed by Colombians there is an acknowledged lack of these professional skills in Colombia. Training is generally obtained abroad (sometimes under scholarship) and most frequently from Switzerland. Most hotels have on-the-job training schemes and most managers claimed to have been the sole source of training for their staff. Though Bogota was better, on the north coast the quality of service was poor. The problem seems to be a complex one with educational and training programs as presently designed.

Training.   The present source of training in the hotel and catering industries is the Servicio Nacional de Aprendizaje (SENA), which in 1969 began training apprentices for lower level jobs in cooperation with the hotels. The training program, based on the 1966 manpower survey, showed shortages of over 15,000 skills in the hotel and related services industries. SENA has a program in most centers and currently has an ambitious program for a large and fully equipped training center to serve all Colombia but situated in Bogota. The center would teach some 378 apprentices per year by 1972, compared with less than 100 being given full-time training in Bogota during the past two years. Part time training is planned for some 6,000 working pupils by that date also. Evaluation of SENA's activities varied among different hotel managers, but

---

5. ADELA: The Adela Investment Company, a multinational investment company incorporated in Luxembourg which has participated in private investment projects throughout Latin America and the Caribbean.

most of the apprentices in the current course in Bogota had found permanent employment in Bogota hotels before the end of their training. On-the-job training is likely to continue to be the main source of acquisition of skills at the lower to medium hotel employee level.

Related Tourist Services

Entertainment and Recreation.   Outside Bogota, very few related tourist services are available to the visitor. The casinos in Cartagena and Santa Marta are very poor relations to those in other areas of the Caribbean. There is a shortage of good restaurants and night clubs. Colombia's many cultural assets are not accessible outside Bogota to any other than the dedicated specialist. Automobiles or passenger vehicles generally are not produced or assembled locally and their availability is made prohibitive by exchange control regulations. As yet, although authorized under the 1968 legislation, no special vehicle imports have been authorized for the tourist sector. Restrictions apply equally to the import of recreational equipment. If the potential of the north coast and San Andres area is to be fully realized, these resorts must be supplied with the sporting equipment for which the Caribbean area is famous. Public sector support for tourism development must take account of its import requirements and understand that imports which in another context are luxury consumer goods, in the tourist context are the industry's raw materials. Net foreign exchange revenues from tourism are likely to be higher with these import concessions than without them, as will be the public sector's revenues from hotel and airport taxes, without considering the multiplier effects of increased tourist expenditures.

The Role of Travel Agencies.   Trade commissions were several times stated to restrict tourism to Colombia. This problem has several facets: high occupancy rates make hotel managers reluctant to accept block bookings from agents, because the acceptance of the booking implies rejection of the same number of individual guests not subject to commission payments; agents abroad were reluctant to accept the delays in remittance of commissions and fees for promoting travel to Colombia, which were attributed locally to the red tape of strict exchange control; the high commissions charged by local agencies in Colombia for services rendered, were said to be out of line with international averages and as such raised the costs to promoters abroad. With **certain outstanding exceptions the quality, responsibility and efficiency of the local travel agents was often criticized. The profitability and comparative ease of organizing tourism outside Colombia (mainly to the United States and Europe) was given as one reason for lack of attention by local travel agencies to the needs of incoming tourists. Another factor may be that legislation for travel agencies was only introduced in April 1969 and a strict professional code has not yet evolved.**

Investment Requirements

Infrastructure Requirements

No comprehensive assessment of Colombia's infrastructure requirements for tourism purposes presently exists. The entity charged with making that assessment, the Corporacion Nacional de Turismo (CNT), awaits the results of the preinvestment studies discussed in a later section. Pending these results, some indication, however rough and incomplete, will help establish an idea of the magnitudes involved. It is based on estimates for several specific areas (Cartagena, San Andres and Santa Marta); also it draws on those estimated requirements in other sectors which directly benefit tourism. (Most of the infrastructure requirements, although they may be stimulated by tourism demand, are generally also required for social or other purposes, such as industrial expansion in Cartagena). Although all major hotels in Bogota have their own generating plants and water storage tanks, these are mostly used or maintained for emergency purposes and the city is unlikely to have specific infrastructure requirements for tourism purposes.

Cartagena

In December 1968 a tourism seminar was held in Cartagena, under the auspices of the Asociacion Nacional de Industriales de Colombia (ANDI), for which a summary of investment already undertaken by the municipality of Cartagena for basically tourism purposes and a list of requirements for the future were prepared. Investments already undertaken at that time amounted to some Col\$283 million (US\$16 million) and consisted mainly, and in declining order of importance, of programs for electrification, for water supply and sewerage, for water filter plants, aqueducts and road paving. Investment requirements for the future amounted in the estimate of those conducting the seminar to nearly Col\$700 million, i.e., some US\$39 million.

The breakdown on these investment requirements was as follow:

(a)   restoration of colonial buildings (Col\$153 million);
(b)   public services including sewerage, paving, water supply, power lines; markets, parks and landing stages (Col\$112 million);
(c)   first-class hotel (Col\$81 million);
(d)   dredging of water pipes and circumferential highways (Col\$74 million);
(e)   improvement of the area called Cienaga de la Virgen including dredging and other works and establishment of fishing and hunting areas (Col\$69 million);
(f)   development of the island of Baru, including roads, urbanization, aqueducts and energy supply (Col\$48 million);
(g)   airport improvements, including terminal building and runways (Col\$47 million);
(h)   purchases of buses and launches; construction of entertaining facilities, aquariums, an international civic center, a colisseum and others (Col\$40 million);
(i)   development of electric power lines, water supply and roads (Col\$30 million);
(j)   conservation and protection of beaches (Col\$25 million).

These estimates were prepared in December 1968, some investment has been undertaken since then and more recent data are not available. These unofficial estimates should be treated merely as an indication of investment requirements if a tourism sector development program were to be initiated with Cartagena as one of its development poles.

The Island of San Andres

In November 1969 Planeacion completed a study of the tourist investment requirements of San Andres and Providencia whose need to realize their tourism potential is urgent given their lack of comparative advantage in other development sectors. San Andres is the more developed of the islands in the Archipelago, followed by Providencia. The study is summarized below:

(a)   The existing tourism plant results from domestic internal tourism to the island and from tourism from the Central American countries principally Costa Rica and Nicaragua. The main attraction in San Andres is its free port. The largest infrastructure investment being undertaken in the period 1969/70 is for the airport and its terminals. The total cost of the civil work at the airport is Col\$17 million which will include complete paving of the landing strips (Col\$6 million), a passenger terminal building (over Col\$7 million) and a cargo terminal building (Col\$2 million). Additional investments are for radar equipment, parking aprons, access roads and general navigational equipment.
(b)   A difficult problem that San Andres shares with many of its Caribbean island neighbors, is contamination of its water with salt. A short-term solution, the cheapest, is to supply water by drilling of new wells; however, experience has shown that these become rapidly contaminated. A longer term solution, is treatment of the water for salinity but experience on other islands has shown that this is still an extremely costly method of

supply. Investments of Col$2 million are being made for the construction of an aqueduct and the addition of a new storage tank for 400 cubic meters of water. These works are confined to urban areas and rural zones are still waterless.

(c)   The budget for electric energy works has been estimated at Col$4.4 million, for two years with National Government financing of Col$2 million in 1969 and Col$1.5 million in 1970 and additional financing to be provided by local authorities. These works are being carried out by the Instituto Colombiano de Energia Electrica (ICEL).

(d)   Various investments under the National Hospital Plan are to be made in the two islands in 1970. The allocations are small, less than Col$500,000 for four hospitals and medical services. The main health problem on the island, however, arises from lack of water.

(e)   Short-term development plans contain a project to provide the islands with automatic long distance services, specifically three telephone lines to Bogota, one telephone line to Providencia, two to Barranquilla, and a telegraph system with Bogota. Also planned were telephone communications with Panama and Nicaragua. These plans were to be completed by end-1970. Should an intensive tourist development plan be undertaken further extension of these systems would have to be considered.

(f)   The paving of 22 km of circumferential highway on the island of San Andres would cost an estimated Col$13.3 million, would take 12 months to complete and the justification would be basically for tourist purposes. A package of 1,800 kms is being presented for international financing in the period 1970-72, but Planeacion assumes that the low average daily vehicle traffic of 60 on the San Andres circumferential highway will compare unfavorably with other areas in the package.

Infrastructure investment planned for 1969-70 amounts then to some Col$45 million (US$2.5 million) for the islands of San Andres and Providencia. In addition the Corporacion Nacional de Turismo invested Col$1.5 million in a series of minor construction works in 1969 (well below the original budget allocation of Col$3.5 million) and the allocation under the 1970 capital budget is for Col$10 million. No estimate of future investment requirements is available. The mission estimates that these will consist mainly of projects for water supply and most urgently for a sewerage system to replace the present septic tanks; the circumferential highway and some feeder roads; and the provision of better quality hotel accommodation than that presently available on the island; slum clearance and the provision of alternative low-cost housing. A very tentative estimate of these costs would be some Col$70 million (US$4 million).

The Santa Marta Area

In January 1970, a tourism seminar was hurriedly put together by local officials and civic leaders in Santa Marta. The seminar's object was to draw attention to the area's tourism potential in the international market and most particularly from Venezuela. An inventory of the likely infrastructure and superstructure investments required in the future to attract and sustain that demand amounted to some Col$880 million (US$49 million). One component of that investment was water supply and sewerage. During the peak tourist season public utilities are strained beyond their supply capacities, to the extent that lack of sewerage constitutes a danger to health. While in Colombia the Mission was informed that an emergency program, under the direction of INSFOPAL and financed by the Corpracion Nacional de Turismo was to be undertaken before December 1970 to provide adequate water facilities. The other components of the Col$880 million total of investment requirements consisted of electric energy, roads (particularly feeder roads), telecommunications, restoration of historical and archaeological sites, urbanization and slum clearance, air and port facilities and accommodation.

Summary

If these three estimates of investment requirements for infrastructure projects in Cartagena, Santa Marta and San Andres are simply added together their total cost amounts to some Col\$1,655 million or some US\$92 million. Of this total, perhaps as much as 10% could be financed by local government funds. The bulk of the investment would undoubtedly fall on the central government. The total capital budget of the CNT for the period 1970-72 amounts to Col\$248 million; hopefully, this will increase rapidly in subsequent years. Much of the investment though justified for tourist purposes is already urgently required on a more limited scale for social purposes or for the development of other sectors and may already be included in the budgets of non-tourism institutions. The question that arises and cannot be answered at this stage is to what extent the above estimate reflects the true infrastructure requirements of the tourism sector in the immediate future. The inclusion of investment estimates for air and port terminal buildings for example, might not be essential or priority projects to induce a higher growth in demand for tourism facilities. However, to determine the true size of infrastructure requirements and the establishment of priorities among them, two vital parameters must be made available rapidly: preinvestment studies and a quantitative assessment of market demand.

Organization of the Tourist Industry

Measured by most criteria, public sector activity in tourism is below that in other sectors in Colombia. Recently, the situation has been changing. In late 1968,[6] a flood of legislation was introduced to change the character of the main tourism institution and endow it with greater responsibilities. There is still some uncertainty about ways and means to develop the country's tourism potential.

Public Sector Tourism Institutions

The Empresa Colombiana de Turismo.   The institution that preceded the present Corporacion Nacional de Turismo (CNT) which is an autonomous state entity, was the Empresa Colombiana de Turismo, created in 1957. Its principal objectives were defined as the development and industrialization of tourism in Colombia. Initial capital in 1957 amounted to Col\$20 million contributed by the national government, semi-official entities, municipalities, departments and those who subscribed to the company's shares. There were difficulties in determining priorities and probably also shortages of funds. The Government Plan for 1969-72 assesses the problems as follows:[7] "The achievements of the Empresa Colombiana de Turismo in its ten-year existence were limited. The failure of adequate planning in its programs produced a dispersion of its limited budget resources without the achievement of a positive result in national tourism development. Its primary function was directed to promotion through publicity campaigns, publication of posters, support for regional events and international congresses, without criteria on the priority or importance which each one of its programs had in tourism development. As for investments in infrastructure works to develop tourism, they were not considered important and the criteria with which these investments were authorized did not relate to any specific policy for the sector. The result of the above was deficient quality of tourist services and shortages of these, plus their dispersion throughout the country. As a consequence, the private sector because of lack of guidance, invested in urban centers exclusively according to commercial criteria." The Corporacion Nacional de Turismo (CNT) was created at the end of 1968 to remedy the above deficiencies.

6. 1968 became a base year in tourism development, most probably because the Eucharistic Congress was held in Bogota in that year and gave Colombia a first experience of large-scale international tourism.
7. Free translation by the mission.

Corporacion Nacional de Turismo. Details of the functions of the Corporacion Nacional de Turismo are laid down in Decree No. 2700 of 1968. Briefly, they comprise: the preparation of tourism development programs for submission to the central government; a study by area of infrastructure necessities to be carried out in coordination and cooperation with all other entities involved in the sector; the promotion and authorization of credits for tourist development; the raising of funds in the national and international capital markets; the formation of technical personnel for tourism; the promotion of economic consortia and all types of commercial entities in the public or private sector to promote tourism; the direct administration of funds for superstructures and regional works; and the supervision of tourism projects of all kinds. The CNT is also to be the main source of promotion for the tourist sector abroad and internally. Several offices within Colombia and abroad principally in Venezuela and New York are also administered directly by the CNT. The CNT is also responsible for the classification of all accommodation and related services in tourism and must directly control their operations and if necessary apply sanctions. These myriad functions make the Corporacion in principle an extremely complex and powerful organization. One of the problems in direction of the CNT is the absence from membership of the Board of representatives with specific experience in tourism development.

The main source of funds for the CNT is direct allocations from the Central Government Budget, which in 1970 amounted to some Col\$65 million. However, the CNT has been given the same financial powers as the Financieras: i.e. the CNT is also considered a development bank but specifically for the tourist sector. As such, the Banco de la Republica approved a line of credit in the form of rediscounting facilities for Col\$42 million in early 1970, which would have to be utilized for investment in fixed assets. In addition, the Banco de la Republica was studying a *pro forma* for an issue of shares by the CNT valued at Col\$30 million. Another source of financing under discussion was the acquisition of term deposits from other institutions or private individuals, since the CNT is also authorized to act as a commercial banking institution. Should these measures be approved, the financial resources of the CNT would be expanded by 100% over its 1970 budget allocation and would represent an even greater increase over previous years.

Past Financial Results. The expansion in capital resources described above, implies that the CNT has the ability to absorb and invest those resources. The CNT's record only begins in 1969 and members of the institution declared that the intention was not to begin new investments until the completion of the preinvestment studies, so that any judgments about past performance must be seen in this light. In 1969, the CNT was able to invest only 52% of its capital budget allocation, mostly for investments to continue projects already begun in previous years. This compares with investment performance of the Empresa Colombiana of 72%-82% in 1966-68 (see Table 21-10). Although the absolute level of lending increased in 1969, the methods of operation are similar, there are doubts about the technical and executive capacity to disburse a much higher level of lending, particularly when projects are likely to be more complicated, e.g. a tourism complex or infrastructure investment rather than supervision or construction of a small restaurant or hostels. A new and dynamic role which the CNT will have to play in the future, including that of intermediary for international borrowing, calls for appropriate measures to strengthen its organization and improve its effectiveness.

Other Public Sector Institutions

The Role of Planeacion in Tourism Planning. So far all planning for the sector, organization of preinvestment studies and any project identification and preparation, has been undertaken by Planeacion. The latter are as new to tourism as most others in Colombia but have acquired a theoretical appreciation of the subject's ramification and have adapted to tourism techniques applied in other sectors. The Urban Development and Housing Sector of Planeacion, has produced a very good overall plan for tourism[8] in which priority tourist areas are identified. Planeacion's close contact with other government agencies permits it to act as coordinator in tourism development. A criticism of Planeacion could be that—necessarily—they lack practical experience in tourism and are not closely related to the private sector which is the only source

8. Planes y Programas de Desarrollo, 1969-72, Section V, Pages 155-174.

TABLE 21-10: BUDGET ALLOCATIONS AND EXPENDITURES OF TOURISM CORPORATION 1966-1972
(in Col$ '000)

	1966			1967		
	Allocation	Actual	Actual as % Of Allocation	Allocation	Actual	Actual as % of Allocation
Income						
Current	7,961	7,358	92	10,299	10,413	101
Capital	7,685	6,449	84	4,171	4,503	108
Total:	15,646	13,807	88	14,470	14,916	103
Expenditures						
Current	4,530	4,558	101	2,560	4,141	162
Capital	11,116	8,023	72	11,910	8,774	74
Total:	15,646	12,581	80	14,470	12,915	89
Capital Expenditure						
Promotion Expenditures[1]	4,562	4,402	101	4,340	5,903	136
Construction	2,772	996	36	(		
Loans for construction & contri-				(7,570	2,871	38
butions to funds with tourist	3,782	2,625	69	(		
purposes				(		
Total Capital:	11,116	8,023	72	11,910	8,774	74
Percentage Annual Rates of Growth[4]						
Current Expenditures					neg.	
Capital Expenditures					9	

Notes: 1960-1968 data refer to activities of the Empresa Colombiana de Turismo.

1969-1972 data refer to the Corporacion Nacional de Turismo created in December 1968.

[1] Promotion expenditures comprise promotion internally and promotion and financing of offices abroad.

[2] Of which Col$ 0.7 million were for studies.

TABLE 21-10: BUDGET ALLOCATIONS AND EXPENDITURES OF TOURISM CORPORATION 1966-1972 (Cont.)

1968			1969			Public Investment Plan		
Allocation	Actual	Actual as % of Allocation	Allocation	Actual	Actual as % of Allocation	1970	1971	1972
14,855	15,060	101	43,991					
10,135	9,274	92	22,233					
24,990	24,334	97	66,224					
5,316	4,603	87	8,932			10,000	13,000	14,000
19,674	16,204	82	57,292	(30,000)[5]	52	55,000	87,000	106,000
24,990	20,807	83	66,224			65,000	100,000	120,000
10,735	8,900	83		(7,400)[5]		16,918	18,000	20,000
(				7,598[2]				
(8,939	7,304	82				38,082[3]	69,000	86,000
(								
(				15,000				
19,674	16,204	82	57,292	(30,000)[1]		55,000	87,000	106,000
	11		94			12	30	8
	85				85	83	58	22

[3] Of which Col$ 10 million pesos are for development of St. Andres.

[4] Actual expenditures where possible, allocation of plan data otherwise.

[5] Estimate.

at present of practical tourism experience in Colombia. Nevertheless, Planeacion is presently the main institution in Colombia which has considered the development of the tourist sector in broad economic or even operational terms.

Other Public Sector Institutions.   Various other institutions in the public sector are or could be engaged in the development of the tourist sector. Principal among these are of course the Ministries of Public Works and of Transport; and Aeronautica Civil, municipal water supply projects are carried out by INSFOPAL, energy works by ICEL. Other semiautonomous entities that do or could share in tourist activities are INDERENA (the Institute for protection and development of Colombia's natural resources); the Instituto de Cultura, which is in charge of museums among other projects of tourist interest; the Concejo Nacional de Monumentos; and Artesanias de Colombia which was created in 1969 to develop the handicraft industry. They could make useful contributions in the tourism sector if incorporated into its direction.

The Private Sector

Various private sector trade and professional organizations exist. The travel agencies are formed into a professional group, ANATO, with 100 members comprising 90% of all agencies in Colombia. The Asociacion Lineas Aereas Internacionales en Colombia (ALAICO) groups all international airlines operating in Colombia. The hotels have formed into two groups: FEDEHOTELES and ACOTEL which have developed a relationship of unfortunate rivalry, although no substantive issues seem to divide them. The impression was gained that private sector organization is limited to Bogota and that operations in other cities are conducted by branches of the main office in Bogota. Presumably though, should demand for tourism to the northern coast increase, the private sector would shift its center of operations accordingly.

Coordination

An essential element missing from tourism planning and organization is coordination between public and private sectors. The membership of the Board of the CNT would benefit from inclusion of representatives of private sector professional tourism associations such as those described. Again, public sector institutions mentioned above, are apparently divorced from participation in tourism development. Yet many of them are the only repositories of the technical expertise required to evaluate infrastructure requirements and prepare certain tourism projects such as resort complexes. A regular system of intercommunication between the CNT and agencies directly and indirectly involved in tourism development would be highly useful. A first-hand acquaintance with recent organizational and institutional changes in the tourist sector in neighboring Venezuela would be beneficial. Venezuela has used Planeacion in Colombia as a model for its Planning Department; the compliment could perhaps be reciprocated in the tourism sector.

Preinvestment Studies

The Present Program

A preinvestment study program for tourism has been urgently required because of the sector's development potential, combined with its lack of facilities and the poor state of knowledge about both supply of and demand for its facilities. A preinvestment study series amounting to US$1 million and consisting of six studies has recently been initiated. The funds are provided jointly by FONADE and the Corporacion Nacional de Turismo. Two minor studies begun in 1969 are being undertaken by Colombian consultants in conjunction with public sector institutions.

The three major studies that absorb over 90% of the US$1 million allocation concentrate on the Caribbean area: two are designed for the North Atlantic (i.e. Caribbean) coast and have

Santa Marta and Cartagena as their respective development "poles". The third refers to the archipelago of San Andres (principally the islands of San Andres and Providencia). The priority given these studies accords with the priority given the development of these tourism areas in the National Development Plan. The last study for which terms of reference exist—a minor one in terms of cost—is for the Boyaca area which could form part of a secondary internal tourist circuit and/or be a means of extending the length of stay of travelers to Bogota.

A study, also minor in terms of cost, is already being undertaken of the Santa Marta area, and specifically of the 12,000 acres Parque de los Tayronas, by Colombian consulting firms and its purpose is to evaluate tourist assets and to zone the area. While the Colombians stress "the park's variety of flora and fauna" the international traveler is unlikely to consider the area as more than a backdrop to the really beautiful 11 km. of beach inlets along the 85 km. coast of the park. The important but little excavated Tayrona archaeological remains could provide a nearby point of cultural interest for the beach tourist. The results of this study are to be incorporated within the overall study of the Santa Marta area, to be carried out by a consortium of international consultants. The February 20, 1970 progress report contains a preliminary zoning map of the park which is considered state property. However, a problem crucial to the development of the area is that 6% of land consisting of the best beaches is claimed by "traditional" families who long ago built vacation homes there and who consider "land improvement" compensation offered by the government inadequate. Another study in execution is that for the San Agustin area where important archaeological remains, as yet difficult of access, could eventually constitute a significant cultural tourist attraction.

Comments and Suggestions

All six studies refer to well-chosen priority tourist areas, and the concentration of study resources on the Caribbean coast and islands accords with Colombia's main tourism potential. However, comparative experience suggests that the investment of nearly US$1 million (the likely total cost of the three Caribbean studies) in a single study for the whole of Colombia—with particular emphasis on specific priority tourist areas—would be a more efficient investment of resources than investment in a proliferation of studies that theoretically and in practice fragment the tourist plant. At present six studies have been designed but the implication of Planeacion's identification of even more priority tourist areas (see Map: Priority Tourist Areas in Colombia) than those for which studies presently exist, is that additional preinvestment studies could be planned for these other areas too. While the studies are primarily physical inventories, the evaluation of tourist assets and establishment of development priorities among them depends on availability of complementary or competitive assets within Colombia as much as in nearby areas. Given the present inadequacy of tourism infrastructure and superstructure and the inevitable constraint of lack of investment funds, it is desirable to finance initially a highly selective series of major projects in order to make a promotional impact on the major tourist supplier market. Three groups of consultants presently required for the three major studies, are likely each to produce a project list for their specific area of study with priorities established internally within the geographical area of study but not nationally. Furthermore all three studies purport to include a market study of demand for tourist traffic to the partial area under study. While the different consortia of consultants undertaking the three studies are expected to cooperate closely, in practice the three groups are likely to be professionally highly competitive so that duplication or triplication could easily be a substitute for cooperation. Much of the technical assistance benefits to the CNT that are intrinsic in a preinvestment study, could be lost if three major, uncoordinated studies are presented for consideration. Specifically, no improvement of the statistical base for tourism planning, is likely on a global basis, since collection and collation of techniques must be instituted nationally. Furthermore, the studies virtually ignore the existence of Bogota and the interaction between tourism development on the coast and in the capital.

The most efficient use of study resources would be a global study for all Colombia, consisting of a land use survey of tourist assets and quantitative estimates of infrastructure and superstructure requirements: (a) on the Caribbean coast: Santa Marta and Cartagena would be considered as tourism development centers on this coast, Barranquilla as a dispersion center for international arrivals; (b) in San Andres and Providencia; (c) in Bogota, and (d) in the rest of Colombia, where it would also identify secondary circuits and specialist tourist areas. The survey would be combined with a market study of demand in the United States and Venezuela and in other supplier countries, notably in Central and South America. Internally the consulting firms should study public sector organization and administration of tourism and advise on methods of strengthening existing institutions and policies. Technical assistance should be provided by incorporating Colombian counterparts to work in different aspects of the study. In addition advice on data collection, collation and processing techniques should be given to provide an adequate statistical base for planning.

.While not necessarily as detailed as the partial studies, according to their present terms of reference, the global study would have the compensating advantage of assessing demand for tourism facilities in specific centers in Colombia relative to other competing areas both within and outside the country. The market study of demand is likely to be more effective when related to Colombia as an area rather than to one city within a country with so little history in the international tourist market. Furthermore, the technical assistance benefits of a major and global analytical study of the tourist sector are likely to be high. Rather than a proliferation of consulting firms working in partial aspects of the same sector, a highly selective and worldwide choice of the best consulting firms available would seem to be a better investment of study resources.

Colombia is but one of sixteen developing countries, plus the United States and United Kingdom islands, that border or lie in the Caribbean Sea and that are potential borrowers for tourism projects. Whether tourism is a potential or actual exchange earner, investment requirements for tourism facilities that would sustain demand are unknown because of lack of knowledge of the tourist supplier markets (principally the United States), the likely growth of that market and the likely distribution of demand for tourist facilities among the different Caribbean suppliers. Knowledge of other tourist supplier markets is even more hazy. No complete inventory as yet exists either, of the total supply of facilities according to different price ranges and for the whole of the Caribbean. Individual tourism development plans run the risk of overinvestment (or under-investment) in facilities generally or specifically, while the size of the market and the factors that influence its size remain unknown. Colombia, through consultants, now is attempting a market study of demand, but its scope will be restricted because of the limited time and cost allowed. Others in the Caribbean group have financed similar studies. Perhaps the most useful form of technical assistance with which foreign agencies could provide their Caribbean members would be assistance in the organization and execution of a comprehensive market study of demand for and supply of tourist facilities in the Caribbean. While the inevitable time delay between organization and finalization of such a study prevents it being of immediate assistance to Colombia, its execution should play a vital role in the longer-term development of the tourist sector everywhere in the Caribbean area, including Colombia.

The Employment Effects and Other Economic Benefits of Tourism Development

The Santa Marta area has a population of about 135,000; Cartagena, some 300,000. Unemployment rates are in the region of 18%. Cartagena has an overall population growth rate of 8% per annum composed of a natural population increase of 3% per annum and an additional rate of immigration of 5% per annum. The Santa Marta rate of increase is similar. Underemployment is characteristic of the whole coastal region. Average per capita income on the coast is lower than the US$300 average for Colombia as a whole.

At present the impact of tourism on employment is more significant in Santa Marta than in Cartagena. Column 9 of Table 21-8 shows the number of hotel rooms per 1,000 inhabitants in different centers. This is a useful indicator of the relationship between the hotel trade and employment. The average for Santa Marta is 3.7 rooms per 1,000 inhabitants and for Cartagena 2.1 compared with a national average of 1.0. These ratios are higher than for any other population centers of similar or greater size in Colombia and indicate that the bulk of the tourist plant is located on the north coast. The 26.9 average for San Andres demonstrates the island's heavy dependence on tourism. Because of its large population of over 2.5 million, Bogota shows a ratio of only 0.9 rooms per 1,000 inhabitants, despite having nearly 30% of total accommodation.

The number of rooms per inhabitant is an indicator of the dependence of a community on tourism for employment generation. However, the intensity of employment per room depends on many factors but is determined mainly by the characteristics and efficiency of tourism in a particular area. In highly developed resort areas particularly in Europe and often in underdeveloped areas with high unemployment rates, the ratio of employment to hotel accommodation can be as high as 1 per bed. In city hotels and in United States-type hotels where standardization is a rule, the ratio tends to be 1 employee per room; in these hotels there tend to be about 2 beds per room but the bed occupancy rate tends to be much lower than the room occupancy rate. In Colombia no firm data exist on the number employed in hotels—let alone the total employed by the tourist sector as a whole. However, from conversations with hotel managers, it appears that the ratio is near the 1 employee per room estimate in city hotels and may reach it on the coast in the peak domestic tourist season which is a maximum of ten weeks per year. During the rest of the year less staff are employed because of lower occupancy rates. Labor laws prevent drastic reductions in numbers employed—the dismissal of any employee retained for longer than the two months probationary period becomes extremely costly in terms of termination payments. Given, in addition, that even minimum hotel skills are unknown and their inculcation requires at least on-the-job training if not special courses, hotel managers tend to retain rather larger staff than is economically justified in the low season, to retain a minimum efficiency. Only a 'guesstimate', based on individual inquiries at each hotel visited, of numbers employed in relation to number of rooms available, is feasible at this time. These inquiries indicate that the present ratio of employment to available rooms in the north coast area is 0.8 to 1.0. (A firm estimate could be obtained very easily if the CNT were to collect data on numbers employed by the hotels.)

Current tourism experience tends to indicate a minimum 1:1 relationship between labor employed in hotels and those in related tourist services. A higher ratio for hotel employment could indicate the inadequacy of the latter. In countries with heavy unemployment, the probabilities are that more are employed in related services than in hotels, especially if the employed include underemployed who would otherwise have been unemployed. If, furthermore, the underemployed include those offering services which are paid not by wages but by tips, then the numbers of those in related services should definitely be higher than those in hotels. However, because of lack of restaurants and similar facilities, guides, internal local transport, recreation equipment, shops etc., and other related tourist services on the north coast, the ratio of employment in tourist services to that in hotels, on an annual average basis, cannot be more and could even be less than 1:1, even despite the low employment per hotel room ratio.

The question of what amount of additional employment is generated by tourism depends very much on the individual economic circumstances of the tourism sector in a particular country. The Mexican Fondo de Promocion de Infraestructura Turistica (INFRATUR) has recently estimated that in Mexico a 1:1 relationship exists between numbers employed in hotels and those in related services and that more than an equivalent number of this total is employed in sectors of production such as: agriculture, livestock and fisheries, textiles, food processing and others. Since comparisons abstracted from their original economic context are dangerous, there is no reason to suppose that necessarily the ratio is the same in Colombia as in Mexico. Indications that employment in productive services generated by tourism is likely to be high are that Colombia is virtually self-sufficient in food production: imports of foodstuffs for tourism are and would be, minor and confined to luxury items; wines and spirits would be the only exceptions and would have to be imported in quantity. The local textile industry acts as an incentive for travel to Colombia by other Latin Americans, especially Venezuelans, so that some employment effect is likely from purchases by tourists. Given the very low import content in hotel construction (5% maximum) tourism is likely to stimulate demand for furniture, furnishings, fixtures and hotel equipment generally. At present, the relationship is likely to be weak, but given greater development of the tourist sector the potential employment generation of one hotel room could be at least two in the productive sectors, unless the expenditures resulted in an increase in income for those already employed rather than an increase in employment. A further assumption is that employment created in the construction industry is very approximately the same as that created in hotels after they are opened. This employment will be continuous as long as the tourist industry continues to expand. When expansion slows down incomes are expected to have been raised to a point where demand for private residential construction has been built up.

These estimates are highly tentative. While it is not too difficult to estimate the employment effects in related tourist services and in construction, the estimation for productive sectors must be very imprecise, because the effect is so dispersed throughout the economy and frequently so difficult to relate causally to tourism. In the Colombian context of high unemployment, mainly unskilled labor and low wage rates, ratios higher than those that are the norm in more developed economies, should be expected, since many of the so-called employed will be under-employed rescued from unemployment. As an indication of general orders of magnitude, a summary of the above would give a tentative indication of the potential employment effects of tourism. The resort areas of the north coast and San Andres might be expected to employ directly a higher total number per hotel room, while the greater variety of economic activity in Bogota (and lower unemployment rates) means that tourist services will also be used and therefore employment generated by, other sectors e.g. internal transport. Table 21-11 shows employment generated by a hotel room and the effect of tourist demand on employment in other sectors.

TABLE 21-11: POTENTIAL JOB CREATION OF ONE HOTEL ROOM

1-2		per hotel room
1-2		for related services
2-4		per hotel room and for related services
2-4		in production sectors
1-2		in construction industry
Total	5-10	per hotel room

Based on these estimates, employment generated by all present hotel accommodation used by both foreign and domestic visitors on the north coast, San Andres and Bogota, should range from 25,000 to 50,000 jobs, using a ratio of from five to ten jobs per room. However given the present inter-related restrictions of limited tourist numbers, poor hotel service, seasonality and lack of supporting tourist facilities, the mission doubts whether present hotel accommodation generates more than three jobs per hotel room. Therefore actual employment is probably as follows:

TABLE 21-12: TENTATIVE ESTIMATE OF PRESENT JOB CREATION FROM EXISTING ACCOMMODATION IN SELECTED CENTERS[1]

	Number Employed From Existing Accommodation	Number Employed as % of Population
Cartagena	2,000	0.7
Barranquilla	2,500	0.4
Santa Marta	1,500	1.1
San Andres	1,500	8.6
Bogota	7,500	0.3
Total	15,000	

[1] Based on a "guesstimate" that 3 jobs are presently generated per hotel room. This is made up as follows: 0.8 hotel room; 0.8 related service; 1.0 productive sector; and, presently a minimal amount in construction. Number of rooms in each center is shown on Table 21-8.

In order to maximize job and income generation from existing accommodation, numbers of tourists must be increased. Accordingly new improved facilities must be provided not only in related services but also in new accommodation. The provision of new and better quality accommodation to attract more tourists and increase both their length of stay and average spending, should eventually create between five and ten jobs per new hotel room and raise the level of employment generation from three to at least five for existing accommodation, assuming some of these are now underemployed, particularly in agriculture and services. While hotel construction is likely to be undertaken by the private sector, some investment—and probably promotion expenditure—will be required from the public sector for infrastructure and conservation both of the city of Cartagena and the natural resources of the whole coastal area. The required matching public sector investment in the north coast area will only reach the level of investment necessary for accommodation, should considerable investment be undertaken in airport and port development, which does not at present seem essential on the north coast.

The construction costs per room of new first class resort hotels on the coast are not likely to exceed US$10,000, according to the best estimates of architects, builders and hotel managers interviewed. (A luxury high-rise hotel with large areas of public space could cost up to 50% more, but the question arises whether this type of hotel—rather than a lower cost first class resort-type hotel—is really suitable for the north coast area.) As a general order of magnitude therefore, an assumption will be made that for each private sector investment of US$10,000 in a new hotel room a matching public sector investment in infrastructure (e.g. highways, water supply and sewerage, feeder roads, etc.), conservation of natural and historic resources, and promotion of very roughly US$5,000 will be required. The aggregate public and private investment of US$15,000 should generate at least two to four jobs in hotels and related services per annum; and the more intensive development of the tourist sector should generate some two more jobs in existing accommodation, because of higher occupancy rates there. For an unquantified further amount which will probably be low, an additional two to four jobs in productive sectors, plus one to two in construction should be created. Taking the least optimistic estimate of five jobs, their average and very tentative investment cost would be about US$3,400 per job. This is a relatively low figure, by both international and Colombian standards. There are also two further points to be considered.

The type of infrastructure investment required to develop the tourist sector on the north coast area and in San Andres would be of immediate economic and social benefit to the resident population and might induce the development of light manufacturing industry in the region with its consequent effect on income and employment. Mainly required are public utilities: principally water supply and sewerage and to a lesser degree power and telecommunications. With the completion of the Troncal del Caribe, only feeder rather than major trunk roads would seem necessary. Other public sector investments that would be required for tourism, but would be of direct benefit to the north coast and San Andres as a whole would be slum clearance and the provision of alternative low-cost housing and investment in urbanization. Direct investment for tourism that would be of indirect benefit to the resident population would be for the conservation and preservation of natural resources such as beaches, flora and fauna. The public sector direct expenditures especially for tourism would be current expenditures on promotion and the cost of recreational and additional transport equipment.

A second point to be considered is that the presently foreseeable development opportunities in other sectors are unlikely to generate a sufficient number of new jobs. New industries currently being considered for the north coast area are: steel, salt-chemicals, petrochemicals and ship-building. The employment to be generated in these industries in the next five years can be counted in thousands rather than in tens of thousands. In agriculture, the major development possibilities are in livestock, cotton, bananas and rice. The three latter are only seasonally labor-intensive while livestock has at all times limited employment effects. At least over the short and the medium term, tourism development seems an essential and relatively low-cost ingredient of an overall regional policy. Tourist facilities and industrial and agricultural development do not compete for the same land, although in Cartagena a carefully designed land use plan and effective zoning regulations are needed to prevent pollution of tourism resources from the proposed chemical complex.

Other Benefits

Direct central government revenues from the tourism sector are currently obtained from a 5% tax on hotel bills and on international travel tickets. These revenues have grown progressively from nearly Col$10 million in 1965 to Col$20 million in 1969. Airport taxes, taxes on incomes generated from tourism and indirect taxes on consumer goods purchased by tourists are some of the other unquantified sources of revenues from tourism. Although tourism's present share in foreign exchange earnings is small (3%-6%), it is among the leading earners after coffee. The contribution of tourism to further export diversification should be substantial as investment is stepped up, in view of the low import content of tourism operations and of a short gestation period.

Projections

Market Prospects

Lack of promotion has previously handicapped Colombia in the international tourist market. Private sector investments that are now being made in accommodation are accompanied by efficient professional and widely distributed promotional material organized by Pan American, Braniff and the Hilton chain. Should the Club Mediterranee confirm their letter of intent to construct a resort complex in the Santa Marta area, another source of promotion for Colombia and probably with emphasis on the European supplier market, will be added to the existing ones. During the mission's stay in Colombia, Dutch journalists representing important European periodicals were making an exhaustive inventory of Colombia's tourist assets for promotion in the European market.

Venezuelan Traffic. The IDB feasibility study[9] for the Troncal del Caribe Highway, estimates that in 1972, a total of 100 cars, with an average occupancy rate of 4 (a family unit), will arrive during 100 days of the year and will remain an average of 10 days in Santa Marta, i.e. a total of 100,000 tourist family days (4 people per family). Probably this is the best measure of claim on accommodation resources, since the family unit could use 1 room with 4 beds. Possibly not all these Venezuelan tourists will demand this new accommodation; some will prefer existing and cheaper facilities, but demand for Santa Marta's facilities will also come from supplier markets as described below. The data abstracted from the feasibility study may seem unduly optimistic. However, the recent IBRD Tourism Sector Review of Venezuela states that authorities there estimate that no less than 2.5 million Venezuelans have income levels that permit taking a domestic vacation. Given the relatively low costs of road or air transport between Colombia and Venezuela, the Colombian resorts may share in this market. At present 200,000 or 2% of the population travel abroad (excluding travel to Colombia) presumably for more expensive vacations. Should Santa Marta provide a luxury type sporting resort, some of these 200,000 could also be attracted.

9. Estudio de Factibilidad Carretera Cienega-Santa Marta Riohacha-Paraguachon,Restrepo y Uribe, Ltda., November 1967.

Several factors confirm the optimistic outlook for Santa Marta for tourist demand from Venezuelan traffic.

(a)   Per capita income in Venezuela at US$900 for a population of 9.5 million compares with average income of US$300 per capita for the 20 million Colombians. Average income in Maracaibo, the nearest tourist supplier market, where the population amounts to some 450,000 is known to be considerably above the country average.

(b)   The cost of hotel accommodation in Colombia is approximately one-half of that in Venezuela—food prices are roughly two-thirds of those in Venezuela. There is there-fore, a very strong price incentive for Venezuelans to visit the Colombia coast rather than their own. They also have a shopping incentive for visiting Colombia. The remark-able quality of the local textile industry attracts the Venezuelans whose local alternative is much more costly imported material, and who are reputed to outfit themselves during their visits to Colombia.

(c)   While scenic and coastal attractions are very similar between Venezuela and Colombia, ethnic and cultural similarities act as inducements to the Venezuelans to visit Colom-bia—and vice versa of course, except that Venezuela's high prices are a disincentive to Colombians. Santa Marta is of specific interest to Venezuelans as the death-place of Simon Bolivar, one of Latin America's greatest heroes.

The United States Market.   Little information presently exists in Colombia on the size of US demand, on its dispersion in Colombia and on its length-of-stay and expenditure characteristics. US tourist traffic has been growing at an average rate of 13% over the past nine years, while the traffic to the Caribbean has increased at 15% annually. An increase of 13% per annum implies approximately an increase of 6,000 tourists from the United States to Colombia per annum. The Carib Inn project alone, on the basis of 200 beds and an average stay of 5 days, could absorb all that number with only a 42% occupancy rate. Lack of adequate accommoda-tion and promotion have been the main constraints on growth of United States travel to Colombia, and a rate of growth considerably higher than 13% may be expected in the future. The actual growth can only be determined once the new projects have begun to make an impact on the market and once analytical records of tourist behavior patterns are consistently main-tained.

Other Supplier Markets.   Another source of supply for Santa Marta will be well-off Colombi-ans and residents of nearby areas, as well as longer distance resort tourists from other areas including the southern cone of South America. Estimates of growth from these other foreign supplier markets are difficult given the present lack of history, trend or statistics. Once the size of non-Venezuelan and non-United States traffic is known over a period of time, promotional efforts can be directed at these main secondary supplier markets. Should the Club Mediterranee establish a 600-bed resort in the Santa Marta area, these tourists might be European or United States—since the Club has recently become affiliated with American Express and is advertising its other resorts in the United States market. This is highly organized and 'enclave-type' tourism with a danger of a lower net benefit to Colombia than that of straight commercial hotels. However, given such small import expenditures on current and capital account in Colombia, the remaining danger of large remittance of profits can be controlled, as presently, by legislation. The inclusion of Colombia in Club Mediterranee literature should undoubtedly provoke more general interest in the European supplier market.

Methodology of Projections

Given the lack of history and trend in tourism development, the inadequate statistical data base and the poor state of knowledge about international supplier markets, the mission has not attempted to forecast growth quantitatively from the demand side. Instead it has calculated the potential size of tourist traffic using present and expected supply of accommodation facilities,

TABLE 21-13: PROJECTION OF FOREIGN VISITOR BEDNIGHTS IN 1975; BASED ON INCREASES IN SUPPLY OF ACCOMMODATION IN SELECTED CENTERS

		Bogota	Santa Marta	Cartagena	San Andres	Barranquilla, Cali, Medellin	Leticia and Cucuta	Total Selected Centers
1. Number of first and second class hotel rooms	1969	1,322	185	396	79	1,024	106	3,112
2. Percentage room occupancy rates	1969	85	60	70	65	60	60	(72)
3. Implicit number of bednights	1969	615,226	60,773	151,767	28,114	336,384	34,821	1,227,085
4. Tentative estimate of proportion of nationals	%	45	80	60	90	60	50	(46)
5. Implicit foreign bednights	1969	338,374	12,155	60,707	2,811	134,554	17,411	566,012
6. Additions to room capacity	1970/71	644	142	—	—	567	50	1,403
7. Percentage room occupancy rates	1970/71	60	60	—	—	60	60	(60)
8. Implicit number of bednights	1970/71	211,554	46,647	—	—	186,260	16,425	460,886
9. Tentative estimate of proportion of nationals	%	40	10	—	—	60	20	(56)
10. Additional foreign tourist bednights	1970/71	126,932	41,982	—	—	74,504	13,140	256,558
11. Total foreign bednights	1970/71	465,306	54,137	60,707	2,811	209,058	30,551	822,570
(% increase)	1969-1970/71	37	345	—	—	55	75	45
12. Assumed higher percentage occupancy rates	1973	85	80	80	75	75	75	(79)
13. Total foreign tourist bednights	1973	512,359	71,613	69,379	3,244	261,322	38,435	956,352
(% increase)	1970/71-1973	10	32	14	15	25	26	(16)
14. Tentative and feasible additions to room capacity by	1975	1,000	600	800	500	—	—	2,900
15. Occupancy rates of new capacity	%	70	70	70	70	—	—	70
16. Additional foreign bednights	1975	214,620	114,975	122,640	172,463	—	—	624,698
17. Total foreign bednights	1975	726,979	186,588	192,019	175,707	261,322	38,435	1,581,050
(% increase)	1973-1975	42	160	177	5,316	—	—	65
18. Increase in foreign bednights	1969-1975	388,605	174,433	131,312	172,463	126,768	21,024	1,015,038
19. % increase	1969-1975	115	1,435	216	6,135	94	121	179
20. Average annual rate of growth in foreign bednights 1969-1975	%	14	58	21	99	12	14	19

Note: This table is a reproduction of the mission's work-sheet. On other tables where these data are used they have been rounded, where appropriate, to the nearest thousand.

Notes to Projections of Foreign Visitor Bednights
Assumptions and Methodology

Row 1   These data are obtained from Table 21-9.

Row 2   Occupancy rates for existing accommodation obtained from CNT.

Row 3   Assuming 1.5 bed occupancy per room:
                   bednights = Row 1 x 365 x 1.5 x Row 2.

Row 4   Based on Missions questions to Hotel Managers.

Row 5   Row 3 x $\left(\dfrac{100 - \text{Row } 4}{100}\right)$

Row 6   Mission estimates shown on Table 21-9.

Row 7   Based on investor's expectations.

Row 8   Row 6 x 365 x 1.5 x Row 7.

Row 9   Mission assumption.

Row 10   Row 8 x $\left(\dfrac{100 - \text{Row } 9}{100}\right)$

Row 11   Row 10 + Row 5.

Row 12   Qualitative Mission assumption that foreign tourist numbers will grow to
                   limits of supply capacity in 1973; No change assumed in percent of
                   nationals using these facilities.

Row 13   (Row 1 + Row 6) x 365 x 1.5 x Row 12 x $\left(\dfrac{100 - \begin{array}{c}\text{weighted average of}\\ \text{Row 4 and Row 9}\end{array}}{100}\right)$

Row 14   Tentative projects mentioned to Mission.

Row 15   Mission assumption.

Row 16   Row 14 x 365 x 1.5 x Row 15 x $\left(\dfrac{100 - \text{weighted average of Row 4 and Row 9}}{100}\right)$

Row 17   Row 16 + Row 13.

Row 18   Row 17 - Row 5.

Row 19   Row 18 as % of Row 5.

and subsequently has compared the feasibility of the results with supplier market potential. The worksheet for this statistical exercise is shown in Table 21-13, with details of the methodology and assumptions about individual components. Basically, number of rooms in each of the main tourist centers and their rates of occupancy, were given; from this the mission calculated bednights and assumed the proportion of foreigners using the supply facilities. This exercise was undertaken for the base year 1969. Significantly, and perhaps even surprisingly since the methodologies are completely different, the mission's estimate of foreign visitor bednights for 1969 was slightly higher than that of the Banco de la Republica for 1968. (See Table 21-6). Specific projects for completion in 1970/71 and tentative future projects which had been mentioned to the mission and that were located in areas where only temporary constraints prevent development of potential, were added to present capacity for later years. Assumptions were then made both about occupancy rates and about the proportion of foreigners that would use these facilities. The exercise is obviously highly tentative and rests on the following three general assumptions:

(a)   The public sector will effectively implement a development plan for the tourist sector that results from a preinvestment study program as discussed in the previous section and,

(b)   Colombia will maintain a comparative price advantage vis-a-vis the rest of the Caribbean. Emphasis has been frequently laid in this report on the need for Colombia to maintain her comparative price advantage over other areas of the Caribbean. Tax incentive construction and management help to maintain this advantage. A further measure that might be considered by the Colombian Government if necessary in the future to maintain price advantage, is the granting to tourism of the 15% export tax certificate, the Certificado de Abono Tributario (CAT). The export subsidy is presently granted for "minor" exports, i.e. those non-traditional exports which the authorities wish to encourage; as yet, the privilege has been confined to commodity exports. If granted to tourism the effect would be to apply to tourists' sale of exchange a rate about 12% more favorable than that currently in force.

(c)   No significant change in the pattern of demand for resort-type tourism from the major supplier markets will take place.

Summary of Forecasts, 1969-75.

As shown in Table 21-13, present *accommodation* suitable for tourists is projected to increase from 3,112 rooms in 1969 to 4,515 in 1971 and to 7,400 in 1975, with the main increases located in Bogota (1,640 rooms), Cartagena (800 rooms), Santa Marta (740 rooms), San Andres and Providencia (500 rooms), Leticia (50 rooms) and some 570 distributed between Barranquilla, Cali and Medellin.[10] Average occupancy rates are not expected to fall below the present level for these areas of about 70%. Both Santa Marta and San Andres (and/or Providencia) are expected to have one large resort complex of from 300 to 500 beds, managed by international resort chains whose organization for mass tourism would ensure high occupancy rates immediately. The projections shown in Table 21-14 suggest that total bednights will increase from the base year estimate of nearly 600,000 in 1969 to over 1.6 million in 1975, i.e. an average annual rate of growth of 19% for all Colombia. This rate is compatible with the qualitative forecasts of the market made earlier, which suggested that the long-term growth rate of 14% in tourist numbers would be exceeded.

Tourist numbers are derived from tourist bednights via a divisor which is average length of stay. Length of stay is variously assumed by different official organizations at from 4 to 6 days average. Applying both factors to the estimate of bednights, on a 4-day average length of stay, tourist numbers would grow from 148,000 in 1969[11] to about 410,000 in 1975; on the 6-day

10. Obviously in an exercise as tentative as this one, all data are rounded and treated merely as indications of magnitude rather than precise numbers.

11. This independent mission estimate is very similar to CNT estimates of numbers of arrivals of 143,000 in 1969 (Table 21-6).

TABLE 21-14: SUMMARY OF MISSION'S PROJECTIONS[1] ON FOREIGN VISITORS TO SELECTED CENTERS IN COLOMBIA: 1969-1975

Foreign Bednights ('000)	1969	1970	1971	1972	1973	1974	1975
Bogota	338	297	465	489	512	610	727
Santa Marta	12	27	54	62	72	115	187
Cartagena	61	61	61	65	69	115	192
San Andres & Providencia	3	3	3	3	3	176	176
Barranquilla, Cali, Medellin	135	168	209	234	261	261	261
Leticia & Cucuta	17	23	31	34	38	38	38
Total Selected Centers	566	679	823	888	956	1,234	1,581
Rest of Colombia	27	31	35	40	46	52	59
Total Colombia	593	710	858	928	1,002	1,286	1,640

Annual Rates of Growth	1970	1971	1972	1973	1974	1975	Average Annual Rates of Growth (1969-1975)
Bogota	17	17	5	5	19	19	14
Santa Marta	120	120	15	15	60	60	58
Cartagena	0	0	7	7	65	65	21
San Andres & Providencia	0	0	7	7	–	–	99
Barranquilla, Cali, Medellin	25	25	12	12	0	0	12
Leticia & Cucuta	33	33	12	12	0	0	14
Selected Centers	20	20	8	8	29	29	19
All Colombia	20	21	8	8	28	28	19

Notes: Sub-totals add to totals for 1969, 1971, 1973 and 1975 and are obtained from Table 21-13. Intermediate years are derived from average implicit growth rates between each set of terminal points (except for 1974 San Andres which is the same as the 1975 estimate) and therefore do not add to totals. Estimates are in all cases rounded to nearest thousand.

Data for rest of Colombia in 1969 are obtained by deducting total rooms in Selected Centers from the total in Colombia and assuming (from CNT data) a 45% room occupancy rate, a 1.5 bed per room occupancy rate and that only 5% of occupants are foreigners. The long term overall growth rate of 14% has been extrapolated for other years.

1 Bednights as estimated by official agencies in Colombia are shown on Table 21-6. The mission's independent estimate is close to that of the Banco de la Republica and well below that of the CNT.

TABLE 21-15: FURTHER ASSUMPTIONS FROM MISSION'S PROJECTIONS OF FOREIGN VISITOR BEDNIGHTS 1969-1975

		1969	1970	1971	1972	1973	1974	1975
Arrivals								
Projected bednights	No.	593,000	710,000	858,000	928,000	1,002,000	1,286,000	1,640,000
Number of arrivals, assuming average stay of: 4 days	No.	148,000	178,000	215,000	232,000	251,000	322,000	410,000
6 days	No.	99,000	118,000	143,000	155,000	167,000	214,000	273,000
Annual rate of growth	%		19	21	8	8	28	28
Average annual growth-rate, 1969-75	%				18.5			
Effect on Employment								
Number of rooms plus projected additions	Rooms	3,112	3,112	4,515		4,515		7,400
Number employed per room (assumed increasing)[1]	No.	3	3	5		6		6-7
Employment generated[2]	No.	9,300	9,300	22,600		27,000		44,000-52,000
Effect on Direct Tax Returns[3]								
Projected bednights	No.	593,000	710,000	858,000	928,000	1,002,000	1,286,000	1,640,000
Revenue	Col$ mn.	11	13	15	17	18	23	30

[1] Increase due to progressive development of related services.

[2] These estimates are subject to all the qualifications described in the last two sections and are so tentative that certain intervening years have been omitted.

[3] This calculation includes only revenues from the 5% tax on the hotel bill which is assumed to average US$20 hotel expenditure per bednight. Other tax revenues would arise from international passages bought in Colombia, airport taxes, taxes on incomes directly generated from tourism and indirect taxes on consumer items purchased by tourists.

Table 21-16: PROJECTED VISITOR EXPENDITURES, 1969-1975
(In millions of US dollars)

	1969	1970	1971	1972	1973	1974	1975
Bogota	10.2	11.9	14.0	14.7	15.4	18.3	21.8
Santa Marta	0.2	0.5	1.1	1.2	1.4	2.3	3.7
Cartagena	1.2	1.2	1.2	1.3	1.4	2.3	3.8
San Andres and Providencia	0.1	0.1	0.1	0.1	0.1	3.5	3.5
Barranquilla, Cali, Medellin	3.4	4.2	5.2	5.9	6.5	6.5	6.5
Leticia and Cucuta	0.3	0.5	0.6	0.7	0.8	0.8	0.8
Total Selected Centres	15.4	18.4	22.2	23.9	25.6	33.7	40.1
Rest of Colombia	0.5	0.6	0.7	0.8	0.9	1.0	1.2
All Colombia	15.9[1]	19.0	23.0	24.7	26.5	34.7	41.3
Annual Percent Increase		19.0	21.0	7.0	7.0	31.0	19.0
Average Annual Percent Growth Rate 1969-1975				17.0			

[1]Table 21-6 shows various estimates of receipts from tourist expenditures. The mission estimate is arrived at both indirectly and independently of these estimates, but is close to that of the Banco de la Republica and well below that of the CNT.

Note: Total Expenditures are obtained by multiplying total bednights on Table 21-14 by an assumed daily average expenditure as follows: Bogota: US $30; Barranquilla, Cali, Medellin: US $25; other areas: US $20.

average basis, numbers of tourists would increase from nearly 99,000 in 1969[12] to 273,000 in 1975 (See Table 21-15). In both cases, the average annual rate of growth is nearly 19%. This increase in numbers would be spread over three major and two minor tourist centers and four major cities in Colombia. The increase forecast in tourist arrivals (on a 4-day length of stay) over a period of six years is exactly similar to that achieved from the same base by Mexico between 1945 and 1951. Although tourist assets, including geographical location, are superior in Mexico, the growth took place at an arguably less favorable time in economic history for tourism development. From 425,000 in 1951, Mexico received 1.8 million tourists in 1969. At present Colombia receives more tourists than Barbados (90,000) and the number of arrivals forecast for 1975 (412,000 at 4 days average length of stay or 275,000 at 6 days) compares with present levels of 374,000 tourists to Jamaica in 1969 and to over one million visitor arrivals each to Hawaii, Puerto Rico and Bahamas in 1969. Total tourism traffic to the Caribbean islands alone, presently amounts to 2.5 million and despite the large base has been expanding at an average of 13% per annum. Foreign exchange income from this tourism is estimated by IUOTO[13] at US$400 million. An average annual growth of 19% per annum in tourist arrivals given the present base, the physical and economic size of Colombia, on-going supply projects, an effective public sector development plan and varied tourist assets, is feasible from 1969 to 1975.

Projections of *tourist expenditures* from 1969 to 1975 are shown on Table 21-16. The estimated average annual increase of 17% would raise foreign exchange revenues from an estimated US$16 million in 1969 to over US$41 million in 1975. The implicit average daily expenditure is between US$26 and $28. These estimates are necessarily very tentative. If resort-complex tourism were to be introduced on a large scale and for middle income tourists, average daily expenditure for food and accommodation would be considerably lower in these tourist centers than the US$26 to $28 overall average used in the projection. However, if Colombia attracts tourists away from much higher priced areas in the Caribbean, an average expenditure of US$28 per day, including purchases, would be a relatively modest expectation. While the impact of foreign exchange revenues on the balance of payments would be significant in relation to earnings from non-coffee exports, the impact of these expenditures on the actual tourist centers in which they are spent would be even greater in terms of employment generation and tax revenues.

Table 21-15 shows the projection of the *employment* to be generated by foreign tourism development. From an estimated 9,000 in 1969, the projected additions to accommodation used by foreign visitors and development of related facilities could generate jobs in all sectors of economic activity amounting to between 44,000 and 52,000 in 1975. *Tax Revenues* from 5% tax on hotel bills of foreign visitors are projected to increase from an estimated Col$11 million in 1969 to Col$30 million in 1975.

The Longer-Term Perspective.   The potential of the Caribbean coast or of Colombia's tourist assets is by no means exhausted by investment plans incorporated into the projections. However, the public sector investment costs of extending the tourist centers on that coast, e.g., to the La Guajira peninsula and of opening up new areas such as the Pacific beaches south of Buenaventura or of making specialized tourist areas such as San Agustin or Leticia more accessible to general tourists, are likely to be very high. Experience over the next few years will determine whether demand from the tourist sector warrants these investments. The potential for sustained growth of the tourism sector exists, the economic size to which that potential should be developed depends on returns to be expected from tourism versus other economic development alternatives.

---

12. The Banco de la Republica estimates tourist numbers at 95,000 in 1968 (Table 21-6).
13. IUOTO: International Union of Official Travel Organizations.

CHAPTER 22
EDUCATION AND TRAINING

The declared policy of the Colombian government in the last decade has been the transformation of the education system to make it a more responsive instrument of economic and social development policies. This meant expansion, redirection and reform of the system. A great deal of headway has been made. Overall quantitative objectives have been achieved. Political and social realities in the sixties directed the major effort to expansion and to the beginning of redress of the extreme disparities of educational opportunity. Resources appeared to be too limited to permit simultaneous application of both the expansion program and improvement measures on a large scale. Redirection and quality improvement programs have moved at a slower pace but are now gathering momentum. The basic work in reform ideas and measures has created a climate more conducive to acceptance of change and an appreciation of the need to use resources more rationally in support of economic and social development policies. It is also more widely realized that improving the quality, the efficiency and the productivity of the system would help to effect economies and thereby indirectly support the expansion program.

The Administration of Education

In the administration of education, historical and political factors have brought about a sharing of responsibilities among the central government, the departments, municipal and university authorities, and the private education sector. The public and private sectors of the formal education system fall within the jurisdiction of the Minister of Education. His control over private education, however, is tenuous; under the Constitution, private bodies may establish schools without seeking the authority of the minister. This leads to difficulties when the location, level, type and capacity of schools have to be planned on a national and local basis. During the 1960s, the private sector increased its effort but, for reasons of economy and tradition, concentrated on the more academic types of education. This explains why general secondary education has shown a higher rate of growth than technical secondary education. The local and private authorities have been slow in accepting the proposed reform of the secondary education. The implementation of the ministry's consolidation program, which would lead to substantial economies of resources, has not progressed rapidly, and small secondary schools and non-accredited new universities continue to be established and the universities continue to start up small new faculties.

Public schools are established and administered by the national authority (the Ministry of Education), the departments and the municipalities. This degree of decentralization could become a more positive development force provided there is adequate communication between the partners. The local authorities have been disinclined to plan their contribution to the educational effort in a national context. Recently, the Ministry of Education has made vigorous efforts to convey to the local authorities the requirements at department level consistent with national policies and plans. The ministry proposes to hand over routine administration of the national schools to the department authorities. In addition, a delegate of the ministry has been assigned to each Department Secretariat of Education, and some departments have made progress in setting up small planning units.

To improve management capability the Ministry of Education has further decentralized some of its functions by establishing a number of semi-autonomous agencies and expanding the functions of existing decentralized agencies. Some of these agencies, such as the Colombian Institute for Education (ICOLPE), are to engage in and sponsor educational and scientific research, which have been neglected hitherto. ICOLPE has been set the tasks of (a) carrying out and initiating and coordinating educational research throughout the country, and (b) research and design of teaching and learning aids and materials, including textbooks. It will work closely with the university faculties of education and in particular with the National University of Pedagogy to which it is annexed.

Another agency, the School Construction Institute (ICCE), has architects and engineers in the departments and builds national schools; it has been **entrusted** with administering and staffing the secondary comprehensive schools (INEM)[1] built with IBRD assistance, and also the agricultural institutes reorganized under the sponsorship of UNDP/Unesco; it has carried out competent studies of curriculum development and related facilities planning.

Another semiautonomous agency, the Institute for Education Credit for Technical Studies Abroad (ICETEX), has provided credits to over 19,000 Colombians for graduate and advanced **studies abroad in the following fields in the period 1965-68: engineering (20.4 %), health (14.7 %), education (10.7%), the sciences (10.6%), agriculture (7.7%) and the social sciences, humanities and law (27.6%). In 1969, there were 900 fellows abroad and 9,000 students were receiving assistance in Colombia.**

The education supervisory services have been understaffed and their responsibilities have not been sufficiently clear. The plans to reinforce, reorient, retrain and integrate the service may aim at it becoming: (a) a mobile counseling service to promote quality improvements in the schools; (b) the liaison unit between the education authorities and the schools; and (c) a pool of expertise to provide the planning services with essential information on schools and teachers.

The Ministry of Education Planning Bureau has been understaffed and constrained by inadequate information on economic growth possibilities and policies, skilled manpower needs, and financial plans. Attention has now been directed to reinforcing it and redrafting its functions, particularly in relation to the education section of the Human Resources Unit of the National Planning Department, the planning group of the Institute for Development of Higher Education (ICFES) and the planning offices of the departments.

The Structure and Operations of the Formal System

The structural pattern is depicted in Chart 22-I. It is basically the three-tiered system:

(a) *Primary Education* of five years, nominally for the age group 7-11 (Grades 1-5);

(b) *Secondary Education* of 4/6 years, for the age group 12-15/17, and normally divided into first cycle (Grades 6-9) and diversified or second cycle (Grades 10-11/12);

(c) *Higher Education* of 1/2/3 years for non-degree courses, and 4/5/6 years for university degree courses.

The statutory obligatory primary education has not been enforced, especially since the public authorities have been unable to provide five-year schooling opportunities throughout the country.

Secondary education is open to all primary school graduates provided places can be made available, and is offered in academic, primary teacher training and technical[2] schools. All types have a first and second cycle. The first cycle in technical education is terminal in character, but graduates may enter the second cycle for more advanced work.

The reform to make first cycle general secondary education terminal as well as open-ended has not been. applied, and all first cycle graduates may automatically move to the second cycle. Similarly, it is taken for granted that second cycle secondary education leading to the bachillerato[3] is simply a preparatory course for university education, and the content is oriented accordingly. Transferability is possible only between general secondary and primary teacher-training schools at the end of the first cycle.

Higher education is provided in thirty accredited and eight unrecognized universities, offering first degree and also non-degree technician level courses. Technical level courses are also provided in 27 other higher education institutes or polytechnics.

1. INEM comprehensive secondary schools: secondary schools which admit on a non-selective basis all pupils of a given age group of a given catchment area, and offer a curriculum that integrates practical and academic subjects.

2. "Technical" applies throughout the chapter to industrial, commercial, agricultural and girls' vocational education and training.

3. Award on completion of six years of secondary school.

CHART 22-I

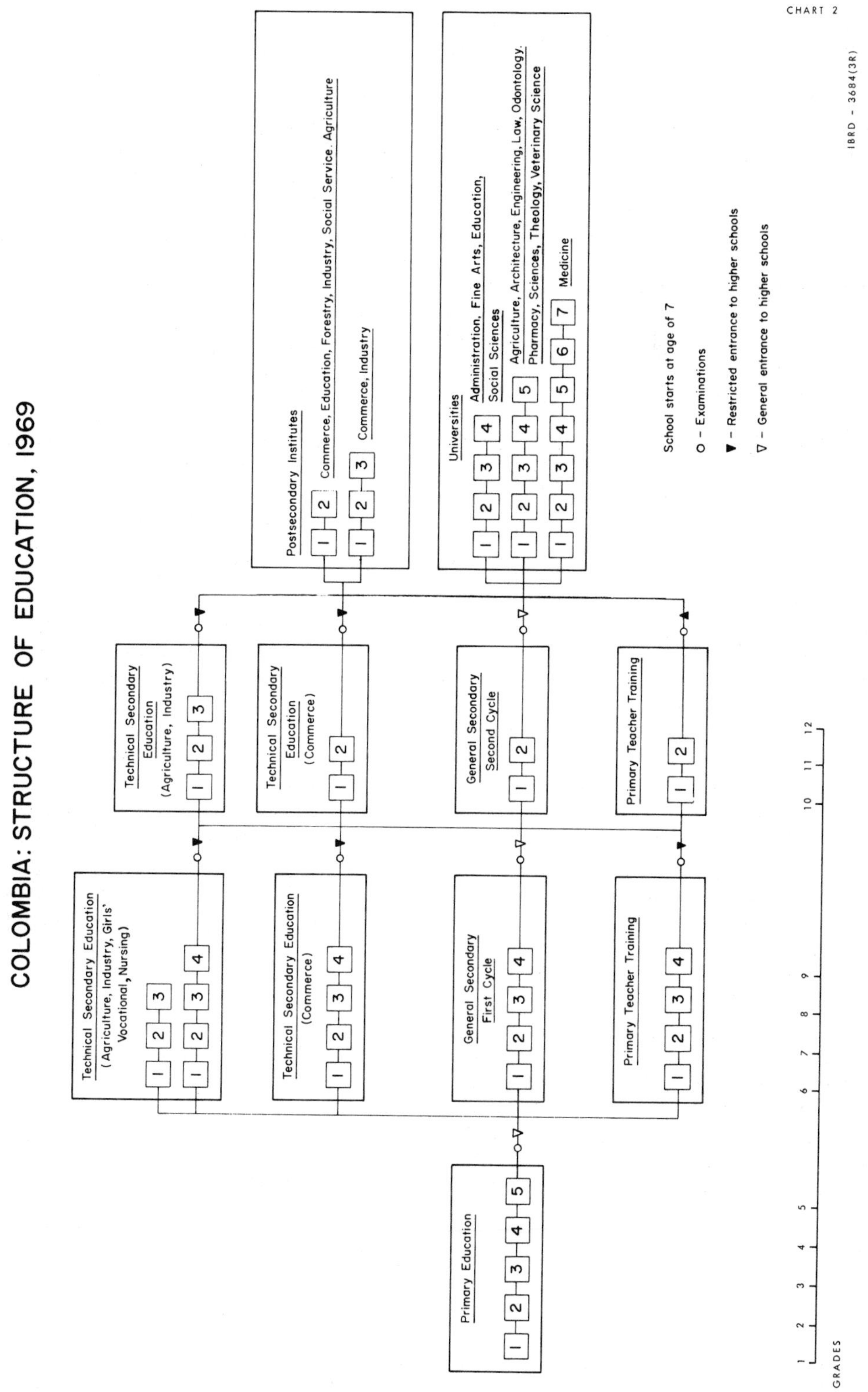
CHART 2
IBRD - 3684(3R)
COLOMBIA: STRUCTURE OF EDUCATION, 1969
Primary Education
Technical Secondary Education (Agriculture, Industry, Girls' Vocational, Nursing)
Technical Secondary Education (Commerce)
General Secondary First Cycle
Primary Teacher Training
Technical Secondary Education (Agriculture, Industry)
Technical Secondary Education (Commerce)
General Secondary Second Cycle
Primary Teacher Training
Postsecondary Institutes
Commerce, Education, Forestry, Industry, Social Service, Agriculture
Commerce, Industry
Universities
Administration, Fine Arts, Education, Social Sciences
Agriculture, Architecture, Engineering, Law, Odontology, Pharmacy, Sciences, Theology, Veterinary Science
Medicine
School starts at age of 7
O - Examinations
▼ - Restricted entrance to higher schools
▽ - General entrance to higher schools
GRADES

Enrollment Growth

Enrollment growth details are summarized in Table 22-1.

This rapid growth in enrollments has required the introduction of emergency measures to provide places. Various forms of the shift-system are used in a growing number of schools and the student work-load has been reduced. The shift system has been accepted with little demur despite its social inconvenience and educational inadequacy.

The private sector has increased its share in primary and higher education enrollments:

	1960 Private Sector	1968 Private Sector
Primary	15.3%	19%
Secondary	60.5%	54%
Higher	39.8%	44%

The main effort of the private sector is made in the larger urban areas. The private sector controls 88% of general secondary education in Bogota, but only 16% in Choco.

Overall enrollments between 1960 and 1968 increased at an average annual rate of 6.2% in primary, 11% in secondary and 14.2% in higher. The increase has been faster in the traditional academic types of education at the secondary and higher levels, particularly in the private sector, than enrollments in the vocational type schools (see Table 22-2).

The proportion of students in second-cycle technical education is only 7.5%, since many students leave after completing the terminal first cycle. As a result the number coming out with middle-level technical skills is seriously low. The establishment of comprehensive secondary schools will help make good this balance, as will also the program for upgrading and rationalizing industrial, agricultural and nursing schools to function only as second-cycle technical schools. The output from first-cycle schools is adequate.

Enrollments in higher education have trebled in the period 1960-68 (Table 22-3), and a further sharp increase took place in 1969. The highest rates of growth have been in fine arts (including architecture), education, the humanities and social sciences (including economics); that is in those areas, apart from the education sciences, in which the private sector is highly involved. The proportion of students in agriculture, engineering, medicine and the sciences has dropped from 62.6% of total enrollments to 40.3%. In some of the faculties, it appears that the more traditional branches are emphasized: civil as compared with mechanical engineering, degree medical studies as compared with nursing. The number of students in graduate courses

TABLE 22-1: ENROLLMENTS ALL LEVELS, 1960 AND 1968

	1960		1968	
	Enrollment In 000's	As Percentage of Appropriate School Age Population	Enrollment In 000's	As Percentage of Appropriate School Age Population
Primary	1,690	77 %	2,733[1]	94 %
Secondary	254	9.8%	587	17 %
Higher	22	1.6%	64	3 %
Total	1,966	32.9%	3,384	40.6%

[1] Including 737,000 over-age pupils; of the total 7 through 11 years age group 69% were enrolled (compared with 59.1% in 1960).

TABLE 22-2: SECONDARY EDUCATION, ENROLLMENT BY TYPE OF EDUCATION, 1960 AND 1968

	1960		1968		1968	
	Total En-rollment	As %	Total En-rollment	As %	Enrollment Second Cycle	As %
General	140,329	55.9%	405,778	69.2%	61,324	72.3%
Industrial	12,243	4.9%	27,808	4.7%	3,329	3.9%
Commercial	40,177	16.0%	69,233	11.8%	1,976	2.3%
Agriculture	2,845	1.1%	7,930	1.3%	317	0.4%
Primary teacher training	28,023	11.1%	54,198	9.2%	16,901	20.0%
Girls' vocational	7,704	3.1%	11,504	2.0%	792	0.9%
Nursing	372	0.1%	1,572	0.3%	34	–
Not stated	13,023	5.2%	–	–	–	–
Art	6,352	2.5%	8,681	1.5%	167	0.2%
	251,068	100 %	586,704	100 %	84,840	100 %

is less than 400, but the courses in medicine and engineering are considered to be of an adequate standard.

In the last three or four years there has been an upsurge in enrollments in the non-degree courses. This may be partly due to students who have failed to win admittance to degree courses using the shorter courses as a stepping stone to university entrance. But there is a growing awareness among secondary school graduates of the value of the shorter technical course. Some 10,000 candidates, over 21% of the total applicants to higher education in 1968, sought admission to the technican level courses.

The shortage of physical places has led to control of intake in the last three years. The biggest difficulties have been experienced in the faculties of agriculture, medicine, engineering and social sciences.

Output and Attrition

Enrollments in primary education include 737,000 over-age pupils. This accounts for 27% of the total, and is almost equivalent to the number of school-age children not enrolled. Theoretically, therefore, Colombia could have achieved universal primary education by 1970 if (a) the children had been induced to enter school at the age of 7, (b) the flow had been smooth, and (c) attendance had been maintained to the terminal point. As it is, the situation is quite different as the education pyramid brings out. Chart 22-II shows the planned 1980 pyramid superimposed over that of actual enrollments in 1968. It will be observed how the base narrows as the flow-through improves, and the pyramid in a regular system opens up to form almost a rectangle at each level of education. At present, however, the age-range in each grade is extremely wide making teaching very difficult, and giving rise to emotional problems. The difficulties are compounded by inadequate learning-teaching aids, rigid promotion and examination procedures and practices, and socio-economic factors affecting learning ability and school retention power.

The rate of attrition—73%—in primary education in the period 1964-68 is very high although it shows improvement over the 85% rate of 1955-1959. Failure rates are also high at

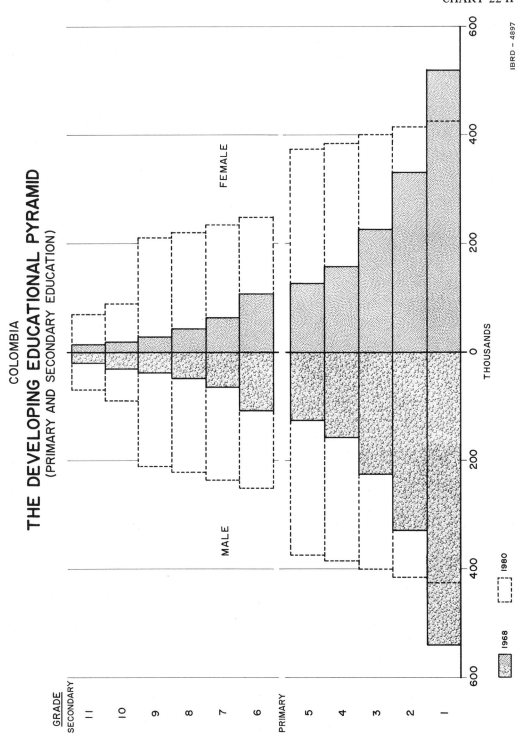

CHART 22-II

COLOMBIA
THE DEVELOPING EDUCATIONAL PYRAMID
(PRIMARY AND SECONDARY EDUCATION)

TABLE 22-3: HIGHER EDUCATION, ENROLLMENT BY FIELD OF STUDY, 1960 AND 1968

	1960		1968					
	All Levels	As %	Middle Level	Post-Secondary Technician	University Level	Post Graduate	Total	As %
Administration and economics			339	798	7,528	169	8,834	12.7
Agriculture and related subjects	1,490	6.7	–	257	3,421	–	3,678	5.7
Engineering and related subjects	5,796	26.1	184	1,949	11,114	334	13,281	20.6
Medicine and related subjects	4,241	19.1	–	782	5,210	49	6,041	9.4
Education	1,079	4.8	329	271	6,074	31	6,705	10.4
Humanities	604	2.7	–	1,569	2,393	67	4,029	6.2
Sciences	2,382	10.7	32	491	2,453	–	2,976	4.6
Social sciences	2,100	9.4	233	146	2,936	–	3,315	5.1
Law	4,180	18.8	27	224	6,280	38	6,569	10.2
Fine arts	309	1.3	885	261	2,925	–	4,071	6.3
Unspecified			490	4,182	34	–	4,706	7.3
Total	22,181	100	2,519	10,930	50,368	388	64,205	100

18%. The regional inequalities are evidenced by the average failure rate of 11% in Bogota as compared with the 22% of Choco.

In secondary education, the attrition rates are about 50% in the first cycle and 20% in the second, and appear to be in part a function of the failure rate (under 10%) and of students entering inappropriate branches of secondary education. In higher education, attrition has averaged about 50%, but engineering, architecture and the humanities fall well below the average. The high failure and drop-out rates, as at all levels, occur in the first two years of the courses. This suggests that the new testing instruments for suitability and ability and guidance services should improve the retention power of the secondary schools and the universities.

Lower outputs as a result of the high drop-out rates defeat the objectives of the system and greatly increase unit costs per graduate. The government is conscious of the problem and is now justifiably preoccupied with regulating flows and reducing dropout. This would also fill up the upper grades in the schools leading to better utilization of teachers, space and available equipment, and so achieve expansion at minimal cost.

The composition of the output of secondary schools reflects the predominance of academic education. Whereas output of general secondary schools at bachillerato level in 1968 was 23,800, the output of the technical schools was only 1,119. The 71 graduates from agricultural technical schools are only a small fraction of university graduates in agriculture. Second-cycle technical education would have to be expanded and also reinforced by the technical branches of the multi-option curriculum of the comprehensive schools.

Since outputs were severely restricted by attrition within each cycle, it was possible to provide fully the educational opportunities in the higher cycles to the successful graduates. Enrollments in first year secondary, grade 6, in 1968 were 93% of the 1967 enrollments in primary grade 5; enrollments in first year higher education in 1968 were 74% of the last year of all types of secondary education in 1967. As the attrition within each cycle is reduced and the system expands, it will not be possible to maintain these high educational opportunity indices. In applying the controls recognition might be given to the special problems of the rural and rural-urban areas which are presently at a disadvantage; also the controls would have to ensure a distribution of students in second cycle secondary and higher education in closer alignment with overall development needs.

Teachers and Teacher Training

There has been an improvement in the qualification of teachers, mainly in the primary schools, between 1960 and 1968. However, the proportion of teachers which can be considered adequately qualified remains low—56% in primary schools and 33% in secondary schools.

In primary schools in 1968 there were between 28 and 34 students per full-time teacher. (The range depends on the assumptions regarding full-time equivalency, of part-time teaching.) In secondary and higher education, the teacher-student ratio appears to be within the range of 1:10 to 1:15. The statistical basis for this estimate is weak. If correct, this is a low ratio for secondary schools and points to under-utilization of teachers. This may be due partly to the rather light teaching load of the teachers, and partly to the uneconomic size of some of the classes in the attenuated upper grades. Centralization and consolidation of secondary school facilities can lead to a more rational and economic use of teachers.

An estimated output of about 5,500 new primary teachers is required annually from 1970 to 1980 to meet expansion needs, make good wastage and gradually replace unqualified teachers. This could be assured with an enrollment of about 15,000 in a two-year course after allowing for attrition and for 20% of graduates not entering the teaching profession. These enrollments would need some 50 schools each accommodating 250 to 500 students, depending on the primary school enrollment in the department concerned. The best teacher-trainers could be concentrated in these schools rather than dispersed, as at present, around 239 teacher training schools where the average school has only 70 students in the second-cycle professional course.[4] This would mean that 180-190 existing establishments could be converted for other purposes

TABLE 22-4: TEACHERS BY QUALIFICATIONS, 1960 AND 1968

Primary Education	1960		1968	
	Number	% of Total	Number	% of Total
Qualified primary teachers	17,044	38 %	34,886	51.5%
University education	1,583	3.5%	3,097	4.5%
Not qualified	26,283	58.5%	29,781	44 %
Total	44,910	100 %	67,764	100 %
Secondary Education				
Qualified secondary teachers	2,127	10 %	5,301	12.5%
Other university degree	4,302	20 %	8,633	20.3%
Qualified primary teachers	5,024	23.4%	11,747	27.6%
Not qualified	10,026	46.6%	16,884	39.6%
Total	21,749	100 %	42,565	100 %
Higher Education				
University first degree	. . . . .		7,368	
Post-graduate degree	. . . . .		796	
Unqualified	. . . . .		976	
No information	. . . . .		1,764[1]	
Total	4,782		10,734[2]	

[1] Figures are incomplete and apply mostly to teachers in public schools. Information on private schools in particular is scanty.

[2] Of whom 3,989 full time, and 359 foreigners.

4. They have more than twice as many in the first-cycle (non-professional).

within the education plan. It would not be easy to carry out such rationalization in view of the large redeployment of teachers, the adverse effects on particular localities and the possible resistance of the private sector school authorities. However, the difficulties would not be unsurmountable if timely alternative developments are made for the teachers and students being displaced.

Secondary teacher training has been the responsibility of the university faculties of education. Total enrollments in regular courses have increased from about 1,000 in 1960 to over 6,000 in 1968; the National University of Pedagogy, exclusively dedicated to teacher training, and 21 faculties participate, nine with enrollments of less than 300. Further fragmentation of secondary teacher training will occur unless expansion is planned. Attrition has been almost 50%, so that in the period 1958-67 there have been only 3,643 graduates: 40% in mathematics and sciences, 26% in social studies and economics, 21% in literature and languages and 13% in pedagogy, administration and psychology. This is a satisfactory distribution, but it does not include the technical specialisms of the secondary comprehensive school or of the technical schools of the existing system. One institute at Zipaquira, has been training workshop instructors, with 60 enrollments in teacher training courses. The Agricultural Institute of Pamplona has been expanded for an output of 30 agricultural teachers annually as from 1972. Expansion in both cases would be highly desirable.

Measures have already been taken to improve the secondary teacher output which is now about 1,200 annually. Faculties of education have restructured other courses to improve retention rates and to permit entry at various points of transferees from other faculties and from other specialist courses within the faculty itself. Special courses have been organized for graduates of other faculties and for professionals in public service and private enterprises who wish to take up teaching. Intensive courses have been conducted for some 2,000 practicing teachers, with USAID assistance, in industrial arts, agriculture, handicrafts, commerce and home economics, or as counsellors or administrators, in response to the requirements of the IBRD-assisted INEM project. However, now that the immediate needs of the project schools are being met, regular courses are needed to prepare teachers of the technical subjects. The teachers of the technical subjects of the first cycle comprehensive schools may be more effectively trained in special technical teacher colleges including the one in Zipaquira (expanded) and in the new polytechnics. Enrollments of about 5,000 on a two-year course (or one-year course for practicing unqualified teachers) would be required to meet the annual need for technical teachers. In addition, the faculties of education could expand and rationalize programs for training administrators, supervisors and teacher-trainers, also, they could combine with engineering, agricultural and economics faculties to offer special courses to train graduates of those faculties as teachers for the technical subjects of the diversified second-cycle secondary schools.

School Facilities

In general, school buildings and equipment are not satisfactory. Many buildings are unsuitable, dilapidated and poorly equipped, the rural and rural-urban schools and smaller technical schools often being the paupers. The shortage of laboratories, workshops and learning-teaching aids and materials is a serious obstacle to adopting modern teaching methods.

The school construction unit (ICCE) has initiated a program to improve school building design and to ensure that practical teaching spaces are provided and equipped. The two IBRD-assisted education projects have required ICCE to review the relationships between school objectives, capacity, organization, curricula, programs of study, teaching methodology and techniques, school design and costs, economic utilization factors, schedules of accommodation and equipment, and relevant teacher training. ICCE has also established satisfactory design norms for the multiple-grade primary school. The principles developed could be applied in all new construction and technical assistance provided by ICCE for this purpose to local and private education authorities on request.

From 1969, the government began distributing textbooks to the public primary schools on a restricted scale with priority given to the rural schools. It proposes to extend the program and to include secondary education. Acceleration of the program is desirable; particularly important to the successful operation of a multiple-grade school is that it have a generous supply of textbooks and supplementary reading and other work material. Costs might be reduced by developing a rental system for secondary schools provided distribution is free to the needy and able students.

Another program which has improved the quality of education is the use of instructional television (ITV) in primary schools. This was started experimentally in 1964 and now reaches 16% of primary school children. The technical difficulties which restricted its use mainly to urban schools can be overcome; and the expansion proposed for the next four years could give more attention to the less-endowed rural schools. Two universities are experimenting with closed-circuit ITV programs. The proposal to introduce closed-circuit ITV into the 19 INEM schools is to be revised in the framework of the longer-term program of full secondary school coverage. It is suggested that the scope of the project be widened into a feasibility study to consider the possible role of new technological media in helping meet the total medium-term and long-term educational, instructional and information requirements of all government and para-government authorities. Such a preinvestment study may take into consideration the present and proposed telecommunications facilities and network, and the resolution taken by the ministers of education of the Andean countries (Caracas, January 1970) to explore the possibilities on a regional basis of satellite communication for educational and other purposes.

Redirection and Rationalization

With technical assistance from the Federal Republic of West Germany, a thorough review has been undertaken of the primary schools curriculum and particular attention has been given to the operation of the multiple-grade school.[5] Guides to teachers have been published, embodying some of the proposed new content and teaching techniques. ICOLPE (the Colombian Institute of Education) has started its own studies on primary school curriculum reform, while the ITV authorities have presented their material and approach to the schools. Coordination and integration of these excellent efforts would be very useful.

At secondary levels, structural reform is envisaged, as shown in Chart 22-III. Its implementation could increase the number graduating and ensure that because of the oriented curricula, they would either be ready for direct productive employment or have sound bases for on-the-job training. The same purpose is served by the introduction of clear terminal points. Consolidation policies are part of the reform, with the purpose of reducing investment and operating costs. Restructuring has begun with the INEM program for construction in the major cities of 19 large well-equipped and appropriately staffed comprehensive schools and the UNDP/UNESCO-sponsored program for reorganization and upgrading of agricultural schools. However, the benefits of restructuring will be limited to the large cities if the reform is not extended into the smaller towns serving the rural areas. This could be done by remodeling and reequipping, and converting where necessary, existing schools to function as first-cycle comprehensive secondary schools. Selected students at the end of the course would be directed into the more centralized institutions of second-cycle diversified education. New first-cycle schools for this purpose can be constructed and equipped in areas where facilities are inadequate or unsuitable for rehabilitation. The school would be sited to serve the needs of its feeder primary schools.

The INEM project indicates the economies of scale in operational and capital expenditures which are made possible by consolidation and capacity utilization of facilities. Operational expenditures of a 1,500 capacity school are 18% higher per unit than those of a 3,000 capacity school, and unit capital expenditures 40% higher. The Colombian secondary schools are very small and uneconomical at present: average size of the public school is 207 pupils, and of private schools, 133 (Table 22-5). While rural and rural-urban areas cannot carry large capacity schools, there is no doubt that the possibilities of consolidation are substantial elsewhere. In order to prepare the action program and estimate the resulting savings in current and investment expenditures, it would be necessary to carry out a technical survey of all existing public

5. A school which provides a full course of studies, but which, because of small enrollment per grade, has not one teacher per class; classes are combined so as to form an economic-sized group to be handled by one teacher.

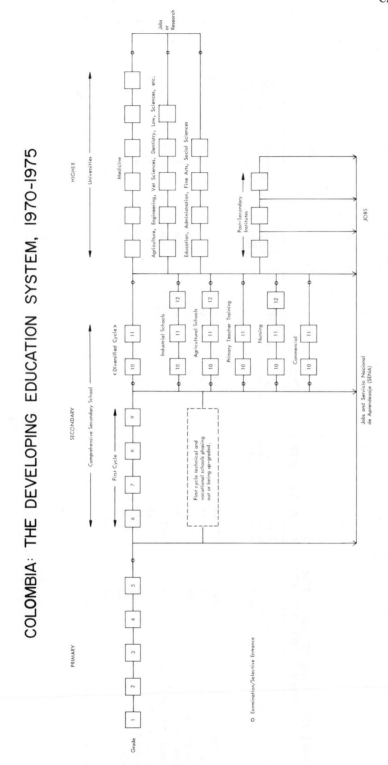

COLOMBIA: THE DEVELOPING EDUCATION SYSTEM, 1970-1975

TABLE 22-5: SECONDARY EDUCATION, 1968
AVERAGE SIZE OF SCHOOLS, BY TYPE, BY CONTROLLING AUTHORITY

Type	Public			Private			Total		
	No. of Schools	Enrollments in '000s	Average Size	No. of Schools	Enrollments in '000s	Average Size	No. of Schools	Enrollments in '000s	Average Size
General secondary	799	177,554	220	1,408	228,224	162	2,207	405,778	183
Industrial	97	22,819	235	79	4,989	63	176	27,808	158
Commercial	69	16,270	235	569	52,963	93	638	69,233	108
Agriculture	65	6,179	95	16	1,751	109	81	7,930	98
Primary teacher training	154	38,588	250	85	15,610	184	239	54,198	227
Girls vocational	77	6,415	83	101	5,089	50	178	11,504	65
Nursing	20	847	42	15	725	48	35	1,572	45
Art	33	4,122	125	77	4,559	59	110	8,681	50
Total	1,314	272,794	207	2,350	313,910	133	3,664	586,704	160

educational institutions as a basis for a comprehensive plan of school facilities requirements (see Preinvestment Study Program in chapter 5).

Programs such as the one to rationalize and upgrade agricultural second-cycle secondary schools, could be extended and implemented for industrial, commercial and primary teacher training at second-cycle level. In addition, the government could require that private schools be established only after government approval has been granted to ensure that private schools offer adequate service and fit into the planned pattern of school facilities.

The success of the reform of the formal education systems is closely related to the activities of training institutions outside the system, especially SENA (Servicio Nacional de Aprendizaje). They are discussed in the next section.

Education and Training Outside the Formal System

A number of ministries, official bodies, para-official bodies and private enterprises organize technical activities usually related to their needs. The Ministry of Agriculture, together with its decentralized agency, ICA, conducts agricultural extension courses and has a program for preparation of community leaders (in agricultural activities). ICA also cooperates with the university schools of agriculture in graduate agricultural studies. The Banco Cafetero and the Caja Agraria plan to augment their training involvement by closer cooperation with existing extension agencies. The Ministry of the Interior organized the Accion Comunal to involve communities in self-help projects which include school construction and literacy programs. The Ministry of Health conducts courses in public health improvement and also subsidizes the university schools of medicine. The Ministry of Defense runs its own secondary and higher education establishments, and military personnel assist in school construction and teaching activities in the rural areas. The Higher School of Public Administration holds courses in political science, administration and planning for civil servants. The National Institute of Nutrition provides relevant courses for school teachers. The Association of the University Faculties of Medicine organizes courses in family planning. The Ministry of Education runs the adult education campaign which aims at reaching 900,000 illiterates of over 13 years of age in the next four years and is considering organizing accelerated full primary level courses for adults. A television program has been inaugurated with telecenters in eight departments.

Semi-public agencies involved in specialized training activities also include the railway, telecommunications and aeronautical authorities and the Empresa Colombiana de Turismo. The coffee, tobacco and cotton growers' associations, in addition to providing schooling for the children of their employees, maintain courses in farm management and improved crop production. The program of the Coffee-Growers' Federation, in particular, is not confined to improving coffee growing techniques but attempts to guide farmers to diversification of crops and to promotion of minor industries. Some of the major enterprises, such as COLTEJER (textiles), conduct systematic upgrading courses for their employees.

The major agency in providing training outside the formal education system is SENA. It provides courses at two levels: three-year courses for apprentices on a system of six months in the SENA training center and six months at work, and courses of varying duration for upgrading adult employees either in the training center or on the job.

SENA is affiliated to the Ministry of Labor but is considered a decentralized agency of the Ministry of Education. It enjoys a great deal of freedom and adequate resources. Consequently, it has the flexibility to meet the needs of local industry as these needs appear. It cooperates closely with the agrarian reform projects of INCORA and with the Ministry of Defense to provide skills to national servicemen about to complete their service. It has also assisted the Ministry of Education with accelerated technical teacher training programs.

SENA is financed by a 2% tax on the payroll of industry. Its recent budgets show its healthy financial position:

	1967	1968	1968 Source of Revenue		
			Industry	Commerce, Other Services	Agri-culture
	Millions Col$	Millions Col$			
Revenue	223.5	330.9	46%	40%	14%
Expenditures	181.9	218.3			
Surplus	41.6	112.6			

TABLE 22-6: ENROLLMENTS IN SERVICIO NACIONAL
DE APRENDIZAJE (SENA), 1965-69

	1965		1968		1969	
	Number	%	Number	%	Number	%
Agriculture	5,331	16	37,320	35	61,536	40
Industry	14,625	45	32,316	31	41,561	27
Commerce and services	13,002	39	36,134	34	50,960	33
	32,958	100	105,770	100	154,057	100

Enrollments have shown a sharp increase with the major emphasis turning to agriculture. The 50% enrollment increase in one year reflects the capability of SENA to meet situations as they arise; SENA's effort in vocational training is, consequently, greater than that of the Ministry of Education in technical education (cf. Table 22-2).

One reason for the success of SENA has been the keen support employers have given it. SENA will cooperate with management in devising suitable programs for workers. Employers also speak well of the product of these courses; the quality and relevance of training is satisfactory since the objectives and the content of the courses are closely related, accommodations and equipment are ample, and SENA is able to attract and train able technicians as teachers. In addition, SENA has received a great deal of assistance from UNDP/ILO, FAO and French, British, German and Swiss sources. Criticism has been leveled at SENA principally on grounds of high administrative costs. With the upsurge in enrollments the overheads should be reduced as a proportion.

SENA has been instructed to spend 10% of its revenues on courses for the unemployed. This is a new departure for SENA since hitherto its mandate was to serve adults and youths in employment. In planning the new activities, SENA could build up two types of programs: providing a variety of accelerated courses for training or retraining of unemployed adults and adolescents and in each case to include functional literacy as necessary, and providing elements of employable skills to over-age primary school dropouts and graduates and to secondary school dropouts. The latter programs could help make up the deficiency of the system. SENA expansion can be expedited and savings effected by handing over to SENA for conversion and modernization some of the formal schools made redundant by the rationalization program.

SENA is the instrument most competent and capable to rapidly promote government employment policies, meet immediate needs for lower and middle level skills, and complement the formal education system.

Financing

The main sources of financing education are:(a) the central government revenues through the Ministry of Education and, to a lesser extent, through other ministries and autonomous government agencies; (b) the local education authorities (departments and municipalities); (c) the private education sector, made up of religious and secular authorities which include large industrial enterprises and associations such as the Federation of Coffee Growers; and (d) international and bilateral agencies. The Ministry of Education supports the department and municipal budgets, makes transfers to ICFES for channeling to higher education, and subsidizes some private higher and secondary education institutions.

In support of its program to decentralize administration, the Ministry of Education has established a Regional Education Fund in each department. The fund will be operated by the local public education authorities under the supervision of the Ministry of Education representatives attached to the local governments. The funds will comprise the contributions of the national, department and municipal government for the operation and expansion of public primary and secondary education.

The Ministry of Education exercises no control over the appropriations to the autonomous universities. The new higher education coordinating and planning agency, (ICFES) has some indirect powers of control, and is also responsible for seeking new sources of finance for higher education.

Public primary education is basically free. Students have to pay an enrollment fee of Col$10-$20 per annum (US$0.50-$1.00) and pay for their books. The fees are low also in public secondary (Col$40-$400) and higher (Col$400-$2,000) education. However small, fees may be prohibitive to the rural population and the low-income urban dwellers who have large families, especially when other costs (books, clothing, transportation) and possible foregone earnings are taken into account. This may be one cause of attrition and irregular school attendance.

Fees at the private secondary schools range from Col$8,000-$18,000 per annum. These, it has been estimated, can be met by only about 10% of the population. This implies that about 90% of candidates for secondary education have to compete for 46% of the total places, since the private schools control 54% of total secondary enrollment. Colombia is not exploiting to the full its latent pool of talent.

Total Expenditures

Total central and local government education expenditures were about Col$3 billion in 1968. With an additional estimated Col$1 billion expended by the private sector, expenditures on education amounted to 4% of gross domestic product. This proportion is below that of Chile which has a higher per capita income and below Guyana with a lower income, but above Brazil and Ecuador at comparable incomes.

Ministry of Education Budget

Expenditures by the Ministry of Education accounted for 61% of total public education expenditures in 1968. This proportion has been rising because of the increasing role of the central authority in the system: in 1960, it mounted to 44%. The ministry budget for 1970 for a total of almost Col$2 billion represented 13.8% of total Central Government expenditures. Its composition is shown in Table 22-8.

Primary education accounts for 78% of all enrollments, but absorbs only 32% of the

TABLE 22-7: COMPARATIVE EXPENDITURES ON EDUCATION, SELECTED COUNTRIES

		Per Capita Income US$	Total Expenditure on Education as % of GDP	Education Expenditure per Capita US$
Colombia	1968	290	4.0	12
Chile	1969	530	5.4 (1968)	34
Venezuela	1969	1,035	4.8	49.50
Brazil	1969	310	3.4	10.50
Guyana	1967	240	5.0	15
Ecuador	1966	235	3.2	7.60
Spain	1968	770	3.0	23.50

TABLE 22-8: MINISTRY OF EDUCATION BUDGET FOR 1970
(In millions of Col$)

	Recurrent	Investment	Total	%
By Levels of Education and other Services				
Administration	108.9		108.9	5.5
Primary education	574.5	52.3	626.8	31.7
Secondary general and teacher training	317.9	189.4	507.3	25.7
Secondary technical	18.4	10.0	28.4	1.5
Higher	347.3	107.4	454.7	23.0
Culture	34.5	12.4	46.9	2.4
Sports	18.2	33.0	51.2	2.6
Social Security and pensions	103.0	–	103.0	5.2
Others	22.5	25.9	48.3	2.4
Total	1,545.2	430.3	1,975.5	100.0
As % of national budget	20.9	5.9	13.1	–
By Major Categories of Expenditures				
Salaries and wages	316.7			20.5
Materials	23.7			1.5
Transfers (local authorities and ICFES)	1,055.3			68.3
Transfers to private schools	35.3			2.3
International agencies	11.2			0.7
Pensions	103.0			6.7
Total	1,545.2			100.0
Investment Expenditure through ICCE				
Urban primary		43.2		
Rural primary		6.5		
Primary unidentified		2.5		
Secondary general		10.5		
Secondary comprehensive (INEMs)		161.6		
Agricultural institutes		10.0		
Primary teacher training		5.0		
Secondary unidentified		12.3		
Other[1]		29.9		
Total		281.6		

[1] Includes items which are usually classified as recurrent.

ministry's budget. In contrast, higher education, accounting for less than 3% of enrollments, gets 23% of the budgetary funds. The imbalance would be smaller if expenditures by local authorities could be taken into account since they go mainly to primary and secondary schools. Nonetheless, substantial disproportions would still remain.

Other Public Sources

It has not been possible to separate from the recurrent budgets of other ministries the amounts expended on education and training, but in the 1970 investment budget about Col$150 million has been identified as expenditures on education, training and research by ICA, IN-DERENA, and the Ministries of Interior and Health. Four-fifths of this is for agricultural education and research, and rural and community development expenditure.

Foreign assistance to education and training in Colombia has been considerable; particularly important has been the technical assistance aid from the U.N. family and from numerous bilateral agencies. Aid from six major donors in 1960-66 was estimated at about US$48 million (USAID-US$8.4 million, Ford, Rockefeller and Kellogg Foundations $18 million, IDB-US$15.6 million, UNDP and agencies-US$5.5 million). Nearly 60% of this aid was to the universities. In 1967-68 about US$25 million was committed by UNDP/ILO ($5.7 million), UNDP/UNESCO ($3.4 million) and IBRD ($15.2 million). A large measure of technical assistance has been received from the same sources, and also from the Federal Republic of West Germany (primary curriculum and vocational training), Spain (training in handicrafts, fisheries and shipbuilding), United Kingdom (foundry and textile technology), France (vocational training), Holland (engineering education), and the United States (higher education, TV, educational planning).

Imbalances

The amounts included in the 1970 national budget for education as a percentage of the total budget are significant, although relatively lower than appropriations in some Latin American countries. The allocations to recurrent expenditures are particularly encouraging, but those for investment purposes, are inadequate in view of the deficiencies which accumulated during the middle 1960s. The loss of headway at that time was due mainly to the inability of the school construction unit to utilize the funds made available. Its work capacity has now been considerably improved.

The present balance of the education system and its financing system puts able children of the lower income bracket groups at a disadvantage. ICETEX alleviates the difficulties of some students through its educational credit scheme for studies in secondary and higher education. But the resources of ICETEX are unequal to the needs and the government proposes to seek external assistance to expand the fund. In addition, the family welfare fund of the Ministry of Education helps poorer children to defray non-fee costs, and the program to distribute free textbooks has started well with priority for Grades 1 and 2 in rural areas. The other major imbalance is in insufficient amounts for primary schools and for secondary technical education, as compared with allocations for general secondary and higher education; and within the higher education, insufficient amounts are given to technician level education (mostly technical) compared to other types.

Future Programs: Priority Indicators

In the absence of a comprehensive manpower survey measuring market demand and the needs for manpower in each sub-sector of economic activity, the authorities would find it difficult to plan education and training with sufficient certainty and detail. Such survey is urgently required and is suggested in the Preinvestment Study Program. It is possible, however, on the basis of already declared policies and objectives, to identify broad priority areas. They result from the assessment of the existing education services and their potential; from the inequality of educational opportunities in the rural areas compared to urban centers and the social problems this creates; and from a series of recent partial studies on employment policies, skill levels, training requirements and numbers of the economically active working population in relation to the possible needs of a developing economy at Colombia's stage of growth.

Inequality of Educational Opportunities

In 1964, at the time of the census, the average length of schooling of the rural population was 1.7 years as against the 5.1 years of the urban population. This was in part due to the inferior facilities in the rural areas: few schools offer a complete primary school course, and the majority (64%) provide only one or two years of schooling. As a result, only 3% of rural primary school entrants complete the five-grade course as compared with 46% of the urban children. Secondary education and vocational training facilities are virtually non-existent in the rural areas. The literacy rate of the over 15 years of age population increased from 62.3% in 1951 to 73% in 1964, but the absolute number of 2.5 million illiterates also shows an increase, and illiteracy remains almost three times higher in the rural areas (41%) than in the urban ones (15%).

It is likely that the educational situation of the rural population has improved since 1964. It is unlikely that the improvement has been substantial and that the differences in educational opportunities have been narrowed. Similarly, it is unlikely that the educational opportunities available to the lower income groups in the urban areas, many of whom are recent migrants from the rural hinterland, have significantly increased. The implication, dictated by considerations of social and broad development policy is that a major effort is needed to improve primary education with special emphasis on rural education, and secondly to locate first-cycle comprehensive secondary schools to serve the rural and rural-urban areas. This emphasis on primary and then secondary education is supported by the findings of three studies on the returns on investment in education in Colombia.[6] These studies are not conclusive because their scope was limited by the quantity and quality of the data available. However, they indicate that investment is highly profitable in primary (about 21%) and secondary (about 20%) education, but less so in university education (about 7%). A useful sidelight emerges from the studies; the highest economic benefit accrues when a level of education is completed, underlining the importance of measures to reduce dropout rates.

Another factor in determining priorities in education is its possible effect on population growth. A recent study confirms for Colombia direct relationships between education, income, occupation and family size.[7] Income is related to education level both as cause and as effect. As family income increases, the percentage of persons less than 15 years of age decreases sharply. Fertility is inversely related to the level of education reached: the pregnancy rate in women with no schooling is 58% higher than that of women with some secondary education; the pregnancy rates of women whose husbands are farmers or laborers is higher than that of wives of professionals, administrators and skilled workers; and women in the rural areas or of the poorer socio-economic level have a higher fertility rate than those in the urban areas or of the higher socio-economic groups. The implication of these findings is that improving the quantity and quality of educational opportunity in the rural areas and among the lower income groups in the cities could help control population growth.

6. T.P. Schultz, *Returns to Education in Bogota, Colombia* (RAND Corp. memorandum RM-5645-RC/AID, September 1968).
M. Selowsky, *The Effect of Unemployment and Growth on the Rate of Return to Education: The Case of Colombia* (Development Advisory Service, Harvard University, Economic Development Report No. 116, November 1968).
C.R.S. Dougherty, *The Optimal Allocation of Investment in Education.*
7. Carlos Aqualimpia and others, *Demographic Facts of Colombia,* The Milbank Memorial Fund Quarterly, July 1969.

Supply of Skills

The 1964 census showed the following occupational structure of the labor force: 6.5%**high-**level manpower, 10.2% sales and office workers, 47% farmers and related workers, 17% craftsmen and related workers, and the rest in service industries, communications and transport and non-classifiable positions, a breakdown which differs from the partial survey of establishments in 1963 mainly because the latter covered only the modern sector of the economy. In the survey, 13% of the labor force was classified as high level manpower, white collar workers were 22.7% and blue collar workers 64.3%. The census identification of the educational attainments of the labor force showed that 61% had finished primary schools, 9% secondary and about 1% university level education. Information on the remainder is ambiguous. Among the high-level manpower, 64% are shown as completing secondary education and 17% as having university education. The educational profile of the labor force as a whole is not high, but is improving slowly. Generally, the recent experience is that unemployment varies inversely with educational attainments.

There are two imbalances characterizing the labor market. One is the quantitative imbalance, primarily in the urban sector, reflected in large unemployment and underemployment. It has been generated by the slow expansion of the market's labor absorption in wage/salaried jobs at a time of continuous high annual increases in the labor force from migration and from the growth of the indigenous urban population. The other imbalance is of a qualitative nature and the result of the orientation of the graduates of the educational system. There appears to be a serious mismatch of market labor demand and educational output at the secondary level of education, with its emphasis on general secondary education. Corrective action is being taken to reorient the education system toward satisfying manpower demands of a changing economic structure, but lags in supply of some skills are evident.

In the agricultural extension services the stock of high-level manpower appears sufficient for present needs, but there is a substantial shortage of agricultural technicans and middle-level workers. A rational allocation of manpower in such a program would be about one professional to five middle-level workers; the present ratio is 1 : 1.5. It is estimated that the staff of the official extension services and of various other government agencies engaged in similar work is about 2,000 professional and non-professional personnel. Most, however, serve the modern commercial sector. As a result, the staff available for effective work in the small farms is quite insufficient.

In the health field, the universities have an annual output of about 400 doctors; conservative estimates of future needs require an output of about 600. Whereas the estimated needs for professional level nurses is about 900 annually, the output is below 200. Auxiliary nurses and personnel for para-medical services are required at a rate of some 4,000-5,000 a year; present outputs cannot be accurately evaluated, but they are much below the needs.

The solution to the supply lag of technical skills would have to be sought in the acceleration of structural reform, particularly in the secondary education, remodeling and reequipping of existing schools as well as designing new construction on the reform lines. This would ensure an increased output of technically-trained or technically-oriented graduates and help decrease correspondingly the enrollments in the academic branches of secondary education. It would appear that emphasis on expansion-cum-reform of technical education facilities, broadening of the first cycle secondary curriculum, and expansion of out-of-school training agencies, such as SENA, would lead in a faster manner to the needed qualitative and quantitative advance of the labor force.

Future Programs: An Indicative Projection

An indicative planning model for the period 1969-80 is sketched below. The purpose is to explore the quantitative implications of several major policy objectives, not to draw up a long-term educational plan: the latter can be undertaken only by the Colombian authorities. The

TABLE 22-9: FLOW OF STUDENTS IN THE FORMAL EDUCATION SYSTEMS, '000's (ACTUAL 1964-68 and PROJECTED 1969-80)

A. PRIMARY EDUCATION

	Grade 1 Year 1	Grade 2 Year 2	Grade 3 Year 3	Grade 4 Year 4	Grade 5 Year 5	Total Enrollment	Estimated Primary Graduates
1964	938	562	327	221	166	2,215	
1965	922	574	349	243	182	2,270	
1966	955	592	380	273	208	2,408	
1967	1,006	626	414	295	229	2,571	200
1968	1,056	660	449	317	251	2,733	230
1969	1,140	707	470	350	270	2,937	250
1970	1,060	760	526	400	300	3,046	280
1971	1,050	750	580	440	330	3,150	310
1972	1,000	870	650	500	380	3,400	360
1973	800	900	800	600	450	3,550	420
1974	750	750	800	720	530	3,550	500
1975	720	700	720	750	670	3,560	630
1976	750	720	700	720	700	3,590	670
1977	770	720	720	700	700	3,640	670
1978	800	770	750	720	700	3,740	670
1979	883	800	770	750	720	3,870	700
1980	850	830	800	770	750	4,000	700

Notes:

Primary Flow assumes:

(i) improvement of retention rate from 27% in period 1964-1968 to 64% in period 1971-1975

(ii) normal age-grade relationships beginning 1973 and over-age pupils moved out almost entirely by 1975.

Secondary Flows assume:

(i) improvement of retention rates in first cycle from about 50% in 1964-1967 to about 75% in 1972-1975

(ii) control of entry from primary into secondary – Grade 6 enrollment as % of Grade 5 enrollment decreasing from 95% in 1968-1969 to 70% in 1975-1976; and from first cycle secondary into second cycle, i.e., Grade 10 enrollment as % of Grade 9 enrollment from 80% in 1967-1968 to 60% in 1974-1975 and to 45% in 1979-1980.

B. SECONDARY EDUCATION

	Grade 6 Year 1	Grade 7 Year 2	Grade 8 Year 3	Grade 9 Year 4	Total First Cycle	Output First Cycle	Grade 10 Year 5	Grade 11/12 Year 6/7	Total Second Cycle	Output Second Cycle	Grand Total
1964	129	83	60	41	313		27	19	46	18	359
1965	142	93	68	48	351		32	22	54	20	405
1966	171	110	80	58	419		39	29	68	26	487
1967	192	120	85	63	460		44	33	77	29	537
1968	214	129	92	67	502	64	49	36	85	34	587
1969	239	145	106	72	562	68	54	43	97	40	659
1970	230	170	130	90	620	85	57	47	107	47	737
1971	250	190	140	110	690	105	63	52	117	49	807
1972	270	210	160	120	760	114	70	58	128	55	888
1973	320	240	190	140	890	130	80	65	145	62	1,035
1974	344	270	220	180	1014	170	90	75	165	69	1,179
1975	376	300	250	210	1136	200	108	85	193	81	1,329
1976	450	330	280	240	1300	228	120	100	220	95	1,520
1977	490	430	310	270	1500	256	130	110	240	104	1,740
1978	500	460	410	300	1670	287	140	120	260	114	1,930
1979	500	460	440	400	1800	380	150	130	280	123	2,080
1980	500	470	440	420	1830	400	180	140	320	133	2,150

TABLE 22-10: PROJECTION OF TEACHER REQUIREMENTS, FORMAL EDUCATION SYSTEM[1] FULL-TIME EQUIVALENCY, 1980

Level	Projected Enrollments	Teacher-Pupil Ratio	A Teachers Required	B Teachers on Post 1968	C Estimated[3] Wastage 1968-79	Total Additional Qualified Teachers Required 1969-80 A - B + C	Average Annual Requirement of Qualified Teachers
Primary	4,000,000	1:35	112,000	80,000[2]	28,000	60,000	5,500
First Cycle Secondary	1,830,000	1:26	75,000	29,000	17,000	58,000	5,200
Diversified Cycle Secondary	320,000	1:20	16,000	11,000	5,000	10,000	900
Total Secondary	2,150,000	1:25	86,000	40,000[4]	22,900	68,000	6,100
Higher	190,000	1:12	16,000	5,000[5]	3,000	14,000	1,200

1 Excludes requirements for pre-primary, seminaries and special schools.

2 Estimated full-time equivalency of 1968 force of 100,600.

3 Estimated wastage of 4% decreasing to 3%.

4 Estimated full-time equivalency of 1968 force of 58,000.

5 Estimated full-time equivalency of 1968 force of 7,900.

exercise is not comprehensive, and some basic policy options have not been explored, such as: whether extension of compulsory education to 15 years of age was not advisable in terms of social and employment policies; whether there should not be an even greater emphasis on systematic development of training facilities outside the school system than has been put forward in this chapter; whether the present and likely future patterns of skills should be considered to a greater extent in terms of industrial programs keeping pace with every advance in technology.

It is assumed that the major policy objectives in the 1970's would be to:

(a)   redress inequities in educational opportunity as between the rural and urban populations, and the lower and higher socio-economic groups;

(b)   redress imbalances between technical and academic education at all levels and make good gaps in training facilities for certain vocational and high-level skills;

(c)   reconcile expansion and reform demands by ensuring that expansion results from the efforts to implement modernization reforms. This implies some measure of control and direction of expansion.

There are a number of implications of these objectives: an increase in government participation in secondary and higher education, particularly in the technical branches; provision of expanded welfare and guidance services; expansion and extension of training activities outside the formal system and complementarity of the two services; a substantial decline in the attrition rate within each cycle, accompanied by application of controls at entry points into levels or cycles of education other than primary, so that the production of usable skills can expand rapidly.

The main results of this exercise, concerning enrollments, output and teacher requirements, are shown in Tables 22-9 and 22-10 which also contain the specific assumptions on retention rates (i.e., the inverse of attrition rates) and on teacher-pupil ratios. The enrollments projections are summarized in Table 22-11.

The projected rate of growth of total enrollments is 5.4% per annum, lower than the 1960-68 rate of 7.1% per annum. This is a result of the reforms designed to improve flows. The main features of the strategy implied in the model and in the associated projections are:

(a)   smoothing out of the flow of students through the primary education system. This would make possible achievement of universal primary education in the late 1970s , with special emphasis given to fulfilling the needs in the rural areas. The program which

TABLE 22-11: ENROLLMENTS IN '000s AND AS PERCENTAGE OF RELEVANT AGE-GROUP

	1968		1975		1980	
Primary	2,733[1]	94 %	3,560[2]	100 %	4,000	98 %
Secondary First Cycle	502	24.6%	1,136	46 %	1,830	61 %
Secondary Second Cycle	85	6.7%	193	11 %	320	17 %
Higher	64	3.0%	142	5.0%	190	5.5%
Total	3,384	40.6%	5,031	47.6%	6,340	51 %

[1] Includes 737,000 over-age pupils (age-group 12-15).

[2] Still includes some over-age pupils.

has been started to provide at least full primary school education through the multiple-grade schools is accorded the highest priority;

(b)   phasing out of first-cycle technical schools which have proved ineffective, but combining this with increased provisions for first-cycle comprehensive secondary education, and assumption by SENA of increasing responsibility for school leavers and dropouts including the over-age pupils in the rural areas;

(c)   shift in the proportion of students in second-cycle technical education or technically-oriented education (in the diversified cycle of comprehensive schools) as compared with academic branches from 30% of the total second-cycle enrollments in 1968 to 70% in 1980;

(d)   shift in the proportion of students in the technical level courses in higher education as compared with students in the degree courses from 16% of higher education enrollments in 1968 to 30% in 1980,

(e)   giving priority in the process of restructuring and rationalization, whenever more economical, to conversion and re-equipping over new construction and always firstly providing improved and expanded facilities for the rural and rural-urban areas, including upgrading and re-equipping the incomplete schools[8] in these areas.

The expansion projected in the model would, in addition to achieving universal primary education, raise the enrollments in secondary schools from 17% of the relevant age group in 1968 to 45% in 1980—a growth rate in enrollments (11.4% per annum) higher than in the past.

Cost estimates for this kind of expansion and reform can only be illustrative at the present time. Current expenditures per student are assumed to increase in real terms at annual rates ranging from 3% to 7% to allow for quality improvements. Capital expenditures are based on ICCE unit costs for primary and higher education and IBRD project appraisal for comprehensive secondary education.

This level of expenditures should be possible to accommodate. The social and economic benefits would be substantial.

TABLE 22-12: PROJECTION OF PUBLIC EDUCATION BUDGETS
(In Col$ millions at 1969 prices)

	1968	1975	1980
(a) Public education authorities' recurrent budget:	2,300	4,245	7,160
(b) Public education authorities' investment budget:	190	850-1,350[1]	1,040[2]
(c) Total public education authorities' recurrent and investment budgets:	2,490	5,095-5,595[1]	8,200(?)
(d) Total public and private education expenditures as % of GDP	4.0%	4.6-5.0%[1]	5.0%(?)

[1] Lower end of the range assumes a continued large use of double-shift system. The higher end assumes that additional places are established for all additional enrollments.

[2] Expenditure level dependent on investment level in prior years.

8. Schools providing only one or two years of primary tuition.

Preinvestment Studies

To ensure timely and realistic perspective planning and implementation on a sound basis of the first-phase program, the Colombian authorities propose to carry out a number of preinvestment studies in the near future. They comprise: a school facilities' planning study; preparation of a post-secondary technician training program; a feasibility study on the use of the new communications media for education purposes; a manpower survey; planning and establishment of automated data processing for education administration; organization of a teaching aids and text-book center, and a project-oriented program of further development of the secondary education reform. The cost estimates and description of the studies are given in the chapter on the Preinvestment Study Program.

Organization

Most of the decisions affecting the operation and development of water supply and sewerage in Colombia are made by three agencies: the municipal public companies (Empresas) in the larger cities; the National Institute for Municipal Development (INSFOPAL), with jurisdiction over 769 urban communities; and the National Institute for Special Health Programs (INPES), serving the rural population. Their development plans and programs are coordinated by the National Planning Department (Planeacion).

The 1970 population under the jurisdiction of the Empresas, INSFOPAL and INPES is shown in the table below:

TABLE 23-1: POPULATION BY AGENCY JURISDICTION – 1970

Agencies	Population (in millions)
Municipal Empresas	7.2
INSFOPAL	5.8
INPES	8.6
Total	21.6

Municipal Empresas.   There are 21 public companies under municipal control which provide such services as water supply and sewerage, solid waste collection and disposal, public markets, telephone and electric power service. The Empresas in the three major cities of Bogota, Medellin and Cali successfully cope with the problems of these fast-growing urban centers. Barranquilla, the fourth city in size, is having serious problems of administration and financing. The 17 remaining Empresas, in the medium-size and smaller cities, have experienced difficulties in providing adequate services. They have recently been preparing feasibility studies for expansion of their water supply and requesting funds from international lending agencies. Table 23-2 shows the municipal public companies operating in Colombia, the estimated population under the jurisdiction of each, and the percentage of the population connected to the respective water supply system.

National Institute for Municipal Development (INSFOPAL).   Its main functions are to prepare public investment plans in the water/sewer sector for submission to the planning unit of the Ministry of Health (this unit, in turn, must seek the approval of the National Planning Board—Planeacion); build, operate and maintain water supply and sewage disposal systems for communities of more than 2,500 inhabitants; establish, with the approval of the Ministry of Health, sanitary standards for construction and operation of water supply and sewage disposal systems; and submit to the National Tariff Board the water supply and sewerage rate applications for those systems under its jurisdiction.

INSFOPAL has suffered the consequences of frequent changes in general managers and conflicts between the central office and its regional water supply corporations, the ACUAS. With little supervision from the central office, the ACUAS took the initiative and sought political and economic support of the local governments. The larger ACUAS strongly criticized deficiencies in the central office and even defaulted on relending agreements with INSFOPAL of loans from the Inter-American Development Bank to INSFOPAL for expansion of systems. A recent survey of the ACUAS' debts to INSFOPAL revealed that a total of Col$12 million was past due in 1968, thus forcing INSFOPAL to service the IDB loans from its own appropriated funds. At the beginning of 1968, Direcciones Seccionales (Branch Offices of INSFOPAL) were established to replace those ACUAS which presented difficult administrative and financial problems. Of the original 20 ACUAS, only 10 remained in 1970.

TABLE 23-2: MUNICIPAL PUBLIC UTILITIES OPERATING IN THE WATER SUPPLY/SEWAGE DISPOSAL SECTOR

Utility	Estimated Population under Jurisdiction ('000)	% Population Connected
Bogota	2,540	80.0
Medellin	1,025	77.0
Cali	950	80.0
Barranquilla	640	84.0
Bucaramanga	305	82.0
Cartagena	295	50.0
Manizales	270	52.0
Cucuta	205	85.0
Pereira	200	79.0
Armenia	180	67.0
Palmira	145	80.0
Monteria	115	60.0
Neiva	110	83.0
Buga	91	75.0
Tulua	77	72.0
Cartago	72	75.0
Villavicencio	70	70.0
Sugamoso	48	–
Calarca	39	–
Honda	22	–
Garzon	17	–

Six towns—Buenaventura, Giradot, Popayan, Pamplano, Santa Rosa del Cabal and Leticia—have an agreement with INSFOPAL to operate and maintain their systems. The percentages of population served with water in the 10 largest towns under INSFOPAL's jurisdiction are shown in Table 23-3.

National Institute for Special Health Programs (INPES).   This Institute, created by a Decree of April 2, 1968, is part of the Ministry of Public Health. Its main fields of activity are training

TABLE 23-3: PERCENTAGE OF POPULATION WITH WATER SERVICES – TEN LARGEST TOWNS UNDER THE JURISDICTION OF INSFOPAL, 1970

Towns	Estimated 1970 Population ('000)	% Population with Services
Ibague	183	60.0
Santa Marta	133	60.0
Itagui	131	50.0
Pasto	105	80.0
Buenaventura	96	40.0
Valledupar	89	40.0
Barrancabermeja	88	60.0
Giradot	88	60.0
Popayan	77	90.0
Envigado	67	80.0

of professional and auxiliary personnel in the public health sector; rural sanitation, involving water supply and sewerage for communities with less than 2,500 inhabitants; and biomedical and epidemiological research.

Water supply and sewerage systems are constructed by departmental branches of INPES, and priority of investment depends on local interest and willingness to contribute labor and materials. A survey of the particular community's economic condition is made and each family's monthly contribution to the system's costs is determined prior to construction. Part of the revenues are retained locally for salaries and maintenance; the remainder amortizes a pre-established part of the capital investment (about 40%). Although this program has not been in effect long enough to judge whether debt service will be maintained, the approach taken appears appropriate to the problem and the environment in which INPES must operate.

Regional Authorities and Independent Municipalities. Besides the Empresas, INSFOPAL and INPES, there are regional authorities and independent municipalities operating in the sector.

The Autonomous Regional Corporation of the Bogota Plain, Ubate and Chiquinquira Valleys (CAR) is a planning and coordinating agency for Greater Bogota, having jurisdiction in an area of 6,000 sq km. CAR's fields of interest include: water in its several aspects (potable and waste water, flood control, recreation, land reclamation), forestry and erosion control, electric power, highways and telephones. In 1968 CAR financed a regional water supply system for the towns of Zipaquira, Cogua and Nemocon, where salt mines represent an important fiscal resource as well as a source of employment, both in the mines and related industries. A second regional system (Madrid-Mosquera-Funza) is being built, and studies are completed for a large regional aqueduct serving the towns of Tabio, Tenjo, Cota, Chia and Cajica. These systems are independent of INSFOPAL and INPES.

The Cauca Valley Authority (CVC) has developed water supply systems for communities under its jurisdiction. The Institute for Agrarian Reform (INCORA) and the Coffee Federation have likewise built small rural systems in areas of particular interest to their programs.

There is a group of towns where water supply and sewerage are operated directly by the municipality. The only large town in this category is Bello, with a population of 140,000 within the metropolitan area of Medellin. Once affiliated with ACUANTIOQUIA, Bello withdrew from INSFOPAL some years ago; owing to internal difficulties, the ACUA management was not able to cope with the needs of this rapidly growing municipality despite INSFOPAL's intervention.

National Planning Department (Planeacion). There are three sections of Planeacion directly involved in the water supply and sewerage sector: the Infrastructure Unit - Sanitary Engineering Division; the National Public Services Tariff Board; and the National Fund for Development Projects.

The infrastructure Unit acts as a reviewing and coordinating agency for public utility sector investment, and the Sanitary Engineering Division carries out this function in the water supply and sewerage sector. It also supervises feasibility studies financed by FONADE (see below) and follows up projects submitted to external lending agencies.

National Fund for Development Projects (FONADE) was created in late 1967 to finance technical and economic studies for sectors and specific projects. In its first year of operations, loans totaling Col$74.0 million were authorized, out of which Col$18.5 million was used to finance the following water supply and sewerage studies:

Col$8.0 million for feasibility studies for Palmira, Tulua, Pereira, Bogota, Neiva, Cartagena and Manizales;

Col$2.5 million for sewerage and erosion control in Bucaramanga;

Col$3.0 million for studies of a new water source in Medellin; and

Col$5.0 million for expanding Cali's water supply system.

National Public Services Tariff Board reviews requests for rate changes submitted by the water, sewer and electric power utilities. No rate change can be put into effect without the Board's approval and the Board is required to set guidelines for the frequency with which rate increases should be sought by the utilities, as well as the type of data which should be submitted in support of a rate change. Given the generally low level of rates for water and sewer services, most requests have been for increases.

Supply of Service

It is estimated that in 1970 slightly more than one-half of the population was served, i.e. was connected to a system or had access to water services. In 1965, this proportion was about 40%. Table 23-4 gives the relevant data by grouping population into urban and rural, and according to the agency with jurisdiction over water services.

TABLE 23-4: WATER SUPPLY IN RELATION TO POPULATION

	Estimated Population under Agency Jurisdiction (millions)			Estimated Population with Water Services (millions)		
	1965	1970	Increase	1965	1970	Increase
Urban Areas						
Empresas	5.8	7.2	1.4	4.0	5.9	1.9
INSFOPAL	4.6	5.8	1.2	2.0	2.8	0.8
Rural Areas						
INPES	8.0	8.6	0.6	1.5	2.2	0.7
Total	18.4[1]	21.6[1]	3.2	7.5	10.9	3.4

[1] Equals total population of Colombia.

From this table, estimated percentages of population with water service can be derived as shown below:

Agency	Percentages of Total Population		Increase (Percentage Points)
	1965	1970	
Empresas	69	82	13
INSFOPAL	43	48	5
INPES	18	25	7

INSFOPAL is making very slow progress in reducing the backlog of unserved urban population and has not set goals for supplying water to any specific percentage of the population under its jurisdiction. The Empresas have made a substantial advance; however, in some of the smaller cities the situation is not favorable (see Table 23-3).

When one considers the rural population in two groups—concentrated (when a community's population exceeds 100) and dispersed (when a rural settlement has less than 100 people)—then the total rural population of 8.6 million is divided as follows:

Group	Population 1970 (in millions)	Est. Pop. with Water Services (in millions)	Est. % Pop. with Water Services
Concentrated	3.6	1.6	45%
Dispersed	5.0	0.6	12%

The Punta del Este Conference for the Latin American countries set a rural goal of 50% of the population to be served by water supply and sewage disposal by 1971. INPES is still far from this target for total rural population, but is closing the gap for the rural concentrated

TABLE 23-5: INVESTMENT IN WATER SUPPLY/SEWERAGE, 1965-69
(millions of US$ equivalent)

Agency	1965	1966	1967	1968	1969	Total
Empresas	15.1	19.6	20.5	28.0	31.9	115.1
INSFOPAL	6.2	6.9	7.0	6.2	8.0	34.3
INPES	0.3	0.6	1.2	2.1	2.5	6.7
Total	21.6	27.1	28.7	36.3	42.4	156.1

population. Serving the dispersed rural population is extremely difficult because, among other things, they are itinerant and have low incomes.

Comprehensive data for population served with sewer systems are not available. From the information collected it is estimated that about 50% of the urban population has access to sewers and less than 30% of the rural population is connected to septic tanks or latrines. Many systems have deteriorated because of deficient maintenance, and expansion has left many overloaded.

It is likely that investment in sewerage is being made more slowly than population growth requires. This is certainly the case in rural areas and in smaller cities. Figures for INSFOPAL show that expenditure for sewerage construction between 1964 and 1969 ranged from 10% to 14% of the total, particularly in Bogota. It is considered that the cost of investment required for sewer services may be twice as high as the cost of investment needs for water services. Since sewage and industrial wastes are not treated, the receiving bodies of water may become seriously polluted in the near future, particularly in the highly industrialized areas.

Technology

INSFOPAL has provisional design standards for water sources, ground-water use, water quality, pumping stations, transmission pipelines, elevated tanks and distribution systems. These standards have been under review. INPES does not have official standards, even though criteria for design and construction are uniform in the rural water supply and sewerage program.

Standards for construction materials are prepared by the Instituto Colombiano de Normas Tecnicas (INCONTEC), the national bureau of standards. Specifications for construction and equipment are based to a large extent on locally produced goods, while American or European specifications are adopted for the imported components of projects.

Recent studies to increase treatment plant capacity through higher filtration rates have been undertaken in Bogota, Cali, Cucuta and Pereira and one study is programmed for Popayan. The benefits of this type of investigation cannot be overemphasized, since doubling the production of filters, as appears feasible in most plants, is a low-cost way to expand treatment facilities.

Inlet and outlet structures of settling tanks in plants suggest the need for performance studies. Improperly designed perforated walls at the entrance and extremely high discharge rates (ratio of flow/unit length of weir) in outlet weirs may substantially lower sedimentation efficiency. A problem occurring in some towns is the small capacity of storage tanks which fail to meet peak demands.

Bidding procedures for construction in INSFOPAL were set out in official rules dated 1965. A mathematical formula relating INSFOPAL's cost to bidder's cost establishes an "ideal" cost for the particular job. The winning bid is the one closest to this ideal figure. The result is that the lowest evaluated bid may not win the award and a formula is substituted for professional judgment. Difficulties have been experienced in the past, caused by bidders who were not qualified and whom the evaluators did not feel able to eliminate.

Preventive maintenance is not practiced, even in many of the larger Empresas. Because of the lack of maintenance, unaccounted-for water (difference between water produced and billed) ranges from an estimated 30% to 60% . Only Bogota is conducting a leak detection study to locate and prevent excessive losses. A typical example of large-scale loss occurs in the town of Armenia. Out of 1.2 million m^3 of water produced monthly, only 612,000 m^3 are accounted for. The main causes of the situation, in order of importance, are leaks in the system, defective or insufficient meters, and illegal connections. Moreover, laxity in collection has caused an increase in the amount of delinquent accounts.

Production meters are generally not installed and many of those installed do not work properly. Therefore, neither production nor consumption of water is known and losses can only be estimated. This situation should be corrected, particularly in the larger towns, where the sales value of water losses is much higher than the cost of corrective measures.

Water quality control is generally weak, because facilities and staff are lacking and perhaps because insufficient priority is given to this. It is suggested that the agencies concerned seek the collaboration of the United Nations Development Program and the Pan American Health Organization to establish a central control and reference laboratory.

Besides performing normal functions in water quality control, the central laboratory should be a training and research center. The collaborating international agencies might provide the experts, supplies and equipment, while the Colombian Government would provide the local staff and facilities. Regional laboratories also should be established as the need arises, to form a network of water quality control agencies throughout the country.

Colombia has two large rivers, the Magdalena and the Cauca, which drain a large portion of the country and provide readily accessible surface sources of water supply. However, in some regions ground water should be a more economical source as surface waters are distant and/or limited. Ground water potential should be assessed in the States of Guajira, Magdalena, Atlantico, Bolivar and Sucre. So far, only a few studies made by INCORA in the Guajira peninsula, CVC in the Cauca valley and CAR in the Bogota area have explored the possibility of economically feasible ground water use in Colombia.

Staffing and Materials

Skills.   The composition of the membership of the Colombian Water and Sewage Works Association (ACODAL) indicates that the number of sanitary engineers employed in the sector is close to 100, corresponding to a ratio of one sanitary engineer per 200,000 inhabitants. This ratio is close to the average for Latin America, but is only one-tenth the ratio for the United States.

Many of the Colombian sanitary engineers were trained in the United States, Brazil and Mexico. Graduate-level education is now offered at the Universidad Nacional in Bogota, but this course is not a regular one. Some of the professors have left, and this makes high-level training difficult. A four-year course at the undergraduate level, offered by the Universidad del Valle in Cali, has graduated an average of 10 engineers per year in the last three years.

All civil engineers trained in Colombia receive instruction in sanitary engineering, and there are two to three times more civil engineers than sanitary engineers who are active in the water supply and sewerage sector. The Pan American Health Organization is collaborating with three Colombian universities to develop a program of continuing education for civil and sanitary engineers. Since 1967, courses have been offered, covering the administrative and technological aspects of water supply and waste disposal.

Training at the sub-professional level is offered by the National Technical Institute (Servicio Nacional de Aprendizaje, SENA), a highly regarded institution with branches in the larger Colombian towns. Both INSFOPAL and the Bogota Municipal Company have relied on SENA to organize and develop a number of short courses for technicians and administrators.

The Ministry of Public Health trains a small number of water treatment plant operators, since the Colombian Sanitary Code requires all plant operators to have a certificate of qualification issued by the Ministry. Training has not been offered on a regular basis.

A comprehensive plan for training and educating professional and auxiliary personnel is needed if effective service is to be provided. A survey is suggested of the existing manpower and project needs, according to the expansion plans of the Empresas, INSFOPAL and INPES, to help guide the universities and SENA in programming their courses. Assistance may usefully be sought from the Pan American Health Organization to furnish instructors, equipment and supplies, as well as fellowships for international training.

Materials.   A large percentage of the construction materials and equipment used in water and sewage works is manufactured in Colombia. Eternit has a plant producing 40,000 tons of asbestos-cement pipe per year, in diameters ranging from 2 to 24 inches. The plant capacity is greater than present internal demand, and exports have been made to Costa Rica, Ecuador and Panama. The pipes are manufactured according to acceptable standards and prices are competitive in the international market, because of the low cost of cement, which constitutes 85% of the pipe's raw material. The remaining 15% is a mixture of asbestos fibers.

A Medellin company, Apollo, produces cast iron fittings used with Eternit pipes. American Pipe has a plant in Colombia, manufacturing medium and large-size cement pipe, reinforced with imported steel plate. For diameters between 12 and 24 inches, prices are comparable to those of asbestos-cement pipe. For diameters larger than 24 inches American Pipe is the sole supplier of the market. Plastic PVC and polyethylene pipe is made by four domestic firms; their prices are 40% higher than those for equivalent imported materials.

Also manufactured locally are small centrifugal pumps and electric motors, drive mechanisms for flocculators, and dry feeders for alum and lime. This equipment needs improvement as quality control is in early stages and industrial standards are tentative. Water meters made by Kent Colombiana are not competitive in price with those imported from Kent of England. Chlorinators of the V-notch type have begun to be made by a local subsidiary of Wallace and Tiernan of New Jersey and appear to be of good quality.

Investment

The level of investment in water supply and sewerage in 1969 was about double the level in 1965—an annual growth rate of 19% (Table 23-5).

Three of the largest Empresas—Bogota, Medellin and Cali—are expanding investments at a rate which will provide adequate services to cover population growth. Most of the smaller municipal public companies, on the other hand, face a difficult problem since present levels of investment are not reducing the current deficit of population served. INSFOPAL has maintained a fairly constant rate of investment in the past five years, resulting in modest increases in the percentage of population with water services. INPES is steadily increasing direct investments in rural communities. In 1965 INPES's expenditures were 5% of INSFOPAL's; in 1969 they were 32%, whereas the INSFOPAL to Empresas ratio of expenditures fell from 40% in 1965 to 25% in 1969.

The total investment for improvement and expansion of water supply and sewerage for 1970, distributed among the three main responsible agencies, is shown below:

Agency	Amount US$ millions
Municipal Public Utilities	37.5
INSFOPAL	7.1
INPES	3.4
Total	48.0

Bogota and Medellin account for 77% of the total investment of US$37.5 million by municipal public utilities. Investment in these two cities also accounts for 52% of the total sector investment of US$48 million. The 3.5 million population of Bogota and Medellin is 49% of the total population under the jurisdiction of municipal public utilities and 27% of the entire urban population of the country.

The 1970 INSFOPAL budget request to the central government for direct investment was Col$260.3 million, but only Col$99.8 million was approved. Also approved was Col$25.0 million for administration and Col$16.5 million for debt service. INSFOPAL counted on a special supplemental appropriation of Col$30 million, to be used in the construction of new

TABLE 23-6: INSFOPAL – ACTUAL AND BUDGETED INVESTMENT 1966-1969
(In millions of Col$)

	1966	1967	1968	1969
Actual	93.5	103.0	102.2	139.0
Budgeted	124.8	113.9	125.9	150.4
Ratio of Actual/Budgeted	74%	90%	81%	92%

systems. Thus, the 1970 budget for direct investments would be of Col$130.0 million. Operational costs should be covered by the ACUAS and Direcciones Seccionales, but past experience has revealed a number of cases where INSFOPAL was forced to cover their operation and maintenance costs with budget appropriations. This appears to be the case in 1970 also, at least with respect to the debt service.

INSFOPAL still has not been able to spend all the funds appropriated for investments in recent years, as shown in Table 23-6.

Firm expansion plans were not available in 1970 from either INSFOPAL or INPES. INSFOPAL has prepared a tentative four-year plan to benefit 49 communities that do not have water supply systems, 64 towns where services are extremely deficient, and 254 in need of sewerage. INPES has studied a 10-year plan involving construction of 3,150 water supply and 1,915 sewage disposal systems for concentrated rural communities, as well as 10,000 rudimentary water systems (wells and public hydrants) and 200,000 latrines for the dispersed population, with a total cost of US$50 million. An alternative four-year plan was also considered, having the same objectives as the 10-year plan. A six-year plan was in preparation in 1970 along the same lines as the other two plans.

Table 23-7 shows tentative projections of expenditures in 1971-75. Expenditure estimates for INSFOPAL are based on the tentative four-year plan (1971-74) and the extrapolation for 1975. The estimate for INPES reflects the possibility of carrying out the 10-year plan in six years involving an average annual investment of US$8.5 million. Since firm engineering or investment plans are not yet prepared, actual investments may fall below the amounts projected. Projections for most Empresas are more realistic than those for INSFOPAL and INPES, due to the

TABLE 23-7: PROJECTED INVESTMENTS IN WATER SUPPLY/SEWERAGE, 1971-75
(In millions of US$ equivalent)

Agency	Actual		Budgeted	Projected				
	1965	1969	1970	1971	1972	1973	1974	1975
Empresas	15.1	31.9	37.5	41.0	44.5	45.5	49.0	53.0
INSFOPAL	6.2	8.0	7.1	14.0	17.0	22.0	25.0	27.0
INPES	0.3	2.5	3.4	5.0	6.0	8.0	10.5	13.5

existence of specific expansion plans and investment programs. There is a moderate increase in their rate of expenditures for the period 1971-1975, compared with the 1965-1969 period.

Financing

Three major sources of investment financing have been available: contributions from the government budget, internal cash generation of the companies, and foreign loans.

The Inter-American Development Bank, USAID and the World Bank have been the chief sources of external finance. IDB made loans in 1961 and 1962 to the cities of Medellin, Cartagena, Cucuta and Cali, and to INSFOPAL. Cucuta and INSFOPAL experienced a series of administrative difficulties that resulted in long disbursement periods. Medellin, on the other hand, obtained a second loan in 1965 and a third in 1969, indicating efficient loan administration. Total IDB lending to the sector during 1961-69 amounted to US$43.2 million.

USAID has financed both water and sewerage projects and preinvestment studies leading to projects to be financed by multilateral and bilateral credit institutions. The total lent in 1961-69 was US$13.3 million.

The World Bank made a US$14 million loan in 1968 to expand Bogota's water supply system. This project was financed jointly with the Export-Import Bank (loan of US$3 million) and with Kreditanstalt fuer Wiederaufbau (loans of US$1 million). The Bank also made a loan in June 1970 of US$18.5 million for Cali's water supply and sewerage systems. In 1971, loans were made to Palmira (US$2 million) and again to Bogota (US$88 million).

Based on project studies already completed or under way, further external financing for water supply and sewerage will be sought by a number of larger cities during the next five years, including Cali, Barranquilla, Bucaramanga, Pereira, Armenia, Villavicencio, Manizales, Tulua, Neiva, Cartagena and Medellin. In addition, INSFOPAL has a program for 19 smaller towns, but the needs are larger. In the case of INPES (rural water supply), the policy of the central government is to finance the investments with budget appropriations, and no external loans are contemplated.

An efficient mechanism for financing expansions of the smaller Empresas depends on the possibility of channeling loan funds through a single national agency, acting as an intermediary between international credit institutions and individual recipients of funds. INSFOPAL would be a convenient agency for this purpose, but some time will be required to achieve the required standards of administration and management.

The capacity to finance the needed investment, including the ability to provide local currency needed to supplement foreign loans, is closely related to internal cash generation of the sector. This has been its weak spot: cash generation has been low. The larger Empresas have been able to generate up to 25% of investment needs, while the smaller ones have used practically all their internally produced resources for administration, operation or maintenance expenses and for debt service. In the case of INSFOPAL, budget appropriations (government grants) and capital contributions by subscribers (e.g., connection fees) have been used to cover administration, operation and maintenance costs. Some of the Empresas have financed the expansion of the water supply systems with funds generated from other services, such as electric energy or telephone service; frequently, the result has been to reduce the investment in these sectors below priority needs or to request additional assistance from the central government.

A few small short-term loans have been extended by local banks for improvement and expansion of services, and some long-term loans have been made by the Instituto de Fomento Industrial (IFI). In a few cities, the Instituto de Credito Territorial (ICT) also has financed water supply/sewerage systems. In the aggregate, internal borrowing has been small.

Water Tariffs

Low internal cash generation has been the result of low effective charges for water supply and sewerage services. This has been recognized, in principle. When the National Public Services Tariff Board was established as part of Planeacion in December 1968, it was instructed to follow two criteria in setting the tariffs:

Insure the protection of the entity's assets and generate national saving through tariff levels that cover real costs of services and provide a rate of return on assets, with the objective of facilitating financing of future programs;

set tariffs which take into account the ability to pay for services in the different sectors of society, particularly those with low incomes.

The practical result of applying both these criteria to urban water/sewer systems is a complex multiple-tariff system under which a minimum amount (usually 15-30 m^3/month) of potable water is subsidized as a necessary social good; amounts above the minimum are considered an economic good, with the tariff set to cover the total cost of production.

In the rural areas, with their very low per capita incomes, only a portion of a system's capital cost is to be recovered from charges for services. Depending on per capita income in each case, the element of subsidy ranges between 60% and 100%.

The basic mechanism for determining each class of consumer's tariff classification continues to be the assessed value of his property. Three classes of consumers are generally established: domestic, commercial/industrial, and special consumers (official and non-profit institutions). For each class a number of categories is defined, according to the property valuation. The number of categories varies widely among different towns. Sewer tariffs are based on a variable percentage of the water bill, ranging from 10% to 60%.

Adoption of new tariffs has been slow, particularly in the systems under INSFOPAL jurisdiction. Of 300 to 400 tariff studies expected to be prepared by INSFOPAL in 1969, not one was submitted to the Board. The Board took the initiative to collect information in 86 systems of the Cundinamarca Sectional Branch of INSFOPAL, as well as in 40 other communities. The lag is regrettable in the light of the fact that the critical portion of the sector is in the towns and smaller cities under INSFOPAL where the backlog of population not served is increasing (Table 23-4).

After studying proposed tariff increases, the Board recommends them to the National Council for Economic and Social Policy, which is empowered by law to authorize the new tariffs. Implementation, however, is left to the discretion of the municipal councils.

Some delegation of tariff-setting power to at least the larger Empresas might be considered. Delegation of authority might be granted to make changes within certain limits, with the Board retaining its right to review all changes.

The National Board's tariff policy would have to be geared to the attainment of positive return on net revalued assets in order to finance expansion without excessive budgetary assistance. To achieve this objective, the central government would have to limit construction subsidies to the agencies and eliminate operation and maintenance subsidies. The power to authorize external and internal financing could be used by the government as a means to obtain adequate tariffs. Exceptions from this policy could apply to cases where for reasons peculiar to the locality operating costs are unusually high. This may be expected to occur primarily in the rural areas.

Introduction

This and the next chapter assess the major health problems of Colombia, describe the present health care system, analyze the institutional resources available for health, and appraise the national Ten-Year Health Plan. For this survey the health sector has been broadly defined to include all planned and organized public endeavor toward the promotion of health, prevention of illness and disability, the care of the sick and the restoration to useful work or activity of all those whose health status has been impaired. It also includes public measures affecting population growth. In Colombia, as elsewhere, health care has become an integral part of a rising tide of national aspirations for the interdependent goals of better health, education, housing, and job opportunities.

So defined the scope of public health activity has been enlarged in many directions. It involves a national network of programs and activities reaching down through every jurisdiction of government to the local level where people live and work. It must engage the efforts of every ministry of the national government, and must incorporate the resources of professional groups and private enterprise outside the framework of government. Public health today includes the protection of the human population against all of the hazards of its environment, whether these hazards arise from naturally occurring noxious agents, or from dangerous pollutants of the environment created by man himself; it includes the fortification of man's own resistance to disease by the application of the developing sciences of nutrition, immunization, and chemoprophylaxis; the provision of the institutional resources required to care for the sick (hospitals, dispensaries, health centers, etc.); and the training and development of health personnel—both professional and auxiliary—required to staff the complex services demanded in a modern health and medical care system.

Two other essential ingredients of such a system should not be overlooked. First, it is widely recognized—and will be documented here—that an illiterate population is an unhealthy population, and a health-illiterate population cannot, or will not, take those measures which it alone must apply to safeguard or promote its own well-being, nor will it utilize effectively and efficiently the public health resources available to it to meet those needs which the individual alone cannot provide. Thus, a national public education system, adapted to the special need for increasing enlightenment in matters of health, is an indispensable requirement of a sound national public health program. Secondly, there must be clearly defined leadership within the national government—appropriately within the Ministry of Health—to take stock of the ever-changing health situation, to plan and promote the needed programs, and to mobilize all resources—governmental and private—to the end that the services required by the public are provided within the resources available.

In a developing country, such as Colombia, the burden of public health endeavor falls heavily on the national government, and particularly, on the national Ministry of Health. Despite its nominal designation and its legal authorities, the Ministry of Health does not always provide the sole, or even the major channel for the expenditure of funds for public health activity. Funds available for public health are at best limited and other areas of national development are in severe competition for the resources of the national treasury. The tax base of local and state (departmental) governments is severely limited and may be nonexistent; private enterprise in health and medical care is rudimentary, and public philanthropy which has pioneered so extensively in expanding the scope of public health endeavor in the more advanced countries, is episodic and essentially unorganized.

Despite the above assessment, the public health system in Colombia is an extensive one, and many organizations within and outside of government, and at national, departmental and local levels are vigorously engaged in a modern public health program in Colombia that clearly meets the definitions and criteria set forth in this section. A unique attribute of the public health movement in Colombia is the availability of an extensive array of basic data on the health situation and the available health resources within the country. These were assembled in 1965-66 through a cooperative enterprise of the Ministry of Health and the Association of Colombian Medical Schools with financial and other assistance provided by the Milbank Memorial Fund of New York and the Pan American Health Organization (Regional Office for the Americas, World Health Organization).[1] Many of these data were of fundamental value in the formulation by the Ministry of Health of a Ten-Year Health Program for Colombia (1968-77).[2]

In reviewing the health problems of a developing country such as Colombia, the observer is immediately made aware of the wide discrepancies that exist in the major health indicators of that country when these are compared with similar indicators for the more advanced nations of the world, as for example, those in Western Europe or in North America. A direct comparison of such data is frequently odious and sometimes hazardous. For example, matching the infant mortality rate for all of Colombia and the U.S. national rate, fails to reflect the variable components within each set of data or that approximately half of the Colombian population resides in a rural setting where levels of literacy are low and family income meager. The infant mortality rates of rural Negro communities in the Mississippi Delta are of the same order of magnitude as those for a local population in a rural Colombian village. Similar direct compari-sons could be made for a Bogotan barrio with an urban ghetto area in any one of several major U.S. cities.

Again, in Colombia the ratio of physicians to total population is low, about 4:10,000, whereas, in the U.S. this ratio is 16.4:10,000.[3] The uneven distribution of physicians in the U.S. has evoked much concern but nowhere does it approach the maldistribution recorded in Colombia where almost 3 out of 4 doctors reside in the principal cities, and serve less than 1/3 of the total population; only 10% of the medical manpower in Colombia is available to the 2/3 of the population residing in places of 20,000 population or less.[4] Probably of even greater significance is the observation that with the resources at present in sight, it would take no less than 100 years for the medical training institutions of Colombia to produce the number of physicians required to approach current U.S. physician/population ratios. Herein lies an im-portant inference for Colombian health planners: it would be folly for them to set as their goal the uncritical adoption of health care patterns and norms observed in the developed countries of the world. Rather, by applying innovative approaches they must devise new techniques and new concepts appropriate to their own health problems and their available or potential re-sources. For example, impressive evidence is rapidly accumulating in Colombia and elsewhere demonstrating that the skills and professional knowledge of a limited number of physicians can be extended to serve a larger segment of the population. This can be accomplished by the greater utilization of auxiliary workers trained to work as members of an integrated health care team. The role of the physician remains a dominant one. However, his functions assume more of a directing and supervising nature and he becomes more the manager of health ser-vices than the sole provider of medical care. Thus, in utilizing data presented in this report the purpose to be served is less to compare the Colombian situation unfavorably with that of the more advantaged areas of the world, but more to provide suitable starting points or bench marks to Colombian health planners, and those who would assist them in their tasks, to devel-op unique and even experimental approaches to realistic goals.

1. See International Conference on Health Manpower and Medical Education, Maracay, Venezuela, June 1967, *Study on Health Manpower and Medical Education in Colombia,* Ministry of Public Health of Colombia and the Colombian Association of Medical Schools, three Volumes, and also Ministerio de Salud Publica, Associacion de Facultades de Medicina, *Estudio de Recursos Humanos para la Salud y Educacion Medica en Colombia, Investigacion Nacional de Morbilidad.*

2. Ministerio de Salud Publica *Plan Nacional de Salud 1968-1977,*Bogota, November 1967.

3. Pan American Sanitary Bureau, Regional Office of the World Health Organization, *Health Conditions in the Americas, 1961-64,* Scientific Publication No. 138, Second Printing, October 1967.

4. Associacion de Facultades de Medicina, *La Profesion Medica, 1968* Investigacion Nacional de Morbilidad, Ministerio de Salud Publica.

The Health Care System

Governmental Programs

Governmental health activities are conducted on each of three administrative levels— national, departments and intendancies or comisarias[5] and at the local level where services to the public are provided through 1500 health centers and health posts, dispensaries, and similar facilities for ambulatory medical care, and through about 500 hospitals offering both inpatient and ambulatory services. These public hospitals[6] with about 42,400 beds comprise 88% of all such facilities available in the country.[7]

At the national level, the Ministry of Health is charged by law with formulating national health policy, "the preparation of national plans and programs, the supervision, coordination and control of all activities relative to health, the establishment of regulations and supervision for their fulfillment." There are other national organizations concerned with the provision of health services for specific population groups and these include the Colombian Institute for Social Security, the Military Health Services, the Ministries of Education, Labor, Public Works, Police, the National Railways, the Ports of Colombia and other agencies with smaller programs which either provide health services directly to their employees or through welfare funds (Cajas). These special health programs, focused on both publicly and privately employed workers, are limited to approximately 1.3 million beneficiaries out of a labor force estimated in 1970 to be about 6.5 million and a total population of 21.6 million.[8]

As a consequence of recent legislation (Decrees 3224, (1963); 1499, (1966); and 2470, (1968)) most, if not all, of these separately administered programs are coordinated through a National Health Council, chaired by the Minister of Health. This legislation also authorized internal reorganizations within the Ministry and provided for the coordination of regional and local health programs and the unification of their financial resources. For the first time a national network of health activity now exists with consolidated mechanisms established within the Ministry for supervision, control, programming and periodic evaluation at all levels. In addition a series of semi-autonomous institutes were either assigned to or created under the aegis of the Ministry with the authority and flexibility to undertake urgent and major health programs of national significance. As a consequence of these recent organizational adaptations the Ministry of Health currently includes the following functional elements:[9]

(a) Policy Determination and National Planning:
Office of the Minister,
Office of Planning,
Office of Human Resources for Health,
Office of the Legal Counsel;
(b) Assigned Agencies:
Colombian Institute for Family Welfare (ICBF) (includes Division of Nutrition— formerly, National Nutrition Institute),
National Institute for Municipal Development (INSFOPAL) (responsible for water

5. Division de Atencion Medica, *Manual para el Adiestramiento de Promotoras Rurales de Salud,* Conocimientos Basicos Minisalud, Enero de 1969.

6. Public hospitals, many of which are governed by independent or semi-autonomous boards of directors, are defined as receiving all or part of their funds from the public treasury; the medical care services they provide are subject to the supervision of the Ministry of Health.

7. Associacion de Facultades de Medicina, *Atencion Medica, 1968,* Investigacion Nacional de Morbilidad, Minesterio de Salud Publica

8. In general, health benefits in these plans are restricted to the employed workers; some provide limited benefits to dependents of insured workers, e.g., maternity care and infant care during the first six months of life. National Planning Department, *Economic Studies*

9. See Ordones Plaja, Antonio, Ministerio de Salud Publica, *Informe al Honorable Congreso de la Republica de Colombia,* ag-jul, 1967/68, 1968/69.

supplies and sewerage systems for communities over 2,500 population),
National Institute for Special Health Programs (INPES) (includes the formerly sep-
arately administered National Institute of Health and is responsible for water supplies
and environmental sanitation in rural areas),
National Hospital Fund (responsible for financing the construction of hospitals and
health centers with funds loaned by the Colombian Institute for Social Security),
National Cancer Institute,
Supplies Corporation for Social Welfare Institutions (CORPAL);
(c) Administrative Divisions:
Medical Care,
Direct Campaigns,
Environmental Sanitation,
General Administration.

The Private Sector

In Colombia, as in many other developing countries, the privately operated and financed health sector is of relatively small magnitude when compared with governmentally directed or controlled operations. Through various channels, however, the private sector exerts considerable influence on national policies and governmental programs. Approximately 20% of all hospitals, with about 12% of the available beds, are privately operated. Yet, the vast majority of the public hospitals throughout the country were established by local groups and municipalities and continue to be directed by independent charity or other boards. These institutions are now dependent in preponderant degree for support from the public treasury, and the medical care provided is subject to the supervision of the Ministry of Health; yet they still retain considerable autonomy and independence in their operations.

As for the medical profession, private practice appears to be the ambition of most physicians, though this may be as much due to lower remuneration and less satisfactory working conditions in salaried positions as to philosophical orientation. Only 14% of physicians in Colombia are engaged exclusively in private practice and 24% exclusively in salaried positions; the majority, 62% combine private and non-private work in various proportions. However, after age 50, two-thirds or more physicians concentrate their efforts on the private sector whereas under age 35, over 75% of doctors are dependent on salaries as the major source of their income.[10] Also in the private sector the drug and pharamaceutical manufacturing and distribution industry appears to be large and profitable.

No discussion of the role of the non-governmental sector in meeting the health needs of the Colombian population would be complete without reference to the Association of Colombian Medical Colleges. This association representing the seven (now nine) university medical schools in Colombia has provided outstanding leadership in the health sector over the 10 years of its existence. It has contributed particularly to the development of public awareness of health as a necessary condition of social and economic development of the country. It has cooperated with the Ministry of Health in the 1965-66 health survey, and has been instrumental in seeing that many of the findings, which are still in process of analysis and publication, are utilized as the basis for new national programs now in process of implementation.

Major Outlays for Health and Medical Care

In the 10-year interval 1961-70 there has been a substantial rise in recorded public health expenditures in Colombia. In 1961, health expenditures represented 1.8% of the gross national product and in 1969, at Col$2,763 million, 2.5%. For 1970 an additional rise is planned to Col$3,507 million, 2.8% of GNP.

Table 24-1 shows the recorded expenditures for public health and medical care for each of the years 1961-69 and budget estimates for 1970. The major sources of these funds are also

10. *La Profesion Medica,* op. cit

TABLE 24-1: EXPENDITURES FOR PUBLIC HEALTH, BY SOURCE OF FUNDS[1], 1961-1970

(in millions of current Col$)

	1961		1962		1963		1964		1965		1966		1967		1968		1969		1970[2]	
	Col$	%	Col$	%	Col$	%	Col$	%	Col$	%	Col$	%	Col$	%	Col$	%	Col$	%	Col$	%
Total	542.9	100	599.5	100	790.6	100	956.4	100	1,101.5	100	1,371.3	100	1,642.4	100	2,017.1	100	2,762.9	100	(3,507.0	100)
1. Internal Sources	538.2	99	589.7	98	781.8	99	942.6	99	1,091.4	99	1,361.1	99	1,632.1	99	2,006.7	99	2,630.1	95	(3,374.1	96)
a) Ministry of Health	162.4	30	181.5	30	178.6	23	203.5	21	208.5	19	307.0	22	346.5	21	406.6	20	578.2	21	671.2	19
b) Other Ministries	23.6	4	37.5	6	35.4	4	57.3	6	63.5	6	(75.6	6	(90.0	5	(107.1	5	(127.4	5	(151.6	4)
c) Social Security and National Cajas	121.9	22	132.0	22	212.4	27	245.4	26	349.2	32	(483.6	35	(669.8	41	(927.6	46	(1,284.7	46	(1,779.3	51)
d) Other Central Agencies	10.2	2	21.5	3	23.6	3	34.9	4	31.6	3	35.9	3	(40.8	2	(46.4	2	(52.8	2	(60.0	2)
e) Lotteries, 5 and 6, Totogol, etc., (Beneficencias)	112.8	21	99.2	17	181.4	23	230.0	24	254.6	23	(287.0	21	(323.0	20	(364.0	18	411.0	15	(463.0	13)
f) Departments and Municipalities	88.3	16	93.1	16	118.1	15	137.0	14	146.0	13	(128.0	9	(112.0	7	(98.0	5	86.0	3	(75.0	3)
g) Payments for Hospital Services	22.0	4	24.9	4	32.3	4	34.5	4	38.0	3	(44.0	3	(50.0	3	(57.0	3	65.0	2	(74.0	2)
h) Taxes on Beer	–	–	–	–	–	–	–	–	–	–	–	–	–	–	–	–	25.0	1	(100.0	2)
2. External Sources[3]	4.0	1	9.8	2	8.8	1	13.8	1	10.1	1	(10.2	1)	(10.3	1)	(10.4	1)	132.8	5	132.9	4
Gross National Product[4]	30,067.0		34,199.2		43,525.5		53,760.3		60,797.6		73,612.3		83,525.2		94,550.5		(109,300.4)		(126,897.8)	
Health Expenditures as percent of GNP	1.8%		1.8%		1.8%		1.8%		1.8%		1.9%		2.0%		2.1%		(2.5%)		(2.8%)	

1 Does not include expenditures for water and sewerage in urban areas.

2 1970 figures represent budget as opposed to expenditures; figures in parentheses are estimates.

3 Included in 1969 and 1970 figures are World Food Program contributions.

4 1969 and 1970 estimated by National Planning Department.

Sources: Study of Human Resources for Health and Medical Education in Colombia - Ministry of Health,
Association of Colombian Medical Schools, 1967; National Hospital Plan, Bank of the Republic;
Economic Investigations - National Planning Department.

Note: The listings for Beneficencias, Departments and Municipalities, Payment for Services and Ministry of
Health take into account data from the historical series up to 1965 and estimates for 1969 prepared
by the Ministry of Health; for other years figures have been developed by interpolation and projection -
Human Resources Unit - Department of National Planning - March 5, 1970.

displayed. It should be noted that expenditures for water and sewerage in urban communities (population 2,500 and over) have been omitted from the tabulation. Some, but probably a minor fraction, of the annual increases in total health expenditures is attributable to improved accounting and reporting procedures. The depreciation in the purchasing value of the peso during this ten-year interval also must be considered. However, the increase is so substantial and the accelerating rise in annual increments so notable in recent years that there can be little question that with improving economic conditions in the country the government of Colombia has established as national policy the earmarking of larger and larger expenditures for public health and medical care services.

Appropriations for the Ministry of Health have risen from Col$162 million in 1961 to Col$578 million in 1969. This represents a rise of approximately 140%, in terms of the 1961 purchasing power of the peso, in the eight-year period. However, during this same interval appropriations for the Ministry of Health have become a significantly smaller fraction of the total expenditures for health and medical care, falling from 30% of the total in 1961 to 20% in 1969. If.expenditures through the National Institute for Social Security, the Cajas and by other national agencies—i.e., costs of providing medical care for special employed groups—are subtracted from the totals it becomes apparent that general health care for the total Colombian population has not been as much the beneficiary of this rising tide of health expenditures as might be initially surmised. In 1961 general health care represented 72% of total costs and about 1% of the gross national product; in 1969 general health care had fallen to 47% of total costs and remained at about 1% of gross national product.

Conversely, the beneficiaries of the social security system and of the Cajas and other special programs are now receiving a substantially higher level of health care than that received by their own dependents and by the balance of the population. It has been estimated that such beneficiaries now number about 1.3 million workers, or about 5% of the total population. They are beneficiaries of over a half (53%) of all public expenditures for health (Table 24-2). Private expenditures for health, though substantial, cannot be readily assessed.

TABLE 24-2: PUBLIC EXPENDITURES FOR HEALTH BY AGENCIES WHICH SERVE THE GENERAL POPULATION, AND WHICH SERVE SPECIAL POPULATION GROUPS, 1961-1970
(in millions of current Col$)

Year	Total	Expenditures for the General Population[1]		Expenditures for Specific Population Groups[2]	
		Col$	Index	Col$	Index
1961	542.2	387.1	100	155.1	100
1962	599.5	409.4	106	190.1	123
1963	790.6	521.1	135	269.5	174
1964	956.4	627.5	162	338.9	219
1965	1,101.5	663.7	171	437.8	282
1966	1,371.3	776.2	201	595.1	384
1967	1,642.4	841.8	217	800.6	516
1968	2,017.1	936.0	242	1,081.1	697
1969	2,762.9	1,298.0	335	1,464.9	944
1970	3,507.0	1,516.1	392	1,990.9	1,284

[1] Includes: Ministry of Health, National Nutrition Institute, National Cancer Institute, Health Services of the Departments, cities, and health care institutions which receive support from the "beneficencias" through lotteries, Totogol, and own income.

[2] Includes: Health services of the Ministry of Defense, Military Hospital, Colombian Institute of Social Security; Medical Services of National Employees, of Ministry of Communications, of the National Telecommunications Corporation, of the Ministry of Labor, of the Ministry of Public Works, of the National Railways, of the Ports of Colombia, and other agencies with smaller programs.

Sources: Study of Human Resources for Health and Medical Education in Colombia-Ministry of Health, Association of Colombian Medical Schools, 1967; Economic Investigations - Department of Natural Planning - March 5, 1970.

Considerable difficulty is encountered in analyzing available Colombian data to differentiate continuing operational expenses from those of an investment nature—expenditures for the construction of new facilities and their initial equipment. This is in part due to recent changes in the organizational structure of national government agencies providing health and medical care and in part to changing patterns of budget formulation, along with changing and tenuous definitions of "investments" as opposed to "operational expenditures".

For example, for 1965, Col$55.5 million—5% of the total Col $1,101.5 million expenditures for health—were allocated to capital investment in construction: Col$50.4 million for hospitals and other facilities, Col$5.1 million for rural water supplies.[11] In 1970, the investment budget of the Ministry of Health amounted to Col$228 million, exclusive of investment in water supply and sewerage services. This was equal to 6.6% of total expenditures on public health. The investment of Col$228 million includes about Col$47 million for hospital and health center construction and equipment, and approximately Col$173 million, for a variety of activities in which construction or the purchase of fixed equipment—the usual basis for inclusion in a capital investment budget—are minor or absent elements in the uses of these funds. Included in such "investments" are the malaria eradication campaign (Col$61 million), mass vaccination programs (Col$24 million), leprosy control (Col$19 million), tuberculosis control (Col$3 million), maternal and child health services (Col$49 million), and education and training of personnel (Col$17 million). In addition, the Colombian Institute for Social Security and the National Hospital Fund were planning to spend about Col$100 million on construction of hospitals and health centers. These investment expenditures would then work out at 10% of total public expenditures on health in 1970.

For the period 1961-68, the recorded financial assistance in the health sector from external sources has been small ranging from Col$4.0 million to Col$13.8 million per year with an average of Col$9.7 million. Such assistance has amounted to well under 2% of total public expenditures for health and for the most part has been earmarked for special projects in the form of stimulatory or initiating grants. These figures undoubtedly under-reflect the amount of external assistance received over the years by Colombia for many of the assisting agencies have, in addition, provided substantial technical consultation and assistance, supplies and fellowships for the training of professional personnel abroad. The Pan American Health Organization and the United Nations Children's Fund have been major donors as has been the U.S. Agency for International Development and its predecessor agencies. In the non-governmental area the Rockefeller Foundation, the Milbank Memorial Fund and the Hope program have been conspicuous for their assistance in recent years. Since 1969, the World Food Program in cooperation with UNICEF and PAHO has been a substantial source of external financial assistance to meet the requirements of the current country-wide nutrition campaign. This aid, amounting to about Col$133 million per year for five years, brings the percentage of foreign aid to the total health expenditures to just under 5% in 1969.

Demographic Variables Associated with Health

Population Characteristics

The Colombian demographic picture is very similar to that of many countries in the process of development (see Table 24-3): a fast growth in size of population, a high fecundity rate, a declining mortality rate, a concentration of population in childhood and young adult years, great movements in the spatial distribution of the population, a rapid growth of the urban nucleus and the incipient formation of a middle class.

In 1970, the population of Colombia is estimated to number 21.6 million individuals. The next national census is planned for 1972; the last, in 1964, which, because of technical problems may have resulted in an under-enumeration, placed the population at 17.5 million inhabitants residing in an area of 439,519 square miles. At that time about 98.7% lived in the Departments making up 53.6% of the national territory. Population density of these Departments was about

---

11. *Study on Health Manpower and Education in Colombia,* op. cit.

TABLE 24-3: DEMOGRAPHIC DATA FOR SOME LATIN-AMERICAN COUNTRIES

Countries	Population	Rate of Increase (per '000)	Years Required to Double	Birth Rate (per '000)	Death Rate (per '000)	Life Expectancy at birth - in years	Population under age 15 (%)	Inhabitants/Km² Total	Inhabitants/Km² In Cultivable Areas
Argentina (1960)	20,010	17	42	23	8	66	31	7	14
Bolivia (1960)	3,696	23	31	44	21	41	42	3	26
Brazil (1960)	70,119	29	25	39	10	56	43	8	44
Colombia (1964)[1]	17,485	32	21	47	15	51	47	15	92
Chile (1960)	7,374	25	28	37	12	57	40	10	57
Ecuador (1962)	4,476	34	21	48	14	53	45	17	88
Mexico (1960)	34,923	33	21	45	12	58	44	18	31
Peru (1961)	9,907	29	24	45	16	52	43	8	46
Uruguay (1963)	2,593	13	54	22	9	69	28	14	16
Venezuela (1961)	7,524	38	18	46	8	–	45	8	39
Latin America	214,000	29	24	40	11	57	42	11	37
Total World (1960)	3,005,000	18	39	34	16	–	–	25	–

[1] Figures for Colombia taken from census data and some estimates based on special studies.

Source: United Nations, *Demographic Yearbooks.*

73 inhabitants per square mile. The remaining 1.3% of the population occupied the 46.4% of the territory included in the Llanos Orientales. The population density of that area is about one inhabitant per square mile.

In 1905 the country had 4.4 million inhabitants; 33 years later, in 1938 the population had doubled (8.7 million); 26 years later, (1964) the phenomenon was repeated (17.5 million) and it is possible that it will double again in 22 years. This period of duplication is in contrast with that of some other countries, such as Italy (117 years), Portugal (100 years), Spain (88 years), Uruguay (58 years) and Argentina (47 years).

This rate of growth varies in different sections of the country. For example, Bogota, the capital city, is doubling its population every 10-15 years, whereas some of the predominantly rural Departments require over 55 years to double their population. Over a brief span of years, the Colombian population has shifted from predominantly rural (69% in 1938) to one almost equally divided between the rural and urban areas.

The economic resources of this population are limited. The average per capita production in 1966 was Col$1,622, representing a 20% rise from the Col$1,300 figure for 1950. (In US dollar equivalents these figures represent a rise in per capita production from $203 in 1950 to $253 in 1966.) Associated with this low per capita production are the uneven levels of family income: one-third of the population earns Col$3,600 or less per year and only 14% Col$12,000 or more. In the rural areas almost half (48%) have family incomes in the lower category and less than 5% in the higher.

The infant mortality rate, deaths under one year per thousand live births, is widely considered as one of the most sensitive indicators of levels of public health accomplishment. In the United States this rate has remained almost constant, around 25, for many years. In Colombia, the infant mortality rate is reported to have declined from 114.4 to 88.5 between 1951 and 1964, a reduction of almost 23%. There is no basis for challenging that a true decline has occurred. On the other hand the under-reporting of deaths suggests that the "corrected" infant mortality rate is still over 100 indicating that one child in ten born alive fails to reach his first birthday.

Age specific death rates have been utilized to calculate life expectancies at birth; these indicate that an infant born in 1965 has a 50-50 chance of surviving to age 57 whereas for children born earlier the comparable figure for 1951 was 53 years and for 1938, 45 years.

Based on the calculated average annual birth and death rates (47.2 and 14.95 respectively), and since immigration and emigration are negligible factors, Colombian authorities have assumed that the gross rate of population increase is in the range of 3%. For 1964 this figure has been set at 3.3%. Obviously this estimate is an approximate one but until a markedly improved system of vital registration is adopted, no better approximations are available. It is suggested that a priority study be undertaken with the purpose to modernize and improve the Colombian national system of registration, tabulation and analysis of essential vital statistics and current morbidity data.

The average size of households for the whole of Colombia is 5.9 members. 24% of the population lived in households with five or six members, 25% in households with seven to eight members, 18% in households with nine to ten members and 17% in households with eleven or more members. Thus only about 1 in 6 Colombians shares living space with 3 or less other household members. In urban households, the average size is 5.8 members in comparison with 6.1 members among their rural counterparts. Although large families are characteristic of both urban and rural areas, small families are more prevalent in towns. Among women who have reached the age of 30, the modal range of previous live births is 6-9, with significant numbers having had 15 or more children born alive.

Morbidity Indices and Their Socio-Economic Relationships

Illness and Restricted Activity

In the 1965-1966 household surveys four out of every ten Colombians reported that they had been ill during the preceding two week period, with more than half of these illnesses (57%) beginning during that period and slightly less than half (43%) of a more prolonged nature. A

TABLE 24-4: SICKNESS DURING TWO-WEEK PERIOD, PER '000
POPULATION, BY AGE AND SEX, 1965

Sex	All Ages	Under 1	1 to 4	5 to 14	15 to 24	25 to 44	45 to 64	65 and over
Males	363	429	403	289	284	389	489	630
Females	410	435	404	300	349	482	472	674
Both Sexes	387	432	403	294	319	439	531	654

TABLE 24-5: RESTRICTED ACTIVITY DURING TWO-WEEK PERIOD,
PER '000 POPULATION, BY AGE AND SEX, 1965

Sex	All Ages 6 and over	6 to 14	15 to 24	25 to 44	45 to 64	65 and over
Males	103	74	74	111	160	250
Females	113	78	90	138	154	198
Both Sexes	108	76	83	125	157	222

TABLE 24-6: DAYS OF RESTRICTED ACTIVITY AND IN BED PER PERSON
PER YEAR, BY AGE AND SEX, 1965

Sex	All Ages 6 and over	6 to 14	15 to 24	25 to 44	45 to 64	65 and over
Restricted Activity Days						
Males	12.7	8.8	9.8	16.2	31.1	57.0
Females	14.5	8.9	11.9	22.8	28.1	50.0
Both Sexes	13.6	8.9	10.9	19.8	29.6	53.0
Days in Bed						
Males	5.8	5.4	4.7	7.5	11.3	20.0
Females	8.6	6.1	7.7	13.8	13.9	28.0
Both Sexes	7.3	5.8	6.3	10.9	12.7	24.0

slightly higher rate of illness occurred in rural areas than in cities (399 versus 378 per 1,000) and women were more prone to reported illness than were men (410 versus 363 per 1,000), a difference which persisted over all ages. For males the minimum sickness rate was in the age group 15-24 years and for females in the age group 5-14; following these minima, the rates rose steadily with age to a maximum for ages 65 and over. Particularly noteworthy is the very high illness rate among infants.

Many of the illnesses reported were mild and caused no disability or restriction of activity. However, the activity of approximately one person out of ten (108 per 1,000) was restricted during this same two week period. Again, the rate for those in the country was higher than for city dwellers. Females had a slightly higher rate of restricted activity than males (113 versus 103 per 1,000) although over age 45 the rates for males were higher; for both males and females, restricted activity rates increased with age. From these data it has been calculated that the average Colombian loses about 13.6 days per year from his usual activity because of illness. The rates for women are slightly higher than for men (14.5 days versus 12.7 days) and there is a sharp increase with age. On the average, those between 25 and 44 years lose 3 weeks per year (19.8 days) those between 45-64 years over four weeks (29.6 days) and those over age 65 years almost two months (53.6 days).

In the course of a year disability in bed due to illness averaged about a week (7.3 days) for every Colombian. Variations by age and sex were similar to those reported for the number of days of restricted activity. As might be expected, the annual average was higher for women than for men (8.6 days versus 5.8) and for both sexes there were sharp increases with age. Although the rural population reports more days of restricted activity they tend to be confined to bed less frequently (6.9 days versus 7.7 days) than city dwellers. Tables 24-4, 24-5 and 24-6 show some of the above illness and restricted activity indices by age and sex.

Utilization of Health Services

How, when and to whom the Colombian population turns for medical attention are questions of more than passing interest. These questions were asked in the 1965 household sample survey for the two week period immediately preceding the interview. Almost 9% of the population (88.6 per 1,000) sought consultation for reasons of health during that period. When persons are not ill they rarely seek consultation for health services (17.1 per 1,000) but even when they are, only about one in five seek such aid (201.3 per 1,000). The overall rate of consulting with a physician is 63.2 per 1,000, constituting 72% of all contacts with health personnel. The rates for visiting a doctor are three times greater for the urban population than the rural.

When the sickness rates, reported above, are further compared with consultation rates it becomes even clearer that only a relatively small proportion of individuals when they are ill are consulting any type of health personnel for their complaints. In urban areas where the sickness rate was 363 per 1,000, the consultation rate was 118, only a third as much, and the consultation rate for physicians was 93, about one-fourth of the sickness rate. Among the rural population, these differentials are even more pronounced. With a sickness rate of 410, the total consultation rate was 57; consultation with a physician, 31 per 1,000. Thus, when an individual living in the country feels ill there is one chance in seven that he will seek any type of health assistance and one chance in thirteen that he will be seen by a physician.

After the physician, the most frequently consulted health workers were pharmacists (9.2 per 1,000) and nurses (2.2 per 1,000). The urban-rural difference in the consultations with health personnel persisted but were less pronounced. It is not possible to differentiate whether nurse consultations were with professionally trained nurses, practical nurses (auxiliary nurses) or aides.

Approximately 13% of the consultations about health are with other types of health workers—the tegua, the midwife and others—unsanctioned and often unrecognized by the medical profession. These groups provide a significant proportion of all medical care available to the population. If patterns of health care consultation with unsanctioned so-called indigenous, practitioners common to other parts of the world apply in Colombia these figures may be gross understatements of the true picture of the population's search for relief from their medical ills.

Hospital utilization.   Almost 23% of the population has had some past experience with hospitals and 5% has been hospitalized within a year. Of the latter group 89% had been hospitalized once, 8.6% twice and over 2% three or more times. More urban residents seek hospitalization than rural dwellers. In a year, more women are hospitalized than men, 64.2 and 35.9 per 1,000 respectively. This differential is even more marked in the age period 15-54 years when women in the child bearing period are hospitalized primarily because of complications of pregnancy, delivery or in the post partum.

Socio-Economic Correlates of Morbidity and the Utilization of Health Care Resources

The close associations of disease, malnutrition, lack of sanitation, poverty, crowding, illiteracy and the other stigmata of underdevelopment are all well recognized and well documented. In Colombia, data are available to demonstrate some of these direct correlations and a few are selected in this section for illustrative purposes.

As shown in Table 24-7 the rate of reported illness is twice as high for individuals with no formal educational experience (411 per 1,000) as for those with education beyond the secondary level (199 per 1,000). Similar differences characterize the association of reported illness with income and occupation. Restricted activity due to illness can also be correlated inversely with these three social variables—education, income and occupational level. Those

TABLE 24-7: RATE OF ILLNESS, PER '000 POPULATION,
BY EDUCATION AND URBAN OR RURAL RESIDENCE, 1965

Education	National	Urban	Rural
Superior	198.7	200.7	161.0
Secondary	323.4	322.4	332.3
Primary	385.8	373.3	400.7
None	411.3	418.9	407.2
Don't Know	436.6	404.1	475.7
No Information	391.4	400.2	383.3
Total	381.1	377.0	397.8

Source: As for Table 24-1.

whose annual income is over Col$30,000 have half of the rate of restricted activity experienced by those who earned less than Col$3,600 (64 versus 126 per 1,000), and just over half the number of days of restriction due to illness (9.4 versus 17.0). The correlation between the rate of restricted activity and education and occupation follows a similar trend as well. Those with high incomes spent on the average fewer days in bed at home because of illness and are hospitalized slightly less than those with more modest incomes.

Social circumstances are also directly correlated with access to health care and the type of consultation sought for illness (Table 24-8). Urban dwellers visit all types of health workers twice as frequently as the rural population (118 versus 57 per 1,000) and the rate of visiting a doctor in the cities is three times that in the country (93 versus 31 per 1,000). Although those

TABLE 24-8: RATES OF CONSULTATION WITH HEALTH PERSONNEL
PER '000 POPULATION, BY INCOME AND ZONE, 1965

Median Income in Col$	M.D.	Pharmacist	Nurse	Tegua	Other	Total
National						
Under 3,600	38.6	8.8	2.7	9.8	9.2	71.1
3,601 to 6,000	47.4	10.9	1.6	7.3	5.6	85.8
6,001 to 12,000	86.9	10.7	2.1	4.1	6.0	112.1
12,001 to 30,000	107.6	10.3	1.9	1.4	3.1	127.7
30,001 and over	105.7	5.5	.8	3.1	3.4	125.0
No information	55.9	6.4	2.2	6.9	5.8	83.4
Total	63.2	9.2	2.2	6.7	5.9	91.0
Urban						
Under 3,600	65.8	14.0	4.5	9.3	9.3	104.3
3,601 to 6,000	85.8	12.9	1.5	4.5	5.6	110.8
6,001 to 12,000	102.5	12.1	1.8	2.2	6.4	125.4
12,000 to 30,000	120.0	10.1	2.1	1.4	3.0	136.7
30,001 and over	116.1	6.2	.9	1.0	3.3	127.6
No information	82.6	7.2	3.2	3.7	6.3	105.3
Total	93.3	11.1	2.5	4.0	6.1	117.7
Rural						
Under 3,600	27.2	6.6	1.9	10.0	6.2	54.0
3,601 to 6,000	32.8	9.2	1.6	9.7	5.5	59.4
6,001 to 12,000	43.0	6.6	2.9	9.2	4.8	67.0
12,001 to 30,000	46.8	11.4	.9	1.7	3.8	66.3
30,001 and over	48.9	1.4	–	14.6	3.8	68.6
No information	29.5	5.7	1.3	10.1	5.3	53.1
Total	31.3	7.1	1.8	9.6	5.7	56.8

Source: As for Table 24-1

with high incomes living in the country see a doctor almost twice as often as the rural poor (49 versus 27 per 1,000), their rate of medical visits is still lower than for the poorest urban dwellers (49 versus 66 per 1,000). The decision to visit a doctor or another type of health worker is influenced by income and place of residence. Those with high incomes living in the city will turn to a physician nine times out of ten when they seek health care. The rural poor utilize other personnel just as often as they turn to doctors when they seek health care. Similar correlations are found with levels of education.

Major Categories of Health Problems in Colombia

Dependable data on the frequency of specific disease entities or other major health problems—either as causes of death or of morbidity—are limited for a variety of reasons. First, there are severe shortages of physicians or other health personnel qualified to reach even reasonably accurate diagnoses. Those who are available are highly concentrated in the few large cities of the country. Secondly, the system for registration of important vital events is poorly manned, inefficient, cumbersome and very tardy in the tabulation and publication of even annual summaries. The National Health Survey of 1965 and other special studies conducted more recently, indicate that this situation is improving, at least in some areas of the country. However, considerable caution must be applied in interpreting currently available data for they undoubtedly underestimate the magnitude of each of the major developmental health problems that confront the health authorities of the country. The following brief summaries of selected major disease categories and health problems are included for illustrative purposes.

Diarrheal Diseases and Related Conditions

This group of conditions is clearly associated with the low levels of environmental sanitation still prevalent in the country particularly outside the major cities and in the rural areas. It can be estimated that no less than one in eight of all deaths are associated with enteric infections. They give rise to almost 8.5% of all consultations with health personnel and comprise the second, or possibly the third, most frequent cause of hospitalization. The toll of diarrheal diseases is greatest in the early years of life but no age group is spared. Linked to these conditions are the parasitic infections of the gastrointestinal tract which in addition to causing their own morbidity and mortality add a significant burden to the nutritional requirements of the population. As a special phase of the National Health Survey it was found that over 80% of the population harbors one or more varieties of pathogenic intestinal worms and other parasites; infestation is heaviest in childhood and the young adult years and in the rural areas where lowest income and levels of education prevail and where there is the least access to sanitation of water supplies and sewage disposal.[12]

The Common Acute Infectious Diseases (of childhood)

Deaths and morbidity in infancy and early childhood remain high in Colombia even though appreciable reductions have been noted in recent years. Underlying malnutrition and gastrointestinal infections are, in all probability, the most significant factors for even in mild form they can also severely increase the toll of the common infections of childhood. Modern medical technology has developed simple and relatively inexpensive immunization procedures to prevent many of these common infections but only limited success has yet been attained in protecting the Colombian population. For example, only 13% of the susceptible population (under age 5) have been immunized against whooping cough, 9% (under 15) against diphtheria and 5% against polio (under age 5). Measles vaccination, one of the newest yet most useful prophylactic procedures, has not yet been supplied through public health channels and tetanus toxoid has been given to about 1% of the general population. On the other hand smallpox vaccination has been given to 56% of all age groups, a level of protection which is considered low were this devastating infection to be reintroduced into the population. The health authorities have adopted the policy of giving BCG vaccination as a means of protection against tuberculosis but efforts to date have not exceeded the immunization of 8% of the population.

12. Associacion de Facultades de Medicina *Parasitismo Intestinal, 1969,* Investigacion de Morbilidad, Ministerio de Salud Publica.

Malnutrition

   Colombian authorities and external assistance agencies have recognized the need for correcting the severe nutritional deficiencies of the Colombian population and currently extensive programs, costing in the range of US$15 million annually, are in progress and will be continued for at least a five year period. No other major health problem in Colombia has been so intensively studied, nor has so well planned or so ambitious a program been devised against other major health problems equivalent to that currently under way in this country-wide attack on malnutrition. Yet the extent of the problem is so great, the factors contributing to it so complex and the implications for the total economic and social development of Colombia so pervasive that measures short of those planned would be ill advised. Table 24-9 shows the categories of nutritional deficiencies identified in sample studies conducted by the Institute of Nutrition, according to urban-rural residence and family income. For all classes of the population only two nutritional requirements are adequately met—those for iron and vitamin C, whereas caloric, protein, mineral and other vitamin needs are significantly deficient. Additional data are available demonstrating that malnutrition is heavily concentrated in early childhood where growth requirements are high and where nutritional deficits are directly reflected in increased susceptibility to intercurrent infections and retarded physical and intellectual development. A second highly vulnerable group is made up of pregnant and lactating mothers. Although direct measurements are lacking in Colombia substantial evidence derived from studies in other countries indicates that the efficiency and productivity of the total working population is reduced when their nutritional requirements are unmet and that absenteeism and learning curves of school children are comparably impaired under similar conditions.

TABLE 24-9: ADEQUACY, PERCENT, OF DAILY PER CAPITA INTAKE OF CALORIES AND NUTRIENTS FOR URBAN AND RURAL ZONES AND FOR SOCIO-ECONOMIC CLASSES[1]
1963-1965

Zone and Socio-Economic Class	Calories	Proteins	Calcium	Iron	Vitamin A	Thiamine	Riboflavin	Niacin	Vitamin C
URBAN									
Very Low	76	67	39	109	56	82	47	77	91
Low	80	80	43	108	54	67	55	87	101
Average	93	106	69	112	107	77	92	102	148
High	114	126	87	165	135	110	110	124	200
All Classes	88	87	50	126	86	85	71	93	127
RURAL									
Very Low	77	64	40	108	50	81	54	89	174
Low	90	82	54	125	68	77	68	94	192
Average	87	82	49	140	56	88	60	93	161
High	98	97	66	124	84	98	74	95	216
All Classes	83	72	46	115	56	83	61	90	178

1 Figures are for 10 of the 11 localities studied by the National Institute of Nutrition omitting those from the study in El Trebol which did not include tabulations for socio-economic class.

Source: Report on seven years of nutrition programs in Colombia 1963-1970, Division of Nutrition, Colombian Institute of Family Welfare, January 1970.

Tuberculosis and Other Chronic Infectious Diseases

In recent years both the mortality rate from tuberculosis and its prevalence have been following a steadily downward trend. These improvements are reflections, in part, of better case-finding procedures and the institution of modern therapeutic methods, including chemotherapy, BCG immunization and chemoprophylaxis. Current death rates, in the range of 20 per 100,000 can be compared favorably with those of other major Latin American countries but are 5 or more times higher than those currently being observed in North America. Deaths and known cases are heavily concentrated in the older age groups but the true extent of this, as yet uncontrolled, problem is obscured by serious underreporting. In order to make international comparisons, it is still necessary to adopt an arbitrarily selected "corrective factor" and apply this to the reported number of cases or deaths.

Syphilis appears to be on the increase in Colombia and this rise has been noted by some observers as reflecting greater frequency of transmission to new cases and not merely an increase in recognition and larger numbers under treatment. Leprosy and yaws are two other chronic infectious diseases noted in Colombia and though their frequency is not so great as to constitute major health problems they have absorbed significant public health effort to keep them under reasonable control.

Malaria. Beginning in 1958 an extensive program of malaria eradication was initiated in cooperation with PAHO and UNICEF with additional bilateral, technical and financial assistance from the United States. A survey conducted at that time indicated that nearly 8% of the population was infected and that it was the fourth highest cause of illness in the country, producing an annual economic loss estimated in the range of Col$58 million. Initial success permitted the opening up of large areas of the country to exploitation and colonization but by 1962-1963 much of the campaign's momentum was lost because sufficient funds were not available. Since 1966 the program has been reorganized and now is an integral part of the 10-year National Health Program (1968-1977), with concentrated attack operations scheduled for the first five years and the consolidation phase completing the ten-year schedule. At the conclusion of the mass campaign, continued vigilance in the maintenance phase of eradication will rest with the local decentralized health services. The highland areas of the country are essentially free of risk of malaria transmission. (17% of the land area and 44% of the population have been designated as free of malaria). An additional 22% of the land area and 42% of the population are now designated as in the consolidation phase; the balance, with 61% of the land area but only 14% of the population, now fall into the active attack area. (Most of the Llanos Area with less than 3% of the population is excluded from the above analysis.)

As a result of the application of modern case finding methods in the field, it is now believed that less than 3 per 1,000 of the population harbor malaria plasmodia, a significant reduction in the foci and sources of infection which were estimated to approach about 80 per 1,000 about ten years earlier. The cost of this antimalarial program have been substantial with no less than US$36 million having been invested in the period 1958-1967. To bring it to its ultimate fruition in 1977, fund requirements will continue to be large: the National Health Plan requires an additional US$33 million for this purpose.

High Fertility and Abortions

Factors associated with high rates of population increase—a phenomenon commonly identified with early stages of economic and social development—are not well known and even less well understood. The 1965-1966 National Health Survey has provided unique information for critical appraisal of some of these factors. Many of these analyses should have significant implications for health planning not only in Colombia but elsewhere.

The Colombian population is young; 46.6% is less than 15, and only 6.8% more than 54 years of age;[13] but in the urban zone the proportion of females less than 15 years old is less than this and the proportion between 15 and 54 greater. In the lower-income group 49.6% of the population, and in the higher 38.5% is less than 15 years of age. Inversely, the population between 15 and 54 years old amounts to 42% and 52.6% of the lower-income and higher-income groups, respectively. The female population, age 15 to 54 years, is 24.2% of the total population of Colombia. Of that group, 22.7% has not attended school at all and only 16.1% has attended some years of intermediate or higher education.

The annual rate of pregnancies is 198.3 per 1,000 women of fertile age. The rate is higher in the rural zone (237.7) than in the urban zone (168.0), and diminishes as social and economic conditions improve.

Of each 100 pregnancies 11.7 terminate during the early fetal period, 2.0 in the intermediate fetal period and 86.3 in the late fetal period, 77 of which end at normal term. Fetal deaths account for 16.5% of the products of pregnancy.

The specific fertility rate is 165.0 per 1,000 women aged 15 to 54 years; the urban rate is 129.4 and the rural rate is 211.3 The highest fertility by age is among the women aged 25 to 34 years, with a rate of 273.4 (see Table 24-10). According to the specific fertility rates of the country, a woman might have six children during the course of her reproductive life. That figure would vary from 4.7 children in the urban zone to 7.7 in the rural zone. The different indicators of fertility consistently show that the fertility of rural women is 38% higher than that of urban women. In addition, fertility is 50% higher in some regions than in others. The differences are maintained in all age groups by zone and family income, although the differences are more accentuated in the extreme age groups.

The estimated 117,401 abortions among women aged 15 to 54 years amount to a rate of 136.1 abortions per 1,000 pregnancies, or one abortion for every six live births (Table 24-11). The risk of abortion increases with age, is higher in women without children and is reduced as the number of children previously born increases. The abortion rate is lower in women of rural areas with lower family income or little education. The rate is intermediate among women, urban or rural, who have more education or higher income. The highest abortion rate is found in women of the urban zone with a low level of education or low incomes.

The estimated number of induced abortions is 65,600 in one year. That figure corresponds to a rate of 76 per 1,000 pregnancies and is 65% of all abortions that occurred before 20 weeks gestation.

Rural women and women of low socio-economic level have a high fertility rate, probably attributable to their limited use of methods to control fertility. Urban women and women of intermediate socio-economic level have a lower fertility rate achieved by increased rates of induced abortions and prevented pregnancies. Women of high socio-economic level have the lowest fertility rate, a low rate of induced abortion and the highest rate of prevented pregnancies. The comparison by regions reinforces the inverse relation between the fertility rates and abortion rates.

A total of 23,241 still-births were reported; a rate of 26.9 per 1,000 pregnancies or 32.9 per 1,000 live births. The risk of stillbirth increased with age, but no significant differences could be found related to socio-economic level of the mother.

Dental Disease

In most countries, developed or developing, the extent of dental pathology is subject only to gross estimates. In Colombia, however, extensive information has been gathered indicating that 43.5% of the population over the age of three are in need of dental care with the highest prevalence during the age span 5-44, reaching a peak of 55.7% at ages 15-24. No marked

13. These data are derived from the 1965-66 National Health Survey. For age distribution of the population, 1970 population estimates show no essential change; the percentage under age 15 is also 46.6; and for 55 and over, 6.6%.

TABLE 24-10: SPECIFIC FERTILITY RATE BY AGE, ZONE AND ANNUAL FAMILY INCOME
(Income in Col$)

Age (years) and Zone	3,600 or Less		3,601 to 6,000		6,001 to 12,000		12,001 to 50,000		50,001 and More		Unknown or no Information		Total	
	Number	Rate	Number	Rate	Number	Rate	Number	Rate	Number	Rate	Number	Rate	Number	Rate
Urban														
15 to 24	26,042	172.7	17,996	121.1	26,488	110.1	16,076	83.8	4,736	45.4	16,203	120.4	107,541	110.6
25 to 34	25,703	237.4	28,618	267.5	40,472	232.7	19,237	199.3	9,277	158.4	28,262	261.8	151,569	232.4
35 to 44	15,337	138.3	10,158	131.1	18,491	144.0	5,033	72.8	1,811	52.2	7,897	94.6	58,727	116.5
45 to 54														
Total	67,800	153.6	57,165	147.2	85,451	138.0	41,210	97.9	15,824	70.6	52,362	138.6	319,812	129.4
Rural														
15 to 24	74,785	231.8	32,921	224.9	15,735	198.5	2,828	117.1	598	52.7	25,306	113.3	152,173	215.2
25 to 34	86,690	340.3	33,415	333.1	13,231	280.3	5,732	354.2	1,094	238.6	23,182	303.2	163,344	327.0
35 to 44	42,327	216.8	19,405	242.0	7,679	225.4	1,458	98.3	218	50.5	8,903	142.1	80,080	204.3
45 to 54	4,057	25.5									1,151	21.4	6,539	21.4
Total	207,859	223.1	86,573	228.4	37,144	197.4	10,018	157.9	1,910	79.7	58,632	185.0	402,136	211.3
Total														
15 to 24	100,827	212.1	50,917	172.6	42,223	132.0	18,904	87.5	5,334	46.1	41,509	160.9	259,714	154.6
25 to 34	112,393	309.6	62,033	299.3	53,703	242.9	24,969	221.5	10,371	164.3	51,444	279.0	314,913	273.4
35 to 44	57,664	188.4	29,563	187.5	26,170	161.1	6,491	77.3	2,029	52.0	16,890	115.1	138,807	154.9
45 to 54	4,775	20.9	1,225	11.4							1,151	10.9	8,514	13.2
Total	275,659	200.8	143,738	187.3	122,595	151.9	51,228	105.8	17,734	71.5	110,994	159.8	721,948	165.0

In 1965-1966, Col$ 1,000 = US$67.
Rates not shown when based on small number of cases.

Source: Aqualimpia M., Carlos, et al, Demographic Facts of Colombia, 1969

TABLE 24-11: ESTIMATES OF INDUCED ABORTIONS BY ZONE, REGION
ANNUAL FAMILY INCOME AND EDUCATION

Zone	Total Rate Observed	Rate of Induced Abortions (Observed Minus 60)	Induced as Per Cent of Observed
Urban I	159.9	99.9	62.5
Urban II	204.2	144.2	70.6
Rural	79.6	19.6	24.6
Total	136.1	76.1	55.9
Region			
Atlantic	118.3	58.3	49.3
Oriental	60.8	0.8	1.3
Bogota, D.E.	101.0	41.0	40.6
Central	109.1	109.1	64.5
Pacific	211.6	151.6	71.6
Total	136.1	76.1	55.9
Income (Col$)[1]			
3,600 or less	110.0	50.0	45.5
3,601 to 6,000	131.3	71.3	54.3
6,001 to 12,000	174.4	114.4	65.6
12,001 to 30,000	201.5	141.5	70.2
30,001 and over	120.6	60.6	50.3
Total	136.1	76.1	55.9
Education			
None	113.1	53.1	47.0
1-8 years	144.8	84.8	58.6
High school and beyond	128.4	68.4	53.3
Total	136.1	76.1	55.9

[1] In 1965-1966 Col$1,000 = US$67.

Source: As for Table 24-10.

differentials occur with income levels or geographic location although women appear to have a higher need than men.

Not all those who need dental care receive such attention. Only 24.3% of the population consult dental attendants, slightly more than half of those who express need for such care. Those who seek dental assistance average 2.5 visits per year and this attention is concentrated in urban areas, in the higher income groups and in the active working age groups of the population. Extractions account for over two-thirds of services rendered with fillings and dental prostheses making up most of the remainder of care given. Dental prophylaxis, so important in early life, makes up only a small fraction of dental care services.

Mental Illness

Substantial evidence exists that mental illness and psychiatric disorders are serious and important health problems in Colombia. An estimate made in 1967 indicates that about 710,000 persons or almost 4% of the population is disabled or chronically impaired by the psychoses, neuroses, mental deficiency, epilepsy and alcoholism. One in six of all hospital beds are devoted to psychiatric care and almost 2% of all medical consultations arise from mental health problems. About 3% of physicians select psychiatry as their area of specialty practice. Regrettably neither time nor opportunity permitted an appropriate survey of the mental health area or a proper evaluation of the proposed mental health program incorporated in the Ten-Year National Health Plan.

CHAPTER 25
RESOURCES FOR HEALTH AND THE NATIONAL HEALTH PLAN

Hospitals, Health Centers and Health Posts

As of December 31, 1966, there were 658 hospitals in the country providing 46,735 beds (approximately 2.5 beds per 1000 population). 523 of these hospitals, with 87.4% of the beds, receive total or partial support from the public treasury and their medical policies are guided by the Ministry of Health. The remaining 135 hospitals, representing 12.6% of total beds, make up the private sector. About one bed in five is devoted to special health problems: chronic diseases (tuberculosis) and mental illness. (Note: In the last four years the ratio of available beds has fallen slightly; this has been due in part to an increase in the population and to the closing of some hospitals and the deactivation of some beds.) In addition to these hospitals, there are operative about 1,120 health centers and health posts rendering primarily preventive services and ambulatory care.

Although the overall ratio of available beds compares reasonably favorably with resources available in other countries, subdivision of the country reveals serious maldistribution of these essential health care facilities. For example, if we divide the country into three major categories: major towns of over 20,000 population, towns of 1,500 to 20,000 population and smaller communities with less than 1,500 inhabitants interesting disparities of availability of hospital care become apparent (Table 25-1). Whereas 23.2% of the population is judged to lack access to hospital care this proportion rises from 1.1% in the more populous areas to 87.5% in small communities and rural areas. Concurrently the bed/population ratio falls from 3.5 per 1,000 in larger centers to 2.0 per 1,000 in intermediate size communities and to 0.8 per thousand for the rural balance of the country.

Other important comparisons indicate that hospital resources are utilized more efficiently in the more populous areas with shorter average hospital stays (12.3, 10.9 and 15.1 days respectively per admission) and higher occupancy rates (75.4%, 51.5% and 53.3% respectively).

An important adverse feature of the health facilities situation is reflected in the number of partially constructed and unequipped and unutilized hospital (or other health care) facilities scattered throughout the country. A recent inventory of these facilities places the number of such structures in the vicinity of 856 buildings partially erected at various times during a 15 or more year interval. This situation resulted from political pressures and from contributions from local charity boards and other sources, without reference to clearly assessed needs, or national or regional plans and, all too often, with insufficient funds either to complete planned construction and equipment or to initiate and maintain operation. One source estimates the investments already made in these structures at over Col$2,000 million. The new National Hospital Plan has not only assessed these structures but proposes the completion, equipment, and placing in operation of such of these facilities as will contribute to a rational national plan for comprehensive health care coverage of the total population. Also as part of the National Hospital Plan the estimated deficit of additional hospital beds needed by 1975 is in the range of 15,400 (Table 25-2).

Ambulatory care facilities—of the total of 1,120 health centers and health post facilities, 710 fall in the former category and 410 in the latter. In addition, 657 hospitals provide outpatient or ambulatory care services as do 205 offices of the Social Security System and the National Welfare Funds. About 5,500 private physicians' offices and an indeterminate number of private care centers contribute to the ambulatory care services for the population.

On the basis of the above compilation, it has been postulated that for the country as a whole over 94% of the population has reasonable access to ambulatory care resources.

However, the comprehensiveness of available services varies. For example, there are only limited facilities, equipment and personnel in the health centers and health posts which for the country as a whole, render over 30% of all consultations (57% in small towns and 83% in villages and rural areas). Health centers are staffed primarily by nurse auxiliaries with occasional visits by physicians; health posts, many of which are open only on a sporadic basis, are staffed only by nurse auxiliaries. In consequence, as shown in Table 25-3, whereas for the total

445

TABLE 25-1: POPULATION WITH AND WITHOUT ACCESS TO HOSPITALS[1] ACCORDING TO SIZE OF COMMUNITY, 1966

Population Size	With Access to Hospitals			Without Access To Hospitals			Total		
	No. of Communities	Population No.	Population %	No. of Communities	Population No.	%	No. of Communities	Population No.	%
Over 20,000	56	8,529,707	98.9	1	92,678	1.1	57	8,622,385	100.0
1,500 to 20,000	313	5,645,058	70.5	182	2,358,072	29.5	495	8,003,130	100.0
Under 1,500	37	272,605	12.5	306	1,905,086	87.5	343	2,177,691	100.0
TOTAL:	406	14,447,370	76.8	489	4,355,836	23.2	895	18,803,206	100.0

[1] Includes both public and private hospitals.

Source: Colombian Association of Medical Schools, Study of Human Resources for Health.

TABLE 25-2: ESTIMATION OF THE NEED FOR GENERAL HOSPITAL BEDS[2] BY 1975

Strata		1966				1975				Deficit
		Population	%	No. General Beds	Beds per 1,000 Population	Population	%	No. General Beds	Beds per '000 Population	
I.	PC[1]	7,501,099	39.9			14,118,893	57.0			
	PR	1,121,286	6.0				3.0			
	PT	8,622,385	45.9	21,975	2.55	14,861,940	60.0	37,898	2.55	+15,923
II.	PC	2,650,162	14.1			3,220,088	13.0			
	PR	5,352,968	28.4				18.0			
	PT	8,003,130	42.5	14,240	1.78	7,678,672	31.0	13,668	1.78	− 572
III.	PC	243,515	1.3							
	PR	1,934,176	10.3							
	PT	2,177,691	11.6	788	0.36	2,229,292	9.0	802	0.36	+ 14
Total:		18,803,206	100.0	37,003	1.97	24,769,910	100.0	52,368	2.11[2]	15,365

[1] PC = Urban Population.
PR = Rural Population.
PT = Total Population.

[2] Change in total rate resulting from the change in the distribution of the population in each stratum.

Source: Colombian Association of Medical Schools, Study of Human Resources for Health.

TABLE 25-3: COMMUNITIES AND POPULATION ACCORDING TO EXISTING
RESOURCES OF PERSONNEL, BY COMMUNITY SIZE 1967

| Community Size | Permanent Resources | | | | Sporadic Resources | | Without Resources | | Total | |
| | With Medical Assistance[1] | | With Auxiliary Only | | | | | | | |
	No.	%	No.	%	No.	%	No.	%	No.	%
1	9,406,215	100.0	–	–	–	–	–	–	9,406,215	100.0
2	7,711,633	96.8	175,398	2.2	–	–	80,351	1.0	7,967,382	100.0
3	1,139,714	53.8	783,771	37.0	40,902	1.9	154,386	7.3	2,118,773	100.0
Total:	18,257,562	93.7	959,169	4.9	40,902	0.2	234,737	1.2	19,492,370	100.0

[1] Includes communities without health center but with a hospital.

Source: Estimates of Sectional Health Services, Ministry of Health.

population 94% are believed to have access to a doctor when needed, an additional 5% to a nurse auxiliary when needed, and less than 1.5% to only sporadic care or none, this is not the situation that prevails in the smallest communities and rural areas. There, only 54% have access to medical assistance and 37% must depend solely on the resources of a nurse auxiliary; the balance, 9%, are unprovided for or exposed only to sporadic and then severely limited services.

Health Personnel: Supply and Distribution

Physicians[1]

Few countries have as much or as precise information on the number. qualifications, location and other characteristics of its medical profession. Using December 1966 as a reference point there were then 8,100 physicians practicing in the country or a ratio of 4.5 physicians per 10,000 population (1 physician per 2,200 population). Much of the following analysis is based on data received from each of the 6,323 physicians who responded to inquiries incorporated in the 1965-1966 National Survey of Human Resources for Health.

Comparing physician resources in Colombia with those in other countries, Colombia falls slightly below the South American mean of 6.0 physicians per 10,000 population and considerably below the national averages of 15.1 for North American countries; for Brazil the ratio is 4.0; Ecuador, 3.3; Bolivia 2.9; Chile 5.8 and Argentina 14.9. The physician population in Colombia is young with 56% under 40 years of age; 65% have completed their medical training since 1950. The practice of medicine is essentially a male occupation with less than 2% women, a rate even lower than in the U.S. All but 3% are native born although 9% received their medical training abroad.

The distribution of physicians is uneven with 74% located in the principal cities of the country serving the needs of the 31% of the population that resides in such centers. Thus, in these cities there is one physician per 1,000 of the population whereas elsewhere the ratio drops to one per 6,400 persons. Only 9% of physicians are in practice in communities of under 20,000 population, where almost 64% of the population reside. This disparity would be even greater were it not for the fact that since 1957 every graduating physician is required to render obligated service for at least two years, usually in a rural area designated by the Ministry of Health.

Only 27% of physicians devote their energies to general medicine. An additional 53% are involved in the specialized practice of surgery, internal medicine, pediatrics and obstetrics. Only a small fraction of physicians specialize in public health, 4.3%, and an even smaller fraction, 2.5%, specialize in psychiatry.

1. Associacion de Facultades de Medicina, *La Profesion Medica, 1968,* Investigacion Nacional de Morbilitad, Ministerio de Salud Publica.

A significant finding of the 1965-1966 study focused on the utilization of the professional time and skills of the physicians; almost half (47.3%) is consumed in non-medical duties or tasks which in the view of medically trained observers could be done as well, and in some instances better, by other personnel without the long and expensive educational preparation requisite for the awarding of a medical degree. This observation and others to be considered later strengthen the argument for a greater use of auxiliary personnel, thereby extending the availability of physicians for duties that cannot be delegated to less well qualified workers.

The mean income of physicians for the country as a whole in 1965-66 was about Col$92,000 per year (equivalent to US$6,200), this mean varying from Col$93,000 in the largest population centers down to Col$54,000 in communities of under 20,000 population. In the larger centers about one-third of physicians have incomes of over Col$100,000 and only 20% earn less than Col$50,000 annually. In smaller communities 40% fall into the lower category and only 4% in the higher.

A recent development arousing the concern of Colombian authorities is the increasing tendency of Colombian physicians to migrate to other countries, particularly to the United States. In recent years this "professional drain" has averaged about 70 physicians a year equivalent to about 17% of the annual number of physicians graduating from Colombian medical schools. Regrettably, during the last several years this trend has been accelerating and this migration rate may now be approaching 25% of production, a serious economic drain both on the limited educational facilities of the country and on its long-term social resources. Ostensibly the main motivation for this emigration is to seek professional graduate training and experience in US hospitals and institutions and many such trained physicians contemplate return to Colombia at the conclusion of this specialization experience. However, data are incomplete or unavailable in this area and it is commonly believed that a large number remain as expatriates.

Dentists

Studies similar to those summarized above for physicians have recently been completed in Colombia for professional dentists. Unfortunately, delays in the publication of these more recent studies preclude the incorporation of the major findings in this report. However, the 3,400 graduate dentists who have been identified as in professional practice in the country establish a dentist population ratio of 2.1 per 10,000, a figure slightly below the average of 2.8 for all of South America and considerably below the average of 5.4 for the North American countries. Comparable figures for several other Latin American countries are: Argentina, 5.4; Bolivia, 1.6; Brazil, 2.7; Chile, 3.3; Ecuador, 1.2; Peru, 1.5; and Venezuela, 1.9.

Professional Nurses

Data similar to those covering the physician supply are also available for a segment of the nursing resources; namely, the supply and distribution of professional nurses, those who have had training beyond secondary school level, usually, if not exclusively provided in a university medical center setting. In 1965 there were just under 2,000 nurses in Colombia of whom 1,618 responded to the study questionnaire. Of the respondents, 73% were engaged in nursing in Colombia, 21% were inactive and the balance, about 6%, were outside the country. Secular nurses made up 77% of those covered in the survey but the balance, belonging to religious orders, constituted 25% of the active professional nurse supply.

The ratio of nurses surveyed to the population as a whole was 8.2 per 100,000; in the capital cities this ratio was 22.7, 15 times greater than in the rest of the country where it was 1.5 per 100,000. In contrast to some other countries where there are usually twice as many graduate nurses as physicians, (e.g., United States), in Colombia, physicians outnumber nurses about 5.5 to 1. The internal distribution of nurses in Colombia is further remarkable in that about 67% of nurses are concentrated in the three principal cities, Bogota, Medellin and Cali, which make up less than 19% of the total population.

Nurses are not well remunerated with the average monthly income of religious order nurses about Col$800 per month and secular nurses averaging about Col$1,500 per month. In recent years there has been a slightly upward trend in the availability of professional nurses but this trend is paralleled by an increasing emigration of nurses from the country, with about 11% of the graduate nurse supply in foreign residence, about half of these in the United States.

Auxiliary Nurses

Auxiliary nurses or nurse aides provide the bulk of traditional nursing services available in Colombia. However, no inventory comparable to those undertaken in medicine, dentistry and professional nursing has yet been initiated and thus only crude and somewhat contradictory estimates of their number in actual working situations are available. One estimate (1965) places the number of nurse auxiliaries at about 11,000 or 8 for each professional nurse. Another estimate (also in 1965) places the number of employed nurse auxiliaries at just under 4,000 and a more recent assessment (1967) indicates that there were then 3,500 "certified" auxiliary nurses known to health authorities and that an additional 12,000 "untrained" auxiliary nurses are employed by hospitals, health centers, and health posts throughout the country. This estimate would place the total number of "certified" and "untrained" auxiliary nurses in excess of 15,000.

These disparities arise, in part at least, as a consequence of differences in definitions and terminology. Until recently no formal educational requirements were established for nurse auxiliaries and nurse aides, both categories being trained on an in-service basis in hospitals or other health care institutions. In contrast, professional nurse training has been directed by accredited educationally oriented institutions. By-and-large, nurse auxiliaries have completed one or two years of secondary school education and receive two years of supervised practical experience in a hospital setting; nurse aides usually have less formal educational background and receive less than a year of practical training on the job. Accordingly, large numbers of young women employed in hospital or ambulatory care services, many fulfilling complex and highly responsible tasks, cannot now meet newly established standards for certification. Nor would many of the institutions in which they were prepared for work satisfy even modest criteria for training accreditation of nurse auxiliaries or nurse aides.

Other Health Manpower

Modern medical and health care services have become singularly dependent upon a large number of specialized aides, technicians, and other supporting personnel. These skills now represent, in developed countries at least, 40% to 60% of the total supply of specialized health workers. This differentiation of health manpower and the need for delegation of responsible functions by the physician is clearly recognized in Colombia, particularly in the University Medical Centers. However, this recognition is only now reaching the stage at which national authorities are beginning to take inventory of this segment of the health manpower pool and to establish standards and norms of personnel requirements in order to assure the smooth and effective operation of the health care system. Among the categories of health workers that are due for such consideration are: health administrators, pharmacists, opticians and optometrists, laboratory and other technicians, dieticians and nutritionists, medical and dental aides, health educators and health promoters, hospital and clinical attendants, sanitarians and sanitary inspectors and engineers.

Health Personnel: Education and Training

Medical Education

In the 20-year period since 1950 the medical educational system of Colombia has made a remarkable forward thrust. Despite limited internal resources the university medical schools making up the Association of Colombian Medical Faculties, have made major revisions in their organization, teaching programs and objectives and simultaneously have provided unprecedented leadership to the development of progressive national health policies, resources and programs.

Prior to 1949, three medical schools graduated about 200 physicians annually. Enrollment was open, faculties were small and almost entirely part-time and the teaching plan was based largely on the older Continental European pattern. A relatively small fraction of students beginning medical studies completed their course and graduates were uniformly of high caliber. Four additional schools began contributing graduates in the early 1950's and together the seven medical schools have almost doubled the output of physicians. Two newer schools are now accepting students and with planned increments of admission to all schools the number of graduates should approach 600 annually by 1973.

Only two of these university medical schools are sponsored by private institutions. Almost 3,900 medical students are currently matriculated in the seven-year course of education. Admission requirements are not completely uniform although basic entrance standards have been agreed to by all nine institutions. The number of applicants is increasing with an overall average of one in four applicants being accepted. Attrition due to academic failure remains high but has declined to about 30% for the total seven-year period with the greatest loss occurring in the first two years. The enrollment of women has increased from under 2% to 12%.

The educational plan approximates the curriculum in leading US and Canadian institutions with increasing emphasis being given to basic science training and carefully supervised clinical experience. Preventive medicine and public health are recognized as having particular significance in the curriculum—in view of the nature of Colombia's as yet unsolved major health problems. However, this field has not yet achieved the same degree of acceptance among medical students as have the more glamorous and traditional clinical specialities. In general, medical faculties are growing with increasing emphasis on exclusive and full-time staff, although half-time and part-time faculty members continue to represent more than 50% of the total medical school staffs. In addition to providing undergraduate medical education, the faculties of medical schools are engaged in post-graduate education, the care of patients in the university teaching hospitals, research and, increasingly, in community health affairs as well as in the training of allied health personnel.

The cost of maintaining the medical schools is high and the six schools (of a total of nine) for which data are available required over Col$50 million (about US$3 million) a year for operational costs, without reference to capital outlays or those for replacement or purchase of new equipment. None of the schools have income of their own. The two private schools which receive the smallest public contributions are almost entirely dependent on enrollment fees for their support. Only one school has received substantial financial aid from abroad and only three have private funds from Colombian sources. The seven public schools charge an annual enrollment fee scaled to the income declared by the parents of the students; the two private institutions charge a fixed enrollment fee considerably higher than is charged at the public institutions. The degree to which this system affects the choice of medical careers is not clear; yet the sons of merchants represent more than 25% of medical school matriculants.

Projections for the future supply of physicians have been developed by the Association of Colombian Medical Faculties based on current and anticipated resources of the training institutions. The population of Colombia is expected to rise from its 1969 level of 20.5 million to about 29 million in 1980. With medical graduates rising to about 600 annually and with a loss by death of 70 to 90 physicians a year (emigration of physicians is not considered) the physician-population ratio will rise slightly from its present level of 4.3 per 10,000 to about 4.9 in 1980. It is thus apparent that Colombian authorities are not counting on a major improvement in the existing physician-population ratio as the means of overcoming the large backlog of health problems now confronting the Colombian health system.

Nursing Education

Nursing education in Colombia has remained relatively static over a period of years. Seven nursing schools were in operation in 1956, the same number as in 1965 when the survey of this field as well as medical education was made. One of the seven schools is not included in that study; of the six schools providing data three are located in Bogota and one each in Medellin, Cali and Cartagena. Five of the six are integral parts of a university education system.

Between 1955 and 1963 the number of applications for admission to the six schools rose from 150 to 348 and the number of first year students from 134 to 167. However, only one nursing school was able to select one in four of its applicants; the others accepting all or a considerable majority of theirs.

Two-thirds of all students come from major cities and less than one percent from rural areas where half of the country's population resides. Three-quarters of the matriculants completed their secondary education in private schools and though educational fees are low there is evidence to suggest that candidates for nursing education are drawn from the reasonably well-off economic strata of Colombia though perhaps somewhat less so than are students choosing medicine as their career. On a national average 75% of the students entering nursing school complete the program although this figure ranges from 97% in one school down to 57% in another.

The lack of appeal of nursing education appears to be linked with high academic requirements for admission to the schools and more recently to the lengthening of educational requirements. In the past the nursing training program varied from two to three years depending on the individual school. More recently with the introduction of the general studies program in schools of nursing the duration of the required course has been lengthened to four years and on graduation the term "general nurse" has progressively replaced "licenciate in nursing."

The cost of nursing education is also high and is largely borne by the university budget. The range of cost per student per year varies from a low of Col$2,800 in one school to Col$16,600 with an average of Col$6,740 per student (about US$420).

Auxiliary Nurse Education

It is stated that 30 schools of auxiliary nurse education are now in operation in the country. Other information suggests that this figure is low and is limited to "accredited" training institutions. The Ministry of Health estimates the number of "graduates" each year from these "accredited" schools in the range of 700. In all probability twice or three times that number of new recruits annually enter employment as auxiliary nurses without proper training or preparation. By crude calculation it is possible to arrive at an estimate that no less than 100 "accredited" auxiliary nurse training schools are needed with each turning out no less than 30 or 40 graduates annually.

Education for Dental and Other
Health Professions and Occupations

These systems have been or are in the process of being studied but published or other data are not presently available for inclusion here.

The National Ten-Year Health Plan, 1968-77: Origins and Evolution

A number of strong, converging forces have been at work in initiating and consolidating the Ten-Year Health Plan now in effect in Colombia. This document, Plan Nacional de Salud, 1968-1977, critically assesses the significant health problems of the country, catalogs the resources available and needed to resolve these problems and, equally importantly, crystallizes a series of long-term national policies and plans to guide the governmental and private sectors in achieving attainable national goals. In the brief period of time in which it has been in effect many of its innovations have proven feasible. Moreover, though a period of ten years appears to be a short span in which to accomplish its multiple objectives its practical directives have aroused the confidence of the health administrators of the country and have mustered widely based support both within the country and among international authorities and observers.

Among the prominent forces that have given rise to the plan is the clear recognition that economic and social development are inseparably interwoven; advances in the former area cannot proceed at the expense of parallel progress in the levels of health, the educational status and the living conditions of the Colombian people. Stated alternatively the development of modern social institutions is not dependent solely on, and cannot be delayed until, the prior accumulation of industrial capital and economic power. Rather, a healthy population, educated to participate actively in a modern society and living in relative homeostasis with its domestic and working environment is, in fact, an essential condition of full economic development. Such a recognition has also been incorporated in the charter of the Alliance for Progress signed by Colombia in 1961. That document calls for a national health plan as an integral element of a national plan for economic and social development.

But even in advance of the Punta del Este Declaration, the Government of Colombia began in 1956 to draft a long-term public health plan. The technical assistance of the World Health Organization and the Pan American Health Organization was enlisted as was the help of the United Nations Children's Fund. These efforts gave rise to an initial ten-year health plan (1962-1971) but, even more significantly, revealed many of the severe limitations and constraints under which the health authorities in that country were forced to function. Dispersed and fractionated responsibilities were the order of the day, funds from a multiplicity of sources in inadequate amounts were expended without reference to priority needs or national plans and unqualified personnel subject to patronage appointment and removal were devoid of professional guidance and supervision. But not the least of the difficulties identified was the lack of reliable data characterizing even the most prevalent of major health problems and providing a reasonable basis for evaluating the effectiveness of established activities or the shortcomings of traditional organizational patterns some of which dated back to the colonial era. This gap was filled by the scientifically based and successfully carried out National Health Survey of 1965-66. Its findings form an integral part of the National Ten-Year Health Plan, 1968-77. The design and application of this national health planning procedure is being increasingly emulated in other Latin American countries and elsewhere.

Important national legislative enactments have accompanied and paralleled the formulation of the National Health Plan. These have authorized and formalized institutional and administrative reorganizations required for sound development of national, regional and local activities in the health field. Specifically, the above legislation provides for the reorganization of regional (departamento) and local (municipio) health services as a decentralized function of the Ministry of Health; fosters the coordination through a National Health Council, chaired by the Minister of Health, of the efforts of previously dispersed entities of government responsible for fractional health functions, and the unification of their financial resources; organizes and consolidates within the Ministry of Health the mechanisms for supervision, control, programming and periodic evaluation of health activity at all levels of government; and finally, defines the fields of activity as well as creating the new organizational structure required to carry out the new health programs called for in the National Plan (see Chapter 24, the section on Health Care System).

Major Elements of the Plan

The Plan critically assesses current mortality and morbidity rates for Colombia and takes note of recent time trends. Each of the major causes of death and of illness is reviewed for various age groups of the population. An appraisal is then made of the availability and utilization of health care resources in the various geographic zones and among the various social strata of the population. Thus, utilizing the extensive data assembled in the National Health Survey, the health authorities of Colombia have been placed, for the first time, in a position to formulate on defensible grounds a series of health priorities to guide both immediate and long-range programs.

For purposes of planning, diseases or other health problems have been arbitrarily categorized into those that are "reducible" or "non-reducible". Among the former are listed the major communicable diseases in the following order: the diarrheal diseases, intestinal parasitism, tuberculosis, measles, whooping cough, malaria, syphilis and gonorrhea, diphtheria, tetanus, leprosy, poliomyelitis, smallpox, rabies and yellow fever. Two other conditions not of infectious origin, are included in this list of "reducible" conditions—abortions and endemic goiter—and it is somewhat surprising that at least two other conditions known to be highly prevalent in the country, contributing significantly to high morbidity and mortality and also clearly susceptible to preventive measures, are conspiciously omitted from this list. Malnutrition and to a lesser extent, accidents are, in fact, given high priorities in the subsequently developed health plan. The justifications for treating other significant health problems as "non-reducible" can also be challenged; but, in the main, those too are covered in the subsequent development of programmatic plans.

The major programs developed in the Ten-Year Plan are listed as follows:

(a) Reduction of morbidity and mortality from "reducible causes":
  program of basic sanitation (diarrheal disease and intestinal parasitism);
  tuberculosis program (preventive vaccination and treatment of the sick);
  five-year mass vaccination campaign (measles, whooping cough, diphtheria, tetanus, poliomyelitis and smallpox);
  ten-year malaria eradication program;
  venereal disease program;
  family planning program (abortions);
  leprosy control program;
  goiter control program;
  rabies control program;
  aedes aegypti eradication program (yellow fever);
  yaws eradication program.
(b) Reduction of mortality from "non-reducible" causes:
  nutrition and feeding program;
  occupational health program;
  comprehensive health and medical care program (hospitals, health centers and health posts);
  mental health program;
  dental health program.
(c) Organization of the health sector:
  development of health policies and programs;
  evaluation and supervision of decentralized health activities;
  the training and organization of health personnel;
  health investigations and research;
  budgeting for health operations and investments for health.

The Ten-Year Health Plan: Analysis and Comments

Neither space nor time permits a detailed analysis of each of the programs and activities outlined in the Plan, and now being implemented, beyond the observations and discussions provided in earlier sections. In general however, each of the projected programs and activities is based on a sound assessment of the problem's scale and vulnerability to attack, a clear appraisal of the resources needed and available, and reasonable projections of the time and funds required to achieve desirable objectives. Whether the goals sought by the Plan will be achieved or whether it will fail or fall short of its goal—as did earlier Colombian efforts—depends less on its scientific and technical elements (which appear sound) than on the political climate in which this Plan has evolved. A number of items bearing on the prospects for success of the Ten-Year Plan warrant further consideration.

National Support for the Plan

Health, as one of the social sectors in development, has not been in the past, and is not now, assigned a high priority by the governmental, industrial and economic leaders of the emerging nations. Health and medical care expenditures have been considered consumer goods and prevailing policies have tended to favor investment opportunities in physical capital. Only with rising national output has there been a willingness to devote part of the increment to the financing of additional health services.

Since the mid-1950s Colombia has been seeking to formulate a national health plan. Furthermore, the support given to the National Health Survey by the President and other high government officials attest to a revision of priorities that has been in process in Colombia for some time.

More recent legislative enactments implementing the Ten-Year Plan, and others now pending, indicate that this national level support has been maintained and perhaps even strengthened. However, it should be recalled that these developments have all occurred during a period of continuing rises in national productivity when there has been a larger share of the gross national product available for the support of the social institutions of the country.

The National Health Plan has been able to provide reasonable estimates of the direct costs of health and medical care services now available and some approximations of the indirect costs accruing from losses due to premature death and preventable disability within its human capital resources. Unfortunately, technical skills are not yet sufficiently advanced to weigh in exact terms, the relative benefits of equal investments in extending health care services or in, for example, additional industrial plants. Thus, choice or balancing of alternatives remains a political rather than a technical judgement. At present in Colombia, there is every indication that public expenditures for, and that national support of, the national Health Plan will continue to receive favorable consideration.

Support Within the Health Sector.   The Ministry of Health, which has been responsible for the drafting of the Ten-Year Plan and now has primary responsibility for its implementation, is only one of at least a score of national agencies—governmental, quasi-governmental and private—that share major responsibility for the provision of health and medical care services. Moreover, at regional and local levels previously independent and autonomous governmental agencies and their non-governmental counterparts render health care services to a greater or lesser degree. (The National Health Plan identified 22 departamentos, 3 intendencias and 5 conisarias at the regional level and 890 municipios, 865 corregimentos and 1,407 inspecciones de policia at the local level).

The National Health Plan, as one of its major elements, has provided for a total organizational and functional reorientation of this multiplicity of agencies into a unified, yet regionalized, countrywide health program. At the national level a National Health Council chaired by the Ministry of Health, provides representation for each of the national bodies in policy and program formulation. In addition, the Ministry of Health has been transformed into a coordinating entity with clearly defined responsibility for the supervision, evaluation and control of decentralized health activities.

In concept, such a plan fosters the establishment of clear lines of authority and accountability as well as the elimination of costly and wasteful duplication of scarce resources. However, its effectiveness will depend on two major considerations: a) the administrative skill and leadership provided by the top echelons of the Ministry of Health, backed up by a full complement of professional staff within its own organization and b) the support provided by other health organizations and health personnel who have become accustomed to functioning independently and who may have established loyalties to other power structures within the country.

The implementation of the new organizational plan is still too recent to assess its effectiveness. At the national level, however, the observer cannot fail to be impressed by the vigorous support being given the plan by leaders in the medical profession, particularly in academic circles.

Professional leadership within the Colombian Institute of Social Security and associated with the National Welfare Funds, which to some degree compete with the ministry in providing personal medical care services, has strongly endorsed and praised the coordinating machinery provided through the National Health Council.

The ministry itself is unusually fortunate to have at the foremost levels of administration a small group of dedicated health authorities who, having formulated the Ten-Year Plan, are now attempting to make it work. Unfortunately this group is severely limited in number, is overworked and forced to depend on supporting staff far less experienced and subject to excessive turnover in professional assignments. Several high-level posts are currently occupied by individuals relatively recently graduated from basic medical education, whose graduate formal training and experience provide them with meager background for the responsibilities they now hold.

At the regional and local levels, one also observes the unevenness of qualifications of responsible personnel. Even in major population centers, to find an outstanding health professional in a key post is the exception rather than the rule. The principle of integrated and coordinated health services so strongly advocated and endorsed at the national planning level is only now beginning to filter down to operational levels. These shortcomings are recognized by the top levels of administration and their correction depends on rapid implementation of manpower training and organization plans, to be discussed below.

Financing of the Plan: The implementation of the Plan will call for significantly larger resources than those spent in the past. As indicated in Chapter 24, section on Major Outlays for Health and Medical Care, the programs benefiting the general population have been relatively neglected and there is a great backlog of accumulated needs. Virtually all of the increases in appropriation for general health services during the last ten years have been consumed in keeping pace with increases in the population and depreciation of the purchasing power of the peso. Granted that, with the economies and greater efficiency of operation called for in the National Health Plan, additional and improved general health services will be forthcoming at lower cost per unit as the Plan becomes established, it still appears unrealistic to assume that even the most urgent of the country's health problems can be overcome through reallocating available funds, without sizable increments of new funds for general health services for the total population of Colombia. Although the various segments of the Plan indicate, approximately, the funds required to attain their objectives, the presentation does not permit a reasonable **approximation of any one year's total budgetary needs for general health programs under** the Ministry of Health. A crude calculation, which should be refined by further study and analysis, would place this estimate at about Col\$70-80 per capita compared with the present Col\$54.5.

An extension and consolidation of the social security system is under consideration. Because such a system involves contributory mechanisms—contributions by the workers, by the employer and by the government—it has appeal to those who recognize the need for broadening the base for the funding of essential health care services. Such an extension, however, warrants careful study of the current costs and the efficiency of operation of the existing system and its more effective integration with the general health services directed by the Ministry of Health. There are already evidences that a two class system of health and medical care services—one for the employed, the other for the rest of the population—is developing.

An additional parameter for assessing the financial requirements of the Ten-Year Plan and its effective implementation can be derived from a special analysis of 1965 national health expenditures. Therein a dichotomy was developed dividing costs into those for care of the sick—hospitalization and curative or palliative services—and, secondly, all other services, primarily those to prevent diseases or promote health. Of the total of Col\$1,091 million expended that year, 91% was devoted to care of the sick and only 9% to preventive services. There are, of course, serious limitations to so sharp a differentiation, since many duties performed by a physician or other attendant in providing medical treatment have significant preventive implications. However, in a country such as Colombia where so many of its serious health problems are amenable to strictly preventive measures such a differentiation can serve a useful purpose. The Ten Year Plan makes a strong case for the strengthening and reorientation of medical care services to provide a more comprehensive and readily available program for the total population. But sound planning dictates that a larger segment of this program be oriented toward preventing illness and promoting health through such activities as intensified maternal and child health activities, health education including nutrition education, vaccination, and improved environmental health services. It would not be unreasonable to increase expenditures for preventive services to 20% or 25% of health care cost instead of maintaining it at its present level of 9% or less.

Another critical insight into the financial requirements of the Ten-Year Health Plan is provided by its initial recognition of the need for the special funding of capital investments for health facilities.

In the past, the building of health facilities was in almost total measure a responsibility or function of local authorities or of local philanthropic or charitable groups. No national plan or standards existed to guide or control such undertakings and not infrequently appropriations from the national treasury were made to assist local hospital or health center construction with funds awarded largely on the basis of political patronage. The Ten-Year Health Plan establishes for the first time a rational and systematic approach to such long term capital investments in health facilities by creating the National Hospital Fund to set standards, review and approve construction plans and award funds on a competitive basis, according to a National Hospital Plan; also, the National Institute for Municipal Development, now incorporated within the framework of the Ministry of Health, will do the same for the construction of water supply and sewerage systems in communities with populations of over 2,500.

Table 25-4 indicates the funds available in the past at the national level for the building and equipment of hospitals, health centers and health posts.

It may be seen that in recent years funds available from the national level for hospital, health center and health post construction and equipment are increasing substantially. However, the National Hospital Plan, 1970-72, assesses the immediate construction and equipment needs in this area at more than Col$800 million. The Plan envisages the completion and equipment of some of the 860 partially constructed but not at present utilized health structures existing throughout the country (see the earlier section on Hospitals, Health Centers and Health Posts). Future needs, particularly those for facilities required for the training of essential personnel have not yet been firmly established.

As in the recent past both the Ministry of Health and the Colombian Institute for Social Security will allocate from their regular budgets, funds earmarked for capital construction. To these will be added the loan funds available through the National Hospital Fund and borrowed from the I.C.S.S. trust funds. Repayment and the financing of these loans will ultimately be borne by Ministry of Health appropriations. Since the effective life of constructed facilities and fixed equipment is reasonably long, the new financing mechanism created by the National Hospital Fund offers a suitable device for the satisfactory management of external investment funds that would accelerate the construction and equipment of needed health facilities.

TABLE 25-4: FUNDS AVAILABLE AT THE NATIONAL LEVEL FOR CONSTRUCTION
OF HEALTH FACILITIES AND EQUIPMENT

(Col$ '000)

Year	Appropriations Ministry of Health	National Hospital Fund	I.C.S.S.	Total
1962	41,025	–	n.a.	41,025
1963	23,494	–	n.a.	23,494
1964	20,822	–	n.a.	20,822
1965	8,426	–	n.a.	8,426
1966	46,887	–	n.a.	46,887
1967	49,790	26,837	21,106	97,733
1968[1]	48,800	37,508	31,971	118,279
1969	42,500	43,000	34,974	120,474
1970[2]	50,000	50,000	56,000	156,000

[1] National Hospital Fund established.

[2] Preliminary estimates.

Manpower Requirements

The training of higher level personnel is expensive both to the individual and to the society which must underwrite the costs of needed educational facilities and subsidize a large fraction, if not all, of the operating expenses. Large investments of time are required before formal training is completed; for the physician seven to ten years, for the dentist five or more and for the nurse three to four years of university level education are required. In Colombia, the Colombian Association of Medical Schools has given much time and thought to developing ways of improving the educational patterns of all schools of the health professions and also influencing the training of auxiliary and supporting personnel. More recently, and as an out-growth of the Ten-Year Plan, the Ministry of Health has created a high-level administrative unit within its organization to give direction and leadership in finding solutions to the most pressing of the country's health manpower problems.

At the present time, no consolidated and comprehensive plan has yet evolved for the whole health manpower area although there are indications that such an overall blueprint may be forthcoming within the next 12 to 18 months. Nonetheless, a number of important guidelines have already emerged indicating the direction this plan is expected to follow:

(a) The nine medical schools, by increasing the combined number of their graduates from the present level of under 400 per year to 600, will be able to maintain the present physician-population ratio of 4.32 per 10,000 and possibly raise it to close to 5.00 per 10,000 despite the anticipated increase in the total population of the country. Curriculum changes now in process will give even greater attention to preventive medicine and will stress the role of the physician as the health team leader and the responsibility to delegate to and supervise the work of other members of the team.

(b) Education for professional nursing, which has not been an attractive career (with less than 150 graduates annually), must be greatly strengthened to provide at least 900 new trained professional nurses each year. This would ultimately bring the nurse-population ratio from its present level of 1 per 10,000 to 5 per 10,000, a figure comparable to the proposed physician-population ratio though still grossly below the availability of nurses in most developed countries of the world. Concurrently the training of auxiliary nurses will have to be increased and improved to at least double the present numbers of 3,500 certified workers and at least similar augmentation must be achieved in the training of nurse aides and rural health promoters.

(c) Specialized training at all levels of public health activity at the Colombian School of Public Health, University of Antioquia, is already under way and these programs are being strengthened.

(d) Intensive efforts must be made to improve the working environment of health workers in hospitals, health centers and health posts, through augmentation of equipment and facilities and better organization of health staff. Through such efforts and the delegation of tasks to supervised auxiliary workers the efficiency and productivity of the total staff can be enhanced.

(e) Improved salaries, opportunities for career advancement, and other rewards and benefits will have to be developed to attract and retain personnel, at all levels, to fill staff positions, particularly those serving the rural and more remote areas of the country.

(f) In the plan for decentralized and regionalized comprehensive health services the nine university medical centers are already assuming, and will have to assume even greater, responsibility for supervising the quality of health care provided as well as offering continuing educational opportunities for the health staff.

The cost of instituting, developing and maintaining this health manpower training program is as yet undefined and is probably well beyond the present or anticipated resources of the educational institutions concerned or of the Ministry of Health. Moreover, to date, those grappling with the problem have largely, if not exclusively, been limited to the health profession-als working within the confines of the health sector itself. There is little evidence of collateral effort. Neither the Ministry of Education, nor any of the educational institutions, other than the nine universities which operate university medical schools, has yet considered the roles they ultimately must play in the preparation and training of auxiliary and supporting health person-nel.

The above considerations suggest that the time is right for a concerted extension of the analysis and planning activities of the Association of Colombian Medical Colleges and the Ministry of Health to a new level of national planning for essential health manpower training and development. Essential data are now available, reasonable goals and objectives have been determined but the means for meeting these educational needs and requirements have not been fully mobilized nor have the minimum costs and the appropriate sources of funds for meeting these costs been clearly identified. It is clear that the medical schools alone, or even the nine universities which sponsor them, cannot by themselves find adequate solutions to all of the problems or meet all the needs. Even the Ministry of Health working with these institutions is not capable of mustering all of the required resources. The overall problem is a national one involving several ministries and agencies of government and many other institutions. A tentative plan for an immediate and direct attack on these problems calls for a large-scale developmental study over a period of eighteen months to two years. This is outlined in a suggested Preinvest-ment Study Program.

Suggested Areas for Further Development of the Plan

During the period when the Plan was being prepared it was clearly recognized that neither all of the major health problems nor all of the possible approaches to their solution could be fully explored. Priorities had to be established, based on data then available, or the likelihood of achieving reasonable goals in limited time spans, leaving open for future consideration areas that might then warrant or be amenable to intensive study, analysis and planning efforts. Thus, the plan was offered not as a static or fixed set of proposals, but rather as an initial effort, capable of extension and revision as circumstances and opportunities permitted. Several areas touched on but not fully explored or developed in the original Plan, published in November 1967, now appear to merit special attention, after some years have elapsed.

Health Advances Arising from Advances in Other Economic and Social Development.
Throughout the various segments of the Plan extensive attention is given to the positive correla-tions found in the National Health Survey of a wide range of social and economic variables with the frequency of illness and its severity and the equally significant negative correlations of these same variables with the availability or the utilization of health services. Such correlations do not always establish cause and effect relationships but they do, at least, confirm the inextricable bonds that make it impossible for the health planner to depend solely upon his own limited resources. They also reinforce the need for those responsible for planning at the overall level or in other sectors to consider carefully the implications of their own planning efforts for the health of the population.

Since 1968, the Ministry of Health has been cooperating with the Ministry of Justice under special legislation in tackling the multiplicity of problems arising from the special need to protect the welfare of mothers and children. Working through the Colombian Institute of Family Welfare, a semi-autonomous agency attached to the Ministry of Health, they are now making a concerted effort to bring together the previously uncoordinated and dispersed institutions of social assistance under the policy guidance of the Colombian Council for Social Protection of Minors and the Family. The former National Institute of Nutrition is now merged as an integral part of the new entity.

However, similar innovative approaches appear worthy of exploration in the fields of education, housing and community development—both urban and rural—and conjointly with agriculture, industry, public works and other sectors of economic and social development. In education two significant areas of activity deserve high priority. Even in developed countries health instruction in the school system has been sadly overlooked and downgraded. Content and teaching methods have completely escaped the attention or concern of qualified health experts. Health instruction materials devised 50 years ago, lacking relevance to modern day problems and neglecting notable advances in technical knowledge, are being used by unqualified teachers who do not fully understand the implications of the instruction they are trying to transmit. This problem is serious enough in an advanced society where deficiencies in the school may be made up by instruction and example in the home. In a developing country such as Colombia this augmentation of school instruction does not exist. The system does not capitalize on one of the few channels of bringing health instruction, via the children, into the home. Health care and the proper utilization of community health resources have always depended on an informed and sufficiently motivated public to do as much for their own health protection as possible and to use reasonable discrimination in turning to available resources for those measures which they cannot provide for themselves. The transplantation of modern and more complex health systems to a developing society will not take hold unless concerted efforts are made to inform and motivate, through public education, the people who are expected to benefit from improved health knowledge and health resources. These opportunities offer a special challenge to both educational and health leaders.

A second opportunity for conjoint health and educational effort lies in the training of sorely needed health manpower. Traditionally such educational needs have been left to and assumed by the health profession and particularly by the small fraction of those professionals identified with a specialized educational program. Colombian leaders have now recognized that the health problems of the country cannot be resolved merely by intensified training of more physicians, dentists, nurses or other highest level personnel. Far more auxiliaries must be recruited and trained, and specified tasks—within their competence to perform under supervision—must be assigned to them. It could be argued that the ideal locus for such training of supporting personnel is in the same environment in which higher level personnel are also being educated. However, the large numbers of auxiliary workers now needed in Colombia and the tremendous cost involved in adding requisite facilities in a medical school dictate that many other educational institutions in the country, reaching down to the secondary and vocational school level, become engaged in health manpower training commensurate with their educational capacities. To move in this direction appears to be the most promising next step in resolving the health manpower problems of Colombia. An outline of a suggested developmental plan is included as an integral part of the Preinvestment Study Program.

The above are offered as examples of multi-sectoral planning and conjoint activity involving the health sector with other prominent social and economic sectors. In agriculture, both the protection of the health of the large number of workers engaged in this essential occupation and the augmented and improved production, distribution and use of essential food resources offer special problems that cannot be resolved by efforts in either sector alone. In the area of nutrition interesting innovative approaches are currently being explored and the Preinvestment Study Program suggests ways in which the amplification of these efforts might be attempted. In the industrial area, the Ten-Year Plan refers to the increasing problems of industrial and occupational illness and accidents. The plan suggests a minimum program within the Ministry of Health's own operations designed to combat the most serious of these problems. But the need will not be met until industry itself recognizes the magnitude of the burden of ill health and loss of productivity identified with industrial operations and joins with health authorities in seeking jointly solutions to these problems. Closely associated with this area are the problems of air and water pollution and of the disposal of industrial wastes. Colombia has not yet reached the stages now faced by the advanced countries of the world where the costs of correcting mistakes in environmental sanitation in the past are reaching staggering proportions. A preventive approach initiated early in Colombia's industrial development is certainly indicated.

Population Policy. The Ten-Year Plan itself did not elaborate any specific program directed toward family planning *per se* nor refer to the already initiated national efforts to reduce or limit the rate of population increase. However, shortly after the issuance of that Plan, the Ministry of Health collaborated in the preparation of a special report and statement of policy on population issued by the National Department of Planning which reports directly to the Office of the

President. This more recent document[2] is highly sensitive to the cultural, religious and political framework in which the government of Colombia must function and also takes into critical account the vast array of economic and social consequences of uncontrolled population growth in a developing society. These consequences are not only observable in the health sector but have direct bearing on the educational, housing and community development needs, and also serious implications for employment, the per capita gross national product and other components of the general standard of living. It can be stated, without reservation, that no single developmental problem basically identified with health and medical services has received so comprehensive a consideration from a multisectoral vantage point. It is of interest, however, that the major burden of effort to alter the rate of population increase still rests on the shoulders of the health sector which, as has been shown throughout this report, is seriously handicapped by severely limited financial, physical, manpower, organizational and even political resources.

Family planning activities in Colombia are not new. Since 1964 the Association of Colombian Medical Colleges has made family planning services available through university hospitals and affiliated health centers. In addition it has undertaken rather extensive educational programs at the professional level and has been largely responsible for such research, primarily of an operational research nature, as has been carried on in the country. Almost simultaneously a private group, the Association for the Welfare of the Colombian Family, started to provide family planning consultations and services on an extensive scale through the offices of private medical practitioners and through independent clinics. These services are also almost entirely restricted to urban centers.

More recently, the Ministry of Health, concentrating on the less urbanized and rural population of the country, has begun a family planning program based largely on increasing the availability of information and appropriate medical consultations to those women who voluntarily seek such services through its established maternal and child health programs. Even more recently, the Colombian Institute for Social Security and the National Welfare Funds have similarly improved their capability to respond to requests for family planning assistance sought by their beneficiaries. A reasonable estimate of funds currently being spent on these family **activities is in the range of US$2.5 million to US$3 million annually with all but minor amounts being derived from external sources, primarily from the United States. It is apparent that lack of funds, earmarked specifically for family planning purposes, is not inhibiting progress in these programs.**

Consolidated data on the exact nature and types of services rendered are meager as is information on the number of women reached and retention rates or on other indices essential for adequate appraisals of the success of these programs. This is not surprising in the light of the paucity, delayed nature and unreliability of all vital statistics data for Colombia except those derived from special studies such as those conducted in the National Morbidity Survey of 1965-1966.

Barring the availability of far more accurate and current birth registration information and associated data, a critical reviewer of family planning activities in the present Colombian scene is unable to forecast, with any degree of confidence, future trends in the rate of natural increase of the population. This rate appears to be high, in the range of 3% per year. It is either stable or gradually declining but whether present family planning efforts will or will not have a demonstrable impact on the rate is highly conjectural.

The above assessment of present family planning activity in Colombia does not controvert the sound national policies recently adopted nor the sincere determination and efforts of national leaders both within and outside the government to apply available technical knowledge and capability to such ends within the social and political framework of the country. Other and perhaps even more important constraints on these efforts are the limitations imposed by the sources of supporting funds which restrict expenditures to those which can be directly identified with the immediate process of prevention of pregnancy.

On superficial analysis the strategy of reaching between 700,000 and 750,000 additional women with family planning services over the next five years (increments of approximately 3% of the women of the country, age 15-49, per year for each of the next five years) appears to be

2. Departaments Nacional de Planeacion, *Planes y Programas de Desanollo* Documents DNP-417J, Diciembre 1969, "Politica de Poblacion".

a reasonable one. Calculations have been made indicating that such efforts would cumulatively reduce the birth rate at least 4.4 per thousand and possibly as much as 12.5 per thousand. A substantial number of physicians and nurses have been or are being brought up to date on modern family planning techniques, health "promoters" are being recruited and given short training courses to prepare them to carry maternal and child health instruction into the homes and ample funds are available to support salaries and to purchase family planning commodities for the program. Questions can be raised as to the reliability of the above predictions since these depend not only on the number of acceptors—those who initially volunteer to accept these services—but (of equal and perhaps crucial importance) the number of women who are successful in adopting and continuing over long periods of time effective contraceptive procedures. Such prevention of conception requires medical instruction and supervision on a continuous basis and only time and experience will demonstrate whether the programs now initiated can meet these requirements.

The programs also appear vulnerable to serious shortfalls on other accounts. It remains to be seen whether the necessary responses can be obtained from the child-bearing segment of the population in a social and cultural milieu in which only 9% of the total population seeks aid when it believes it needs health care for illness and in rural areas only 3% turn to a physician for such assistance; less than half of the pregnant women receive care during pregnancy; only 37% have a physician in attendance at delivery, a figure dropping to 18% in rural areas. Even in the serious circumstances of a pregnancy terminating in an abortion (about 1 in 7.5 pregnancies) only slightly more than half (56%) are seen by a physician.

A strong case can be made for the view that an effective family planning program must be not only part of an inclusive maternal and child health program but linked with a comprehensive and total health and medical care program for the entire country. It is highly problematical that the infrastructure required for an effective family planning program can be established for this purpose alone or can prepare the way for the building of the same infrastructure required for more comprehensive services. Thus, it seems reasonable to question whether present family planning activities in Colombia will really take hold until and unless far more adequate provision is made for supplying the facilities and manpower resources required for the comprehensive health and medical care program called for in the Ten-Year National Health Plan and now in process of implementation. Moreover, as has been clearly demonstrated by the data available for Colombia, marked differentials in the acceptance and effective utilization of family planning practices can be identified with rising levels of education and family income. It follows, then, that augmented efforts to improve educational and job opportunities in Colombia also offer direct avenues to the effective slowing of the overall rate of population increase in the country.

STATISTICAL ANNEX

Table

Table 1: GROSS DOMESTIC PRODUCT OR EXPENDITURE, 1958-69[1]
(In millions of Col $)

Year	Total Gross Domestic Product	Personal Consumption Expenditures	Gross Fixed Domestic Investment	Change in Inventories	Government Current Purchases of Goods & Services	Net Exports of Goods & Services
1958	20,682.5	15,004.9	3,338.8	523.8	1,196.1	618.9
1959	23,648.8	17,198.2	3,907.9	487.7	1,369.5	685.5
1960	26,746.7	19,589.3	4,844.9	649.9	1,659.3	13.3
1961	30,421.0	22,584.5	5,580.3	754.7	2,016.0	-514.5
1962	34,199.2	25,699.7	6,136.9	267.8	2,356.0	-261.2
1963	43,525.5	33,024.8	7,167.5	677.0	3,149.0	-492.8
1964	53,760.3	41,467.6	8,653.8	948.2	3,483.6	-792.9
1965	60,797.6	45,482.1	9,504.2	1,238.0	3,954.3	619.0
1966	73,612.3	55,842.6	12,303.6	2,736.8	4,910.4	-2,181.1
1967	83,082.7	61,596.0	14,729.1	611.9	5,716.8	428.9
1968	96,421.7	70,695.6	18,815.1	1,591.1	6,579.8	-1,259.9
1969	110,953.3	81,230.1	21,230.1	1,932.4	7,832.8	-1,272.1

[1]Data as of June 1971. The data for 1967 and 1968 in this and other national accounts tables are revised and differ from those in Chapter 3. The differences are negligible and do not influence the analysis.

Source: Banco de la Republica.

Table 2: IMPLICIT PRICE DEFLATORS FOR GROSS DOMESTIC PRODUCT, 1958-69[1]
(Index Numbers, 1958 = 100).

Year	Total Gross Domestic Product	Personal Consumption	Gross Fixed Domestic Investment	Change in Inventories	Government Current Purchases of Goods & Services	Gross Exports of Goods & Services	Gross Imports of Goods & Services
1958	100.0	100.0	100.0	100.0	100.0	100.0	100.0
1959	106.6	109.0	108.9	100.5	112.8	90.2	99.7
1960	115.7	118.7	114.7	118.9	123.9	92.1	103.5
1961	125.2	128.5	121.7	109.5	142.7	92.9	106.0
1962	133.5	135.0	133.4	121.2	153.9	90.9	101.8
1963	164.5	165.2	169.3	138.7	194.5	116.2	131.0
1964	191.4	190.3	181.6	160.8	212.3	135.4	132.5
1965	208.9	211.2	211.3	172.6	226.6	138.4	143.2
1966	240.1	237.4	253.2	197.2	269.4	180.8	189.2
1967	260.1	258.4	284.2	245.6	298.1	185.5	206.7
1968	284.4	279.7	315.8	245.5	331.6	215.5	238.6
1969	307.7	299.7	347.6	255.1	366.0	241.2	260.1

[1]Data as of June 1971.

Source: Banco de la Republica.

Table 3: GROSS DOMESTIC PRODUCT OR EXPENDITURE, IN 1958 PRICES, 1958-69[1]
(In millions of 1958 Col $)

Year	Total Gross Domestic Product	Personal Consumption Expenditures	Gross Fixed Domestic Investment	Change in Inventories	Government Current Purchases of Goods & Services	Net Exports of Goods & Services
1958	20,682.5	15,004.9	3,338.8	523.8	1,196.1	618.9
1959	22,176.9	15,774.2	3,587.7	485.2	1,214.3	1,115.5
1960	23,123.4	16,509.2	4,225.6	546.6	1,339.6	502.4
1961	24,300.2	17,579.1	4,584.7	689.3	1,413.2	33.9
1962	25,615.3	19,031.4	4,602.0	220.9	1,531.2	229.8
1963	26,457.2	19,989.0	4,234.0	488.1	1,619.4	126.7
1964	28,088.8	21,795.0	4,764.2	589.8	1,641.2	-701.4
1965	29,100.0	21,538.9	4,498.9	717.1	1,744.8	600.3
1966	30,658.2	23,522.9	4,859.7	1,387.9	1,822.7	-935.0
1967	31,947.0	23,840.5	5,182.6	249.1	1,917.7	757.1
1968	33,902.2	25,276.8	5,958.0	648.0	1,984.1	35.3
1969	36,060.6	27,103.7	6,106.8	757.5	2,140.0	-47.4

[1]Data as of June 1971.

Source: Banco de la Republica.

Table 4: GROSS DOMESTIC PRODUCT BY INDUSTRY, 1958 and 1969.

	1958		1969	
Industry	Value at Current Factor Cost, in Millions of Col $[1]	Percentage Share of Total GDP	Value at Current Factor Cost, in Millions of Col $[1]	Percentage Share of Total GDP
Agriculture	7,086.1	36.7	29,453.6	29.0
Fishing and Hunting	31.5	0.2	347.0	0.3
Forestry	79.3	0.4	408.0	0.4
Mining	736.5	3.8	2,514.0	2.5
Manufacturing	3,127.0	16.2	17,208.1	16.9
Construction	659.8	3.4	5,427.7	5.3
Commerce	2,334.8	12.1	13,776.4	13.5
Transportation	1,109.8	5.7	6,282.8	6.2
Communications	127.5	0.7	1,027.9	1.0
Electricity, Gas, Water	144.5	0.7	1,515.0	1.5
Personal Services	1,496.2	7.7	7,740.6	7.6
Government Services	997.9	5.2	6,631.9	6.5
Other	1,380.1	7.2	9,403.2	9.3
Total Gross Domestic Product	19,311.0	100.0	101,736.2	100.0

[1]Valuation at factor cost differs from the more common measurement at market prices by the exclusion of indirect business taxes and the inclusion of subsidies.

Source: Banco de la Republica.

Table 5: COMPOSITION OF GROSS DOMESTIC INVESTMENT, 1958-69[1]
(In millions of Col $)

Year	Gross Fixed Domestic Investment			Inventory Change	Gross Domestic Investment	Percentage Share of GDI	
	Construction	Transportation Equipment	Machinery and Other Equipment			Private Sector	Government
1958	1,951.6	356.5	1,030.7	523.8	3,862.6	83.8	16.2
1959	2,486.5	480.2	941.2	487.7	4,395.6	83.1	16.9
1960	2,697.1	691.6	1,456.2	649.9	5,494.8	85.3	14.7
1961	3,272.1	746.9	1,561.3	754.7	6,335.0	81.8	18.2
1962	3,841.9	506.1	1,788.9	267.8	6,404.7	79.7	20.3
1963	4,421.1	691.7	2,054.7	677.0	7,844.5	82.3	17.7
1964	5,247.8	931.1	2,474.9	948.2	9,602.0	83.6	16.4
1965	5,976.8	840.5	2,686.9	1,238.0	10,742.2	82.6	17.4
1966	7,468.5	1,126.6	3,708.5	2,736.8	15,040.4	79.7	20.3
1967	9,738.3	1,457.3	3,533.5	611.9	15,341.0	71.7	28.3
1968	11,723.9	2,231.3	4,859.9	1,591.1	20,406.2	73.7	26.3
1969	13,873.2	2,318.7	5,038.2	1,932.4	23,162.5	71.3	28.7

[1]Data as of June 1971.

Source: Banco de la Republica.

Table 6:   CIF IMPORTS, BY PRINCIPAL PRODUCT GROUPS, 1958-69
(In thousands of US dollars)

Year	Machinery and Electrical Equipment	Chemicals and Pharmaceuticals	Metals and Products	Transport Vehicles and Equipment	Food-Stuffs and Beverages	Textiles and Manufactures	Paper Materials and Products	Minerals	Rubber and Products	Other	Total
1958	101,238	66,557	55,726	32,151	44,210	24,924	20,325	15,572	9,955	29,274	399,932
1959	103,309	67,838	53,160	54,772	37,207	23,412	22,032	15,651	8,387	29,820	415,588
1960	146,357	78,644	68,238	77,326	31,373	23,425	26,176	17,495	13,256	36,295	518,585
1961	158,700	87,794	64,620	89,664	43,842	21,609	27,552	20,762	9,890	32,696	557,129
1962	169,402	87,425	62,644	61,134	31,752	20,221	26,311	21,848	12,323	47,291	540,351
1963	148,717	97,557	60,956	63,983	22,071	22,080	21,988	18,112	12,917	37,642	506,023
1964	172,632	99,877	78,964	84,085	35,996	24,255	21,677	14,328	11,576	42,901	586,291
1965	140,327	62,042	46,615	63,864	28,145	20,808	21,943	9,936	22,274	37,098	453,502
1966	169,116	128,819	83,765	89,443	49,691	25,775	32,280	14,128	31,807	49,268	674,092
1967	142,969	76,531	54,483	84,072	26,737	13,550	26,554	12,258	20,530	39,171	496,855
1968	187,515	100,793	64,916	117,351	38,850	14,936	35,938	10,403	25,603	46,942	643,247,
1969	181,499	103,073	88,946	119,156	44,541	15,253	40,479	13,282	33,427	45,581	685,237

Source: Banco de la Republica.

Table 7: MERCHANDISE EXPORT EXCHANGE SURRENDER, 1958-69[1]
(In thousands of US dollars)

Commodity	1958	1959	1960	1961	1962	1963	1964	1965	1966	1967	1968	1969
Bananas	8,955	8,969	5,031	5,564	4,195	4,957	17,548	25,384	23,729	19,173	15,571	18,559
Cattle and meat	40	.....	.....	.....	.....	.....	202	6,079	6,378	4,072	4,471	10,970
Cement	.....	1,960	1,757	2,021	1,925	1,323	2,006	1,463	1,996	3,269	3,978	3,229
Cotton	.....	.....	13,293	10,770	20,230	6,212	9,296	6,662	4,954	19,607	33,695	36,413
Hides and skins	1,014	1,144	539	884	2,105	2,523	3,868	3,668	3,051	3,635	6,276	8,658
Live animals, excluding cattle	.....	1,143	1,560	1,537	1,865	1,596	1,728	3,478	1,639	1,627	1,514	6,524
Mechanical manufactures	.....	.....	.....	791	488	650	1,030	949	1,866	2,154	2,409	4,657
Metal manufactures	.....	.....	.....	.....	.....	.....	.....	.....	2,388	3,470	3,322	4,063
Minerals	.....	.....	.....	.....	.....	1,029	2,568	1,528	170	1,818	6,090	13,931
Paper and cardboard	.....	.....	.....	.....	.....	.....	.....	3,864	2,707	5,283	8,419	6,333
Pharmaceuticals	.....	.....	.....	.....	.....	1,626	2,085	.....	1,741	1,695	2,378	8,081
Sugar	4	.....	.....	5,233	7,451	5,038	3,282	7,696	10,043	15,947	22,035	17,495
Textiles	.....	.....	183	1,110	4,336	3,840	6,645	11,842	8,450	8,923	16,043	15,132
Tobacco	1,812	2,246	2,212	3,069	5,111	8,609	10,904	5,332	4,441	5,072	7,072	9,145
Wood	.....	1,920	2,279	2,195	2,508	3,861	4,145	3,688	3,877	4,526	5,647	7,204
Other minor exports	6,931	5,668	3,397	3,668	3,798	3,919	7,210	17,140	18,299	16,792	39,514	36,803
Sub-Total	(18,756)	(23,069)	(30,251)	(36,842)	(54,012)	(45,183)	(72,517)	(98,773)	(95,729)	(117,063)	(178,434)	(207,197)
Coffee	350,562	370,729	325,641	326,939	300,089	312,455	439,830	346,675	302,302	318,813	314,144	332,853
Total	369,318	393,798	355,892	363,781	354,101	357,638	512,347	445,448	398,031	435,876	492,578	540,050

[1]Excludes petroleum.

Source: Banco de la Republica.

Table 8:   OFFICIAL MARKET RATES OF EXCHANGE, BY QUARTER, 1967-71
(Col$ per US dollar)

End of Period	Dollar Purchase			Dollar Sale	
	Exchange Certificate Rate[1]		Petroleum Capital Rate[2]	Exchange Certificate Rate[1]	Preferential Rate[3]
1967-March	13.53		7.67	13.53	9.00
1967-June	14.46		7.67	14.51	9.00
1967-September	15.30		7.67	15.30	9.00
1967-December	15.76		16.25	15.82	9.00
1968-March	15.98		16.25	16.03	9.00
1968-June		16.29		16.33	9.00
1968-September		16.55		16.57	9.00
1968-December		16.88		16.91	9.00
1969-March		17.10		17.14	9.00
1969-June		17.27		17.31	9.00
1969-September		17.55		17.59	9.00
1969-December		17.85		17.90	9.00
1970-March		18.15		18.20	9.00
1970-June		18.41		18.48	9.00
1970-September		18.76		18.81	9.00
1970-December		19.09		19.13	9.00
1971-March		19.48		19.52	9.00
1971-June		19.98[4]		19.93[4]	20.00

[1]Decree-Law 444 of March 22, 1967, created this flexible Exchange Certificate Rate which remains in force today.

[2]Monetary Board Resolution 8 of March 10, 1965, established a rate of Col $7.67 for the purchase of dollars brought into Colombia as capital importation by oil companies. Resolution 13 of March 22, 1967, continued this rate and specified precisely the types of activities and outlays to which the rate applied. Resolution 58 of November 10, 1967, ruled that a Capital Market buying rate would be used for petroleum company conversions. This rate existed from November 1967 through May 1968 at a constant Col $16.25. On June 1, 1968, Resolution 24 transferred petroleum capital transactions to the Certificate Market.

[3]The Preferential Rate for domestic purchases of crude petroleum was held at Col $9.00 from 1962 to June 25, 1971, when it was raised to Col $20.00.

[4]Estimate.

Source: Banco de la Republica.

Table 9:   EXCHANGE RATE DEPRECIATION AND WHOLESALE PRICE INCREASES, BY QUARTER, 1967-71

	Certificate Market Selling Rate of Exchange		Wholesale Prices, Excluding Foodstuffs		
	Quarterly Percentage Increase[1]	Cumulative Percentage Increase[1]	Index, 1952 = 100	Quarterly Percentage Increase	Cumulative Percentage Increase
1967-March	.....	.....	449.2	.....	.....
1967-June	7.2	7.2	458.4	2.0	2.0
1967-September	5.4	13.1	467.5	2.0	4.1
1967-December	3.4	16.9	471.1	0.8	4.9
1968-March	1.3	18.5	479.0	1.7	6.6
1968-June	1.9	20.7	483.8	1.0	7.7
1968-September	1.5	22.5	489.9	1.3	9.1
1968-December	2.0	25.0	494.6	1.0	10.1
1969-March	1.4	26.7	513.1	3.7	14.2
1969-June	1.0	27.9	526.4	2.6	17.2
1969-September	1.6	30.0	535.9	1.8	19.3
1969-December	1.8	32.3	547.5	2.2	21.9
1970-March	1.7	34.5	565.8	3.3	26.0
1970-June	1.6	36.7	576.4	1.9	28.3
1970-September	1.8	39.0	585.8	1.6	30.4
1970-December	1.7	41.4	593.5	1.3	32.1
1971-March	2.0	44.3	609.8	2.7	35.8
1971-June[2]	2.1	47.3	625.0	2.5	39.1

[1]Exchange rate percentage changes are based on last day of March 1967, using end-of-period values.

[2]Estimate.

Source: Banco de la Republica.

Table 10:   NET INTERNATIONAL MONETARY RESERVES OF THE CENTRAL BANK, 1968-71
(In millions of US dollars)

	End-of-period positions:						
	1st Half 1968	2nd Half 1968	1st Half 1969	2nd Half 1969	1st Half 1970	2nd Half 1970	1st Half 1971
Gross Reserves[1]	163.1	217.7	212.1	257.4	317.1	257.5	219.8
Gold	32.8	30.6	28.7	26.5	26.1	16.9	
IMF Gold Tranche	31.2	31.3	31.2	31.2	31.2	39.2	
Foreign Exchange	83.0	141.2	132.8	190.8	247.4	180.2	
Net Bilateral Agreements	15.0	13.6	16.4	4.9	5.3	12.1	
IDB & IBRD Bonds	1.0	1.0	3.0	4.0	7.0	9.0	
Liabilities[1]	173.0	182.5	161.8	160.8	131.8	105.5	79.4
IMF	126.6	143.9	130.4	137.5	116.3	94.1	
Foreign Banks	43.1	38.1	31.4	23.3	15.5	10.4	
Other	3.2	0.6	.....	.....	.....	1.0	
Net Reserves	-9.9	35.2	50.3	96.6	185.3	152.0	140.4

[1] Figures may not add to totals because of rounding. Liabilities refer to short-term and medium-term external obligations (10 years or less).

Source: Banco de la Republica.

Table 11: FOREIGN ASSISTANCE, COMMITMENTS BY AGENCY, 1961-69
(In millions of US dollars)

	1961	1962	1963	1964	1965	1966	1967	1968	1969	1961-1969 Total
AID	20.0	89.9	26.2	65.9	65.0	16.5	100.0	73.0	95.0	551.5
EXIMBANK	54.4	3.4	2.5	22.0	3.9	3.4	25.5	.....	19.5	134.6
IDB	12.4	35.6	24.9	8.1	37.7	27.4	35.6	48.9	102.3	332.9
IBRD	41.5	50.0	73.8	45.0	.....	41.7	25.0	105.6	60.3	442.9
IDA	19.5	.....	.....	.....	.....	.....	.....	.....	.....	19.5
OTHERS	n.a.	n.a.	8.6	20.5	15.1	27.9	30.7	41.7	41.0	185.5
Sub-total	147.8	178.9	136.0	161.5	121.7	116.9	216.8	269.2	318.1	1,666.9
PL-480	.....	.....	6.9	13.4	.....	16.9	.....	13.0	.....	50.2
Total	147.8	178.9	142.9	174.9	121.7	133.8	216.8	282.2	318.1	1,717.1

Source: National Planning Department.

Table 12: FOREIGN ASSISTANCE, COMMITMENTS BY SECTOR, 1961-69
(In millions of US dollars)

	1961	1962	1963	1964	1965	1966	1967	1968	1969	1961-1969 Total	1961-1969 Percentage
Agriculture	8.0	....	12.5	11.0	....	46.3	21.2	14.8	59.8	173.6	11
Industry	0.7	4.1	44.9	30.7	10.2	25.0	5.0	10.0	65.1	195.7	12
Mining	....	....	2.0	....	....	....	....	....	....	2.0	....
Transportation	48.5	....	40.0	....	5.0	....	25.5	52.0	3.8	174.8	11
Power	22.0	50.0	13.8	46.3	....	8.1	....	59.4	82.6	282.2	18
Communications	....	....	....	....	....	....	16.0	2.2	9.2	27.4	2
Education	....	....	....	1.1	0.5	6.3	18.4	14.2	....	40.5	3
Housing	12.0	15.2	7.5	....	....	....	....	9.1	....	43.8	3
Water and sewerage	11.2	19.1	3.7	1.9	26.0	3.3	....	14.0	12.6	91.8	6
Preinvestment	0.5	0.6	3.0	....	....	....	....	3.0	....	7.1	1
Sub-total, project loans	102.9	89.0	127.4	91.0	41.7	89.0	86.1	178.7	233.1	1,038.9	67
General imports	44.9	89.9	....	50.0	65.0	....	100.0	78.0[2]	85.0	512.8	33
Total	147.8	178.9	127.4	141.0	106.7	89.0	186.1	256.7	318.1	1,551.7	100

[1] The series in this and following tables exclude the item Others for the years 1961 to 1967 and PL-480 from Table 19 in this Annex.

[2] Includes 5.0 million for the Justice Palace.

Source: National Planning Department.

Table 13:   IBRD LOANS AND IDA CREDITS COMMITTED TO COLUMBIA 1949-71
(In millions of US dollars)

	Loan or Credit No.	Purpose	Date of Loan Agreement		Original Principal Amount	Cumulative Original Amount
1949-60					178.7	178.7
1961	282	Power	May 12		22.0	
	295	Roads	August 28		19.5	
	IDA-5	Roads	August 28		19.5	
				Sub-total	61.0	239.7
1962	313	Power			50.0	289.7
1963	339	Power	June 3		8.8	
	343	Railways	June 21		30.0	
	345	Steel	June 28		30.0	
	347	Power	July 16		5.0	
				Sub-total	73.8	363.5
1964	369	Power			45.0	408.5
1965					--	
1966	448	Agriculture	May 16		16.7	
	451	Industry	May 31		25.0	
				Sub-total	41.7	450.2
1967	499	Telecom.	June 15		16.0	
	502	Agriculture	June 29		9.0	
				Sub-total	25.0	475.2
1968	534	Industry	May 22		12.5	
	536	Water	June 3		14.0	
	537	Power	June 3		18.0	
	550	Roads	July 25		17.2	
	551	Railways	July 25		18.3	
	552	Education	July 31		7.6	
	575	Power			18.0	
				Sub-total	105.6	580.8
1969	624	Agriculture	June 27		17.0	
	625	Industry	June 27		25.0	
	651	Agriculture	Dec. 29		18.3	
				Sub-total	60.3	641.1
1970	679	Education	June 4		6.5	
	680	Roads	June 4		32.0	
	681	Power	June 4		52.3	
	682	Water	June 4		18.5	
				Sub-total	109.3	750.4
1971 First Semester	738	Water	May 28		2.0	
	739	Agriculture	May 28		8.1	
	740	Telecom.	May 28		15.0	
	741	Water	May 28		88.0	
	742	DFC	May 28		40.0	
				Sub-total	153.1	903.5

Source: IBRD.

Table 14: EXTERNAL PUBLIC DEBT OUTSTANDING AS OF DECEMBER 31, 1970[1]
Debt Repayable in Foreign Currency
(In thousands of US dollars)

Source	Debt outstanding December 31, 1970	
	Disbursed only	Including undisbursed
TOTAL EXTERNAL PUBLIC DEBT	1,229,650	1,721,914
Privately-held Debt	134,319	201,320
Publicly-issued Bonds	20,616	20,616
Suppliers	94,503	110,868
Financial Institutions	18,868	69,504
Privately-placed Bonds	332	332
Loans from International Organizations	437,936	713,242
IBRD	354,064	577,921
IDA	19,500	19,500
IDB	64,372	115,821
Loans from governments	634,509	784,466
United States	601,902	710,817
Others	32,607	73,649

[1]Debt with an original or extended maturity of over one year.

Source: Economic and Social Data Division, Economic Program Department, July 6, 1971.

Table 15: CENTRAL GOVERNMENT OPERATIONS, 1966-70
(Cash flows in millions of Col $)

	1966	1967 Actual	1968	1969 Estimate	1970 Projected
Current Account Income	6,027	6,688	8,057	9,250	11,623
Income Taxes	2,310	2,862	3,578	4,467	5,310
Inheritance Tax	109	119	150	159	170
Customs duties	1,911	1,117	1,372	1,573	2,125
3% import surcharge	.....	73	184	218	300
Special exchange account	346	371	428	534	1,303
Sales taxes	644	724	783	883	1,010
Fuel taxes	62	649	694	731	780
Stamp taxes	311	410	477	538	615
Other	334	363	529	478	510
Tax Credit Certificates (CAT)	.....	.....	-138	-331	-500
Current Account Expenditure	4,120	4,293	5,122	6,418	7,668
Personal services	2,150	2,440	2,474	2,950	3,378
General expenditures	409	418	485	590	675
Transfers	1,227	1,122	1,794	2,465	2,782
Interest on public debt	334	313	369	413	833
External	(84)	(100)	(130)	(171)	(350)
Internal	(250)	(213)	(239)	(242)	(483)
Current Account Surplus	1,907	2,395	2,935	2,832	3,955
Investment	1,852	2,626	3,646	3,987	5,300
Current account surplus	1,907	2,395	2,935	2,832	3,955
Surplus or deficit (-)	-55	-231	-711	-1,155	-1,345
Financed by Credit	-55	231	711	1,155	1,345
External, net	79	367	1,063	1,272	1,976
(amortization)	(-187)	(-286)	(-261)	(-252)	(-317)
Internal, net	-132	-136	-352	-117	-631

Source: Banco de la Republica; Ministry of Finance.

Table 16:   CENTRAL GOVERNMENT TOTAL EXPENDITURE BY ECONOMIC CLASSIFICATION, 1966-70
(In millions of Col $; allotments 1966-69, budget 1970)

	1966	1967	1968	1969	1970
General Services	2,123.6	2,327.7	2,962.7	3,384.7	3,997.2
Administration	508.4	512.8	659.7	870.9	1,090.2
Police and Justice	910.2	1,010.2	1,221.9	1,442.0	1,609.2
Defense	705.0	794.7	1,068.5	1,071.8	1,297.8
Other general services	.....	10.0	12.6	.....	.....
Economic Services	1,251.4	1,971.4	2,850.6	3,209.7	4,276.1
Agriculture	270.2	477.7	746.9	844.2	1,202.0
a. Administration and technical services	8.1	.....	7.7	5.0	.....
b. General agricultural development	34.0	2.1	33.6	20.6	29.0
c. Livestock development	9.7	110.7	67.6	39.2	47.0
d. Extension services	5.4	.4	86.6	119.9	274.8
e. Agricultural research	55.2	81.8	1.8	88.4	24.9
f. Renewable natural resources	45.4	63.4	89.5	42.0	138.2
g. Storage of agricultural products	11.3	.....	20.0	29.0	46.8
h. Agricultural education	1.1	13.4	1.0	3.5	5.1
i. Agrarian reform	100.0	205.5	439.0	486.5	636.2
j. Development of agrobased industries	.....	.4	.1	.1	.....
k. Animal health	.....	.....	.....	10.0	.....
Industry	20.7	84.8	220.9	153.7	111.5
Mining	6.1	10.7	13.6	36.6	43.3
Tourism	10.1	10.0	32.6	51.9	65.2
Energy	129.9	161.9	295.8	331.8	383.2
Transport	760.4	1,115.3	1,340.2	1,629.6	2,251.2
a. Administration and technical services	23.8	12.1	15.9	2.4	88.0
b. Maritime and river transport	17.5	34.9	34.6	26.4	30.0
c. Railways	55.0	97.0	116.3	125.0	113.9
d. Roads	643.7	873.9	1,088.3	1,354.3	1,915.7
e. Air transport	17.4	49.4	79.1	115.5	95.6
f. Other transport	3.0	48.0	6.0	6.0	8.0
Communications	20.0	40.0	51.6	48.5	53.7
a. Administration and technical services	1.7	1.7	1.9	3.9	.7
b. Radio communications	18.1	5.0	20.7	5.2	14.0
c. Postal services	.2	19.0	22.5	20.0	27.2
d. Telephone and telegraph	.....	4.3	.....	11.6	1.3
e. Radio and television	.....	10.0	6.5	7.8	10.5
Studies	34.0	71.0	22.4	23.9	36.0
Regional Development	.....	.....	88.3	.....	.....
Promotion of exports	.....	.....	38.3	89.5	130.0
Cultural and Social Services	1,614.9	1,893.3	2,678.4	3,235.0	3,713.0
Education and Culture	874.2	1,014.4	1,300.4	1,570.1	1,927.5
Administration and technical services	6.0	8.0	11.9	32.6	67.3
Primary education	356.8	404.4	493.2	591.3	626.8
Secondary education	69.6	100.0	228.6	205.4	509.0
University education	218.3	255.4	316.8	435.9	454.7
Industrial and commercial training	25.3	35.4	45.5	50.9	18.4
Vocational training	19.3	22.5	24.4	36.2	10.0
Adult education and cultural activities	70.1	95.0	121.7	144.2	83.7
Sports	1.4	1.1	7.4	4.7	52.1
Other educational services	103.0	87.9	43.0	62.8	100.4
Educational services for natives	1.4	1.7	4.9	.1	.....
Training in public administration	3.0	3.0	3.0	6.0	5.1
Social Security	328.9	413.9	708.5	921.7	904.2

Table 16 (Cont.): CENTRAL GOVERNMENT TOTAL EXPENDITURE BY ECONOMIC CLASSIFICATION, 1966-70
(In millions of Col $; allotments 1966-69, budget 1970)

	1966	1967	1968	1969	1970
Cultural and Social Services (Cont.)					
Public Health	309.3	367.0	405.3	617.4	777.4
Administration and technical services	62.1	62.6	20.0	16.6	96.6
Hospitals	132.9	170.7	230.0	285.5	347.9
Preventive medical services	34.6	29.3	31.9	13.9	.....
Mother and child care	.5	.5	.5	10.0	48.7
Environmental health	18.3	28.2	30.9	59.8	85.9
Epidemiology	56.1	68.5	72.8	140.2	174.9
Other services	4.8	7.2	19.2	91.4	23.4
Housing	102.5	98.0	264.2	125.8	103.9
Community Services	118.5	202.5	320.2	425.1	403.0
Sanitary Services	61.1	66.0	146.3	212.2	206.4
Water and sewerage	61.1	66.0	144.2	201.0	206.4
Slaughterhouses, markets, fairs	.....	.....	2.1	11.2	.....
Other Community Services	57.4	136.5	173.9	212.9	196.6
Other Expenditures	1,959.2	1,441.1	1,352.2	1,486.0	2,131.7
Public debt	1,930.8	1,398.4	1,320.5	1,369.7	1,921.5
Reimbursement, indemnifications, etc.	28.0	19.0	26.7	110.1	205.2
State of emergencies	.4	23.7	5.0	6.2	5.0
Total Expenditures	7,067.6	7,836.0	10,164.1	11,740.5	14,521.0
(Excluded accounting items)	(-)	(-)	(-)	(1,702.4)	(500.0)
In constant prices	7,067.6	7,248.8	8,754.0	9,303.3	10,756.0

Source: Ministry of Finance.

Table 17: INCOME AND EXPENDITURES OF THE DECENTRALIZED AGENCIES[1], 1966-70
(In millions of Col $)

	1966	1967	1968	1969	1970
		Actual		Estimate	Projected
Current Account Income	3,715	4,860	6,068	7,470	8,715
Sale of goods and services	1,269	1,507	1,828	2,200	2,590
Transfers	1,269	1,842	2,470	2,820	3,350
Central government	1,090	1,698	2,327	2,585	
Departments	61	50	73	80	
Municipalities	2	3	3	5	
Other decentralized agencies	88	61	27	100	
Other	28	30	40	50	
Taxes or dues	865	1,241	1,551	1,730	2,035
Other income	205	202	358	700	840
Loss (-) of profit of commercial operations	(+107)	+68	-139	+20	-100
Current Account Expenditures	2,403	3,085	3,853	5,375	6,500
Personal services	1,185	1,376	1,750	2,400	2,800
Goods and services	437	767	901	1,170	1,500
Transfers	597	806	1,035	1,555	1,915
Public sector	123	147	180	225	
International organizations	29	41	58	70	
Private sector	418	570	699	1,140	
Social security	27	48	98	120	
Interest on debt	184	136	167	250	285
External					
Internal					
Current Account Surplus	1,312	1,775	2,215	2,095	2,215
Excl. Central Govt. transfers	(222)	(77)	(-112)	(-490)	
Direct Investment	1,348	2,023	2,548		
Indirect investment	262	482	732		
Total	1,610	2,505	3,280	3,875	
Financial investments	40	184	558	750	

[1]Excluding the Fondo Vial.

Source: Ministry of Finance.

Table 18:   DEPARTMENTS: TOTAL EXPENDITURE BY ECONOMIC CLASSIFICATION, 1966-69
(In millions of Col $, Budget Executions)

DEPARTMENTS	1966	1967	1968	1969
Administration	265.5	300.4	335.6	338.2
Police and justice	90.1	107.8	128.4	116.2
Public services	1.7	2.9	3.1	3.3
Labor and social security	147.2	178.1	195.4	205.3
Public health	84.3	96.1	106.8	117.1
Education and culture	889.4	1,136.1	1,169.3	1,165.0
Economic Development	447.4	293.5	291.8	503.7
Public works	316.9			
Agriculture	26.8			
Industry and commerce	82.7			
Others	21.0			
Other services	46.9	47.1	47.8	48.9
Public debt	82.5	124.7	157.3	214.8
Total Expenditures	2,055.0	2,286.7	2,435.5	2,712.5

Source: Ministry of Finance; accounts of the Empresas of the bigger cities, mission estimates.

Table 19:   MUNICIPALITIES: TOTAL EXPENDITURE BY ECONOMIC CLASSIFICATION, 1966-69
(In millions of Col $, Budget Executions)

	1966	1967	1968	1969
Municipalities				
Administration	138.3	153.9	180.0	220.0
Police and justice	112.3	127.6	145.0	165.0
Public services	618.7	735.2	1,040.0	1,380.0
Labor and social security	146.3	269.0	355.0	410.0
Public health	82.8	89.3	140.0	185.0
Education and culture	143.8	160.6	195.0	250.0
Economic development	856.0	1,209.3	1,380.0	1,590.0
Other services	91.2	140.8	190.0	230.0
Public debt	345.5	399.0	460.0	600.0
Total Expenditures	2,534.9	3,284.7	4,085.0	5,030.0

Source: Mission estimates.

Table 20: PUBLIC INVESTMENT PLAN 1970-72, ADJUSTMENTS AND MISSION'S SUGGESTIONS
(In millions of Col $ and Percentages)

ADJUSTMENTS — Millions of Col $

Sector	1970 Plan	1970 Adjusted Plan	1971 Plan	1971 Adjusted Plan	1972 Plan	1972 Adjusted Plan
Transport	3,134	3,321	2,746	2,931	2,937	3,076
Energy	2,117	1,951	1,657	1,671	1,864	1,909
Communications	390	661	155	474	170	533
Water and sewerage	892	765	1,348	1,095	1,423	1,335
Housing	554	724	587	720	705	861
Education	433	478	515	567	610	649
Health	1,238	228	1,152	326	1,354	303
Agriculture	11,087	1,884	12,606	2,293	14,251	2,694
Industry	1,174	1,166	1,164	1,141	1,051	1,001
Tourism	65	55	100	87	120	106
Studies and research	165	101	203	132	225	146
Other	871	664	742	661	820	682
Total	22,120	11,998	22,975	12,098	25,530	13,295

ADJUSTMENTS — Percentages

Sector	1970 Plan	1970 Adjusted Plan	1971 Plan	1971 Adjusted Plan	1972 Plan	1972 Adjusted Plan
Transport	14.2	27.7	11.9	24.2	11.5	23.1
Energy	9.6	16.3	7.2	13.8	7.3	14.4
Communications	1.8	5.5	0.7	3.9	0.7	4.0
Water and sewerage	4.0	6.4	5.9	9.1	5.6	10.0
Housing	2.5	6.0	2.6	5.9	2.8	6.5
Education	2.0	4.0	2.2	4.7	2.4	4.9
Health	5.6	1.9	5.0	2.7	5.3	2.3
Agriculture	50.1	15.7	54.9	18.9	55.7	20.3
Industry	5.3	9.7	5.1	9.4	4.1	7.5
Tourism	0.3	0.5	0.4	0.7	0.5	0.8
Studies and research	0.7	0.8	0.9	1.1	0.9	1.1
Other	3.9	5.5	3.2	5.5	3.2	5.1
Total	100.0	100.0	100.0	100.0	100.0	100.0

MISSION PROPOSAL — Millions of Col $

Sector	1970 Adjusted Plan	1970 Mission Proposal	1971 Adjusted Plan	1971 Mission Proposal	1972 Adjusted Plan	1972 Mission Proposal
Transport	3,321	2,974	2,931	2,989	3,076	3,139
Energy	1,951	2,226	1,671	1,959	1,909	2,473
Communications	661	661	474	474	533	533
Water and sewerage	765	888	1,095	1,187	1,335	1,422
Housing	724	724	720	720	861	861
Education	478	504	567	634	649	690
Health	228	228	326	326	303	303
Agriculture	1,884	1,884	2,293	2,293	2,694	2,784
Industry	1,166	977	1,141	1,041	1,001	1,018
Tourism	55	55	87	87	106	106
Studies and research	101	101	132	132	146	146
Other	664	664	661	661	682	682
Total	11,998	11,886	12,098	12,503	13,295	14,157

MISSION PROPOSAL — Percentages

Sector	1970 Adjusted Plan	1970 Mission Proposal	1971 Adjusted Plan	1971 Mission Proposal	1972 Adjusted Plan	1972 Mission Proposal
Transport	27.7	25.0	24.2	23.9	23.1	22.2
Energy	16.3	18.7	13.8	15.7	14.4	17.5
Communications	5.5	5.6	3.9	3.8	4.0	3.8
Water and sewerage	6.4	7.5	9.1	9.5	10.0	10.0
Housing	6.0	6.1	5.9	5.7	6.5	6.1
Education	4.0	4.2	4.7	5.1	4.9	4.9
Health	1.9	1.9	2.7	2.6	2.3	2.1
Agriculture	15.7	15.9	19.0	18.3	20.3	19.7
Industry	9.7	8.2	9.4	8.3	7.5	7.2
Tourism	.5	.5	.7	.7	.8	.7
Studies and research	.8	.8	1.1	1.1	1.1	1.0
Other	5.5	5.6	5.5	5.3	5.1	4.8
Total	100.0	100.0	100.0	100.0	100.0	100.0

Source: Development Plan 1969-72: National Planning Department estimates; mission estimates. For the concepts and methods of adjustment see Chapter 1, The Overall View, section on Public Investment and Finance and Table 1-16.

Table 21:   INCOME AND EXPENDITURES OF THE PUBLIC SECTOR, 1966-72
(In millions of current Col $)

	1966	1967	1968	1969	1970	1971	1972
		Actual		Estimate		Projected	
Current Accounts							
Direct taxes	2,953	3,545	4,552	5,706	6,650	7,507	8,730
Indirect taxes	4,434	4,570	5,264	5,937	7,763	8,860	9,790
Other taxes and dues	865	1,241	1,551	1,730	2,035	2,395	2,820
Sale of goods and services	2,346	2,966	4,208	5,245	6,110	7,120	8,285
Other income	1,208	1,568	1,828	2,169	2,570	2,925	3,335
Profit or loss (-) of commercial operations	107	68	-139	20	-100	-100	-100
Tax credit certificates (CAT)	.....	.....	-138	-331	-500	-675	-915
Total current account income	11,913	13,958	17,126	20,476	24,528	28,032	31,945
Personal services	5,041	5,793	6,690	7,970	9,188	10,530	12,055
General expenditures	1,274	1,862	2,316	3,030	3,655	4,400	5,315
Transfers to the private sector	1,179	1,248	1,447	2,256	2,672	3,245	3,850
Interest on debt	628	581	701	868	1,348	1,530	1,750
Total current account expenditures	8,122	9,484	11,154	14,124	16,863	19,705	22,970
Current account surplus	3,791	4,474	5,972	6,352	7,665	8,327	8,975
Investments (by sectors)							
Transport	1,205	1,826	1,957	2,300	2,974	2,989	3,139
Energy	596	776	944	1,180	2,226	1,959	2,473
Communications	144	206	256	335	661	474	533
Water and sewerage	365	422	591	737	888	1,187	1,422
Housing	269	385	577	640	724	720	861
Education	180	241	374	365	504	634	690
Health	69	142	148	260	228	326	303
Agriculture	498	784	1,127	1,260	1,884	2,293	2,784
Industry	162	199	392	590	977	1,041	1,018
Tourism	.....	.....	10	30	55	87	106
Studies and research	4	13	25	50	101	132	146
Other	229	273	423	465	664	661	682
Total	3,721	5,267	6,824	8,212	11,886	12,503	14,157
Financial investments	40	184	558	750	500	500	600
Total investments	3,761	5,451	7,382	8,962	12,386	13,003	14,757
Current account surplus	3,791	4,474	5,972	6,352	7,665	8,327	8,975
Deficit	+30	-977	-1,410	-2,610	-4,721	-4,676	-5,782
Financing:							
Net external credit	770	808	1,554	1,922	2,760	3,150	3,495
Other sources	342	348	559	663	935	800	800
Change in cash balances (increase minus)	-411	-33	-300	178	862	.....	.....
Net internal credit	-731	-146	-403	-153	.....	.....	.....
To be financed (+)					164	726	1,487
Amortization (non BOR)					1,110	1,270	1,450
Total financing required					1,274	1,996	2,937

Source: Development Plan 1969-72; National Planning Department estimates; mission estimates. For the assumptions underlying the projections see Chapter 1, The Overall View, Section on Public Investment and Finance and Table 1-17.

Table 22:   COMPOSITION AND GROWTH OF THE MONEY SUPPLY, 1958-71
(In millions of Col $)

End of Period	Currency Outstanding	Money with the Public	Demand Deposits	Total Money Supply	Percentage Increase during Period
1958	1,459	1,360	1,958	3,318	.....
1959	1,605	1,486	2,230	3,716	12.0
1960	1,724	1,606	2,497	4,103	10.4
1961	1,983	1,846	3,267	5,112	24.6
1962	2,287	2,115	4,054	6,169	20.7
1963	2,743	2,537	4,386	6,923	12.2
1964	3,385	3,115	5,255	8,370	20.9
1965	3,872	3,595	6,085	9,680	15.6
1966	4,358	4,104	6,931	11,035	14.0
1967	5,051	4,759	8,691	13,450	21.9
1968	5,898	5,548	9,887	15,435	14.8
1969	7,015	6,554	11,894	18,448	19.5
1970	8,357	7,866	13,761	21,627	17.2
1968-I	3,715	3,303	10,208	13,510	0.4
1968-II	3,928	3,527	10,492	14,019	3.8
1968-III	3,963	3,442	10,944	14,386	2.6
1968-IV	5,898	5,548	9,887	15,435	7.3
1969-I	4,566	3,982	11,859	15,840	2.6
1969-II	4,620	3,993	12,127	16,120	1.8
1969-III	4,613	3,985	13,046	17,031	5.6
1969-IV	7,015	6,554	11,894	18,448	8.3
1970-I	5,306	4,543	14,205	18,748	1.6
1970-II	5,741	5,179	14,391	19,570	4.4
1970-III	5,505	4,777	15,210	19,987	2.1
1970-IV	8,357	7,866	13,761	21,627	8.2
1971-I	6,134	5,358	16,249	21,607	0.0

Note: Currency Outstanding less cash holdings of banks equals Money with the Public. Adding Demand Deposits to Money with the Public gives Total Money Supply, defined to exclude deposits of the government and official entities in the central bank.

Source: Banco de la Republica.

Table 23:   ANNUAL PERCENTAGE INCREASES IN GDP AND MONEY SUPPLY, 1965-70

Year	Real GDP	GDP Deflator	Nominal GDP	Money Supply[1]	Money Supply[2]
1965	3.6	9.1	13.1	15.6	15.1
1966	5.4	14.9	21.1	14.0	15.4
1967	4.2	8.3	12.9	21.9	17.0
1968	6.1	9.3	16.0	14.8	19.9
1969	6.4	8.2	15.1	19.5	16.4
1970	6.8[3]	9.5[3]	17.0[3]	17.2	18.9

[1] Year-end to year-end.
[2] Change in annual average computed from monthly data.
[3] Estimate.

Source: Banco de la Republica.

Table 24: WHOLESALE PRICE INDICES, BY MAIN COMMODITY GROUP, 1958-70 (1952-100)

Period	Foodstuffs	Beverages and Tobacco	Raw Materials Excluding Fuels	Fuels and Lubricants	Oils and Fats	Chemical Products	Manufactured Products	Machinery and Transport Equipment	Various Manufactured Products	Total Index	Total Index Excluding Foodstuffs
1958	174.7	175.2	175.0	217.3	220.2	187.8	176.1	224.0	178.2	180.3	187.8
1959	191.5	186.5	203.9	228.6	253.7	201.6	191.2	260.4	190.4	197.6	205.7
1960	199.1	193.9	201.8	234.6	301.0	205.9	199.8	278.8	198.3	205.9	214.9
1961	214.7	199.1	214.6	239.6	302.2	211.2	205.2	310.7	212.1	219.4	225.1
1962	217.2	211.5	226.8	244.5	344.1	219.4	214.7	320.1	220.3	225.2	235.7
1963	277.1	281.5	255.8	313.4	456.7	269.1	267.9	379.2	279.7	284.4	294.1
1964	344.0	329.4	272.3	334.8	537.0	289.6	288.1	412.3	294.7	334.1	320.7
1965	366.4	370.2	299.6	356.4	754.3	313.0	311.7	455.1	331.4	361.7	355.3
1966	426.9	420.9	349.8	393.6	1,265.8	367.3	365.8	542.4	395.2	424.6	421.3
1967	449.2	466.6	405.7	446.6	1,292.0	404.5	398.2	587.9	415.3	453.6	459.4
1968	479.4	492.2	456.5	464.5	1,238.1	444.8	428.3	613.3	431.4	482.1	485.6
1969	505.3	506.6	490.3	497.1	1,256.1	476.2	462.6	682.1	502.1	514.3	526.3
1970	536.2	531.8	507.6	551.8	1,267.7	496.7	499.4	816.5	558.4	553.5	576.7

Source: Banco de la Republica.

Table 25: CONSUMER PRICE INDICES FOR SALARY EARNERS AND WAGE EARNERS, 1958-70
(July 1954-June 1955 = 100)

Period[1]	Bogota[2]		Medellin[3]		Nation	
	Salary Earners	Wage Earners	Salary Earners	Wage Earners	Salary Earners	Wage Earners
1958	137.6	141.3	135.7	137.6	137.9	140.4
1959	147.9	151.5	148.2	150.0	149.6	151.9
1960	155.3	157.3	160.0	161.2	158.6	160.5
1961	167.4	171.0	171.9	175.1	171.1	174.1
1962	176.4	175.2	182.9	185.9	180.6	181.6
1963	221.9	231.2	227.8	236.2	224.9	231.1
1964	252.6	272.0	259.3	274.3	260.1	272.1
1965	269.1	281.6	280.4	288.1	282.8	291.3
1966	318.3	337.5	327.3	333.5	330.2	339.9
1967	348.9	365.0	359.8	364.2	359.6	367.3
1968	372.3	386.3	391.1	395.3	386.8	394.5
1969	402.4	425.5	422.7	423.7	414.0	421.9
1970	429.2	454.6	455.9	451.5	444.0	450.2

[1]Annual figures are simple averages of monthly data.

[2]Bogota has a weight of 20.2 percent in the national total.

[3]Medellin has a weight of 23.5 percent in the national total.

Source: National Statistics Department (DANE).

Table 26: GROSS VALUE OF PRODUCTION IN MANUFACTURING INDUSTRIES (CURRENT PRICES)
(In millions of current Col$)

	1953	1958	1960	1961	1962	1963	1964	1965	1966	1967
Non-durable Consumer Goods	2,862.6	5,591.7	7,143.1	7,822.8	8,913.5	11,204.6	13,988.6	15,936.8	18,916.2	21,178.5
Food	1,575.3	2,694.6	3,223.8	3,440.3	3,894.7	4,713.4	6,641.7	7,403.3	8,950.5	10,346.6
Beverages	470.0	819.2	1,124.3	1,260.3	1,414.8	1,945.0	2,235.1	2,631.0	2,867.2	3,125.9
Tobacco products	94.8	295.1	347.4	377.4	449.4	505.7	690.9	804.8	791.0	829.2
Textiles	273.8	645.5	914.4	1,014.7	1,122.2	1,437.2	1,557.9	1,730.4	2,062.5	2,194.7
Clothing and footwear	251.2	501.3	631.6	697.7	847.9	1,030.5	1,068.4	1,332.3	1,572.4	1,575.8
Printing and publishing	71.2	184.4	254.0	307.5	364.5	465.4	525.8	573.6	738.4	864.3
Pharmaceuticals and related products	126.3	451.6	647.6	724.9	820.0	1,107.6	1,268.8	1,461.4	1,934.2	2,242.0
Durable Consumer Goods	140.2	428.1	633.0	771.0	859.2	1,312.6	1,466.8	1,655.5	2,008.2	2,261.9
Furniture and fixtures	24.2	63.5	74.4	89.3	108.0	117.4	130.3	146.3	177.9	186.1
Rubber products	64.0	187.9	254.4	302.9	387.8	542.3	549.0	623.5	811.7	840.8
Ceramic products	9.4	16.4	36.2	55.6	60.9	74.8	83.1	97.0	141.7	134.4
Non-electrical appliances	2.0	10.3	16.6	30.1	35.2	34.2	39.1	45.9	48.4	54.5
Electrical appliances	12.0	57.8	102.6	124.5	170.4	247.7	265.7	324.3	400.9	408.1
Motor vehicles	28.6	92.2	148.8	168.6	96.8	296.2	399.6	418.5	427.6	638.0
Intermediate Goods	771.1	2,597.0	3,719.2	4,283.8	4,948.5	6,443.8	7,362.1	8,645.3	10,990.1	11,912.0
Textiles	273.8	645.5	914.3	1,014.7	1,122.3	1,437.2	1,557.9	1,730.4	2,062.5	2,194.7
Wood and products	41.5	93.0	117.6	117.9	145.1	191.2	215.4	259.9	329.6	330.3
Paper and products	30.3	141.2	227.5	288.8	421.9	612.8	673.5	794.7	1,224.4	1,177.4
Leather and products	71.5	137.1	183.5	199.9	233.4	263.4	276.2	346.6	427.1	431.5
Chemicals other than pharmaceuticals	40.9	190.5	265.9	308.6	420.3	589.5	865.3	1,173.2	1,704.9	1,967.3
Petroleum and coal products	88.8	506.3	636.3	710.0	760.6	944.9	1,071.8	1,204.8	1,305.9	1,472.8
Non-metallic mineral products	146.7	304.8	458.1	530.3	614.1	877.9	1,003.4	1,170.9	1,477.5	1,491.7
Basic metals	21.1	360.8	554.3	677.7	659.4	745.7	796.4	865.0	1,039.5	1,434.1
Metal products	56.5	217.8	361.7	435.9	571.4	781.2	902.2	1,099.8	1,418.7	1,412.2

Capital Goods	39.5	204.3	322.9	395.4	632.4	629.4	782.5	955.5	1,241.9	1,266.1
Mechanical machinery	15.1	50.6	80.4	102.2	145.5	174.0	219.2	253.1	309.8	330.3
Electrical machinery (except appliances)	8.1	89.2	165.2	216.9	263.9	327.6	414.1	529.1	731.3	720.0
Transport equipment (except motor vehicles)	16.3	64.5	77.3	76.3	223.0	127.8	149.2	173.3	200.8	215.8
Other	26.9	118.5	201.0	232.1	282.6	364.8	447.0	552.8	689.7	783.4
Total	3,840.3	8,939.6	12,019.2	12,505.1	15,636.2	19,955.2	24,047.0	27,745.9	33,846.1	37,401.9

Notes:
Data for the textile industry do not permit a clear distinction between textiles for consumer and industrial uses. The mission estimated that about half of the textiles produced in Colombia are for consumer use. Totals may not add up because of rounding.

The statistics on manufacturing generally cover the period ending 1967. This was the last year for which detailed data from the manufacturing sample survey were available during the mission's stay in Colombia in the spring of 1970.

Source: 1953, 1958, 1961, 1963-1966: DANE. *Boletin Mensual de Estadistica*, Numbers 67, 117, 148, 170, 180, 201 and 207; 1960, 1962 and 1967: unpublished DANE data.

Table 27: GROSS VALUE ADDED IN MANUFACTURING INDUSTRIES (CURRENT PRICES)
(In millions of current Col$)

	1953	1958	1960	1961	1962	1963	1964	1965	1966	1967
Non-durable Consumer Goods	1,010.7	1,977.9	2,683.4	3,066.9	3,676.6	4,814.4	5,730.4	6,637.3	7,535.0	8,429.8
Food	273.0	517.9	658.3	785.8	941.6	1,208.2	1,574.4	1,759.6	2,251.0	2,442.3
Beverages	340.7	480.6	693.7	794.0	945.9	1,326.9	1,509.4	1,829.0	1,809.4	2,072.4
Tobacco products	55.9	225.6	259.4	279.9	344.7	355.2	515.4	583.4	559.1	609.7
Textiles	133.4	267.3	364.3	391.7	461.6	654.3	682.8	797.5	876.9	1,001.1
Clothing and footwear	99.6	175.1	233.8	259.0	333.3	422.5	443.6	538.3	647.8	643.8
Printing and publishing	42.7	94.7	132.6	162.6	195.5	245.4	289.4	316.1	395.9	477.7
Pharmaceuticals and related products	65.4	216.7	341.3	393.8	454.0	601.9	715.4	813.4	994.9	1,182.8
Durable Consumer Goods	79.7	193.9	304.3	381.4	433.1	709.1	706.0	811.7	900.8	1,003.7
Furniture and fixtures	14.2	33.5	38.6	49.2	61.6	66.6	72.8	81.9	99.9	94.1
Rubber products	35.6	75.7	114.2	147.9	200.6	297.0	275.4	317.4	361.4	380.1
Ceramic products	6.8	19.1	21.1	31.2	37.2	47.5	52.6	59.0	74.4	54.9
Non-electrical appliances	1.2	6.6	8.5	16.1	17.9	17.3	18.6	20.9	22.8	25.6
Electrical appliances	5.8	24.9	46.9	52.9	82.7	137.9	122.0	162.1	171.1	157.8
Motor vehicles	16.1	45.1	75.0	84.1	33.1	142.8	164.6	170.4	171.2	291.3
Intermediate Goods	369.0	903.5	1,418.9	1,652.3	1,902.4	2,721.8	3,022.6	3,418.8	4,414.1	4,939.9
Textiles	133.4	267.3	364.3	391.7	461.6	654.3	682.8	797.5	876.9	1,001.1
Wood and products	16.9	33.1	44.3	48.7	62.0	88.2	95.8	117.3	151.7	150.3
Paper and products	15.5	45.7	85.0	103.8	155.5	249.5	277.7	274.2	416.0	392.5
Leather and products	26.2	47.0	67.4	73.3	90.0	102.4	111.2	144.6	171.1	167.6
Chemicals other than pharmaceuticals	23.6	72.9	132.1	148.7	197.3	273.7	342.1	469.0	725.0	865.6
Petroleum and coal products	24.7	108.7	163.0	182.8	214.6	254.2	295.5	282.3	389.8	571.6
Non-metallic mineral products	92.0	171.4	248.5	293.8	336.5	489.9	539.8	644.6	816.1	794.2
Basic metals	8.3	71.3	157.4	212.5	117.7	236.1	244.8	161.9	223.9	323.2
Metal products	28.4	86.1	156.9	197.0	267.2	373.5	432.9	541.4	643.8	673.8

Capital Goods	23.4	97.1	147.9	193.8	317.3	320.7	410.0	487.7	625.0	621.0
Mechanical machinery	6.9	25.9	40.8	56.3	80.9	98.5	127.3	144.1	170.2	181.9
Electrical machinery (except appliances)	4.8	39.7	64.6	92.6	111.9	144.0	190.1	245.2	348.5	334.4
Transport equipment (except motor vehicles)	11.7	31.5	42.5	44.9	124.5	78.2	92.6	98.4	106.3	104.7
Other	15.9	61.5	94.1	120.4	151.9	202.7	232.4	306.3	348.8	412.0
Total	1,498.7	3,233.9	4,648.6	5,414.8	6,481.3	8,768.7	10,101.4	11,661.8	13,823.7	15,406.4

Notes: Data for the textile industry do not permit a clear distinction between textiles for consumer and industrial uses. The mission estimated that about half of the textiles produced in Colombia are for consumer use. Totals may not add up because of rounding.

Source: 1953, 1958, 1961, 1963-1966: DANE, *Boletin Mensual de Estadistica*, Numbers, 67, 117, 148, 170, 180, 201 and 207; 1960, 1962 and 1967: unpublished DANE data.

Table 28: WAGES AND SALARIES AND GROSS VALUE ADDED PER MAN BY INDUSTRIAL SUB-GROUP AND SIZE OF FIRM, 1967

Firm Size (Number of Workers)	Firms	Employment	Value Added (millions current Col$)	Wages ('000 current Col$)	Wages, Salaries and Social Benefits ('000 current Col$)	Value Added per man ('000 current Col$)	Wages and Salary per man	Wages, Salaries and Social Benefits per Man ('000 current Col$)	Share of Wages Salaries and Social Benefits in Value Added %
Non-durable Consumer Goods									
1 – 14	4,866	20,551	559.8	127,533.1	145,360.6	27.4	6.2	7.1	26.0
15 – 19	287	4,610	145.0	37,281.8	44,164.5	31.5	8.1	9.6	30.5
20 – 49	662	20,051	795.1	188,029.7	233,084.0	39.7	9.4	11.6	29.3
50 – 99	265	18,277	958.6	210,450.3	269,186.7	52.5	11.5	14.7	28.1
100 – 199	156	21,734	1,906.9	318,552.2	398,734.2	87.7	14.7	18.4	20.9
200 and over	133	72,225	5,065.6	1,239,357.4	1,678,848.6	70.1	17.2	23.2	33.1
Durable Consumer Goods									
1 – 14	855	4,218	81.4	32,964.7	36,788.2	19.3	7.8	8.7	45.2
15 – 19	75	1,196	27.8	11,234.0	13,161.4	23.2	9.4	11.0	47.3
20 – 49	168	4,908	116.8	51,932.5	63,181.3	23.8	10.6	12.9	54.1
50 – 99	49	3,461	109.6	32,313.7	42,372.4	31.7	9.3	12.2	38.7
100 – 199	22	2,645	96.2	31,977.4	40,275.3	36.4	12.1	15.2	41.9
200 and over	20	10,998	593.5	195,996.4	293,332.4	54.0	17.8	26.7	49.4
Intermediate Goods									
1 – 14	1,714	8,887	191.1	59,477.2	67,830.8	21.5	6.7	7.6	35.5
15 – 19	168	2,659	61.5	23,020.8	27,498.4	23.13	8.7	10.3	44.7
20 – 49	367	10,737	420.2	106,527.2	132,697.4	39.1	9.9	12.4	31.6
50 – 99	144	9,944	490.1	141,092.3	179,404.4	42.3	14.2	18.0	36.6
100 – 199	77	10,766	640.6	163,567.4	230,626.9	59.5	15.2	21.4	36.0
200 and over	67	28,697	2,110.4	527,245.7	748,720.4	73.5	18.4	26.1	35.5

Capital Goods

1 – 14	225	1,462	32.8	12,724.2	14,390.0	22.4	8.7	9.8	43.9
15 – 19	35	533	13.2	4,736.5	5,557.0	24.8	8.9	10.4	42.1
20 – 49	71	1,925	60.0	20,543.5	25,133.7	31.2	10.7	13.1	41.9
50 – 99	31	2,124	108.4	37,822.5	44,722.0	51.0	17.8	21.1	41.3
100 – 199	13	1,813	74.6	29,710.8	40,760.6	41.2	16.4	22.5	54.6
200 and over	19	9,236	335.2	148,724.8	198,556.8	36.3	16.1	21.5	59.2

TOTAL

1 – 14	7,829	36,045	891.7	240,358.5	273,339.5	24.7	6.7	7.6	30.6
15 – 19	584	9,295	255.3	78,954.4	93,546.3	27.5	8.5	10.1	36.6
20 – 49	1,338	39,782	1,485.7	390,966.8	483,932.0	37.4	9.8	12.2	32.6
50 – 99	525	36,293	1,766.3	450,995.7	573,218.8	48.7	12.4	19.8	32.4
100 – 199	283	38,939	2,827.5	571,405.5	749,522.9	72.6	14.7	19.3	26.5
200 and over	244	122,629	8,179.9	2,137,083.6	2,956,149.8	66.7	17.4	24.1	36.1

Notes: All textile production is shown under non-durable consumer goods.
    Employment figures refer to paid workers.
    Further breakdown by industry branch, e.g. food, beverages, textiles, etc., is available in IBRD files.

Source: Unpublished DANE data.

Table 29: COMPARISON OF IMPORTED AND DOMESTIC PRICES FOR SELECTED MANUFACTURED PRODUCTS

| | IMPORTS | | | | DOMESTIC MANUFACTURES | | | | | | (F.O.B. plant ÷ C.I.F. Barranquilla) |
| | | Delivered to | | | | | | Delivered to | | | |
	C.I.F. Barranquilla	Barranquilla	Medellin	Bogota	F.O.B. Plant	Name of Plant	Location	Barranquilla	Medellin	Bogota	
Steel											
1/4 dia. wire rod	3,149	3,648	3,848	3,908	3,480	Paz del Rio	Belancito	3,715	3,660	3,545	1.10
3/8 dia. bars	3,176	3,679	3,879	3,939	3,240	Paz del Rio	Belancito	3,475	3,420	3,305	1.02
3/4 dia. bars	2,719	3,050	3,250	3,310	3,100	Paz del Rio	Belancito	3,335	3,280	3,165	1.14
Channels and beams	2,902	3,370	3,570	3,630	3,960	Paz del Rio	Belancito	4,195	4,140	4,025	1.36
9-gauge bright wire	3,085	3,577	3,777	3,837	3,740	Paz del Rio	Belancito	3,975	3,920	3,805	1.21
8-gauge galvanized wire	3,436	3,973	4,173	4,233	4,490	Paz del Rio	Belancito	4,725	4,670	4,555	1.30
Galvanized barbed wire	3,795	4,521	4,721	4,781	4,980	Paz del Rio	Belancito	5,215	5,160	5,045	1.31
16-gauge hot-rolled sheet	3,158	3,659	3,859	3,919	3,760	Paz del Rio	Belancito	3,995	3,940	3,825	1.19
Electrolytic tinplate (107 lb)	4,400	4,900	5,100	5,160	5,390	Emp. Siderurgica	Medellin	5,510	5,390	5,540	1.22
Aluminum (Pesos/kg)											
.0089 mm foil x 500-760mm wide	27.06	27.22	27.42	27.48	33.90	Al. Reynolds	Barranquilla	33.90	34.10	34.16	1.25
Corrugated sheets 4mm thick, 6 ft. long x 32 in. wide (Pesos/lineal foot)	5.65	5.70	5.76	5.78	6.34	Al. Reynolds	Barranquilla	6.34	6.40	6.42	1.12
Class 150 irrigation pipe, 2 in. dia.	4.33	4.36	4.39	4.40	4.56	Al. Reynolds	Barranquilla	4.56	4.59	4.60	1.05
					4.80	Al. Alcan	Cali	4.84	4.81	4.83	1.10
Class 150 irrigation pipe, 3 in. dia.	6.07	6.11	6.16	6.17	6.95	Al. Reynolds	Barranquilla	6.95	7.00	7.01	1.14
					7.31	Al. Alcan	Cali	7.37	7.32	7.35	1.20
Class 150 irrigation pipe, 6 in. dia.	15.05	15.14	15.26	15.29	19.57	Al. Alcan	Cali	19.72	19.76	19.81	1.30
Synthetic Fibers (Pesos/kg)											
Nylon yarn	32.89	33.63	34.03	34.13	52.00	Colnylon	Medellin	52.40	52.00	52.26	1.58
					57.75	Enka	Medellin	58.15	57.75	58.01	1.75
					57.00	Vanylon	Barranquilla	57.00	57.40	57.26	1.73
Nylon tire canvas	34.79	35.55	35.95	36.05	46.00	Enka	Medellin	46.40	46.00	46.26	1.32

Product						Company	City				
Polyester filament	59.22	60.23	60.63	60.73	76.40	Polymeros Col.	Medellin	76.80	76.40	76.66	1.29
					76.50	Enka de Col.	Medellin	76.90	76.50	76.76	1.30
Polyester staple	23.22	23.87	24.27	24.37	41.80	Polymeros Col.	Medellin	42.20	41.80	42.06	1.80
						Enka de Col.					
					44.00	Celanese	Cali				1.89
Chemicals				(Pesos/kg)							
P.V.C.	7.06	7.54	7.96	8.07	8.07	Petroquimica	Cartagena	8.11	8.25	9.24	1.14
Carbon black	4.09	4.54	4.94	5.04	4.28	Phillips	Cali				1.04
				(Pesos/ton)							
Complex fertilizer 20-20-0	1080-1440				1150	Monomeros Colombianos					.79-1.06
Caustic soda	720				1200	Planta de Soda					1.66
Chlorine	954				1468	Planta de Soda					1.53
Cardboard boxes (bananas)	5.94			(Pesos/unit)	8.46	Carton de Colombia					1.42
Automobiles											
Dodge Dart	44200				178,949	Chrysler	Bogota	178,949		4.04	4.04
Dodge truck – 5 tons	65000				156,989			156,989			2.41

Note: The difference between imports "c.i.f. Barranquilla" and imports "delivered Barranquilla" are port handling charges, based on figures given to the mission by Acerias Paz del Rio. The "delivered" figures, both for domestic and imported manufactures, exclude taxes. Imported manufactures exclude tariffs. The figures on internal transport should be taken as rough estimates rather than definite quotations. The steel rates were supplied by Acerias Paz del Rio. The aluminum rates were estimated on the basis of steel rates. Internal transport costs of synthetic fibers are based on figures given in *Board Report on Enka de Colombia* (Reference: IFC/t-40, dated July 30, 1969). The internal transport costs exclude insurance during transit which can be quite high. Internal insurance during transit for synthetic fibers, for example, was estimated in the ENKA Report to be about $80 per ton. All dollar quotations were converted into Col $ at the rate of Col$ 18 per US $1.

Sources: Domestic prices from company price lists or direct communication with companies; international prices were, in most cases, calculated from f.o.b. quotations in principal selling markets plus allowance for freight, insurance and consular fees.

Table 30: DISTRIBUTION BY SIZE OF THE CAJA LOANS FOR THE YEAR JULY 1967-JUNE 1968

Size Range of Loans in Col $	Number	Percentage Distribution	Cumulative Percentage	Value ('000 Col $)	Percentage Distribution	Cumulative Percentage
Less than 100	46	0.01	0.01	4	0.00	0.00
From 101 to 250	834	0.25	0.27	173	0.00	0.00
From 251 to 500	9,677	2.92	3.19	4,604	0.19	0.20
From 501 to 1,000	40,386	12.19	15.38	35,707	1.50	1.70
From 1,001 to 5,000	199,541	60.23	75.61	546,615	22.91	24.61
From 5,001 to 10,000	41,846	12.63	88.24	318,970	13.37	37.97
From 10,001 to 20,000	19,620	5.92	94.16	305,602	12.81	50.78
From 20,001 to 30,000	6,954	2.10	96.26	181,385	7.60	58.38
From 30,001 to 40,000	3,242	0.98	97.24	115,298	4.83	63.21
From 40,001 to 50,000	2,420	0.73	97.97	107,586	4.51	67.72
From 50,001 to 100,000	4,451	1.34	99.31	295,340	12.38	80.10
From 100,001 to 150,000	864	0.26	99.57	80,976	3.39	83.50
Greater than 150,000	1,411	0.43	100.00	393,820	16.50	100.00
TOTAL	331,292	100.00		2,386,081	100.00	

Note: Components may not add to totals due to rounding.

Source: Caja de Credito Agrario Industrial Y Minero.

Table 31: DISTRIBUTION BY SIZE OF THE NEW LIVESTOCK LOANS OF THE BANCO GANADERO IN 1968
(In '000 of Col $)

Size Range (In Col $)	Law 26 of 1959		Alliance for Progress		I.D.B.[1]		Fondo Rotatorio		Total Number	Cumulative Percentage	Total Value	Cumulative Percentage
	Number	Value	Number	Value	Number	Value	Number	Value				
Less than 30,000	1,503	15,926	77	1,647	–	–	1,303	23,833	2,883	53.41	41,405	16.26
From 30 – 50	576	25,708	95	4,240	–	–	548	21,079	1,219	75.99	51,027	36.30
From 50 – 70	174	11,500	34	2,172	–	–	230	13,624	438	84.11	27,296	47.02
From 70 – 100	318	29,118	77	7,112	–	–	86	6,594	481	93.02	42,824	63.84
From 100 – 130	51	6,101	20	2,414	–	–	1	102	72	94.35	8,617	67.22
From 130 – 170	97	14,384	25	3,721	1	145	5	766	128	96.72	19,016	74.69
From 170 – 200	71	13,986	6	1,160	2	347	4	779	83	98.26	16,272	81.08
From 200 – 250	17	4,185	1	250	2	473	2	452	22	98.67	5,360	83.19
From 250 – 300	20	5,890	–	–	2	558	1	251	23	99.09	6,700	85.82
From 300 – 400	14	4,830	–	–	1	311	5	1,775	20	99.46	6,916	88.53
From 400 – 500	5	2,436	–	–	–	–	3	1,288	8	99.61	3,724	90.00
From 500 – 600	6	3,430	–	–	1	507	–	–	7	99.74	3,937	91.54
From 600 – 700	2	1,358	–	–	–	–	1	689	3	99.80	2,047	92.35
From 700 – 800	–	–	–	–	–	–	–	–	–	–	–	–
From 800 – 900	–	–	–	–	–	–	–	–	–	–	–	–
From 900 – 1,000,000	3	3,000	2	2,000	–	–	2	1,860	7	99.93	6,860	95.04
Greater than 1,000,000	2	9,558	–	–	1	1,520	1	1,555	4	100.00	12,632	100.00
TOTAL	2,859	151,410	337	24,715	10	3,861	2,192	74,647	5,398		254,633	

[1] I.D.B.—Inter-American Development Bank.

Note: Loans over Col $ 800,000 have only been granted to Fondos Ganaderos and Agricultural Cooperatives.

Source: Banco Ganadero.

Table 32:   FERTILIZERS USED[1], BY CROPS AND REGIONS, 1969
(In thousands of metric tons)

Department	Potatoes	Rice	Wheat	Barley	Sugar Cane	Banana	Coffee	Tobacco	Cotton	Corn	Oil Palm	Sorghum	Other	Total	% of Total
Cundinamarca	50		7	10			3			1			5	76	22
Antioquia	12				2 [a]	6	18			4			8	50	15
Caldas	4						30			b			4	38	11
Boyaca	25		3	6									2	36	11
Valle		3			12		12		2	1		a	3	33	10
Tolima	1	20					3		4	1		a	1	30	9
Narino	18		5	1										24	7
Meta		11				4	1		2		b		1	15	4
North Coast		6							5		1		b	16	5
Huila		7					1	b	1	b			b	9	3
Santanderes					1		1	1	2	1			1	7	2
Cauca	3	b			1		b							4	1
Total	113	47	15	17	16	10	69	1	16	8	1	1	25	338	100
% of total	33	14	4	5	5	3	20	b	5	2	b	b	7	98	

[a] Estimate.

[b] Less than 500 tons.

Source: Calculations provided by W. Gregory from estimates made by fertilizer trade, principally P.Q. Esso, ABOCOL and Caja.

Table 33: SUPPORT PRICES (COL$ PER METRIC TON) OFFERED BY IDEMA, 1963-1970[1]

Products	1963	1964	1965	1966	1967	1968	1969	1970
Rice (unhulled)[2]	1,260	1,260	1,260	1,720	2,050	2,050	2,000	2,250
	680	680	680	1,170	1,170	1,310	1,150	1,240
Yellow corn	–	925	925	1,020	1,250	1,020	1,300	1,300
White corn	–	887.50	925	1,020	1,250	1,020	1,350	1,300
Beans[2]	2,300	3,600	3,600	3,600	3,600	8,200	5,400	5,400
	2,100	3,000	3,000	3,000	3,000	5,800	4,500	4,500
Wheat	1,098	1,428	1,428	1,714	1,714	2,100	2,100	2,100
Soybeans	1,200	1,460	1,460	1,460	1,680	1,680	2,000	2,000
Sesame	2,100	2,100	2,100	2,900	3,500	3,700	3,700	3,700
Sorghum	700	700	700	700	980	980	1,170	1,170
Barley	–	–	–	–	–	–	2,000	2,000
Anis	–	–	–	–	20,000	20,000	11,450	11,450

[1] Prices for 1963-68 are those of IDEMA's predecessor, INA.

[2] IDEMA currently specifies 22 grades of rice and 3 grades of beans. This table shows prices only for the lowest and the highest grades for which prices were listed during any given year.

Source: IDEMA.

Table 34: SUPPORT PRICES (US $ EQUIVALENT PER METRIC TON) OFFERED BY IDEMA, BY CROPS, 1963-70[1]

Products	1963	1964	1965	1966	1967	1968	1969	1970[2]
Rice (unhulled)[3]	140	140	93	127	130	121	112	123
	76	76	50	87	74	77	64	68
Yellow corn	–	103	68	76	79	60	73	71
White corn	–	99	68	76	79	60	75	71
Beans[3]	256	400	266	267	228	484	301	296
	233	333	222	222	190	342	251	246
Wheat	122	159	106	127	108	124	117	115
Soybeans	133	162	108	108	106	99	112	109
Sesame	233	233	155	215	221	218	206	203
Sorghum	78	78	52	52	62	58	65	64
Barley	–	–	–	–	–	–	112	109
Anis	–	–	–	–	1,264	1,179	639	627

[1]Prices for 1966-68 are those of IDEMA's predecessor, INA. Figures were converted from Colombian pesos by using the principal selling rate at the end of each year.

[2]Converted by using the principal exchange rate at the end of March, 1970.

[3]IDEMA currently specifies 22 grades of rice and 3 grades of beans. This table shows prices only for the lowest and the highest grades for which prices were listed during any given year.

Source: IDEMA. The exchange rates were obtained from the IMF, *International Financial Statistics,* May 1970, and the *Supplement to 1964s65 Issues.*

Table 35: INDICATIVE AVERAGE PRICES RECEIVED BY FARMERS FOR SELECTED PRODUCTS, 1950-68
(Col $ per ton)

Item	1950	1955	1960	1961	1962	1963	1964	1965	1966	1967	1968
Sesame	588	686	1,519	1,617	2,250	2,650	2,850	3,783	3,682	3,750	3,800
Onions	1,330	2,025	2,337	2,055	2,641	2,694	2,866	6,440	3,826	3,436	3,525
Seed cotton	807	858	1,726	1,753	1,844	2,236	2,567	3,506	3,550	3,750	3,830
Rough rice	350	475	883	954	919	1,046	1,347	1,703	1,884	2,505	2,106
Banana (export)	192	256	440	444	438	607	701	987	808	875	929
Cacao (grain)	2,150	2,700	5,759	5,480	5,575	6,589	7,053	7,179	7,938	8,160	9,504
Coffee	1,476	2,472	3,104	3,281	3,209	3,966	4,990	5,004	5,867	6,000	6,754
Sugarcane	7.4	12	30	33	37	44	66	62	70	59	74
Barley	300	400	624	637	562	828	898	999	1,284	1,350	1,490
Copra	589	665	1,983	1,688	1,739	2,302	2,417	2,584	3,006	3,020	3,235
Beans	1,180	1,070	2,000	2,277	2,006	2,419	4,151	3,477	3,662	4,130	5,230
Corn	290	300	474	629	526	794	1,040	903	1,104	1,150	1,294
Potatoes	337	211	350	504	291	730	1,054	612	983	855	822
Plantain	128	185	224	305	368	459	672	668	801	860	747
Leaf Tobacco	1,290	1,360	1,989	2,009	2,706	3,000	4,067	4,858	5,060	5,488	5,800
Wheat	610	650	880	975	957	1,052	1,394	1,525	1,755	1,756	1,956
Yuca	110	193	303	378	338	398	755	658	691	688	954
Panela	184	217	392	377	541	993	1,133	885	1,003	1,015	1,127

Source: Banco de la Republica; unpublished data.

Table 36: NATIONAL RAILROADS: FREIGHT TRAFFIC
(Million Ton-km)

	1965	1966	1967	1968	1969
Rice	18	14	9	16	16
Corn	14	16	14	19	23
Wheat	81	109	74	140	101
Banana	12	10	9	6	4
Coffee	93	91	135	147	147
Cotton	....	20	25	24	25
Cattle	21	27	29	28	30
Timber	12	13	15	16	14
Limestone	19	13	10	7	4
Salt	43	36	36	33	39
Sand & gravel	11	13	11	10	11
Coal	29	31	30	26	27
Other minerals	17	19	28	29	36
Petroleum products (excluding asphalt)	108	106	98	89	87
Asphalt	18	16	22	43	33
Sugar	44	52	70	90	74
Molasses	6	11	13	12	8
Fodder	....	....	....	20	28
Beer	10	23	10	8	7
Fertilizer	60	86	98	74	93
Cement	29	22	25	21	20
Newsprint	30	26	36	28	38
Iron and steel	55	82	24	52	81
Wire	....	....	....	10	18
Sub-total	730	836	821	948	964
Miscellaneous	160	278	175	177	195
Total	890	1,114	996	1,125	1,159

Source: F.C.N. *Los Ferrocarriles en Cifras, Boletin Anual.*

Table 37: OUTPUTS OF THE FORMAL EDUCATION SYSTEM, 1960, 1964, 1968-1969

Overall

	1960	1964	1968	
Primary	75,900	130,000	230,000	
Secondary	11,633	18,547	34,141	
Higher	2,872	3,998	5,707	

Graduates Secondary Education by Type of Education

	1960	1964	1968	Rate of Increase
General secondary	8,070	13,902	23,728	14.5
Industrial[1]	199	445	1,223	25.5
Commercial[1]	725	873	1,200	6.5
Agriculture[1]	90	92	220	11.8
Girls vocational[1]	450	529	675	5.2
Primary teacher training	2,099	2,706	7,095	16.4
	11,633	18,547	34,141	

Graduates Higher Education by Specialization
(University and Non-degree Level)

	1964	1966	1969	Rate of Increase
Agriculture and related studies	271	460	717	21.4
Sciences	478	300	426	——
Social sciences	488	1,070	1,832	30.2
Law	793	771	739	——
Education	426	773	765	11.2
Humanities	100	456	518	39.0
Fine Arts	15	254	333	17.3
Engineering & related studies	718	809	1,748	19.5
Medicine & related studies	699	955	448	8.6
	3,998	5,848	7,526	

[1] Both cycles.

Source: Compiled from data supplied by Ministry of Education (1969 figures incomplete).

Table 38: HIGHER EDUCATION OUTPUT BY LEVEL AND TYPE OF STUDIES, 1966 AND 1967.

	Post-Secondary Technician Level		University Level	
	1966	1967	1966	1967
Administration & Economics	136	187	670	659
Agriculture & related studies	55	24	405	316
Engineering & related studies	66	123	800	812
Medicine & related studies	171	215	616	509
Education	73	14	745	694
Humanities	15	27	289	326
Sciences	51	27	302	236
Social sciences	48	16	249	236
Law	43	39	715	821
Fine Arts	12	24	221	115
Others	3	51	–	25
	673	747	5,012	4,749

Table 39: HIGHER EDUCATION ENROLLMENTS AND TEACHERS IN SELECTED FACULTIES, 1968
(Degree Level Courses)

Faculty and Course	No. of[1] Applications	Enrollments		Teachers[1]	
		1st Year	Total	Total	of whom full-time
Agriculture					
Agriculture & agri. engineering		128	857		
Forestry		84	194		
Veterinary Sciences		56	447		
Animal Husbandry		68	164		
Total	3,616	336	1,662	353	314
Health Education					
Medicine		780	2,964		
Preventive medicine		--	99		
Microbiology		26	49		
Dentistry		194	487		
Nursing		59	434		
Nutrition & dietetics		95	262		
Total	8,391	1,154	4,295	1,109	822
Engineering					
Basic studies		173	499		
Civil engineering		1,242	3,392		
Electrical engineering		319	1,493		
Electrical & telecommunications		163	596		
Electro-mechanical		313	406		
Electronics		368	865		
Mechanical		239	1,285		
Engineering administration		136	270		
Industrial engineering		568	1,669		
Geographical engineering		214	464		
Mining & metallurgy		228	619		
Geology and petroleum		50	197		
Sanitary engineers		30	255		
Transport and roads		32	132		
Naval engineering		93	163		
Chemical engineering		168	1,030		
General engineering		302	762		
Surveying		138	249		
Total	10,635	4,776	14,346	928	650

[1] Also includes for non-degree courses.

Source: Compiled from incomplete data supplied by ICFES and DANE: Boletin Mensual de Estadistica, June 1969.

MAP ANNEX

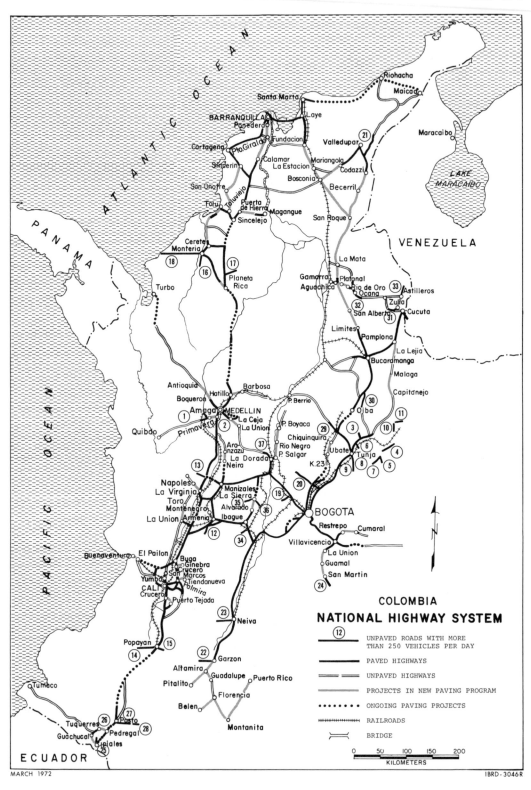

COLOMBIA
NATIONAL HIGHWAY SYSTEM

(12)	UNPAVED ROADS WITH MORE THAN 250 VEHICLES PER DAY
	PAVED HIGHWAYS
	UNPAVED HIGHWAYS
	PROJECTS IN NEW PAVING PROGRAM
••••••	ONGOING PAVING PROJECTS
	RAILROADS
	BRIDGE

0   50   100   150   200
KILOMETERS

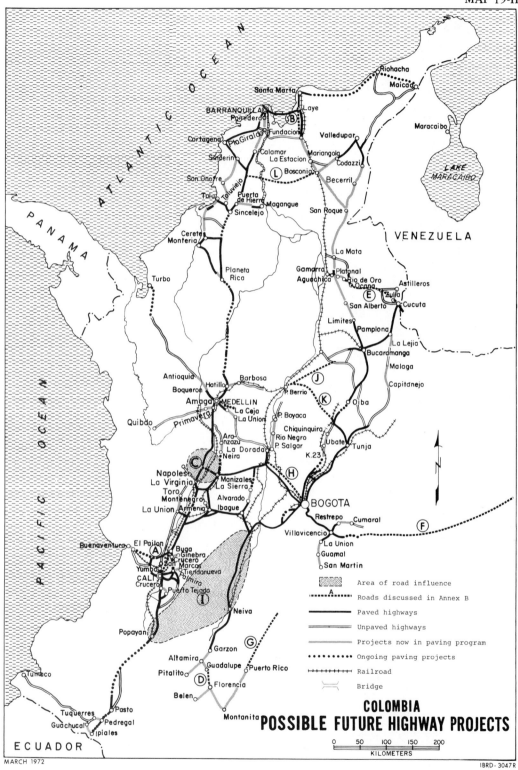

COLOMBIA
POSSIBLE FUTURE HIGHWAY PROJECTS

Area of road influence	
Roads discussed in Annex B	
Paved highways	
Unpaved highways	
Projects now in paving program	
Ongoing paving projects	
Railroad	
Bridge	

0   50   100   150   200
KILOMETERS

MARCH 1972   IBRD- 3047R

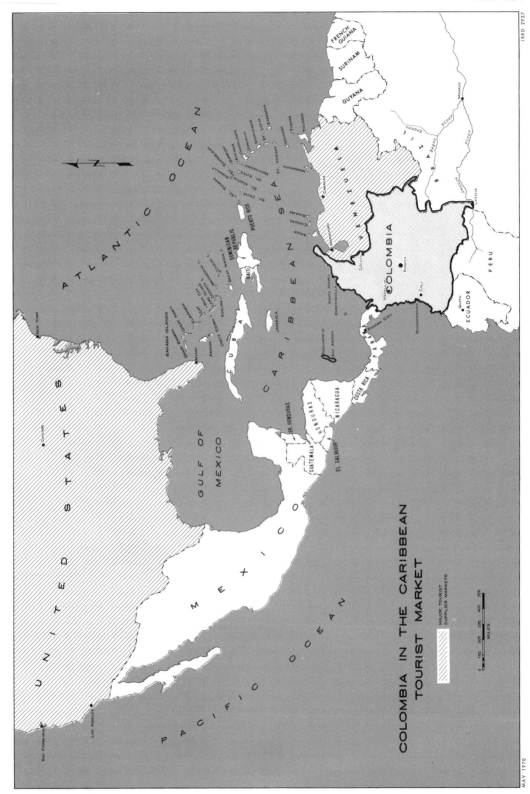

COLOMBIA IN THE CARIBBEAN
TOURIST MARKET

MAJOR TOURIST
SUPPLIER MARKETS

0 100 200 300 400 500
MILES

IBRD 2937

MAY 1970

MAP 21-II

CARIBBEAN
SEA

PANAMA

PACIFIC
OCEAN

VENEZUELA

BRAZIL

ECUADOR

PERU

RIOHACHA
SANTA MARTA   BURITICA   TRONCAL DEL CARIBE
BARRANQUILLA   PARAGUACHON
CARTAGENA   MARACAIBO
VALLEDUPAR
TOLU
SINCELEJO
MONTERIA
CUCUTA
MEDELLIN
BOYACA TOURIST CIRCUIT
MANIZALES   TUNJA
BOYACA
BOGOTA
GIRARDOT
MELGAR   VILLAVICENCIO
BUENAVENTURA   CALI
NEIVA
POPAYAN
ARCHAEOLOGICAL CIRCUIT
SAN AGUSTIN
PASTO
LETICIA

SAN ANDRES
PROVIDENCIA
MALPELO

0   100   200   300   400   500
KILOMETERS

N

COLOMBIA
PRIORITY TOURIST
DEVELOPMENT AREAS

PRIORTY RECEPTIVE
TOURIST AREA

SPECIALIZED TOURIST
ASSETS E.G. ARCHAEOLOGICAL
AREAS

TOURIST CENTERS WITH
DISPERSION AREAS

TOURIST DEVELOPMENT 'POLES'

MAY 1970   IBRD 2938

THE JOHNS HOPKINS UNIVERSITY PRESS

This book was printed by Universal Lithographers, Inc.
on 55-lb. Sebago and bound in Holliston Roxite
cloth by L. H. Jenkins, Inc.